# Sustainable Economy: The Indonesian Pathways

Solikin M. Juhro • Cicilia Anggadewi Harun
Arnita Rishanty • Danny Hermawan
Editors

# Sustainable Economy: The Indonesian Pathways

Springer

*Editors*
Solikin M. Juhro
Bank Indonesia
Jakarta, Indonesia

Cicilia Anggadewi Harun
Bank Indonesia
Jakarta, Indonesia

Arnita Rishanty
Bank Indonesia
Jakarta, Indonesia

Danny Hermawan
Bank Indonesia
Jakarta, Indonesia

ISBN 978-981-92-1214-9 ISBN 978-981-92-1215-6 (eBook)
https://doi.org/10.1007/978-981-92-1215-6

This work was supported by Bank Indonesia Institute.



This Springer imprint is published by the registered company Springer Nature Singapore Pte Ltd.
The registered company address is: 152 Beach Road, #21-01/04 Gateway East, Singapore 189721, Singapore

If disposing of this product, please recycle the paper.

"Sustainable Economy: The Indonesian Pathways" is very timely. Environmental, economic, and social sustainability are key priorities for contemporary society. Indonesia has achieved rapid economic growth in recent years; however, to sustain this momentum, it must avoid the middle-income trap. If income disparities continue to widen despite economic growth, political and social sustainability will be undermined. Digital technologies should be fully leveraged to expand credit access for start-ups and small businesses and to improve credit assessment. These technologies can also significantly enhance efficiency, especially in the public sector. Well-designed incentive mechanisms can help improve productivity among public sector workers and ensure that efficiency gains are fully realized.

Climate protection is also the key to maintaining a sustainable world. Environmental challenges have often been treated as economic "externalities," with no explicit cost assigned to $CO_2$ emissions or plastic pollution. Addressing these issues requires effective pricing mechanisms, such as carbon pricing or carbon taxes. However, such policies to be effective and fair, coordinated global implementation is necessary; otherwise, countries acting alone may face competitive disadvantages. Urgent global dialogue and cooperation are therefore needed to advance climate protection. This book covers timely topics for achieving global sustainability, and I hope it will be widely read not only by academics and business leaders but also by the general public".

—**Prof. (Emeritus) Naoyuki Yoshino**, *Keio University, Japan,*
Former Dean/CEO, *Asian Development Bank Institute*

"In a world transformed by new technologies, rising green ambitions, and profound demographic change, the journey toward sustainability is the defining task of our time. The search for shared vision and collective action from markets, businesses, scholars, policymakers, and society as a whole to follow a sustainable path is not just a challenge but a calling. "Sustainable Economy: The Indonesian Pathways" is an invitation to imagine an economy that safeguards tomorrow while honoring today. It is a gentle summon for social planners, including those in the financial domain, to look inward, to question familiar pathways, and to dare to rethink what they once held certain. May the efforts woven through this book kindle the shift from aspiration to action, and from action to a legacy worthy of the future".

—**Prof. Iwan Jaya Azis**, *Cornell University, USA.*

"The book *Sustainable Economy: The Indonesian Pathways* is timely and insightful—bringing together the collective wisdom and experiences of Indonesia's leading policymakers and researchers on how to move to a more sustainable economy. Its pages reflect the nation's commitment to forging a green and just transition and embedding long-term sustainable development into the heart of economic policy, identifying next steps and challenges. This is also relevant for Central Banks, as price and financial stability can only be preserved if the climate and nature are stable. The forward-looking vision showcased here will undoubtedly serve as an inspiration for policymakers and practitioners worldwide who are striving for a sustainable future".

—**Irene Heemskerk**, Head of Climate Change Centre, *European Central Bank*

# Governor's Remarks

It is with great pleasure that I present Sustainable Economy: The Indonesian Pathways. This book comes at a pivotal moment when the world, including Indonesia, is facing increasingly complex challenges that demand a careful balance between economic growth, social progress, and environmental stewardship. For Indonesia, the pursuit of a sustainable economy is not merely a strategic choice, but a necessity to ensure long-term stability and resilience.

Today, resilience must be understood more broadly—not only as the ability to withstand financial shocks, but also as the capacity to navigate long-term structural challenges such as climate change, demographic transitions, and technological transformation.

In fulfilling its mandate, Bank Indonesia has consistently emphasized the importance of price stability and financial system stability as the foundation of sustainable economic growth. Yet, in the face of climate change, demographic shifts, and global uncertainties, it has become evident that these foundations must be broadened. Stability must be understood not only in macroeconomic terms but also in its contribution to sustainable development and intergenerational welfare. Stability must ultimately serve the people by ensuring that economic progress translates into shared prosperity and intergenerational welfare. The pursuit of a sustainable economy, therefore, is inseparable from our responsibility as a central bank.

Central banks around the world are increasingly expected to play roles beyond their traditional mandates. Increasingly, they are called upon to contribute to solutions "beyond stability," including sustainable finance, inclusive growth, and climate resilience. For Indonesia, this evolution represents both a challenge and an opportunity. Our task is to adapt these global discussions to our unique national context as an archipelagic nation rich in resources, cultures, and aspirations. In Indonesia, this means strengthening our role in advancing sustainable finance, encouraging green innovation, and supporting inclusive growth while maintaining stability as our anchor. A truly sustainable economy is one in which stability and development reinforce each other for the prosperity of all Indonesians.

This book offers valuable perspectives on how Indonesia can navigate this transformative journey. This publication reflects practical yet rigorous insights into how

Indonesia can balance economic progress with environmental stewardship and social equity. They highlight that sustainability is not a single pathway but a multi-dimensional agenda requiring coherence across policies, institutions, and communities. In particular, they remind us that Indonesia's path must be distinctively our own—grounded in national realities yet aligned with global aspirations such as the Sustainable Development Goals (SDGs) and Vision Indonesia 2045.

I commend the authors and contributors for their dedication and thoughtful reflections in presenting these important and timely insights. In my view, this volume is more than a collection of scholarly works; it is a call for collaboration. Achieving a sustainable economy cannot be accomplished by any single institution alone. It requires governments, financial institutions, businesses, and society to move in unison. I hope this book inspires broader collaboration and shared commitment among policymakers, academics, financial institutions, and the public to building an Indonesia that is resilient, competitive, and sustainable—for this generation and the generations to come.

Bank Indonesia
Jakarta, Indonesia

Perry Warjiyo

# Senior Deputy Governor's Remarks

Indonesia's experience highlights that financial stability and sustainability are most durable when growth is inclusive. An inclusive economy and financial system ensure that the transition toward a more sustainable development model benefits not only large firms and financial institutions, but also MSMEs, local enterprises, and communities across the archipelago. By expanding access to finance, strengthening financial literacy, and promoting participation in formal markets, inclusive finance reduces structural vulnerabilities while supporting social cohesion and environmental responsibility.

Indonesia has made progress in strengthening the resilience of its financial system while advancing a more inclusive and sustainable economic and financial landscape. Through sustained reforms in banking, financial market deepening, and digitalization, Indonesia's financial system has become more stable, adaptive, and better equipped to support long-term and sustainable economic growth. This resilience has helped safeguard macroeconomic stability, maintain confidence, and enable the financial system to allocate resources more effectively toward productive and sustainable activities.

In my role, I have had the opportunity to engage directly with markets and communities throughout Indonesia, and I have seen how inclusive and sustainable finance can transform resilience into opportunity. When banking and financial markets support MSMEs and local innovators in adopting sustainable business practices, integrating into value chains, and managing risks, they contribute to stronger productivity, more resilient supply chains, and a greener growth trajectory. Embedding sustainability considerations into financial intermediation is therefore essential to ensure that growth remains robust, balanced, and future-oriented in support of achieving Golden Indonesia 2045.

This book offers timely insights into how Indonesia can further align financial system development with sustainability and inclusivity objectives. By embedding environmental, social, and governance (ESG) principles into banking, markets, and policy frameworks, Indonesia can mobilize finance in ways that strengthen financial system resilience, support inclusive economic participation, and advance a just and sustainable growth path. We must ensure that the financial system serves the people—elevating competitiveness, enhancing social welfare, and safeguarding the environment—so that economic progress translates into shared prosperity and long-term well-being.

I thank the authors for their valuable contributions to this important book. May it serve as a reference, a source of inspiration, and a catalyst for collective action. Building a sustainable economy and financial system is not a task for tomorrow; it is a responsibility we must embrace today. I trust that the ideas presented here will enrich our collective efforts to build a resilient, competitive, and inclusive Indonesian economy, and I am confident that Indonesia will chart a pathway of sustainability and inclusivity that strengthens both our economy and the well-being of our people.

> Let's build a future that is not only green—but just.
> Not only fast—but fair.
> Not only transformative—but inclusive.
>
> *—António Guterres, Secretary-General of the United Nations*

Bank Indonesia
Jakarta, Indonesia

Destry Damayanti

# Foreword

In the dynamic landscape of modern economics, the pursuit of economic growth and short-term profit is unsustainable given finite resources. Natural disasters, degradation of nature, poverty trap, and social unrest are among the problems in the economy that runs with business-as-usual mode. Dealing with this, the definition of economic resilience is constantly evolving. It is no longer sufficient to view stability solely through the lens of financial metrics. The utility can not only be measured by monetary gain, but also the ability to sustain the monetary gain and social welfare in the long term. We are increasingly called to understand resilience as a holistic capacity—the ability of a nation to thrive amid structural shifts, environmental challenges, and the imperative for social equity.

It is with this spirit of inquiry and dedication that the Bank Indonesia Institute presents *Sustainable Economy: The Indonesian Pathways.*

This volume serves as a dedicated effort to map out the practical terrain of sustainable development. It seeks to ground our economic journey in a framework that prioritizes justice and shared prosperity, translating high-level ideas into actionable strategies for the nation. This work humbly attempts to chart a course that upholds these values while addressing the tangible realities of our economic landscape.

While the inspiration for this pathway is rooted in the ideals of inclusivity, the execution requires rigorous structural transformation. The essays contained herein explore how Indonesia can navigate the complex intersection of green growth, technological transition, and demographic change. The authors, led by the insights of Dr. Solikin M. Juhro (Assistant Governor and the Head of Macroprudential Policy Department of Bank Indonesia) and his co-editors, move beyond theoretical aspirations to offer concrete perspectives on how policy can foster an economy that is not only strong but also enduring and kind to its environment.

At the Bank Indonesia Institute, we view our role not merely as a repository of knowledge, but as a facilitator of the intellectual dialogue necessary for national progress. We recognize that the challenges ahead—from climate change to global fragmentation—are immense. Therefore, we offer this book not as a final answer, but as a modest contribution to a much larger, collective effort. It is an invitation to policymakers, academics, and practitioners to think deeply about how we can build an economy that serves the present without compromising the future.

We extend our deepest gratitude to the editors for their intellectual rigor and to the diverse contributors who have lent their voices to this volume. It is our sincere hope that these pages provide a spark for further discussion and action, guiding Indonesia toward a pathway that is as sustainable as it is prosperous.

Bank Indonesia Institute
Jakarta, Indonesia

Clarita Ligaya Iskandar

# Deputy Governor's Remarks

Indonesia has made significant progress in embedding sustainability within its economic and financial architecture. What began as a forward-looking initiative has evolved into a coherent agenda that is reshaping how the financial system manages risks, allocates capital, and supports structural transformation. Sustainability is no longer a peripheral consideration; it is becoming an organizing principle that guides how we build resilience, foster inclusive growth, and prepare the economy for future challenges.

In this evolving landscape, the financial sector holds a strategic role. Banks, capital markets, and financial intermediaries are no longer only providers of liquidity and stability, they are critical enablers of transformation. By mobilizing finance toward productive, green, and inclusive activities, the financial system strengthens economic fundamentals while supporting long-term national development objectives. This requires not only stronger risk management, but also a mindset that views sustainability as an opportunity to innovate, diversify, and enhance competitiveness.

Meaningful progress has already been made. Regulatory direction is clearer, sustainable financial instruments are developing, and risk management frameworks are becoming more forward-looking. Yet the journey ahead demands more: stronger implementation, credible data and analytics, deeper market capacity, and tighter policy coordination so that financial policy moves in step with national development priorities, the energy transition, and structural reforms.

Against this backdrop, Sustainable Economy: The Indonesian Pathways arrives at a timely moment. This volume offers a thoughtful synthesis of ideas, evidence, and policy reflections that enrich our understanding of sustainability from multiple dimensions: economic, financial, social, and institutional. It highlights not only the complexity of the transition, but also the pathways through which Indonesia can move forward with confidence, coherence, and pragmatism.

Ultimately, the message is clear: sustainability and stability must reinforce each other. A forward-looking financial system strengthens resilience while enabling progress; financing renewable energy and innovation, empowering micro, small, and medium enterprises, broadening inclusion, and supporting sectors that build long-term productivity. In doing so, finance becomes not only a guardian of stability, but also a driver of transformation.

I hope this work will inform thinking, sharpen policy execution, and encourage deeper collaboration among policymakers, financial institutions, academics, and the wider community. Let us continue to build a financial system that is resilient, competitive, and firmly aligned with Indonesia's sustainable development aspirations.

Bank Indonesia
Jakarta, Indonesia

Juda Agung

# Preface

*Sustainable Economy: The Indonesian Pathways* explores sustainable economic development through integrated theoretical and policy perspectives, addressing growth challenges, climate risks, energy transition, and inclusivity in Indonesia's development path. It highlights the need to redefine economic development and finance to achieve Golden Indonesia 2045, emphasizing inclusive growth, climate-resilient policies, and institutional strengthening. By combining empirical analysis, policy strategies, and accessible discussion, the book shows that growth, stability, and inclusivity are mutually reinforcing, underscoring the importance of policy coherence, institutional credibility, and a just transition in delivering durable welfare gains and sustainability.

The completion of this book stands as a testament to the collective dedication, intellectual rigor, and shared vision of numerous individuals and institutions committed to shaping a resilient future for Indonesia. This volume would not have been possible without the profound support and guidance of many to whom we owe our deepest gratitude.

First and foremost, we extend our sincere appreciation to Dr. Perry Warjiyo, Governor of Bank Indonesia, for his visionary leadership and for entrusting us with the mandate to explore the complex intersections of stability and sustainability. His opening remarks set the tone for this book, reminding us that our pursuit of a sustainable economy is not merely a strategic choice, but a necessity for the welfare of future generations. We are also deeply grateful to Mrs. Destry Damayanti, Senior Deputy Governor of Bank Indonesia, for her steadfast leadership and invaluable perspectives in advancing policy coherence, financial system resilience, and inclusivity. We are equally grateful to Dr. Juda Agung, Deputy Governor of Bank Indonesia (2022–2026), whose insights on the strategic role of the financial sector in driving the green transition, enhancing productivity, and contributing to economic growth have significantly enriched the narrative of this publication. We wish to express our heartfelt thanks to Ms. Clarita Ligaya Iskandar, Head of the Bank Indonesia Institute, for her unwavering support and for fostering an environment where intellectual dialogue can thrive.

This book is the fruit of intense collaboration among a diverse group of experts whose intellectual backgrounds and ability to synthesize rich economic theories and empirical insights with practical policy applications were instrumental in bringing this volume to fruition. To the authors and contributors—ranging from policymakers and researchers at Bank Indonesia, the Ministry of Finance of the Republic of Indonesia, the Indonesia Financial Services Authority (Otoritas Jasa Keuangan/OJK), the Ministry of National Development Planning of the Republic of Indonesia (Badan Perencanaan Pembangunan Nasional/Bappenas), the National Research and Innovation Agency (BRIN), as well as distinguished academics from the University of Indonesia, Airlangga University (Surabaya), and Lambung Mangkurat University (Banjarmasin)—we extend our sincere gratitude for your expertise, time, and critical perspectives. Your contributions have ensured that this book offers not only theoretical frameworks, but also actionable pathways for Indonesia's development.

Finally, we would like to express our deepest gratitude to our families for their unwavering support, patience, and understanding throughout the long hours of research, writing, and revision, which provided the personal strength required to complete this work. We extend special recognition to Ms. Ragil Pri Hartati and Ms. Ave for their crucial support in coordinating the arrangements for the book's completion. We also gratefully acknowledge the quiet but essential support of our colleagues at Bank Indonesia. It is our shared hope that this volume serves not as a final conclusion, but as a spark for continued collaboration and collective action toward a Golden Indonesia 2045—one that is prosperous, inclusive, and enduringly sustainable.

Jakarta Pusat, Indonesia
January 9, 2026

Solikin M. Juhro
Cicilia Anggadewi Harun
Arnita Rishanty
Danny Hermawan

# Contents

# Contributors

**Arlyana Abubakar** Bank Indonesia, Jakarta, Indonesia

**Donni Fajar Anugrah** Bank Indonesia, Jakarta, Indonesia

**Bambang Arianto** Bank Indonesia, Jakarta, Indonesia

**Prayudhi Azwar** Bank Indonesia, Jakarta, Indonesia

**Salman Fathoni** Bank Indonesia, Jakarta, Indonesia

**Bayu Arie Fianto** Universitas Airlangga, Surabaya, Indonesia

**Djoni Hartono** Universitas Indonesia, Jakarta, Indonesia

**Cicilia Anggadewi Harun** Bank Indonesia, Jakarta, Indonesia

**Danny Hermawan** Bank Indonesia, Jakarta, Indonesia

**Muhammad Handry Imansyah** Universitas Lambung Mangkurat, Kalimantan, Indonesia

**Solikin M. Juhro** Bank Indonesia, Jakarta, Indonesia

**Dhaha Praviandi Kuantan** Bank Indonesia, Jakarta, Indonesia

**Anastuty Kusumowardhani** Bank Indonesia, Jakarta, Indonesia

**Dong Li** University of Liverpool, Liverpool, England

**Charvin Lim** Bank Indonesia, Jakarta, Indonesia

**Satwika Lulu** Bank Indonesia, Jakarta, Indonesia

**Unang Mulkhan** Universitas Lampung, Bandar Lampung, Indonesia

**Muzdalifah** Universitas Lambung Mangkurat, Kalimantan, Indonesia

**Mohammad Marza Naufal** Universitas Indonesia, Jakarta, Indonesia

**Rio Novandra** National Research and Innovation Agency of Indonesia (BRIN), Jakarta, Indonesia

**Ratna Oktriyani** Bank Indonesia, Jakarta, Indonesia

**Riris Shanti Fransiska Pardede** Bank Indonesia, Jakarta, Indonesia

**Titi Muswati Putranti** Universitas Indonesia, Jakarta, Indonesia

**Heru Rahadyan** Bank Indonesia, Jakarta, Indonesia

**Ramdani** Bank Indonesia, Jakarta, Indonesia

**Henry Rialdi** Financial Services Authority (OJK), Jakarta, Indonesia

**Masagus M. Ridhwan** Bank Indonesia, Jakarta, Indonesia

**Arnita Rishanty** Bank Indonesia, Jakarta, Indonesia

**Irman Robinson** Bank Indonesia, Jakarta, Indonesia

**Amanda Sarina Rumbaf** Financial Services Authority (OJK), Jakarta, Indonesia

**Maxensius Tri Sambodo** National Research and Innovation Agency of Indonesia (BRIN), Jakarta, Indonesia

**Joko Siswanto** Financial Services Authority (OJK), Jakarta, Indonesia

**Egi Suarga** World Resources Institute, Jakarta, Indonesia

**Gerry Pramudya Sulaiman** Ministry of Finance (Kemenkeu), Jakarta, Indonesia

**Jarot Suroyo** Financial Services Authority (OJK), Jakarta, Indonesia

**Asep Suryahadi** The SMERU Research Institute, Jakarta, Indonesia

**Ferry Syarifuddin** Bank Indonesia, Jakarta, Indonesia

**Evie Sylviani** Bank Indonesia, Jakarta, Indonesia

**Jati Waluyo** Bank Indonesia, Jakarta, Indonesia

**Rizky Wibisono** World Resources Institute, Jakarta, Indonesia

**Prama Wiratama** Ministry of Finance (Kemenkeu), Jakarta, Indonesia

**Yuki Yasarani** Financial Services Authority (OJK), Jakarta, Indonesia

**Vivi Yulaswati** The Ministry of National Development Planning (BAPPENAS), Jakarta, Indonesia

# Part I
# Perspective of Sustainable Economic Development

# Chapter 1
# A Sustainable Economy: Key Perspectives

**Solikin M. Juhro**

**Abstract** This introductory chapter explores key perspectives of sustainable economy, covering the context of issues, opportunities, and challenges. It also provides in-depth salient theoretical insights into the importance of pursuing sustainable growth and prosperity, including synthesizing recent theoretical developments that have placed environmental sustainability as a key driver of long-term growth. From a more tactical perspective, global and national campaigns—supported by institutional strengthening and joint efforts from all stakeholders, including the government, financial sector authorities, and the public—are critical aspects in delivering sustainable economic development.

**Keywords** Sustainable economy · Sustainable economic development · SDGs

## 1 Opportunities and Challenges

Over the past three decades we have witnessed significant changes in the global economic-social landscape. Indiscriminately blighting advanced and emerging economies alike, economic and financial crises have prompted further exploration of more suitable, stronger economic concepts and systems. Economic development has hitherto failed to manifest a significant impact on poverty alleviation and social inequality, thus fostering the application of an economic and development strategy approach that prioritises inclusive welfare. In line with these changes, global development priorities have steadily shifted towards addressing sustainable economic issues. The global initiative of the Millennium Development Goals (MDGs), followed by the Sustainable Development Goals (SDGs), is a response to the failure of the outdated trickle-down theory approach to development. The MDG/SDG approach employs a modern development style with a direct impact on achieving poverty alleviation targets, reducing inequality, environmentally responsible, and

S. M. Juhro (✉)
Bank Indonesia, Jakarta, Indonesia
e-mail: solikin@bi.go.id



S. M. Juhro et al. (eds.), *Sustainable Economy: The Indonesian Pathways*,
https://doi.org/10.1007/978-981-92-1215-6_1

ameliorating welfare for all through economic empowerment and financial inclusion programmes (microfinance).

Literally, a sustainable economy is a system of economic practices that promotes long-term growth and well-being without depleting natural resources or causing social or environmental harm. It is a strategic approach that seeks to balance profitability, innovation, and success with broader societal and ecological goals. The concept of a sustainable economy is rooted in the broader framework of sustainable development, first popularized by the 1987 Brundtland Report (Brundtland Commission, 1987). It moves beyond short-term profit motives to consider the long-term impact of economic activity on all stakeholders and the planet.

A sustainable economy is represented by three interrelated pillars or dimensions, namely economic sustainability, environmental sustainability, and social sustainability (United Nation, 2025a). Economic sustainability primarily refers to achieving long-term economic growth and involves transitioning away from unsustainable practices and creating an economic system that is resilient to shocks. Environmental sustainability primarily refers to efforts to conserve natural resources, protect ecosystems, and minimize pollution for the benefit of future generations. Meanwhile, social sustainability primarily refers to efforts to promote social well-being and equity by providing fair employment practices, reducing poverty, and ensuring equal access to resources and opportunities. A sustainable economy, therefore, is not about halting growth, but about redefining growth so it improves quality of life, protects ecosystems, and ensures opportunities for future generations.

Achieving a sustainable economy provides several opportunities or benefits, such as significant economic growth and innovation from green jobs and new markets, social progress through improved health, equity, and well-being, and environmental protection via resource conservation and climate actions. These interconnected opportunities also create more resilient organizations, stronger communities, and a more stable future for everyone. Together, they cultivate innovation, investment, job creation, resilience, and global leadership, while ensuring fairness and environmental protection; and thus create a balanced foundation for long-term welfare and resilience (Hermundsdottir and Aspelund, 2022; Hill, 2025).

Achieving a sustainable economy, however, requires profound changes in technology, infrastructure, legislation, markets, behavior, and the underlying institutions and values. Slowly evolving, long-term sustainability issues affecting many people and the entire world are ultimately becoming megatrends that require serious attention in policy discussions. The main megatrend of a sustainable economy involves a fundamental shift away from traditional, resource-intensive economic models towards a more sustainable system driven by accelerated green transitions (like renewable energy and circular economies), stronger regulations and reporting standards, technological innovation (including AI for sustainability), a focus on social responsibility and human rights, and adapting to broader societal shifts like climate change and population dynamics (Nikula and Honkonen, 2024; Loughlin, 2025). The journey towards sustainability is ultimately a shared endeavor, requiring collective actions from governments, businesses, communities, and individuals/societies.

While it is understandable that achieving a sustainable economy requires efforts that are not easy, balancing economic, environmental, and social sustainability is another story. Balancing economic, environmental, and social sustainability is challenging due to inherent conflicts between short-term gains and long-term goals, competing interests and power imbalances, a lack of awareness of interconnectedness, significant investment costs for sustainable transitions, complex progress measurement, and the widespread prevalence of issues such as poverty, inequality, and climate change, which require an integrated and comprehensive approach to address (Vivien, 2023; Asghar et al., 2024; Lee et al., 2023).

In line with this view, institutional strengthening is crucial for achieving sustainable economic development consistently, inclusively, and resiliently. Without strong institutions, sustainable policies often remain at the level of discourse or planning documents, and are difficult to implement consistently due to conflicts of interest and a lack of long-term commitment. Several views have been expressed regarding the importance of institutional aspects, namely those related to political harmony and cooperation, in supporting sustainable economic development (Kaiwa, 2012; Singh, 2012; and Shirakawa, 2010). In other words, institutional aspects can be another dimension of sustainability, beyond economic, environmental, and social sustainability. This is in line with the thesis of Acemoglu and Robinson (2012) which emphasizes that strengthening economic and political institutions, carried out inclusively, is the foundation for a nation's success in achieving prosperity.

Ultimately, achieving a truly ideal sustainable economy is difficult, but moving in a better direction is entirely possible. In other words, while an ideal state may be elusive, moving toward a more realistic and progressive sustainable economy is certainly possible, and can be achieved gradually. These challenges require an integrated approach, one that takes into account policy innovations, technological advances, and social support mechanisms; and collaboration between governments, businesses, and community to create inclusive strategies that balance economic growth with social and environmental sustainability. International cooperation also plays a crucial role in overcoming technological and financial constraints, particularly for developing countries. It is important to note that a one-size-fits-all approach to sustainable development may not be adequate to address the unique cultural, economic, and geographic contexts of developing countries.

## 2 Salient Theoretical Perspectives

Sustainable economic development has a strong foothold in economic theory. It is rooted in classical, neoclassical, endogenous and welfare economic theories, and has evolved through integration with environmental and ecological economics. Sustainability itself can be seen as the evolution of welfare economics when we extend its scope across time, equity, and the environment. Therefore, it is not a stand-alone theory, but rather an evolution of economic theory that adapts to sustainability issues. In this context, established economic growth theories generally provide frameworks to understand long-run prosperity. However, their treatment of sustainability differs significantly.

It is generally understood that in the long run, a country's economic growth depends on total factor productivity, which in turn is determined by the rate of technological progress. One of the prominent early thoughts as put forward by J.A. Schumpeter (1934), who viewed innovation as the main factor driving economic growth with entrepreneurs as the actors. The existence of innovation has several influences, including innovation causing the introduction of new technology, bringing greater profits and the existence of innovation will then be followed by a process of imitation of new technology. The foundation of economic growth theory became stronger with the emergence of the neo-classical view, explained that economic growth is influenced by the growth of production factors (population, labor and capital accumulation) and the level of technological progress (Solow, 1956; Swan, 1956).

While classical and neo-classical models focus on capital accumulation and technological progress (i.e. exogenous growth models), more recent frameworks incorporate innovation, human capital, and environmental considerations, such as endogenous growth models and green endogenous growth models. A more recent framework, namely the Endogenous Growth Models (EGMs)—developed in the 1980s–1990s, explains long-run growth as driven by factors within the economy—such as human capital, knowledge, R&D, and innovation—rather than just external technological shocks (Romer, 1994; Romer, 1986; Lucas, 1988).

Does it address sustainability issues? The answer is partially, but not fully. On one hand, the EGMs portrait the relevance of growth strategic drivers to sustainability. The model highlights how knowledge creation, education, and technological progress drive growth. These mechanisms are directly relevant to green technologies, renewable energy, and eco-innovation, which are crucial for sustainability. The model also suggests that government policies (like R&D subsidies, education investment, or carbon pricing) can influence long-term growth paths, which aligns with sustainability strategies. However, the EGMs still pose some limitations, as it generally focuses on growth drivers but rarely on social inclusion, inequality, or intergenerational equity, which are central to sustainability. It also ignores natural capital and negative externalities.

Amidst these limitations, the EGMs core framework is still very useful for sustainability when extended to include environmental factors and policy interventions. In this context, the EGMs can be adapted for sustainable development by incorporating environmental factors into their core concepts of human capital, innovation, and knowledge accumulation. These models can demonstrate how policies promoting green technologies, resource efficiency, and pollution reduction can foster economic growth while minimizing environmental degradation. By treating the environment as a form of "natural capital" that can regenerate, these models provide a framework for understanding and achieving sustainable growth that decouples economic progress from irreversible environmental harm.

The Green Endogenous Growth Models (GEGMs) are economic frameworks that extend endogenous growth theory to include environmental sustainability by integrating factors such as green innovation, environmental quality, and population green behavior into the dynamics of economic growth. These models demonstrate how innovation can drive economic expansion and environmental improvement, leading to conditions for sustainable growth. Green endogenous growth models offer a comprehensive framework, showing how innovation, policy, and environmental resources can interact to support long-run sustainable growth (Zhou et al., 2023; Wan et al., 2018; Aghion et al., 2025). Thus, the evolution of growth theory reflects a shift from growth at all costs toward a sustainability-oriented paradigm, aligning more closely with global challenges like climate change and the Sustainable Development Goals (SDGs).

Viewed from a broader perspective, the three-sustainability dimensions—growth, inclusion, and environmental—are necessary, but not sufficient to optimize welfare. To truly optimize welfare, additional dimensions beyond the three are needed, namely institutional quality and well-being. Institutional quality requires transparent and accountable practices to ensure the effective use of resources. Welfare also depends on health, education, security, dignity, cultural values, and social trust. In this context, therefore, we need a broader, multidimensional approach to capture the full picture of human welfare.

The state of welfare should therefore be both improving and inclusive, with every effort of public and government policy directed toward enhancing welfare in all its dimensions, which are vital for the continuity of life. The realisation of the desired welfare, therefore, is not "pareto" (non-Pareto optimal) in nature. Non-Pareto optimal condition implies that the achievement or improvement of a person's welfare will not reduce the welfare of others; in contrast to the Pareto optimal condition, where the improvement in the welfare of a person or group will certainly reduce the welfare of other people or groups. This spirit of inclusive welfare is basically inherent to Islamic teachings and laws (sharia), which strongly encourage adherents to live in global prosperity, fairly and equitably, in this life and the hereafter in accordance with wisdom, or main purposes of human creation. The spirit of inclusive welfare is indeed in line with the goal of sustainable development (Juhro et al., 2025).

## 3 Global and National Campaign on Sustainability

Sustainable economy serves as a key strategy and a practical framework for achieving sustainable development by integrating balanced economic growth, environmental protection, and social well-being into economic activities and policies. Sustainable development is therefore not a single pathway, but a multi-dimensional approach that integrates economic progress, environmental stewardship, and social equity. Achieving this vision requires collective action by governments, businesses, communities, and individuals to ensure prosperity today while safeguarding the future. At the same time, the world faces increasingly complex and interconnected challenges across the economic, environmental, and political spheres. For decades, the global community has sought universal and integrated solutions to address critical issues such as poverty, hunger, poor health, climate change, and biodiversity loss.

Global campaigns have been pursued to foster sustainable development, as reflected in the Millennium Development Goals (MDGs). The MDGs comprised eight international development goals for 2015, established at the Millennium Summit of the United Nations in 2000 following the adoption of the United Nations Millennium Declaration. As challenges grew more onerous, the international community continued the momentum of the MDGs, which concluded in 2015, by launching a new initiative: the Sustainable Development Goals (SDGs). The SDGs are a framework of 17 interlinked global goals set by the United Nations General Assembly in 2015, involving 193 member states and civil societies globally, known as the 2030 Agenda. The SDGs provide a common framework for all countries to achieve a more peaceful, prosperous, and sustainable future for all, by ensuring that no one is left behind in development (United Nation, 2025b).

Global progress on the Sustainable Development Goals (SDGs) remains below expectations, with the UN estimating that less than 20% of the targets will be achieved by 2030. While there have been successes in areas such as poverty alleviation and electricity access, these gains have been hampered by challenges, particularly following the Covid-19 pandemic. Despite these obstacles, the SDGs continue to serve as a relevant reference point for development across countries, as they provide a clear, inclusive, and measurable roadmap for building a world that is prosperous, fair, and environmentally sustainable. By linking local actions with global outcomes, ensuring that development today does not compromise the well-being of future generations. Achieving a sustainable economy is therefore central to the SDGs because it requires balancing economic progress with social equity and environmental protection. Moreover, the concept of a sustainable economy is cross-cutting within the SDG framework, serving not only as a goal in itself but also as an enabler of the entire Agenda.

It is worth noting that the key to achieving sustainable economy also lies on accelerating the scale-up of sustainable finance. Despite the significant role central banks play in fostering sustainable economic development, a robust framework to guide the integration of central bank policy with environmental considerations is still lacking. The main mandate or responsibility of most central banks worldwide is to maintain low and stable inflation in both the short to longer term, as well as to safeguard financial stability. Over the past three decades, however, there has been a notable shift in how academics and central bankers view the role of central banks in addressing several issues "beyond stability", particularly those related to sustainable development and climate change. Many central banks now pursue 'implicit' goals to support sustainable economic growth, i.e. through regulations that promote sustainable development financing (Juhro, 2025).

The issue of welfare and economic sustainability is inseparable from the role of central banks in fulfilling their mandate to achieve and maintain price and financial system stability, while also addressing related concerns such as economic growth, full employment and income equality, and environmental/climate change challenges. Throughout the evolution of modern central banking, there has often been a conflict between the role of maintaining stability and that of promoting growth. However, strong empirical evidence suggests that central banks should not neglect their role in fostering economic growth. Demand-side management (short term) must be integrated with supply-side management (medium to long term) to address structural challenges. From a policy perspective, stability should therefore be understood in the broader context of supporting sustainable economic growth—in other words, stability for sustainability. This requires central banks to design and implement policies in a more complex and forward-looking manner to ensure national objectives are met.

Indonesia has been actively engaged in the Sustainable Development Goals (SDGs) initiative since its adoption in 2015, as reflected in the Indonesian SDGs Roadmap toward 2030 (Bappenas, 2021). This engagement demonstrates both commitment and the challenges of implementation as a developing, archipelagic nation with diverse economic and social conditions. Indonesia's progress in SDGs has been notable among upper-middle-income countries: by 2024, approximately 61.4% of the targets had been achieved. With these achievements, Indonesia is in a progressive position and has the highest commitment and achievement in Asia for the SDGs targets, ranking seventh globally. Despite this progress, Indonesia continues to face major challenges, particularly in financing the 2030 SDGs targets, as the post-pandemic period has left a substantial funding gap (Bappenas, 2025).

Collaboration and joint efforts from all stakeholders—including the government, financial sector authorities (Bank Indonesia and the Financial Services Authority/ Otoritas Jasa Keuangan), and the wider public—are essential to achieving the 2030 targets. The Indonesian Government has adopted a range of national strategies to support SDGs implementation, embedding them in the National Medium-Term Development Plan (RPJMN) and strengthening cross-sectoral coordination. The SDGs are also aligned with Nawa Cita and Indonesia's Vision 2045, ensuring that economic development in Indonesia is pursued not only through growth, but also through social inclusion and environmental sustainability. These efforts reinforce with Indonesia's commitment to solution-based action in response to global disruptions, ranging from climate change and financial crises to geopolitical conflicts and technological divides.

Ultimately, the pursuit of sustainable development and SDGs attainment in Indonesia must be mutually reinforcing. The SDGs provide a global framework to guide the country in navigating sustainability challenges, while Indonesia's own development path represents the concrete, localized implementation of that vision, tailored to the national context, regional potential, and domestic constraints. In other words, the SDGs are the roadmap, while Indonesia's sustainable development is the journey. Indonesia aims to become a developed country with high per capita income by 2045; therefore, Indonesia must pursue an integrated strategy for sustainable economic growth that remains adaptive to global developments.

## 4 About This book

### *4.1 Structure*

Various explanations and dynamics concerning sustainability issues as mentioned above require deeper discussion. As such, it is essential to know in greater details, among others, on broader perspectives of sustainable economic development (both theory and policy), climate change and green economy, energy transition and inclusivity, and integrated national policy strategy.

As with any book integrating various essays, the exploration of this book's substance is quite extensive. Therefore, the structure of each essay's discussion is also relatively rich; it covers not only the context of the problems that arise, but also the theories and concepts underlying the assessment, both qualitatively and quantitatively. Several policy challenges, in-depth explotrations in the form of benchmarking, and empirical results also enrich the discussion, although all attempts are made to be presented in a more accessible or more popular language. Policy implications and future development and directions conclude each chapter.

The first few chapters in part one of the book explore the achievement of Golden Indonesia 2045 which require a redefinition of economic development and finance. Part two examines how climate risks—both transition risks and physical risks—can disrupt economic activities, weaken industrial resilience, and increase the vulnerability of the financial system. These conditions demand a transformation of central bank policies to integrate the central bank's policy mix with climate policy responses. Thus, later discussed on Part three of the book that highlights the justice dimension in the energy transition (just transition), which relates to the need for sectoral orchestration of sustainable economic development and the opportunities for green jobs. Part four outlines the national economic policy strategies required to strengthen the foundations of Indonesia's sustainable economy and finance. All the contents of the book will be summarized into a comprehensive set of lessons learned in the epilogue.

### *4.2 Goals*

Literature concerning the sustainable economy is incomplete, particularly concerning policy perspectives, enriched with the perspective of the Indonesian economy and implementation therein, making this a highly anticipated book. Therefore, there are three overarching goals associated with publishing this book.

*First*, academically, to generate frontier thinking and stimulate scientific development, while providing teaching materials concerning materials on sustainable economic development from a broad perspective, including theory and policy. Thus, the book is expected to enrich reference materials on sustainable economics as teaching material for lecturers and students, particularly postgraduate students studying macroeconomics, development economics, and public policy.

*Second*, from a policy perspective, to enrich the discussion and support public policy innovation. To that end, the book identifies the challenges, opportunities and recommendations concerning the direction of economic development policy. This book provides comprehensive understanding concerning the policy theories and practices in sustainability issues based on the aspects of philosophy, economic role, institutions, instruments, regulations and infrastructure as well as the implications or impact on the economy.

*Third*, from a practical standpoint, to contribute and complement current understanding concerning the application and purview of sustainable economy, including popular topics such as the SDGs, climate change, circular economy, and related policy strategy. Therefore, this book is a vehicle to increase understanding and insight for practitioners, stakeholders and regulators.

Based on those goals and contributions, the scope of target readers is broad, including tertiary students, regulators, practitioners, business players and all related stakeholders.

## 5 Closing

In closing, this is a living document. The authors are aware that the material in this book will be adjusted to current needs and developments over time in terms of public policy practices and recommendations from readers and teachers in line with the issues developing in the public space and academic community. To that end, comments, recommendations and suggestions from the readers are warmly welcomed to help hone the contents of this book. Hopefully, this book not only meets the needs of readers wishing to obtain deeper understanding concerning the salient aspects of sustainability but also expands our scientific knowledge.

## References

Acemoglu, Daron and Robert A. Robonson (2012), *Why Nations Fail: The Origins Of Power, Prosperity and Poverty*, Crown Archetype, a division of Random House, Inc.

Aghion, P., Boppart, T., Peters, M., Schwartzman, M., and Zilibotti, F. (2025), A Theory of Endogenous Degrowth and Environmental Sustainability, NBER Working Paper 33634, Issue Date 2025, https://doi.org/10.3386/w33634

Asghar, M., Leghari, S., Ullah, S., and Nobanee, H. (2024), Balancing environmental sustainability: Socio-economic drivers and policy pathways in oil-importing nations, *Energy Strategy Reviews*,Volume 55, September.

Bappenas (2021) Peta Jalan Tujuan Pembangunan Berkelanjutan 2023–2030, October.

Bappenas (2025), Voluntary National Review (VNR) of the Republic of Indonesia 2025 Indonesia's 2025, June.

Brundtland Commission (1987), Brundtland Report, the United Nations and the Oxford University Press, October, ISBN: 019282080X

Hill, L.G. (2025), Economic Sustainability: Benefits & Challenges Explained, GREEner Insight, Updated on July 10.

Hermundsdottir, F. and Aspelund, A. (2022), Competitive sustainable manufacturing - Sustainability strategies, environmental and social innovations, and their effects on firm performance, Journal of Cleaner Production, Volume 370, October.Jinda, Priya (2025), 'Economic, social, and environmental aspects of sustainable development-direct and indirect effects on business practices", *Greening Our Economy for a Sustainable Future.* Science of Sustainable Systems, 2025, Pages 227-240

Juhro, S.M. (2025) 'Future central banking in emerging market economies', in *Encyclopedia of Monetary Policy, Financial Markets and Banking*. Elsevier, pp. 189–198. Available at: https://doi.org/10.1016/B978-0-44-313776-1.00118-5

Juhro, S.M., Syarifuddin, F., & Sakti, Ali (2025), *Inclusive Welfare: On The Role of Islamic Social-Public Finance and Monetary Economics,* Springer Publishing. Available at: https://doi.org/10.1007/978-981-96-0051-9

Kaiwa, Masahiro (2012), "Asia's Sustainable Economic Development", A Keynote Address at USM-AUT International Conference 2012 "Sustainable Economic Development: Policies and Strategies" Penang, November.

Lee, M., Stinson, D. D., and Ma, Lina (2023), The Challenge of Balancing Economic Sustainability with Environmental Sustainability, *International Journal of Strategic Management* 23(1):64-77. https://doi.org/10.18374/IJSM-23-1.7

Loughlin, Bronagh (2025), Sustainability trends 2025 shaping the future of business, Institute of Sustainability Studies, January.

Lucas, R.E.J. (1988), On the mechanics of economic development, Journal of Monetary Economy, 22, 3–42.

Nikula, M., and Honkonen, E. (2024), Megatrend: The Crumbling of the Economic System – Towards a More Sustainable Future, *Blic analyst,* Oct.

Romer, P. M. (1994), The Origins of Endogenous Growth, *Journal of Economic Perspectives*, vol. 8, no. 1, Winter 1994.

Romer, P. M. (1986). Increasing returns and long-run growth, *Journal of Political Economy*, 94, 1002–1037.

Schumpeter, J. (1934). *The Theory of Economic Development.* Cambridge, MA: Harvard University Press

Shirakawa, Masaaki (2010), Future of Central Banks and Central Banking, speech on International Conference, hosted by the Institute for Monetary and Economic Studies, Bank of Japan, Tokyo, May.

Singh, Sukhdave (2012), "Role of Central Banks in Supporting Growth in a Low Growth Environment", The SEACEN-CeMCoA/BOJ High-level Seminar on "Finding Asia's New Sustainable Growth Model Post GFC: The Role of Central Banks", Kuala Lumpur, November.

Solow, R.M. (1956). A contribution to the theory of economic growth. Quarterly Journal of Economics. 70. 65–94.

Swan, T.W. (1956). Economic growth and capital accumulation. Economic Record. 32: 334–61.

United Nation (2025a), The Sustainable Development Goals, Available at: https://www.un.org/sustainabledevelopment/development-goals/

United Nation (2025b), The Sustainable Development Goals, Available at: https://www.un.org/sustainabledevelopment/development-goals/

Vivien, Shuo (2023), Sustainable Development: Balancing Economic Prosperity and Environmental Concerns, *Journal of Economics and Economic Education Research* Volume 24, Issue 4.

Wan, B., Tian, L., Zhu, N., Gu, L., Zhang, G. (2018), A new endogenous growth model for green low-carbon behavior and its comprehensive effects, *Applied Energy*, Volume 230, November.

Zhou, Y., Tian, L., Yang, X. (2023), Schumpeterian endogenous growth model under green innovation and its enculturation effect, *Energy Economics*, November.

# Chapter 2
# Theoretical Foundation of Sustainable Development Goals

**Bayu Arie Fianto and Unang Mulkhan**

**Abstract** This chapter provides a comprehensive review of the theoretical, global, and national foundations underpinning the Sustainable Development Goals (SDGs), situating sustainable development as an integrated paradigm encompassing economic, social, and environmental dimensions. Tracing the historical evolution of sustainability thinking, the chapter highlights how contemporary sustainability governance has emerged through the interaction of science, policy, and institutional reform. It systematically reviews key theoretical frameworks, including the Triple Bottom Line, justice theory, human rights–based and capability approaches, ecological modernization, stakeholder and institutional theories, risk governance, and policy coherence for sustainable development.

**Keywords** Sustainable development goals · Triple bottom line · Sustainability theory · Sustainability history · Global development agenda

## 1 Introduction

### *1.1 History of Sustainable Development*

A common misconception is to equate sustainable development with either ecology or environmentalism. However, these three terms are not interchangeable. Ecology is a scientific discipline within biology, dedicated to the study of natural systems and their interactions. Environmentalism, on the other hand, is a social and political movement. Its focus lies in raising awareness of environmental pollution and advocating for solutions. While environmentalism draws on ecological principles, it is not a branch of ecological science and therefore must be clearly distinguished from it.

B. A. Fianto (✉)
Universitas Airlangga, Surabaya, Indonesia
e-mail: bayu.fianto@feb.unair.ac.id

U. Mulkhan
Universitas Lampung, Bandar Lampung, Indonesia



S. M. Juhro et al. (eds.), *Sustainable Economy: The Indonesian Pathways*,
https://doi.org/10.1007/978-981-92-1215-6_2

Both the rise of ecology as a scientific field and the growing importance of environmental protection studies in the latter half of the twentieth century played a pivotal role in shaping the modern concept of sustainable development. Today, the concept is structured around three interrelated pillars: environmental sustainability, social sustainability, and economic sustainability. None of these pillars can be pursued in isolation; instead, they function together in a dynamic balance. This leads to the question of whether development and sustainability are in conflict. Many scholars equate development primarily with economic growth. According to Romer's endogenous growth theory, knowledge creates a snowball effect in the marketplace of ideas: "The more we know, the easier it gets to discover." His theory emphasizes that economic growth originates within internal systems, where knowledge and innovation serve as the driving forces of a creative economy. In the literature most often the following meanings of the term development are emphasized: (1) development as structural transformation; (2) human development; (3) development of democracy and governance; (4) development as environmental sustainability (Vázquez & Sumner, 2013).

The history of sustainable development grows out of a long-standing realization that what people do can inflict lasting damage on nature. Many writers trace early calls for prudent, long-term stewardship to practices in the Roman Empire or to eighteenth-century forestry, which is often described as the cradle of the idea. By the 1700s in Europe and Japan, foresters recognized the direct link between cutting timber and planting new trees, making forestry one of the first fields to acknowledge the need to manage resources sustainably (Grober, 2007). For nearly two centuries, "sustained yield" served as international forestry's guiding doctrine. Its roots lie in the early European Enlightenment, when German cameralists began planning princely woodlands so they could be handed down to future generations without being diminished (Grober, 2007).

Good stewardship also depends on tracking progress. Indicators help set direction in decision-making and reveal whether development goals are being met. The Compendium of Initiatives Indicators of Sustainable Development listed 669 indicators in 2005 and 836 by 2007, reflecting a rapid expansion of measurement efforts. Because sustainable development is closely linked to ecology, it is often associated with ecological sustainability, understood as maintaining the environmental conditions necessary to support human well-being in both present and future generations (Lélé, 1991). This is a holistic way of thinking. Mainstream theory brings these strands together, viewing sustainable development as social change that pursues familiar development aims while staying within ecological limits (Lélé, 1991). The major milestones that shaped the evolution of sustainable development from the rise of modern environmental awareness to the adoption of the SDGs are summarized in Fig. 2.1.

## The First Period

The history of the sustainable development concept is divided into three periods. The first phase from the classical economic theories of Smith, Marx, Malthus, Ricardo, and Mill, several of whom acknowledged resource constraints and limits

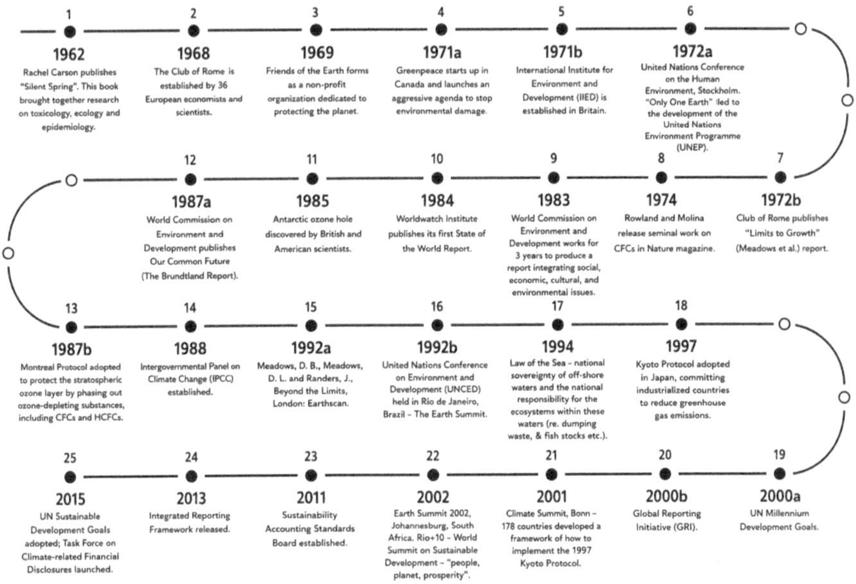


**Fig. 2.1** Timeline of Key Milestones in Sustainable Development (1962–2015)

to development, to the warnings issued by the Club of Rome and the 1972 United Nations Conference on the Human Environment in Stockholm (Mebratu, 1998; Drexhage & Murphy, 2010).

1962 marked the publication of Rachel Carson's Silent Spring, which synthesized toxicology, ecology, and epidemiology to argue that agricultural pesticides were accumulating to catastrophic levels. Carson linked these accumulations to harm in wildlife and human health, puncturing the belief that nature could indefinitely absorb pollutants. By 1968, the Club of Rome had taken shape with 36 European economists and scientists. Aiming to understand the "world problematique" holistically, it commissioned a global study to model interactions among industrial production, population, environmental damage, food consumption, and natural resource use.

The next years, 1969, brought the creation of Friends of the Earth, a non-profit committed to preventing environmental degradation, safeguarding biological, cultural, and ethnic diversity, and empowering citizens to influence decisions affecting environmental quality and human well-being. Two years later, 1971, two milestones stood out: Greenpeace began in Canada, pursuing an assertive strategy of civil protest and non-violent direct action to halt environmental harm; and the International Institute for Environment and Development (IIED) was established in Britain with a mandate to seek ways to make economic progress without destroying the environmental resource base.

The following year, 1972 with the Stockholm conference "Only One Earth", which led to the creation of the United Nations Environment Programme (UNEP). Stockholm also ushered the idea of sustainable development into global discussion;

while it did not fully integrate environment and development, it pressed for shifts in economic development policy (Mebratu, 1998; Drexhage & Murphy, 2010). That same year, the Club of Rome's Limits to Growth became a best seller in several languages that described the use of a computer model World 3 to study the implications of continuing exponential growth in five interconnected trends of global concern: industrialization, population, growth, widespread malnutrition, depletion of non-renewable resources and ecological damage, and the report adopted a pessimistic view of development, warning of severe resource shortages if development were to maintain its current momentum, while being extremely controversial Northern countries criticizing it for not including technological solutions and Southern countries criticizing it because it advocates abandonment of economic development. Mid-decade, 1974 saw Rowland and Molina release seminal work on CFCs in Nature magazine, calculating that if human use of CFC gases was to continue at an unaltered rate the ozone layer would be depleted by many percent after some decades.

## The Second Period

The years following the Stockholm conference make up the second phase of the concept. Terms such as "development and environment," "development without destruction," and "development in accordance with the environment" appeared with growing frequency in the literature, while "eco-development" was first outlined in a 1978 United Nations Environment Programme (UNEP) edition (Mebratu, 1998). Momentum continued into 1983 with the formation of the World Commission on Environment and Development, which spent 3 years crafting a report that wove together social, economic, cultural, and environmental concerns. The Worldwatch Institute's first State of the World (1984) tracked shifts in the global resource base especially their economic implications and concluded that "we are living beyond our means, largely by borrowing against the future." Scientific alarms intensified in 1985 with the discovery of the Antarctic ozone hole by British and American researchers.

The year 1987 delivered two landmarks as the World Commission on Environment and Development published Our Common Future (The Brundtland Report) in response to the request from the UN general assembly to propose long-term environmental strategies for achieving sustainable development by the year 2000, and as the report elaborated, sustainable development is "development that meets the needs of the present without compromising the ability of future generations to meet their own needs," while the Montreal Protocol focused on the depletion of the stratospheric ozone layer and eliminating substances that cause this (HCFCs), was since strengthened twice London and Copenhagen and production of CFCs in the North stopped by 1996 with countries in the South (China and India) to end production by 2006. Shortly thereafter, 1988 established the Inter-Governmental panel on Climate Change, which resulted in the framework convention on climate change signed by 153 countries plus the then EU, dealing with the threat of global warming, and though thought to lack firm agreements on targets, it did aim to stabilise 1990 levels of CO2 and other greenhouse gases.

### The Third Period

The third, "After Brundtland" period extends to the present and opens in 1992, when Meadows, D. B., Meadows, D. L., and Randers, J. released Beyond the Limits. Using a computer model to trace growth patterns, they argued that if trends in world population, industrialization, pollution, food production, and resource depletion were left unchanged, the planet's limits would likely be reached within roughly a century. In parallel, preparatory work that began in 1989 culminated in the United Nations Conference on Environment and Development (UNCED) in Rio de Janeiro, the Earth Summit, where 179 countries sought to reconcile the impacts of human socio-economic activity on the environment, even as environmental concerns were often sidelined in economic decision-making and overall conditions had deteriorated (UNCED, 1992a, b; Mebratu, 1998; Drexhage & Murphy, 2010).

That summit adopted the Rio Declaration on Environment and Development, Agenda 21, a non-legally binding statement of forest principles, the Climate Change Convention, and the Convention on Biological Diversity (UNCED, 1992a, b). Two of these texts proved foundational. The Rio Declaration sets out 27 principles that guide future policy and decision-making, balancing socio-economic development with environmental stewardship, affirming a right to development alongside a duty to protect the environment, and underscoring the need for cooperation among the public sector, private sector, and civil society (UNCED, 1992b). Agenda 21, meanwhile, is a comprehensive global program: 40 chapters of objectives, action plans, and resources that provide detailed guidance for aligning socio-economic development with environmental conservation. It stresses international cooperation and a consensus between development and protection, with governments playing a central role in adopting and implementing policies, plans, and programs while participation from all other stakeholders remains essential.

Progress then moved through a sequence of milestones. The year 1994 affirmed the Law of the Sea national sovereignty over offshore waters and national responsibility for the ecosystems within them (e.g., waste disposal and fish stocks). By 1997, negotiations produced the Kyoto Protocol, committing industrialized economies to limit and reduce greenhouse-gas emissions $CO_2$, $CH_4$, NO, plus three types of fluorinated gases according to agreed targets. The turn of the century brought the UN Millennium Development Goals (eight goals to be achieved by 2015) alongside the Global Reporting Initiative, which set guidelines for public reporting on a firm's economic, environmental, and social impacts. At the heart of sustainable development lie three elements: the concept of development, the concept of needs, and the concept of future generations. The trajectory continued with the 2001 Climate Summit in Bonn, where 178 countries devised a framework for implementing Kyoto; the 2002 World Summit on Sustainable Development in Johannesburg (Rio + 10), framed around "people, planet, prosperity".

The creation of the Sustainability Accounting Standards Board in 2011 to help companies identify, measure, and manage ESG components; the 2013 Integrated Reporting Framework to explain to providers of financial capital how an organization creates, preserves, or erodes value over time; and, in 2015, the UN Sustainable Development Goals a set of 17 interlinked objectives to be achieved by 2030, described as a "blueprint to achieve a sustainable future for all" together with the Task Force on Climate-Related Financial Disclosures, which guides the reporting of the risks and opportunities associated with climate change. Within this landscape, "strong sustainability" aligns with the green economy and robust environmental protection (Davies, 2013), emphasizing that safeguarding total capital is not enough: certain critical natural resources are irreversible and cannot be substituted by other forms of capital, so their loss undermines all other capital stocks (Turner, 1993; Neumayer, 2003).

## 2 Theory of Sustainable Development

### *2.1 Triple Bottom Line (3P) by Elkington*

The term triple bottom line (TBL) was introduced in the 1990s by business consultant John Elkington to capture the broader economic, environmental, and social value generated by investments, which may extend beyond a company's financial outcomes (Elkington, 2004). The TBL framework seeks to provide a more comprehensive approach to valuing assets and utilizing resources effectively, ensuring that capital is used in the most efficient manner possible. This idea is also known by other terms such as the 3Ps people, planet, profit triple value adding (Roberts & Cohen, 2002), and blended value (Emerson, 2003).

Triple bottom line thinking is closely aligned with the concept of sustainable development, which emphasizes that progress should meet the needs of the present generation while preserving the resources and opportunities for future generations to do the same (World Commission on Environment and Development, 1987). Embedded in this definition are the principles of environmental stewardship and fairness both within and between generations. The need to redefine sustainability emerged from the understanding that current development patterns cannot continue without threatening the environmental systems that sustain life and economies. Moreover, significant inequalities between and within generations are unsustainable, unethical, and misaligned with development goals.

The concepts of the triple bottom line and sustainability have gained increasing importance in fields related to economic development, including business, finance, planning, and real estate. This shift is evident in the growing number of publications, conferences, and professional organizations dedicated to topics like impact investing, responsible property investment, and corporate social responsibility (Hammer & Pivo, 2017).

## 2.2 *Justice Theory (John Rawls)*

John Rawls' A Theory of Justice is a seminal work in social philosophy that aims to outline principles of social justice within a liberal society. Rawls critiques utilitarianism and proposes a model where justice is regarded as a fundamental virtue that should underpin social institutions. A central idea in his theory is the "social contract," in which rational individuals, in ideal conditions, determine the principles that should govern their society. He introduces the concept of the "original position," a hypothetical scenario in which people choose principles of justice without any knowledge of their future social standing, thus ensuring fairness through what Rawls calls the "veil of ignorance" (Rawls, 1971).

Rawls outlines two main principles of justice: the first asserts that every individual should enjoy equal basic liberties, while the second allows for economic inequalities only if they benefit society's least advantaged members (this is known as the difference principle). His theory underscores that justice is not only about individual rights but also about how society's structure and resources are distributed. He advocates for systems that foster fairness and cooperation among all members of society. By placing his theory within a framework of cooperation, Rawls addresses issues of distributive justice, striving for a balance between individual freedom and collective welfare, all while respecting the dignity and rights of each person (Rawls, 1971).

## 2.3 *Rights-Based Approach*

Development does not automatically advance human rights; many "development" activities can even undermine them. To improve outcomes, strategies must be explicitly tied to promoting and respecting rights throughout the entire process—needs assessment, design, implementation, monitoring, and evaluation—with human-rights training for all actors and the state fulfilling its duty-bearer role. Development must be people-centered, participatory, and environmentally sustainable. Growth alone is insufficient; it must be paired with fair distribution, capacity building, and real choices. Priorities include reducing poverty, integrating women into development, strengthening community and governmental self-reliance and self-determination, and protecting indigenous peoples' rights.

Needs-based approaches are narrow and short-term, often creating downstream problems. A human rights–based approach (HRBA) can: (a) ground strategies in rights; (b) reform misaligned policies and institutions; (c) expand civil and political rights to empower participation; (d) affirm economic, social, and cultural rights as binding, not aspirational; (e) flag regressions or failures to meet minimum obligations; (f) legitimize meaningful participation by all; and (g) build accountability mechanisms. Adopting an HRBA advances civil, political, economic, social, and cultural rights by driving changes in policy, law, resource allocation, attitudes and practices, institutions, monitoring, participation, and empowerment (Komnas HAM, 2013).

## 2.4 Capabilities Approach (Sen & Nussbaum)

The capability approach (Sen, 1999) centers on expanding people's real freedoms to live lives they value, urging social policy to build human capabilities—education, health, and access to basics—rather than merely giving economic support or regulating markets. It stresses human agency and diverse needs, so policies should help individuals develop the capabilities they themselves prize (Nussbaum, 2011). Applied to education, health, and disability, it shifts focus from minimal provision to enabling people to flourish—for example, supporting life-enabling skills, community well-being, and full participation (Nussbaum, 2011; Sen, 2002; Shakespeare, 2006). Misapplications that reduce "capabilities" to narrow capacities (e.g., employability training) undermine the approach (Nussbaum, 2011; Sen, 1999; Robeyns, 2017). Common flaws include overvaluing economic competencies, neglecting social context and inequalities, and adopting a too-limited view that overlooks personal freedoms, political participation, control over one's environment, and individual preferences (Nussbaum, 2011; Robeyns, 2017; Comim et al., 2020).

## 2.5 Ecological Modernization Theory

Ecological modernization theory (EMT) emerged during the 1990s as a different way of approaching environmental reform, in contrast to earlier ideas rooted in the "de-growth" perspective and the "small is beautiful" movement. The de-growth approach emphasized the need for deep societal transformation, arguing that capitalist industrial systems and the inability of nation-states to prevent ecological decline revealed a fundamental flaw within modernity itself (Jänicke, 1990). By contrast, EMT suggested that rather than abandoning modern institutions, it is possible to redirect the core features of modernity, such as capitalism and state governance, toward more sustainable forms of production and consumption (Mol, 1996; Spaargaren, 2000). Instead of focusing narrowly on short-lived, technology-based fixes, EMT highlights a broader transition in which ecological knowledge and priorities become central to the ongoing development and organization of society (Mol, 2002; Spaargaren, 1997).

## 2.6 Resilience Thinking & Systems Theory

Resilience thinking is, by nature, a form of systems thinking, much like the concept of sustainable development. As Walker and Salt (2006, p.38) note, when analyzing social–ecological systems, it is essential to view them as integrated wholes because human and biophysical domains are mutually dependent. Within this perspective, resilience and systems thinking intersect around three key ideas: (1) human societies exist within and are inseparable from the ecological systems that sustain them; (2) these social–ecological systems function as complex adaptive systems, meaning they do not evolve in straightforward, linear, or gradual ways; and (3) resilience thinking provides a lens for understanding these systems as interconnected across multiple spatial and temporal scales, with an emphasis on how they respond to shocks and disturbances.

To grasp resilience theory more fully, it is important to unpack several central concepts, including thresholds, the adaptive cycle, panarchy, resilience itself, adaptability, and transformability (European Sustainable Development Network, 2012).

The close interconnection between people and ecosystems underscores why adopting a resilience-thinking approach is vital for governance. Unlike traditional policies that aim to control change in supposedly stable systems, a resilience-based perspective emphasizes managing the capacity of social–ecological systems to withstand, adapt to, and shape change (Berkes et al., 2003; Smit & Wandel, 2006). Advocates argue that by prioritizing resilience, societies are better positioned to sustain desirable development pathways, particularly in dynamic environments where uncertainty and unexpected events are inevitable (Walker et al., 2004; Adger et al., 2005).

## 2.7 *Stakeholder Theory*

Stakeholder theory (ST) is a framework in business ethics and organizational management (Schaltegger et al., 2019). It argues that companies should create value not just for shareholders but for a wide range of stakeholders—defined as individuals or groups who can influence, or are influenced by, the organization, such as governments, employees, customers, suppliers, shareholders, communities, and civil society (Freeman, 1984). The idea dates back to the 1960s, when the Stanford Research Institute introduced the notion of stakeholders, stressing that a company's survival depends on the support of more than just its investors. This shifted attention from focusing solely on shareholder returns to also meeting stakeholder needs. Despite its early roots, research on ST only began gaining strong visibility in leading business journals in the early 2000s (Laplume et al., 2008). Since then, the literature has expanded significantly. In essence, ST can be seen as a perspective that (1) calls on organizations to recognize and engage both internal and external stakeholders, (2) emphasizes the importance of identifying and addressing their expectations and concerns, and (3) provides a more comprehensive and responsible decision-making approach that extends beyond shareholder interests. Ultimately, this enables firms to act strategically, enhance value creation, and strengthen their long-term sustainability and success (Mahajan et al., 2023).

## 2.8 Institutional Theory

Institutional theory is identified as the second most commonly applied theoretical framework in the visualization analysis. This perspective examines organizational forms and seeks to explain why companies operating within the same sector often develop similar structures. It suggests that organizations function within established norms, values, and assumptions that define what is considered acceptable economic behavior. Since institutional theory views organizations as part of the broader society (Scott, 1987), it connects corporate practices—such as CSR and accounting—with prevailing social standards and expectations. Researchers frequently adopt this theory in sustainability studies to explore how socially responsible movements drive institutional changes toward CSR (Avetisyan & Hockerts, 2017), to investigate the factors influencing ESG performance (Brammer et al., 2012), and to analyze practices in integrated reporting (Aouadi & Marsat, 2018).

## 2.9 Risk Governance Theory

Risk governance refers to a set of academic concepts and frameworks that guide collective decision-making in contexts where actions or events carry uncertain outcomes. The model advanced by the International Risk Governance Council in Geneva offers direction for developing comprehensive strategies to assess and manage risks effectively. This framework draws on three types of scientific contributions: traditional curiosity-driven research, strategic research focused on defined objectives, and catalytic investigations that emphasize processes (Glückler et al., 2020).

## 2.10 Global Governance Theory

Global governance is often understood as a form of management in the absence of a central world government. While no single governing authority exists at the global level, different mechanisms of governance do operate, though with varying degrees of effectiveness. Recent studies, however, suggest a continuing decline: a system of global governance that was already fragile appears to be weakening further. Legal and institutional frameworks for global governance are even described as becoming increasingly fragmented (Ruggie, 2014).

## 2.11 Policy Coherence for Sustainable Development (PCSD)

Acknowledging that the SDGs are interconnected and should be pursued as a whole, as emphasized in the 2030 Agenda, this chapter uses the Policy Coherence for Sustainable Development (PCSD) framework to examine key linkages among the SDGs highlighted in the 2019 HLPF review. PCSD serves both as an approach and a

**Table 2.1** Summary of Theory for Sustainable Development

| No | Theory | Core idea (brief) | Key principles |
|---|---|---|---|
| 1 | Triple Bottom Line (3P) | Performance on People–Planet–Profit | Stewardship; intergenerational equity |
| 2 | Justice Theory (Rawls) | Fairness; veil of ignorance; difference principle | Equal basic liberties; pro–least-advantaged |
| 3 | Rights-Based Approach (HRBA) | Rights-anchored development; duty-bearers vs rights-holders | Participation; non-discrimination; accountability |
| 4 | Capabilities (Sen–Nussbaum) | Expand real capabilities; agency | Plural values; social context |
| 5 | Ecological Modernization | Reform within modernity; decoupling | Clean innovation; market instruments |
| 6 | Resilience & Systems | Adaptive SES; thresholds; panarchy | Adaptive learning; diversity; modularity |
| 7 | Stakeholder Theory | Value for all stakeholders; engagement | Identification–prioritization–materiality |
| 8 | Institutional Theory | Isomorphism; legitimacy | Coercive–normative–mimetic pressures |
| 9 | Risk Governance | Risk decision framework | Transparency; inclusiveness; precaution |
| 10 | Global Governance | Polycentric governance without a world government | Multi-level; subsidiarity; partnerships |
| 11 | PCSD | Policy coherence across SDGs | Whole-of-government; cross-border/long-term |

policy instrument to integrate economic, social, environmental, and governance aspects of sustainable development throughout the policymaking process. Its main objectives are to: (1) create synergies and manage trade-offs between different policy areas, (2) align national policies with internationally agreed goals, and (3) consider the cross-border and long-term effects of policies. In today's highly interconnected world, countries influence one another through multiple channels, including financial flows, trade in goods and services, migration, and the transfer of knowledge (OECD, 2019). Taken together, the theoretical perspectives discussed above provide complementary normative, human-centered, ecological, organizational, and governance foundations for sustainable development, as summarized in Table 2.1.

# 3 Global and National Frameworks of Sustainable Development

## *3.1 Global Frameworks of Sustainable Development*

**Agenda 2030: Transforming Our World (Sustainable Development Goals)**

The 2030 Agenda for Sustainable Development, endorsed by the United Nations General Assembly in 2015, serves as the central normative and political framework guiding global sustainability governance. It establishes 17 Sustainable Development

Goals (SDGs) and 169 targets as an integrated roadmap, grounded in the principles of universality, integration, and inclusivity through the commitment to "leave no one behind" (United Nations, 2015). These principles not only enhance the political legitimacy of the agenda but also direct policy prioritization across member states. Crucially, Goal 17 emphasizes multi-stakeholder partnerships as indispensable for mobilizing finance, technology, knowledge, and capacity, underscoring the agenda's reliance on collaborative global action.

Operationally, progress toward the SDGs is assessed through the Global Indicator Framework, developed by the Inter-Agency and Expert Group on SDG Indicators and coordinated by the United Nations Statistics Division (UNSD). This framework enables comparability across countries while permitting contextual adaptation through proxies or modified indicators (United Nations, 2015; Global Reporting Initiative [GRI], 2023). Nevertheless, critical challenges persist, particularly data scarcity in low- and middle-income countries, where many indicators remain under Tier II or III classifications. Bridging these gaps requires investment in statistical systems, integration of geospatial and administrative data, and the development of disaggregated datasets to realize the LNOB principle. Equally pressing is the need for policy coherence, as advances in one goal may undermine others. In this context, Voluntary National Reviews (VNRs) and international review platforms have become essential mechanisms for fostering accountability, transparency, and mutual learning on the pathway toward 2030.

### Paris Agreement (UNFCCC)

The Paris Agreement, adopted in 2015 under the United Nations Framework Convention on Climate Change (UNFCCC), represents the cornerstone of global climate governance. It commits Parties to limit global temperature rise to well below 2 °C above pre-industrial levels, while striving to cap warming at 1.5 °C. Central to this framework is the submission and progressive strengthening of Nationally Determined Contributions (NDCs), which institutionalize an iterative cycle of ambition, implementation, and review. The Agreement rests on three mutually reinforcing pillars—mitigation, adaptation, and finance—while placing differentiated obligations on developed countries to mobilize resources, transfer technology, and support capacity-building for developing economies. Its scope transcends climate policy, intersecting with energy, food security, water, and health, thereby embedding climate action within the broader sustainable development agenda (UNFCCC, 2015).

In practice, the Paris Agreement has catalyzed major policy and market shifts. Governments are required to translate NDCs into domestic measures, such as renewable energy regulation, carbon pricing, and subsidy reform, while capital markets and corporations have embraced science-based targets, climate-related financial disclosures, and portfolio alignment strategies. These efforts have stimulated the creation of frameworks like the Task Force on Climate-related Financial Disclosures (TCFD) and IFRS S2, alongside the expansion of carbon markets and just transition mechanisms. Yet, persistent shortcomings remain: aggregated NDC pledges fall short of the 1.5–2 °C goal, climate finance remains inadequate, and challenges of emissions accounting and carbon market integrity persist (UNFCCC, 2015, 2022). Thus, while the Paris Agreement sets a critical global direction, its effectiveness ultimately hinges on ambitious domestic policies, credible monitoring, and robust accountability mechanisms that reinforce its alignment with the Sustainable Development Goals, particularly SDG 7, SDG 11, and SDG 13.

### Global Reporting Initiative (GRI Standards)

The Global Reporting Initiative (GRI) Standards stand as the most widely embraced global framework for sustainability reporting, enabling organizations to systematically identify, measure, and reveal their economic, environmental, and social footprints. Beyond the narrow lens of investor-focused disclosure, GRI insists on stakeholder inclusivity—ensuring that workers, local communities, suppliers, and regulatory bodies have their concerns reflected in reporting (GRI, 2021, 2023). Its modular construct—comprising Universal, Sector, and Topic Standards—allows firms to address issues material both to their operations and to broader Sustainable Development Goal (SDG) priorities (e.g., emissions & energy use tied to SDG 13; labor & worker well-being to SDG 8; procurement & inequality to SDGs 1 & 10) (Global Reporting Initiative, 2021, 2024a, b).

Notwithstanding its strengths, GRI faces structural constraints. The voluntary nature of its adoption in many jurisdictions permits significant discretion in how organizations define scope and boundaries, which may lead to selective disclosure or even greenwashing in the absence of external assurance (Bais et al., 2024; Du Toit et al., 2024). Furthermore, comparability across industries remains difficult due to divergent materiality assessments and methodological choices. To maximize its potential, the GRI framework benefits substantially when paired with independent verification, outcome- rather than process-focused metrics, and explicit alignment with SDG targets—ensuring reporting is not merely performative but anchored in accountability and strategic value (Bais et al., 2024; Du Toit et al., 2024).

### IFRS/ISSB Sustainability Disclosure Standards (IFRS S1 & S2) and SASB Consolidation

The establishment of the International Sustainability Standards Board (ISSB) under the IFRS Foundation in 2021 marked a critical step toward harmonizing sustainability and financial reporting at the global level. Its two flagship standards—IFRS S1 on general sustainability disclosures and IFRS S2 on climate-related disclosures—seek to enhance transparency, comparability, and decision-usefulness of corporate reporting across capital markets. Anchored in financial materiality, both standards require companies to disclose governance structures, strategies, risk management practices, and performance metrics relevant to enterprise value, thus aligning sustainability with investor decision-making (IFRS Foundation, 2023). Importantly, the ISSB consolidates earlier frameworks, notably the Sustainability Accounting Standards Board (SASB) and the Task Force on Climate-related Financial Disclosures (TCFD), thereby reducing long-standing fragmentation in disclosure regimes and supporting more forward-looking, quantitative reporting (KPMG, 2023).

Nevertheless, the adoption of IFRS S1 and S2 remains uneven, particularly in developing countries where data limitations, high assurance costs, and institutional gaps constrain full compliance (World Bank, 2023). To address these barriers, jurisdictions such as Indonesia have pursued phased implementation: the Indonesian Institute of Accountants (IAI), through its Sustainability Standards Board (DSK IAI), has issued PSPK 1 and 2 as transitional instruments aligned with IFRS S1 and S2, with full enforcement expected by 2027 (IAI, 2023). At the conceptual level, however, the ISSB's investor-oriented focus on financial materiality has provoked debate about its limited attention to "impact materiality"—the social and environmental consequences of corporate activity more central to frameworks like the Global Reporting Initiative (GRI). Reconciling these approaches remains a critical challenge for embedding sustainability disclosures not only as instruments for investor confidence but also as vehicles for advancing the Sustainable Development Goals (Adams & Abhayawansa, 2022; IFRS Foundation, 2023).

## Task Force on Climate-related Financial Disclosures (TCFD) and CDP

The Task Force on Climate-related Financial Disclosures (TCFD), launched in 2015 by the Financial Stability Board, has become a cornerstone of climate-related financial reporting. Its recommendations, structured around governance, strategy, risk management, and metrics and targets, emphasize forward-looking scenario analysis to assess firms' exposure to climate risks and transition opportunities (TCFD, 2017). By promoting standardized and decision-useful disclosures, TCFD has reshaped how corporations and investors evaluate climate risk, while influencing regulators to integrate climate considerations into financial oversight. Complementing this framework, the Carbon Disclosure Project (CDP) functions as the world's largest environmental disclosure platform, collecting corporate data on emissions, water security, and deforestation that are widely used by institutional investors for benchmarking, investment screening, and capital allocation (CDP, 2023). Together, TCFD and CDP reinforce climate transparency by combining disclosure guidance with large-scale data dissemination.

Despite their influence, persistent challenges remain. Many firms—particularly in emerging economies—struggle with the technical demands of scenario analysis, Scope 3 emissions measurement, and data assurance, which undermines comparability and investor confidence. Concerns about verification further highlight the need for stronger assurance mechanisms and harmonization across jurisdictions. Nevertheless, the integration of TCFD recommendations into binding disclosure regimes and their formal consolidation within IFRS S2 Climate-related Disclosures by the ISSB represents a critical step toward mainstreaming climate-related reporting across global markets (TCFD, 2021; IFRS Foundation, 2023). This institutionalization signals a broader shift toward embedding climate risk within financial decision-making and aligning disclosure practices with global sustainability agendas.

### Taskforce on Nature-related Financial Disclosures (TNFD)

The Taskforce on Nature-related Financial Disclosures (TNFD) was created to address the growing urgency of embedding biodiversity, ecosystem services, and natural capital dependencies into financial and corporate decision-making. Modeled on the TCFD, the TNFD framework provides recommendations across governance, strategy, risk management, and metrics, but extends its scope to capture geospatial dependencies, ecological integrity, and resource rights (TNFD, 2023). Its ambition is twofold: to integrate nature-related risks into mainstream financial practices such as credit pricing and capital allocation, and to align business disclosures with global biodiversity commitments, particularly the Kunming–Montreal Global Biodiversity Framework (CBD, 2022). A distinctive contribution of TNFD lies in its explicit recognition of human rights and Indigenous knowledge, underscoring that ecological disclosures cannot be divorced from the social systems that sustain them (Reuters, 2024).

Yet, the operationalization of TNFD remains complex. The absence of robust ecological baselines, methodological diversity in natural capital valuation, and the spatial heterogeneity of ecosystems challenge both comparability and independent assurance. Despite these limitations, TNFD has rapidly gained traction among global financial institutions, signaling its potential to redirect capital flows away from biodiversity-destructive activities toward "nature-positive" investments (TNFD, 2023). For biodiversity-rich countries such as Indonesia, where forests, marine ecosystems, and other natural assets underpin economic resilience, the adoption of TNFD offers a strategic pathway to embed ecological value in financial governance while advancing the Sustainable Development Goals.

### Science Based Targets initiative (SBTi)

The Science Based Targets initiative (SBTi), launched through a collaboration between WRI, WWF, CDP, and the UN Global Compact, has emerged as a central mechanism for aligning corporate climate commitments with the temperature goals of the Paris Agreement. By providing standardized methodologies and an independent validation process, SBTi ensures that corporate greenhouse gas reduction targets are credible, transparent, and consistent with 1.5–2 °C pathways (SBTi, 2023a, b). Its scope has expanded from corporates to the financial sector through the Net-Zero Standard, requiring banks and investors to integrate climate ambition into portfolio strategies. A distinctive strength of SBTi lies in its comprehensive requirement to account for Scope 1, 2, and 3 emissions, thereby embedding accountability across entire value chains and reducing risks of greenwashing or "greenhushing" (WRI, 2023; WWF, 2023).

Nevertheless, the initiative faces persistent challenges. Scope 3 measurement remains methodologically complex in industries with diffuse supply chains such as agriculture, transport, and heavy industry. Moreover, tensions between the ambition of net-zero benchmarks and the structural realities of carbon-intensive sectors—most visibly in oil and gas—have triggered debates over feasibility, credibility, and the potential role of carbon credits (Reuters, 2024). These dilemmas illustrate the dynamic interplay between scientific integrity, market expectations, and political pressures. In response, SBTi continues to refine sectoral guidance and methodological updates, seeking to balance rigor with practicality while maintaining its position as a cornerstone of corporate climate accountability (SBTi, 2023a, b).

## ISO 26000: Guidance on Social Responsibility

ISO 26000 provides an internationally recognized framework for embedding social responsibility into organizational strategies and operations. Unlike ISO 9001 or ISO 14001, it is not a certifiable management system but a guidance standard that promotes ethical conduct, human rights, labor rights, environmental stewardship, and responsible governance. By addressing seven core subjects—ranging from fair operating practices to community involvement—ISO 26000 advances a values-driven approach to corporate social responsibility (CSR) and reinforces the alignment of business conduct with broader sustainable development objectives (ISO, 2010; Hahn, 2013). Its contributions are particularly relevant to SDGs related to health, equality, decent work, and institutional integrity, positioning it as a strategic instrument for fostering social inclusion and accountability.

However, the voluntary and non-binding nature of ISO 26000 limits its enforceability, with effectiveness largely dependent on organizational commitment and leadership capacity. Inconsistent interpretation across industries and jurisdictions has also created risks of symbolic compliance or fragmented application. To enhance its credibility, ISO 26000 is most effective when integrated with complementary frameworks such as the GRI Standards, the UN Global Compact, or independent third-party assurance mechanisms (Moratis & Cochius, 2011; Castka & Balzarova, 2008). Such integration transforms CSR from a rhetorical exercise into a substantive governance tool, enabling organizations to demonstrate measurable contributions to sustainable development.

## UN Guiding Principles on Business and Human Rights (UNGPs)

The UN Guiding Principles on Business and Human Rights (UNGPs), unanimously endorsed by the UN Human Rights Council in 2011, constitute the leading global framework for addressing corporate human rights responsibilities. Structured around the Protect–Respect–Remedy framework, the UNGPs define the duty of states to protect individuals, the responsibility of businesses to respect human rights, and the right of victims to effective remedy (UN, 2011; Ruggie, 2013). While not legally binding, they provide authoritative guidance for embedding human rights due diligence (HRDD) into corporate governance and supply chains, aligning directly with the Sustainable Development Goals (SDGs), particularly SDG 8, SDG 10, and SDG 16. Their influence is evident not only in voluntary corporate initiatives but also in the rise of regulatory frameworks such as the EU Corporate Sustainability Due Diligence Directive (CSDDD) and national legislation in Germany and France (European Commission, 2022; BHRRC, 2023).

Despite their normative authority, the implementation of the UNGPs has been uneven. Many small and medium-sized enterprises (SMEs) lack the capacity to conduct comprehensive HRDD, while access to remedy remains limited in jurisdictions with weak judicial and regulatory systems. Furthermore, enforcement challenges persist in contexts where governments are reluctant to impose corporate accountability (De Schutter, 2016). Strengthening institutional capacity, harmonizing regulatory approaches, and expanding remedy mechanisms are therefore essential to move the UNGPs beyond voluntary guidance and ensure they function as effective instruments of corporate accountability. Such measures would not only enhance protection against business-related human rights abuses but also reinforce the UNGPs' role in advancing sustainable and inclusive development.

### OECD: Policy Coherence for Sustainable Development (PCSD)

The OECD's Policy Coherence for Sustainable Development (PCSD) framework provides a systemic approach to aligning national and international policies with the Sustainable Development Goals (SDGs). By addressing trade-offs, mitigating cross-border spillovers, and countering "policy silos," PCSD seeks to ensure that fiscal, trade, and investment policies do not undermine long-term sustainability outcomes (OECD, 2019). The framework emphasizes whole-of-government approaches through policy screening tools, impact assessments, and coherence indicators, while also recognizing the extraterritorial effects of domestic decisions on global public goods (Nilsson et al., 2018). Central planning institutions—particularly ministries of finance and development agencies—play a critical role in integrating these mechanisms into fiscal and regulatory processes.

In practice, however, PCSD implementation has been constrained by political and institutional barriers. Many countries face limited analytical capacity, weak inter-ministerial coordination, and insufficient political incentives to sustain cross-sectoral governance. Evidence shows that PCSD is most effective where integrated governance structures are already in place (Weitz et al., 2018). For developing economies, the direct transplantation of OECD member-state models is often impractical; instead, PCSD methodologies must be tailored to local institutional realities to ensure scalability and context-sensitive application. Strengthening institutional capacity, fostering political commitment, and embedding coherence mechanisms into national planning remain crucial to transforming PCSD from a normative framework into an operational driver of sustainable development (OECD, 2019).

## EU Taxonomy for Sustainable Activities (and the Global Taxonomy Discourse)

The European Union (EU) Taxonomy for Sustainable Activities represents the world's most advanced science-based classification system for identifying environmentally sustainable activities. Its technical framework requires that an economic activity make a substantial contribution to at least one of six environmental objectives, do no significant harm (DNSH) to others, and comply with minimum social and governance safeguards (European Commission, 2020a). By embedding these criteria, the taxonomy provides transparent market signals, curbs greenwashing, and directs capital flows toward activities compatible with the low-carbon transition. Companies and financial institutions operating in the EU must also disclose the share of their operations aligned with the taxonomy, thereby strengthening accountability and comparability across markets (European Commission, 2021).

The EU model has become a global reference point, inspiring the development of taxonomies in China, the United Kingdom, ASEAN, and Indonesia's Taksonomi Keuangan Berkelanjutan Indonesia (TKBI) (ASEAN, 2021; OJK, 2022). Its reliance on scientific and technical thresholds reduces ambiguity around "green" classifications, yet implementation faces challenges: sectoral data requirements are complex, political pressures shape the treatment of transitional activities such as natural gas and nuclear, and the proliferation of divergent national taxonomies risks market fragmentation. As a result, international platforms such as the International Platform on Sustainable Finance (IPSF) have prioritized taxonomy interoperability, recognizing that global convergence is essential to reduce transaction costs and ensure cross-border capital alignment with sustainability objectives (IPSF, 2022; European Commission, 2021).

## Natural Capital Protocol (Capitals Coalition)

The Natural Capital Protocol, introduced by the Capitals Coalition, provides a structured framework for identifying, measuring, and valuing organizational dependencies and impacts on ecosystems, services, and biodiversity through a stepwise methodology of scoping, measurement, valuation, and application (Capitals Coalition, 2016). By embedding natural capital into corporate strategy and financial planning, the Protocol seeks to internalize environmental externalities and align business practices with planetary boundaries, making it particularly relevant to SDG 14 (Life Below Water) and SDG 15 (Life on Land), while also contributing to SDG 2, 6, and 7. Its application by multinational corporations demonstrates its utility in mapping supply-chain risks, guiding mitigation and restoration strategies, and incorporating both monetary and non-monetary ecological values, including cultural and ethical dimensions, into decision-making (Natural Capital Coalition, 2016; Vardon et al., 2019).

Despite these strengths, the Protocol faces persistent methodological challenges, especially in valuing ecosystem services across data-scarce contexts or reconciling divergent disciplinary approaches. Excessive reliance on monetization can marginalize ethical, socio-spiritual, and Indigenous perspectives, limiting inclusivity (Kenter et al., 2015). Hence, its effectiveness is maximized when implemented through multi-metric approaches that integrate quantitative, qualitative, and participatory methods, complemented by independent verification. Such integration enhances both the credibility and legitimacy of natural capital assessments, reinforcing their contribution to sustainable finance and corporate accountability.

#### Planetary Boundaries Framework

The Planetary Boundaries framework, introduced by Rockström et al. (2009) and further refined by Steffen et al. (2015) and Richardson et al. (2023), identifies nine Earth-system processes—such as climate change, biodiversity, land-system change, and biogeochemical cycles—each with thresholds that define a "safe operating space" for humanity. By establishing absolute rather than relative limits, it has reshaped sustainability discourse and informed global policy and corporate commitments, including net-zero targets, deforestation-free supply chains, and agricultural reforms to reduce nitrogen and phosphorus inputs (Stockholm Resilience Centre, 2025). Evidence indicates that critical boundaries, notably climate change, biodiversity loss, and biogeochemical flows, have already been breached, underscoring the urgency of systemic rather than incremental interventions (Steffen et al., 2015; Richardson et al., 2023).

Despite its scientific rigor, operationalizing the framework remains complex. Its global orientation raises difficulties in translating thresholds into national or sectoral contexts, particularly in distributing carbon budgets, nitrogen loads, or freshwater use equitably (Downing et al., 2019). As such, it is best seen as a guiding compass rather than a prescriptive tool, with its greatest value realized when combined with spatially explicit and sector-specific instruments that render planetary limits actionable for policymakers and businesses (Stockholm Resilience Centre, 2025).

### 3.2 National Frameworks of Sustainable Development

#### Presidential Regulation No. 59/2017 on the Implementation of the Sustainable Development Goals

Presidential Regulation No. 59/2017 represents Indonesia's core legal framework for institutionalizing the 2030 Agenda. It appoints Bappenas as the national coordinator, mandates the integration of SDG targets into the RPJMN and RPJMD, and requires the preparation of a National Roadmap alongside national and regional action plans (RAN/RAD SDGs). By embedding SDGs into the country's legal and planning architecture, the regulation provides political legitimacy and administrative authority, ensuring that sustainable development is treated not as an auxiliary agenda but as a central component of national development policy (Government of Indonesia, 2017; Bappenas, 2020).

The regulation also establishes multi-level coordination mechanisms involving ministries, subnational governments, and multi-stakeholder platforms, while aligning national indicators with the UN Global Indicator Framework and allowing contextual adaptations. However, its implementation faces persistent challenges, including weak inter-ministerial coordination, regional disparities in planning capacity, financing gaps, and limited disaggregated data—critical for realizing the "leave no one behind" principle. Consequently, the regulation functions primarily as an enabling framework whose effectiveness depends on capacity-building, innovative financing, and robust accountability systems such as Voluntary National Reviews, independent audits, and civil society monitoring (Pramono et al., 2021; OECD, 2021a, b, c).

### Indonesia's SDG Roadmap and Integration into RPJMN/RPJMD

Indonesia's SDG Roadmap, prepared by Bappenas in consultation with diverse stakeholders, translates the 17 goals and 169 targets of the 2030 Agenda into nationally relevant objectives, indicators, and programs. Serving both as a mapping and planning instrument, it aligns global commitments with domestic priorities while informing the formulation of the National and Regional Action Plans (RAN/RAD SDGs). Its design emphasizes localization through the integration of SDG targets into RPJMD at provincial and municipal levels, recognizing that the provision of basic services such as health, education, and sanitation is largely decentralized. Budget tagging mechanisms further strengthen the coherence between planning, budgeting, and monitoring, ensuring that fiscal allocations can be tracked against SDG-relevant programs (Bappenas, 2019; OECD, 2021a, b, c).

Nevertheless, implementation has been constrained by disparities in local planning capacity, persistent data gaps, and programmatic fragmentation that weaken inter-sectoral coordination. To address these challenges, the Roadmap—supported by partners such as UNDP and OECD—calls for enhancing the role of Statistics Indonesia (BPS), improving data systems, and investing in capacity-building for subnational governments. It also advocates the use of simplified national indicators consistent with global standards to promote feasibility while safeguarding the "leave no one behind" principle (Bappenas, 2021; Pramono et al., 2021).

### PROPER (Program for Corporate Performance Rating in Environmental Management)

The Corporate Performance Rating Program on Environmental Management (PROPER), managed by the Ministry of Environment and Forestry (KLHK), is Indonesia's flagship instrument for advancing corporate accountability in environmental governance. Through a five-color rating system—ranging from Black to

Gold—it evaluates compliance, management practices, and community engagement, with the Gold rating reserved for companies that demonstrate performance beyond regulatory requirements, such as adopting advanced emission-reduction technologies, water conservation measures, and community empowerment initiatives (KLHK, 2023a, b). By combining compliance auditing, environmental performance assessment, and dissemination of best practices, PROPER leverages transparency and reputational incentives, applying a "naming and shaming" mechanism that not only compels firms to improve but also encourages industry-wide diffusion of green technologies and sustainable practices.

Despite these achievements, PROPER continues to face limitations, including uneven evaluator capacity, inconsistent criteria across sectors, and restricted accessibility for SMEs with limited resources. Nevertheless, empirical studies show that it has effectively promoted continuous environmental improvements in high-impact industries such as mining, oil and gas, and manufacturing (Suharto et al., 2019). Recent enhancements, notably the integration of life-cycle assessment (LCA) principles, have further aligned PROPER with the Sustainable Development Goals, particularly SDG 12 on responsible production and consumption, SDG 13 on climate action, and SDGs 14 and 15 related to biodiversity conservation (KLHK, 2023a, b).

**Financial Services Authority (OJK): Sustainable Finance Roadmap, POJK Regulations, and the Indonesia Taxonomy for Sustainable Finance (TKBI)**

The Financial Services Authority (OJK) has played a pivotal role in advancing Indonesia's sustainable finance ecosystem through a phased roadmap, regulatory instruments (POJK), and the Indonesia Taxonomy for Sustainable Finance (TKBI). The first roadmap (2015–2019) focused on awareness and pilot initiatives, while Phase II (2021–2025) emphasizes mainstreaming practices through climate risk management tools, scenario analysis, and incentives for green capital markets (OJK, 2021). Complementing this, POJK regulations mandate sustainability reporting and provide guidelines for green bonds and sukuk, positioning Indonesia as a frontrunner in Islamic green finance (OJK, 2022). Central to these reforms, the Indonesia Taxonomy for Sustainable Finance (TKBI) was introduced through TKBI Version 1 in 2024 and subsequently expanded through TKBI Version 2 in 2025. The framework classifies economic activities according to their contribution to Indonesia's environmental objectives, covering sectors such as energy, transportation and storage, construction and real estate, agriculture, forestry and fisheries, as well as water supply and waste management. By establishing clearer science-based classification criteria and promoting interoperability with regional frameworks, including the ASEAN Taxonomy for Sustainable Finance, TKBI is expected to reduce greenwashing risks, strengthen market transparency, and direct capital flows toward Indonesia's climate and sustainable development priorities (ASEAN, 2021; OJK, 2024, 2025).

Notwithstanding these advances, implementation remains constrained by limited sectoral data, institutional capacity gaps, and the need for interoperability with international taxonomies to avoid market fragmentation. Many financial institutions face difficulties in applying technical screening criteria and conducting robust due diligence.

To address these barriers, OJK has pursued capacity-building initiatives, accelerator schemes, and cross-agency coordination with the Ministry of Finance, Bank Indonesia, and sectoral ministries, ensuring greater coherence between sustainable finance policies and Indonesia's broader development agenda (OECD, 2021a, b, c).

## Sustainability Disclosure Standards (PSPK): National Adoption of IFRS S1 & S2

Indonesia has advanced its sustainability reporting agenda through the issuance of Sustainability Disclosure Standards (PSPK 1 and PSPK 2) by the Indonesian Institute of Accountants, mirroring IFRS S1 and S2 from the International Sustainability Standards Board. Released in 2023 with a transition period until 2027, these standards represent a milestone in embedding sustainability into corporate governance and capital market practices. Anchored in the principle of financial materiality, PSPK requires firms to disclose governance, strategy, risk management, and performance metrics relevant to sustainability risks and opportunities, thereby enhancing transparency and comparability in reporting. By aligning with OJK regulations and the Indonesia Sustainable Finance Taxonomy (TKBI), PSPK strengthens regulatory coherence in areas such as emissions disclosure, scenario analysis, and eligibility for green financial instruments (OJK, 2021; IAI, 2023; IFRS Foundation, 2023).

Nevertheless, implementation presents notable challenges. Technical difficulties in measuring Scope 3 emissions, gaps in historical data, and the costs of independent assurance hinder smooth adoption. Conceptual tensions also persist between PSPK's investor-oriented materiality focus and the stakeholder-inclusive "double materiality" model of the Global Reporting Initiative, raising the likelihood of dual reporting requirements for many firms (Adams & Abhayawansa, 2022). Future policy developments—such as OJK mandates or stock exchange listing rules—will be decisive in determining whether PSPK becomes a mandatory standard, shaping the evolution of sustainability disclosure in Indonesia.

## Green Sukuk and Sovereign Sustainable Finance Instruments

Indonesia has positioned itself as a global pioneer in sovereign green sukuk, using Islamic finance to mobilize capital for renewable energy, water management, climate adaptation, and sustainable infrastructure. Since the inaugural issuance in 2018, the government has raised billions of US dollars, with cumulative issuances expanding significantly through 2023. The introduction of retail sukuk (ST-series) has further broadened domestic participation, democratizing access to sustainable investment opportunities and strengthening the role of green sukuk as a key instrument for financing the SDGs (Ministry of Finance, 2023). Their credibility is reinforced by a governance framework that integrates the ICMA Green Bond Principles with the Indonesia Sustainable Finance Taxonomy (TKBI), requiring transparent allocation of proceeds, external verification, and impact reporting, thereby enhancing investor confidence while aligning shariah-compliant financing with international standards (ICMA, 2021; OECD, 2021a, b, c).

Nevertheless, challenges persist in ensuring independent verification, harmonizing impact measurement methodologies, and sustaining long-term monitoring of developmental outcomes. The risk of greenwashing highlights the need for rigorous reporting and continuous alignment with global best practices (UNDP, 2022). Looking forward, Indonesia's sovereign strategy is expected to evolve toward social and sustainability sukuk, integrating poverty reduction and gender equality with environmental objectives. This diversification not only strengthens developmental impact but also consolidates Indonesia's leadership in aligning Islamic capital markets with the SDGs.

# 4 Global and National Best Practices

## 4.1 *Global Best Practices*

### European Green Deal and the European Climate Law

The European Green Deal, reinforced by the European Climate Law and the "Fit-for-55" package, stands as the EU's most ambitious supranational framework to achieve climate neutrality by 2050, mandating a 55% reduction in emissions by 2030 relative to 1990 levels through reforms to the Emissions Trading System, stricter efficiency and emission standards, and substantial fiscal and industrial financing instruments (European Commission, 2020b). By 2022, EU emissions had already declined by 31%, though projections warn that without stronger national alignment and sectoral commitments, the 2030 target may remain unattainable (European Environment Agency, 2024). While the framework has catalyzed large-scale decarbonization and renewable energy investment, it continues to face structural challenges such as uneven national capacities, industrial resistance, risks of carbon leakage, and the pressing need for a just transition for vulnerable communities, ultimately illustrating both the transformative power and the inherent limitations of binding legal governance in balancing environmental imperatives with socio-economic resilience (Climate Action Tracker, 2024; Tagliapietra & Wolff, 2021).

### Microsoft: Science-Based Targets and the Climate Innovation Fund

Microsoft has positioned itself as a frontrunner in corporate climate governance by pledging to become carbon negative by 2030 and to eliminate its entire historical footprint by 2050, anchoring this ambition in science-based targets and a USD 1 billion Climate Innovation Fund that invests in technologies such as BECCS and DAC (Microsoft, 2024). By 2023, the company reported a 6.3% reduction in Scope 1 and 2 emissions from its 2020 baseline, while expanding long-term contracts for carbon removal. However, its trajectory reveals systemic tensions: the rapid growth of AI and data centers has fueled rising Scope 3 emissions (IEA, 2023a), and reliance on costly, uncertain carbon removal technologies risks substituting offsets for genuine reductions (Anderson & Peters, 2016).

#### Unilever: Supplier Climate Programme and Operational Decarbonization

Unilever has integrated leading sustainability frameworks such as GRI, TCFD, and SBTi into its Supplier Climate Programme, targeting around 300 suppliers responsible for 44% of its Scope 3 emissions while simultaneously reducing Scope 1 and 2 emissions by 70% ahead of its 2025 goal (Unilever, 2024a; Unilever, 2024b). The programme combines co-financed capacity building, supplier adoption of science-based targets, and product-level data monitoring, amplified through partnerships with global retailers like Walmart, thereby extending decarbonization efforts across value chains. Yet, Scope 3 emissions remain the most persistent challenge, as SMEs often lack resources for low-carbon transitions and inconsistencies in accounting methodologies risk greenwashing (SBTi, 2023a, b; TCFD, 2021).

#### Apple: Supplier Clean Energy Program

Apple's Supplier Clean Energy Program, one of the largest corporate-led renewable energy initiatives globally, engages over 300 suppliers through technical assistance, collective procurement, and direct investment to facilitate a transition to 100% renewable energy, particularly in developing economies. By 2023, hundreds of suppliers had committed to full renewable adoption, contributing to significant emissions reductions and systemic energy transitions through Apple's role as an aggregator of renewable demand, which creates economies of scale and lowers transaction costs (Apple, 2023a; Apple, 2023b; Chen et al., 2021). Nonetheless, persistent barriers—including grid limitations, complex power purchase negotiations, and the need for independent verification—challenge the program's scalability and credibility, especially as global demand for digital devices intensifies.

#### Global Reporting Initiative (GRI)

The Global Reporting Initiative (GRI) is the world's most widely adopted sustainability reporting framework, used by the majority of the G250 and thousands of SMEs to disclose emissions, resource use, labor practices, and social responsibility metrics, thereby strengthening corporate accountability and supporting evidence-based policymaking and investment aligned with the SDGs (GRI, 2022, 2024a, b; KPMG, 2022). Yet, its operation within a fragmented reporting landscape—alongside IFRS S1 and S2, SASB, VRF, and the EU's CSRD—creates duplicative requirements, raises compliance costs, and limits cross-framework comparability (Adams & Abhayawansa, 2022).

## 4.2 *National Best Practices*

### Green Sukuk (Government of Indonesia)

Since its debut in 2018, Indonesia's Green Sukuk has emerged as a pioneering sovereign instrument to finance environmentally sustainable projects in sectors such as public transport, renewable energy, water management, and land restoration. Backed by clear eligibility criteria, rigorous allocation and impact reporting, and external verification, it aligns closely with international green bond and sukuk principles, enhancing investor confidence (Ministry of Finance, 2022). By 2023, cumulative issuances reached IDR 185.6 trillion—including IDR 21.8 trillion from retail sukuk—helping reduce an estimated 10.5 million tons of $CO_2e$ between 2018 and 2021 (World Bank, 2021; Antara, 2025). Beyond its climate impact, the sukuk has broadened Indonesia's investor base and strengthened its pipeline of green projects. Yet, challenges persist around data consistency, scope expansion to transitional energy, and sustaining credibility through robust reporting and alignment with global taxonomies (UNDP & World Bank, 2022).

### PROPER (Ministry of Environment and Forestry—KLHK)

Administered by the Ministry of Environment and Forestry, PROPER evaluates corporate environmental performance through a five-tier color-coded system that combines compliance auditing with public disclosure to leverage reputational pressure as a governance tool (KLHK, 2023a, b). Its impact is evident in 2023, when Pertamina alone secured 34 Gold and 76 Green ratings—43% of all Gold awards nationwide—through innovations in waste-to-energy, corporate governance, and community programs (Pertamina, 2024). While effective in promoting best practices and rewarding environmental leadership, PROPER faces limitations, including uneven verification, limited SME participation, and risks of "label formalism" where compliance may not translate into real ecological improvements (Republika, 2023). Strengthening the framework through outcome-oriented indicators—such as water quality, emission reductions, and ecosystem restoration—would enhance its legitimacy as a comprehensive sustainability instrument (Afsah et al., 2013).

### OJK: Indonesia Taxonomy for Sustainable Finance (TKBI) and Sustainable Finance Roadmap

The Financial Services Authority (OJK) has positioned itself as a central driver of Indonesia's sustainable finance transition through its Sustainable Finance Roadmap Phase II (2021–2025), which mainstreams sustainability into financial sector governance via mandatory reporting requirements and guidelines for green bonds and sukuk (OJK, 2021). Complementing this, the Indonesia Taxonomy for Sustainable

Finance (TKBI)—launched in 2024 and expanded in 2025—classifies sustainable economic activities in sectors such as construction, transport, and AFOLU, thereby mitigating greenwashing risks, enhancing transparency, and channeling capital toward verifiable environmental and social outcomes. Despite measurable growth in sustainable finance portfolios, significant challenges remain, including data and capacity gaps, limited fiscal incentives, and the need for interoperability with international frameworks to secure cross-border investment. Addressing these constraints will require a robust pipeline of bankable projects, stronger institutional capacities, and policy instruments that align private finance with national climate and development goals (OECD, 2021a, b, c).

### PLN: RUPTL as an Energy Transition Instrument

Indonesia's Electricity Supply Business Plan (RUPTL) 2021–2030 represents a strategic pivot from fossil fuels toward renewable energy, targeting an additional 20.9 GW of capacity to raise total renewables from 8.2 GW in 2021 to 28.9 GW by 2030, or 51.6% of new capacity additions (PLN, 2021). The plan serves as a blueprint for investment, IPP tenders, and grid expansion aligned with SDG 7 on clean energy. However, the RUPTL 2025–2034 signals reduced ambition, retaining coal and gas as significant contributors, reflecting structural reliance on fossil industries and challenges of financing, integration, and policy coherence. As both a pipeline for renewable deployment and a contested policy space, the RUPTL underscores the tension between long-term transition goals and short-term economic pressures. Safeguarding its role in Indonesia's decarbonization will depend on mobilizing domestic and international capital, deploying de-risking instruments, and leveraging global initiatives such as the Just Energy Transition Partnership (JETP) to accelerate a resilient low-carbon power system (IEA, 2023b; Climate Investment Funds, 2023).

### BRI: Green Financing and SME Inclusion

Bank Rakyat Indonesia (BRI) has positioned itself as a pioneer of inclusive sustainable finance by integrating green financing instruments with its microfinance expertise, extending climate-aligned finance to SMEs through green micro-loans, green bonds, and the expansion of sustainable portfolios in line with POJK 51/2017 (BRI, 2023; OJK, 2017). By early 2025, its sustainable finance portfolio reached IDR 89.9 trillion, funding renewable energy, resource management, and bond issuances (BRI, 2025). This dual approach demonstrates how green credit can democratize access to sustainable finance, empowering small-scale entrepreneurs while advancing national SDG progress and strengthening socio-ecological resilience (UNEP FI, 2021). Yet, challenges persist, including limited micro-level impact reporting, product mismatches for smaller enterprises, and the need for technical assistance to ensure tangible sustainability outcomes. Addressing these gaps is critical to enhance credibility, mitigate greenwashing risks, and ensure that inclusive green finance delivers measurable contributions to climate action, adaptation, and social equity (ADB, 2022).

## 5 Conclusion

The review of international and national frameworks on Sustainable Development Goals (SDGs) highlights the inherently multidimensional architecture that underpins global sustainability governance. At the global level, instruments such as the 2030 Agenda for Sustainable Development, the Paris Agreement, the Global Reporting Initiative (GRI), the IFRS/ISSB Sustainability Standards, the Task Force on Climate-related Financial Disclosures (TCFD), the Taskforce on Nature-related Financial Disclosures (TNFD), the Science Based Targets initiative (SBTi), ISO 26000, the UN Guiding Principles on Business and Human Rights (UNGPs), the OECD Policy Coherence for Sustainable Development (PCSD), the EU Taxonomy, the Natural Capital Protocol, and the Planetary Boundaries framework collectively provide the normative, scientific, and technical foundations of sustainable development. Taken together, these frameworks integrate legal, policy, financial, and scientific instruments, establishing a global governance ecosystem that seeks to operationalize sustainability principles across states, markets, and corporations.

At the national level, Indonesia has institutionalized sustainability commitments through Presidential Regulation No. 59/2017, the Indonesia SDG Roadmap, the PROPER program, the OJK Sustainable Finance Roadmap and the Indonesia Taxonomy for Sustainable Finance (TKBI), PSPK Sustainability Disclosure Standards, Green Sukuk issuances, Green Building certification systems, and national reporting mechanisms such as the Voluntary National Reviews (VNRs) and the SDG Dashboard. Collectively, these initiatives create an enabling environment for mainstreaming the SDGs into national development planning, fiscal policy, capital markets, and corporate governance practices.

Despite these advancements, the effectiveness of sustainability frameworks—both global and national—ultimately hinges on three interrelated dimensions. First, policy coherence is required to minimize trade-offs and manage synergies across competing development priorities. Second, data and measurement capacity must be strengthened to ensure robust monitoring, accountability, and comparability of outcomes. Third, sustainable financing mechanisms and incentive structures are essential to mobilize the large-scale investments needed to achieve SDG targets. Experiences from international and domestic contexts alike underscore that institutional capacity, independent verification, and multi-stakeholder engagement are critical to move beyond superficial compliance and generate transformative impact. Table 2.2 synthesizes the key international and Indonesian sustainable development frameworks discussed in this chapter by comparing their principal features, strengths, and implementation challenges.

**Table 2.2** Summary of Key Frameworks for Sustainable Development

| Level | Framework | Key Features | Strengths | Challenges |
|---|---|---|---|---|
| International | Agenda 2030 (SDGs) | 17 goals, 169 targets, leave no one behind | Universal, integrated, normative legitimacy | Data gaps, trade-offs, coherence issues |
| | Paris Agreement | Net-zero, NDCs, mitigation–adaptation–finance | Legal-political binding, global climate governance | Ambition gap, uneven finance, double counting risks |
| | GRI Standards | Universal & sector-specific sustainability reporting | Stakeholder inclusivity, SDG alignment | Voluntary, risk of selective disclosure |
| | IFRS/ISSB (S1, S2) | Investor-focused disclosure, climate metrics | Global baseline, financial materiality | Data intensity, Scope-3 challenges |
| | TCFD & CDP | Climate-risk disclosure + data platform | Forward-looking, investor relevance | Scenario analysis capacity, verification limits |
| | TNFD | Nature-related risks, biodiversity & ecosystems | Extends beyond climate, nature-positive finance | Complex valuation, data scarcity |
| | SBTi | Science-based emission targets | Credible validation, investor trust | Scope-3 difficulties, sectoral feasibility |
| | ISO 26000 | Guidance on social responsibility | Holistic CSR, human rights focus | Non-binding, varied implementation |
| | UNGPs | Protect–Respect–Remedy for human rights | Widely accepted, HRDD practices | Enforcement gaps, SME capacity |
| | OECD PCSD | Policy coherence for SDGs | Trade-off analysis, whole-of-gov tools | Political will, institutional heterogeneity |
| | EU Taxonomy | Classification of green activities | Reduces greenwashing, capital alignment | Complexity, political disputes |
| | Natural Capital Protocol | Business-natural capital integration | Internalizes ecosystem value | Valuation challenges, data limits |
| | Planetary Boundaries | Scientific thresholds for Earth systems | Science-based, systemic perspective | Global–local translation difficulty |

| | | | | |
|---|---|---|---|---|
| National (Indonesia) | Perpres 59/2017 | Legal adoption of SDGs into RPJMN/RPJMD | Institutional legitimacy | Coordination & funding gaps |
| | SDG Roadmap | National targets & localization to RPJMD | Planning–budgeting–monitoring linkage | Data & local capacity limits |
| | PROPER (KLHK) | Corporate environmental performance rating | Reputation pressure, best practice diffusion | SME reach, verification consistency |
| | OJK Roadmap & TKBI | Sustainable finance regulation & taxonomy | Capital mobilization, anti-greenwashing | Data gaps, international harmonization |
| | PSPK (IAI) | Local adoption of IFRS S1/S2 | Investor comparability, standardized reporting | Dual materiality tension, transition cost |
| | Green Sukuk | Sovereign green Islamic bonds | Mobilizes public capital, global role model | Impact verification, greenwashing risk |
| | Green Building (GREENSHIP, EDGE) | Certification for sustainable construction | Reduces energy demand, urban resilience | Cost barrier, limited adoption |
| | National Reporting & VNR | Bappenas–BPS dashboard & UN reporting | Transparency, peer learning | Local disaggregation, interoperability |

# References


Adams, C. A., & Abhayawansa, S. (2022). Connecting the SDGs and sustainability reporting: The role of the GRI Standards. *Sustainability Accounting, Management and Policy Journal, 13*(1), 1–23. https://doi.org/10.1108/SAMPJ-09-2021-0370

Adger, W. N., Hughes, T. P., Folke, C., Carpenter, S. R., & Rockström, J. (2005). Social-ecological resilience to coastal disasters. *Science, 309*(5737), 1036–1039. https://doi.org/10.1126/science.1112122

Afsah, S., Blackman, A., García, J. H., & Sterner, T. (2013). *Environmental regulation and public disclosure: The case of PROPER in Indonesia.* Routledge.

Anderson, K., & Peters, G. (2016). The trouble with negative emissions. *Science, 354*(6309), 182–183. https://doi.org/10.1126/science.aah4567

Antara. (2025, January 12). Green sukuk issuance reaches IDR 185.6 trillion by 2023. *Antara News.* https://en.antaranews.com/

Aouadi, A., & Marsat, S. (2018). Do ESG controversies matter for firm value? Evidence from international data. *Journal of Business Ethics, 151*(4), 1027–1047. https://doi.org/10.1007/s10551-016-3213-8

Apple. (2023a). Apple's Supplier Clean Energy Program overview. *Apple Inc.* https://www.apple.com/

Apple. (2023b). Environmental progress report 2023. *Apple Inc.* https://www.apple.com/environment/

ASEAN. (2021). *ASEAN taxonomy for sustainable finance (Version 1).* ASEAN Finance Ministers and Central Bank Governors' Meeting. https://asean.org/

Asian Development Bank. (2022). *Green and inclusive finance: Scaling sustainable microfinance for SMEs.* ADB. https://www.adb.org/

Avetisyan, E., & Hockerts, K. (2017). The consolidation of the ESG rating industry as an enactment of institutional retrogression. *Business Strategy and the Environment, 26*(3), 316–330. https://doi.org/10.1002/bse.1919

Bais, B., et al. (2024). Global Reporting Initiative: Literature review and research directions. *Journal of Cleaner Production, 471,* 143428. https://doi.org/10.1016/j.jclepro.2024.143428

Bappenas. (2019). *Roadmap of SDGs Indonesia: A pathway to achieve the 2030 Agenda.* Ministry of National Development Planning, Republic of Indonesia. https://sdgs.bappenas.go.id/

Bappenas. (2020). *Voluntary National Review (VNR) 2020: Sustainable Development Goals.* Ministry of National Development Planning, Republic of Indonesia. https://sdgs.bappenas.go.id/

Bappenas. (2021). *Voluntary National Review (VNR) 2021: Sustainable Development Goals.* Ministry of National Development Planning, Republic of Indonesia. https://sdgs.bappenas.go.id/

Bank Rakyat Indonesia. (2023). *Sustainability report 2023.* PT Bank Rakyat Indonesia (Persero) Tbk. https://bri.co.id/

Bank Rakyat Indonesia. (2025). *Quarterly financial and sustainability disclosure Q1 2025.* PT Bank Rakyat Indonesia (Persero) Tbk. https://bri.co.id/

Berkes, F., Colding, J., & Folke, C. (Eds.). (2003). *Navigating social–ecological systems: Building resilience for complexity and change.* Cambridge University Press.

Brammer, S., Jackson, G., & Matten, D. (2012). Corporate social responsibility and institutional theory: New perspectives on private governance. *Socio-Economic Review, 10*(1), 3–28. https://doi.org/10.1093/ser/mwr030

Business & Human Rights Resource Centre. (2023). *Mandatory human rights due diligence laws.* BHRRC. https://www.business-humanrights.org/

Capitals Coalition. (2016). *Natural Capital Protocol.* Capitals Coalition. https://capitalscoalition.org/

Carbon Disclosure Project. (2023). *Disclosure data factsheet 2023.* CDP.

Castka, P., & Balzarova, M. A. (2008). The impact of ISO 9000 and ISO 14000 on standardisation of social responsibility—An inside perspective. *International Journal of Production Economics, 113*(1), 74–87. https://doi.org/10.1016/j.ijpe.2007.02.048

Chen, L., Li, Z., & Wang, Y. (2021). Corporate renewable energy procurement in global supply chains: Opportunities and challenges. *Journal of Cleaner Production, 315,* 128163. https://doi.org/10.1016/j.jclepro.2021.128163

Climate Action Tracker. (2024). *EU policies and action.* Climate Analytics & NewClimate Institute. https://climateactiontracker.org/

Climate Investment Funds. (2023). *Indonesia Just Energy Transition Partnership (JETP) country platform.* CIF. https://www.climateinvestmentfunds.org/

Comim, F., Qizilbash, M., & Alkire, S. (Eds.). (2020). *The capability approach: Concepts, measures and applications.* Cambridge University Press.

Convention on Biological Diversity. (2022). *Kunming–Montreal Global Biodiversity Framework.* CBD Secretariat. https://www.cbd.int/gbf/

Davies, G. R. (2013). Appraising weak and strong sustainability: Searching for a middle ground. *Consilience: The Journal of Sustainable Development, 10*(1), 111–124. https://doi.org/10.7916/consilience.v0i10.4635

De Schutter, O. (2016). Towards a new treaty on business and human rights. *Business and Human Rights Journal, 1*(1), 41–67. https://doi.org/10.1017/bhj.2015.5

Du Toit, E., et al. (2024). Thirty years of sustainability reporting: Insights, gaps and future research. *Sustainability, 16*(23), 10750. https://doi.org/10.3390/su162310750

Downing, A. S., Steffen, W., Häyhä, T., Cornell, S. E., & Fetzer, I. (2019). We need an integrated assessment of planetary boundaries. *Nature Ecology & Evolution, 3*(5), 744–747. https://doi.org/10.1038/s41559-019-0858-5

Drexhage, J., & Murphy, D. (2010). *Sustainable development: From Brundtland to Rio 2012. Background paper prepared for the United Nations High-Level Panel on Global Sustainability.* International Institute for Sustainable Development.

Elkington, J. (2004). Enter the triple bottom line. In A. Henriques & J. Richardson (Eds.), *The triple bottom line: Does it all add up?* (pp. 1–16). Earthscan.

Emerson, J. (2003). The blended value proposition: Integrating social and financial returns. *California Management Review, 45*(4), 35–51. https://doi.org/10.2307/41166187

European Commission. (2020a). *The European Green Deal.* European Commission. https://ec.europa.eu/

European Commission. (2020b). *Regulation (EU) 2020/852 on the establishment of a framework to facilitate sustainable investment (EU Taxonomy Regulation).* Official Journal of the European Union. https://eur-lex.europa.eu/

European Commission. (2021). *EU Taxonomy: Delegated acts and technical screening criteria.* European Commission. https://finance.ec.europa.eu/

European Commission. (2022). *Corporate sustainability due diligence directive (CSDDD).* European Commission. https://ec.europa.eu/

European Environment Agency. (2024). *Trends and projections in Europe 2024: Tracking progress towards climate and energy targets.* EEA. https://www.eea.europa.eu/

Freeman, R. E. (1984). *Strategic management: A stakeholder approach.* Pitman.

Glückler, J., Herrigel, G., & Handke, M. (2020). *Knowledge for governance.* Springer Nature.

Global Reporting Initiative. (2021). *Universal standards: GRI 1, GRI 2, GRI 3 (Foundational, general disclosures, material topics).* Global Reporting Initiative. https://www.globalreporting.org

Global Reporting Initiative. (2022). *Consolidated set of GRI Standards 2021.* GRI. https://www.globalreporting.org/

Global Reporting Initiative. (2023). *GRI sustainability reporting trends 2023.* GRI. https://www.globalreporting.org/

Global Reporting Initiative. (2024a). *GRI standards overview: Universal, sector, and topic standards.* Global Reporting Initiative. https://www.globalreporting.org/standards/standards-development/universal-standards/

Global Reporting Initiative. (2024b). *GRI sustainability reporting trends 2024.* GRI. https://www.globalreporting.org/

Government of Indonesia. (2017). *Presidential Regulation No. 59/2017 on the Implementation of the Achievement of Sustainable Development Goals.* Jakarta: Government of Indonesia.

Grober, U. (2007). Deep roots: A conceptual history of "sustainable development" (Nachhaltigkeit). WZB Discussion Paper P 2007–002. Wissenschaftszentrum Berlin für Sozialforschung.

Hahn, R. (2013). ISO 26000 and the standardization of strategic management processes for sustainability and corporate social responsibility. *Business Strategy and the Environment, 22*(7), 442–455. https://doi.org/10.1002/bse.1751

Hammer, J., & Pivo, G. (2017). The triple bottom line and sustainable economic development theory and practice. *Economic Development Quarterly, 31*(1), 25–36. https://doi.org/10.1177/0891242416674808

Indonesia Financial Services Authority (OJK). (2024). *Indonesia Taxonomy for Sustainable Finance (TKBI)*, Version 1. Indonesia Financial Services Authority (OJK).

Indonesia Financial Services Authority (OJK). (2025). *Indonesia Taxonomy for Sustainable Finance (TKBI)*, Version 2. Indonesia Financial Services Authority (OJK).

Indonesian Institute of Accountants. (2023). *Pernyataan Standar Pelaporan Keberlanjutan (PSPK 1 & 2).* IAI. https://iaiglobal.or.id/

International Capital Market Association. (2021). *Green Bond Principles: Voluntary process guidelines for issuing green bonds.* ICMA. https://www.icmagroup.org/

International Energy Agency. (2023a). *Indonesia Energy Transition Outlook 2023.* IEA. https://www.iea.org/

International Energy Agency. (2023b). *Data centres and data transmission networks.* IEA. https://www.iea.org/

International Organization for Standardization. (2010). *ISO 26000:2010 Guidance on social responsibility.* ISO. https://www.iso.org/standard/42546.html

International Platform on Sustainable Finance. (2022). *Common Ground Taxonomy—Climate change mitigation: Instruction report.* European Commission.

IFRS Foundation (ISSB). (2023). *IFRS S1 General requirements for disclosure of sustainability-related financial information and IFRS S2 Climate-related disclosures.* IFRS. https://www.ifrs.org/

Jänicke, M. (1990). *State failure: The impotence of politics in industrial society.* Penn State University Press.

Kementerian Lingkungan Hidup dan Kehutanan. (2023a). *Program Penilaian Peringkat Kinerja Perusahaan dalam Pengelolaan Lingkungan Hidup (PROPER).* KLHK. https://www.menlhk.go.id/

Kementerian Lingkungan Hidup dan Kehutanan. (2023b). *Laporan PROPER 2023.* KLHK. https://www.menlhk.go.id/

Kenter, J. O., Reed, M. S., & Fazey, I. (2015). The deliberative value formation model: Integrating non-monetary values into ecosystem service assessments. *Ecological Economics, 114,* 32–44. https://doi.org/10.1016/j.ecolecon.2015.03.018

Komisi Nasional Hak Asasi Manusia. (2013). *Pembangunan berbasis hak asasi manusia: Sebuah panduan.* Komnas HAM. https://www.komnasham.go.id/files/20131117-pembangunan-berbasis-hak-asasi-%24SLP7PE.pdf

KPMG. (2022). *The time has come: The KPMG survey of sustainability reporting 2022.* KPMG International. https://kpmg.com/

KPMG. (2023). *ISSB Standards: A new global baseline for sustainability disclosures.* KPMG International. https://home.kpmg/

Laplume, A. O., Sonpar, K., & Litz, R. A. (2008). Stakeholder theory: Reviewing a theory that moves us. *Journal of Management, 34*(6), 1152–1189. https://doi.org/10.1177/0149206308324322

Lélé, S. M. (1991). Sustainable development: A critical review. *World Development, 19*(6), 607–621. https://doi.org/10.1016/0305-750X(91)90197-P

Mahajan, R., Lim, W. M., Sareen, M., Kumar, S., & Panwar, R. (2023). Stakeholder theory. *Journal of Business Research, 166,* 114104. https://doi.org/10.1016/j.jbusres.2023.114104

Mebratu, D. (1998). Sustainability and sustainable development: Historical and conceptual review. *Environmental Impact Assessment Review, 18*(6), 493–520. https://doi.org/10.1016/S0195-9255(98)00019-5

Microsoft. (2024). *Microsoft sustainability report 2024.* Microsoft Corporation. https://www.microsoft.com/sustainability

Ministry of Finance of the Republic of Indonesia. (2022). *Green Sukuk Allocation and Impact Report 2022.* Directorate General of Budget Financing and Risk Management. https://www.djppr.kemenkeu.go.id/

Ministry of Finance of the Republic of Indonesia. (2023). *Indonesia's Green Sukuk Report 2018–2023.* Ministry of Finance. https://www.djppr.kemenkeu.go.id/

Mol, A. P. J. (1996). Ecological modernisation and institutional reflexivity: Environmental reform in the late modern age. *Environmental Politics, 5*(2), 302–323. https://doi.org/10.1080/09644019608414266

Mol, A. P. J. (2002). Ecological modernization and the global economy. *Global Environmental Politics, 2*(2), 92–115. https://doi.org/10.1162/15263800260047844

Moratis, L., & Cochius, T. (2011). *ISO 26000: The business guide to the new standard on social responsibility.* Greenleaf Publishing.

Natural Capital Coalition. (2016). *Natural Capital Protocol: Food and beverage sector guide.* Capitals Coalition. https://capitalscoalition.org/

Neumayer, E. (2003). *Weak versus strong sustainability: Exploring the limits of two opposing paradigms* (2nd ed.). Edward Elgar Publishing.

Nilsson, M., Chisholm, E., Griggs, D., Howden-Chapman, P., McCollum, D., Messerli, P., … Stafford-Smith, M. (2018). Mapping interactions between the sustainable development goals: Lessons learned and ways forward. *Sustainability Science, 13*(6), 1489–1503. https://doi.org/10.1007/s11625-018-0604-z

Nussbaum, M. C. (2011). *Creating capabilities: The human development approach.* Harvard University Press.

OECD. (2019). *Policy Coherence for Sustainable Development 2019: Empowering people and ensuring inclusiveness and equality.* OECD Publishing. https://doi.org/10.1787/a90f851f-en

OECD. (2021a). *OECD SDG Review of Indonesia 2021.* OECD Publishing. https://www.oecd.org/

OECD. (2021b). *Green, social, sustainability and sustainability-linked bonds: Policy considerations for Indonesia.* OECD Publishing. https://www.oecd.org/

OECD. (2021c). *Developing sustainable finance markets in emerging economies: Policy considerations for Indonesia.* OECD Publishing. https://www.oecd.org/

Otoritas Jasa Keuangan. (2017). *POJK No. 51/POJK.03/2017 on the implementation of sustainable finance for financial institutions, issuers, and public companies.* OJK. https://www.ojk.go.id/

Otoritas Jasa Keuangan. (2021). *Sustainable Finance Roadmap Phase II (2021–2025).* OJK. https://www.ojk.go.id/

Otoritas Jasa Keuangan. (2022). *Taksonomi Keuangan Berkelanjutan Indonesia (TKBI) 2.0.* OJK. https://www.ojk.go.id/

Pertamina. (2024). *Pertamina raih 34 PROPER emas dan 76 PROPER hijau tahun 2023.* PT Pertamina (Persero). https://www.pertamina.com/

Pisano, U. (2012). *Resilience and sustainable development: Theory of resilience, systems thinking and adaptive governance.* ESDN Quarterly Report No. 26. European Sustainable Development Network.

Pramono, A., Nugroho, A., & Fitriani, E. (2021). Localizing the Sustainable Development Goals in Indonesia: Institutional challenges and policy opportunities. *Sustainability, 13*(19), 10823. https://doi.org/10.3390/su131910823

PT PLN (Persero). (2021). Rencana Usaha Penyediaan Tenaga Listrik PT PLN (Persero) 2021–2030. PT PLN (Persero).

Rawls, J. (1971). *A theory of justice: Original edition*. Cambridge, MA: Belknap Press of Harvard University Press.
Republika. (2023, June 15). Evaluasi PROPER: Perlu penguatan indikator hasil lingkungan. *Republika Online*. https://www.republika.co.id/
Reuters. (2024, March 7). *The new frontier of nature-related financial disclosures: What the finance industry needs to know*. Reuters.
Richardson, K., Steffen, W., Rockström, J., Lenton, T. M., Lamontagne, J. R., Chaves, R. M., ... Donges, J. F. (2023). Earth beyond six of nine planetary boundaries. *Science Advances, 9*(37), eadh2458. https://doi.org/10.1126/sciadv.adh2458
Roberts, B., & Cohen, M. (2002). Enhancing sustainable development by triple value adding to the core business of government. *Economic Development Quarterly, 16*(2), 127–137. https://doi.org/10.1177/0891242402016002003
Robeyns, I. (2017). *Well-being, justice, and development ethics: The capability approach*. Oxford University Press.
Rockström, J., Steffen, W., Noone, K., Persson, Å., Chapin, F. S., Lambin, E. F., Lenton, T. M., Scheffer, M., Folke, C., Schellnhuber, H. J., Nykvist, B., de Wit, C. A., Hughes, T., van der Leeuw, S., Rodhe, H., Sörlin, S., Snyder, P. K., Costanza, R., Svedin, U., ... Foley, J. A. (2009). A safe operating space for humanity. *Nature, 461*(7263), 472–475. https://doi.org/10.1038/461472a
Ruggie, J. G. (2013). *Just business: Multinational corporations and human rights*. W. W. Norton & Company.
Ruggie, J. G. (2014). Global governance and "new governance theory": Lessons from business and human rights. *Global Governance, 20*(1), 5–17. https://doi.org/10.5555/1075-2846-20.1.5
Schaltegger, S., Hörisch, J., & Freeman, R. E. (2019). Business cases for sustainability: A stakeholder theory perspective. *Organization & Environment, 32*(3), 191–212. https://doi.org/10.1177/1086026617722882
Science Based Targets initiative. (2023a). *SBTi Corporate Net-Zero Standard (Version 2.0)*. SBTi. https://sciencebasedtargets.org/
Science Based Targets initiative. (2023b). *Foundations for science-based net-zero target setting in the corporate sector*. SBTi. https://sciencebasedtargets.org/
Scott, W. R. (1987). The adolescence of institutional theory. *Administrative Science Quarterly, 32*(4), 493–511. https://doi.org/10.2307/2392880
Sen, A. (1999). *Development as freedom*. Oxford University Press.
Sen, A. (2002). Health: Perception versus observation. *BMJ, 324*(7342), 860–861. https://doi.org/10.1136/bmj.324.7342.860
Shakespeare, T. (2006). *Disability rights and wrongs*. Routledge.
Smit, B., & Wandel, J. (2006). Adaptation, adaptive capacity and vulnerability. *Global Environmental Change, 16*(3), 282–292. https://doi.org/10.1016/j.gloenvcha.2006.03.008
Spaargaren, G. (1997). *The ecological modernization of production and consumption: Essays in environmental sociology* (Doctoral dissertation). Wageningen University and Research.
Spaargaren, G. (2000). Ecological modernization theory and domestic consumption. *Journal of Environmental Policy and Planning, 2*(4), 323–335. https://doi.org/10.1080/714038561
Steffen, W., Richardson, K., Rockström, J., Cornell, S. E., Fetzer, I., Bennett, E. M., Biggs, R., Carpenter, S. R., de Vries, W., de Wit, C. A., Folke, C., Gerten, D., Heinke, J., Mace, G. M., Persson, L. M., Ramanathan, V., Reyers, B., & Sörlin, S. (2015). Planetary boundaries: Guiding human development on a changing planet. *Science, 347*(6223), 1259855. https://doi.org/10.1126/science.1259855
Stockholm Resilience Centre. (2025). *Planetary boundaries research*. Stockholm University. https://www.stockholmresilience.org/research/planetary-boundaries
Suharto, R., Pramudianto, A., & Sari, D. (2019). Environmental rating programs and industrial compliance: Evaluating Indonesia's PROPER scheme. *Environmental Science and Policy, 101*, 260–268. https://doi.org/10.1016/j.envsci.2019.08.007

Tagliapietra, S., & Wolff, G. B. (2021). The European Union recovery plan: An opportunity to foster the green transition. *Intereconomics, 56*(2), 99–104. https://doi.org/10.1007/s10272-021-0965-x

Task Force on Climate-related Financial Disclosures. (2017). *Final report: Recommendations of the Task Force on Climate-related Financial Disclosures.* Financial Stability Board. https://www.fsb-tcfd.org/

Task Force on Climate-related Financial Disclosures. (2021). *Final report: Recommendations of the TCFD.* Financial Stability Board. https://www.fsb-tcfd.org/

Taskforce on Nature-related Financial Disclosures. (2023). *TNFD recommendations: Final framework and guidance.* TNFD Secretariat. https://tnfd.global/

Turner, R. K. (Ed.). (1993). *Sustainable environmental economics and management: Principles and practice.* Belhaven Press.

Unilever. (2024a). *Climate Transition Action Plan 2024.* Unilever PLC. https://www.unilever.com/

Unilever. (2024b). *Supplier Climate Programme report 2024.* Unilever PLC. https://www.unilever.com/

United Nations. (1973). *Report of the United Nations Conference on the Human Environment, Stockholm, 5–16 June 1972.* United Nations.

United Nations. (2011). *Guiding principles on business and human rights: Implementing the United Nations "Protect, Respect and Remedy" framework.* Office of the High Commissioner for Human Rights. https://www.ohchr.org/

United Nations. (2015). *Transforming our world: The 2030 Agenda for Sustainable Development (A/RES/70/1).* United Nations General Assembly. https://sdgs.un.org/2030agenda

United Nations Conference on Environment and Development. (1992a). *Agenda 21.* United Nations.

United Nations Conference on Environment and Development. (1992b). *Rio Declaration on Environment and Development.* In Report of the United Nations Conference on Environment and Development, Rio de Janeiro, 3–14 June 1992 (A/CONF.151/26/Rev. 1, Vol. I, Annex I). United Nations.

United Nations Development Programme. (2022). *Sovereign green bonds and sukuk: Unlocking sustainable finance for development.* UNDP. https://www.undp.org/

United Nations Development Programme, & World Bank. (2022). *Scaling up sustainable finance through green bonds and sukuk: Opportunities and challenges for emerging markets.* UNDP & World Bank. https://www.worldbank.org/

United Nations Environment Programme Finance Initiative. (2021). *Principles for responsible banking—Guidance on SME inclusion in sustainable finance.* UNEP FI. https://www.unepfi.org/

United Nations Framework Convention on Climate Change. (2015). *Adoption of the Paris Agreement (FCCC/CP/2015/L.9/Rev.1).* UNFCCC. https://unfccc.int/process-and-meetings/the-paris-agreement/the-paris-agreement

United Nations Framework Convention on Climate Change. (2022). *Nationally determined contributions under the Paris Agreement: Synthesis report by the secretariat (FCCC/PA/CMA/2022/4).* United Nations.

Vardon, M., Castaneda, J.-P., Nagy, C., & Schenau, S. (2019). The accounting push and the policy pull: Balancing environment and economic decisions. *Ecological Economics, 161,* 1–8. https://doi.org/10.1016/j.ecolecon.2019.03.018

Vázquez, T. S., & Sumner, A. (2013). Revisiting the meaning of development: A multidimensional taxonomy of developing countries. *The Journal of Development Studies, 49*(12), 1728–1745. https://doi.org/10.1080/00220388.2013.822071

Walker, B., & Salt, D. (2006). *Resilience thinking: Sustaining ecosystems and people in a changing world.* Island Press.

Walker, B., Holling, C. S., Carpenter, S. R., & Kinzig, A. (2004). Resilience, adaptability and transformability in social–ecological systems. *Ecology and Society, 9*(2), 5. https://doi.org/10.5751/ES-00650-090205

Weitz, N., Carlsen, H., Nilsson, M., & Skånberg, K. (2018). Towards systemic and contextual priority setting for implementing the 2030 Agenda. *Sustainability Science, 13*(2), 531–548. https://doi.org/10.1007/s11625-017-0470-0
World Bank. (2021). *Green and sustainable sukuk: Leveraging Islamic finance for climate action.* World Bank Group. https://www.worldbank.org/
World Bank. (2023). *Sustainability reporting in emerging markets: Challenges and opportunities.* World Bank Group. https://www.worldbank.org/
World Commission on Environment and Development. (1987). *Our common future.* Oxford University Press.
World Resources Institute. (2023). *The role of SBTi in driving corporate climate action.* WRI. https://www.wri.org/
World Wide Fund for Nature. (2023). *SBTi progress and pathways report 2023.* WWF International. https://www.wwf.org/

# Chapter 3
# Sustainable and Green Economy: A Systematic Review

**Arlyana Abubakar, Prayudhi Azwar, Riris Shanti Fransiska Pardede, and Salman Fathoni**

**Abstract** This chapter reviews the concept of the green economy within the broader sustainability discourse using a systematic literature review of Scopus-indexed studies from 2016–2025. It shows that, despite growing prominence after the SDGs and the Paris Agreement, the green economy remains conceptually diverse and context-dependent. Bibliometric analysis identifies key linkages with technology, finance, governance, and the circular economy. The chapter suggest that effective implementation requires coherent measurement frameworks, sector-specific pathways, institutional coordination, and alignment between economic growth, environmental limits, and social equity, particularly in developing-country contexts.

**Keywords** Green economy · Sustainability · Systematic literature review (SLR) · Green concept · Green strategy

## 1 Introduction

The concept of a green economy gained momentum with the onset of the global economic and financial crisis at the end of 2007. But in fact, this idea has been around for more than half a century in academic discussions (Pearce et al., 1989; Jacobs, 1991). However, policymakers showed little interest in this early research. In the middle of the continually evolving classification of the relationship between the green economy and sustainable development, the most crucial question is how the concept, stance, and connection of the green economy relate to social and environmental justice. Equity must be at the center of any debate on transitional development models (Reiff, 2013). The transition must take into account how policies aiming at developing a greener economy might take into account the impact and possibilities for overall equity.

A. Abubakar (✉) · P. Azwar · R. S. F. Pardede · S. Fathoni
Bank Indonesia, Jakarta, Indonesia
e-mail: arlyana@bi.go.id; yudhi@bi.go.id; riris@bi.go.id; salman_f.i@bi.go.id



S. M. Juhro et al. (eds.), *Sustainable Economy: The Indonesian Pathways*,
https://doi.org/10.1007/978-981-92-1215-6_3

At the same time, the green economy is closely connected to the broader idea of sustainability. While the green economy provides specific strategies to reduce carbon intensity and foster eco-friendly innovation, sustainability offers the overarching paradigm that balances three interconnected pillars: economic viability, social equity, and environmental integrity. Recent bibliometric evidence confirms that research is increasingly linking the green economy with sustainability frameworks, reflecting a global shift toward integrative approaches that position the green economy not merely as an environmental tool but as a pillar of long-term sustainable development (Apriantoro et al., 2024). Positioning the green economy within the sustainability agenda ensures that it is not seen merely as an environmental initiative, but as part of a long-term transformation toward inclusive and equitable development that benefits both present and future generations.

Shifting to a green economy requires clear measurements and indicators to guide its implementation. The Green Growth Knowledge Platform (2013) highlights the need to track economic opportunities and transitions, as well as to assess the tools and policy limits connected to the green economy. Similarly, the United Nations (2014) stresses the importance of having agreed rules and boundaries. This means the scope of the green economy must always be reviewed and understood within its core concept.

In this study, we analyze and define green economy principles to establish green economy constraints. The article then considers the consequences of adopting a green economy. This study, which employs a systematic literature review (SLR) methodology, aims to provide new insights and understanding into the concept of the "green economy." To achieve this, the purpose of this research is to determine how the concept of a green economy may be implemented globally.

The use of an SLR for this study aims to look at empirical evidence related to several aspects contained in the green economy concept. This makes it possible to compare the results of the findings of other researchers to identify similarities, connections, differences, and gaps that allow for further research. A thorough examination of the green economy and its evolution process is important and required. This study examines many modalities and evolutionary trajectories of the green economy. Thus, it provides a solid theoretical foundation for a more relevant and comprehensive conceptual framework of green economy that is required in implementing green economy policy, research, and activity to build a new ecological civilization.

The remainder of this chapter is divided into the following sections. A theoretical foundation for green economic ideas is provided in the second section. The third section explains the approach utilized to investigate the subject (literature-based analysis). The fourth section provides the results and discussion. The last section ends the article by giving suggestions for future agendas.

## 2 Literature Review

The Brundtland Report (1987) supplied the normative foundation—"needs" and intergenerational justice—upon which later "green economy" ideas were built. In the late 1980s, Pearce et al., (1989) established the concept of a green economy for the first time in their renowned report "Blueprint for a Green Economy," in which they recommend that the government of the United Kingdom add the term "sustainable development" and investigate its implications for measuring economic success and evaluating projects and programs. The concept of a green economy is not thoroughly explained in the "Blueprint for a Green Economy."

Jacobs (1991) made the first attempt to describe a green economy in his book The Green Economy, where he established the identification of the term through a rigorous theoretical explanation of the ideology and academic discipline of the green economy. Pearce (1991, 1993) published Blueprint 2: Greening the World Economy (1991) and Blueprint 3: Measuring Sustainable Development (1993), respectively. In these two publications, Pearce developed the first blueprint for a green economy, focusing on climate change, ozone depletion, tropical deforestation, and the degradation of natural resources to support environmental laws.

During the 1990s and early 2000s, the concept lost attention, but it was revived in 2008 by the UN Environment Programme (UNEP) as a response to the global financial crisis (Bina & la Camera, 2011; Death, 2015). According to UNEP (2008), the principles of a green economy include: recognizing the value of natural resources and investing in them, increasing the efficiency of resource and energy use, encouraging low-emission and sustainable lifestyles, diverting the use of fossil fuels to renewable and low-emission energy, growing faster while conserving natural resources, reducing poverty, boosting employment, and promoting social equity.

The green economy is a future operating approach that encourages economic recovery and more sustainable growth (Barbier, 2012; Georgeson et al., 2017). During the financial crisis and fears of a global recession, UNEP championed the concept of green stimulus packages and highlighted industries in which large-scale public investment might adopt green economy principles (AtKisson, 2012). As a result, some governments have launched extensive "green stimulus" programs as part of their economic recovery attempts.

In the years following the 2008 financial crisis, the concept of the green economy gained significant momentum. When the World Bank and the Organization for Economic Cooperation and Development (OECD) began promoting the green economy more strongly at the global level, the idea once again sparked wide debate. The OECD's 2009 Green Growth Declaration and the 2011 Green Growth Strategy Package showed its clear commitment to advancing and applying the concept. These two key reports soon became influential references, shaping how many nations developed their own approaches to the green economy.

In 2012, the United Nations Conference on Sustainable Development (UNCSD, often known as Rio + 20) had the green economy as one of its focus areas. There was some hope in the build-up to Rio + 20 that it could generate enough consensus to create political and financial backing for the green economy (Damon & Sterner, 2012). In 2015, the world adopted the 2030 Agenda (17 SDGs) and the Paris Agreement, targeting temperature rise "well below 2°C" and pursuing 1.5 °C—placing decarbonization at the core of the green economy. Since then, the green economy has been understood as a development pathway compatible with both SDGs and Paris-aligned temperature goals (UNFCCC, 2016; United Nation, 2015). The SDGs and Paris Agreement reframed green economy as an enabler linking societal goals (poverty, resilience, shared prosperity) to outcomes, provided measurement frameworks capture economy–society–environment interactions and move beyond GDP (Georgeson, 2024).

The definition of a green economy is typically defined as having a broad reach (Bigg, 2011; Loiseau et al., 2016a), being ambiguous (Jänicke, 2012), and sparking disputes (PEP, 2012; Jakob & Edenhofer, 2014; Faccer et al., 2014; Buseth, 2017; Speck & Zoboli, 2017). Some economists say that the inherent difficulties of the concept of a green economy contribute to the lack of consensus regarding the definition of a green economy (Georgeson et al., 2017; Merino-Saum et al., 2020). Some additional viewpoints assert that the conceptual uncertainty is a result of the existing political problems surrounding the green transition and highlights differences in international governance over the green economy (Brown et al., 2014).

Since 2012, the green economy has been presented as a model for mitigating climate change, a driver of economic growth, and a tool for reducing poverty. In general, the achievement of sustainable development is inextricably related to the green economy (UNEP, 2011a). However, this method was severely criticized by other scientists whose fields of research intersected with this one. First, according to some academics, sustainable development is too wide and difficult to operationalize; therefore, the deployment of a green economy would encounter the same difficulty (Borel-Saladin & Turok, 2013). Additionally, the green economy is an instrument for achieving sustainable development. The green economy should be viewed as an adjunct to sustainable development, not a replacement (OECD, 2011). Third, the green economy and sustainable development are identical. According to these individuals, the terms are interchangeable. The green economy, according to Halle (2011), is a rebranding of sustainable development. Likewise, Abaza et al. (2011) demonstrate that a green economy contributes nothing novel to the concept of sustainable development.

The agreement of international organizations on the notion of a green economy includes the following: (1) a clear link with the concept of sustainable development; and (2) the concept of a green economy as a tool for growth that blends economic benefits with environmental and social outcomes (Speck & Zoboli, 2017). Faccer et al. (2014) describe three identify three unique concepts of the green economy: (1) an incrementalist perspective, Focuses on continuous economic growth, values technology and market solutions, but pays little attention to environmental limits.; (2) a reformist perspective, which also Also prioritizes economic growth and technology, but recognizes the tension between growth and environmental protection; and (3) a transformative perspective, which emphasizes a paradigm shift from economic growth to environmental protection.

## 3 Data and Methodology

In this study, we conduct an SLR to assess the impact of the green economy concept. An SLR can be described as the location, synthesis, assessment, and combination of results of existing studies on a particular topic (Fink, 2019). The process involves identifying, evaluating, and interpreting all available articles to provide answers to specific research questions (Kitchenham & Charters, 2007; Staples & Niazi, 2007).

There are substantial data and capacity constraints that must be surmounted to measure all aspects of the green economy. However, there are reasons to be concerned about the availability of official data assessing the green economy. A lack of data can affect the measurement of progress toward diverse green economy objectives and might lead to reliance on less robust models of such an economy. In this study, we carry out a thorough literature review to identify datasets concerning the green economy.

The accurate sampling and identification of the data from the literature review was ensured by adopting an appropriate methodology (Webster & Watson, 2018). Scopus is one of the world's major databases, indexing scientific journals, books, and conference papers, containing data used by academics, governments, and corporations for their analysis. This study uses a mix of Boolean search and Bibliometric network analysis utilizing various combinations of search phrases related to the notion of the green economy to boost the effectiveness of the sample search. As described by Eck & Waltman (2014), a bibliometric network consists of the vertices and edges that demonstrate the correlation and strength of the relationships between words. The database uses keywords for sorting sources by title, abstract, and keywords. SLR can randomly rank articles according to the research's keywords; hence, keywords must be determined beforehand to restrict the research's scope. In this study, the keywords used are (concept AND green AND economy). Existing studies use different terms to refer to the concept of the green economy, and the search terms here are broad to reflect this fact: (sustainab* AND green economy).

In the SLR process, articles are selected if the green economy concept is raised. In addition, additional complementary inclusion and exclusion criteria are applied to obtain the best results. Only articles published between 2016 and August 2025 are included.

The results obtained from this search yielded 20.730 articles in which the concept of the green economy is discussed. The specified eligibility criteria are employed in the sorting process to ensure the correct studies are selected. The search was limited to articles and reviews indexed in the Scopus database and published in English. Subsequent sorting is based on the number of interconnections overall and between individual articles. The final sorting step involves reading each study identified in its entirety and sorting the sample according to the extent of their focus on green-economy concepts. This multi-stage selection process resulted in a final dataset comprising 144 articles.

# 4 Discussion

## *4.1 The Green Economy Concept*

Guided by the abovementioned understandings and theories, the concept of the green economy continues to evolve, improve, and innovate, deepening the possibilities of its practical application. Transforming current modes of economic development requires understanding the green economy's evolutionary path and trends; there has, to date, been no specialized and comprehensive study conducted on this topic. In the first stage of the SLR, the findings are in line with Bigg (2011) and Loiseau et al. (2016b), who argue that the concept of the green economy is too broad and ambiguous. This can be seen from the word cloud, which reflects research topics related to the green economy discussed in the sample.

This ambiguity results in different interpretations and limits the extent to which the concept can be applied and implemented; as a logical corollary, the boundaries between the concept of a green economy and other related terms are fuzzy and contested. Indeed, although international organizations insist that a green economy is not a mere substitute for sustainable development (OECD, 2011; UNEP, 2011a), observers have wondered whether there is any difference between them.

The green economy is alternatively presented as "the child of" (Jacobs, 2013), "the intellectual cousin of" (Fiorino, 2014), "a key vehicle for" (ten Brink, 2012), "a way to operationalize" (GGKP, 2016), "a pathway to" (UNEP, 2011b), "a support of" (UNDESA, 2012), or still "an enabler of" sustainable development (Georgeson et al., 2017; UNCTAD, 2011). As these examples illustrate, the green economy and sustainable development are most often articulated using teleological reasoning, with the former a means to achieve the latter. The green economy is also usually presented as "narrower in scope" (OECD, 2011) and "more focused" (Brown et al., 2014; Ferguson, 2015), "practical" (Choi, 2015), or "operational" (GGKP, 2016) as a concept than sustainable development.

## *4.2 The Sustainability and Green Economy*

### Framing Sustainability and Green Economy

Fundamentally, the link between sustainability and the green economy combines normative goals with practical tools: sustainability defines the aim of protecting ecological integrity and social well-being across generations, while the green economy activates technologies, markets, and institutions that address environmental externalities and adjust incentives. Research on "values–growth-relationships" highlights the need to rethink current growth models through systems thinking, ensuring that economic expansion does not undermine ecological resources or social cohesion (Dalei & Heggde, 2021). Putting this into practice calls for governance that values ecosystem services, uncludes the true social and environmental costs of production, and outlines the changes required to scale up agroecology and other low-impact strategies (Andres & Bhullar, 2016), social criteria must sit alongside techno-economic metrics from the outset—e.g., green-hydrogen assessment frameworks that elevate equity, basic needs, and project-planning justice—so that cost is never the sole decision rule in green transitions (Blohm & Dettner, 2023).

For this to work, measurement tools are essential. Indicators such as the Environmental Human Index (EHI), which combines the Human Development Index (HDI) and Environmental Performance Index (EPI), help show whether human development is progressing at the cost of environmental damage (Y. Zhang & Wu, 2022). When making decisions with limited or mixed evidence, tools like Bayesian Decision Nets can combine numbers and expert judgment. These tools help estimate the overall benefits of development options across social, economic, and environmental aspects. In some cases, they even challenge the usual assumptions about projects such as irrigation and infrastructure (Crossman & Pollino, 2018). Downstream, procurement-ready methods such as CEACE operationalize this framing by combining ecological, carbon, and water footprints with economic and social criteria—plus explicit accounting of construction and demolition waste—so that "green public procurement" becomes a measurable lever for circularity and decarbonization (Solís-Guzmán et al., 2024).

Finally, the framing must be institutionally and politically literate. Business-model innovation in the circular bio-economy shows that technological options scale only when embedded in cross-sector partnerships and value co-creation logics, not linear supply chains (Donner & de Vries, 2021). Participatory, spatially explicit scenario processes that reconcile local knowledge with national data improve the social license and policy relevance of green pathways (Capitani et al., 2016), while political-economy evidence reminds us that perceived effectiveness, trust, and communication can make or break otherwise successful environmental policies at the ballot box (Gainza & Montes-Nebreda, 2023). A credible approach to sustainability and the green economy must be at once normative (values), diagnostic (metrics and models), and institutional (governance and legitimacy)—bringing ecological limits together with human development and lasting policy action.

## Sectoral Pathways: Energy, Industry, and Infrastructure (Technology)

Coal remains a structural hinge in many energy systems, yet its life-cycle burdens underscore why phasing it down is central to a credible green economy. A mine-level life cycle assessment (LCA) in China shows that coal extraction and its auxiliary processes (steel and electricity inputs, ventilation) dominate impacts across fossil depletion, ecotoxicity, climate change, eutrophication and human toxicity, with efficiency improvements and activity reductions identified as the primary levers (Tao et al., 2022). Resource-dependent cities reliant on coal likewise demonstrate persistently low green development scores, with strong regional disparities between eastern and western regions (Long et al., 2021). These findings indicate that a credible green economy requires not only the systematic phasing down of coal but also transition strategies that are sensitive to geographic, economic, and social contexts. Without such place-based approaches, cities at different life-cycle stages risk remaining locked in environmentally damaging growth trajectories.

A diverse portfolio of alternative energy pathways is emerging to displace coal in power and heat generation. Hydrogen occupies a central role, with production routes expanding beyond canonical electrolysis to include solar-driven processes (Kalaiselvan & Mathimani, 2024), direct-air electrolysis that harvests atmospheric moisture at ~95% Faradaic efficiency in arid regions (Guo et al., 2022), and biohydrogen generated from waste streams, thereby strengthening circular economy linkages (Ahmad et al., 2024; S. Li et al., 2024; A. K. Sharma et al., 2025a). Waste-to-energy pathways demonstrate further potential by converting municipal burdens into hydrogen (Okedu et al., 2022), while reimagining coal as a precursor for graphitic nanomaterials offers a materials-economy trajectory that reduces combustion demand (B. Zhang et al., 2024). Such diversification minimizes the risk of technological lock-in and enhances resilience, though challenges related to cost, efficiency, and scale-up remain significant.

Yet technology alone cannot deliver the transition. Policy design, including environmental taxation, subsidy reform, and green finance, shapes the trajectory of energy markets by realigning fiscal incentives and accelerating low-carbon adoption (Cao et al., 2025; Y. Cheng et al., 2024b). For example, in Indonesia, annual variation in green finance dedicated to the power sector remains modest at only 3.1%, highlighting the need for deeper fiscal realignment (Cao et al., 2025). Just transition modelling in South Africa's coal heartland (Mpumalanga) further warns that without rapid reinvestment, regional economies may shrink relative to baseline, though well-sequenced financing can yield a long-run "double dividend" of growth and environmental gains (Bohlmann et al., 2023). Coordinated hydrogen supply chains likewise demand multi-stage planning under uncertainty (Sgarbossa et al., 2022, 2023), while digital infrastructures such as blockchain, Logistics 5.0, and Industry 4.0 enhance sustainability and transparency (Huang et al., 2024; Machado & Rodríguez, 2025; Umar et al., 2022). Ultimately, community micro-grids with hydrogen storage, cooperative market hubs, and governance frameworks that prioritize social acceptance, safety, and planning justice (Blohm & Dettner, 2023; C. Cheng et al., 2024a). illustrate how enabling infrastructures, market rules, and policy can together anchor the green economy.

## Circular Economy and Waste Valorization

Bibliometric signals across the sustainability corpus converge on circularity as both a design paradigm and a systems-governance challenge: moving from end-of-pipe control to "waste-as-resource" requires new business models, multi-actor coordination, and place-based policy toolkits (Donner & de Vries, 2021; Skripnuk et al., 2023). Municipal strategies that pair technical programs with citizen participation—zero-landfill roadmaps, door-to-door sorting, donation networks, and community training—consistently raise diversion rates but also surface social trade-offs where political contestation and perceived effectiveness shape outcomes as much as engineering (Cannavò et al., 2019; Gainza & Montes-Nebreda, 2023; Tantanee & Hantrakul, 2019). At the national level, research has moved beyond simply measuring waste tonnages to linking circular economy indicators with wider sustainability goals like footprints, equity, and procurement. This shift helps policy account for external costs in project evaluations and public purchasing (Solís-Guzmán et al., 2024). Recent bibliometric reviews also show that since 2020 there has been a strong move toward digital tools (AI, platforms) and sector-specific studied (hospitality, supply chains), marking progress from broad ideas to real-world applications (Gál et al., 2025).

Technological pathways now span catalytic upcycling, green materials, and bio-valorization. Waste-derived functional materials—from cornstalk-based bifunctional oxygen reduction/oxidation reaction (ORR/OER) electrocatalysts that outperform Pt/C and $IrO_2$ to wood-sawdust/magnetite Fenton catalysts optimized via response-surface methods—demonstrate performance parity with incumbent, high-impact inputs while closing agricultural loops (Y. Li et al., 2022; Nour et al., 2022). Construction ecosystems are particularly dynamic: agricultural residues (almond skins, straw, pigeon-pea ash), agro-industrial by-products (rice husk ash, coconut fiber), and hazardous process wastes (bypass cement dust) are entering cementitious and insulation applications with verified mechanical, durability, and hygro-acoustic gains, alongside low-temperature geopolymerization routes that cut energy and toxicity (Hassan et al., 2025; Krishnan & Senthil Selvan, 2025; Liuzzi et al., 2020; Morato et al., 2024; Peterková et al., 2025). Circular mining backfill engineered with trace graphene oxide and fly ash reduces $CO_2$ per unit strength by ~48% while improving permeability and strength, illustrating micro-to-macro performance coupling (Yu et al., 2025). Beyond the built environment, bio-based products are scaling: cellulose-reinforced bioplastics from bagasse and corn cobs exhibit rapid biodegradation (≈85% mass loss in 50 days) and antimicrobial shelf-life extension, while citrus and celery peel streams yield value-added pectin/limonene and functional food ingredients when solvent systems and extraction routes are optimized by LCA (Askin-Uzel, 2023; Latif et al., 2024). Wastewater and e-waste round out the portfolio: integrated precipitation/advanced oxidation can remove >90% chloride from industrial effluents, and biomass-based leaching recovers 80–90% of lithium (Li), cobalt (Co), nickel (Ni), and iron (Fe) from spent lithium-ion batteries (LIBs), aligning circular chemistry with critical-materials security (He et al., 2023; Iqbal et al., 2025). Complementary nano-enabled routes convert agro-waste into green energy carriers and storage media, reinforcing a waste-to-energy nexus consistent with circular bioeconomy principles (Sonu et al., 2023).

Expanding these pathways relies on market design, information, and governance. Long-term econometric studies show clear links between waste generation, recycling, and new renewable combustion and national emission trends. This evidence highlights that recycling by itself is not enough to counter growing municipal solid waste unless there are upstream changes in demand and product design. (Sasmoko et al., 2022). In resource-intensive digital trade, incentives for extraction and even "combustible renewable waste" can raise mineral footprints unless countered by transparency and information systems, highlighting the demand-side of circularity (Dong et al., 2024). Standards and procurement matter: integrating footprint-based assessments (ecological, carbon, water) into green public procurement generates reliable demand for low-impact materials and advances efforts in construction and demolition (C&D) waste prevention and reuse (Solís-Guzmán et al., 2024). Industrial practice is moving forwards as well Recycled Concrete Aggregates (RCA)/ Recycled Concrete Sand (RCS)/ Recycled Concrete Powder (RCP) can replace up to about 50% in structural concrete mixes without weakening performance, while full substitution is suitable for non-structural applications. However, incentives for disclosure remain uneven, with evidence of "under-reporting" sustainability innovations when firms perceive risks to their competitive advantage (Baldania et al., 2025; Rossetto, 2025). Ultimately, a successful circular transition requires overcoming barriers to adoption, such as ROI uncertainty, regulatory gaps, and high upfront costs, through targeted policy, financial tools, and capacity building that reduce investment risks and help scale pilot initiatives to urban-industrial levels (Raja et al., 2025).

## Finance, Trade, and Geopolitics

Studies show that geopolitical risk (GPR) can affect green bond prices (GBP) in different ways. Sometimes GBP rises when investors see them as safe assets, but in other cases, demand falls when risks scare investors away. Green bonds can also send signals back to geopolitics, since countries compete for renewable resources (Liu, Qin, et al., 2024b). Because of this two-way link, governments and central banks play an important role. They can read market signals and create policies—like financial buffers and disclosure standards—to keep green finance stable during uncertain times. Beyond bonds, other tools like sustainable insurance and green loans also influence decisions. For example, giving subsidies for green loans is more effective than strict caps in encouraging renewable adoption. On the other hand, overly tough caps can reduce both company and stakeholder value (S. Chen et al., 2024). In cross-border trade, similar issues appear. For instance, in China–Russia trade, green insurance has slowed export growth when not paired with proper policies. This shows that risk-transfer tools alone can harm green trade unless they are combined with tax incentives and common standards for green finance (Xie et al., 2025).

Trade and competitiveness in the green economy hinge on digitalization, innovation, and factor footprints. In China, digital trade, financial development, and green innovation jointly improve ecological performance with rapid convergence toward a stable low-carbon equilibrium, positioning digital trade as a lever for decoupling growth from emissions (Fu et al., 2023). Cross-country analysis further indicates that digital trade and technological innovation lift green total factor productivity, while high material footprints and certain FDI profiles suppress it; education quality conditions these effects asymmetrically across developed and developing economies (T. Zhang & Choi, 2025). Inside global value chains, executive "green awareness" accelerates firms' upgrading in the global green value chain, especially where production is digitally intensive and human capital is strong, highlighting micro-level leadership as a meso-level trade advantage (Huang & Xie, 2025). Yet composition matters: agricultural imports (and in some cases exports) raise per-capita $CO_2$ via embedded logistics and production externalities, underscoring the need to green trade structures, not merely expand volumes (Sirel Öztürk, 2025).

Geopolitics intersects materially with technology and resources. In BRICS economies, GPR directly increases $CO_2$ emissions, but green technological innovation moderates and can ultimately reverse the net impact, arguing for pro-growth R&D policies as climate-security instruments (Zhao et al., 2024). Rare-metal supply chains, which are crucial for clean technologies, face major risks. They are concentrated in only a few regions, raise ethical concerns, and create environmental impacts. Research suggests building more resilient and ethically managed networks that share responsibility across countries and sectors (Marty & Ruel, 2025). Macroeconomic headwinds also matter: panel dynamic ordinary least square (OLS) estimates show inflation curtails green energy consumption over the long run, while geopolitical uncertainty exerts no systematic short-run effect, implying that monetary stability is a prerequisite for sustaining the energy transition (Mishra & Sahu, 2025). Sectoral cases crystallize these forces: blue hydrogen can bridge Colombia's transition, but the binding constraints are $CO_2$ capture capacity (15–180 $MtCO_2$/yr. by 2050) and investment envelopes beyond current roadmaps, necessitating credible carbon capture, utilization, and/or storage (CCUS) policy and finance (Domınguez et al., 2022). For Norway, exporting low-carbon hydrogen (as ammonia) to the EU is techno-economically viable in select scenarios (≈3.5–7.3 €/kg) but constrained by land use, Carbon Capture Storage (CCS) infrastructure, and international cost competition; broad stakeholder engagement and offshore decarbonization can improve feasibility (C. Cheng et al., 2024a). Uruguay's strong renewable base yields levelized cost of hydrogen (LCOH) of 2.11–4.12 USD/kg, yet competitiveness as a net exporter still hinges on electricity and electrolyzer cost reductions (Bouzas et al., 2024).

The way policy is designed at the finance-trade interface will shape both the pace and fairness of green technology adoption. In closed-loop supply chains, carbon taxes and cap-and-trade performs better when permit prices stay below a certain threshold and quotas are matched to abatement efficiency, but when trading prices rise above that level, the advantage shifts toward carbon taxation (Pal, 2025). When embedded within circular supply chains with trade credit, shorter credit periods (compared to replenishment times) cut costs and increase investment in green technology under both systems. This shows that working-capital policies can strengthen carbon policies (Vandana & Cerchione, 2025). Public procurement that internalizes ecological, carbon, and water footprints into budgeting creates durable market pull for low-impact solutions and improves C&D waste prevention outcomes (Solís-Guzmán et al., 2024). Finally, green trade strategies must align with information and social acceptance: sustainability criteria for green hydrogen projects require integrating social and basic-needs metrics alongside energy and environmental indicators to avoid ecological and justice backfires (Blohm & Dettner, 2023), and national hydrogen supply-chain roadmaps should prioritize regulatory clarity, infrastructure, and public acceptance as first-order risks (Ghasemian Sahebi et al., 2025).

## Organizational and Human Drivers

Across the corpus, people and organization centric capabilities emerge as the principal levers that translate green intentions into measurable performance. At the micro–meso interface, green human resource management (GHRM) coupled with organizational learning builds the routines that support circular practices: interpretive structural modelling in Indian manufacturing SMEs shows "green separation" and an "organizational learning culture" as dominant drivers, while green performance management and green health-and-safety depend on these upstream enablers (Subramanian & Suresh, 2022). These HR architectures work through pro-social behaviors: organizational citizenship toward the environment mediates the effects of CSR and GHRM on triple-bottom-line outcomes in multi-firm evidence (Malik et al., 2021). Consistent with a resource-based view of the firm, specific HR levers—green recruitment and training—exhibit positive effects on sustainability in Malaysian large manufacturers, underscoring the role of skill pipelines and capability building (Yong et al., 2020). More broadly, sustainable HR practices correlate with higher organizational performance, strengthening the business case for embedding green criteria across recruitment, development, appraisal and rewards (Cherian et al., 2019).

Leadership, engagement, and knowledge flows shape how these systems perform in context. In Saudi manufacturing SMEs, GHRM improves sustainable performance directly and indirectly by activating green work engagement, a partial mediator that operationalizes employees' energy and persistence on environmental tasks (Alfadel et al., 2025). In Zimbabwean SMEs, GHRM's effect is amplified when green innovation mediates and green knowledge sharing moderates, indicating that social learning and collaborative problem-solving are essential complements to formal HR policies (Makumbe, 2024). Organizational development itself follows discernible phases: cluster analysis across 100 manufacturers identifies maturity patterns of "green organizations" spanning production, HR, marketing, environmental management, supply chain, and circular design—criteria that managers can target to accelerate progression (Graczyk-Kucharska, 2023). Sector-specific governance like a nickel mine in an Islamic economy, GHRM supports a culture of health, safety, and environmental responsibility. Recommended practices include supervised recruitment, focused training, ISO certification, and audit systems to embed safe and eco-efficient operations (Maskuroh et al., 2023).

Upgrading human capital is just as crucial when new low-carbon technologies intersect with existing skills. In Australia, for instance, gasfitters—essential for installing and maintaining household hydrogen appliances, demonstrate limited initial awareness but a high willingness to upskill. To turn this intent into accredited, large-scale capability, effective national programs must coordinate plumbers, employers, vocational training providers, and regulators (Sandri et al., 2024). Multi-stakeholder planning methods help reconcile top-down targets with local knowledge: a participatory scenario framework in Tanzania synthesizes national spatial data with subnational stakeholder inputs to steer land-use toward a "green economy" pathway, illustrating how inclusive processes de-risk implementation and improve policy fit (Capitani et al., 2016). At the societal scale, composite metrics that link human development with environmental outcomes, such as the Environmental human Index, highlight uneven progress and regional faps. These finding remind policy makers that lasting transitions depend on advancing social welfare and ecological quality together (Y. Zhang & Wu, 2022). Finally, managers must navigate paradoxes inside sustainable HRM—efficiency versus responsibility and present versus future—by integrating pillars of socially responsible HRM, GHRM, the common-good perspective, and the triple-bottom-line, supported by organizational and policy scaffolding to resolve trade-offs rather than defer them (Ahmad Giran et al., 2025).

## Green Strategy: Metric-Led, Place-Based Governance

Effective green strategy begins by aligning human development with ecological performance using robust, decision-ready metrics and spatial planning. The Environmental Human Index (EHI)—which integrates the Human Development Index (HDI) with the Environmental Performance Index (EPI)—exposes regional imbalances and helps prioritize interventions where welfare gains are most likely to degrade ecosystems unless policy course-corrects (Y. Zhang & Wu, 2022). Scaling from measurement to action requires participatory, spatially explicit scenario design that connects local knowledge with national targets; Tanzania's green-development scenario demonstrates how stakeholder co-production can reduce deforestation and degradation while lifting productivity through payments for ecosystem services (Capitani et al., 2016). To institutionalize such choices in markets, green public procurement must translate footprints into contracting; Spain's CEACE method operationalizes ecological, carbon, and water footprints—plus social costs and construction-demolition waste—so authorities and firms can rank projects against circularity and equity objectives (Solís-Guzmán et al., 2024).

## Hydrogen-First Decarbonization with Water, Risk, And Capability Constraints In View

Hydrogen should support deep decarbonization where direct electrification is hard, but strategies must reflect water scarcity, infrastructure maturity, and workforce readiness. Direct-air electrolysis (DAE) shows how to decouple green hydrogen from freshwater by harvesting atmospheric moisture and sustaining ~95% Faradaic efficiency even at 4% relative humidity, a pivotal option for arid regions and remote nodes (Guo et al., 2022). Country pathways will differ: Colombia's "blue-to-green" bridge could leverage coal with CCS to reach 0.7–8 Mt. $H_2$ by 2050, provided capture capacity (15–180 $MtCO_2$/yr) and policy finance materialize (Domınguez et al., 2022); Brazil can mobilize ethanol-reforming "green hydrogen" to accelerate jobs and GDP while preparing for renewable-powered electrolysis at scale (Martins et al., 2024). At system level, hydrogen supply-chain (HSC) planning must move beyond legacy tools to manage interdependencies in production, storage, distribution, and end-use under high uncertainty; a dedicated planning matrix tied to technology maturity and market adoption offers a research and practice agenda for resilient build-out (Sgarbossa et al., 2022, 2023). Safety and social license must be given equal importance: probabilistic risk graphs help assess leakage scenarios and rank cost-effective mitigations (such as pressure relief valves), while weighing safety, environmental, and economic impacts (Seiti et al., 2025). Equally, strong talent pipelines are essential surveys of plumbers and gasfitters in Australia reveal positive attitudes but limited hydrogen knowledge, showing that upskilling needs to be aligned with suppliers, regulators, and clients to reduce risks in household hydrogen adoption (Sandri et al., 2024).

## Circular Re-Industrialization and Waste Valorization at Scale

A credible green strategy internalizes circular economy principles in materials, buildings, and energy. Business-model innovations that valorize agricultural by-products succeed when supported in cross-sector partnerships and combined organizational-technological change rather than when a single firm tries to scale up alone (Donner & de Vries, 2021). Lab-to-market evidence is accumulating: orange-peel biocomposites deliver low-frequency acoustic performance comparable to commercial insulation, creating rural income streams while avoiding field burning (Balbay et al., 2024); almond-skin panels hit market-level thermal–acoustic benchmarks (Liuzzi et al., 2020); citrus-waste biorefinery yields limonene and pectin, with LCA revealing solvent selection as the dominant hotspot and a 73.4% footprint reduction via greener alternatives (Midolo et al., 2024). In construction, cemented waste-rock backfill enhanced with trace graphene oxide and fly ash cuts cradle-to-gate $CO_2$ per unit strength by ~48% while improving mechanical performance (Yu et al., 2025); recycled concrete aggregates and powders can replace up to 50% of virgin inputs with acceptable strength for many applications (Baldania et al., 2025).

Municipal levers matter too: "zero-landfill" pathways show that multi-year programs coupling technical assistance, citizen training, and city-to-city knowledge transfer can embed community-based waste systems (Tantanee & Hantrakul, 2019). For energy–waste integration, dark/photo-fermentation and bio-routes turn biowaste into $H_2$, advancing a 5R waste-to-energy nexus within circular bioeconomy policies (Ahmad et al., 2024; A. Sharma et al., 2025b).

#### Finance, Trade, and Geopolitics as Enablers (and Constraints)

Green finance must be designed for resilience under geopolitical volatility. Rolling-window causality shows that green-bond prices both protect against and transmit shocks from geopolitical risk; investors and governments can co-monitor bond and risk dynamics to anticipate turbulence, but elevated risk can also depress green-bond demand (Liu, Qin, et al., 2024b). Digital trade and green innovation, in turn, are associated with improved long-run environmental outcomes. However, the pace and fairness of transition differ by region, meaning digital, financial, and R&D policies must be carefully sequenced (Fu et al., 2023). On hydrogen markets, techno-economic modeling suggests Norway's blue exports could be cost-competitive to the EU if CCS and offshore decarbonization scale, whereas green exports face stiffer competition from low-cost solar geographies; public acceptance, land use, and security concerns must be integrated into siting and diplomacy (C. Cheng et al., 2024a). Uruguay's path underscores that electricity cost (>40% of LCOH) and electrolyzer CAPEX (>30% in polymer electrolyte membrane (PEM)) dominate competitiveness, making renewables expansion and equipment cost curves the strategic hinge for export viability (Bouzas et al., 2024). Trade composition is greening as well: China–ASEAN aquatic trade competitiveness and demand effects are now conditioned by blue-economy sustainability criteria, pressing exporters to upgrade product environmental performance (Kong et al., 2025).

#### Organizational and Human Capital for Execution

Firms drive the transition, and their people determine its success. In manufacturing SMEs, practice like "green separation" (hiring and exits based on environmental criteria) and fostering a strong learning culture act as core enablers. On top of these foundations, green performance management and green health-and-safety systems can be effectively built (Subramanian & Suresh, 2022). Evidence from Malaysia shows green recruitment and training positively affect sustainability, even when other HR levers are neutral (Yong et al., 2020). Organizational citizenship behavior toward the environment mediates the impact of CSR and green HRM on triple-bottom-line performance, signaling the need to cultivate voluntary pro-environmental behaviors (Malik et al., 2021). In emerging-market SMEs, green innovation partially mediates the GHRM–performance link, and green knowledge sharing amplifies it—pointing to knowledge platforms and peer learning as cost-effective accelerants (Makumbe, 2024). Engagement also matters: in Saudi manufacturing SMEs, green work engagement partially mediates GHRM's effect on sustainability performance (Alfadel et al., 2025). Finally, managers must navigate paradoxes (efficiency–responsibility; present–future) by integrating SHRM pillars in decision routines so short-term efficiency does not crowd out substance (Ahmad Giran et al., 2025).

## Systems Engineering, Innovation, and Standards to De-Risk Scale-Up

Green strategy should leverage process-systems engineering and standards to compress the lab-to-market gap. For $CO_2$ circularity, early-stage evaluation and optimal sizing under renewable intermittency help triage electrified $CO_2$-to-fuels routes (direct electroreduction vs. $H_2$-hydrogenation) along sustainability and scale-up criteria (Chung et al., 2023). Materials breakthroughs—such as ohmic $NiS_2$/g-$C_3N_4$ photocatalysts that simultaneously exploit oxidizing holes and reducing electrons to boost $H_2O_2$ photosynthesis ~4.5×—illustrate how device-level advances can cascade into greener chemistries and storage value chains (Z. Zhang et al., 2025). For energy communities, PV-to-$H_2$ microgrids with solid-oxide cells can meet seasonal demand at community scale with compelling abatement per household when paired with tax incentives and extended lifetimes (Enaloui et al., 2025). Across hydrogen projects, measurable sustainability criteria spanning energy transition, environment, basic needs, socio-economy, electricity supply, and project planning should be hard-wired into approvals to avoid social and ecological injustices (Blohm & Dettner, 2023).

## Policy Sequencing and Market Design

Sequencing matters: start with credible measurement and procurement (EHI, CEACE), target early wins in circular materials and municipal waste, and build hydrogen where it is water-secure, system-ready, and socially licensed. Market design should combine certification of green hydrogen, targeted support for hubs and shared infrastructure, and risk-informed safety regulation (R. Chen et al., 2025; Seiti et al., 2025). Internationally, strategies must reduce geopolitical risks in green-bond markets and base export plans on renewable energy costs and CCS readiness (Bouzas et al., 2024; C. Cheng et al., 2024a; Liu, Chen, et al., 2024a). Organizationally, mandate green HRM baselines (recruitment, training, learning culture), measure engagement and citizenship behaviors, and fund sectoral upskilling for hydrogen and circular technologies (Malik et al., 2021; Sandri et al., 2024; Yong et al., 2020). This integrated playbook ties macro-metrics to micro-capabilities, ensuring that finance, technology, and human systems co-evolve toward a just, competitive, and science-based green transition.

## 4.3 Use Case: China and the EU

### China

China's green policy mix is evolving through a layered approach that integrates structural instruments, targeted pilots, and new measurement frameworks. At the city level, smart supply-chain pilots act as quasi-natural experiments that lower coal reliance by diffusing green technologies and upgrading industries, with evidence from 2012–2022 showing measurable declines in coal's energy share where they are deployed (Yang et al., 2025). In coal-resource-based cities, dynamic performance tracking across economic, social, resource, and environmental dimensions (TOPSIS method) has enabled region-and stage-specific interventions, with eastern and "regenerative" coal cities leading in transition outcomes (Long et al., 2021). At the macro scale, the Environmental Human Index (EHI) exposes the imbalance between human welfare gains and ecological pressures, guiding fiscal support, differentiated provincial strategies, and tax or transfer mechanisms to better align human development with environmental performance (Y. Zhang & Wu, 2022).

Industry-level transformation further anchors this trajectory, with firm capabilities and sectoral reconfiguration determining the pace of change. State subsidies and innovation mandates have proven most effective when paired with digitization, catalyzing low-carbon technology adoption among coal firms (X. Li & Wu, 2024). Broader evidence confirms that managerial green awareness and digitization accelerate integration into global green value chains, though effects vary by ownership form and human capital intensity (Huang & Xie, 2025). The solar-hydrogen sector exemplifies these tensions: input-output analyses show strong financial-to-performance linkages but governance fictions, with state-owned enterprises investing more yet underperforming private peers in profitability (Song et al., 2025). Process-systems studies underscore that scaling hydrogen and $CO_2$ conversion requires stable regulation, certification, and storage innovation, while price signals alone are insufficient to drive sectoral R. Chen et al., 2025; Chung et al., 2023).

China's external economic ties increasingly braid sustainability with trade strategy. Under a "blue economy" lens, China–ASEAN aquatic trade growth has been driven primarily by competitiveness on the China-to-ASEAN side and by demand scale on the ASEAN-to-China side, yet both flows now face product-sustainability requirements that will reshape market composition (Kong et al., 2025). With Russia, green finance instruments show uneven real-economy traction—green insurance, in particular, dampens provincial export growth—suggesting that policy design and burden-sharing must be recalibrated to avoid unintended trade frictions while advancing green transformation (Xie et al., 2025). Taken together, China's best practices feature a sequence that combines data-driven regional targeting (EHI, TOPSIS), digital-green pilots to cut coal dependence, innovation-conditioned finance tied to verifiable upgrades, and hydrogen-centric industrial policy that integrates certification, infrastructure, and ownership-neutral competition to unlock system-wide scale.

## European Union

In Europe, hydrogen sits at the core of decarbonization roadmaps, but supply-chain planning and geography matter. A systematic supply-chain planning matrix tailored to renewable hydrogen highlights the interdependencies among production, storage, distribution and multi-sectoral demand, and cautions against transplanting legacy planning methods into a high-uncertainty $H_2$ context (Sgarbossa et al., 2022, 2023). On the import side, scenario modeling positions Norway as a potential EU supplier via ammonia shipping, with blue hydrogen appearing cost-competitive but constrained by CCS infrastructure and natural-gas reliance, while green exports face tougher cost competition and land-use trade-offs—making policy support, stakeholder engagement and careful spatial planning prerequisites for viable EU market integration (C. Cheng et al., 2024a).

The EU's circular economy agenda translates into tangible material innovations and procurement governance. Business-model cases across Europe show that valorizing agricultural by-products hinges on cross-sector partnerships and combined organizational–technological innovation, rather than linear scaling of single-firm solutions (Donner & de Vries, 2021). Laboratory and pilot studies in Italy demonstrate how citrus waste streams can yield pectin and limonene, with life-cycle assessment pinpointing solvent choice as a dominant hotspot and documenting a 73% footprint reduction through greener solvents; likewise, almond-skin panels achieve market-comparable acoustic–thermal performance, illustrating viable substitution pathways in construction materials (Liuzzi et al., 2020; Midolo et al., 2024). To mainstream such choices, Spain's CEACE method operationalizes green public procurement for housing by combining ecological, carbon and water footprints with social and economic metrics and explicit accounting of construction–demolition waste, creating a practical decision tool for authorities and firms (Solís-Guzmán et al., 2024).

Yet European implementation also hinges on social acceptance and political economy. A natural experiment in the Basque Country shows that door-to-door waste collection—despite measurable gains in sorting—incurred sizable electoral penalties amid controversy and information gaps, implying that perceived effectiveness, participatory mechanisms and trust are co-determinants of green policy durability (Gainza & Montes-Nebreda, 2023). These lessons reverberate back to hydrogen siting and renewables build-out: large-scale land and sea use must be balanced with local consent and transparent benefit-sharing (C. Cheng et al., 2024a). In parallel, supply-chain planning guidance for renewable hydrogen underscores the need for phased adoption strategies aligned to technology maturity and market development—linking EU industrial policy, procurement, and infrastructure finance to de-risk first-of-a-kind projects while building public legitimacy (Sgarbossa et al., 2022, 2023).

## 4.4 Indonesian

Indonesia's green economy is anchored in a coherent climate policy framework. The Enhanced NDC 2030 raises emission-reduction targets to 31.89 percent unconditional and 43.20 percent conditional against business-as-usual, aligned with the LTS-LCCR 2050 pathway to net-zero by 2060 or sooner (UNFCCC, 2022). Forestry plays a central role through the FOLU Net Sink 2030, while in the power sector the Just Energy Transition Partnership (JETP) commits to an emissions cap of 290 $MtCO_2$ by 2030 and net-zero power by 2050 (IESR, 2023). Yet implementation remains off-track, with renewable shares at only 13.1 percent in 2023 against the 23 percent target by 2025, and investment needs for the transition estimated at USD 97.1 billion compared to the USD 20 billion JETP package (IESR, 2024).

Indonesia's Nationally Determined Contribution (NDC) targets commit to greenhouse gas emission reductions of 31.89% under the unconditional scenario and 43.2% under the conditional scenario by 2030, with the total mitigation financing requirement estimated at IDR 4002 trillion (Ministry of Environment and Forestry, 2022). However, the country's projected public financing capacity remains substantially below this level. Between 2016 and 2020, government budget allocations for climate change mitigation and adaptation averaged IDR 89.6 trillion per year, representing only 3.9% of total annual public expenditure (Ministry of Finance, 2022). Consequently, an estimated financing gap of approximately 70% must be bridged through private-sector participation. Addressing this substantial funding shortfall requires a comprehensive understanding of green financial policies. Within the green economy framework, fiscal instruments play a critical role in mobilizing and reallocating financial resources toward sustainable activities. Beyond fiscal measures, green-economy policy increasingly emphasizes the role of monetary and macro-micro prudential instruments in steering financial systems toward climate-aligned investment (Abubakar et al., 2025).

Market instruments and sectoral practices are beginning to operationalize this policy architecture. Financing mechanisms include green sukuk issuance, village funds channeled to green micro-enterprises, and emerging ESG-oriented banking platforms (Ali et al., 2024; Gunawan et al., 2022; Ronaldo & Suryanto, 2022). The launch of IDXCarbon in September 2023 marked the start of domestic carbon trading, reaching 1.60 million $tCO_2e$ cumulative volume by August 2025 (IDX, 2025). The Circular Economy Roadmap and Action Plan 2025–2045 further targets 39 percent emission reduction and 52 percent waste reduction by 2030 (Bappenas, 2024). At the sectoral level, pilots in circular ports, industrial residue valorization, and EV ecosystem development show pathways for low-carbon restructuring (Fathoni et al., 2025; Gurning & Tangkau, 2022; Hendrik et al., 2022). Firm-level studies also indicate that green process innovation and shared value strategies can simultaneously improve profitability and environmental performance, though stronger disclosure and consumer education remain necessary (Lindawati et al., 2023; Wedari & Alfian, 2024).

Governance and political economy dynamics ultimately shape outcomes. In palm oil, a new structural-equation model finds that job creation and no-deforestation are key to sustainability, with domestic actors exerting direct influence and green consumer behavior acting as a latent lever (Purnomo et al., 2024). By contrast, contested projects such as ultra-supercritical coal framed as "green" highlight tensions among state, transnational capital, and civil society, underscoring the need for transparent and conflict-sensitive transition management (Wijaya, 2022). Resource diagnostics reveal unsustainable green water footprints in wood-product supply chains, pointing to the importance of basin-level allocation and sustainable procurement (Cazcarro et al., 2022). The overarching policy implication is that Indonesia's instruments and roadmaps can deliver real decarbonization and inclusive growth only if barriers to renewable investment are removed, the nickel-EV build-out is managed as a just transition, and circular-economy execution matches economic expansion (IEEFA, 2024).

## 5 Conclusion

This bibliometric synthesis positions sustainability and the green economy as a systems problem that links metrics, markets, technology, and human capabilities. Metric-led, place-based governance (e.g., the Environmental Human Index and participatory, spatial scenario design) enables decision-makers to align human development with ecological performance and to hard-wire circularity into procurement and planning. Across sectoral pathways, hydrogen emerges as a keystone option for hard-to-abate segments when built with rigorous water accounting, probabilistic safety management, and workforce upskilling; solutions now range from direct-air electrolysis in arid regions to country-tailored "blue-to-green" bridges and ethanol-reforming routes.

The circular economy is moving from concept to deployable practice: agricultural and industrial wastes are being valorized into materials for buildings, acoustics, and mining backfill with demonstrated LCA benefits and mechanical performance, while bio-routes create a waste-to-hydrogen nexus consistent with 5R principles. Finance and trade can catalyze or constrain the transition: green-bond prices both hedge and transmit geopolitical risk, digital trade and green innovation support ecological outcomes, and hydrogen export strategies hinge on renewables costs, CCS readiness, and social license. Ultimately, organizations and people make the transition real—evidence shows green HRM, organizational learning cultures, citizenship behaviors, engagement, and knowledge sharing are reliable levers of firm-level sustainability.

Comparative insights suggest China and the EU are converging on complementary strengths: China's digital-finance-innovation engine and hydrogen industrialization require tighter governance of emissions and safety, while the EU's procurement- and standards-driven model must reconcile cost, land use, and public acceptance as it scales hydrogen and circularity. A coherent green strategy therefore blends (i) metric-led, place-based governance, (ii) hydrogen-first decarbonization with water-risk-capability constraints, (iii) circular re-industrialization, (iv) risk-aware green finance and trade, (v) organizational and human capital development, and (vi) systems-engineering standards to de-risk scale-up.

**The Study Provides some Recommendations are as Follows**

*Clarify and standardize the definition of the green economy.*

The green economy remains a contested and often ambiguous concept, with blurred boundaries between it and sustainable development. Such definitional uncertainty has created barriers to effective implementation and left room for political contestation. Henceforth, policymakers, international organizations, and research communities must collaborate on a clear, standardized, and operational definition that integrates economic, social, and environmental dimensions. A shared definition would reduce conceptual fragmentation, build political legitimacy, strengthen public trust, and create a consistent framework for adoption across countries and sectors.

*Develop comprehensive indicators and data systems.*

Relying solely on GDP might potentially fail to capture the interdependencies between human welfare, ecological integrity, and long-term economic growth. As highlighted in the literature, there is a pressing need for composite and multidimensional metrics, such as the Environmental Human Index (EHI), which combines the Human Development Index with the Environmental Performance Index to reveal trade-offs and imbalances between development and environmental outcomes. However, data gaps remain a major challenge, particularly in developing countries, where official statistics often lack the granularity to track progress. Building robust, open, and decision-ready data systems should therefore be a policy priority to enable more informed planning, monitoring, and evaluation.

*Promote cross-sectoral and interdisciplinary research.*

The transition to a green economy is inherently multi-dimensional, involving intersections between energy, trade, finance, governance, technology, and social systems. Siloed approaches within single disciplines may not adequately address such complexity. Instead, interdisciplinary research, combining systems thinking, socio-economic analysis, environmental science, and policy studies can generate more holistic and actionable insights. Cross-sectoral collaboration, for example between technology developers, social scientists, and policymakers, is essential for identifying synergies, mitigating trade-offs, and ensuring that green economy transitions are socially inclusive as well as ecologically sound.

*Support green and sustainable economic capacity building and policy alignment in developing countries.*

Developing nations face systemic barriers to implementing a green economy, including financing gaps, limited institutional capacity, and insufficient technical expertis. International cooperation should focus on strengthening capacity building, knowledge transfer, and equitable access to green technologies. Initiatives such as

Just Energy Transition Partnerships (JETP) demonstrate the importance of coordinated global support in bridging investment shortfalls and accelerating renewable adoption. By aligning policy frameworks with sustainable development goals and strengthening institutional resilience, capacity building can empower underrepresented countries to both contribute to and benefit from the global transition, ensuring fairness and inclusivity in the process.

*Frame the green economy as a pragmatic path toward sustainable development.*

The green economy should not be treated as an alternative to sustainable development but as the inherent element in achieving it. Framing the green economy as the pragmatic driver of long-term development, aligned with the Paris Agreement and the 2030 Agenda for Sustainable Development, can help build stronger political legitimacy and broaden public support. This requires linking the green economy narrative directly to tangible benefits such as job creation, poverty reduction, and social equity in addition to eco-friendly environment. In doing so, the green economy can shift from being perceived as a niche environmental agenda to becoming a mainstream strategy for building inclusive and resilient societies.

## References

Abaza, Hussein., Saab, Najib., Zeitoon, Bashar., & Muntadá al-ʻArabī lil-Bīʼah wa-al-Tanmiyah. (2011). *Green economy : sustainable transition in a changing Arab world*. Arab Forum for Environment and Development (AFED).

Abubakar, A., Azwar, P., Pardede, R. S. F., Fathoni, S., & Triandini, N. A. (2025). Financial Policy for a Green Economy in a Resource-Rich Emerging Economy. *Buletin Ekonomi Moneter Dan Perbankan/Monetary and Banking Economics Bulletin*, *28*(2), 229–260. https://doi.org/10.59091/2460-9196.2328

Ahmad, A., Rambabu, R., Hasan, S. W., Loke Show, P. L., & Banat, F. (2024). Biohydrogen production through dark fermentation: Recent trends and advances in transition to a circular bioeconomy. *International Journal of Hydrogen Energy*, *52*, 335–357. https://doi.org/10.1016/j.ijhydene.2023.05.161

Ahmad Giran, A. H., Muhamad Tamyez, P. F., & Fauzi, M. A. (2025). The paradoxes of sustainable HRM: Insights through the perspective of common good, green, social responsibility, and triple bottom line. *Human Systems Management*, *44*(4), 691–709. https://doi.org/10.1177/01672533251320795

Alfadel, A., Al-Kahtani, S. M., Almekhlafi, A.-W. A.-G. S., Alhebry, A., & Ahmed, A. (2025). Fostering sustainable development: the role of green HRM and green work engagement. *Discover Sustainability*, *6*(1). https://doi.org/10.1007/s43621-025-01167-z

Ali, Q., Rusgianto, S., Parveen, S., Yaacob, H., & Zin, R. M. (2024). An empirical study of the effects of green Sukuk spur on economic growth, social development, and financial performance in Indonesia. *Environment, Development and Sustainability*, *26*(8), 21097–21123. https://doi.org/10.1007/s10668-023-03520-6

Andres, C., & Bhullar, G. S. (2016). Sustainable intensification of tropical agro-ecosystems: Need and potentials. *Frontiers in Environmental Science*, *4*(FEB). https://doi.org/10.3389/fenvs.2016.00005

Apriantoro, M. S., Widyastuti, H., Ashfahany, A. El, & Murtadla, A. A. (2024). Sustainability and Green Economy in Developmental Paradigms: A Bibliometric Analysis of Scholarly Trends and Transformations. *Indonesian Interdisciplinary Journal of Sharia Economics (IIJSE)*, *7*(2), 4587–4610.

Askin-Uzel, R. (2023). Sustainable green technology for adaptation of circular economy to valorize agri-food waste: celery root peel as a case study. *Management of Environmental Quality*, *34*(4), 1018–1034. https://doi.org/10.1108/MEQ-03-2022-0087

AtKisson, A. (2012). *Life Beyond Growth*. Annual Survey Report of the Institute for Studies in Happiness, Economy, and Society — ISHES.

Balbay, S., Gün, A. R., Ucgun, H., & Balbay, A. (2024). Green Composite Sound Absorber Production from Orange Peel Waste for Efficient Sound Insulation. *Journal of Vibration Engineering and Technologies*, *12*(3), 3719–3728. https://doi.org/10.1007/s42417-023-01080-7

Baldania, M. B., Bhogayata, A. C., & Somaiya, P. B. (2025). Utilization of Recycled Concrete Materials in Concrete Production: Methodology, Characterization, and Performance Evaluation. *SSRG International Journal of Civil Engineering*, *12*(5), 142–155. https://doi.org/10.14445/23488352/IJCE-V12I5P112

Bappenas. (2024). *Peta Jalan& Rencana Aksi Nasional Ekonomi Sirkular Indonesia 2025-2045.*

Barbier, E. B. (2012). The green economy post Rio+20. In *Science* (Vol. 338, Issue 6109, pp. 887–888). American Association for the Advancement of Science. https://doi.org/10.1126/science.1227360

Bigg, T. (2011). RPR Review of Policy Research Development Governance and the Green Economy: A Matter of Life and Death? In *Review of Policy Research* (Vol. 28, Issue 5).

Bina, O., & la Camera, F. (2011). Promise and shortcomings of a green turn in recent policy responses to the "double crisis." *Ecological Economics*, *70*(12), 2308–2316. https://doi.org/10.1016/j.ecolecon.2011.06.021

Blohm, M., & Dettner, F. (2023). Green hydrogen production: Integrating environmental and social criteria to ensure sustainability. *Smart Energy*, *11*. https://doi.org/10.1016/j.segy.2023.100112

Bohlmann, H. R., Bohlmann, J. A., Chitiga-Mabugu, M., & Inglesi-Lotz, R. (2023). Just Energy Transition of South Africa in a Post-COVID Era. *Sustainability (Switzerland)*, *15*(14). https://doi.org/10.3390/su151410854

Borel-Saladin, J., & Turok, I. (2013). The Green Economy: Incremental Change or Transformation? *Environmental Policy and Governance*.

Bouzas, B., Téliz, E., & Díaz, V. (2024). Green hydrogen production in Uruguay: a techno-economic approach. *International Journal of Chemical Reactor Engineering*, *22*(7), 783–795. https://doi.org/10.1515/ijcre-2024-0066

Brown, E., Cloke, J., Gent, D., Johnson, P. H., Hill, C., Brown, E., Johnson, J., & Hill, P. H. (2014). GREEN GROWTH OR ECOLOGICAL COMMODIFICATION: DEBATING THE GREEN ECONOMY IN THE GLOBAL SOUTH. *Swedish Society for Anthropology and Geography*.

Buseth, J. T. (2017). The green economy in Tanzania: From global discourses to institutionalization. *Geoforum*, *86*, 42–52. https://doi.org/10.1016/j.geoforum.2017.08.015

Cannavò, D., Cigna, G., Manzoni, S., Mazzi, A., & Saporito, S. B. (2019). Policies for the disposal of agri-food waste in the green economy sphere: Sustainable management of food waste in large-scale organized distribution. *Procedia Environmental Science, Engineering and Management*, *6*(1), 45–50. https://www.scopus.com/inward/record.uri?eid=2-s2.0-85078130877&partnerID=40&md5=86e6387d521f29eb19c324cf7e23f286

Cao, W., Zhang, X., & Iqbal, K. (2025). Using green finance to study energy elasticity, coal subsidy, energy transition and energy dependence in E7 economies: an efficiency analysis with data envelopment analysis. *Energy Strategy Reviews*, *60*. https://doi.org/10.1016/j.esr.2025.101794

Capitani, C., Mukama, K., Mbilinyi, B., Malugu, I. O., Munishi, P. K. T., Burgess, N. D., Platts, P. J., Sallu, S. M., & Marchant, R. (2016). From local scenarios to national maps: A participatory framework for envisioning the future of Tanzania. *Ecology and Society*, *21*(3). https://doi.org/10.5751/ES-08565-210304

Cazcarro, I., Schyns, J. F., Arto, I., & Sanz, M. J. (2022). Nations' water footprints and virtual water trade of wood products. *Advances in Water Resources*, *164*. https://doi.org/10.1016/j.advwatres.2022.104188

Chen, R., Abdalla Adam, N., Israilova, F., Shen, Q., & Yan, X. (2025). Economic and technological innovations in hydrogen production, storage, and utilization for sustainable energy systems and industrial applications. *International Journal of Hydrogen Energy*, *147*. https://doi.org/10.1016/j.ijhydene.2025.05.392

Chen, S., Bai, H., Wang, B., & Lin, J.-H. (2024). Social enterprise, renewable energy, and cap-and-trade under sustainable insurance. *Energy Economics*, *133*. https://doi.org/10.1016/j.eneco.2024.107535

Cheng, C., van Greevenbroek, K., & Viole, I. (2024a). The competitive edge of Norway's hydrogen by 2030: Socio-environmental considerations. *International Journal of Hydrogen Energy*, *85*, 962–975. https://doi.org/10.1016/j.ijhydene.2024.08.377

Cheng, Y., Zhao, G., Meng, W., & Wang, Q. (2024b). Resources utilization, taxation and green education: A path to sustainable power generation. *Resources Policy*, *88*. https://doi.org/10.1016/j.resourpol.2023.104389

Cherian, J., Jacob, J., & Farouk, S. (2019). Impact of green hr practices on environmental sustainability of a UAE based organization. *Ecology, Environment and Conservation*, *25*(2), 1–10. https://www.scopus.com/inward/record.uri?eid=2-s2.0-85100755354&partnerID=40&md5=e8e64b13ed56d6d268051a453ace4316

Choi, Y. (2015). Intermediary propositions for green growth with sustainable governance. *Sustainability (Switzerland)*, *7*(11), 14785–14801. https://doi.org/10.3390/su71114785

Chung, W., Jeong, W., Lee, J., Kim, J., Roh, K., & Lee, J. H. (2023). Electrification of CO2 conversion into chemicals and fuels: Gaps and opportunities in process systems engineering. *Computers and Chemical Engineering*, *170*. https://doi.org/10.1016/j.compchemeng.2022.108106

Crossman, N. D., & Pollino, C. A. (2018). An ecosystem services and Bayesian modelling approach to assess the utility of water resource development in rangelands of north Australia. *Journal of Arid Environments*, *159*, 34–44. https://doi.org/10.1016/j.jaridenv.2018.02.007

Dalei, N. N., & Heggde, G. S. (2021). The economics of value, growth and relationship in a green prospective. *Rivista Di Studi Sulla Sostenibilita*, *1*, 29–41. https://doi.org/10.3280/RISS2021-001003

Damon, M., & Sterner, T. (2012). Policy Instruments for Sustainable Development at Rio +20. *Journal of Environment and Development*, *21*(2), 143–151. https://doi.org/10.1177/1070496512444735

Death, C. (2015). Four discourses of the green economy in the global South. *Third World Quarterly*, *36*(12), 2207–2224. https://doi.org/10.1080/01436597.2015.1068110

Domınguez, S., Cifuentes, B., Bustamante, F., Cantillo, N. M., Barraza-Botet, C. L., & Cobo, M. (2022). On the Potential of Blue Hydrogen Production in Colombia: A Fossil Resource-Based Assessment for Low-Emission Hydrogen. *Sustainability (Switzerland)*, *14*(18). https://doi.org/10.3390/su141811436

Dong, W., Niu, X., Nassani, A. A., Naseem, I., & Zaman, K. (2024). E-commerce mineral resource footprints: Investigating drivers for sustainable mining development. *Resources Policy*, *89*. https://doi.org/10.1016/j.resourpol.2023.104569

Donner, M., & de Vries, H. (2021). How to innovate business models for a circular bio-economy? *Business Strategy and the Environment*, *30*(4), 1932–1947. https://doi.org/10.1002/bse.2725

Eck, N. J. van, & Waltman, L. W. (2014). Visualizing Bibliometric Networks. *Measuring Scholarly Impact*, 285–320.

Enaloui, R., Sharifi, S., Faridpak, B., Hammad, A., Al-Hussein, M., & Musílek, P. (2025). Techno-economic assessment of a solar-powered green hydrogen storage concept based on reversible solid oxide cells for residential micro-grid: A case study in Calgary. *Energy*, *319*. https://doi.org/10.1016/j.energy.2025.134981

Faccer, K., Nahman, A., & Audouin, M. (2014). Interpreting the green economy: Emerging discourses and their considerations for the Global South. *Development Southern Africa*, *31*(5), 642–657. https://doi.org/10.1080/0376835X.2014.933700

Fathoni, F., Kesidou, E., Rifansha, M. M., & Tiftazani, A. (2025). Drivers and barriers of eco-innovation in electric vehicle diffusion: Evidence from Indonesia. *Journal of Environmental Management*, *389*. https://doi.org/10.1016/j.jenvman.2025.126021

Ferguson, P. (2015). The green economy agenda: business as usual or transformational discourse? *Environmental Politics*, *24*(1), 17–37. https://doi.org/10.1080/09644016.2014.919748

Fink, A.,. (2019). *Conducting Research Literature Reviews: from the Internet to Paper*. SAGE Publications.

Fiorino, D. (2014). The green economy: mythical or meaningful? *Policy Q, 10*(1), 26–34.
Fu, H., Huang, P., Xu, Y., & Zhang, Z. (2023). Digital trade and environmental sustainability: the role of financial development and ecological innovation for a greener revolution in China. *Economic Research-Ekonomska Istrazivanja, 36*(2). https://doi.org/10.1080/1331677X.2022.2125889
Gainza, X., & Montes-Nebreda, A. (2023). The Waste War: on the electoral costs of local sustainability policies. *Journal of Environmental Policy and Planning, 25*(5), 625–641. https://doi.org/10.1080/1523908X.2023.2238638
Gál, T., Kovács, S., & Buglyó-Nyakas, E. (2025). A comprehensive analysis of food waste through historical context: A bibliometric study from 2019 to 2024. *Cleaner Waste Systems, 11*. https://doi.org/10.1016/j.clwas.2025.100318
Georgeson, L. (2024). Green economy definitions: recent trends and developments. In *Research Handbook on the Green Economy* (pp. 13–33).
Georgeson, L., Maslin, M., & Poessinouw, M. (2017). The global green economy: a review of concepts, definitions, measurement methodologies and their interactions. In *Geo: Geography and Environment* (Vol. 4, Issue 1). Blackwell Publishing Ltd. https://doi.org/10.1002/geo2.36
Ghasemian Sahebi, I. G., Masoomi, B., Gholian-Jouybari, F., & Hajiaghei-Keshteli, M. (2025). Overcoming challenges in the path to a hydrogen economy for energy supply chain transition. *Applied Energy, 393*. https://doi.org/10.1016/j.apenergy.2025.126084
Graczyk-Kucharska, M. (2023). Sustainability in the Development of Green Organizations Based on the Example of Manufacturing Companies. *Sustainability (Switzerland), 15*(20). https://doi.org/10.3390/su152014705
Green Growth Knowledge Platform (GGKP). (2016). *Measuring Inclusive Green Growth at the Country Level*.
Gunawan, J., Permatasari, P., & Sharma, U. (2022). Exploring sustainability and green banking disclosures: a study of banking sector. *Environment, Development and Sustainability, 24*(9), 11153–11194. https://doi.org/10.1007/s10668-021-01901-3
Guo, J., Zhang, Y., Zavabeti, A., Chen, K., Guo, Y., Hu, G., Fan, X., & Li, G. K. (2022). Hydrogen production from the air. *Nature Communications, 13*(1). https://doi.org/10.1038/s41467-022-32652-y
Gurning, R. O. S., & Tangkau, D. I. (2022). The Analysis of the Conceptual Framework of Green Port Implementation in Indonesia Using Circular Economy: The Case Study of Benoa Public and Fishing Terminals. *Sustainability (Switzerland), 14*(10). https://doi.org/10.3390/su14106083
Halle, M. (2011). Accountability in the green economy. *Review of Policy Research, 28*(5), 473–477.
Hassan, H. S., Shi, C., Hashem, F. S., Abu El-Magd, S., Maged, A., Abdel-Gawwad, H. A., & Pfeiffer, H. (2025). Industrial waste recycling approach: An ecofriendly geopolymer binder for clean and sustainable environments (A 24-h green recycling process). *Journal of Environmental Management, 377*. https://doi.org/10.1016/j.jenvman.2025.124568
He, Y., Li, X., Li, T., Srinivasakannan, C., Li, S., Yin, S., & Zhang, L. (2023). Research progress on removal methods of Cl-from industrial wastewater. *Journal of Environmental Chemical Engineering, 11*(1). https://doi.org/10.1016/j.jece.2022.109163
Hendrik, Y., Fauzi, A., Suryaningtyas, D. T., Firdiyono, F., & Yao, Y. (2022). Determination of the Red Mud Industrial Cluster Sites in Indonesia Based on Sustainability Aspect and Waste Management Analysis through PROMETHEE. *Energies, 15*(15). https://doi.org/10.3390/en15155435
Huang, X., Ullah, M., Wang, L., Ullah, F., & Khan, R. (2024). Green supply chain management practices and triple bottom line performance: Insights from an emerging economy with a mediating and moderating model. *Journal of Environmental Management, 357*. https://doi.org/10.1016/j.jenvman.2024.120575
Huang, X., & Xie, J. (2025). Sustainability of Global Trade: The Impact of Executive Green Awareness on the Global Green Value Chain of Enterprises. *Sustainability (Switzerland), 17*(4). https://doi.org/10.3390/su17041510

IDX. (2025, July 15). *Press Release Details: IDXCarbon Received Carbon Positive Award 2025 as the Best Official Carbon Exchange in an Emerging Economy.*

IEEFA. (2024). *Indonesia's Nickel Companies: The Need for Renewable Energy Amid Increasing Productio.*

IESR. (2023). *Indonesia Energy Transition Outlook 2023.*

IESR. (2024, January 17). *Pursuing the Target of a 23% Renewable Energy Mix in 2025 Requires an Acceleration Strategy and Political Commitment.*

Iqbal, S. S., Ramadan, N., Dagwar, P. P., Dutta, D., & Abdo, D. M. (2025). Recovery of metals from spent lithium-ion batteries using agricultural waste, applications and circularity framework. *Separation and Purification Technology, 376*. https://doi.org/10.1016/j.seppur.2025.133860

Jacobs, M. (1991). *The Green Economy: Environment, Sustainable Development and the Politics of the Future*. Pluto Press.

Jacobs, M. (2013). *Green growth. Handbook of Global Climate and Environment Policy* (Falkner, R.). Oxford.

Jakob, M., & Edenhofer, O. (2014). Green growth, degrowth, and the commons. *Oxford Review of Economic Policy, 30*(3), 447–468. https://doi.org/10.1093/oxrep/gru026

Jänicke, M. (2012). "Green growth": From a growing eco-industry to economic sustainability. *Energy Policy, 48*, 13–21. https://doi.org/10.1016/j.enpol.2012.04.045

Kalaiselvan, N., & Mathimani, T. (2024). Solar-driven green hydrogen generation for revolutionizing the future of zero-carbon energy. *Fuel, 375*. https://doi.org/10.1016/j.fuel.2024.132538

Kitchenham, B., & Charters, S. (2007). *Guidelines for performing Systematic Literature Reviews in Software Engineering.*

Kong, X., Zhou, Y., Yao, W., Zhang, J., Ma, S., Wang, X., Chen, M., Zhang, L., Wang, Y., & Dang, Z. (2025). Research on China's Aquatic Product Export Trade to ASEAN from the Perspective of the Blue Economy: An Empirical Analysis Based on the Modified Constant Market Share Model. *Water (Switzerland), 17*(4). https://doi.org/10.3390/w17040487

Krishnan, A., & Senthil Selvan, S. S. (2025). An investigation on the mechanical and microstructural properties of pigeon pea stalk ash concrete: an approach towards environmental sustainability. *Environmental Science and Pollution Research, 32*(11), 6732–6749. https://doi.org/10.1007/s11356-025-36147-3

Latif, S., Ahmed, M., Ahmed, M., Ahmad, M., Al-Ahmary, K. M., & Ali, I. (2024). Development of Plumeria alba extract supplemented biodegradable films containing chitosan and cellulose derived from bagasse and corn cob waste for antimicrobial food packaging. *International Journal of Biological Macromolecules, 266*. https://doi.org/10.1016/j.ijbiomac.2024.131262

Li, S., Tabatabaei, M., Li, F., & Ho, S.-H. (2024). A review of green biohydrogen production using anoxygenic photosynthetic bacteria for hydrogen economy: Challenges and opportunities. *International Journal of Hydrogen Energy, 54*, 218–238. https://doi.org/10.1016/j.ijhydene.2022.11.014

Li, X., & Wu, C. (2024). Influence mechanism of government subsidy on the green transformation of coal company in China. *International Journal of Mining Science and Technology, 34*(7), 1033–1040. https://doi.org/10.1016/j.ijmst.2024.07.013

Li, Y., Qu, Y., Liu, C., Cui, J., Xu, K., Li, Y., Shen, H., Lu, Z., Pan, H., & Xu, T. (2022). Processing Agricultural Cornstalks toward High-Efficient Stable Bifunctional ORR/OER Electrocatalysts. *Advanced Sustainable Systems, 6*(1). https://doi.org/10.1002/adsu.202100343

Lindawati, A. S. L., Agata, Y. D., & Handoko, B. L. (2023). Instructions Green Innovation and Creating Shared Value on Achievement of Environmental Development Pillar in Indonesian Energy Sector. *International Journal of Sustainable Development and Planning, 18*(7), 2213–2221. https://doi.org/10.18280/ijsdp.180726

Liu, F., Chen, Y., Zhu, J., & Zhai, G. (2024a). Enhancing sustainable urban economies: A statistical investigation of transitioning from fossil fuel-dependent industries to green innovation hubs. *Sustainable Cities and Society, 101*. https://doi.org/10.1016/j.scs.2023.105161

Liu, F., Qin, C., Qin, M., Ştefea, P., & Norena-Chavez, D. (2024b). Geopolitical risk: An opportunity or a threat to the green bond market? *Energy Economics, 131*. https://doi.org/10.1016/j.eneco.2024.107391

Liuzzi, S., Rubino, C., Stefanizzi, P., & Martellotta, F. (2020). Performance characterization of broad band sustainable sound absorbers made of almond skins. *Materials*, *13*(23), 1–20. https://doi.org/10.3390/ma13235474

Loiseau, E., Saikku, L., Antikainen, R., Droste, N., Hansjürgens, B., Pitkänen, K., Leskinen, P., Kuikman, P., & Thomsen, M. (2016a). Green economy and related concepts: An overview. *Journal of Cleaner Production*, *139*, 361–371. https://doi.org/10.1016/j.jclepro.2016.08.024

Loiseau, E., Saikku, L., Antikainen, R., Droste, N., Hansjürgens, B., Pitkänen, K., Leskinen, P., Kuikman, P., & Thomsen, M. (2016b). Green economy and related concepts: An overview. *Journal of Cleaner Production*, *139*, 361–371. https://doi.org/10.1016/j.jclepro.2016.08.024

Long, R., Li, H., Wu, M., & Li, W. (2021). Dynamic evaluation of the green development level of China's coal-resource-based cities using the TOPSIS method. *Resources Policy*, *74*. https://doi.org/10.1016/j.resourpol.2021.102415

Machado, N. T., & Rodríguez, C. M. T. (2025). LOGISTICS 5.0 MATURITY MODEL: A HUMAN-CENTRIC AND SUSTAINABLE APPROACH FOR THE SUPPLY CHAIN OF THE FUTURE. *Journal of Engineering and Technology for Industrial Applications*, *11*(51), 164–170. https://doi.org/10.5935/jetia.v11i51.1407

Makumbe, W. (2024). Green Human Resources Management and Green Performance: A Mediation–Moderation Mechanism for Green Innovation and Green Knowledge Sharing. *Sustainability (Switzerland)*, *16*(24). https://doi.org/10.3390/su162410849

Malik, S. Y., Mughal, Y. H., Azam, T., Cao, Y., Wan, Z., Zhu, H., & Ramayah, R. (2021). Corporate social responsibility, green human resources management, and sustainable performance: is organizational citizenship behavior towards environment the missing link? *Sustainability (Switzerland)*, *13*(3), 1–24. https://doi.org/10.3390/su13031044

Martins, P. H. D. S., Marques-Serrano, A. L. M., Pimenta Rodrigues, G. A. P., Vergara, G. F., Saiki, G. M., Borges, R. V, Bispo, G. D., Peixoto, M. G. M., & Gonçalves, V. P. (2024). Brazil's New Green Hydrogen Industry: An Assessment of Its Macroeconomic Viability Through an Input–Output Approach. *Economies*, *12*(12). https://doi.org/10.3390/economies12120333

Marty, J., & Ruel, S. (2025). Unpacking the interconnected challenges of rare metals supply chains: A systematic literature network analysis and conceptual framework. *Resources Policy*, *106*. https://doi.org/10.1016/j.resourpol.2025.105624

Maskuroh, N., Widyanty, W., Nurhidajat, R., Wardhana, I. W., & Fahlevi, M. (2023). Green human resource management and green supply Chain Management on Sustainable performance of nickel mining companies in Indonesia. *Uncertain Supply Chain Management*, *11*(1), 203–212. https://doi.org/10.5267/j.uscm.2022.10.006

Merino-Saum, A., Clement, J., Wyss, R., & Baldi, M. G. (2020). Unpacking the Green Economy concept: A quantitative analysis of 140 definitions. In *Journal of Cleaner Production* (Vol. 242). Elsevier Ltd. https://doi.org/10.1016/j.jclepro.2019.118339

Midolo, G., Cutuli, G., Porto, S. M. C., Ottolina, G., Paini, J., & Valenti, F. (2024). LCA analysis for assessing environmenstal sustainability of new biobased chemicals by valorising citrus waste. *Scientific Reports, 14*(1). https://doi.org/10.1038/s41598-024-72468-y

Ministry of Environment and Forestry. (2022). *ENHANCED NATIONALLY DETERMINED CONTRIBUTION REPUBLIC OF INDONESIA 2022.*

Ministry of Finance. (2022). *Menkeu: Indonesia Rentan terhadap Dampak Perubahan Iklim.* Ministry of Finance.

Mishra, A., & Sahu, P. K. (2025). Do geopolitical uncertainty and inflation transmit opportunities or threats to green energy consumption? *International Journal of Energy Sector Management*, *19*(4), 1045–1060. https://doi.org/10.1108/IJESM-08-2024-0006

Morato, B. N., Guedes, V. S., Barbosa, R. A., Nunes Branco, L. A. M., Campos Ribeiro, S. E., Flor, J. M., de Oliveira, D. M., & Almeida, M. L. (2024). INFLUENCE OF COCONUT FIBER WASTE AND RICE HUSK ASH ON GREEN CONCRETE. *Revista de Gestao Social e Ambiental*, *18*(3). https://doi.org/10.24857/rgsa.v18n3-033

Nour, M. M., Tony, M. A., & Nabwey, H. A. (2022). Immobilization of Magnetic Nanoparticles on Cellulosic Wooden Sawdust for Competitive Nudrin Elimination from Environmental Waters as a Green Strategy: Box–Behnken Design Optimization. *International Journal of Environmental Research and Public Health, 19*(22). https://doi.org/10.3390/ijerph192215397

OECD. (2011). *Towards green growth: A summary for policy makers.*

Okedu, K. E., Barghash, H. F., & Al Nadabi, H. A. (2022). Sustainable Waste Management Strategies for Effective Energy Utilization in Oman: A Review. *Frontiers in Bioengineering and Biotechnology, 10.* https://doi.org/10.3389/fbioe.2022.825728

Pal, B. (2025). Optimizing pricing, greening, recycling, and emission reduction in a policy-driven sustainable closed-loop supply chain. *Journal of Cleaner Production, 519.* https://doi.org/10.1016/j.jclepro.2025.145824

Pearce, D. (1991). *Blueprint 2: Greening the World Economy.*

Pearce, D. (1993). *Blueprint 3: Measuring Sustainable Development.*

Pearce, D., Markandya, A., & Barbier, E. B. (1989). *Blue Print for a Green Economy.* Earthscan.

PEP. (2012). *Building an Inclusive Green Economy for All.* www.povertyenvironment.net/pep

Peterková, J., Korjenic, A., Zach, J., Bydžovský, J., Halásová, S., & Sesto, E. (2025). Analysis of the Possible Use of Straw from Agriculture as an Environmental Insulation Material in Buildings. *Sustainability (Switzerland), 17*(8). https://doi.org/10.3390/su17083589

Purnomo, H., Kusumadewi, S. D., Ilham, Q. P., Kartikasara, H. N., Okarda, B., Dermawan, A., Puspitaloka, D., Kartodihardjo, H., Kharisma, R., & Brady, M. A. (2024). Green Consumer Behaviour Influences Indonesian Palm Oil Sustainability. *International Forestry Review, 25*(4), 449–472. https://doi.org/10.1505/146554823838028210

Raja, K. S., Maliha, A., Paul, S., Shakur, M. S., & Bari, A. B. M. M. (2025). Unraveling the obstacles to transform agro-wastes into value-added bioproducts: Implications for sustainability. *Sustainable Operations and Computers, 6,* 171–188. https://doi.org/10.1016/j.susoc.2025.05.002

Reiff, M. R. (2013). *Exploitation and economic justice in the liberal capitalist state.* Oxford: Oxford University Press.

Ronaldo, R., & Suryanto, T. (2022). Green finance and sustainability development goals in Indonesian Fund Village. *Resources Policy, 78.* https://doi.org/10.1016/j.resourpol.2022.102839

Rossetto, D. (2025). Relationships between sustainability disclosure, environmental innovation and performance: an examination of practice within the Australian construction and demolition waste sector. *Environment, Development and Sustainability, 27*(4), 9427–9446. https://doi.org/10.1007/s10668-023-04291-w

Sandri, O., Holdsworth, S., Wong, P. S. P., & Hayes, J. (2024). Upskilling plumber gasfitters for hydrogen: An empirical study using the Theory of Planned Behavior. *Renewable Energy, 221.* https://doi.org/10.1016/j.renene.2023.119800

Sasmoko, S., Akhtar, M. Z., Khan, H. U. R., Sriyanto, S., Jabor, M. K., Rashid, A., & Zaman, K. (2022). How Do Industrial Ecology, Energy Efficiency, and Waste Recycling Technology (Circular Economy) Fit into China's Plan to Protect the Environment? Up to Speed. *Recycling, 7*(6). https://doi.org/10.3390/recycling7060083

Seiti, H., Ghasemi Pirbalouti, R., Elkamel, A., Selvik, J., & Makui, A. (2025). Developing a new framework for techno-economic hydrogen energy risk management through probabilistic R. Graph. *International Journal of Hydrogen Energy, 136,* 1198–1218. https://doi.org/10.1016/j.ijhydene.2024.03.199

Sgarbossa, F., Arena, S., Tang, O., & Peron, M. (2022). Reprint of: Renewable hydrogen supply chains: A planning matrix and an agenda for future research. *International Journal of Production Economics, 250.* https://doi.org/10.1016/j.ijpe.2022.108712

Sgarbossa, F., Arena, S., Tang, O., & Peron, M. (2023). Renewable hydrogen supply chains: A planning matrix and an agenda for future research. *International Journal of Production Economics, 255.* https://doi.org/10.1016/j.ijpe.2022.108674

Sharma, A. K., Ghodke, P. K., Chen, W.-H., Shah, S. V, & Patel, A. K. (2025a). Circular economy in biohydrogen: A state-of-the-art review on advances in sustainable production, storage, and transportation. *Journal of Cleaner Production, 500.* https://doi.org/10.1016/j.jclepro.2025.145305

Sharma, A., Kumar, K., & Dwesar, R. (2025b). "Keenly aware of environmental issues, yet wavering in conviction": Understanding the factors influencing the consumers' willingness to pay for green energy. *Sustainable Futures, 9*. https://doi.org/10.1016/j.sftr.2024.100427

Sirel Öztürk, N. (2025). Decarbonizing Agriculture: The Impact of Trade and Renewable Energy on CO2 Emissions. *Economies, 13*(6). https://doi.org/10.3390/economies13060162

Skripnuk, D., Didenko, N., Gazizulina, A., Kikkas, K. N., & Skripniuk, K. (2023). Methodology of a Circular Economy in a Specific Territory. *Sustainability (Switzerland), 15*(13). https://doi.org/10.3390/su151310363

Solís-Guzmán, J., Garzón-González, P., González-Vallejo, P., & Marrero, M. (2024). Sustainability Evaluation of Residential Buildings Based on the Footprint Family: Application to Case Studies in Andalusia. *Buildings, 14*(4). https://doi.org/10.3390/buildings14041131

Song, J., Ye, W., & Hou, Q. (2025). Economic analysis of solar-hydrogen energy industry in China: A PLS-SEM approach to financial performance and input-output dynamics. *International Journal of Hydrogen Energy, 136*, 546–562. https://doi.org/10.1016/j.ijhydene.2025.04.425

Sonu, S., Rani, G. M., Pathania, D., Umapathi, R., Rustagi, S., Huh, Y. S., Gupta, V. K., Kaushik, A., & Chaudhary, V. (2023). Agro-waste to sustainable energy: A green strategy of converting agricultural waste to nano-enabled energy applications. *Science of the Total Environment, 875*. https://doi.org/10.1016/j.scitotenv.2023.162667

Speck, S., & Zoboli, R. (2017). *The Green Economy in Europe: In Search for a Successful Transition* (pp. 141–160). https://doi.org/10.1007/978-3-319-38919-6_7

Staples, M., & Niazi, M. (2007). Experiences using systematic review guidelines. *Journal of Systems and Software, 80*(9), 1425–1437. https://doi.org/10.1016/j.jss.2006.09.046

Subramanian, N., & Suresh, M. (2022). The contribution of organizational learning and green human resource management practices to the circular economy: a relational analysis – evidence from manufacturing SMEs (part II). *Learning Organization, 29*(5), 443–462. https://doi.org/10.1108/TLO-06-2022-0068

Tantanee, S., & Hantrakul, S. (2019). Municipal waste management challenge of urbanization: Lesson learned from Phitsanulok, Thailand. *Geographia Technica, 14*, 39–46. https://doi.org/10.21163/GT_2019.141.17

Tao, M., Cheng, W., Nie, K., Zhang, X., & Cao, W. (2022). Life cycle assessment of underground coal mining in China. *Science of the Total Environment, 805*. https://doi.org/10.1016/j.scitotenv.2021.150231

ten Brink, P., M. L., B. T., K. M., W. S. (2012). Nature and its Role in the Transition to a Green Economy. *TEEB Discussion Paper.*

Umar, M., Khan, S. A. R., Yusliza, M., Ali, S., & Zhang, Z. (2022). Industry 4.0 and green supply chain practices: an empirical study. *International Journal of Productivity and Performance Management, 71*(3), 814–832. https://doi.org/10.1108/IJPPM-12-2020-0633

UNCTAD. (2011). *United Nations Conference on Trade and Development THE GREEN ECONOMY: TRADE AND SUSTAINABLE DEVELOPMENT IMPLICATIONS.*

UNDESA. (2012). *A Guidebook to the Green Economy Issue 3: Exploring Green Economy Policies and International Experience with National Strategies.* United Nations Department of Economic and Social Affairs.

UNEP. (2008). *Climate of Change.* www.unep.org/governingbodies.

UNEP. (2011a). *Investing in energy and resource efficiency.*

UNEP. (2011b). *Towards a Green Economy: Pathways to Sustainable Development and Poverty Eradication - A Synthesis for Policy Makers.* www.unep.org/greeneconomy

UNFCCC. (2016). *THE PARIS AGREEMENT.* https://treaties.un.org/Pages/ViewDetails.aspx?src=TREATY&mtdsg_no=XXVII-7-

UNFCCC. (2022). *ENHANCED NATIONALLY DETERMINED CONTRIBUTION REPUBLIC OF INDONESIA 2022.*

United Nation. (2015). *70/1. Transforming our world: the 2030 Agenda for Sustainable Development Transforming our world: the 2030 Agenda for Sustainable Development Preamble.*

Vandana, & Cerchione, R. (2025). Managing energy resources, carbon emissions and green technology adoption in circular economy transition: A mathematical approach. *Journal of Cleaner Production, 501*. https://doi.org/10.1016/j.jclepro.2025.145105

Webster, J., & Watson, R. T. (2018). Analyzing the Past to Prepare for the Future: Writing a Literature Review. *Theoretical Economics Letters*, *8*(5).

Wedari, L. K., & Alfian, H. (2024). Does Green Innovation Impact on Profitability of Indonesian Consumer Non-Cyclicals Companies? *International Journal of Sustainable Development and Planning*, *19*(7), 2805–2812. https://doi.org/10.18280/ijsdp.190738

Wijaya, T. (2022). Conditioning a stable sustainability fix of 'ungreen' infrastructure in Indonesia: transnational alliances, compromise, and state's strategic selectivity. *Pacific Review*, *35*(5), 821–852. https://doi.org/10.1080/09512748.2021.1884123

Xie, W., Bi, C., & Kuznetsova, N. P. (2025). Towards a Sustainable Future: The Emerging Role and Far-Reaching Impact of Green Finance Instruments in Russia-China Trade Relations. *Финансы: Теория и Практика*, 194–206.

Yang, X., Wang, W., & Yu, M. (2025). Smart supply chain adoption and urban energy transition: Empirical evidence on de-coalization effects. *Journal of Environmental Management*, *390*. https://doi.org/10.1016/j.jenvman.2025.126210

Yong, J. Y., Yusliza, M.-Y., Ramayah, T., Jabbour, C. J., Sehnem, S., & Venkatesh, V. (2020). Pathways towards sustainability in manufacturing organizations: Empirical evidence on the role of green human resource management. *Business Strategy and the Environment*, *29*(1), 212–228. https://doi.org/10.1002/bse.2359

Yu, Z., Jing, H., Gao, Y., Wu, J., Fang, Z., Wang, A., Huang, K., & Liu, Y. (2025). Performance enhancement and environmental impact of graphene oxide-fly ash hybrid on cemented waste rock backfill. *Environmental Research*, *282*. https://doi.org/10.1016/j.envres.2025.122055

Zhang, B., Chen, H., Han, Z., Song, L., Liu, Z., Lau, W.-M., & Zhou, D. (2024). Electrically conductive coals in nature: Their traits, whereabouts, green-exploitations and impacts. *Fuel*, *361*. https://doi.org/10.1016/j.fuel.2023.130741

Zhang, T., & Choi, C. H. (2025). Will digital trade be friend or foe of the green economy? Unveiling the complexities of green growth. *Journal of Applied Economics*, *28*(1). https://doi.org/10.1080/15140326.2025.2464591

Zhang, Y., & Wu, Z. (2022). Environmental performance and human development for sustainability: Towards to a new Environmental Human Index. *Science of the Total Environment*, *838*. https://doi.org/10.1016/j.scitotenv.2022.156491

Zhang, Z., Chen, C., Tayyab, M., Wei, Z., Zheng, X., Shangguan, W., Zhang, S., Chen, S., & Meng, S. (2025). Regulating electron-hole pairs of g-C3N4 efficiently separated and fully utilized for photosynthesis of H2O2 under visible light. *Chemical Engineering Journal*, *509*. https://doi.org/10.1016/j.cej.2025.161409

Zhao, Y., Wang, W., Liang, Z., & Luo, P. (2024). Racing towards zero carbon: Unraveling the interplay between natural resource rents, green innovation, geopolitical risk and environmental pollution in BRICS countries. *Resources Policy*, *88*. https://doi.org/10.1016/j.resourpol.2023.104379

# Chapter 4
# Perspectives on Inclusive Economic Development

**Solikin M. Juhro, Masagus M. Ridhwan, and Arnita Rishanty**

**Abstract** In the aftermath of the global financial crisis 2008/09, which was also colored by the Covid-19 pandemic, the world economy has tended to grow more sluggishly, entering what is often described as a "new normal," characterized by growth rates lower than historical long-term trends, heightened uncertainty, shifts in the global economic power structure, and evolving geopolitical dynamics. Comprehensive and integrated framework is needed to support the implementation of relevant development strategy. Apart from that, in facing the increasingly complex challenges, the perspectives of national economic development also need to be 'reset', or more directed at overcoming socio-economic problems, which runs parallel to deal with health issues due to the pandemic. Holistically, these perspectives should be focused on inclusivity in order to reduce potential disparities in economic development. Several policy strategies should be addressed, namely: (1) developing infrastructure and public services, (2) empowering the economic base for a wider community, (3) accelerating digitalization and strengthening innovation/research activities, (4) developing human capital by taking advantage of demographic dividend, and (5) strengthening inclusive institutional factors.

**Keywords** Economic development · Inclusive economy · Covid-19 pandemic · New normal

## 1 Introduction

Over the past decade following the 2008–2009 Global Financial Crisis, Indonesia's economic performance has shown steady improvement. Despite an unfavorable global economic environment, economic growth remained resilient, supported by sustained macroeconomic stability. Key welfare indicators—including unemployment, poverty, and income inequality—showed improvements during this period.

S. M. Juhro (✉) · M. M. Ridhwan · A. Rishanty
Bank Indonesia, Jakarta, Indonesia
e-mail: solikin@bi.go.id; mha_ridwan@bi.go.id; Arnita_rishanty@bi.go.id



S. M. Juhro et al. (eds.), *Sustainable Economy: The Indonesian Pathways*,
https://doi.org/10.1007/978-981-92-1215-6_4

These positive developments were underpinned by the discipline in macroeconomic management and consistent efforts to strengthen the economic structure. Nevertheless, the challenges facing the Indonesian economy remain substantial. In the aftermath of the global financial crisis, the world economy has tended to grow more sluggishly, entering what is often described as a "new normal," characterized by growth rates lower than historical long-term trends. Global financial markets continue to be marked by heightened uncertainty. Many observers argue that the world has entered a new environment defined by increasing Volatility, Uncertainty, Complexity, and Ambiguity (VUCA). Looking ahead, global economic challenges are expected to intensify further with the rapid pace of technological and digital revolutions, shifts in the global economic power structure, and evolving geopolitical dynamics.

One inevitable challenge is the rapid expansion of digital technology in the global economy, including in Indonesia, through the process of digital transformation. While digitalization has the potential to significantly enhance economic efficiency and productivity, it may also generate economic disruption if not properly managed. In developing countries including Indonesia, challenges stem from the relatively weak performance of the manufacturing sector, limited infrastructure capacity, suboptimal domestic financing sources, and the need for continuous improvement in human capital quality. At the global level, these include heightened financial market uncertainty and the spread of inward-looking policies.

These challenges have been further compounded by a series of overlapping global crises, most notably the unprecedented global health shock triggered by the Covid-19 pandemic, which first emerged in China in late 2019, as well as the ongoing escalating geopolitical tensions that have disrupted the global economic order. Covid-19 represents the first truly global viral pandemic, generating severe losses not only in the health sector but also across almost all economic sectors worldwide. The crisis evolved into a multidimensional shock, accompanied by substantial social and economic costs, and starkly revealed the fragility of one of the most fundamental human-made systems—public health—resulting in widespread infection and historically high fatality rates. Beyond the health crisis, these global shocks have disrupted energy markets, food supply chains, transportation networks, trade flows, and financial conditions through severe and simultaneous supply and demand disturbances. The resulting socio-economic impacts have been profound and multidimensional, posing significant risks to national economic and political stability, particularly through widening economic and social inequalities (Epstein et al., 2008).

The mounting uncertainties and dynamics have the potential to further exacerbate income and social disparities, especially if policy responses are not carefully designed. The informal sector and micro, small, and medium-sized enterprises (MSMEs), which absorb a large share of the workforce, have been among the most severely affected. Contemporary discourse highlights that growing inequality amid persistent global shocks and an accelerating digital transformation has intensified calls for a fundamental restructuring of socio-economic and political systems for the common good—an agenda widely referred to as the "Great Reset" (WEF, 2020).

# 2 Key Challenges in an Evolving Strategic Environment

Various changes in the strategic environment—both economic and non-economic—must be appropriately understood and addressed to enable a country such as Indonesia to progress. An advanced and inclusive Indonesia implies an economy supported by sustained stability, robust economic growth, strong external resilience, and rising social welfare. Macroeconomic stability—encompassing both price stability and financial system stability—constitutes the foundation for sustainable economic growth. Strong external resilience, reflected in a surplus balance of payments and a sound external financing structure, is essential to mitigate risks arising from global uncertainty. At the same time, improvements in social welfare—manifested in declining unemployment and poverty rates, as well as narrowing income and regional disparities—are necessary to ensure that the benefits of development are shared broadly across society.

## 2.1 *Basic Infrastructure and Public Services*

Physical infrastructure plays a strategic role in economic development by facilitating the movement of goods and services and supporting productive activities. From an economic perspective, infrastructure constitutes public capital formed through government investment in assets such as roads, bridges, and irrigation systems (Mankiw, 2003). Infrastructure development is therefore a critical input for enhancing national productivity and improving living standards, with empirical studies consistently showing a positive relationship between infrastructure investment and output productivity (Todaro, 2006).

Despite its widely recognized importance, Indonesia's infrastructure development remains constrained by land acquisition challenges, financing limitations, and regulatory frameworks that are not yet sufficiently investor friendly. Prior to the Covid-19 pandemic, according to the *Global Competitiveness Report 2019* published by the World Economic Forum (WEF), Indonesia ranked 72nd out of 141 countries in infrastructure development, indicating average global performance and relatively lower competitiveness compared with regional peers such as Singapore, Malaysia, and Thailand.

In the face of the global pandemic crisis, infrastructure in the health and public service sectors is essential for human capital development. However, limited access and capacity—particularly in rural areas—were sharply exposed during the Covid-19 pandemic (WHO; Riskesdas, 2018; Ministry of Health, 2020). Access to hospitals and health facilities in Indonesia remains constrained, as the 2018 Basic Health Research (Riskesdas) conducted by the Ministry of Health indicates that, on average, 52.9 percent of the population reported difficulty or extreme difficulty in accessing hospitals and other health services. Significant regional disparities in access to and quality of healthcare further complicated pandemic management, particularly as cases spread beyond urban centers to rural areas.

## 2.2 People-Centered Economic Base

Micro, small, and medium-sized enterprises (MSMEs) play a strategic role in Indonesia's economic growth and inclusive development, accounting for around 99 percent of all enterprises, 62 percent of national output, and nearly 97 percent of employment. Despite their dominance, MSMEs contribute only about 14 percent of total exports, highlighting the policy challenge of transforming their large numbers into higher productivity, stronger regional GDP contributions, and more sustainable job creation.

Indonesian MSMEs—both conventional and Sharia-based—continue to face structural constraints, including limited market (and information) access beyond district or municipal level, weak production and managerial capacity, and persistent financing gaps with formal financial institutions. While government support policies have generally helped ease some constraints, MSME stakeholders identify continued misalignment between policy design and on-the-ground realities, indicating the need for further refinement to accelerate productivity and value creation (Azis, 2022).

MSMEs operating within the Sharia economy hold considerable potential given Indonesia's large Muslim consumer base and the regulatory foundation provided by Law No. 33/2014 on Halal Product Assurance, as well as subsidized halal certification programs. However, uneven consumer awareness, perceived complexity and costs of certification among producers, and weak coordination between policy implementation and MSME perceptions continue to constrain the expansion of Sharia-based MSMEs.

The Covid-19 pandemic disproportionately affected MSMEs through declining demand, rising production and logistics costs, and tightening financing conditions, leading to sharp revenue losses, cash flow failures, and employment reductions. These shocks exacerbated longstanding vulnerabilities in marketing and access to finance, confirming that MSMEs are particularly exposed to systemic crises and underscoring the need for more resilient and adaptive MSME support frameworks. In response to these challenges, the government and relevant institutions have introduced various policies aimed at supporting MSME development. From the perspective of MSMEs, these policies have generally been beneficial in addressing constraints and improving productivity. Nevertheless, MSME stakeholders continue to identify scope for further policy refinement, particularly to bridge gaps between policy design and on-the-ground realities in order to accelerate MSME contributions to economic growth and value creation.

## 2.3 Innovation and Research Activities

Beyond MSMEs, innovation and research are central to long-term productivity growth and economic development, as emphasized by Schumpeter's theory of innovation-led development (Schumpeter, 1911) and endogenous growth theory, which highlights the role of human capital, knowledge, and research investment (Romer, 1987, 1990). For Indonesia, innovation is critical to avoiding the middle-income trap and upgrading resource-based production toward higher value-added activities (Lawrence et al., 2020); however, weak performance—reflected in Indonesia's low ranking in the Global Innovation Index (85th out of 131 countries in 2020), limited R&D spending (0.24 percent of GDP), fragmented institutional coordination, and low private-sector participation—remains a major constraint (WEF, 2019; GII, 2020; Juhro et al., 2020a), even as the Covid-19 crisis underscores the strategic importance of innovation in sectors such as health, food, energy, transport, and infrastructure.

It is therefore evident that innovation serves as a central engine of investment development and productivity growth. Innovation primarily emerges from research activities, which typically require medium- to long-term time horizons and are carried out by highly skilled and competent researchers in science and technology. As stated by the Indonesian Institute of Sciences (LIPI), "Without research, there is no innovation. Without innovation, a nation will be highly dependent on the technological products of other countries." Innovation also enhances economic efficiency, enabling domestically produced goods to become more competitive in global markets. Empirical studies on endogenous economic growth in Indonesia confirm the significant role of innovation and research activities in supporting economic growth over the past five decades (Juhro et al., 2020a).

During the Covid-19 pandemic, innovation and national R&D performance have been particularly vulnerable, especially due to funding pressures, as public resources have been redirected toward pandemic response. Nevertheless, behind the health crisis lies a critical opportunity: innovation and research play a vital role in producing national champions, particularly in the sectors of health, transportation, food, energy, and infrastructure.

## 2.4 Education and Human Capital

From a theoretical perspective, human capital plays a central role in economic development, primarily because it is grounded in knowledge and technological capabilities that can be replicated and expanded without spatial or temporal limits. Building on the Solow (1956), Romer (1987, 1990) developed endogenous growth theory, emphasizing the importance of human capital over physical capital. Accordingly, education has been a key development priority in Indonesia, as reflected in the significant increase in education spending over the past two decades, with 20 percent of the total government budget allocated to education. However, when measured as a share of GDP, Indonesia's education spending has averaged only around 3 percent over the past 5 years, which is relatively low compared with other ASEAN countries.

In quantitative terms, Indonesia's school participation rates are relatively high within ASEAN; however, despite significant increases in education spending and participation, education quality remains a major concern. According to the 2018 Programme for International Student Assessment (PISA), Indonesia ranked 70th out of 78 countries in literacy, mathematics, and science. Without substantial improvements, Indonesia is projected to reach the average OECD performance level only after several decades. Low education quality is closely associated with relatively weak teacher competencies; as of 2018, approximately 20 percent of teachers held qualifications below the undergraduate level, and many lacked adequate subject knowledge and pedagogical skills.

The Covid-19 pandemic has further complicated human capital development. School closures and the shift to online learning introduced new challenges related to internet availability, teacher and student readiness, and increased dropout risks, particularly among students from households affected by layoffs or income loss (Azevedo et al., 2020). Distance learning policies risk exacerbating educational disparities, especially in remote areas with limited connectivity and high costs. In response, the Ministry of Education and Culture introduced measures such as emergency curricula, adjustments to the academic calendar, and free internet data assistance.

Internet access is a prerequisite for effective distance learning, yet significant disparities persist across regions. Many areas, particularly in remote, frontier, and underdeveloped regions (3T areas), lack reliable internet access, electricity, or communication signals. Moreover, the economic impact of Covid-19 increased poverty levels, raising the risk of school dropouts as children are forced to work to support household income. World Bank estimates suggest that approximately 91,000 children may drop out of school as a result of the pandemic-induced income shock.

## 2.5 Institutional Factors

Institutional factors constitute a fundamental pillar of development success. Acemoglu and Robinson (2012) argue that national success or failure is determined not by culture, climate, geography, or religion, but by the quality of economic and political institutions. Sustained economic growth is far more likely to occur under inclusive institutions than under extractive ones. Analytically, four institutional configurations can be identified: (1) extractive economic institutions, characterized by weak legal frameworks, insecure property rights, and market distortions that undermine business activity; (2) extractive political institutions, where power is concentrated among a narrow elite with limited checks and balances; (3) inclusive economic institutions, which ensure property rights, effective legal systems, supportive public services and regulations, openness to new economic activities, and broad access to education and economic opportunities; and (4) inclusive political institutions, which enable pluralism, broad participation, and effective checks and balances, supported by sufficient political centralization to enforce laws collectively.

Strong synergies exist between economic and political institutions. Inclusive institutional synergies create virtuous cycles that promote sustainable economic growth by expanding access to resources, reducing entry barriers, and fostering efficient market functioning. Conversely, extractive institutional synergies generate vicious cycles, whereby political elites control economic institutions to limit opposition and consolidate power, while extractive economic institutions enrich elites and reinforce political dominance.

In practice, extractive institutional dynamics remain observable in Indonesia, often highlighted in media reporting. Political dominance enables elites to shape economic institutions in their favor, weakening law enforcement and accountability. Following decentralization, elite capture has also emerged at the regional level. Another critical institutional challenge lies in weak policy coordination across sectors and between central and local governments. According to the Global Innovation Index (2020), institutional weaknesses significantly contribute to Indonesia's low innovation ranking. Overlapping research agendas across government agencies and reluctance to adopt externally produced research outputs reflect sectoral ego and coordination failures, leading to inefficiencies and low productivity.

Leadership is another crucial institutional dimension. In the early stages of the Covid-19 pandemic, policy responses were relatively slow, and some leaders underestimated the severity of the crisis, generating public confusion. Weak coordination between central and local governments further undermined policy effectiveness. These governance challenges, combined with low public compliance, highlight the importance of strong leadership, effective coordination, and institutional credibility in managing crises and supporting inclusive development.

## 3 National Economic Modalities

### *3.1 Natural Resource Endowment*

Indonesia is endowed with abundant natural resources; however, this substantial potential has not yet been optimally managed. Indonesia's forests constitute one of the world's largest tropical forest areas, characterized by exceptionally rich biodiversity. As the world's largest archipelagic state, comprising more than 17,000 islands, Indonesia also possesses the second-longest coastline globally, extending approximately 95,000 kilometers. Consequently, the country is endowed with vast marine resources, including marine biodiversity, mineral resources, and extractive commodities. Indonesia's coastal ecosystems—such as mangrove forests, coral reefs, and seagrass beds—are among the most diverse in the world. Despite this abundance, Indonesia remains a net importer of fossil energy, particularly crude oil, recording an energy trade deficit. This condition is largely attributable to declining oil production due to aging oil fields and limited development of new wells. Similar challenges affect natural gas, where declining discoveries and underutilized reserves—such as the Natuna gas field, with an estimated 40 trillion cubic feet—continue to constrain domestic supply. In contrast, coal extraction remains relatively inexpensive and technologically less complex, making it economically attractive. Supported by geographic proximity to major emerging markets such as China and India, Indonesia has significantly expanded coal production over the past two decades.

Recognizing the strategic importance of minerals for industrial development—particularly in electronics and advanced manufacturing—the Indonesian government introduced a ban on raw mineral exports in 2014 to promote domestic downstream processing. Key minerals produced in Indonesia include tin, bauxite, nickel, gold, and copper (U.S. Geological Survey, 2014). Downstream industrialization (hilirisasi) of natural resources is expected to increase domestic value added, reduce dependence on raw material exports, and improve the trade balance by minimizing reimports of finished goods. In the short term, downstream development can help reduce trade deficits, while in the medium term it can stimulate economic growth through investment inflows, job creation, and income generation. However, successful downstream industrialization requires strengthened industrial capabilities, including skilled human capital, technological mastery, and the development of industrial zones across regions.

Despite its rich natural resource base, Indonesia's level of economic development remains relatively behind that of comparable resource-rich countries such as Australia, Malaysia, Brazil, and South Africa, which have more effectively leveraged their resources for economic progress and social welfare. Nevertheless, Indonesia has avoided the severe social and security conflicts experienced by some resource-rich African countries, illustrating the paradoxical relationship between natural resource wealth and economic welfare. In economic theory, this phenomenon is known as the "resource curse," whereby resource abundance undermines development through three main channels: structural distortions that weaken competitiveness due to currency appreciation; institutional failure in managing and distributing resource rents; and conflict arising from competition over resource control. In the long term, Indonesia's non-renewable resources—particularly oil and coal—are expected to decline significantly within the next two decades. To mitigate this risk, both central and local governments must prioritize economic diversification, invest resource revenues in human capital, and strengthen governance to avoid the resource curse.

## *3.2 Cultural Heritage and Social Capital*

Indonesia's rich cultural diversity—encompassing ethnicity, religion, language, and tradition—is a fundamental national asset, reflected in the national motto *Bhinneka Tunggal Ika* (Unity in Diversity). This diversity is reinforced by a deeply rooted tradition of mutual cooperation (*gotong royong*), which remains a defining characteristic of Indonesian society.

Historically, the Indonesian archipelago has played a central role in global trade since the seventh century, beginning with the Srivijaya Kingdom's commercial links to China, India, and the Arab world. Cultural diversity and long-standing trade engagement have fostered vibrant creative industries spanning performing arts, fashion, architecture, music, literature, cuisine, and film. These assets provide strong potential for regional economic development, particularly through tourism and the creative economy. Indonesia's maritime culture, supported by extensive territorial waters of approximately 3.2 million square kilometers, further reinforces its historical strengths in navigation and shipbuilding. Globalization presents both opportunities and challenges for preserving Indonesia's local cultural identity (Dwijendra & Mahardika, 2018).

From a theoretical perspective, these traditions constitute social capital. Fukuyama (1995) defines social capital as informal cooperation rooted in shared norms and values, while Putnam (1993) emphasizes trust as its core component. High levels of trust foster cooperation, which in turn reinforces trust in a virtuous cycle. Empirical evidence for Indonesia confirms that social capital—manifested through cultural values such as integrity, honesty, religiosity, and mutual cooperation—plays a significant role in supporting economic growth across provinces (Juhro et al., 2022). These findings underscore the importance of preserving cultural values and strengthening both formal and informal institutions, as culture and institutions interact in a complementary manner to shape economic performance, productivity, and social welfare.

## *3.3 Population and the Demographic Dividend*

Indonesia is the world's fourth-most populous country, with more than 270 million people, providing a vast domestic and potential international market. Over the past 15 years, the middle class has expanded significantly—from 7 percent to approximately 20 percent of the population—representing around 52 million individuals. Urbanization has also accelerated, with 55 percent of Indonesians residing in urban areas, a share projected to rise to 70 percent within the next decade. As of February 2020, Indonesia's labor force totaled 137.9 million people, although workforce quality remains constrained by relatively low educational attainment.

Indonesia is currently experiencing a demographic dividend, expected to peak between 2025 and 2030, driven by a high proportion of working-age population relative to dependents. This demographic structure provides an opportunity to boost savings, investment, and productivity, thereby facilitating escape from the middle-income trap. Millennials constitute a key growth engine through innovation, creative industries, and start-up formation, supported by technology adoption and digital connectivity. However, unequal access to technology, education, finance, and entrepreneurial networks—particularly between urban and rural areas—poses significant challenges. To fully harness the demographic dividend, Indonesia must invest in inclusive entrepreneurship, particularly in agriculture and resource-based sectors, where technology-driven innovation led by younger generations can enhance productivity, food security, and rural economic development.

### *3.4 Potential for Sharia Economy Development*

Over the past two decades, the Islamic economy and finance have expanded rapidly both globally and nationally. As the world's largest Muslim-majority country, Indonesia holds significant potential in the global halal market, which continues to grow alongside the expanding Muslim population. Despite this potential, Indonesia's contribution to the global halal market remains modest. While exports of halal food, Muslim fashion, and halal tourism have increased, Indonesia remains a net importer of halal products, contributing to persistent current account pressures.

Key challenges include inadequate halal industry regulation, limited public literacy, weak integration between halal industries and Islamic finance, insufficient domestic production capacity, and limited global recognition of Indonesia's halal standards. In response, Bank Indonesia—together with government agencies and stakeholders—has adopted a "4C" strategy: strong commitment, concrete and implementable programs, collaborative institutional synergy, and sustained public campaigns promoting halal lifestyles. Bank Indonesia has also supported halal value chain development across agriculture, food, fashion, tourism, and renewable energy. However, Indonesia's non-membership in international halal standard-setting bodies such as SMIIC remains a constraint to global market integration.

Empirical evidence suggests that Islamic finance has strong potential to support Indonesia's economic growth. Islamic financial markets operate under principles prohibiting interest, excessive uncertainty, speculation, and unethical investment, while emphasizing risk-sharing mechanisms. Given Indonesia's demographic profile, Islamic finance should play a more prominent role in economic development. Empirical studies using long-term time-series data indicate that when Islamic finance is incorporated into growth models, the expansion of Islamic capital markets contributes positively to productivity growth and overall economic performance (Juhro et al., 2020a).

## 4 Inclusive Economic Policy Strategies in the New Normal Era

As discussed earlier, the new normal era such as Covid-19 pandemic has affected not only public health but has also led to a significant economic slowdown through simultaneous and mutually reinforcing supply- and demand-side disruptions. These sudden and unexpected shocks have inevitably generated wide-ranging social, economic, and political consequences. Against this backdrop, this section presents a

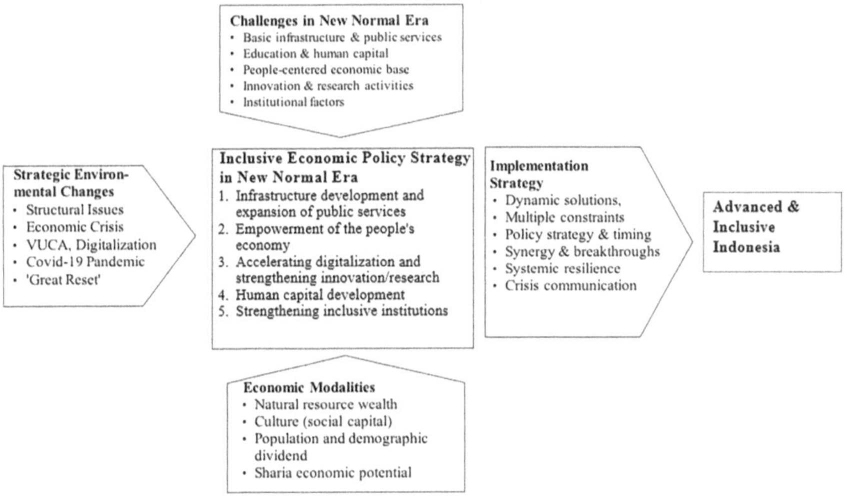


**Fig. 4.1** Inclusive Economic Policy Strategies in the New Normal Era. Source: Authors

framework for inclusive economic growth aimed at guiding the economy through the new normal era.

Taking into account the evolving strategic environment and the underlying modalities of the national economy, the following discussion outlines several priority policy strategies that may serve as inputs for policymakers and relevant stakeholders, particularly in supporting national economic recovery during the pandemic and the transition to the new normal (Fig. 4.1).

## 4.1 *Infrastructure Development and Expansion of Public Services*

Prior to the Covid-19 pandemic, the Government of Indonesia had identified 42 strategic priority projects under the 2020–2024 National Medium-Term Development Plan (RPJMN), designed as integrated initiatives across ministries, levels of government, state-owned enterprises, and communities, with strong multiplier effects. However, the pandemic necessitated substantial budget reallocations toward the National Economic Recovery (PEN) program, requiring infrastructure development to be refocused on projects that directly support economic recovery and employment.

In this context, labor-intensive infrastructure projects are critical for absorbing displaced workers, provided that strict health protocols are enforced to prevent new transmission clusters. Priority infrastructure during the pandemic and recovery phases includes vaccine development and procurement as a key enabler of health and economic recovery; expansion of healthcare capacity through hospitals, laboratories, medical equipment, and incentives for healthcare workers; and strengthened food security infrastructure, including irrigation systems, dams, agricultural land development, and maritime and fisheries support, to reduce reliance on imports during global disruptions.

The pandemic has also underscored the importance of telecommunications infrastructure, as remote working and digital learning have become essential. Given Indonesia's archipelagic geography and persistent digital divides, especially in rural and outer regions, expanding digital connectivity and providing subsidized internet access are critical to ensuring continuity in education and economic activity. In parallel, continued development of physical transport infrastructure—such as toll roads, bridges, and integrated land, sea, and air logistics—is necessary to safeguard the distribution of essential goods and support nationwide vaccine logistics (Suparmi et al., 2018).

Beyond physical infrastructure, the crisis highlights the need for comprehensive reform of the national health system to enhance resilience against future systemic shocks. Key priorities include strengthening the National Health Insurance (JKN) system as a core social protection mechanism to safeguard household welfare and consumption, and accelerating the adoption of digital health technologies, including artificial intelligence, to support early warning systems, risk identification, and more efficient healthcare delivery. Together, these measures are essential to fostering an inclusive and resilient economic recovery in the new normal era.

## *4.2 Empowering the People's Economy*

People-centered economic empowerment should focus primarily on micro, small, and medium-sized enterprises (MSMEs), given their central role in employment generation and economic growth, as well as their heightened vulnerability during the Covid-19 pandemic. Accordingly, MSME policy strategy should combine short-term relief measures to support business survival with medium- to long-term efforts to strengthen competitiveness and global integration.

Building resilient and competitive MSMEs requires improving the quality of human capital, particularly entrepreneurial skills, production and marketing management, financial literacy, and digital capabilities. To this end, the government has introduced targeted training programs aimed at increasing productivity, scale, and market access, including initiatives that promote digital entrepreneurship and technology adoption. Synergies between MSMEs, vocational education institutions, and industrial zones are also essential to enhance workforce readiness, facilitate knowledge transfer, and strengthen MSME operational capacity. Post-pandemic recovery strategies further emphasize mentoring, digital platform adoption, online marketing, and innovation, supported through collaboration among local governments, universities, financial institutions, and digital marketplaces.

Digitalization is a key enabler for transforming MSMEs into new drivers of national growth, particularly when integrated with efficient digital payment systems and digital finance. To address pandemic-related liquidity pressures, the government and financial authorities have implemented credit restructuring policies, including interest rate reductions, maturity extensions, and temporary equity conversion, to ease cash-flow constraints and sustain MSME operations. Complementary measures—such as short-term, subsidized financing for micro-entrepreneurs and newly established businesses, particularly those affected by layoffs—are also critical to accelerate recovery in the new normal era.

Beyond short-term survival, MSME development strategies must prioritize long-term competitiveness and export orientation World Bank (2014). While digital platforms have expanded market access, many MSMEs remain concentrated in low-value-added trading activities and act primarily as resellers of imported goods. This poses risks to the current account balance and limits domestic value creation. Policy support should therefore be carefully targeted to promote MSMEs as producers and exporters of domestic goods, particularly in manufacturing and innovation-driven sectors, and to facilitate their integration into global value chains. This requires improvements in product standardization, export readiness, regulatory compliance, logistics support, and utilization of e-commerce as a bridge to global markets.

Strong and coordinated multi-stakeholder collaboration is essential to enable MSMEs to "scale up" and compete globally. Clear role allocation and synergy among central and local governments, state-owned enterprises, private firms, MSMEs, academia, and aggregators are needed to avoid fragmentation and inefficiency. Strategic partnerships can support skills upgrading, quality assurance, logistics facilitation, and access to export markets, including through the use of state-owned enterprises as aggregators to enhance economies of scale and value-chain integration.

In addition to conventional MSMEs, Sharia-based MSMEs hold substantial growth potential given Indonesia's large Muslim population and expanding global halal markets. Beyond human capital and digitalization, access to Sharia-compliant financing—particularly through Islamic banks and digital Islamic fintech platforms—plays a critical role. Sharia fintech, including equity-based and social finance instruments such as zakat and waqf, offers more flexible, risk-sharing financing options for MSMEs that may not qualify for conventional bank credit. With regulatory support and institutional coordination, Islamic fintech can become a powerful mechanism for MSME recovery, inclusion, and long-term growth in the digital era.

## 4.3 Accelerating Digitalisation and Strengthening Innovation and Research

Accelerating digital transformation through innovation and technology adoption has become increasingly urgent in response to heightened global–domestic uncertainty and complexity, while also supporting Indonesia's medium- to long-term transition toward a competitive and inclusive advanced economy. This requires the rapid integration of digitalisation across economic and social sectors, alongside the development of an innovation ecosystem that is inclusive and socially beneficial. In theory, innovation ecosystems consist of networks of organisations and individuals that combine human creativity, business acumen, scientific discovery, and investment capital to transform ideas into productive enterprises and competitive industries (Lawrence et al., 2020). However, in Indonesia, coordination among government, research institutions, businesses, and other stakeholders remains weak, limiting the downstream commercialisation and practical application of research and innovation outcomes.

Given Indonesia's regional heterogeneity in human capital, business capacity, and sectoral development, innovation cannot be uniformly applied across regions. Instead, innovation strategies must incorporate local conditions and "local wisdom." In this context, frugal innovation—defined as the development of affordable, adaptable, and accessible technologies tailored to local needs—offers a suitable approach. Frugal innovation promotes creativity, entrepreneurship, and inclusive technological diffusion, and is particularly relevant for Indonesia's development context. During and after the Covid-19 pandemic, research and innovation efforts should be prioritised toward addressing health challenges and mitigating the broader social and economic impacts of systemic shocks.

In the health sector, innovation priorities include strengthening healthcare capacity through temporary facilities, expanded testing, medical equipment production, and incentives for healthcare workers. Digital solutions—such as telemedicine, artificial intelligence (AI), mobility data, and community-driven development—can enhance access to healthcare, reduce system burdens, and support effective pandemic management. Over the medium term, public–private investment cooperation is needed to ensure efficient vaccine distribution, while long-term reforms should focus on strengthening physical and non-physical health infrastructure and adopting a "One Health" approach that integrates human, animal, and environmental health systems.

To preserve inclusivity, innovation in social protection is equally critical. Existing programs—including cash transfers, education assistance, and national health insurance—should be expanded in coverage and benefit levels to protect vulnerable groups affected by income loss and unemployment. In the medium term, labour-intensive public works and skills training programs can support economic reintegration, while long-term strategies should focus on digitally enabled social protection systems that are responsive to future shocks and aligned with labour market needs.

In education, the widespread adoption of distance learning has accelerated digital transformation. AI-enabled learning platforms and the rapid growth of education technology (EdTech) firms present opportunities to improve education quality and global competitiveness. However, effective implementation depends on robust data systems. Digital population identity systems are therefore essential to improve service targeting, interoperability across government programs, financial inclusion, and administrative efficiency, while carefully managing cybersecurity, data governance, and digital exclusion risks.

Technology adoption is also critical in productive sectors. In agriculture, digital platforms and appropriate technologies can address scale inefficiencies, improve market access, enhance productivity, and reduce import dependence. In manufacturing, real-time monitoring systems, automation, robotics, and the Industrial Internet of Things (IIoT)—supported by advancements such as 5G—can sustain productivity under constrained working conditions, improve energy efficiency, and strengthen domestic supply chains. These transformations offer a strategic opportunity to reduce import reliance and enhance industrial resilience.

Finally, innovation must be supported by strong research collaboration. The Covid-19 pandemic has accelerated the shift toward a highly connected, low-contact economy, increasing the importance of integrated digital ecosystems across sectors. Government-led research consortia, innovation platforms, and diaspora-based research initiatives have played a vital role in mobilising collective innovation capacity. Strategic research collaboration—particularly in vaccine development, medical technology, and socio-economic resilience—strengthens national innovation sovereignty and enhances Indonesia's preparedness for future systemic shocks.

## *4.4 Human Capital Development*

The Covid-19 pandemic presents a critical opportunity to implement structural policy reforms aimed at improving education quality and human capital development in a more integrated, effective, and efficient manner. In the short term, priority measures include reallocating education budgets to support digital connectivity, enabling continuity of learning through distance education (PJJ). These measures include internet data subsidies for students, teachers, lecturers, and academic staff, as well as continued professional allowances to support educators' welfare during the economic downturn. In addition, public institutions, state-owned enterprises, and high-income communities can contribute through social responsibility initiatives by providing free or subsidised internet access for students from low-income households and families affected by layoffs.

To preserve equity in access to education, the government has expanded quotas for economically disadvantaged students in public schools, although the ad hoc nature of this policy has generated implementation challenges. Limited reopening of schools in low-risk (green zone) areas may be pursued gradually under strict health protocols. Beyond pandemic-related disruptions, long-standing structural issues in education remain, particularly in relation to funding adequacy, teacher quality, and institutional coordination. Although education spending has reached the constitutional threshold of 20 percent of total government expenditure, Indonesia's education expenditure remains relatively low at approximately 3.3 percent of GDP—below regional peers such as Vietnam (6.3 percent) and Thailand (4.1 percent)—indicating the need for increased real per capita investment in education during the recovery and post-pandemic period.

Improving teacher quality is central to strengthening human capital. Policy priorities include competency-based recruitment of new teachers, systematic certification and professional development for existing teachers, and the provision of adequate incentives to attract and retain high-quality educators. Institutional coordination also plays a critical role, particularly under decentralisation. Local governments should ensure that education officials are selected based on competence and integrity, while school committees—although currently underutilised—should be empowered to participate meaningfully in school management, planning, and oversight of public funding such as the School Operational Assistance (BOS) program.

The pandemic has further underscored the need for more flexible learning models. While distance learning has been widely implemented, certain educational activities—such as laboratory work, community service (KKN), and internships—require physical presence. Blended learning models that combine online and face-to-face instruction offer a viable solution, particularly in higher education, while also supporting cross-institutional credit mobility. At the same time, curriculum reform has become increasingly urgent, as Indonesia's education system remains overly focused on rote learning and insufficiently oriented toward higher-order thinking skills (HOTS). This weakness is reflected in Indonesia's consistently low performance in international assessments such as PISA.

Labour market outcomes further highlight skills mismatches. According to Statistics Indonesia (BPS), the unemployment rate (of total open unemployment) among university graduates rose from 5.89 percent in 2019 to 12.1 percent in 2023, reflecting inadequate job-relevant skills and weak alignment between education providers and labour market needs. Indonesia also lacks an integrated labour market information system to guide curriculum design, particularly in vocational and technical education. Moreover, higher education accreditation remains uneven—especially outside Java–Bali—limiting the relevance of many institutions to industry demand.

To address these challenges, comprehensive education reform is required, with a stronger focus on science, technology, engineering, and mathematics (STEM) skills, as well as competencies such as complex problem-solving, critical and creative thinking, social skills, and lifelong learning (Deming, 2017). In the digital era, soft skills and digital literacy—including basic ICT competencies—are increasingly essential as routine tasks decline and automation expands. These priorities align with the government's *Kampus Merdeka* program, which grants greater autonomy to universities, redefines credit systems based on learning activities, and promotes experiential learning through internships, research, student exchanges, and community engagement. This approach aims to ensure that graduates are not only theoretically proficient but also practically skilled and labour-market ready.

## 4.5 Strengthening Inclusive Institutions

Future development will be shaped by increasing uncertainty and complexity, driven not only by the Covid-19 pandemic but also by widening socio-economic inequality resulting from economic recession and climate change. As discussed earlier, extractive economic and political institutions—those that benefit narrow groups at the expense of broader society—tend to generate long-term instability and collective welfare losses. Addressing these challenges requires a strong commitment to collaboration among government, the private sector, and society, both domestically and internationally. Collaborative interactions are most effective when they are guided by shared objectives, symmetrical governance structures, and high levels of negotiation, interdependence, and trust, enabling collective problem-solving and innovation toward inclusive prosperity.

Inclusive development further depends on leadership that is capable not only of taking calculated risks but also of institutionalising innovation. As emphasised by Juhro and Aulia (2019), the central challenge is often not resistance to innovation per se, but the failure to embed innovation processes within organisational structures. Strategic leadership therefore determines whether innovation becomes episodic or continuous and sustainable, particularly in environments characterised by short performance evaluation cycles and limited leadership tenures—conditions common in both public and private institutions.

In this context, *catalytic collaboration* has emerged as a critical leadership approach for navigating complex, multidimensional challenges. According to Juhro et al. (2020b), catalytic collaboration enables organisations to work collectively toward outcomes that exceed individual institutional goals. This approach is characterised by four key elements: prioritising continuous learning, adopting systems thinking, maximising shared access to information and assets, and building diverse, long-term, and transformational relationships. Such collaboration is particularly relevant for Indonesia, as it can integrate regionally dispersed growth potentials and strengthen national economic performance amid global uncertainty.

The Covid-19 crisis has underscored the importance of catalytic collaboration as both a response mechanism and a strategic opportunity. Systematic, learning-based policy responses—supported by transparent information sharing—enhance public accountability and trust, while cross-institutional coordination enables more coherent and sustainable crisis management. Transformational leadership is essential in this process, as it enhances institutional adaptability and innovation capacity in addressing the multidimensional impacts of the pandemic (Juhro et al., 2020b). Crucially, innovation should not depend on a small number of creative individuals, but instead be supported by structured, institutionalised processes that translate ideas into scalable and sustainable solutions. This logic underpins the growing importance of dedicated strategic leadership roles—such as Chief Innovation Officers or Chief Networking Officers—tasked explicitly with fostering innovation ecosystems rather than treating innovation as an auxiliary function.

Beyond formal institutions, inclusive development also requires strong informal leadership and social cohesion, particularly in rural and underserved communities with limited access to education, information, and digital infrastructure. Religious and community leaders play a vital role as informal change agents in facilitating behavioural adaptation, social trust, and collective resilience. At the societal level, effective institutions must be supported by strong followership—characterised by trust, social capital, and civic discipline. Countries such as Singapore, South Korea, and Japan illustrate how high social trust and education levels contribute to societal resilience. In Indonesia, the pandemic has created momentum to reinforce trust and *gotong royong* (mutual cooperation) as core components of social capital. A combination of transformational leadership and strong followership can therefore accelerate adaptation in the new normal and support Indonesia's long-term transition toward an advanced and inclusive economy.

Finally, institutional strengthening must extend to Indonesia's engagement with the global economy. As global economic dynamics evolve, Indonesia is required to improve its business climate, reduce barriers to trade, enhance infrastructure and economic governance, and respond proactively to global trends. Revitalising regional and global economic partnerships is thus a strategic priority to strengthen competitiveness and export market access. Deeper integration into global supply chains—through both backward and forward linkages—can stimulate new sources of growth, particularly in priority sectors, and reinforce Indonesia's position within regional and global production networks.

## 5 Conclusion

This closing section presents the implementation strategy, built on the five core strategies for inclusive economic development in the new normal era. First, policy responses must be guided by a **dynamic optimisation approach under multiple constraints**. The Covid-19 pandemic has simultaneously triggered a global health crisis and a deep economic shock, exposing economies—including Indonesia—to heightened risks of poverty and unemployment. These intertwined crises require carefully sequenced, integrated, and evidence-based decision-making. Health and economic policy responses must therefore proceed in parallel, as effective health crisis management depends on economic capacity, while sustainable economic recovery requires successful containment of the health crisis.

Second, **policy strategy and timing must address simultaneous supply and demand shocks**. The pandemic generated parallel disruptions on both sides of the economy, reinforced by feedback loops. In the short term, policy priorities should focus on stimulating aggregate demand to prevent deeper contraction, with the expectation that demand recovery will subsequently support supply-side adjustment. In this context, fiscal policy plays a critical role in jump-starting economic activity through timely and well-targeted budget execution, expanded spending on public goods, and social assistance programs. Over time, accommodative monetary and financial policies are expected to reinforce real-sector recovery, supported by active participation from businesses and households.

Third, **stronger policy synergy and breakthrough-oriented approaches** are essential to restoring productivity and sustaining recovery in the new normal. The transition to new behavioural and economic norms requires coordinated action among policymakers, businesses, and society at both central and regional levels (Juhro, 2013). While economic reopening is necessary to revive growth, it must be accompanied by continued efforts to control virus transmission. Given the multidimensional nature of the crisis, sectoral and regionally fragmented approaches are insufficient; instead, recovery strategies must be comprehensive, well-coordinated, and supported by strong leadership and innovative policy instruments capable of generating meaningful breakthroughs (Juhro, 2019).

Fourth, the crisis underscores the urgency of developing **systemic resilience strategies**. In an increasingly interconnected and dynamic global system, even small shocks can propagate rapidly and generate large-scale systemic impacts. Resilience-oriented strategies therefore require a multidisciplinary perspective that recognises economies as "systems of systems" and emphasises the capacity to absorb shocks, recover lost functionality, and adapt to new realities—including shifting global economic conditions, social needs, behavioural changes, and escalating climate risks (OECD, 2020). Importantly, resilience strategies should focus not only on prevention, but also on recovery and adaptation, acknowledging that future large-scale disruptions are likely. Crises such as Covid-19 should be leveraged as opportunities to "bounce forward" by addressing broader systemic vulnerabilities, rather than merely restoring pre-crisis conditions (Linkov et al., 2018). International cooperation and data-sharing—covering prevention measures, treatment options, vaccines, and public health practices—are critical components of this approach.

Finally, **effective strategic communication** is a vital pillar of crisis management and recovery. Clear, timely, and credible communication by leaders is essential not only for transparency, but also for maintaining public trust and policy effectiveness. In crisis situations, communication failures often arise from excessive early optimism or delayed disclosure while awaiting complete information. Although no single communication blueprint exists, leaders must communicate consistently and adapt messages as new information emerges, demonstrating responsiveness and accountability. Addressing public concerns and sustaining dialogue beyond the immediate crisis phase are equally important. A balanced narrative—combining realism with optimism—can mobilise collective support, strengthen stakeholder confidence, and foster broad-based participation in the economic recovery process.

## References


Acemoglu, D., dan Robinson, J. A. (2012). *Why nations fail: the origins of power, prosperity and poverty*. New York: Crown Publishers.

Azevedo, J. P., Hasan, A., Goldemberg, D., Iqbal, S. A., dan Geven, K., (2020). Simulating the Potential Impacts of COVID-19 School Closures on Schooling and Learning Outcomes, World Bank, Jakarta.

Azis. (2022). https://link.springer.com/book/10.1007/978-981-16-6831-9

Deming D. J. (2017). The Growing Importance of Social Skills in the Labor Market. *Quarterly Journal of Economics*. 132 (4):1593–1640.

Dwijendra, N. K. A., & Mahardika, M. (2018). The Influence of Globalization on The Existence of Local Culture In Indonesia. *Asian Academic Research Journal of Multidisciplinary*. 5.

Epstein, J. M., Parker, J., Cummings, D., dan Hammond, R. A. (2008). Coupled Contagion Dynamics of Fear and Disease: Mathematical and Computational Explorations. *PLoS ONE*, 3(12): e3955.

Fukuyama, F. (1995). *Trust: The social virtues and the creation of prosperity*. New York: Free Press.

GII. (2020). https://www.wipo.int/edocs/pubdocs/en/wipo_pub_gii_2020.pdf

Juhro S. M. (2013). Penguatan Peran Bank Indonesia dan Optimalisasi Strategi Bauran Kebijakan untuk Mendukung Pertumbuhan Ekonomi yang Berkelanjutan, Makalah SESPIBI, Bank Indonesia, Jakarta.

Juhro, S. M. (2019). *Transformational Leadership: Konsep, Pendekatan, dan Peran dalam Pembangunan*. Bank Indonesia Institute, February.

Juhro, S. M. dan Aulia, A.F. (2019). New Sources of Growth: The Role of Frugal Innovation and Transformational Leadership. *Bulletin of Monetary Economics and Banking*. Vol. 22, No. 3 (2019), pp. 383–402

Juhro, S. M., Narayan, P. K., Iyke, B. N, & Trisnanto, B. (2020a). Is There a Role for Islamic Finance and R&D in Endogenous Growth Models in the Case of Indonesia? *Pacific Basin Finance Journal*, Elsevier.

Juhro, S. M., Aulia, A.F., Hadiwaluyo, D., Aliandrina, D., dan Lavika, E. (2020b). The Role of Catalytic Collaboration in Leveraging Transformational Leadership Competencies to Generate Sustainable Innovation. *International Journal of Organizational Leadership*. 9(2020) 48-66

Juhro, S. M., Narayan, P. K., Iyke, B. N., & Trisnanto, B. (2022). Social capital, R&D and provincial growth in Indonesia. *Regional Studies*, *56*(12), 2117–2132. https://doi.org/10.1080/00343404.2022.2042469

Lawrence, S., Hogan, M., Brower, A., dan Zayed, S. (2020). Global Practices for Building Innovation Ecosystems. https://www.ksi-indonesia.org/en/knowledge/detail/1827-global-practices-for-building-innovation-ecosystems

Linkov, I., Trump, B.D., & Keisler, J. (2018). Risk and resilience must be independently managed. *Nature*. 555(7694), 30–30.

Mankiw, N.G. (2003). *Macroeconomics*. New York: Worth Publishers.

Ministry of health. (2020). https://infeksiemerging.kemkes.go.id/document/pedoman-pencegahan-dan-pengendalian-covid-19/view

Organisation for Economic Co-operation and Development. (2020). A systemic resilience approach to dealing with Covid-19 and future shocks. http://www.oecd.org/coronavirus/policy-responses/

Putnam, R.D. (1993). What makes democracy work?. National Civic Review. Vol.82(2) 101-107.

Ridhwan, M.M., dan Pratama, R. (2016). Analisis Pertumbuhan dan Daya Saing Manufaktur Nasional serta Implikasinya terhadap Jebakan Kelas Menengah. Background Paper RDG, Bank Indonesia.

Riskesdas. (2018). https://repository.badankebijakan.kemkes.go.id/id/eprint/3514/1/Laporan%20Riskesdas%202018%20Nasional.pdf

Romer, P. M. (1987). Growth Based on Increasing Returns Due to Specialization. *American Economic Review*. American Economic Association, vol. 77(2) 56-62, May.

Romer, P. M. (1990). Endogenous Technological Change. *Journal of Political Economy*. University of Chicago Press, vol. 98(5) 71-102, October.

Schumpeter, J.A. (1911). *The Theory of Economic Development*. Cambridge: Harvard University Press.

Solow, R. M., (1956). A Contribution to the Theory of Economic Growth. *The Quarterly Journal of Economics*, Oxford University Press, vol. 70(1), pages 65-94.

Suparmi, Kusumawardani, N., Nambiar, D., Trihono dan Hosseinpoor, A.R. (2018). Subnational Regional Inequality in the Public Health Development Index in Indonesia. *Global Health Action* 11 (sup1): 1500133.

Todaro, P. M. dan Smith, S.C. (2006). *Economic Development*. Boston: Pearson Addison Wesley.

U.S. Geological Survey. (2014). *Mineral commodity summaries 2014*. U.S. Geological Survey.

WEF. (2019). https://www.weforum.org/publications/how-to-end-a-decade-of-lost-productivity-growth/in-full/chapter-one/

WEF. (2020). https://www.weforum.org/press/2020/09/the-great-reset-a-global-opening-moment-to-turn-crisis-into-opportunity/

World Bank (2014). *Indonesia Development Policy Review 2014*. Jakarta: World Bank Office

# Chapter 5
# Golden Indonesia 2045 in the Context of Sustainable Development

**Solikin M. Juhro, Cicilia Anggadewi Harun, Arnita Rishanty, and Danny Hermawan**

**Abstract** This chapter examines Indonesia's pathways toward Golden Indonesia 2045, emphasizing some key perspectives on sustainable development. It explores key central macroeconomic challenges, such as climate change and environmental degradation, that shape productivity, welfare, and financial resilience. Exploring a "sustainability trilemma"; growth–stability–welfare trilemma, and drawing on salient international country experiences, the chapter underscores the critical role of coordinated fiscal, monetary, and financial policies in fostering inclusive and sustainable economic growth.

**Keywords** Golden Indonesia · Indonesia Emas 2045 · Sustainable development

## 1 Introduction

Golden Indonesia is a vision for Indonesia to achieve the status of a high-income country by 2045. Indonesia's long-term vision, popularly known as *Indonesia Emas 2045*, articulates the nation's aspiration to achieve the status of a high-income country by the 100th anniversary of its independence.[1] This ambition is not merely a matter of attaining higher per capita income; it embodies the broader goals of ensuring social welfare, economic resilience, and environmental sustainability.

Indonesia has the potential to emerge as a major nation by 2045. Indonesia, the world's fourth most populous country and the 16th largest economy by GDP (Worldometer, n.d.), is endowed with abundant natural wealth, including precious metals, minerals, biodiversity, and a strategic maritime geographical location. Combined with its rich cultural diversity and a strong sense of unity / *Bhineka*

[1] https://indonesia2045.go.id/

S. M. Juhro (✉) · C. A. Harun · A. Rishanty · D. Hermawan
Bank Indonesia, Jakarta, Indonesia
e-mail: solikin@bi.go.id; charun@bi.go.id; Arnita_rishanty@bi.go.id; danny_h@bi.go.id



S. M. Juhro et al. (eds.), *Sustainable Economy: The Indonesian Pathways*,
https://doi.org/10.1007/978-981-92-1215-6_5

*Tunggal Ika* (Syahputra et al., 2023), these invaluable assets provide Indonesia with great potential not only to achieve high-income status but also to emerge as a major global nation. Suryahadi et al. (2024) argues that across Indonesia's diverse ethnic groups, participation in communal activities and trust in government are the most important forms of social capital needed to improve people's welfare.

Yet, significant challenges continue to hinder this trajectory. Indonesia has remained in the middle-income trap for three decades, with only modest economic growth. Its greatest asset—human capital—faces persistent weaknesses. The country's low PISA scores reflect limited competencies in science, mathematics, and literacy (OECD, 2023). Similarly, Indonesia's Human Capital Index stands at 0.54, far below Singapore's 0.88, underscoring capacity gaps that directly affect innovation, economic growth, and overall prosperity. The domestic business environment also struggles to reach its potential, as indicated by a low public service index, constraining productivity and competitiveness.

At the global level, structural shifts compound the domestic challenges. The world is becoming increasingly protectionist and less globalized (Zahoor et al., 2023; Sugihartono, 2024), marked by rising geopolitical and economic tensions. Generational transitions, technological disruptions, and the emergence of political multipolarity are reshaping global trade structures and market dynamics (Gopinath, 2025; Al Midfa, 2024; Özdilek, 2025; UNCTAD, 2025). These pressures are further intensified by the accelerating planetary crisis, which continues to unfold along an exponential trajectory (OECD, 2025). In navigating these multifaceted domestic and international dynamics, Indonesia must leverage its inherent strengths and undertake bold structural reforms.

The vision of Indonesia as a great sovereign, advanced and sustainable nation in 2045 is translated through The National Long-Term Development Plan. The Indonesian Ministry of National Development Planning (Bappenas) has formulated Law No. 59 of 2024 concerning the National Long-Term Development Plan for 2025–2045 to support the realization of the Golden Indonesia 2045 Vision: a United, Sovereign, Advanced, and Sustainable Unitary State of the Republic of Indonesia. The long-term development plan was designed to ensure synergy among development actors, enabling the achievement of national goals in a coherent and consistent manner across successive periods of Indonesia's leadership. The realization of such vision is reflected in five key vision targets, namely: achieving per capita income equivalent to that of advanced economies, reducing poverty and inequality, strengthening Indonesia's leadership and influence in the international arena, enhancing the competitiveness of human resources, and reducing greenhouse gas emission intensity towards achieving net zero emissions (Bappenas, 2024).

Achieving a Golden Indonesia in 2045, therefore, requires a careful balance between growth, stability, and structural transformation. One of the critical challenges for Indonesia in its pathway to 2045 is how to maintain stability while enabling the structural reforms necessary for transitioning into a high-income economy. Stability, in this sense, goes beyond the traditional notions of price stability and financial system soundness. It encompasses macroeconomic, social, and environmental stability, which together form the foundation upon which sustainable development can be realized. Structural transformation involves shifting the economy from reliance on natural resources and low-value manufacturing toward higher productivity sectors such as advanced manufacturing, services, and digital industries. This transformation is inherently disruptive, often accompanied by sectoral dislocations, labor market adjustments, and distributional consequences.

This chapter examines Indonesia's pathways toward Golden Indonesia 2045, with a focus on key perspectives on sustainable development. It is organized as follows. The next two sections review the relevant literature on the pillars of development and a "sustainability trilemma", as well as salient international country experiences. Section 4 discusses the key macroeconomic challenges facing Indonesia and the associated policy perspectives. Section 5 concludes.

## 2 Literature Review

### *2.1 Four Pillars of Development*

The Government of Indonesia has established four pillars of development to achieve a Golden Indonesia by 2045.

- **The first pillar is "Human Development and Science & Technology".** It emphasizes the importance of human capital as the fundamental of the Indonesian development as a nation. It is conducted through equitable education, health improvements, and labor reforms. Culture, science, and technology are positioned as drivers of productivity and innovation, ensuring the population's well-being and readiness for future challenges.
- **The second pillar is "Sustainable Economic Development".** It highlights the need for robust yet sustainable growth. Priorities include expanding investment and trade, accelerating industrialization, advancement of tourism and the maritime economy, while ensuring food and water security. A strong commitment to environmental protection will align economic progress with long-term sustainability.
- **The third pillar is "Equitable Development".** It focuses on reducing poverty and inequality while promoting regional balance. This requires promoting equal business and income opportunities, spatial development equality across regions, and building integrated infrastructure to connect the archipelago.
- **The fourth pillar is "National Resilience and Governance".** It underscores the importance of strong institutions and governance. Key measures include strengthening democracy, reforming bureaucracy, enforcing the rule of law, and combating corruption. At the global level, Indonesia will uphold its "free and active" foreign policy, while enhancing defense and security to safeguard national sovereignty.

## 2.2 Triple Planetary Crisis: Externalities on the Path to Golden Indonesia 2045

**The triple planetary crisis**—climate change, biodiversity loss and pollution trigger different ecological changes and existential crisis for humanity. The "triple planetary crisis" unifies the ecological and social problems caused by (I) climate change, (II) biodiversity loss and (III) pollution worldwide (UN, 2022). These three major challenges feed into each other through different mechanisms and represent critical threats to the survival and well-being of species on Earth and the stability of different ecosystems. The consequences of the triple planetary crisis include, among others, loss of food security, infrastructural damage, waves of forced migration, decay of genetic resources, and global health problems related to anomalous temperature changes and extreme weather events. Concerning public health, climate change, biodiversity loss and pollution individually and synergistically facilitate the emergence and spread of infectious diseases, especially those caused by pathogens that affect both human and animal species. Emerging zoonoses are projected to increase as the climate crisis intensifies (Carlson et al., 2022), with biodiversity loss and pollution aggravating the problem (Ellwanger & Chies, 2025).

**Climate change**—atmospheric pollution from greenhouse gases drives climate change, as documented in reports by the Intergovernmental Panel on Climate Change (IPCC) and illustrated in the real world by the increasing frequency and intensity of extreme weather events observed across many regions. Climate change results in significant losses in human lives, deteriorates public health, destabilizes economies and financial systems, damages natural ecosystems, and affects millions of people in hundreds of cities worldwide. The burden of vector-borne diseases such as dengue and malaria is projected to rise as global average temperatures increase, particularly in endemic regions. By 2070, an additional 4.7 billion people could be at risk of these mosquito-borne diseases (Colón-González et al., 2021).

**Biodiversity loss**—driven by climate change, chemical pollution, and wildlife exploitation—heightens the risk of pathogens crossing species barriers, a process through which new diseases are transmitted from wildlife to humans (Plowright et al., 2024). The decline of biodiversity undermines the stability of ecological mechanisms that ordinarily contain diseases within wildlife populations. For example, ecosystems with greater biodiversity are generally less prone to widespread disease transmission (Khalil et al., 2016). Beyond health risks, biodiversity loss also weakens agricultural and economic foundations (Dasgupta & Levin, 2023; Notte, 2025; Santoro et al., 2023). Healthy ecosystems protect land from degradation, sustain fertile soils, pollination, and natural pest regulation, which are essential for stable crop yields. As biodiversity declines, soils become less fertile, agricultural productivity diminishes, and the supply of food and raw materials contracts. This reduction in output exerts upward pressure on prices, fueling volatility in essential goods and services. Such dynamics can trigger inflationary pressures, erode household purchasing power, and challenge central banks and policymakers seeking to maintain price and financial stability.

The economic consequences extend beyond food systems. Reduced biodiversity and declining ecosystem services can increase production costs for industries reliant on natural inputs, creating supply-side shocks that ripple across value chains. This not only undermines competitiveness but also heightens vulnerability to external shocks, exacerbating price instability and threatening sustainable growth. The COVID-19 pandemic demonstrated how ecological imbalances can disrupt global supply chains and financial systems, reinforcing the urgency of embedding biodiversity preservation into strategies for economic resilience and sustainable development.

**Pollution**—industrial activities and consumer habits associated mainly with urbanized societies also have important impacts on the spread of pathogens. The huge production of plastic products around the world has a high energy demand that fuels climate change, and the disposal of these materials in the environment leads to plastic pollution even in the most remote places on the globe. The plastisphere, meaning the physical association of microorganisms with plastic waste, allows the easy spread of diseases between different environments, increasing the risk of infection in humans and animals (Amaral-Zettler et al., 2020). Pollution from plastics, tires and other manufactured products that retain water also increases artificial breeding grounds for disease-carrying mosquitoes (Obame-Nkoghe et al., 2023). Pollution by persistent organic pollutants harms metabolism, the immune system and genetic stability, impairing the survival and reproduction of different species and potentially facilitating the emergence and spread of infectious diseases due to the combination of biodiversity decay with compromised immune function (Ziliotto et al., 2024). Antimicrobial pollution caused by medical and veterinary medicines, alone or in association with climate change, are selective pressures that contribute to the emergence of multidrug-resistant diseases that may affect human populations (Baker et al., 2022).

Externalities are especially evident in the triple planetary crisis. In classical economics, externalities arise when the actions of entities (individuals or businesses) create costs or benefits for others, but those effects are not reflected in market prices (Pigou, 1920). These environmental damages generate social and economic costs—ranging from health care burdens and agricultural productivity losses to disaster-related fiscal pressures and economic and financial instability (D'Orazio, 2025; Noordwijk et al., 2023). For instance, the economic cost of annual haze episodes from peatland fires has been estimated at billions of dollars, reducing GDP growth, straining household income, and creating cross-border diplomatic frictions (Tacconi, 2016). Similarly, climate-induced flooding in urban areas disrupts financial transactions, damages critical infrastructure, and amplifies fiscal pressures for reconstruction.

When environmental externalities are linked to financial risks, they are identified as climate- and nature-related financial risks, commonly classified into two categories: physical risks and transition risks (NGFS, 2019). Physical risks stem from acute weather events—storms, floods, droughts—and chronic changes such as rising sea levels and temperature shifts. Transition risks emerge from the structural adjustments required to move toward a low-carbon economy, including changes in global trade rules, carbon pricing mechanisms, and shifts in investor sentiment. For Indonesia, both risks are deeply relevant. As a resource-rich economy dependent on coal exports and land-based commodities, Indonesia faces vulnerabilities if global demand pivots away from carbon-intensive goods (Ordonez et al., 2021). At the same time, physical risks such as rising sea levels pose existential challenges for low-lying regions, threatening livelihoods and financial stability simultaneously.

Generational shifts further complicate this landscape. Younger generations of Indonesians are increasingly vocal about sustainability, climate justice, and inclusive growth. Their preferences as consumers, workers, and investors will influence market dynamics, demanding more transparency and accountability from firms and financial institutions (Inglehart & Norris, 2016).

Indonesia's idiosyncratic characteristics add further complexity to the sustainability challenge. As a developing, archipelagic nation with vast natural resources, diverse economic structures, and significant regional disparities, Indonesia cannot adopt a "one-size-fits-all" approach. Unlike advanced economies with deep capital markets and fiscal space, Indonesia, like many other developing countries, faces tighter resource constraints, competing development priorities, and higher sensitivity to global capital flows (Patunru & Resosudarmo, 2024). These factors limit the scope for aggressive fiscal interventions and highlight the importance of monetary and financial policies that carefully balance stability, growth, and sustainability.

Indonesia's heavy reliance on micro, small, and medium enterprises (MSMEs) creates unique policy considerations in addressing environmental externalities (Satpathy et al., 2024; Tambunan, 2019). Azis et al. (2021) argues that regulators policy and instrument is not what matters the most of effective collective action; rather, social capital plays a critical role. Within this, active participation—particularly in accessing information through transparent and informal coordination—is considered the most important factor. Indonesia's MSMEs—which account for more than 60% of GDP and employ the majority of the labor force—are both highly vulnerable to climate risks (due to limited adaptive capacity) Higuera Roa et al. (2025) and crucial actors in advancing inclusive and sustainable growth (IESR, 2025). By promoting digital literacy, fostering partnerships between MSMEs and larger organizations, and strengthening government regulations that support long-term recovery and sustainability initiatives, such as circular economy practices, MSMEs can achieve greater stability, sustained growth, and enhanced competitiveness (Satpathy et al., 2024).

The significant consequences of triple planetary crisis highlight that unsustainability directly feeds into macro-financial instability. Hence, central banks cannot afford to treat environmental concerns as external to their mandate. Stability cannot be preserved in isolation from sustainability; instead, the two must be understood as mutually reinforcing (Fig. 5.1).

The chart conceptualizes sustainability as both a **growth engine** and a **stability guardrail**, linking climate challenges to sustainable growth outcomes through two interacting channels. On the opportunity side, climate challenges catalyze the development of a sustainable economy and finance, which can unlock new growth engines—capital accumulation, innovation, productivity gains, and integration into international trade. Green investment, sustainable finance instruments, and low-carbon industrial upgrading enhance allocative efficiency and crowd in private capital, thereby strengthening medium- to long-term growth potential.

On the risk side, unmanaged climate and nature risks—including physical risks from extreme weather and transition risks from abrupt policy shifts—threaten

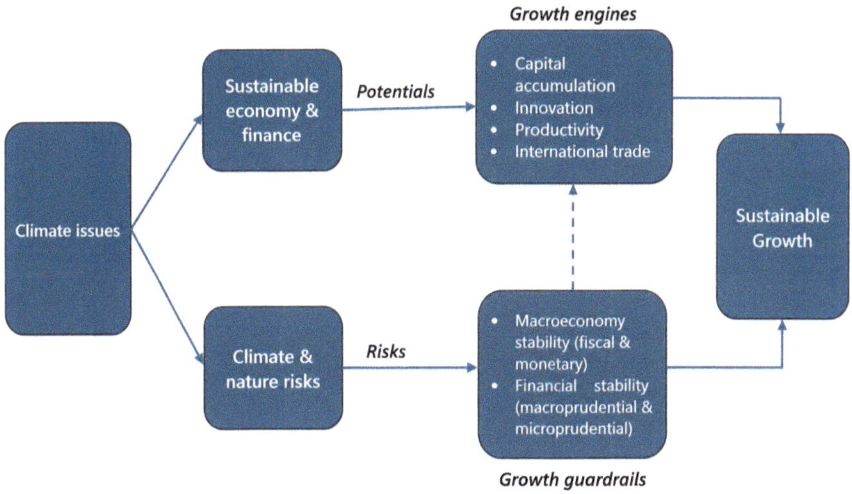


**Fig. 5.1** Sustainability as a growth engine. Source: Author's own identification

macroeconomic and financial stability. These risks transmit through inflation volatility, fiscal pressures, credit deterioration, and asset repricing, ultimately constraining growth. Hence, macroeconomic stability (fiscal and monetary) and financial stability (macroprudential and microprudential) function as guardrails that ensure growth remains durable rather than fragile.

Crucially, the two channels are interdependent. Sustainable finance enhances growth potential only if macro-financial stability is preserved, while stability itself cannot be sustained if environmental risks accumulate unchecked. This bidirectional relationship reframes sustainability not as a trade-off with stability, but as a prerequisite for it.

## 2.3 *Resolving a "Sustainability Trilemma": Growth, Stability, and Welfare*

Indonesia's development challenge can be framed as a "sustainability trilemma", a growth–stability–welfare trilemma. Stability without growth results in insufficient welfare improvements and risks entrenching inequality. Growth without stability produces economic fragility, boom–bust cycles, and social vulnerability. Growth and stability without sustainability, meanwhile, generate long-term welfare losses through environmental degradation, health costs, and climate shocks.

Resolving this trilemma requires embedding sustainability within both growth and stability objectives. From a macroeconomic perspective, sustainable growth enhances welfare by raising productivity, creating quality employment, and stabilizing real incomes. At the same time, sustainability-oriented policies reduce tail risks that threaten price stability and financial soundness. Climate-related supply shocks—such as food price spikes from floods or droughts—illustrate how environmental instability directly undermines monetary policy objectives.

Inclusive growth is central to this resolution. Indonesia's economic structure—dominated by micro, small, and medium enterprises (MSMEs)—means that sustainability transitions must be designed to support, rather than marginalize, vulnerable economic actors. Access to green finance, capacity-building, digitalization, and social protection mechanisms are essential to ensure that sustainability-driven transformation enhances welfare broadly rather than concentrating benefits among large firms or urban elites.

## 3 Country Experiences

Sustainability should embed, not hinder, in the journey towards a high-income country. There are lessons to be learnt from developing countries who are early adopters of green growth strategies. A growing empirical literature showing that green industrial policies, financial market development, and institution building are essential—while financing gaps, institutional quality, and trade/technological constraints remain key barriers for many developing countries. The experiences of Chile, South Korea, and China illustrate the importance of industrial policy, institutional capacity, and tailored environmental strategies.

### *3.1 Chile*

Chile's trajectory demonstrates how resource-based economies can move up the value chain with industrial policy and sustainability integration. Sato & others (2020) highlight how Chile used fiscal incentives, R&D support, and export assistance to upgrade industries like mining, forestry, salmon, and wine. These policies allowed Chile to escape the middle-income trap by creating value-added exports. Recent research (2025) on the lithium industry shows the limits of Chile's approach, where business power and institutional constraints have hindered technological upgrading. This underlines the need for strong regulatory frameworks alongside state capacity. An OECD (2020) transition finance study emphasized Chile's strategy for mobilizing domestic resources and private investment to finance green growth as it graduates from ODA eligibility.

### *3.2 South Korea*

South Korea offers a different path, relying on innovation, green stimulus, and regulatory institutions. Hille et al. (2021) show how regional environmental regulations reduced air pollution while maintaining growth, demonstrating that green growth is achievable with strong governance. Han & Lee (2023) analyze South Korea's Green

Growth and Green New Deal, highlighting how large-scale fiscal stimulus supported renewable energy, green infrastructure, and eco-friendly innovation. A systematic review (Lee & Kim, 2022) shows South Korea's success in promoting sustainable urban infrastructure through green building policies and technology adoption.

### 3.3 China

China's industrial policy has combined green subsidies with innovation-driven growth. Cai et al. (2023) show how subsidies for new energy vehicles (NEVs) significantly improved adoption, reduced emissions, and fostered green innovation. Wu et al. (2019) highlight how industrial policies embedded in Five-Year Plans shaped structural change, with implications for how green growth can be scaled in large emerging economies.

The country experiences demonstrate that policy sequencing, institutional adaptability, industrial policy coordination and technological innovation, are critical for advancing sustainability during economic transformation. Chile's success in leveraging environmental taxation and regulatory reforms shows that robust fiscal instruments, when aligned with a long-term development vision, can strengthen both environmental protection and macroeconomic stability. Chile's example suggests that environmental taxation and fiscal reforms could be harnessed more systematically, provided that enforcement institutions are strengthened. However, the Chilean case also reveals that effective enforcement mechanisms and strong monitoring institutions are essential to prevent regulatory capture and ensure environmental goals are met.

South Korea's trajectory illustrates how coordinated industrial policy, and technological innovation can integrate sustainability with rapid economic growth. The establishment of strong state-led institutions, such as the Ministry of Trade, Industry, and Energy, created a governance framework that enabled targeted investments in renewable energy and green innovation. The Korean model also underscores the importance of linking sustainability to national competitiveness, where investments in education, R&D, and clean technology became a central pillar of industrial upgrading.

China provides an example of scaling sustainability through institutional experimentation and policy decentralization. China's approach highlights the value of gradual policy experimentation and institutional learning. Pilot programs, such as regional emissions trading systems, were gradually scaled up to form a national framework, allowing for policy learning while avoiding systemic risks. China's experience demonstrates the importance of institutional flexibility in responding to local challenges, while simultaneously maintaining strong central coordination. Yet, it also highlights the risks of uneven implementation across provinces, suggesting that institutional capacity building at the subnational level is indispensable for long-term success.

## 4 Discussion

Aligning sustainability with economic competitiveness is essential. As South Korea's case demonstrates, green growth can be a driver of technological advancement and global market integration. Indonesia can learn that should therefore focus on fostering innovation ecosystems, enhancing human capital, and supporting industries such as renewable energy, green manufacturing, and digital services. For Indonesia, piloting innovative financing tools, green industrial policies, or carbon markets at the provincial level could create tailored solutions while minimizing systemic risks. Over time, these pilots could inform a coherent national framework, ensuring that sustainability transitions are inclusive and adaptive to Indonesia's diverse economic and geographic landscape. These sectors can position Indonesia as a leader in sustainable value chains, while simultaneously reducing dependence on resource-based exports.

Furthermore, the relationships between external debt, financial globalization, environmental taxes, and green growth in emerging economies are highly uneven. Given the escalating climate change, economies are concerned for the attainment of sustainable economic improvements. Hence, abiding by the objective of sustainability while stressing the conception that increasing financial progress should not subside the country's environmental advancements (Afshan et al., 2023). Afshan et al. (2023) argues that environmental taxes are an important tool for promoting green growth in emerging economies. However, when it comes to external debt, the findings show that higher levels of debt tend to reduce green growth. This suggests that many emerging countries are not using external borrowing effectively to support sustainable development.

The study also highlights an asymmetric relationship between financial globalization and green growth. At higher levels of green growth, financial development supports further improvements. But at lower levels (lower quantiles), financial development can actually reduce green growth. Similarly, while rising external debt may boost financial development at lower levels, it tends to weaken financial advancement at higher levels. Financial globalization also shows mixed effects: it can improve financial development in some contexts, but the impact varies depending on a country's stage of growth. For environmental taxes, the results reveal another asymmetry. At lower levels of financial development, environmental taxes are linked to weaker outcomes. In contrast, at medium to high levels, they have a positive effect.

Indonesia's vulnerability to climate and nature risks—ranging from sea-level rise to biodiversity loss—creates asymmetric impacts across regions and income groups. Without targeted interventions, these risks could exacerbate inequality and undermine social cohesion, threatening the political and economic foundations of long-term growth. Embedding inclusion within sustainability strategies is therefore essential. MSMEs, which account for the majority of employment, require tailored financial instruments, technical assistance, and risk-sharing mechanisms to participate in green value chains. Social protection systems play a complementary role by cushioning transitional costs, enabling labor mobility, and maintaining aggregate demand during structural shifts.

From a welfare perspective, sustainability-oriented growth strategies generate co-benefits that extend beyond GDP. Reduced pollution lowers health expenditures, resilient infrastructure mitigates disaster losses, and stable ecosystems support food security—all of which reinforce long-term productivity and social stability.

Referring the above perspectives, Indonesia's aspiration to become a high-income, resilient, and sustainable economy by 2045 requires more than accelerating growth rates. The pathway toward *Golden Indonesia 2045* demands a coherent macroeconomic architecture that simultaneously delivers productivity-led growth, macro-financial stability, and social welfare while internalizing environmental constraints. The challenge is not merely technical but conceptual: growth strategies that neglect sustainability generate hidden fragilities, while stability-focused policies that suppress transformation risk stagnation and welfare shortfalls.

In this context, climate change and environmental degradation are no longer peripheral concerns but central macroeconomic issues. They shape investment decisions, productivity dynamics, fiscal sustainability, and financial system resilience. Consequently, central banks and financial authorities—traditionally focused on price and financial stability—are increasingly required to engage with sustainability as a core determinant of long-term macroeconomic stability. For Indonesia, this reorientation is essential to bridge the remaining gaps on the path to 2045.

## 5 Conclusion

Despite significant progress in development planning and climate commitments, important gaps remain along Indonesia's pathway to 2045—particularly in aligning macroeconomic management with sustainability objectives. The Government policy, i.e. fiscal policy, sectoral policy, alone cannot shoulder the transition burden, given limited fiscal space and competing development priorities. This elevates the role of central banks and financial regulators in shaping incentives, managing risks, and safeguarding stability during structural transformation.

Central bank policies contribute through three main channels. *First*, monetary policy credibility anchors inflation expectations amid climate-induced supply shocks, preventing temporary price pressures from becoming entrenched. *Second*, macroprudential frameworks that incorporate climate, and environmental risks enhance financial system resilience by discouraging excessive exposure to carbon-intensive and climate-vulnerable sectors. *Third*, sustainable finance development—through taxonomies, disclosure standards, and risk-based supervision—supports capital reallocation toward productive and resilient sectors. Importantly, central banks do not replace growth or climate policy; rather, they fill coordination gaps by ensuring that the transition does not destabilize the macro-financial system. In this sense, sustainability becomes a *means* to preserve policy effectiveness over the long term.

The pathway toward Golden Indonesia 2045 underscores a central lesson, that sustainable growth cannot be achieved by sequencing growth, stability, and sustainability separately. They must be pursued simultaneously through an integrated policy framework. The conceptual framework presented highlights how sustainability acts both as a catalyst for new growth engines and as a safeguard against systemic risks.

For Indonesia, resolving the growth–stability–welfare trilemma requires embedding sustainability within macroeconomic and financial policy mandates, strengthening institutional coordination, and ensuring that growth remains inclusive. Central banks and financial authorities play a critical supporting role by preserving stability during transition and enabling capital to flow toward productive, resilient activities. Ultimately, sustainability is not a constraint on Indonesia's ambition to become a high-income nation by 2045; it is the condition that makes such ambition achievable, durable, and socially legitimate.

## References


Afshan, S., Yaqoob, T., Kee, H. W., & Yien, L. K. (2023). Achieving sustainable growth in emerging economies: Insights from advance method moment of quantile regression. *Gondwana Research*. https://doi.org/10.1016/j.gr.2023.08.003

Al Midfa, N. (2024, November 29). The future of global trade in a multipolar world: Evaluating how emerging economic powers and shifting alliances are reshaping global trade patterns. *TRENDS Research & Advisory*. https://trendsresearch.org/insight/the-future-of-global-trade-in-a-multipolar-world-evaluating-how-emerging-economic-powers-and-shifting-alliances-are-reshaping-global-trade-patterns/

Amaral-Zettler, L. A., Zettler, E. R., & Mincer, T. J. (2020). Ecology of the plastisphere. *Nature Reviews Microbiology, 18*(3), 139–151. https://doi.org/10.1038/s41579-019-0308-0

Azis, I. J., Rishanty, A., & Can, C. (2021). Interplay of Policy and Social Capital. Bank Indonesia working papers *2021*. https://www.bi.go.id/id/publikasi/kajian/PublishingImages/Pages/Interplay-of-Policy-and-Social-Capital/Interplay_of_Policy_and_Social_Capital.pdf

Baker, R. E., Mahmud, A. S., Miller, I. F., Rajeev, M., Rasambainarivo, F., Rice, B. L., Takahashi, S., Tatem, A. J., Wagner, C. E., Wang, L. F., Wesolowski, A., & Metcalf, C. J. E. (2022). Infectious disease in an era of global change. *Nature Reviews Microbiology, 20*(20). https://doi.org/10.1038/s41579-021-00639-z

Bappenas. (2024). UU no. 59 tahun 2024. https://peraturan.bpk.go.id/Details/299728/uu-no-59-

Cai, Q., Ji, Z., Ma, F., & Liang, H. (2023). The green effects of industrial policy—Evidence from China's new energy vehicle subsidies. *Energies, 16*(19), 6811. https://doi.org/10.3390/en16198811

Carlson, C. J., Albery, G. F., Merow, C., Trisos, C. H., Zipfel, C. M., Eskew, E. A., Olival K. J., Ross, N., & Bansal, S. (2022). Climate change increases cross-species viral transmission risk. *Nature, 607*(607), 1–1. https://doi.org/10.1038/s41586-022-04788-w

Colón-González, F. J., Soares Bastos, L., Hofmann, B., Hopkin, A., Harpham, Q., Crocker, T., Amato, R., Ferrario, L., Moschini, F., James, S., Malde, S., Ainscoe, E., Nam, V. S., Tan, D. Q., Khoa, N. D., Harisson, M., Tsarouchi, G., Lumbroso, D., Brady, O. J., & Lowe, R. (2021). Probabilistic seasonal dengue forecasting in Vietnam: A modelling study using superensembles. *PLOS Medicine, 18*(3), e1003542. https://doi.org/10.1371/journal.pmed.1003542

Dasgupta, P., & Levin, S. A. (2023). Economic factors underlying biodiversity loss. *The Royal Society Publishing, 378*(1881). https://doi.org/10.1098/rstb.2022.0197

D'Orazio, P. (2025). Climate risks and financial stability: Evidence on the effectiveness of climate-related financial policies. *International Review of Financial Analysis, 105*, 104304. https://doi.org/10.1016/j.irfa.2025.104304

Ellwanger, J. H., & Chies, J. A. B. (2025). Triple planetary crisis and emerging zoonotic diseases: Consider degrowth as a solution. *Earth Critical Zone*, 100030. https://doi.org/10.1016/j.ecz.2025.100030

Gopinath, G., Gourinchas, P.-O., Presbitero, A. F., & Topalova, P. (2025). Changing global linkages: A new cold war? *Journal of International Economics, 153*, 104042. https://doi.org/10.1016/j.jinteco.2024.104042

Han, H., & Lee, T. (2023). Varieties of green stimulus policies: Comparative analysis of the green growth and green new deal policies in South Korea. *Journal of Environment & Development*. https://doi.org/10.1177/10704965221139303

Higuera Roa, O., Bachmann, M., Mechler, R., Šakić Trogrlić, R., Reimann, L., Mazzoleni, M., Aerts, J. C. J. H., Buskop, F. E., Pirani, A., & Mysiak, J. (2025). Challenges and opportunities in climate risk assessment: Future directions for assessing complex climate risks. *Environmental Research Letters, 20*, 053003. https://doi.org/10.1088/1748-9326/adc756

Hille, E., Lambernd, B., & Tiwari, A. K. (2021). Any signs of green growth? A spatial panel analysis of regional air pollution in South Korea. *Environmental and Resource Economics, 80*(3), 719–760. https://doi.org/10.1007/s10640-021-00607-4

IESR. (2025). White paper: Unveiling the future of sustainable business through empowering green MSMEs – IESR. In *IESR*. https://iesr.or.id/en/pustaka/white-paper-unveiling-the-future-of-sustainable-business-through-empowering-green-msmes/

Inglehart, R., & Norris, P. (2016). Trump, brexit, and the rise of populism: Economic have-nots and cultural backlash. *HKS Faculty Research Working Paper Series, 16*(026), 1–52. https://dx.doi.org/10.2139/ssrn.2818659

Khalil, H., Ecke, F., Evander, M., Magnusson, M., & Hörnfeldt, B. (2016). Declining Ecosystem Health and the Dilution Effect. *Scientific Reports 6*, 1–11. https://www.nature.com/articles/srep31314

Lee, W., & Kim, K. (2022). Systematic review of green building trends in South Korea from 2001 to 2023. *Sustainability, 16*(5), 1772. https://doi.org/10.3390/su16051772

NGFS. (2019). *Network for greening the financial system first comprehensive report a call for action climate change as a source of financial risk*. https://www.ngfs.net/system/files/import/ngfs/medias/documents/ngfs_first_comprehensive_report_-_17042019_0.pdf

Noordwijk, M., Leimona, B., Amaruzaman, S., Pascual, U., Minang, P. A., & Prabhu, R. (2023). Five levels of internalizing environmental externalities: Decision-making based on instrumental and relational values of nature. *Current Opinion in Environmental Sustainability, 63*, 101299. https://doi.org/10.1016/j.cosust.2023.101299

Notte, L. A., Marques, A., Petracco, M., Paracchini, M. L., Zurbaran-Nucci, M., Grammatikopoulou, I., & Tamborra, M. (2025). The assessment of nature-related risks: From ecosystem services vulnerability to economic exposure and financial disclosures. *Ecological Economics, 235*, 108636. https://doi.org/10.1016/j.ecolecon.2025.108636

Obame-Nkoghe, J., Roiz, D., Ngangue, M.-F., Costantini, C., Rahola, N., Jiolle, D., … Paupy, C. (2023). Towards the invasion of wild and rural forested areas in Gabon (central Africa) by the asian tiger mosquito aedes albopictus: Potential risks from the one health perspective. *PLOS Neglected Tropical Diseases, 17*(8), e0011501–e0011501. https://doi.org/10.1371/journal.pntd.0011501

OECD. (2020). Transition finance country study of Chile. *OECD Development Co-Operation Working Papers*. https://doi.org/10.1787/608cbf6d-en

OECD. (2023). PISA 2022 results: Volume I and II – Country notes: Indonesia. Retrieved from https://www.oecd.org/en/publications/pisa-2022-results-volume-i-and-ii-country-notes_ed6fbcc5-en/indonesia_c2e1ae0e-en.html

Organisation for Economic Co-operation and Development. (2025). Environmental outlook on the triple planetary crisis: Stakes, evolution and policy linkages. *OECD Publishing*. https://doi.org/10.1787/257ffbb6-en

Ordonez, J. A., Jakob, M., Steckel, J. C., & Fünfgeld, A. (2021). Coal, power and coal-powered politics in Indonesia. *Environmental Science & Policy, 123*, 44–57. https://doi.org/10.1016/j.envsci.2021.05.007

Özdilek, Ü. (2025). Digitally melting cities under climate stress. *Discover Cities, 2*(1). https://doi.org/10.1007/s44327-025-00099-7

Patunru, A. A., & Resosudarmo, B. P. (2024). Climate change policies in Indonesia: Challenges and economic consequences. *New Frontiers in Regional Science: Asian Perspectives*, 97–121. https://doi.org/10.1007/978-981-97-0122-3_6

Pigou, A. C. (1920). *The Economics of Welfare*. London: Macmillan and Co.

Plowright, R. K., Ahmed, A. N., Coulson, T., Crowther, T. W., Ejotre, I., Faust, C. L., Frick, W. F., Hudson, P. J., Kingston, T., Nameer, P. O., O'Mara, M. T., Peel, A. J., Possingham, H., Razgour, O., Reeder, D. M., Ruiz-Aravena, M., Simmons, N. B., Srinivas, P. N., Tabor, G. M., Tanshi, I., Thompson, I. G., Vanak, A. T., Vora, N. M., Willison, C. E., & Keeley, A. T. H. (2024). Ecological countermeasures to prevent pathogen spillover and subsequent pandemics. *Nature Communications, 15*(1), 2577. https://doi.org/10.1038/s41467-024-46151-9

Santoro, A., Piras, F., Bazzurro, A., Fiore, B., & Romano, F. (2023). Assessment of ecotone changes over the last six decades in two cultural landscapes: The case of the prosecco hills of Conegliano and valdobbiadene unesco site and of the olive groves of the slopes between assisi and spoleto giahs site. *Biodiversity and Conservation, 34*(9), 3193–3210. https://doi.org/10.1007/s10531-023-02725-5

Sato, T., et al. (2020). Local-foreign technology interface, resource-based development, and industrial policy: How Chile and Malaysia are escaping the middle-income trap. Journal of Technology Transfer. https://doi.org/10.1007/s10961-020-09808-3

Satpathy, A. S., Sahoo, S. K., Mohanty, A., & Mohanty, P. P. (2024). Strategies for enhancements of MSME resilience and sustainability in the post-COVID-19 era. *Social Sciences & Humanities Open, 11*, 101223. https://doi.org/10.1016/j.ssaho.2024.101223

Sugihartono, S. (2024, September 20). The current trend of de-globalization: Protectionism and resource nationalism. Modern Diplomacy. Retrieved from https://moderndiplomacy.eu/2024/09/20/the-current-trend-of-de-globalization-protectionism-and-resource-nationalism/

Suryahadi, A., Rishanty, A., Sparrow, R., *"Social Capital and Economic Development in a Large Multi-Ethnic Developing Country: Evidence from Indonesia."* Asian Development Review, Volume 41, Issue 2, 1 September 2024: Pages 301-323. https://doi.org/10.1142/S0116110524500082. https://www.scopus.com/record/display.uri?eid=2-s2.0-85202869164&origin=inward&txGid=326a8dec7cefe456b2c5b43eecf41993

Syahputra, W., Dhowi, B., Sianipar, S. M., Ali, M. M., & Sriherlambang, B. (2023). The psychological perspective of Bhinneka Tunggal Ika and its measurements. The Open Psychology Journal, 16. https://doi.org/10.2174/0118743501260487231122043601

Tacconi, L. (2016). Preventing fires and haze in Southeast asia. *Nature Climate Change, 6*(7), 640–643. https://doi.org/10.1038/nclimate3008

Tambunan, T. (2019). Recent evidence of the development of micro, small and medium enterprises in Indonesia. *Journal of Global Entrepreneurship Research, 9*(1). https://doi.org/10.1186/s40497-018-0140-4

UN. (2022). What is the triple planetary crisis? https://unfccc.int/news/what-is-the-triple-planetary-crisis

UNCTAD. (2025). Trade and development report 2025: On the brink - trade, finance and the reshaping of the global economy. https://unctad.org/publication/trade-and-development-report-2025

Worldometers. (n.d.). Indonesia population. Retrieved from https://www.worldometers.info/world-population/indonesia-population/

Wu, Y., Zhu, X., & Groenewold, N. (2019). The determinants and effectiveness of industrial policy in China: A study based on Five-Year Plans. China Economic Review, 53, 225–242. https://doi.org/10.1016/j.chieco.2018.11.005

Zahoor, N., Wu, J., Khan, H., & Khan, Z. (2023). De-globalization, international trade protectionism, and the reconfigurations of global value chains. Management International Review, 63, 823–859. https://doi.org/10.1007/s11575-023-00522-4

Ziliotto, M., Chies, J. A. B., & Ellwanger, J. H. (2024). Toxicogenomics of persistent organic pollutants: Potential impacts on biodiversity and infectious diseases. *Anthropocene, 48*, 100450. https://doi.org/10.1016/j.ancene.2024.100450

# Part II
# Climate Challenges, Stability and Growth

# Chapter 6
# Central Bank Climate Regulatory Framework

**Solikin M. Juhro, Irman Robinson, Arnita Rishanty, and Heru Rahadyan**

**Abstract** This chapter proposes an integrated central bank climate regulatory framework, by exploring the transmission mechanisms of central bank policies to support the establishment of just transition targets and promote sustainable economic growth. The framework delineates three strategies, namely: (1) data, tools, and research, (2) regulation and supervision, and (3) climate transition policy. This paper shows that the central bank's climate policies can navigate just transition and support the achievement of sustainable economic growth. These strategies extend beyond the traditional purview of central bank activities, necessitating a collaborative and synergistic approach among regulators and industry stakeholders.

**Keywords** Central bank policy · Climate regulatory framework

## 1 Introduction

The concerning rise in global temperatures is acknowledged to stem primarily from the increase in greenhouse gas (GHG) concentrations resulting from anthropogenic activities over the years (IPCC, 2023). As a result, severe and disastrous weather events create physical risks to the economy and are increasing in frequency, intensity, and geographic spread. They disrupt the continuity of production and the supply of goods and services, which causes market imbalances.

Climate change is a barrier to economic development as it poses a formidable threat to the economy and society, requiring urgent and coordinated action to mitigate its impacts. According to a report by AON (2021), extreme weather events have caused economic losses of US$ 5.1 trillion in the past two decades, and this figure could rise to 18% of global GDP by 2050 if no effective measures are taken (Guo,

S. M. Juhro (✉) · I. Robinson · A. Rishanty · H. Rahadyan
Bank Indonesia, Jakarta, Indonesia
e-mail: solikin@bi.go.id; irman_r@bi.go.id; Arnita_rishanty@bi.go.id; heru_rahadyan@bi.go.id



S. M. Juhro et al. (eds.), *Sustainable Economy: The Indonesian Pathways*,
https://doi.org/10.1007/978-981-92-1215-6_6

Kubli, & Saner, 2021). In its recent report, the WEF (2023) shows that climate and environmental risks are the core focus of global risk perceptions over the next decade.

Such awareness is increasingly spreading across the globe, affecting consumers and investors behavior. Investors and consumers are increasingly favoring more sustainable activities or products (Hoffman & Nayak, 2021). There is an urgent necessity for a rapid global transition away from high-emitting sectors to prevent the significant dangers of climate change from both environmental and socio-economic standpoints. Consequently, high-emitting sectors are expected to peak by 2030 and then decline steadily (International Energy Agency, 2023). The policies, particularly from the advanced economy, implemented to address climate change, are increasingly impacting the global economy (NGFS, 2024). The raising awareness, the changing behavior and policies create transition risks for firms, jobs and the national economy. These risks are further intensified by the responding disruptive technological innovations.

The physical and transition risks of climate change could potentially hinder the central bank's achievement of its inflation target and increase the risk of financial instability (Dikau & Volz, 2018). This underscores the need for the central bank to ensure that the financial system is resilient to the transition toward a low-carbon economy and is able to finance the transition efficiently (Mark Carney BOE, 2015). This eventually crystallized new wisdom regarding the important role of central banks in realizing sustainable economic development.

As the initial response to climate risks are considered insufficient (United Nations, 2024), the need to achieve green growth sustainably is pressing as the window to avoid global catastrophe is shrinking. The key to achieving sustainable growth lies in accelerating the scale-up of sustainable finance and ensuring that the transition process is managed properly to enable a just transition—leaving no one behind in the move toward a more sustainable world. Nevertheless, given the significant role central banks play in promoting sustainable economic development (Dikau & Volz, 2021), a robust framework to guide the integration of central bank policy with climate risk considerations is still lacking.

This chapter aims to explore the critical tasks to cope with climate risks and propose an integrated central bank regulatory framework to foster sustainable economic growth. Two main issues will be addressed. First, how to establish a pivotal linkage between concerted efforts to mitigate climate risks, on the one hand, and the central bank's responsibility in preserving financial system stability and supporting sustainable economic growth, on the other hand. Second, the impact of climate-related policies on transition risk management in supporting the achievement of sustainable economic growth.

This chapter provides several contributions of thought and novelty, which can be seen from several strands. First, it seeks to bridge this gap by proposing a comprehensive framework designed to craft an optimal sustainable regulatory framework. Such a framework is envisaged not only to preclude the emergence of systemic risks associated with climate change but also to mitigate the challenges arising from the transition to a low-carbon economy. Second, by integrating climate risk into the broader regulatory framework, this proposed architecture aims to optimally fortify financial systems against the perils associated with climate change, ensure their resilience amid the transition to a low-carbon economy, and optimize the benefit of the transition to sustainability. Lastly, by addressing the current void in the literature and policy discussion, it also aspires to guide policymakers, financial regulators, and stakeholders toward proactive and effective strategies to navigate the complexities of climate-related risks and transitions.

## 2 Literature Review

### *2.1 Contextualizing Central Bank Mandates on Climate-Related Risks*

The main mandate or responsibility of most central banks in the world is to maintain low and stable inflation in the short to longer term, as well as maintain financial stability. However, in the last two decades we have noted a significant shift in the perceptions of academics and central bankers regarding the role of central banks in addressing several issues "beyond stability", particularly those related to sustainable development and climate change. Many central banks have 'implicit' goals to support the achievement of sustainable economic growth, i.e. through regulations for sustainable development financing (Juhro, 2016).

Climate change directly impact the prices of goods and services and poses risks to financial system stability, thereby affecting the central bank's objectives of ensuring price stability, financial stability, and sustainable growth. These challenges have expanded expectations for central banks to address climate change, even beyond their traditional mandates (Eichengreen, 2021). Carney (2015) highlights the link between climate change, price volatility, and financial system stability, emphasizing the urgency of managing climate-related risks to prevent significant losses.

Some central banks in emerging markets and developing countries (EMDCs) have made significant progress in greening the financial system and addressing climate-related risks. They have achieved this by adapting existing policy tools and introducing new instruments to strengthen macroprudential regulation. This aligns with the broader mandates of many EMDC central banks, which include supporting sustainable development and aligning with government economic policies, in addition to their tradition focus on price stability (Juhro, 2025).

Those countries typically approach green finance and climate change through three main strategies. The first involves green credit allocation instruments, designed to channel credit towards green sectors. The second focuses on green regulatory instruments, such as prudential and macroprudential measures, aimed at safeguarding financial stability. Lastly, some countries implement other green central banking initiatives, such as developing green finance guidelines or establishing green bond markets (Dikau & Ryan-Collins, 2017).

Dikau and Ryan-Collins (2017) and (Dikau & Volz, 2021) also explore how existing traditions of financial intervention have influenced the approach of emerging markets toward green growth and credit allocation. Central banks in countries like India and Bangladesh, which historically engaged in centralized credit allocation policies, have incorporated green project categories—particularly renewable energy initiatives—into their priority loan programs. For example, Bangladesh's central bank green refinancing program has supported approximately 10% of the population to install home solar power systems.

In countries such as South Korea, Brazil and China, national development banks have played a more central role by providing credit support to green sectors, while the central banks focus on suppressing credit to carbon-intensive sectors. In Brazil, the central bank requires commercial banks to stress-test their lending portfolios against environmental and social risk criteria and to maintain additional capital reserves to cover these risks (Dikau & Ryan-Collins, 2017).

The growing need for sustainable financing further underscores the imperative for central banks and other financial regulators to assume a leadership role in this endeavor (Anwar, et al., 2020). By regulating the banking sector, central banks can proactively influence private investment decisions, promoting green finance through incentives for sustainable projects while limiting funding for carbon-intensive industries.

Furthermore, several cases demonstrate that environmental regulations imposed by environmental institutions are often weak or even ignored by economic actors. Consequently, environmental damage persists and worsens. In this context, central banks, with their substantial influence on the economy, are well-positioned to encourage economic actors to integrate environmental considerations into their profit-seeking activities within financial markets (Dikau & Ryan-Collins, 2017).

These above empirical and practical discourse has emphasized the important role of central banks in realizing sustainable economic development. However, this also poses a challenge for central banks, as they must encourage other financial institutions to actively support sustainable finance initiatives.

The execution of the 'wider' mandates, however, requires a judicious approach, given the unique challenges posed by climate-related risks (Lamperti, Bosetti, Roventini, & Tavoni, 2021). In the dynamic landscape of climate-related financial risks, the efficacy of conventional microprudential policies becomes questionable due to the inherent uncertainty surrounding the complete realization of climate risks. The evolving nature of these risks challenges the suitability of traditional measures, necessitating a forward-thinking, well-defined regulatory framework and a strategic alignment (Pfister & Valla, 2021). Moreover, the limitations of microprudential policies are underscored by their exclusive focus on individual firms, failing to consider the broader systemic implications and intricate feedback loops triggered by climate shocks (Coelho & Restoy, 2023). Given the prolonged time horizon and the systemic nature of climate risks, the adoption of monetary and macroprudential policies emerges as a more apt and comprehensive strategy for effectively managing and mitigating these multifaceted threats, thereby enhancing the resilience of the financial system and the economy. Regrettably, the existing landscape reveals a dearth of a robust framework guiding the integration of central bank policy with climate risk considerations.

## 2.2 *Contesting The Generic Concept of "Just" Transition*

In response to the exigency of climate change, nations globally have committed to curtailing their emissions under the Paris Agreement—a pivotal accord aspiring to confine the escalation of global temperatures to well below 2 °C, with a preference for limiting the increase to 1.5 °C, relative to pre-industrial levels (UNFCCC, 2015). Each country's commitment to achieve their climate target is articulated through a Nationally Determined Contribution (NDC), delineating specific emission reduction targets and corresponding plans.

In making the transition, each country's context will be different and no two national transitions will be alike. Countries' economic structures and emissions profiles necessarily influence the policies their government implements and the most affected sectors. As a result, the relative impacts of the transition on sectors in each region will vary considerably. For example, concerns over energy access in the context of energy transition, will appear different in countries rich in energy resources (whether fossil fuels or renewables) and those relying more heavily on imports (Montague, Raiser and Lee, 2024).

A just transition is conceptually broad and context-specific, tailored to the unique needs of each region, sector, and community. Justice is a multi-faceted concept (Koirala & Montague, 2024). The uneven distribution of transitionary costs and benefits is an issue in all countries but can manifest differently in developing countries. In industrialized nations, the focus is often on managing the decline of carbon-intensive industries like coal mining, while in developing countries, due to financing and data gaps, human capacity constraints, and governance challenges, the transition may involve tackling energy poverty and creating new opportunities in renewable energy sectors. Without careful planning, the transition could hinder growth and compromise competitiveness in some countries. Regardless of the context, a successful just transition requires a balance between environmental sustainability and social equity.

At the national level, a just transition acknowledges that the impacts of climate change—and the costs of carbon mitigation and adaptation—are unevenly distributed. It involves all affected parties and addresses these inequities to ensure political support for climate action, ultimately helping to avoid delays in achieving global net-zero goals. As recognized at the international level through its inclusion in the 2015 Paris Agreement, a just transition not only advances climate action but also contributes to progress on all Sustainable Development Goals (SDGs), particularly those related to affordable and clean energy, sustainable economic growth, reducing inequalities, and responsible production and consumption.

The transition to a low-carbon economy is essentially a global challenge that requires cooperation across borders. Developed countries, which have historically been the largest contributors to greenhouse gas emissions, have a responsibility to support developing countries in their transition. This includes providing financial and technical assistance, as well as addressing the potential spillover effects of their climate policies on developing economies. To address this, policies such as border carbon adjustments must be also carefully designed to ensure that they do not disadvantage developing countries (UNFCCC, 2023).

Climate action is a global undertaking, and supporting a just transition for developing countries requires a global perspective. Establishing fair emission reduction targets, however, is a complex process (Lo & Cong, 2022). Given that carbon emissions are presented as the global metric for tracking NDC achievements and progress (UNFCCC, 2024a), we argue that using absolute emissions alone fails to capture the true responsibility and impact differences between Advanced Economies (AEs) and Emerging Market Economies (EMEs). While acknowledging that the absolute emissions metric[1] aligns with global carbon budget constraints and offers simplicity, we propose that a carbon intensity metric would provide a more comparable measure across jurisdictions and promote a more equitable and effective approach to climate action. This shift would create a more transparent framework that balances the rights and responsibilities of each nation, enabling the international community to make meaningful progress toward the Paris Agreement's long-term goals, advancing toward a low-carbon economy and achieving net-zero emissions.

The NDCs under the Paris Agreement, often rely on total annual figures in absolute terms (UNFCCC, 2024b). The discrepancy arises from the fact that AEs with extensive industrialization may exhibit high per capita carbon emissions, yet their absolute total annual figures could be low due to smaller populations. Conversely, EMEs might have low per capita emissions but high absolute total emissions due to larger populations. Recognizing that carbon emissions are an inherent outcome of essential human activities (Canadell, et al., 2010), it is crucial to account for emissions on an individual basis to uphold the fundamental right of each person to emit. This perspective highlights the need for a more nuanced approach to carbon accounting—one that considers a global framework for individual rights to emit, promoting equity and fairness in addressing climate challenges worldwide.

Industrialization, however, has precipitated emissions beyond natural levels, exacerbating global warming and climate change. Therefore, the optimal instantiation of carbon objectives should penalize activities engendering carbon emissions, particularly those associated with environmentally deleterious industrial practices. Consequently, a pivotal strategy for effectuating a fair and efficacious transition lies in measuring carbon emissions as carbon intensity—a metric indicative of the amount of carbon emitted per unit of measurement. In the context of a nation,

[1] Two prevalent approaches to presenting carbon emissions are: absolute total carbon emissions and carbon intensity. While absolute total emissions represent the total annual figures of carbon emissions, carbon intensity divides these emissions by a unit of measurement, such as carbon emissions per capita or financed emissions per million dollars of financing (UNFCCC Regional Climate Week, 2023).

greenhouse gas emissions should be evaluated on a per capita basis. This approach recognizes the fundamental right of each individual to produce emissions necessary for survival, while concurrently penalizing excessive emissions resulting from environmentally detrimental industrial practices.

There is growing recognition that a just transition must consider impacts not only within individual countries but also across borders and along international value chains. Carbon leakage is a key example of a potential spillover effect; this occurs when emissions rise abroad as a result of implementing or strengthening domestic climate policies (OECD, 2020). Leakage from developed to developing countries may happen through trade and investment channels if stricter climate policies in developed nations increase business costs and reduce returns on investment, while similar policies are absent in developing nations.

Other climate actions with potential spillover effects include recent large-scale green industrial policy initiatives in advanced economies, such as the United States' Inflation Reduction Act and the European Union's Green Deal Investment Plan (Koirala & Montague, 2024). These policies offer significant potential for advancing low-carbon industries and supporting domestic jobs and industries from a political economy perspective. However, their domestic benefits may come at a cost to developing countries, which often lack the resources and capacity to finance similar large-scale programs (with exceptions like China, Indonesia, and some other large emerging economies). This dynamic raises the risk that low-carbon investments may favor advanced economies, widening the already substantial investment gap between developed and developing nations (Montague, Raiser, and Lee, 2024). Additionally, there is a risk that developing countries may face increasing exclusion from supply chains if they cannot meet the standards required to benefit from these government-supported industrial policies.

Consistent with the aforementioned perspectives, the adoption of carbon intensity as the pivotal metric in formulating and assessing environmental targets and achievements should also be applied to Financial Institutions (FIs) settings (PCAF, 2022). To optimize the role of FIs in achieving net-zero emissions while enhancing their business sustainability, it is recommended that FIs: (1) initiate climate actions by implementing measures to reduce their overall carbon emissions. This includes adopting resource efficiency strategies and other sustainable practices; (2) align their financial reporting with the guidelines established by the GHG Protocol (2001) and to acknowledge their financed emissions. These actions would help reduce reputational risks for FIs and potentially increase profitability by enhancing their resilience to the evolving landscape of climate-related risks and regulatory frameworks. Unlike the absolute measure of carbon emissions, adopting a carbon intensity metric would not restrict financial institutions (FIs) in expanding their role to mobilize funds for sustainable projects. Larger FIs would not be penalized for having a more extensive financing portfolio if their carbon emissions per million dollars of financing are lower than those of smaller FIs.

Considering the developments and perspectives outlined above, the discourse of a generic just transition is challenged and lead to the complexities surrounding the narrative establishment of the transition targets and operations. The formulation of a well-defined regulatory framework and a strategic alignment the just transition targets emerge as indispensable for the attainment of climate-centric objectives and fostering sustainable economic growth. These foundational components should serve as catalysts, prompting businesses to harmonize their operational blueprints with the overarching transition agenda. Furthermore, the dissemination of these regulatory imperatives by authoritative bodies imbues them with credibility, enabling the persuasive influence necessary for inducing corporate entities to undertake transformative measures, irrespective of any explicit regulatory mandates or incentivization, which then explains prospective strategies for seamless integration within corporate organizational frameworks.

## 2.3 Conceptual Frameworks of The Roles of The Financial Sector Players in Achieving Just Transition

Transitions are complex (World Economic Forum, 2024); many mistakes can be made even with the best of intentions and the best of international best practice to hand. What works well in one region can backfire in another. Due to the complex nature of transitions, a long-term, place-based and multi-pronged policy approach may be best suited to the task. This approach is best founded on an iterative and innovative learning process, informed by constant monitoring through inclusive social dialogue and thus changes flexibly to suit regional needs. However, these challenges also present opportunities for innovation and collaboration. The transition to a low-carbon economy opens avenues for research and development, particularly in clean energy and sustainable practices, which can enhance national competitiveness in the global market. By investing in new technologies and aligning thiss process with just transition targets, countries can create jobs in emerging industries and foster economic growth.

The financial sector is instrumental in enabling a just transition by providing capital for sustainable investments and facilitating risk-sharing mechanisms. To accelerate the scale-up of sustainable finance, financial institutions (FIs) play a pivotal role in mobilizing funds and acting as central counterparties to connect investors with firms. Given the significant opportunities in global sustainable investments, FIs can leverage their position to drive the transition through efficient sustainable financing. This emphasizes the importance of concerted efforts to develop a robust sustainable finance ecosystem. FIs, including banks, investment funds, and development banks, are crucial in directing investments toward green projects that not only reduce carbon emissions but also create jobs and promote social welfare (Fig. 6.1).

A growing number of financial institutions are incorporating environmental, social, and governance (ESG) criteria into their investment decisions to align with sustainability goals (Selvaraju et al., 2024). To maximize impact, FIs must integrate just transition principles into their operations, supporting projects that create equitable opportunities for affected communities, ensuring transparency, and promoting

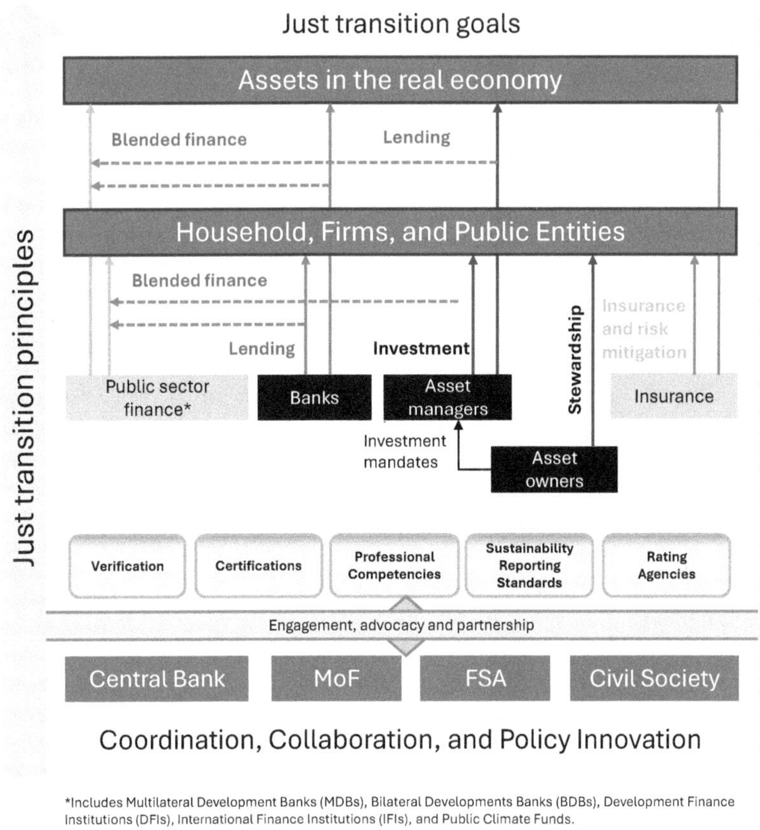


**Fig. 6.1** The roles of the financial sector players in achieving just transition. Source: Authors, adjusted from (ILO & LSE Grantham Research Institute, 2022)

accountability in fund allocation. By doing so, the financial sector can help manage risks such as stranded assets and job losses in fossil fuel-dependent industries while advancing sustainable development.

Innovative financial instruments such as green bonds and sustainability-linked bonds and blended finance are gaining traction as mechanisms to raise capital for projects that support the transition to a low-carbon economy (OECD, 2024). These financial products not only attract environmentally conscious investors but also help mobilize resources for initiatives that contribute to a just transition. However, it is essential to ensure that these instruments are aligned with rigorous sustainability standards to prevent greenwashing and ensure real environmental and social benefits (UNFCCC, 2023).

Coordination and collaboration between public and private sector players is key to achieve a just transition. Public and private sector players need to increase the supply of capital for a just transition by consciously allocating capital to just transition-aligned projects and activities, promoting engagement, advocacy and partnerships and establishing and maintaning a robust sustainable finance ecosystem. They should also accelerate the demand for capital by influencing companies to align with just transition objectives through corporate engagement and stewardship.

Private sector investment is key to mobilising the necessary funds to transition to a net zero economy. Banks, investors, insurers and asset owners have levers at their disposal to allocate capital for a just transition and influence the transition process taking place in the real economy. On top of that, public finance is fundamental for channeling capital toward just transition goals. The mandates of national and international public finance institutions often explicitly include social and environmental sustainability goals, positioning them to lead just transition initiatives. Development finance institutions are key in emerging markets, where investment needs are greatest, social safeguards tend to be weaker, and access to capital can be challenging. Given the complementary mandates, roles, and tools to drive change, cooperation and partnerships between public and private actors are essential to ensuring sufficient investment for a just transition. Development finance institutions, with their ability to provide patient capital and absorb higher levels of risk, play a catalytic role by attracting additional private sector capital through blended finance solutions (ILO & LSE Grantham Research Institute, 2022).

International cooperation, therefore, is crucial in addressing the challenges of a just transition. Developed nations can share best practices and provide financial support to developing countries, enabling them to leapfrog to cleaner technologies without repeating the mistakes of the past. This cooperation can take the form of technology transfer, capacity building, and financing for sustainable development projects (UNFCCC, 2023).

The discussions on some major country experiences, such as China, India, Latin America countries, and Central-Eastern European countries, bring to light the general adoption of three principal strategies as their approach to achieving just transition to support sustainable economic (Juhro et al., 2025). The three principal strategies are as follow.

- *First*, a strong commitment from the government and other authorities is vital for the ongoing efforts for a just transition. It provides clear vision and goals, policy coherence across various sectors, investment prioritization including just transition dedicate funds that can be used to support affected workers and communities, providing social safety nets and retraining programs. Investments in education and training programs can help workers adapt to new job opportunities in the green economy.
- *Second*, effective governance and institutions. Robust institutions are needed to develop and implement effective policies, regulations, and standards. Engaging with workers, businesses, and civil society organizations is crucial for building trust and ensuring a fair transition. Transparent and inclusive decision-making processes can help build public support for the transition. Regular monitoring

and evaluation of policies and programs are essential to ensure accountability and adjust strategies as needed.

- *Third,* collaborative partnerships. Partnerships between governments, businesses, and civil society organizations can leverage resources and expertise to accelerate the transition. International cooperation is essential to share best practices, facilitate technology transfer, finance flows, and capacity building, particularly for developing countries.

Therefore, a just transition is essential to ensuring that the global shift toward a low-carbon economy is fair, inclusive, and sustainable. By balancing environmental, social, and economic considerations, governments, businesses, and financial institutions can work together to create a future that benefits both people and the planet. The transition will not be without its challenges, particularly for workers and communities reliant on fossil fuels, but with the right policies and support systems in place, it can create new opportunities for sustainable growth and development. The role of international cooperation, the financial sector, and sector-specific strategies cannot be understated. These stakeholders must work collaboratively to ensure that the transition to a green economy leaves no one behind and that the benefits of a sustainable future are shared equitably. The transition is complex, but it is also an opportunity to build a more resilient, just, and inclusive global economy.

## 3 An Integrated Central Bank Regulatory Framework for Climate Risks

The issues of welfare and economic sustainability are basically inseparable from the role of the central bank in discharging its duties to achieve and maintain price stability, such as economic growth, full employment, and income equality, as well as environmental/climate change issues. From a central bank policy perspective, the meaning of achieving stability needs to be directed in the context of supporting sustainable economic growth, "stability for sustainability" (Juhro, 2025). Dikau & Volz (2018) distinguish five central bank policy strategies in different areas to achieve several sustainability goals, through microprudential and macroprudential policies, financial market development, credit allocation, as well as soft power and guidelines.

While central banks globally are recognized for their roles in climate actions—that integrating climate considerations into monetary and macroprudential policies could be the game-changer for sustaining economic growth, concrete initiatives are still a work in progress. The Green Central Bank scorecard of Green Central Bank initiatives (Eames & Barmes, 2022) shows that the adoption of groundbreaking green monetary and financial policies is lagging.[2] The absence of a well-defined

[2] The green central banking scorecard in 2024 ranked Bank Indonesia ninth among the G20 countries. The Green Central Banking Scorecard, produced by Positive Money, scores and ranks the full

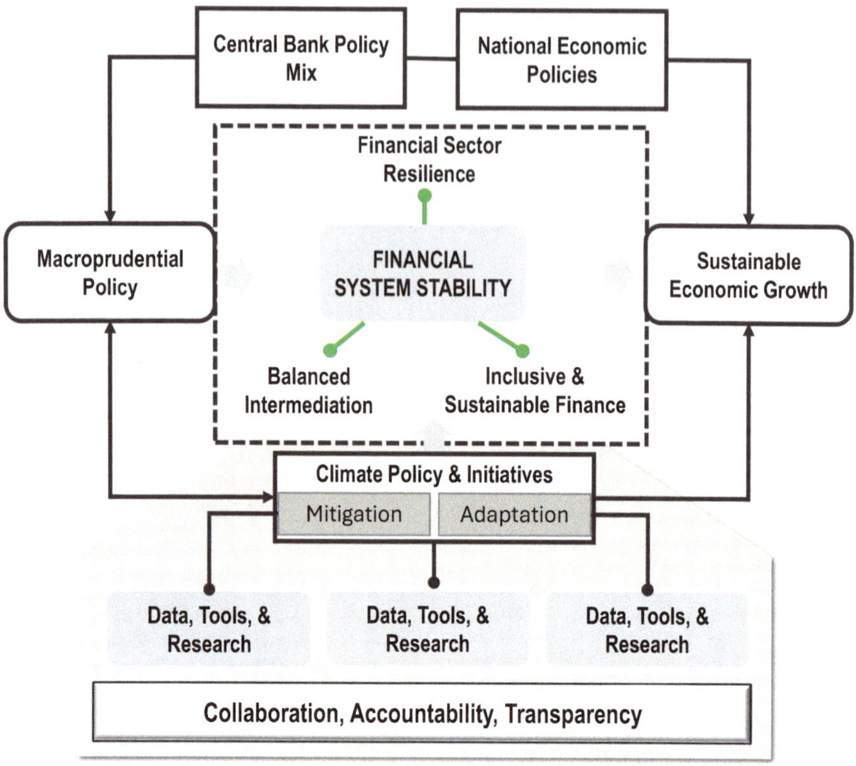


**Fig. 6.2** Central Bank Climate Regulatory Framework. Source: Authors

climate-related regulatory framework is further underscored by the Financial Stability Board (FSB), which designates supervisory and regulatory practices as the final piece in its roadmap (FSB, 2021).

Figure 6.2 depicts an integrated climate regulatory framework with the goal of preserving financial system stability in order to support sustainable growth. There are two blocks of thinking underlying this framework. *First*, this framework is based on the premise that climate-related policies and initiatives are integrated parts of a macroprudential policy framework. Therefore, this strategy should address financial system stability from several policy domains, e.g. time-varying, countercyclical, and structural perspectives, which become the anchor for the implementation of the central bank policy mix. The central bank policy mix emphasizes that the central bank should assess not only the macroeconomic and risk outlooks but also detect macro-financial imbalances in the financial system. Monetary policy responses still need to be directed toward achieving price stability taking into account the financial instability and risk outlook looking ahead, complemented with macroprudential

range of green policies and initiatives adopted by G20 central banks. The analysis is based on a literature review, expert consultations, and bilateral interactions with central bankers and supervisors (https://greencentralbanking.com/scorecard/)

policy and capital flow management. Beyond the central bank, the policy mix is extended by strengthening coordination with the government and related agencies to ensure financial system stability and support overall macroeconomic stability and structural reforms of the nation (Warjiyo & Juhro, 2019).

It is worth noting that safeguarding financial system stability is the objective for macroprudential policy (MPP) calibration, whereby for the case of Indonesia, Bank Indonesia utilizes the three-pronged macroprudential strategies—(1) maintaining financial resilience by mitigating risk propagation from interconnectedness and contagion; (2) managing balanced and sustainable intermediation to tackle procyclicality; and (3) supporting financial inclusion and sustainable finance; which are considered more appropriate approach for emerging market economies. The three-pronged strategies complement each other and will not contradict as the ultimate objective is to achieve financial stability.

*Second*, a pivotal linkage between the financial system stability framework and the support of climate policies and initiatives, given climate-related risk drivers (transition and physical) that impact economies. In the fast-evolving landscape of climate change, two main strategies take the spotlight, namely climate mitigation and climate adaptation. Climate mitigation involves the active reduction or prevention of greenhouse gas emissions to curb the impact of climate change (IPCC, 2022). On the flip side, climate adaptation calls for adjustments in processes, practices, and structures to either cushion potential damages or seize opportunities arising from the changing climate (IPCC, 2022b).

The framework delineates three essential strategies for addressing climate risks, namely: (1) data, tools, and research, (2) regulation and supervision, and (3) climate transition policy. The operationalization of these strategies extends beyond the traditional purview of central bank activities, necessitating a collaborative and synergistic approach among regulators and industry stakeholders to guide the global economy toward sustainability.

## 3.1 Data, Tools, and Research

Despite the comprehensive collection and publication of financial and economic data by central banks worldwide, a glaring gap exists in the availability of data relevant to climate risk assessment and strategy formulation. Hence, the collection of data related to climate risk is integral to the development of robust financial strategies that can withstand the economic impacts of climate change (G20 SFWG, 2021). As shown in Fig. 6.3, we propose several initiatives that central banks could undertake to address this deficiency.

*First*, central banks can facilitate a just transition by advocating for the widespread availability of comprehensive climate-related data (Calice & Demekas, 2024). In doing so, central banks could spearhead the acceleration of the development of the International Financial Reporting Standards (IFRS)-aligned Sustainability Disclosure Standards (IFRS Foundation, 2023). By mandating

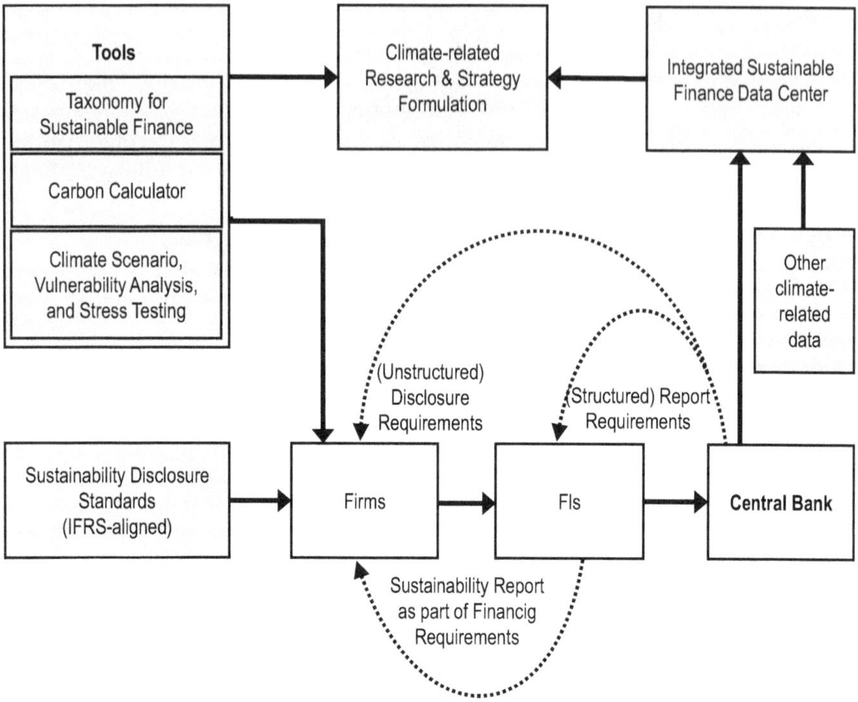


**Fig. 6.3** Sustainable Finance Data, Tools, and Research Framework. Source: Authors

Financial Institutions (FIs) to submit structured climate-related financing reports, central banks could indirectly encourage FIs to require firms' sustainability reports as part of their financing requirements. This initiative could significantly enhance the transparency and accountability of firms in their climate-related activities. Furthermore, central banks could also play a crucial role in facilitating the development of a blockchain-based integrated & open-access data center. This initiative could enhance data reliability and trust, stimulate the growth of the voluntary carbon market, and foster the expansion of the green financial market. The data center should integrate various climate-related data maintained by other agencies. For instance, in Indonesia, the national climate observatory system managed by the Meteorological, Climatological, and Geophysical Agency (BMKG), and the national natural disaster data center managed by the National Agency for Disaster Countermeasure could provide essential data for assessing climate-related risks.

*Second*, central banks could take a central role in developing tools to assist firms in preparing sustainability reports. These tools are crucial in providing comparable and high-quality climate-related data. A taxonomy for sustainable finance could help firms classify their activities, a vital component in sustainability reporting. Furthermore, some central banks, such as HKMA and Bank Indonesia, are developing a carbon calculator that could assist firms in calculating their carbon footprints, enabling them to set, track, and achieve emissions targets. The availability of climate scenarios and analysis could also aid firms in assessing climate-related risks and developing mitigation and adaptation strategies (NGFS, 2018).

Climate stress testing is also an important tool for assessing the banks' resilience to the physical and transition risks. Unlike the usual financial stability stress testing, climate stress testing does not focus on short-term shocks that may result in a financial crisis, but more on forward-looking scenarios with different rates of transition that result in various levels of severity. The central banks and FIs can take insight from this exercise by knowing the pocket of vulnerabilities in terms of sectors, types of FIs as well as individual FIs that have gaps to mitigate physical and transition risks, and finally achieve climate transition goal.

Furthermore, despite the extensive contributions of central banks in various fields of research, a noticeable gap persists in climate-related research (Care, Fatima, & Boitan, 2023). Strengthening climate-related assessments involves leveraging existing global initiatives and actively engaging in knowledge-sharing and collaboration with academia, research institutions, and relevant stakeholders. This collaborative approach could significantly enhance our understanding of climate-related risks and inform the development of effective mitigation and adaptation strategies.

### 3.2 *Regulation and Supervision*

The role of central banks in addressing climate risks has been a topic of debate, especially considering that most of these institutions were established before the emergence of climate-related concerns. Consequently, their existing mandates do not explicitly include climate considerations. According to Anwar et al. (2020), while did not directly relate to sustainable finance, 70 out of 135 central banks worldwide have a "sustainable" mandate, with approximately 47 central banks already implementing green measures. In 2023, Indonesia enacted a law mandating the Ministry of Finance, Financial Services Authority, and Central Bank to support sustainable finance. Specifically, the law authorizes Bank Indonesia to regulate and develop sustainable finance and empowers the Financial Services Authority to regulate and supervise carbon exchange. Presuming that central banks are endowed with a climate mandate; they can implement three distinct types of regulations as depicted in Fig. 6.4.

*Firstly,* it is imperative to enhance the macroprudential instruments to bolster climate mitigation and adaptation strategies, including both price and non-price instruments. Instruments such as liquidity incentives, in terms of reducing reserve requirements for banks that lend to the green sector, are examples of instruments that relate to the pricing of credit. For instance, Bank Indonesia has implemented this type of instrument through its Macroprudential Liquidity Incentive policy (or KLM), which reduces banks' reserve requirements based on the bank's achievement in providing loans to green activities. Other instruments such as Green Loan-To-Value (LTV), Green Down Payment, and Green Credit Allocation, are prevalent as non-price instruments in this domain. The Green LTV serves as an incentive

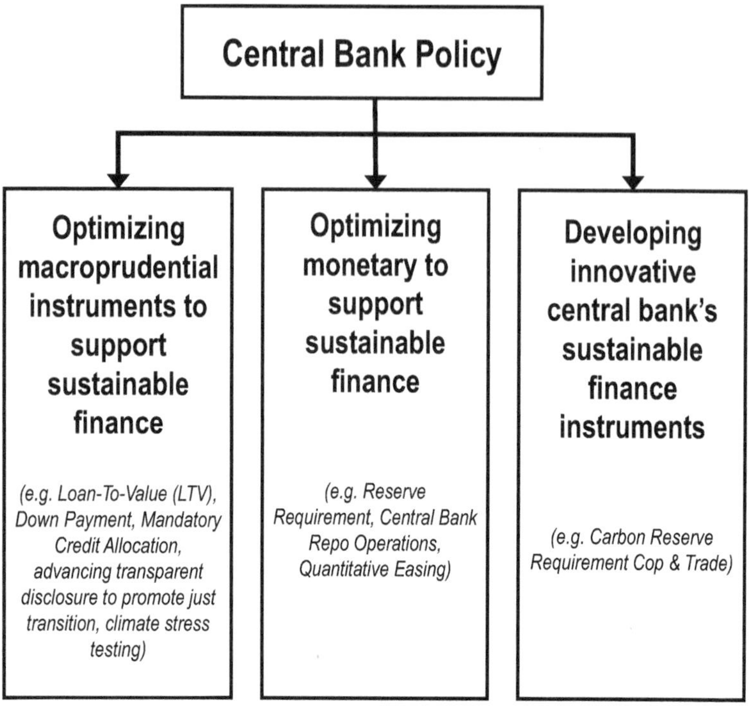


**Fig. 6.4** Central Bank Policy Options. Source: Authors

mechanism instituted by central banks that permits banks to offer mortgages for eco-friendly houses with a higher loan-to-value ratio than mortgages for non-green properties. Similarly, a Green Down Payment allows a lower down payment for electric vehicle ownership loans than automotive ownership loans for non-green alternatives. Green Credit Allocation mandates banks to designate a specific fraction of their loans towards environmentally friendly activities. This instrument is frequently incorporated as a component of a more extensive credit allocation scheme, typically associated with priority sector lending. This approach encourages financial institutions to increase their green lending practices, thereby promoting environmentally sustainable activities.

The central banks can also promote a just transition in the financial sector by advocating the implementation of standardized disclosure of green transition plans for firms and FIs. For instance, the regulation can obligate firms and FIs to disclose not only the transition plan that aligned with the national plan toward net zero emission but also require transparent information on how the firms and FIs reduce the inequality impact on their employees, suppliers, and other relevant stakeholders. Such requirements can provide a comparison between firms and FIs that may shed light on the credibility of each transition plan, particularly in supporting a just transition toward sustainable goals.

*Secondly*, the optimization of monetary instruments to bolster climate mitigation and adaptation is crucial. The Green Reserve Requirement, Green Central Bank Repo Operations, and Green Quantitative Easing are typical examples of such instruments. The Green Reserve Requirement serves as an incentive, offering a relaxation of reserve requirements for banks engaged in green lending. On the other hand, Green Central Bank Repo Operations incentivize banks by providing lower repo rates for those involved in green lending. In the context of Green Repo Operations, central banks can also consider green bonds as collateral that are subject to a favorable rate. Incorporating climate-related criteria into collateral eligibility frameworks can encourage financial institutions to hold more sustainable assets. In another case, central banks may permit the refinancing of green mortgages, combined with standard central bank repo collaterals, with lower rates. Other variations of Green Repo Operations are employed by limiting brown securities as eligible repo transactions. Furthermore, central banks can conduct Green Quantitative Easing by prioritizing the purchase of green bonds and other sustainable assets as part of their quantitative easing programs, supporting the growth of green finance markets.

*Thirdly*, the introduction of an innovative mechanism to enhance green lending is imperative. Currently, the amalgamation of a carbon tax and carbon trading is perceived as a fundamental component of climate mitigation strategies. This regulatory framework can be adapted and implemented within the financial sector. In this regard, central banks could instigate a carbon reserve requirement cap and trade as the primary climate instrument. Under this proposed initiative, banks would be mandated to maintain a reserve in central banks, calculated on the basis of their environmental sustainability. This reserve could be diminished by purchasing credit points from other banks, which have been awarded by central banks for their green initiatives. Given the comparative financial advantage of acquiring credit points as opposed to maintaining a non-interest-bearing carbon reserve, the envisaged model envisions the establishment of a novel carbon reserve market. The functioning of this market, in conjunction with a transparent central bank roadmap governing the cap (e.g., gradual reduction of the cap each year), is anticipated to exert a guiding influence on banks' lending preferences. Furthermore, it is expected to foster heightened competition among banks, resulting in more favorable interest rates for loans extended in support of environmentally sustainable initiatives.

While the green initiatives of central banks could significantly contribute to the attainment of climate targets, it is crucial to recognize that poorly crafted initiatives may yield adverse consequences. Such initiatives could disrupt the prevailing business model and increase non-performing loans. Consequently, central banks must strive to uphold a balance between quality and sustainable financing. Moreover, the adoption of robust climate supervision principles, as outlined by the Basel Committee on Banking Supervision (BIS, 2022), is also recommended.

### 3.3 Climate Transition Policy

Climate-related risks present a long-term challenge with repercussions that transcend the financial system. Given the systemic nature and protracted timeline of these risks, it is posited that a macroprudential policy approach is most suitable. However, for the realization of optimal outcomes, it is imperative to synchronize the central bank's transition policy with national transition strategies. As shown in Fig. 6.5, we propose three pivotal areas where central banks, in conjunction with other agencies, can make substantial contributions.

*First*, identification of transitional activities and investments. Central banks should elucidate guidelines for the identification of transitional activities and investments. The G20 Sustainable Finance Working Group (SFWG) has delineated two primary transition approaches: the principle-based and the taxonomy-based (G20 SFWG, 2022). The principle-based approach offers a framework for identifying green firms predicated on transition objectives rather than sectors. For instance, a firm could be classified as green if it demonstrates the capacity to reduce carbon emissions beyond a certain threshold, as per the transition roadmap, in contrast to a business-as-usual scenario. This approach maintains sector neutrality, thereby averting abrupt disruption in any specific sector. It advocates for the application of technology for sustainable practices across sectors, inclusive of brown sectors, and

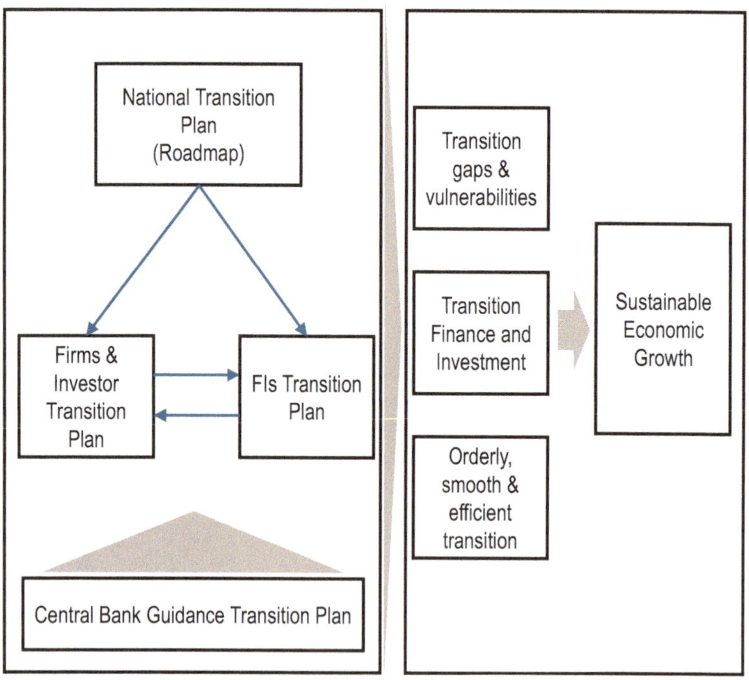


**Fig. 6.5** Central Bank's Role in Promoting Climate Transition Plan. Source: Authors

facilitates comparable carbon measurement across jurisdictions. In contrast, the taxonomy-based approach is reliant on a predefined list of specific activities that bolster climate transition, typically categorized by sector. However, these taxonomies lack comparability among nations and, if not meticulously designed, could precipitate a disorderly transition for a specific sector and decelerate economic growth.

*Second*, the development of a transition roadmap. Central banks should formulate a transition roadmap that aligns with the national transition agenda. This roadmap, replete with clear targets, can serve as a blueprint for FIs in the creation of their transition roadmap and strategy. The existence of a credible roadmap could incentivize FIs to metamorphose into green FIs in anticipation of prospective actions from central banks. Consequently, the green transformation of FIs may transpire even prior to the enforcement of central bank regulations.

*Third*, evaluation of green investment needs and their funding. With a credible transition plan at the national and individual levels, central banks could conduct a more robust assessment of the need for green investment and their funding, the analysis of the structural consequences emanating from the transition, and the advancement of the macroeconomic modeling framework with an emphasis on climate aspects (GFANZ, 2022). This step is instrumental in ensuring a smooth, orderly, and efficient transition to a green economy, minimizing any potential disruptions to the economy.

## 4 Discussion on Transmission Mechanism of Climate Policies

While economists acknowledge that climate change may hinder sustainable economic growth, there is also concern that the shift toward a low-carbon economy could adversely affect economic growth and social well-being. For instance, in Indonesia, the coal and power sector face an increased risk of default due to the energy transition (Rishanty, et al., 2023). Additionally, Rishanty et al. (2022) and Rishanty et al. (2024) demonstrate that adopting circular economy practices can mitigate these challenges and contribute to a more sustainable future. Therefore, it is imperative to develop a just and orderly climate transition strategy to minimize potential economic and social disruptions, and *thus* to deliver fairer outcomes, as the world transitions towards a low-carbon economy.

Even though a just transition is essential to avoid disruption, however, the public sector's financial contributions are anticipated to fall short of the sustainable investment requirements needed to attain the just transition. Thus, the majority of climate change financing is projected to originate from the financial sector. Consequently, the successful financing of the transition heavily relies on the active participation of financial institutions (FIs). As shown in Fig. 6.6, the central bank climate regulatory framework which delineates three essential strategies—namely: (1) data, tool, and research, (2) regulation and supervision, and (3) climate transition policy—plays a pivotal role in the work of just climate transition, by incentivizing FIs to scale up

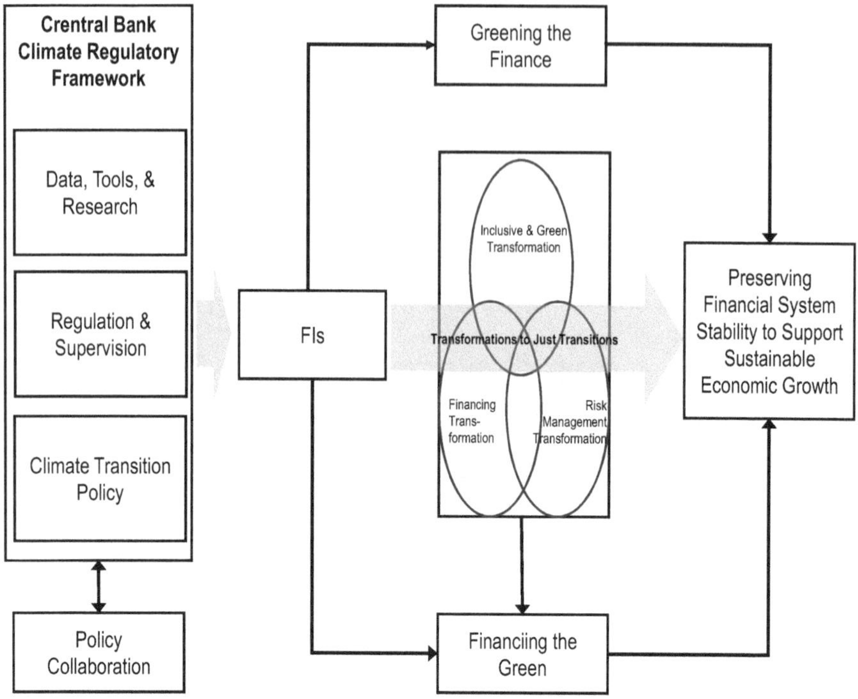


**Fig. 6.6** Transmission Mechanism of Central Bank Climate Policy. Source: Authors

their green financing and, in doing so, encouraging their debtors to become greener in order to get easier access to financing.

In line with global emission quantification standards, FIs are required to proportionally calculate and acknowledge the emissions emanating from the activities or projects they finance, known as financed emissions (Scope 3). Considering that the majority of FIs' assets are in the form of financing, each of which has associated carbon emissions that FIs must acknowledge, FIs are among the largest contributors to carbon emissions. Hence, the reduction of FIs' carbon emissions is integral to the success of national emission reduction.

Since the source of FIs' carbon emissions is financing, the most effective way to reduce their carbon emissions is to increase the share of low-emission financing. Thus, banks are expected to offer incentives to low-emission debtors and disincentives to high-emission debtors to reduce emissions. While this will help FI to build resilience by mitigating physical and transition risk, this will also accelerate the green ecosystem by stimulating firms to transition towards greener operations to secure easier and more affordable access to financing. Consequently, the carbon emission reduction actions of FIs can trigger a positive domino effect on other sectors to collectively achieve the national emission reduction target.

Furthermore, to align FIs' operations with the just transition agenda optimally, we identify three essential transformation agendas that FIs need to adopt.

- *First*, FIs should transform their financing portfolio by increasing the share of sustainable financing. FI is expected to provide incentives and disincentives to sustainable-friendly vs non-sustainable-friendly debtors and accelerate industry transformation toward a sustainable ecosystem.
- *Second*, FIs should transform their risk management practices by integrating climate-related risk considerations into the strategy formulation. In this area, FIs need to consider necessary actions when developing their own transition scenarios and inform FIs about the credibility of their transition plans.
- *Lastly*, FIs need to adopt inclusive and green transformation. In this area, FIs need to align their financing strategies with the social and climate aspects to sustain their long-term growth. The growing concern about the just transition, thus social inequality and other sustainable development issues, is expected to boost the market growth.

Ultimately, the operationalization of three policy strategies, along with the adoption of a transformation agenda, to navigate just transition extends beyond the traditional purview of central bank activities, necessitating a collaborative and synergistic approach among regulators and industry stakeholders. We believe that this mechanism fulfills sufficient conditions in managing financial system stability, and is thus, in line with efforts to pave the way towards sustainable economic growth.

## 5 Conclusion

Climate change poses major challenges to the global economy and society, requiring immediate and coordinated efforts to alleviate its impacts. Given the extended time horizon and systemic nature of climate risks, the adoption of a more integrated policy strategy offers a more holistic strategy for managing and mitigating these complex threats, thereby bolstering macroeconomic and financial system resilience. The urgency for sustainable financing underscores the pivotal role central banks and financial regulators must play in this endeavor. While central banks are globally recognized for their roles in climate action, tangible initiatives are still in the developmental stage. The Green Central Bank scorecard (Eames & Barmes, 2022) indicates that pioneering green monetary and financial policies are lagging. With climate-related risks yet to fully materialize, traditional climate adaptation safeguards such as capital and liquidity requirements are deemed sub-optimal (Coelho & Restoy, 2023). Thus, central banks will have a pivotal role in developing a state-of-the-art climate policy to support the just transition agenda.

This paper proposes a climate regulatory framework for central banks, which includes three primary strategies aimed at achieving climate objectives. The first strategy involves the development of a data collection, tools, and research framework specifically designed for central banks. The second strategy focuses on identifying policy options for central banks that would encourage traditional banks to transition into green banks. The final strategy delves into the climate transition policy, discussing three crucial actions: the transition approach, the transition roadmap, and climate assessment.

This paper shows that the central bank's climate policies to manage transition risks can navigate just transition and support the achievement of sustainable economic growth. Given that FIs are among the largest carbon emitters globally due to financed emissions, reducing FIs' carbon emissions is a critical step in achieving the transition agenda. The central bank climate regulatory framework is expected to play a vital role in this process by incentivizing FIs to increase green financing and thereby facilitating the transformation of firms into green entities. To optimize the transmission mechanism, FIs should adopt a three-pronged transformation agenda: inclusive and green transformation, risk management transformation, and financing transformation. This approach, necessitating a collaborative and synergistic approach among regulators and industry stakeholders, will ensure a comprehensive and effective transition towards sustainable practices.

In this regard, providing guidelines by central banks and other regulators, such as transition plan guidelines for financial institutions and businesses in the real sector, which outline how these entities can develop effective mitigation and adaptation financial strategies to remain resilient amid intensifying climate and nature-related risks, is vital. Central banks and other regulators can also be active in promoting climate-related capacity-building initiatives to support the development of a sustainable finance ecosystem within the country. Last but not least, given the limitations of this study in addressing the research question qualitatively, further research using various approaches to complement this study is essential to understand the nature of problems and related policy interlinkages more comprehensively.

## References

Anwar, R., Mohamed, M., Hamzan, S., Malek, N., Zain, M., Jaafar, M., ... Hong, J. (2020). *Report on the Roles of ASEAN Central Banks in Managing Climate and Environment-related Risks.* Kuala Lumpur.

AON. (2021). *2020 Annual Report: Weather, Climate & Catastrophe Insight.* Chicago, Illinois: AON.

BIS. (2022). *Principles for the Effective Management and Supervision of Climate-related Financial Risks.* Basel: BIS.

Calice, P., & Demekas, D. (2024). Just Transition: Issues for Central Banks and Financial Regulators. *World Bank Policy Research Paper 10685.*

Canadell, J., Ciais, P., Dhakal, S., Dolman, H., Friedlingstein, P., Gurney, K., Raupach, M. (2010). Interactions of the Carbon Cycle, Human Activity, and the Climate System: A Research Portfolio. *Current Opinion in Environmental Sustainability.*

Care, R., Fatima, R., & Boitan, I. (2023). Central Banks and Climate Risks: Where We Are Going? *International Review of Economics and Finance.*

Carney, M. (2015). *Breaking the Tragedy of the Horizon – climate change and financial stability.*

Coelho, R., & Restoy, F. (2023). Macroprudential Policies for Addressing Climate-related Financial Risks: Challenges and Trade-Offs. *FSI Briefs, No. 18*, 1-9.

Dikau, S., & Ryan-Collins, J. (2017). *Green Central Banking in Emerging Market and Developing Country Economies.*

Dikau, S., & Volz, U. (2018). Central Banking, Climate Change and Green Finance. *ADBI Working Paper Series, 867*, 1-19.

Dikau, S., & Volz, U. (2021). Central bank mandates, sustainability objectives and the promotion of green finance. *Ecological Economics, 184*. https://doi.org/10.1016/j.ecolecon.2021.107022

Eames, N., & Barmes, D. (2022). *The Green Central Banking Scorecard 2022 Edition*. Positive Money.

Eichengreen, B. (2021, January 9). *New-Model Central Banks*.

FSB. (2021). *FSB Roadmap for Addressing Climate-Related Financial Risks*. FSB.

G20 SFWG. (2021). *G20 Sustainable Finance Roadmap*.

G20 SFWG. (2022). *2022 G20 Sustainable Finance Report*.

GFANZ. (2022). *Financial Institution Net-Zero Transition Plans: Fundamentals, Recommendations, and Guidance*.

GHG Protocol. (2001). *Green House Gas Protocol: A Corporate Accounting and Reporting Standard*. Washington: WRI and WBCSD.

Guo, J., Kubli, D., & Saner, P. (2021). *The Economics of Climate Change: No Action not an Option*. Zurich: Swiss Re Institute.

Hoffman, A., & Nayak, A. (2021). Sustainable and Responsible Investing: The Next Frontier of Responsible Business. *Academy of Management Perspectives, 35(2)*, 181-198.

IFRS Foundation. (2023). *IFRS S2 - Climate Related Disclosures*. London: IFRS.

International Energy Agency. (2023). *World Energy Outlook 2023*. Paris: IEA.

ILO, & LSE Grantham Research Institute. (2022). *Just Transition Finance Tool for banking and investing activities*. International Labour Organization and LSE Grantham Research Institute for Climate Change and the Environment. www.ifrro.org

IPCC. (2022). *Climate Change 2022: Mitigation of Climate Change*. IPCC.

IPCC. (2022b). *Climate Change 2022: Impacts, Adaptation and Vulnerability*. IPCC.

IPCC. (2023). https://www.ipcc.ch/report/ar6/syr/downloads/report/IPCC_AR6_SYR_LongerReport.pdf

Juhro, S. M. (2016). The Role of Central Bank in Promoting Sustainable Growth: Perspective on the Implementation of Flexible ITF in Indonesia. *Afro Eurasian Studies Journal, 4(1)*.

Juhro, S.M. (2025) 'Future central banking in emerging market economies', in *Encyclopedia of Monetary Policy, Financial Markets and Banking*. Elsevier, pp. 189–198. https://doi.org/10.1016/B978-0-44-313776-1.00118-5

Juhro, S., Robinson, I., Rahadyan, H., & Rishanty, A. (2025). *Climate Risks, Just Transition, and Central Bank Policy for Sustainable Economic Growth*. Retrieved from Jurnal Ekonomi Indonesia: https://jurnal.isei.or.id/index.php/isei/article/view/587

Koirala, S., & Montague, C. (2024). *Developement Cooperation Report 2024: Lessons from OECD countries on just climate transitions*. OECD. https://doi.org/10.1787/57616eb4-en

Lamperti, F., Bosetti, V., Roventini, A., & Tavoni, M. (2021). Three Green Financial Policies to Address Climate Risks. *Journal of Financial Stability*.

Lo, A., & Cong, R. (2022). Emission Reduction Targets and Outcomes of the Clean Development Mechanism (2005-2020). *Plos Climate*.

Montague, C., Raiser, K., & Lee, M. (2024). *Bridging the clean energy investment gap* (OECD Environment Working Papers, Vol. 245). https://doi.org/10.1787/1ae47659-en

NGFS. (2018). *First Progress Report*.

NGFS. (2024). *Network for Greening the Financial System Technical document: Climate change, the macroeconomy and monetary policy*.

OECD. (2020). https://www.oecd.org/en/publications/how-different-climate-policies-affect-carbon-leakage-throughtrade_5819ce91-en.html

OECD. (2024). https://www.oecd.org/content/dam/oecd/en/about/directorates/cfe/CFE-Climate-Policy-Perspectives-2024.pdf

PCAF. (2022). *The Global GHG Accounting and Reporting Standard Part A: Financed Emissions. Second Edition*.

Pfister, C., & Valla, N. (2021). Financial Stability is Easier to Green than Monetary Policy. *Intereconomics*, 154-159.

Rishanty, A., Sambodo, M., Hambali, E., & Silalahi, M. (2024). Zero-Waste Bioenergy to Lower Energy Transition Risks in Indonesia — A Circular Economy Practice on Methane Capture in Biogas Production from POME. *BioEnergy Research.*

Rishanty, A., Sambodo, M., & Wicaksono, R. (2022). "Green Transition Risks On Export Competitiveness: Circular Economy Approach," Working Papers WP/14/2022, Bank Indonesia.

Rishanty, A., Wicaksono, R., Yudawinata, R., Rizkiah, S., Aquary, R., & Arfita, A. (2023). Navigating Climate Transition: Evaluating Exposure And Resilience Of Indonesian Banks' Portfolios Across High-emitting Sectors. A Bottom-up Analysis. *Bank Indonesia Working Paper No. RP/Mon/x/2023.*

Selvaraju et al. (2024). https://justtransitionfinance.org/wp-content/uploads/2024/07/Sustainable-finance-for-a-just-transition-in-India-Role-of-investors.pdf

UNFCCC. (2015). *The Paris Agreement.*

UNFCCC. (2023). *Forum Report of the Standing Committee on Finance*. Retrieved December 3, 2024, from https://unfccc.int/sites/default/files/resource/UNFCCC_SCF_2023_web.pdf

UNFCCC Regional Climate Week. (2023). *Introduction to Article 6 Accounting*. UNFCCC.

UNFCCC. (2024a, March 5). *NDC Registry*. Retrieved from https://unfccc.int/NDCREG

UNFCCC. (2024b). *Nationally determined contributions under the Paris Agreement Synthesis report.*

United Nations. (2024). *Sustainable Development Goals. Goal 13: Take urgent action to combat climate change and its impacts*. Https://Www.Un.Org/Sustainabledevelopment/Climate-Change/.

Warjiyo, P., & Juhro, S. M. (2019). *Central Bank Policy: Theory and Practice.* Emerald Publishing Ltd. London.

World Economic Forum. (2024, January 16). *Putting people at the centre of the green transition.* https://www.weforum.org/stories/2024/01/putting-people-at-the-centre-of-climate-action/

WEF. (2023). *The Global Risks Report 2023.* Geneva: World Economic Forum.

# Chapter 7
# Advancing Climate Action Through Improved Data Governance

**Solikin M. Juhro, Irman Robinson, Heru Rahadyan, and Charvin Lim**

**Abstract** This chapter analyzes the role of climate-related data governance in supporting climate action and financial stability in Indonesia. Drawing on global frameworks such as the Paris Agreement, TCFD, IFRS Sustainability Disclosure Standards, and the NGFS, it assesses Indonesia's progress using a three-pillar framework covering data infrastructure, standards and methodologies, and institutional coordination. While advances have been made through mandatory sustainability reporting, the Sustainable Finance Roadmap, and Bank Indonesia's expanded mandate, challenges remain in data fragmentation, assurance, and global alignment. Strengthening data governance is essential to enhance resilience, attract sustainable investment, and meet climate commitments.

**Keywords** Climate change · Climate action · Sustainability disclosure

## 1 Introduction

Climate change is increasingly recognized as the defining challenge of our century. Its impacts are not limited to environmental degradation but extend to economic performance, social stability, and financial resilience (Juhro, 2025). Scientific assessments consistently confirm that anthropogenic activities have intensified greenhouse gas (GHG) concentrations in the atmosphere, leading to rising global temperatures, extreme weather patterns, biodiversity loss, and profound disruptions to food, energy, and water systems (IPCC, 2021). For many countries, these consequences are not abstract risks but lived realities that threaten livelihoods, undermine economic progress, and exacerbate inequalities.

From an economic perspective, climate change constitutes both a physical risk—manifested in damages from floods, droughts, storms, and sea-level rise—and a transition risk, arising from the global shift toward low-carbon technologies and

S. M. Juhro (✉) · I. Robinson · H. Rahadyan · C. Lim
Bank Indonesia, Jakarta, Indonesia
e-mail: solikin@bi.go.id; irman_r@bi.go.id; heru_rahadyan@bi.go.id; charvin_lim@bi.go.id



S. M. Juhro et al. (eds.), *Sustainable Economy: The Indonesian Pathways*,
https://doi.org/10.1007/978-981-92-1215-6_7

regulatory adjustments that could reprice assets and disrupt industries (BIS, 2021). These risks are increasingly recognized as systemic, with the potential to destabilize financial systems if not adequately assessed and managed. As such, climate change is no longer a peripheral environmental issue but a central concern for policymakers, financial authorities, and businesses (Figs. 7.1 and 7.2).

Despite its destructive potential, climate change also presents unprecedented opportunities to reorient development pathways. The transition toward renewable energy, sustainable agriculture, and circular economy models offers a dual dividend: reducing emissions while fostering innovation, investment, and employment (UNEP, 2020). Global initiatives, such as the United Nations Sustainable

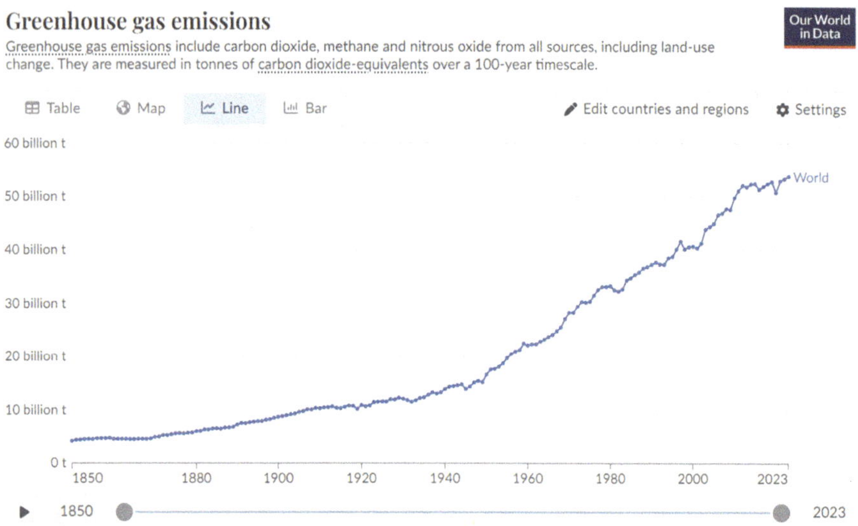


**Fig. 7.1** Global Greenhouse Gas Emissions (in CO2e). Source: Jones et al. (2024), Our World in Data

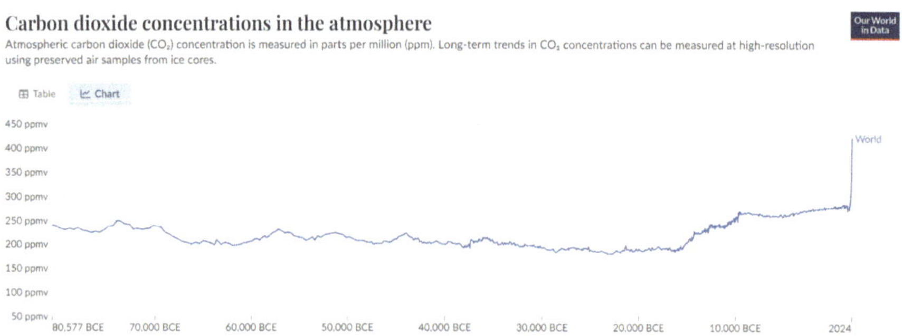


**Fig. 7.2** Atmosphere Carbon Dioxide Concentrations in the Atmosphere. Source: NOAA Global Monitoring Laboratory—Trends in Atmospheric Carbon Dioxide (2025), Our World in Data

Development Goals (SDGs) and the Paris Agreement, embody this dual imperative by emphasizing mitigation, adaptation, and the promotion of sustainable growth (UNFCCC, 2015). For governments and businesses alike, success in this transition depends on the capacity to align economic decision-making with climate objectives while maintaining social inclusivity.

At the heart of these efforts lies the role of climate-related data. Reliable, transparent, and accessible data is indispensable for assessing risks, guiding investments, formulating regulations, and measuring progress. Governments depend on accurate data to design evidence-based climate policies, establish nationally determined contributions (NDCs), and track implementation. Financial institutions use climate-related data to evaluate exposures, stress-test portfolios, and comply with disclosure requirements (TCFD, 2017). Investors, civil society, and the public likewise rely on credible information to hold actors accountable and mobilize support for sustainable initiatives.

However, the availability, quality, and comparability of climate-related data remain uneven across jurisdictions. Many developing countries face substantial data gaps, including insufficient emissions inventories, fragmented reporting systems, and limited technical capacity for data analysis (UNEP, 2019). The interdisciplinary nature of climate data—encompassing meteorology, finance, ecology, and social science—further complicates integration and interpretation (WMO, 2020). Lack of harmonized standards also creates inconsistencies in corporate disclosures, limiting comparability across firms and jurisdictions (IFRS Foundation, 2023). These challenges undermine transparency, discourage investment, and weaken the capacity of policymakers to address climate risks effectively.

The need for enhanced data governance is therefore urgent. Data governance refers to the institutional arrangements, regulatory frameworks, and technical standards that ensure data is collected, managed, and disseminated in a way that is accurate, consistent, and accessible (G20, 2020). In the climate context, robust data governance involves harmonizing sustainability reporting standards, mandating structured disclosures, ensuring independent assurance, and investing in infrastructure for data sharing and interoperability. Without such governance, even the most ambitious climate policies risk being undermined by incomplete or unreliable information.

Indonesia represents a compelling case study for advancing climate action through enhanced data governance. As an archipelagic nation with more than 17,000 islands and one of the world's largest tropical forest areas, Indonesia is highly vulnerable to climate change. The financial system is not immune. Indonesian banks and capital markets are increasingly exposed to climate-related risks, whether through direct physical impacts on assets or through transition risks in carbon-intensive industries. Recognizing this, Indonesian regulators—Bank Indonesia, the Financial Services Authority (OJK), and the Ministry of Finance—have begun integrating sustainability into their mandates. Recent reforms under the Financial Sector Omnibus Law (FSOL) explicitly empower Bank Indonesia to advance sustainable finance as part of its macroprudential policy toolkit (Juhro et al., 2025). These developments underscore the critical role of data in ensuring that climate considerations are embedded within financial decision-making and regulatory oversight.

Indonesia faces challenges as its climate data landscape remains fragmented, with multiple agencies and institutions producing datasets that are not fully interoperable. Corporate sustainability reporting, while mandated under OJK Regulation No. 51/POJK.03/2017, still varies widely in scope, quality, and assurance (OJK, 2020). Moreover, aligning domestic reporting practices with emerging global standards, such as the IFRS Sustainability Disclosure Standards, requires significant capacity building and institutional coordination (IAI, 2023). Addressing these gaps is essential not only for national resilience but also for ensuring investor confidence and maintaining financial system stability.

The central research question guiding this inquiry is:

> *"How to strengthen Indonesia's climate-related data governance to mitigate risks, mobilize finance, and advance its climate action agenda?"*

This chapter argues that enhancing data governance is a prerequisite for Indonesia to fully realize its climate and sustainable finance objectives. By building a robust institutional framework for climate-related data, investing in infrastructure and tools, and harmonizing disclosure standards with international benchmarks, Indonesia can strengthen transparency, accountability, and policy effectiveness. More broadly, improving data governance can help the country mobilize resources for climate action, safeguard financial stability, and contribute meaningfully to global sustainability efforts.

The remainder of this chapter is structured as follows. Section 2 reviews the literature on the conception and role of climate data governance, examines international efforts and standards, and benchmarks global best practices. Section 3 outlines the methodology and data. Section 4 presents the analysis of Indonesia's climate data ecosystem, highlighting both achievements and challenges. Section 5 concludes with key findings and policy recommendations to advance Indonesia's climate action agenda through strengthened data governance.

## 2 Literature Review, Concept, and Benchmarking

### *2.1 Climate Change, Systemic Risks, and the Role of Data*

The relationship between climate change and the global financial system has increasingly been conceptualized through the lens of systemic risk. Climate change generates both physical risks (e.g., damages from extreme weather events, sea-level rise, biodiversity loss) and transition risks (e.g., stranded assets, reallocation of capital due to regulatory or technological changes) that can destabilize economies and financial markets (BIS, 2021). These risks are non-linear, long-term, and highly uncertain, making them particularly challenging to integrate into traditional risk management frameworks (NGFS, 2019).

A growing body of literature highlights that data availability and quality are essential for identifying, measuring, and managing these risks. Climate-related data—spanning emissions inventories, energy use, financial exposures, and adaptation investments—forms the foundation for risk assessment and scenario analysis (WMO, 2020). Without credible data, policymakers and investors risk underestimating climate vulnerabilities or misallocating resources, leading to inadequate mitigation and adaptation strategies (UNEP, 2019). FSB (2021) further develop a roadmap for addressing climate-related risk focusing on the financial sector (Fig. 7.3) and identified a broad set of climate related metrics to be considered by central banks (Table 7.1).

To address the non-linear and uncertain nature of climate impacts, scenario analysis has emerged as a critical tool in assessing systemic risks. The design of scenarios must reflect a diverse set of severe but plausible pathways, incorporating both global megatrends and country-specific idiosyncrasies. Constructing such scenarios requires comprehensive and reliable datasets—ranging from climate science projections to sectoral financial exposures—so that assumptions are transparent, reproducible, and grounded in evidence. Equally important is the institutional preservation of scenarios: once developed, they must be systematically documented, archived, and updated to form a repository of knowledge that supports stress-testing, policy learning, and cross-country comparability over time. As Battiston et al. (2017) argue, scenario analysis not only supports the identification of systemic risk transmission channels but also provides a structured basis for developing mitigation and adaptation plans that safeguard both financial stability and long-term sustainability.

Underlying this analytical framework is the need for strong data governance and institutional arrangements. Climate-related financial data spans multiple jurisdictions, sectors, and reporting standards, requiring coordination among regulators, statistical agencies, financial supervisors, and international organizations. Establishing common taxonomies, harmonized disclosure requirements, and

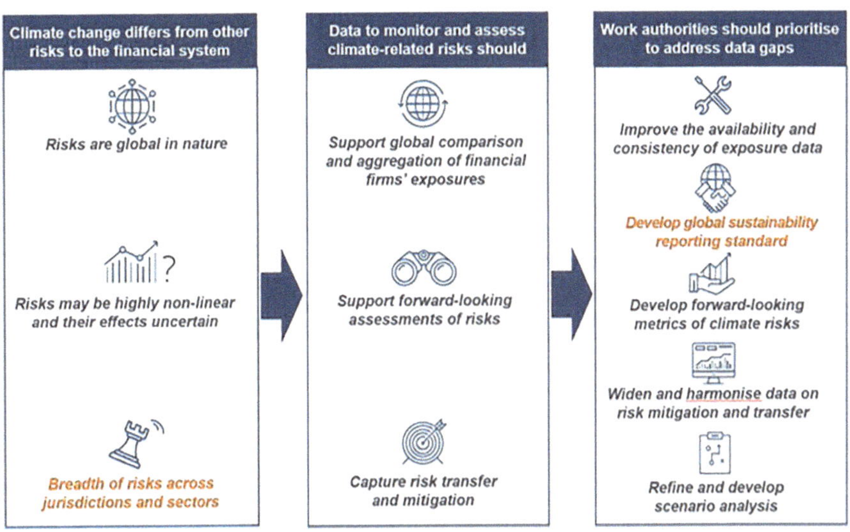


**Fig. 7.3** FSB Roadmap for Addressing Climate-Related Financial Risks. Source: FSB (2021)

**Table 7.1** IFC Climate Related Metrics for Central Bank

| Environment | Forward-looking | Governance | Social | Broad sustainability |
|---|---|---|---|---|
| Emission footprint | Climate target for companies/ countries | Adequate management control | Diversity issues | ESG ratings |
| Exposure to extreme weather | Climate targets related to GHG emissions | Quality and transparency of financial communication and reporting | Labour practices | Green/ sustainable bond holdings and issuance |
| Environmental tax and subsidies | Indicators reflecting transformation and enabling efforts | Diversity of board members | Microcredit indicators | Green/ sustainable lending |
| Energy prices | Companies' scenario analyses | Inclusion of ESG objectives | Banking inclusion indicators | Green/ sustainable stock/ bonds market indices |
| Loan exposures to carbon-intensive industries | Climate value-at-risk | Training of employees and executives integrating ESG criteria | Human capital indicators | Global reporting frameworks used by corporates |
| Environmental-related labels for real estate | Specific measures over next 15 years and intermediate targets | Stock ownership by board and management | Indicators related to the supply chain | Independent green bonds verifier |

Source: adapted from IFC (2021)

interoperable databases ensures that data is comparable, transparent, and reliable. Moreover, embedding climate data governance into the broader financial stability mandate of central banks and supervisory authorities strengthens the system's resilience to shocks. In this sense, data governance is not merely a technical concern but encompasses institutional arrangements, regulatory frameworks, and technical standards that ensure climate data is reliable, comparable, and accessible across jurisdictions. This perspective aligns with the growing recognition that addressing climate change requires not only policy ambition but also robust infrastructure for evidence-based decision-making (IFC, 2021).

## 2.2 *The Paris Agreement and Global Commitments*

The Paris Agreement (UNFCCC, 2015) marked a turning point in global climate governance by introducing a framework for nationally determined contributions (NDCs), transparency mechanisms, and collective ambition toward limiting global temperature rise. Central to the Agreement is the requirement that countries collect, and report standardized data on emissions, mitigation actions, and adaptation progress. Transparency frameworks, such as the Enhanced Transparency Framework (ETF), further underscore the importance of harmonized data to build trust, ensure accountability, and facilitate comparison among countries.

The sectoral classification embedded in NDCs provides an important backbone for national data collection, as it enables governments to structure emissions inventories and mitigation efforts across energy, agriculture, industry, transport, and land-use sectors. This structure helps policymakers monitor progress and prioritize interventions. However, significant challenges arise in aligning sector-level NDC data with micro-level firm disclosures, particularly in the context of environmental, social, and governance (ESG) reporting. While national-level data informs the trajectory of mitigation and adaptation strategies, firm-level data underpins credibility in capital markets and investor confidence. Therefore, differentiated approaches are needed: national datasets should guide collective mitigation and adaptation priorities, whereas firm-level ESG disclosures must demonstrate accountability and alignment with broader climate goals.

Further, a critical dimension of the global climate commitments is the establishment of international initiatives on climate data. Several noteworthy initiatives have been established on the global stage to address the critical need for consistent climate-related data across different countries. Two leading examples include the IMF's global dashboard on climate change indicators and the NGFS data repository for climate data. The IMF dashboard provides a centralized and user-friendly platform for key climate metrics, including greenhouse gas emissions, mitigation and adaptation policies, transition pathways, climate finance, and climate and weather data on a global level and across a range of countries. In contrast, the NGFS repository serves as a comprehensive archive of diverse climate-related datasets, providing information regarding climate data sources and fostering informed decision-making among researchers and policymakers. The NGFS extends its value by providing data on transition pathways.

## 2.3 *Disclosure Standards and Reporting Frameworks*

Corporate disclosure is another critical dimension of climate data governance. Several major international initiatives have shaped the discourse:

- The Task Force on Climate-related Financial Disclosures (TCFD, 2017) established a voluntary framework for companies to disclose governance, strategy, risk management, and metrics related to climate risks and opportunities. Its recommendations have become widely adopted by regulators and stock exchanges.
- The IFRS Sustainability Disclosure Standards (IFRS Foundation, 2023), particularly IFRS S1 (general sustainability disclosures) and IFRS S2 (climate-specific disclosures), provide a globally harmonized framework, ensuring consistency and comparability across jurisdictions.

- The European Union's Corporate Sustainability Reporting Directive (CSRD) expands the scope of mandatory sustainability disclosures and incorporates double materiality, highlighting both financial and environmental/social perspectives (European Commission, 2022).

The common thread among these frameworks is the emphasis on structured, comparable, and assured data. Disclosure is no longer seen as a matter of corporate social responsibility but as a financial and regulatory necessity.

## *2.4 Conceptualizing Climate Data Governance*

The concept of climate data governance has evolved in recent years to capture the complex interplay between institutions, regulations, and technology in managing climate-related information. Scholars identify three key pillars (Fig. 7.4):

1. Data Infrastructure—physical and digital systems for data collection, storage, and dissemination (e.g., national greenhouse gas inventories, centralized databases).
2. Standards and Methodologies—harmonized frameworks for measurement, reporting, and verification (e.g., GHG Protocol, IFRS standards).
3. Institutional Coordination—mechanisms to align different stakeholders, including governments, regulators, private sector actors, and civil society, around shared data objectives (G20, 2020).

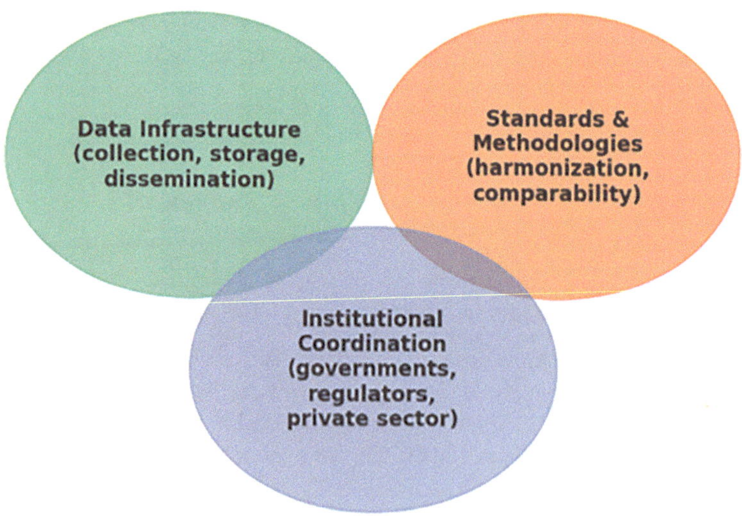


**Fig. 7.4** Three Pillars of Climate Data Governance

**Fig. 7.5** TCFD Sustainability Reporting Guideline. Source: TCFD (2017)

Effective governance requires balancing transparency and accountability with usability and accessibility. For instance, while mandatory reporting ensures comprehensiveness, overly complex requirements may impose high compliance costs on smaller firms. Similarly, while interoperability across jurisdictions enhances comparability, it requires significant investment in standardization and capacity building (UNEP, 2019). In this context, efforts have been made to standardize sustainability reporting, including the Task Force on Climate-related Financial Disclosures (TCFD) recommendations (Fig. 7.5), which have subsequently informed the development of the International Sustainability Standards Board (ISSB) Sustainability Disclosure Standards.

## 2.5 *Benchmarking Global Best Practices*

A review of international experiences offers valuable insights for Indonesia and other emerging economies. Several cases stand out:

- European Union: The EU has established a comprehensive framework combining the CSRD, the EU Taxonomy for Sustainable Activities, and mandatory climate-related disclosures. This integrated approach demonstrates the value of aligning regulatory, financial, and statistical frameworks under a single sustainable finance agenda (European Commission, 2022).
- United States: While the U.S. has traditionally relied more on voluntary disclosure, recent moves by the Securities and Exchange Commission (SEC) toward mandatory climate-related reporting illustrate a shift toward greater regulatory intervention (SEC, 2022).

- China: China has developed national taxonomies and green bond standards while simultaneously mandating disclosure for listed companies. Its centralized governance model allows for rapid policy implementation, although questions remain about enforcement consistency (PBoC, 2021).
- ASEAN: Regional initiatives, such as the ASEAN Taxonomy for Sustainable Finance, highlight the importance of interoperability and cross-border harmonization, especially for countries with integrated financial markets (ASEAN, 2021).

These experiences reveal that while contexts vary, successful climate data governance often combines three elements: mandatory disclosure, harmonized standards, and strong institutional coordination.

# 3 Data and Methodology

## *3.1 Research Design and Analytical Framework*

The methodological foundation of this chapter rests on a qualitative, descriptive, and comparative approach. Unlike quantitative studies that rely on statistical testing or econometric modeling, this approach is particularly suited to exploring a subject as multifaceted as climate-related data governance. The decision to adopt a qualitative framework stem from the recognition that climate change intersects with diverse domains—environmental science, economics, finance, and governance—that cannot be fully captured through numerical indicators alone. Instead, the emphasis is placed on examining institutional arrangements, regulatory frameworks, and international benchmarks, and on assessing how these interact in the case of Indonesia.

The analytical framework for this chapter is built on the three-pillar concept of climate data governance:

1. Data Infrastructure, encompassing the physical and digital systems for collecting, storing, and disseminating climate-related information. This includes greenhouse gas inventories, disaster risk maps, corporate disclosures, and financial supervisory databases.
2. Standards and Methodologies, which provide the measurement and reporting rules that ensure data is consistent, comparable, and credible across different sectors and jurisdictions. Examples include the GHG Protocol, IFRS Sustainability Disclosure Standards, and national sustainability reporting guidelines.
3. Institutional Coordination, referring to the mechanisms through which multiple actors—governments, regulators, private firms, and civil society—collaborate in developing, sharing, and enforcing climate-related data.

These three pillars are not isolated silos but interconnected dimensions. Strong data infrastructure is of little use without harmonized standards, while both remain ineffective without coordination among institutions responsible for generating and using the data. In practice, climate data governance must therefore be understood as a system, one in which weaknesses in one pillar undermine the effectiveness of the others. The analysis followed three sequential stages. The first stage involved mapping international frameworks. Here, documents such as the Paris Agreement, IFRS standards, and NGFS reports were reviewed to identify key requirements, principles, and benchmarks relevant to climate data governance. This stage established the global standards against which Indonesia would later be evaluated.

The second stage consisted of assessing Indonesia's policies. Domestic regulations, reports, and official statements were examined to determine how Indonesia's institutions—Bank Indonesia, OJK, and the Ministry of Finance—are addressing data governance issues. Particular attention was given to the design of mandatory disclosure rules, the development of taxonomies for sustainable finance, and the introduction of stress testing frameworks. The third stage involved comparative benchmarking, where Indonesia's practices were systematically compared with those of other jurisdictions, notably the European Union, the United States, China, and ASEAN. This step was crucial for identifying gaps, such as the absence of comprehensive assurance mechanisms, and for drawing lessons from international best practices that could inform Indonesia's trajectory.

### *3.2 Data Sources*

This chapter draws from three categories of sources, each contributing distinct insights into the subject of climate data governance.

1. First, international reports and frameworks form the backbone for understanding global best practices;
2. Second, national policy and regulatory documents provide the basis for evaluating Indonesia's specific case; and
3. Third, literature and academic works to enrich the analysis with theoretical insights and critical perspectives regarding comparison to global practices.

The study based primarily on document analysis, which involves systematically reviewing and synthesizing conclusion based on available information to provide an integrated understanding of a complex phenomenon (Bowen, 2009).

### *3.3 Scope and Limitations*

The scope of the study is explicitly focused on the intersection of climate-related data governance and financial sector policy. Broader aspects of environmental monitoring—such as biodiversity indices, water quality data, or local community adaptation practices—are acknowledged but remain outside the central scope.

Limitations stem primarily from data availability and comparability. While international frameworks such as IFRS standards and TCFD recommendations are well-documented, domestic data in Indonesia is often fragmented or inconsistent. Another limitation arises from the timing of reforms. Many global initiatives, including IFRS S1 and S2, are relatively new and not yet fully implemented in Indonesia. Thus, the analysis captures a transitional moment rather than a mature system.

# 4 Discussion

## *4.1 Global Drivers of Climate Data Governance*

Climate change has increasingly been framed in international policy and academic discourse as both an existential environmental crisis and a systemic economic risk. The scientific consensus, reflected in the Intergovernmental Panel on Climate Change (IPCC) assessments, demonstrates that anthropogenic emissions are accelerating extreme weather events, biodiversity loss, and rising sea levels, all of which carry severe social and economic consequences (IPCC, 2021). These environmental pressures have direct financial implications, from the physical destruction of assets due to natural disasters to the transitional risks faced by carbon-intensive industries as economies move toward decarbonization.

At the global level, this dual recognition has elevated the importance of climate-related data governance. On the one hand, governments need reliable information to design effective mitigation and adaptation policies, set emissions reduction targets, and monitor compliance with international agreements such as the Paris Agreement (UNFCCC, 2015). On the other, financial institutions require credible, standardized, and comparable data to assess risks, stress-test portfolios, and direct capital flows toward sustainable projects. In this sense, climate-related data becomes the bridge between ambitious commitments and their practical implementation. Without it, policy targets risk becoming rhetorical statements, while financial markets lack the ability to price risks and opportunities accurately.

This recognition explains the rapid proliferation of international initiatives that emphasize data transparency and disclosure. The Task Force on Climate-related Financial Disclosures (TCFD, 2017) created a global framework for voluntary reporting, which has since influenced regulators and corporations worldwide. The IFRS Sustainability Disclosure Standards (IFRS Foundation, 2023), particularly IFRS S1 and S2, go further by introducing harmonized, mandatory requirements to ensure comparability across jurisdictions. Meanwhile, the Network for Greening the Financial System (NGFS, 2019, 2020) has urged central banks and supervisors to integrate climate data into their stress testing frameworks and financial oversight.

Despite these advances, significant disparities remain. Advanced economies such as the European Union have built sophisticated systems that integrate taxonomies, mandatory disclosures, and assurance requirements. By contrast, many developing countries struggle with fragmented data systems, limited institutional coordination, and insufficient technical capacity. Indonesia, while demonstrating leadership among emerging economies, exemplifies these tensions: it is highly vulnerable to climate risks, has taken important regulatory steps, but still faces structural challenges in data governance.

## 4.2 Analysis Through the Three-Pillar Framework

### Data Infrastructure

Indonesia has taken important steps in developing climate-related data infrastructure. The Ministry of Environment (MEF) compiles greenhouse gas inventories and publishes them through Biennial Update Reports to the United Nations Framework Convention on Climate Change (UNFCCC). The National Agency for Disaster Countermeasures maintains a detailed disaster database that documents the frequency, type, and geographic distribution of natural hazards. In the financial sector, Bank Indonesia has introduced reporting requirements that oblige banks to disaggregate loan data by economic sector, project location, and collateral type, while OJK has piloted taxonomy-based reporting frameworks designed to capture sustainable finance flows (OJK, 2020).

Despite this progress, the system remains fragmented. Environmental data is collected by MEF, financial data by Bank Indonesia and OJK, and corporate disclosures by individual companies. These datasets are rarely interoperable, creating silos that limit their usefulness for integrated risk assessments. Unlike the European Union, which has developed the European Single Access Point (ESAP) to centralize sustainability data, Indonesia lacks a unified platform. As a result, policymakers, investors, and researchers face difficulties in accessing consistent datasets that span environmental and financial dimensions.

Another critical gap lies in the measurement of scope 3 emissions, which include the indirect emissions from lending and investment portfolios—also known as financed emissions. These account for the majority of financial institutions' climate impact, yet data availability is extremely limited. Bank Indonesia's initiative to develop a standardized carbon calculator for banks and their debtors represents a promising step toward addressing this gap. However, the success of such tools will depend on significant investments in IT infrastructure, human resources, and inter-agency coordination.

### Standards and Methodologies

Indonesia's regulatory framework for sustainability reporting is anchored in OJK Regulation No. 51/POJK.03/2017, which mandates financial institutions, listed companies, and issuers to produce sustainability reports. This regulation positioned Indonesia as an early mover in Southeast Asia, signaling its recognition that transparency is essential to sustainable finance. Nevertheless, the regulation predates the

IFRS Sustainability Disclosure Standards, creating a gap between Indonesia's reporting practices and global benchmarks (IFRS Foundation, 2023). Many Indonesian companies continue to provide qualitative descriptions rather than standardized quantitative indicators, particularly regarding climate scenario analysis and value-chain emissions.

To bridge this gap, Indonesia has recently advanced its sustainability reporting architecture. The Indonesian Institute of Accountants (IAI) has established the Indonesian Sustainability Standards Board (ISSB Indonesia), which in 2025 launched the first set of Sustainability Reporting Standards (ISRS), aligning them with the IFRS Sustainability Disclosure Standards. The issuance of these standards represents a milestone in harmonizing Indonesia's practices with global disclosure frameworks, ensuring that Indonesian firms' reports are comparable, consistent, and decision-useful for international investors. Such comparability not only enhances investor confidence but also deepens Indonesia's integration into global capital markets.

Another important step has been the introduction of assurance standards for sustainability reporting. The Indonesian Institute of Certified Public Accountants (IAPI), together with IAI, has begun developing assurance frameworks to verify sustainability disclosures, in line with international practices. These assurance standards are crucial to strengthening the credibility, reliability, and accountability of reported data. While in the past only a few leading firms voluntarily sought external verification, the existence of a formal assurance framework creates an institutional pathway toward broader adoption. This mirrors developments in other jurisdictions, such as the European Union's Corporate Sustainability Reporting Directive (CSRD), where mandatory external assurance has become central to ensuring data integrity (European Commission, 2022).

Some critical challenges still remain. Firms require substantial capacity building to adopt more rigorous reporting methodologies, particularly in quantifying greenhouse gas (GHG) emissions across Scopes 1, 2, and 3. Auditors and assurance providers must also upgrade their technical competencies to assess complex climate-related data. In this regard, multi-stakeholder cooperation—including regulators, industry associations, academia, and international partners—will be essential to support effective implementation. By strengthening both reporting and assurance standards, Indonesia can position itself at the forefront of sustainable finance in emerging markets, ensuring that its sustainability disclosures are not only compliant but also credible and globally comparable.

## Institutional Coordination

Institutional coordination is another critical pillar. Climate finance data governance in Indonesia involves multiple actors: the Ministry of Finance (MoF), Bank Indonesia (BI), Otoritas Jasa Keuangan (OJK). Each plays an important role—whether in fiscal policy, macroprudential oversight, microprudential supervision, or environmental monitoring. The enactment of the Financial Sector Omnibus Law (FSOL) has further strengthened coordination by granting Bank Indonesia an explicit mandate on sustainable finance and establishing a Sustainable Finance Committee to facilitate collaboration among regulators (Juhro et al., 2025).

FSOL frames sustainable finance as an ecosystem that integrates policy, regulation, norms, standards, products, transactions, and services. Within this framework, BI is authorized to regulate and develop sustainable finance as part of its policy mix strategy, while OJK holds authority to regulate and supervise the carbon exchange. Meanwhile, the MoF plays a pivotal role in mobilizing fiscal instruments. The establishment of the Sustainable Finance Committee institutionalizes the coordination among these agencies, with a mandate to formulate strategies, align fiscal–monetary–macro- and micro-prudential instruments, facilitate sustainable finance databases, and develop Indonesia's sustainable taxonomy. This committee represents a step toward formalized governance, bringing coherence to what has long been a fragmented institutional landscape.

Coordination persists as major challenge. Databases remain siloed, mandates overlap, and communication channels are not fully institutionalized. The contrast with China is instructive: the People's Bank of China has centralized authority to embed environmental data directly into credit allocation and green bond policies, whereas Indonesia's more pluralistic institutional structure requires extensive inter-agency negotiation. This institutional fragmentation risks undermining the credibility and timeliness of climate-related financial data.

Strengthening coordination requires both horizontal integration across financial and environmental regulators and vertical integration linking national authorities with private sector reporters. The introduction of sustainability disclosure standards and the development of the carbon calculator by BI represent initial efforts to create this vertical linkage, but systematic integration into regulatory databases remains incomplete. Regional cooperation, such as through the ASEAN Taxonomy for Sustainable Finance, offers further opportunities for harmonization, yet domestic systems must first be consolidated to ensure consistency and credibility. Building interoperable databases, standardizing reporting methodologies, and embedding climate data into financial stability assessments will be key to ensuring that institutional coordination translates into effective governance.

### *4.3 Comparative Benchmarking*

Benchmarking Indonesia against other jurisdictions provides a clearer picture of its achievements and remaining challenges. Comparative analysis can be stratified across four key dimensions: regulatory architecture, disclosure and assurance standards, data integration, and regional cooperation.

On the regulatory architecture aspect, The European Union (EU) represents the most advanced model, with its unified and binding regime under the European

Green Deal, including the EU Taxonomy, the Sustainable Finance Disclosure Regulation (SFDR), and the Corporate Sustainability Reporting Directive (CSRD). This integration ensures that sustainability considerations are mainstreamed into investment decision-making across member states. In comparison, Indonesia's regulatory architecture remains fragmented, with overlapping mandates between Bank Indonesia (BI), OJK, and the Ministry of Finance. Nevertheless, Indonesia has shown early regulatory initiative through OJK Regulation No. 51/POJK.03/2017, which made sustainability reporting mandatory well before most emerging economies. Further, Indonesia ratified the Financial Sector Omnibus Law (FSOL), which explicitly mandates coordination among financial regulators to support the development of a green economy and sustainable finance.

On Disclosure and Assurance Standards, The EU has moved decisively toward harmonized sustainability disclosure standards aligned with the European Financial Reporting Advisory Group (EFRAG) and mandatory external assurance under the CSRD. Indonesia, while ahead of the United States in terms of mandating sustainability reporting, still struggles with ensuring comparability and reliability. The United States, until recently, relied heavily on voluntary frameworks such as the Task Force on Climate-related Financial Disclosures (TCFD), though the U.S. Securities and Exchange Commission (SEC) is now advancing rules for mandatory climate reporting. Indonesia's transition to IFRS-based sustainability standards and the development of assurance frameworks by the Indonesian Institute of Accountants (IAI) and Indonesian Institute of Certified Public Accountants (IAPI) represent steps in the right direction but remain in early stages of adoption.

On the Data and Supervisory Integration aspect, China offers a contrasting model characterized by centralized and top-down governance. The People's Bank of China (PBoC) has integrated green credit guidelines and mandatory disclosures directly into banking supervision, and environmental data are embedded into credit allocation and bond issuance frameworks. This centralization allows for rapid policy diffusion and supervisory enforcement. Indonesia's system, by contrast, is participatory, involving multiple agencies and stakeholders. While this pluralism promotes inclusivity and broader legitimacy, it also results in slower implementation, fragmented databases, and weaker coherence in climate-related financial supervision.

At the regional level, ASEAN countries are gradually adopting the ASEAN Taxonomy for Sustainable Finance, which provides a common classification system while allowing for country-specific flexibilities. Indonesia has played an active role in shaping this taxonomy and aligning it with its domestic taxonomy. However, domestic implementation remains uneven, with significant capacity gaps at both institutional and corporate levels. Ensuring alignment between the ASEAN Taxonomy, Indonesia's national taxonomy, and the forthcoming IFRS-aligned disclosure standards will be critical to strengthening cross-border comparability and investor confidence.

### 4.4 *Emerging Opportunities and Challenges*

Indonesia's current trajectory reveals both opportunities and challenges. On the positive side, the establishment of a Sustainability Standards Board, the integration of sustainable finance into Bank Indonesia's macroprudential mandate, and the piloting of structured data tools such as the carbon calculator represent significant steps forward. These initiatives align Indonesia with global trends and create the potential for greater transparency, comparability, and accountability.

Yet challenges remain formidable. Technical capacity among regulators, auditors, and firms remains limited, slowing the adoption of IFRS-aligned standards. Assurance practices are still weak, leaving sustainability reports vulnerable to criticism regarding their credibility. Data systems remain fragmented, with little interoperability between environmental and financial databases. Without addressing these structural issues, Indonesia risks undermining both its financial stability and its credibility in international markets.

The opportunity, however, lies in Indonesia's ability to leapfrog. By leveraging ongoing reforms and international cooperation, the country could build a more coherent data governance ecosystem that not only serves domestic needs but also positions Indonesia as a regional leader among emerging economies. Centralizing data platforms, mandating assurance, and investing in capacity building could create a robust system that underpins both financial stability and sustainable development.

## 5 Conclusion

The analysis presented in this chapter underscores the centrality of climate-related data governance in addressing the dual challenge of mitigating climate risks and advancing sustainable finance. While climate change is often framed as an environmental crisis, its implications extend deeply into economic performance, financial stability, and development trajectories. For a country like Indonesia—highly vulnerable to climate impacts and reliant on carbon-intensive sectors—the ability to generate, manage, and govern climate-related data is not a technical accessory but a strategic necessity.

Globally, the literature review highlighted the growing recognition of climate change as a systemic risk. International initiatives such as the Paris Agreement, the TCFD, the IFRS Sustainability Disclosure Standards, and the NGFS scenarios have established a normative and regulatory architecture that increasingly demands transparency, comparability, and accountability. Advanced jurisdictions such as the European Union have demonstrated the benefits of comprehensive and integrated approaches that combine mandatory disclosures, taxonomies, and assurance requirements. These global developments set the benchmark against which Indonesia must measure its own progress.

The Indonesian case reveals both important achievements and persistent challenges. On the one hand, Indonesia has positioned itself as a regional leader by mandating sustainability disclosures earlier than many peers, introducing a Sustainable Finance Roadmap, and adopting legislative reforms that expand Bank Indonesia's mandate to include sustainable finance. The establishment of the Sustainability Standards Board under the Indonesian Institute of Accountants reflects an explicit commitment to harmonize national disclosure standards with IFRS-aligned frameworks. Initiatives such as Bank Indonesia's carbon calculator and OJK's taxonomy-based reporting pilots illustrate ongoing innovation in data infrastructure.

On the other hand, critical gaps remain. Climate-related data in Indonesia is fragmented across institutions, with limited interoperability between environmental and financial databases. Disclosure practices, while mandatory, are uneven in quality and rarely assured, limiting their credibility. Methodologies for measuring financed emissions, scenario analysis, and forward-looking risk assessments are still at an early stage of development. Institutional coordination, though strengthened by the Financial Sector Omnibus Law and the creation of the Sustainable Finance Committee, continues to be hampered by overlapping mandates and siloed data systems. Compared to global best practices, Indonesia's framework remains less mature, particularly in terms of standard harmonization, assurance mechanisms, and centralized data platforms.

From this analysis, several strategic implications emerge. First, strengthening data infrastructure must be prioritized, particularly through investments in interoperable platforms that allow environmental and financial data to be integrated into coherent risk assessments. Second, the adoption of IFRS-aligned sustainability standards should be accompanied by comprehensive capacity-building efforts, ensuring that firms, auditors, and regulators can meet the new requirements effectively. Third, Indonesia should move toward mandatory assurance of sustainability reports, following the example of the European Union, to enhance credibility and investor confidence. Fourth, institutional coordination mechanisms need to be deepened, moving beyond ad hoc collaboration toward a truly integrated governance structure that aligns ministries, regulators, and the private sector.

The broader message of this chapter is that data is power. In the context of climate change, data determines whether risks are understood, whether opportunities are identified, and whether resources are allocated efficiently. By strengthening its climate-related data governance, Indonesia can not only safeguard its financial stability and enhance resilience but also unlock new avenues for green investment, technological innovation, and sustainable growth. In doing so, Indonesia will contribute meaningfully to the global climate agenda while advancing its own long-term development objectives.

Ultimately, the chapter argues that enhanced data governance is both a domestic imperative and an international obligation. Domestically, it underpins financial stability, economic resilience, and sustainable development. Internationally, it enables Indonesia to integrate with global markets, attract sustainable finance, and fulfill its commitments under frameworks such as the Paris Agreement and the Sustainable

Development Goals. The pathway forward is demanding, requiring investments in infrastructure, capacity, and institutional reform. Yet, the rewards—in terms of credibility, stability, and sustainability—are equally profound.

## References


ASEAN. (2021). *ASEAN Taxonomy for Sustainable Finance (Version 1)*. Association of Southeast Asian Nations.

Bank for International Settlements (BIS). (2021). *Central banks and climate change: Mapping the financial stability implications*. BIS Papers No. 118.

Battiston, S., Mandel, A., Monasterolo, I., Schütze, F., & Visentin, G. (2017). A climate stress-test of the financial system. *Nature Climate Change, 7*(4), 283–288.

Bowen, G. A. (2009). Document analysis as a qualitative research method. *Qualitative Research Journal, 9*(2), 27–40. https://doi.org/10.3316/QRJ0902027

European Commission. (2022). *Corporate Sustainability Reporting Directive (CSRD)*. Official Journal of the European Union.

Financial Services Authority of Indonesia (OJK). (2020). *Sustainable Finance Roadmap Phase II (2021–2025)*. Jakarta: OJK.

Financial Services Authority of Indonesia (OJK). (2017). *OJK Regulation No. 51/POJK.03/2017 on Implementation of Sustainable Finance for Financial Institutions, Issuers, and Public Companies*. Jakarta: OJK.

Fisher, P. (2019). *Bank of England and climate change: Breaking the tragedy of the horizon*. Bank of England Speech Archive.

FSB (2021). FSB Roadmap for Addressing Climate-Related Financial Risks. https://www.fsb.org/uploads/P140725-2.pdf

G20. (2020). *Data Gaps Initiative: Annual Report 2020*. Group of Twenty.

Indonesian Institute of Accountants (IAI). (2023). *IAI establishes Sustainability Standards Board to harmonize IFRS sustainability standards in Indonesia*. Retrieved from https://web.iaiglobal.or.id

International Finance Corporation (IFC). (2021). *Sustainable finance data for central banks: A survey*. IFC Report No. 14.

International Financial Reporting Standards (IFRS) Foundation. (2023). *IFRS Sustainability Disclosure Standards (S1 and S2)*. IFRS Foundation, London.

International Monetary Fund (IMF). (2020). *Central banking and the transition to a low-carbon economy*. Washington, DC: IMF.

Intergovernmental Panel on Climate Change (IPCC). (2021). *Climate Change 2021: The Physical Science Basis. Contribution of Working Group I to the Sixth Assessment Report of the Intergovernmental Panel on Climate Change*. Cambridge University Press.

Jones et al (2024). Greenhouse gas emissions, 2024. Available at: https://ourworldindata.org/grapher/per-capita-ghg-emissions.

Juhro, S.M. (2025) 'Future central banking in emerging market economies', in *Encyclopedia of Monetary Policy, Financial Markets and Banking*. Elsevier, pp. 189–198. Available at: https://doi.org/10.1016/B978-0-44-313776-1.00118-5

Juhro, S., Robinson, I., Rahadyan, H., & Rishanty, A. (2025). *Climate Risks, Just Transition, and Central Bank Policy for Sustainable Economic Growth*. Retrieved from Jurnal Ekonomi Indonesia: https://jurnal.isei.or.id/index.php/isei/article/view/587

Ministry of Environment and Forestry of Indonesia (MEF). (2021). *Indonesia's Second Biennial Update Report to the United Nations Framework Convention on Climate Change*. Jakarta: MEF.

Network for Greening the Financial System (NGFS). (2019). *A call for action: Climate change as a source of financial risk*. Paris: NGFS.

Network for Greening the Financial System (NGFS). (2020). *NGFS climate scenarios for central banks and supervisors.* Paris: NGFS.
People's Bank of China (PBoC). (2021). *China Green Bond Endorsed Project Catalogue (2021 Edition).* Beijing: PBoC.
Task Force on Climate-related Financial Disclosures (TCFD). (2017). *Recommendations of the Task Force on Climate-related Financial Disclosures.* Basel: Financial Stability Board.
United Nations Environment Programme (UNEP). (2019). *The Emissions Gap Report 2019.* Nairobi: UNEP.
United Nations Environment Programme (UNEP). (2020). *Emissions Gap Report 2020.* Nairobi: UNEP.
United Nations Framework Convention on Climate Change (UNFCCC). (2015). *Paris Agreement.* Bonn: UNFCCC.
World Meteorological Organization (WMO). (2020). *WMO Statement on the state of the global climate in 2019.* Geneva: WMO.

# Chapter 8
# Climate Risk Transmission in Indonesia: A Bayesian Network Approach

**Cicilia Anggadewi Harun, Danny Hermawan, and Arnita Rishanty**

**Abstract** Standard global climate risk models often fail to capture Indonesia's unique archipelagic vulnerabilities. Employing a Bayesian Network approach to map non-linear transmission channels, this study reveals critical asymmetries. Physical risks manifest as acute, "fat-tailed" stressors triggering immediate GDP shocks, while transition risks create chronic economic drag through stranded assets. Thus, "one size fits all" approaches prove inadequate. Findings advocate a bespoke, dual-track policy framework addressing regional rigidities, emphasizing the need to manage acute physical threats alongside the structural friction of decarbonizing a coal-dependent economy.

**Keywords** Climate risk transmission · Financial stability · Bayesian network · Physical risk · Transition risk · Macro-financial linkages · Climate stress testing

## 1 Introduction

### *1.1 The Archipelago at the Crossroads of Climate and Capital*

Indonesia, the world's largest archipelagic state, stands at a precipice where the physical realities of a changing planet collide with the financial imperatives of an emerging economy. Spanning the equator with over 17,000 islands, the nation presents a critical global case study for the intersection of climate change, economic development, and financial stability. The country is acutely exposed to a wide array of natural hazards—a vulnerability now being amplified by the increasing frequency and intensity of climate-related events such as extreme floods, droughts, and rising sea levels CMCC (2021). Simultaneously, as a major coal exporter and consumer, Indonesia faces profound transition risks as the global economy shifts toward decarbonization Climate Action Tracker (2025).

C. A. Harun (✉) · D. Hermawan · A. Rishanty
Bank Indonesia, Jakarta, Indonesia
e-mail: charun@bi.go.id; danny_h@bi.go.id; Arnita_rishanty@bi.go.id



S. M. Juhro et al. (eds.), *Sustainable Economy: The Indonesian Pathways*,
https://doi.org/10.1007/978-981-92-1215-6_8

Rishanty et al. (2023) finds that coal phase-out policies in Indonesia's green transition, if done unjustly, may increase financial burdens on the government, coal companies, and the supply chain, while raising unemployment risks.

The economic stakes are substantial, impacting various sectors and regions, with the heaviest burden falling upon the most vulnerable segments of the population. The World Bank estimates that without significant adaptation, climate change could shave off a significant portion of Indonesia's GDP, potentially up to 7% under severe scenarios, with the poor bearing the brunt of the impact.[2] This is not merely an environmental crisis; it is a financial one. A shock in the climate system acts as an external blow to the financial system, potentially transmitting and propagating risks that can trigger systemic instability. Such instability creates a negative feedback loop, reducing credit supply to the real sector and precipitating broader economic downturns.

## *1.2 The Limitations of Global Standardization*

In response to these growing threats, the Network for Greening the Financial System (NGFS)—a consortium of central banks and supervisors—has developed and adopted climate risk models and scenarios. These tools are designed to assess risks to the financial system, providing a common language for regulators worldwide. However, a critical friction has emerged: these scenarios tend to be "one size fits all," often neglecting the "stylized facts" and unique economic texture of the country in review.

For an emerging market like Indonesia, standardized global models often fail to capture the granular, non-linear, and specific transmission channels through which climate risks materialize. A generic transition risk scenario, for instance, might model a uniform carbon price response across all markets. Such a model fails to account for Indonesia's complex political economy of energy subsidies Argus Media (2022), its distinct reliance on captive coal power for industrial downstreaming, or the specific socio-economic rigidity of labor markets in coal-producing regions like East Kalimantan. Similarly, global physical risk models may average out the acute, localized devastation of tropical cyclones or the chronic, localized economic erosion caused by land subsidence in coastal cities like Semarang and Jakarta Business & Human Rights Resource Centre (2024).

Recognizing this gap, more than half of the world's financial authorities have begun making modifications to NGFS scenarios to better reflect their countries' unique characteristics. For Indonesia, this customization is not a luxury but a necessity. The archipelago's risk profile is dominated by specific hazards—monsoon-driven flooding, El Niño-induced droughts affecting rice production, and the unique geotechnical challenge of sinking cities—that generic models invariably underweight.

### 1.3 A Bespoke Framework for Uncertainty

This report presents the results of a bespoke climate risk assessment framework developed specifically for Indonesia using Bayesian Networks (BN). The choice of the BN methodology is both innovative and deliberate, driven by the nature of the problem itself: the "radical uncertainty" characterizing climate change. Unlike traditional econometric models that rely heavily on historical time-series data to predict future trends, climate change presents us with unprecedented events and non-linear tipping points for which history offers little guidance.

Bayesian Networks are uniquely capable of modeling the transmission of risks in such data-sparse environments. They capture complex, probabilistic, and non-linear dependencies among a wide range of variables, integrating empirical data with expert knowledge (in the form of prior probabilities). This provides a robust structure for "forward-looking" analysis, allowing us to model how risks propagate through the specific arteries of the Indonesian economy.

This research specifically addresses how physical and transition risks can be translated into a climate risk stress test scenario that is appropriate for Indonesia's economy. It focuses particularly on sectors that form the backbone of the archipelago's prosperity yet remain uniquely vulnerable: the food sector, the construction sector, and the "brown industries" of mining and manufacturing. By deconstructing these pathways, we move beyond the monolithic "one size fits all" approach to reveal a nuanced landscape where physical and transition risks exhibit strikingly different behaviors and require distinct policy responses.

## 2 The Climate-Financial Nexus in an Emerging Archipelago

To understand how a flood in Central Java or a carbon tax policy in Jakarta affects the stability of the national banking system, one must map the transmission channels. Climate risk is not a single, isolated shock; it is a cascade. It travels through both **microeconomic** and **macroeconomic** channels before aggregating into systemic financial risks.

### 2.1 Anatomy of Transmission

A climate event is a new class of exogenous shock to the financial system stress test. Whether it is a physical event like a typhoon or a transition event like a technological breakthrough in battery storage, the shock enters the real economy first. The Macroeconomic Transmission Channel refers to the physical or productivity loss affecting key macroeconomic variables such as inflation and economic growth. For example, a nationwide drought reduces agricultural output, which drives up food prices (inflation) and reduces the aggregate output of the economy (GDP contraction) EcoShape (2017).

The Microeconomic Transmission Channel this operates at the level of individual agents—households and corporations. A factory located in a flood-prone coastal area suffers direct property damage and business interruption (loss of income). A coal mining company faces "stranded assets" as its reserves become unburnable due to new global regulations or shifts in investor sentiment. These micro-level losses degrade the balance sheets of borrowers. As illustrated in Fig. 8.1, both channels ultimately translate into five typical financial risks that threaten the stability of banks and insurers (NGFS, 2022) (Table 8.1).

For example, technological innovations (a transition risk) can lower the price of renewable energy, threatening the market share of carbon-intensive companies. This results in declining asset values (market risk) and a higher probability of default

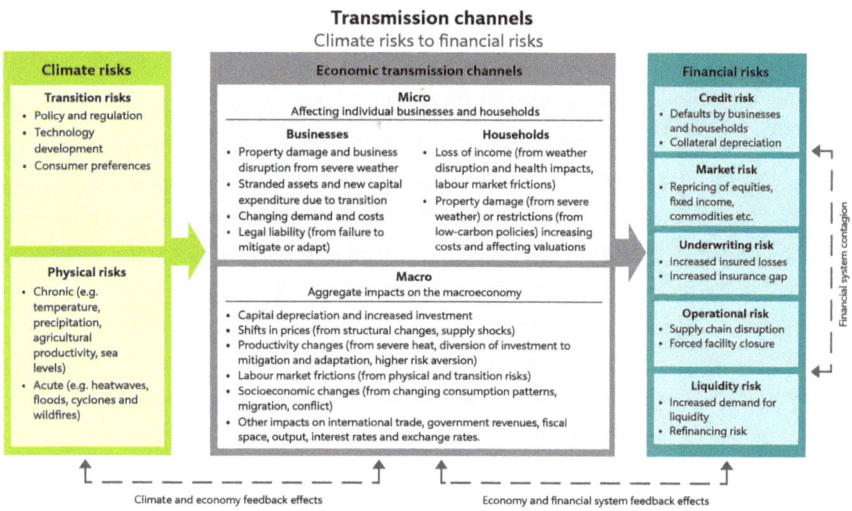


**Fig. 8.1** Transmission channels of climate risks to financial risks

**Table 8.1** Climate transmission to financial risk

| Transmission Channel | Mechanism of Impact | Resulting Financial Risk |
|---|---|---|
| Microeconomic | Physical damage to assets, loss of income, stranded assets, business disruption. | Credit Risk: Borrowers (households/ firms) default on loans.<br>Market Risk: Collateral values (e.g., real estate, coal stocks) decline.<br>Operational Risk: Supply chains break; physical bank assets damaged. |
| Macroeconomic | Inflation volatility, currency depreciation, labor productivity loss, GDP contraction. | Liquidity Risk: Sudden demand for cash; deposit withdrawals.<br>Underwriting Risk: Insurance claims exceed premiums; uninsurability increases. |

(credit risk). Conversely, a physical hazard like a flood can destroy a factory's inventory, leading to an insurance claim (underwriting risk) and an inability to service debt (credit risk).

## 2.2 *The Indonesian Context: Sectoral Vulnerability*

The geographical situation of Indonesia is unique, and as the biggest archipelago in the world, it requires granular mapping of the sectoral niche of each island—even each province. An analysis of provincial Gross Domestic Product (GDP) data reveals which sectors form the backbone of the national and regional economies.

Aggregation of these provincial results reveals that five sectors dominate the Indonesian economy: Agriculture, Manufacturing, Trade, Mining, and Construction. This concentration creates a "double jeopardy" scenario for the nation's financial stability.

1. Transition Risk Exposure: The sectors most crucial to the national and regional economies—Manufacturing and Mining—are also the "brown industries" most exposed to transition risk. The coal mining sector alone contributed significantly to GDP (reaching over 10% in recent high-price years) and is the economic lifeblood of provinces like East Kalimantan and South Sumatra. A global shift away from fossil fuels threatens these regions with structural obsolescence.
2. Physical Risk Exposure: The agriculture sector, the single most important contributor to employment and a key driver of GDP, is acutely vulnerable to physical risks. Changes in rainfall patterns, temperature increases, and extreme weather events directly impact crop yields, threatening food security and farmer incomes.

This structural reality means that Indonesia does not have the luxury of facing one risk at a time. The very engines of its growth are the primary targets of climate risk. The following sections will deconstruct how these risks materialize, using the Bayesian Network results to illuminate the specific pathways of destruction and disruption.

# 3 Data and Methodology

## 3.1 *Empirical Analysis: Deconstructing Physical Risk Pathways*

The application of the Bayesian Network to Indonesia's physical risk landscape reveals a web of dependencies that highlights the acute nature of these threats. The comprehensive BN model for physical risks identifies five primary hazards as the

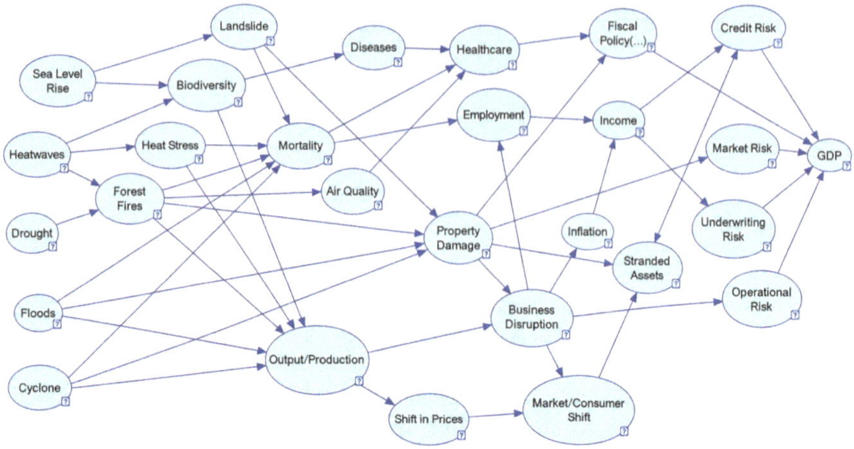


**Fig. 8.2** Bayesian Network transmission of physical risk effects to GDP

"ultimate parent nodes". These are the triggers that set the cascade in motion: Sea Level Rise, Heatwaves, Droughts, Floods, and Typhoons (Fig. 8.2).

In this network, these primary risks impact productivity, cause property damage, and trigger secondary physical risks (e.g., landslides from floods). These impacts then flow through various channels to materialize as credit, market, underwriting, and operational risks, ultimately affecting GDP.

## The Coastal Crisis: Sea Level Rise, Subsidence, and Market Risk

One of the most powerful transmission channels identified in the analysis connects Property Damage to Market Risk and Operational Risk. In Indonesia, this is not a theoretical construct; it is a daily reality for the country's economic centers, exacerbated by a phenomenon unique to its geology and urban development: land subsidence Dwibaskoro (2025).

## The Sinking Capital and Industrial Hubs

Jakarta, the nation's capital, and Semarang, a key industrial hub in Central Java, serve as primary case studies for this transmission. Parts of Jakarta are sinking at a rate of up to 25 cm per year due to the excessive extraction of groundwater, compounded by global sea-level rise. This creates a chronic Market Risk where coastal property values are eroded. Real estate in flood-prone areas faces "price adjustments," and in severe cases, becomes unmarketable, directly impacting the collateral value held by banks.

### Operational Risk Realized in Semarang

The impact on the industrial sector is visceral. In Semarang, tidal floods (rob) have devastated major industrial estates. In May 2022 and again in early 2024, severe tidal floods inundated the Lamicitra industrial zone in Tanjung Emas Port. Factory operations were paralyzed, machinery was submerged, and thousands of workers were evacuated. This is a direct materialization of Operational Risk—factories could not operate, supply chains were severed, and logistics collapsed.

The economic losses from such events are staggering. In Semarang alone, estimates suggest that without intervention, subsidence-related damage could cost trillions of rupiah annually. For the banking sector, this translates into **Credit Risk**: factories unable to operate cannot generate revenue to service their debts. Furthermore, the disruption to the railway network in Semarang during the 2024 floods forced the cancellation of freight trains, severing the logistical artery of Java and illustrating how a localized physical event causes ripple effects throughout the national supply chain (Rusmansar & Tohir, 2025).

### The Insurance Gap and Underwriting Risk

The analysis highlights Underwriting Risk as a critical node influencing GDP outcomes. In Indonesia, the insurance protection gap is significant. Losses from floods often fall directly on households, businesses, or the state budget, rather than being absorbed by insurers. This lack of financial buffering amplifies the shock to the real economy, as capital that could be used for investment is instead diverted to reconstruction, acting as a drag on economic growth (Verisk, 2025).

## 3.2 *The Agricultural Shock: El Niño, Drought, and Inflation*

The Bayesian Network identifies Drought as a key driver affecting Output/Productivity and Inflation.[1] This transmission channel was vividly illustrated during the 2023–2024 El Niño event, providing a real-world validation of the model's structure.

### Productivity Loss

El Niño conditions delayed the monsoon, disrupting the planting calendar for rice, Indonesia's staple crop. Rice production in 2023 dropped by over one million tons compared to the previous year, a decline of approximately 2.28% (Arifin, 2023). In regions like Maluku, farmers reported total crop failures due to water scarcity, with monthly rainfall in late 2023 consistently recording below 100 mm (Barends, 2024).

#### Macroeconomic Transmission via Inflation

This physical shock transmitted directly to the macroeconomy via the Inflation node. As supply tightened, rice prices surged to record highs, topping IDR 14,000/kg and driving up the Consumer Price Index (CPI). For a country where food comprises a large portion of the consumer basket, this erodes the purchasing power of the middle and lower classes, dampening consumption elsewhere in the economy.

#### Financial Consequence

For the banking sector, particularly regional development banks (BPDs) with high exposure to agriculture, this creates heightened Credit Risk. Farmers facing crop failure cannot repay seasonal loans (KUR). The government was forced to intervene with social assistance and massive imports (up to 3.5 million tons), straining Fiscal Policy—another key node in the risk network (United States Department of Agriculture, 2023). This sequence demonstrates how a meteorological anomaly becomes a fiscal and monetary headache.

### 3.3 *The Silent Killer: Heatwaves and Labor Productivity*

While floods and droughts garner headlines due to their visible destruction, the BN framework also incorporates Heatwaves and Heat Stress as critical variables. The transmission here is more insidious, operating through the degradation of human capital.

#### Labor Productivity

Research indicates that Indonesia's outdoor workforce—particularly in Construction and Agriculture—is severely impacted by rising wet-bulb temperatures. Heat stress reduces physical work capacity, leading to "absenteeism" (workers not showing up) and "presenteeism" (workers present but working at reduced capacity).

#### Economic Drag

This loss of labor productivity acts as a drag on Output. Unlike a flood which destroys physical capital (stock), heat stress destroys productive capacity (flow). OECD studies suggests that heat stress leads to substantial productivity losses, particularly in less productive and smaller firms which dominate Indonesia's informal sector (OECD, 2024). In the BN model, this flows into reduced sector outputs and ultimately dampens GDP growth. Furthermore, the health impacts—such as the rising incidence of heat stroke and vector-borne diseases like dengue fever, which spreads faster in warmer temperatures—increase Healthcare Costs, placing further pressure on household incomes and state budgets.

## *3.4 Summary of Physical Risk Findings*

The empirical analysis of physical risks using the BN model leads to a sobering conclusion: Physical risks in Indonesia are "fat-tailed." They are prone to generating high-impact acute events. Sensitivity Analysis: Tornado diagrams derived from the model reveal that Underwriting Risk, Operational Risk, and Market Risk are the most critical nodes influencing GDP outcomes under physical stress. State Change: When physical risks are high, the probability of the economy shifting into a "High Change" (severe GDP contraction) state increases significantly. The economy can shift directly from a low-risk state to a high-risk state without a buffer, reflecting the destructive power of acute disasters.

## *3.5 Empirical Analysis: Transition Risk Transmission*

A similar Bayesian Network analysis was conducted for transition risks. Here, the parent nodes are not weather events, but key transition policy levers: Carbon Tax, Renewable Energy Investment, Fossil Fuel Subsidy Redirection, Adoption of Electric Vehicles (EV), and Coal Phase-out (Fig. 8.3).

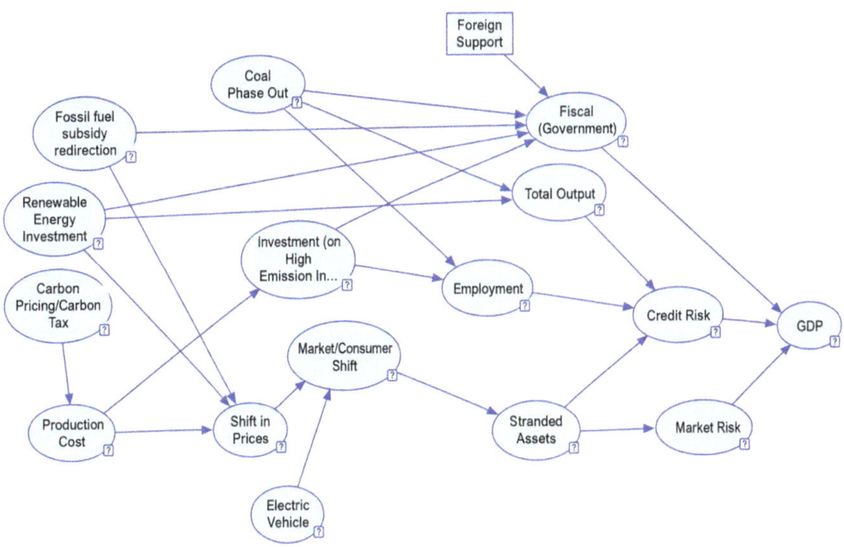


**Fig. 8.3** Bayesian Network transmission of transition risks

This network maps the flow from policy decisions to economic impacts [Production Costs, Investment in High Emission Industries] and finally to financial risks and GDP. It highlights the intricate trade-offs between greening the economy and maintaining industrial stability. These policies influence production costs, investment flows, and consumer behavior, ultimately flowing into credit and market risks. A key finding is that unlike the acute shocks of physical risk, transition risks tend to manifest as a **moderate but persistent drag** on the economy if not managed well—a "disorderly transition".

## *3.6 The Coal Phase-Out: Stranded Assets and Regional Disruption*

The most sensitive nerve in Indonesia's transition network is the Coal Phase-out. Indonesia is the world's largest exporter of thermal coal, and the sector is a massive contributor to GDP, export revenue, and regional employment. Rishanty et al. (2022) argues that Indonesia's low deployment of renewable energy is linked to the financial viability of state-owned enterprises, constraints in human and capital resources, subsidy policies, geographic conditions, and the structural characteristics of the energy sector.

### Stranded Assets

The BN model highlights Stranded Assets as a powerful driver pushing the economy into a high-risk state. This is not hypothetical. The Just Energy Transition Partnership (JETP) has struggled with the early retirement of the Cirebon-1 coal-fired power plant. Despite international pledges, valuations, financial mechanisms, and the fear of asset write-downs have delayed the process. Authorities argue that shutting down younger, supercritical plants like Cirebon-1 is technically and financially irrational compared to older plants, illustrating the immense friction in the system.

### Credit Risk

Indonesian banks have significant exposure to the coal sector. A rapid phase-out threatens to turn these loan books toxic. If global demand for coal collapses (due to transition in China and India) or if domestic regulations force closures without compensation, banks face a wave of defaults. Research indicates that banks continuing to finance coal risk undermining national climate goals and exposing themselves to stranded assets as the energy mix shifts.

#### Regional Inequality

The "stylized facts" of Indonesia show that coal wealth is concentrated in provinces like East Kalimantan and South Sumatra (Ludia et al., 2023). A decline in this sector transmits a shock to regional GDPs that is far more severe than the national average. Local economies dependent on mining royalties and worker consumption would face a recession. Without a "Just Transition" framework that provides retraining and economic diversification, this could lead to social unrest and deepening regional inequality (Bößner et al., 2023).

### *3.7 The Nickel Paradox: Down Streaming and EV Adoption*

Indonesia's strategy to mitigate the loss of coal is to pivot to **Nickel** and **Electric Vehicles (EVs)**. The government has banned nickel ore exports to force downstream processing, aiming to capture the value chain of the green transition (Giwangkara, 2025).

#### Market and Credit Risk

While this strategy attracts investment (e.g., from Hyundai, Wuling, BYD) (International Institute for Sustainable Development, 2024), it introduces new risks. The nickel industry is energy-intensive and currently reliant on captive coal power plants. This creates a "carbon lock-in" risk. If global markets (like the EU or US) penalize "dirty nickel" via mechanisms like the Carbon Border Adjustment Mechanism (CBAM), these investments could themselves become stranded assets (Brookings Institution, 2022).

#### Fiscal Policy Impact

To spur EV adoption, the government has introduced aggressive fiscal incentives, such as VAT reductions (from 11% to 1%) and import duty exemptions for manufacturers committed to local production. This has successfully boosted sales—EV sales hit record highs in 2024, rising 151% year-on-year. However, this impacts the Fiscal Space. The trade-off is between foregone tax revenue today and potential industrial dominance tomorrow. The BN model captures this tension, showing how Fiscal Policy adjustments influence the broader economy.

## 3.8 Carbon Pricing: The Hesitation

The **Carbon Tax** node in the network demonstrates the difficulty of implementation. Indonesia has delayed its carbon tax multiple times (now pushed to 2025/2026) due to fears of economic backlash and inflation (MUC Consulting, 2022, 2023).

**Transmission to Inflation**

The BN model captures the sensitivity of the economy to Production Costs. A carbon tax, if introduced during a period of high energy prices, would pass through directly to consumers, exacerbating inflation and dampening consumption. This fear of a "cost of living crisis" has paralyzed the policy lever, highlighting the dominance of short-term socio-economic stability over long-term climate goals in the current decision-matrix. The government has opted for a cap-and-trade system (ETS) for power plants first, delaying the tax to avoid shocking the broader industrial base.

## 3.9 Summary of Transition Risk Findings

The empirical results for transition risk suggest a different pathology than physical risk. Sensitivity Analysis: Tornado diagrams show that Fiscal Change, Market Risk, and Credit Risk are the most influential variables driving GDP outcomes. State Change: When transition risks are high (a disorderly transition), the probability of a *moderate* GDP change increases. Unlike physical risks which cause crashes, transition risks tend to squeeze the economy—raising costs, tightening credit, and stranding assets over time. The economy can shift states more flexibly, suggesting that policy interventions (like phased implementation) can mitigate the worst outcomes.

## 3.10 Simulating Climate Futures: A Scenario-Based Stress Test

The power of the Bayesian Network lies in its ability to simulate futures. By setting the probabilities of the parent risk nodes, the model provides a "probabilistic stress test" for the Indonesian economy, allowing us to see how different futures might unfold.

### *3.11 Physical Risk Scenarios: The Shock*

When primary physical risk events (floods, droughts, sea-level rise) are set to a High State in the model: The probability of a Low GDP Change (business as usual) decreases significantly (to 37%) and the probability of a High GDP Change (severe contraction) increases to 29%.

**Interpretation**

This suggests a binary fragility. If physical defenses are breached—for example, if the Jakarta seawall fails during a king tide, or if a massive El Niño wipes out the rice harvest across Java—the economy does not just slow down; it suffers a shock (Ludher & Teng, 2023). The transmission is direct, destructive, and difficult to dampen once initiated. The loss of capital stock (factories, roads, crops) leads to an immediate contraction in output.

### *3.12 Transition Risk Scenarios: The Drag*

When transition risks (disorderly policy implementation, rapid coal phase-out, high carbon taxes) are set to a High State: The probability of a Moderate GDP Change increases (from 37% to 39%) and the probability of a High Change increases (from 19% to 23%).

**Interpretation**

Transition risks are more flexible but persistent. The economy can shift between low, moderate, and high change states depending on the "orderliness" of the policy. A disorderly transition (e.g., abrupt carbon taxes without revenue recycling, or a sudden ban on coal exports) creates a structural drag on growth. It raises the cost of doing business and creates uncertainty, but it does not necessarily destroy physical capital overnight. This indicates that while the risk is high, it is more manageable through policy calibration than physical risk.

## 4 Discussion

The convergence of these empirical findings validates the central thesis of this report: a monolithic approach to climate risk management is destined to fail in Indonesia. The "One Size Fits All" global models miss the specific texture of the archipelago's vulnerabilities.

## 4.1 Asymmetric Risk Profiles

The analysis demonstrates that physical and transition risks in Indonesia have asymmetric impact distributions.

- Physical Risk = Tail Risk (Acute Stressor): It is characterized by low-probability but high-impact events (typhoons, massive floods, 100-year droughts). Management requires a focus on Operational and Underwriting resilience—building sea walls, improving insurance penetration, and hardening infrastructure against extremes.
- Transition Risk = Structural Risk (Chronic Stressor): It is characterized by high-probability, moderate-impact shifts (rising carbon prices, shifting energy mix). Management requires a focus on Fiscal and Market resilience—managing the coal phase-out, retraining workers in Kalimantan, and creating liquidity for green investments to prevent credit crunches.

## 4.2 The Regional Dimension

Indonesia is not a single economy; it is a collection of island economies. A policy that fits Java (focused on services and manufacturing) may devastate Kalimantan (focused on coal) or Bali (focused on tourism and dependent on nature).

- East Kalimantan Case Study: A rapid coal phase-out is an existential threat to this province's GDP. A "national" transition plan that does not account for this specific regional reliance will lead to localized economic depressions. The "Just Transition" must be regionally targeted, using fiscal transfers to support the diversification of these specific coal-dependent economies.
- Coastal Cities: Policies for adaptation must prioritize the north coast of Java (Pantura), where the intersection of land subsidence and sea-level rise creates a "hyper-risk" zone does not present in other parts of the country. The economic loss potential in Semarang and Jakarta is of a different magnitude than in inland cities, requiring distinct infrastructure investment strategies.

## 4.3 Policy Implications for Sustainable Finance

To navigate this complex landscape, Indonesian authorities must move beyond generic NGFS scenarios and adopt the bespoke insights generated by frameworks like the Bayesian Network.

1. Targeted Dashboards:

Authorities (OJK, Bank Indonesia) should develop targeted risk dashboards that differ by risk type.

- For **Physical Threats**, the focus must be on **underwriting and operational risk** indicators in vulnerable zones (e.g., credit exposure to Semarang's industrial estates, insurance coverage ratios in flood zones World Bank (2023)).
- For **Transition Threats**, the focus must be on **fiscal and market risk** indicators in high-carbon sectors (e.g., Non-Performing Loan (NPL) ratios in coal mining, collateral value of fossil fuel assets).

2. Gradual vs. Shock Therapy:

The BN results suggest that transition policies like carbon pricing and coal phase-outs should be implemented gradually to mitigate negative impacts on GDP and employment. A "shock therapy" approach increases the likelihood of the economy shifting into a high-loss state. However, "gradual" does not mean "delayed." It means clear, long-term signaling that allows markets to adjust without panicking.

3. Data Sovereignty and Granularity:

There is an urgent need to establish a comprehensive national dataset. The reliance on "hypothetical judgments" in some parts of the BN model highlights the data gap. Indonesia needs granular, localized data on flood frequency, asset locations, and sectoral carbon footprints to refine these models. The protection gap in insurance is partly a data problem; better risk mapping allows for better pricing and product development.

## *4.4 The Role of the Financial Sector*

The financial sector serves as the nervous system for this transition.

- Banks: Must integrate these bespoke scenarios into their stress testing. They need to assess not just the carbon footprint of a borrower, but the *location* of their collateral relative to flood maps (Market Risk) and the *resilience* of their supply chains to heat stress (Operational Risk). The "dirty nickel" issue highlights that banks must also look at the *lifecycle emissions* of their green investments to avoid future transition risks.
- Insurers: The protection gap is a systemic risk. Developing products that transfer climate risk away from the state and households is critical. This involves innovative pricing that incentivizes adaptation (e.g., lower premiums for factories with flood defenses) and parametric insurance for agriculture to handle El Niño shocks.

## 5 Conclusion

This research report has confronted the challenge of assessing climate-related financial risk in Indonesia by developing a novel, country-specific stress-testing framework using Bayesian Networks. The analysis maps the distinct transmission channels for physical and transition risks and provides quantitative evidence that these two risk categories have profoundly different behaviors in the Indonesian context.

High physical risk scenarios are shown to be "acute stressors," likely to trigger sharp, high-impact GDP contractions through the destruction of capital and productivity shocks. Conversely, a disorderly transition acts as a "chronic stressor," creating a moderate but persistent drag on growth through stranded assets and fiscal tightening.

The central conclusion—"No One Size Fits All"—is an evidence-based rationale for a dual-track policy approach. Indonesia cannot simply import climate risk models from Europe or North America. It requires a differentiated toolkit: one that hardens the archipelago against the rising sea while carefully managing the engineered decline of the coal economy.

Ultimately, the resilience of Indonesia's financial system depends on its ability to see these risks clearly—not as generic global trends, but as specific, local realities that demand bespoke, data-driven, and socially just responses.

## References

Argus Media. (2022). Indonesia delays carbon tax scheme again on global risk. https://www.argusmedia.com/en/news-and-insights/latest-market-news/2345415-indonesia-delays-carbon-tax-scheme-again-on-global-risk

Arifin, B. (2023). Navigating the challenge of the "2024 rice economy". Observer ID. https://observerid.com/navigating-the-challenge-of-the-2024-rice-economy/

Barends, J. (2024). Maluku farmers sweat El Niño drought as Indonesia rice prices surge. Mongabay. https://news.mongabay.com/2024/01/maluku-farmers-sweat-el-nino-drought-as-indonesia-rice-prices-surge/

Bößner, S., Fauzi, D., & Rimal, P. (2023). A just coal transition in Indonesia: Actors, framings and future directions (SEI Report No. SEI2023-051). Stockholm Environment Institute. https://www.sei.org/wp-content/uploads/2023/10/sei2023-051-coal-indonesia.pdf

Brookings Institution. (2022). Indonesia's electric vehicle batteries dream has a dirty nickel problem. https://www.brookings.edu/articles/indonesias-electric-vehicle-batteries-dream-has-a-dirty-nickel-problem/

Business & Human Rights Resource Centre. (2024). Indonesia: Workers' homes and vehicles damaged in flood that closed factory. https://www.business-humanrights.org/en/latest-news/indonesia-workers-homes-and-vehicles-damaged-in-flood-that-closed-factory/

Climate Action Tracker. (2025). Indonesia: Policies and action. https://climateactiontracker.org/countries/indonesia/

CMCC. (2021). G20 climate risk atlas: Impacts, policy, economics – Indonesia. CMCC Foundation/G20 Climate Risks. https://www.g20climaterisks.org/indonesia/

Dwibaskoro, A. (2025). Flood impact on property market affects buyers in Indonesia. Seven Stones Indonesia. https://realestate.sevenstonesindonesia.com/flood-impact-on-property-market-affects-buyers-in-indonesia/

EcoShape. (2017). Economic assessment of subsidence in Semarang and Demak, Indonesia. https://www.ecoshape.org/app/uploads/sites/2/2017/08/Economic-assessment-of-subsidence-in-Semarang-and-Demak-Indonesia.pdf

Giwangkara, J. E. (2025). What's next for Indonesia's battery ambitions? Key insights from Climateworks' latest analysis. Climateworks Centre. https://www.climateworkscentre.org/news/whats-next-for-indonesias-battery-ambitions-key-insights-from-climateworks-latest-analysis/

Hamdhi, A. (2025). Mining remains Indonesia's economic backbone amid global uncertainty. Jakarta Globe. https://jakartaglobe.id/business/mining-remains-indonesias-economic-backbone-amid-global-uncertainty

International Institute for Sustainable Development. (2024). Indonesian electric vehicle boom: Temporary trend or long-term vision? https://www.iisd.org/articles/deep-dive/indonesian-electric-vehicle-boom-temporary-trend-or-long-term-vision

Ludia, F., Fermita, B. S., Putri, D. H., & Rahmawati, D. (2023). The impact of coal mining on the socio-economic conditions of the community in Sangatta, East Kutai Regency. Progress in Social Development, 6(2). https://doi.org/10.30872/psd.v6i2.168

Ludher, E. K., & Teng, P. (2023). Rice production and food security in Southeast Asia under threat from El Niño (ISEAS Perspective 2023/53). ISEAS–Yusof Ishak Institute. https://www.iseas.edu.sg/articles-commentaries/iseas-perspective/2023-53-rice-production-and-food-security-in-southeast-asia-under-threat-from-el-nino-by-elyssa-ludher-and-paul-teng/

MUC Consulting. (2022). Once more delayed, government decides to implement the carbon tax in 2025. https://muc.co.id/en/article/once-more-delayed-government-decides-to-implement-the-carbon-tax-in-2025

MUC Consulting. (2023). Carbon tax awaits until 2026. https://muc.co.id/en/article/carbon-exchange-has-already-been-launched-carbon-tax-awaits-until-2026

NGFS. (2022). https://www.ngfs.net/sites/default/files/medias/documents/ngfs_climate_scenarios_for_central_banks_and_supervisors_.pdf.pdf

OECD. (2024). The heat is on: Heat stress and productivity. OECD Publishing. https://www.oecd.org/en/publications/the-heat-is-on-heat-stress-productivity-and-adaptation-among-firms_19d94638-en.html

Reuters. (2025). Indonesia unlikely to move forward with Cirebon-1 early retirement. https://www.reuters.com/business/energy/indonesia-backpedals-retiring-cirebon-coal-power-plant-early-2025-12-05/

Rishanty, A., Anugrah, D. F., & Rahmawati, D. (2023). Coal phase-out: Socioeconomic impact in achieving just energy transition in Indonesia (WP/04/2023). Bank Indonesia. https://ideas.repec.org/p/idn/wpaper/wp042023.html

Rishanty, A., Sambodo, M. T., Anugrah, D. F., & Wicaksono, R. P. (2022). Energy transition risks: Prospect and challenges at ASEAN plus three countries. Bank Indonesia. https://ideas.repec.org/p/idn/wpaper/wp082022.html

Rusmansar, Y. F., & Tohir, M. (2025). The impact of floods on logistics efficiency: A case study of goods delivery via railway in Semarang City. Siber Journal of Transportation and Logistics, 2(2), 69–74. https://doi.org/10.38035/sjtl.v2i2.392

United States Department of Agriculture. (2023). El Niño conditions compel Indonesia to import additional 2 MMT of rice (GAIN Report ID2023-0020). USDA Foreign Agricultural Service. https://usda-indonesia.org/el-nino-conditions-compel-indonesia-to-import-additional-2-mmt-of-rice/

Verisk. (2025). $152 billion and rising: New report shows insurance industry facing growing average annual losses from natural catastrophes. https://www.verisk.com/company/newsroom/152-billion-and-rising-new-report-shows-insurance-industry-facing-growing-average-annual-losses-from-natural-catastrophes/

World Bank. (2023). Indonesia insurance sector assessment (Financial Sector Assessment Program: Technical note). World Bank Group. https://documents.worldbank.org/

# Chapter 9
# Climate Risk Transmission and Stress Test

**Irman Robinson, Jati Waluyo, Arnita Rishanty, and Ramdani**

**Abstract** This study analyzes how climate risks impact Indonesia's economy. It finds that early climate action, like carbon pricing, boosts growth, while delaying it significantly hurts GDP. Although the financial system remains strong, banks face rising risks from lending to polluting sectors like coal. Additionally, physical hazards like floods threaten stability. The findings highlight that immediate, clear policies are essential to protect the economy and manage the shift to green energy.

**Keywords** Climate risk · Climate risk transmission · Climate stress test

## 1 Introduction

Global society has acknowledged climate risk as a nascent issue requiring a strong global concerted initiative. Several global agreements have been established to mitigate and control climate risk; the main challenge in addressing climate risk is comprehending its transmission on the economy and financial system. Network for Greening the Financial System (2024) divides climate risk into transition risk and physical risk to differentiate its transmission mechanism. On one hand, transition risk is triggered by the effort to transcend the economic structure from fossil fuel-based to renewable energy-based by introducing a specific policy measure, such as a carbon tax, which is projected to impact businesses that heavily depend on fossil fuels through a sharp decline in profitability due to a slump in demand. On the other hand, physical risk affect the economy in two ways through chronic impact and acute impact, chronic impact is gradual deterioration of climate condition particularly from increased temperatures and sea levels accretion which may affect economy productivity, meanwhile acute impact is event-based phenomenon such as weather event that inflict staggering cost for the economy through significant damages to property and reduction of agriculture yields.

I. Robinson (✉) · J. Waluyo · A. Rishanty (✉) · Ramdani
Bank Indonesia, Jakarta, Indonesia
e-mail: irman_r@bi.go.id; j_waluyo@bi.go.id; Arnita_rishanty@bi.go.id; ramdani@bi.go.id



S. M. Juhro et al. (eds.), *Sustainable Economy: The Indonesian Pathways*,
https://doi.org/10.1007/978-981-92-1215-6_9

Regarding transmission characteristics, transition risk propagates through the chain of economic processes. For instance, introducing a carbon tax leads to soaring production costs and weakens demand for fossil-based products. This economic shift into a greener economy could significantly impact "brown industries" as global preferences shift (Rishanty et al., 2021, 2023a, b). Conversely, transition policy is expected to have minimal impact on the low-emissions industry due to its low carbon exposure. Therefore, transition risk transmits heterogeneous impact across industries. This complex transmission requires careful scrutiny to measure the precise and accurate economic impact, as each industry could respond differently to transition policies. Industries that already focus on green energy are expected to reap advantages during the transition process as opposed to brown industries that are expected to incur significant financial losses (Battiston et al., 2017). To smooth the transition pathway, the transition policy should be implemented early and gradually, fostering the industry's transition process, including the replacement of old technology with new technology and the substitution of fossil-fuel-based primary inputs with renewable energy inputs. Those transition processes require considerable investment to spur structural economic shifting, especially by promoting transition finance (Zhang et al., 2023). The ultimate objective of the transition is to achieve a just transition guided by just transition principles and just transition targets (Juhro et al., 2025).

Compared to transition risk, physical risk typically has direct transmission and a homogenous impact across the economy through significant damage to capital, as well as reducing economic operationality and productivity. For instance, the Ashizawa et al. (2022) exercised physical risk by focusing on risks such as damage to assets and collateral due to floods. The main challenges in implementing physical risk are the lack of natural disaster data and the difficulty of identifying the regional impact of physical risk, especially for archipelago countries like Indonesia.

Despite having different transmission mechanisms between transition and physical risks, both risks can affect macroeconomic conditions through plummeted productivity, crumbled supply chain, and capital depreciation. Deterioration in macroeconomic conditions affects financial system risks, including credit risk (higher probability of default), market risk (changes in asset values), and liquidity risk (increased cost of funds). Given these potential severe impacts, conducting a climate risk stress test is important to gauge the impact of climate shocks stemming from transition risks and physical risks. Central banks and regulators periodically conduct climate risk stress tests to assess the resilience of the financial systems. Regarding design, climate stress tests consist of three components: scenario, model, and outcome (Acharya et al., 2023).

This research aims to design climate risk transmission, both in the case of transition risk and physical risk, by utilizing publicly used climate scenarios from the NGFS phase V. In order to add country-specific details, it is important to refine the NGFS scenarios to reflect Indonesia's stylized facts better. This process also aligns with a survey conducted by the NGFS, which found that more than half of the 36 financial authorities modified the NGFS scenarios. In modelling transition risk,

Dynamic-Recursive Computable General Equilibrium is used to examine sectoral responses to the impact of carbon tax and to assess the impact on the financial system's resilience. In addition to enriching transition risk analysis from a bottom-up perspective, this research deploys the TRISK framework to evaluate the impact of carbon tax on the banking credit portfolios of high-emitting and energy-producing sectors in Indonesia. Furthermore, in modelling physical risk, the Bayesian Network method captures transmission of climate risks to macroeconomic and financial variables by setting an ad hoc network structure and hypothetical judgments as prior information.

## 2 Literature Review

### *2.1 Climate Scenarios*

Scenarios consist of hypothetical assumptions describing plausible futures and the development path leading to that outcome. According to the NGFS Phase V Scenario (NGFS, 2024), climate scenarios are constructed according to the intertwining of transition and physical risk combinations. High transition risk pertains to a disorderly condition where the introduction of transition policy measures is delayed. In contrast, low transition risk assumes transition policy measures are instigated early and become gradually more stringent. In the context of physical risk, high physical risk implies higher frequency and intensity of natural disasters, followed by rising surface temperature. Due to the transition effort, low physical risk is associated with a lower probability of disaster occurrence. In total, there are seven available scenarios in NGFS Phase V as follows:

*Disorderly Scenario*

a. Delayed Transition assumes no additional climate policies are implemented until 2030. Strong policies are needed to limit warnings to below 2 °C. Negative emissions are limited.

*Orderly Scenario*

b. Net Zero 2050, limit global warming to 1.5 °C through stringent climate policies and innovation, reaching global net zero $CO_2$ emissions around 2050.
c. Below 2 °C, gradually increases the stringency of climate policies, giving a 67% chance of limiting global warming to below 2 °C.
d. Low Demand assumes that significant behavioural changes—reducing energy demand—in addition to (shadow) carbon price and technology-induced effort, would mitigate pressure on the economy to reach global net zero $CO_2$ emissions around 2050.

*Too-Little-too-Late*

e. Fragmented World assumes a delayed and divergent climate policy response among countries globally, leading to high physical and transition risk.

   *Hot House World*

f. Nationally Determined Contributions (NDCs) include all pledges, targets, even if not yet backed up by implemented effective policies.
g. Current Policies assumes that only current implemented policies are preserved, leading to high physical risks.

## 2.2 Climate Risk Stress Testing

Climate Risk Stress Testing is a technique that measures the vulnerability of a portfolio, a financial institution, or an entire financial system to adverse climate-related hazards and scenarios (Reinders et al., 2025). It connects the impact of physical risk and transition risk to the financial system's resilience through multiple channels. Conceptual model in designing Climate Risk Stress Test resembles standard financial system stress test model which consist of at least four elements: (climate) shock scenarios, a model to translate (climate) shock to macroeconomic variables, a model to translate macroeconomic variables to financial sector variables, and a method to assess financial institutions' balance sheet such as solvency ratio (Borio et al., 2014). As mentioned earlier, climate shock scenarios encompass both physical risk and transition risk. The NGFS provides a comprehensive set of climate shock scenarios, comprising transition pathway variables, physical risk variables, and macro-financial impacts (NGFS, 2024).

## 2.3 Source of Shocks

In designing transition risk scenarios, the carbon tax is the most widely used shock to induce the transition pathway (Guth et al., 2021; Reinders et al., 2023; Desnos et al., 2023). Three types of carbon taxes can be levied on different economic activities: intermediate input tax, production tax, and consumption tax (Abe et al., 2023; Matsumura et al., 2024). Intermediate input tax is aimed at reducing dependency on fossil-fuel energy and to induce shifting into renewable energy input, as fossil-fuel energy is priced higher. Furthermore, a consumption tax is imposed on the household's consumption activities at the final consumption stage. For example, the tax will be imposed when a household purchases gasoline. Shock in physical risk is defined as deterioration of climate conditions and sudden economic damages such as severe changes in weather patterns, sea-level rise, or climate-related natural disasters (e.g., typhoons, floods, and droughts).

## 2.4 Computable General Equilibrium (CGE) Model

Computable General Equilibrium (CGE) Model enables interaction between economic agents in an equilibrium setting. The model focuses on policy changes' structural impact, such as subsidies and carbon taxation (Burns et al., 2018; Malahayati & Masui, 2021). The CGE model provides richer sectoral analysis than the macroeconometrics model since it incorporates the Social Accounting Matrix (SAM) that records all transactions and transfers between different production activities, factors of production, and institutions within the economy and with respect to the rest of the world. Another benefit of using the CGE model is the data requirement and the tractable estimation parameters method. Estimating a CGE model entails a calibration method and hypothetical parameter values based on structural interpretation. For instance, the Constant Elasticity of Substitution (CES) production function consists of three parameters to estimate: total productivity factor, substitution parameter, and share parameter. It is conventional to assume a substitution parameter value to a specific number representing the degree of substitutability between inputs, as the remaining parameter can be estimated by a calibration method using information contained in SAM.

Shock specification in the CGE Model is accommodated in the model closure notion, which contains a set of exogenous variables in the CGE model setting. Since the CGE model is a deterministic model forming a nonlinear system of equations, setting up model closure is required to ensure that structural parameters can be estimated uniquely (Babatunde et al., 2017). The Standard CGE Model typically consists of several main blocks as follows:

(i) Production Block

The production function, in the general case, is based on nested functions to minimize production cost given a particular production constraint. For instance, the production function in an activity can be divided into a value-added bundle and an intermediate use bundle through the connection of the CES function. The value-added bundle can be modelled as a bundle of labor and capital. Similarly, an intermediate use bundle can be modelled as a bundle of commodities with CES aggregation. The total output is then aggregated using the CES aggregation between the value-added and intermediate use bundle. In the context of climate modelling, the production nest can be detailed until energy and non-energy bundles are separated to capture the energy transition mechanism, given a set of climate shocks.

(ii) Demand Block

Household demand is derived by solving the utility maximization problem given the budget constraint. The solution captures household consumption behavior, especially in spending allocation, given a set of product prices. Since price is an endogenous variable in the CGE model, incorporating a particular shock affects price, thereby adjusting household spending allocation.

(iii) Trade Block

A trade block typically consists of import demand and export supply. Given the aggregation function, import demand decomposes the demand for a product between domestic and imported goods. A common practice in modelling import demand is assuming an economic agent as an Armington agent with the same preference function for domestic and imported goods. Analogous to import demand, export supply uses a Constant Elasticity of Transformation (CET) structure where domestic output is allocated between the domestic market and the export market.

## 2.5 TRISK Framework

TRISK is an asset-level, bottom-up, and microeconomic climate transition risk stress test methodology designed to estimate potential changes in companies' market valuation (market risk), probability of default, and banks' expected loss (credit risk) across different scenarios. Utilizing the Paris Agreement Capital Transition Assessment (PACTA) alignment approach, TRISK examines the impact of multiple climate scenarios on the company level and calculates the financial risk associated with a delayed and sudden transition. The TRISK framework can be described through three main layers: scenarios, calculation of the real economic impact, and estimation of the impact on financial institutions. Each of these layers is connected through a set of transmission channels, which propagate the climate-adjusted economic impact to the asset value of firms and subsequently translates the impacts into the financial market.

## 2.6 Bayesian Network

Bayesian Network is widely used for risk management and decision-making. The Bayesian Network allows flexible representation of a complex transmission of climate risks to financial risks. Bayesian Networks (BNs) are networks of directed acyclic graphs consisting of 3 components: Nodes, Arrows, and Conditional Probability Tables (CPTs). Since BNs are directed graphs, an arc between two nodes has a specific direction, representing a causal relationship. The application of BNs enables the visual representation of the qualitative relationship between variables, thus capturing interactions between variables and generating predictions based on modifications to the model.

Given an illustrative example below, Heatwaves and Drought variables serve as parent nodes for the Forest Fires variable, where the Forest Fires variable acts as the parent node of the Property Damage variables. In this structure, the probability of Forest Fires is influenced by the interaction between the probabilities of *Heatwaves* and *Drought* according to Bayes' Law. Each node of BN contains a conditional probability table (CPT) that needs to be filled with prior probability. Supposed variables in BNs have two states (High and Low), thus the probability of High *Forest Fire* is calculated by applying the Law of Total Probability (Fig. 9.1).

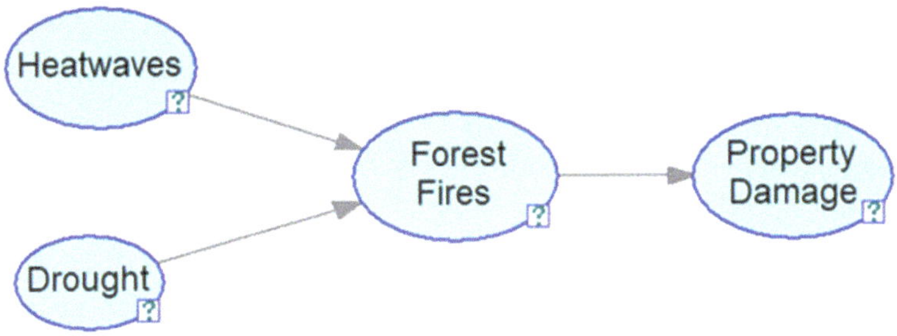


**Fig. 9.1** Bayesian network example

### *2.7 Climate Risk Transmission Channels to the Financial System*

Both transition risk and physical risk affect financial institutions (e.g., banks) through multiple channels, including credit risk, market risk, and liquidity risk. Materialization of physical risk and transition risk leads to lower property and corporate asset values, lower corporate profits, lower household wealth, and lower growth and productivity (Grippa et al., 2019; Bolton et al., 2020). These impacts could increase credit risk through declined residential and corporate repayment capacity, heightened market risk as increased losses in equities, bonds, and commodities, and subsequently trigger liquidity risk through waned ability to refinance themselves due to the impact of rising cost of funds. Numerous literatures aim to capture those impacts through various modelling approaches, such as macro-financial (satellite) risk models (Burns et al., 2021; Vermeulen et al., 2018; Allen et al., 2020; Dunz et al., 2021; Grippa & Mann, 2020), structural credit risk models (Reinders et al., 2023), non-structural empirical models (Jung et al., 2021), and financial impact models (Battiston et al., 2017; Vermeulen et al., 2018; Reinders et al., 2021).

## 3 Data and Methodology

### *3.1 Indonesia's Industrial Emission Data*

In 2022, Indonesia's sectors recorded GHG emissions of 887.232 Gg $CO_2$ e, an increase compared to 2021 of 767.707 Gg $CO_2$ e. Two major emission contributors are the industry sector and the electricity sector, contributing to around 70% of total emissions. In contrast, the mining sector emitted GHG emissions of 29.351 $CO_2$ e or only 3.30% of total emissions. High emissions released in the industry sector and the electricity sector signify high usage of fossil-based energy to fuel the production process. Based on data from the Central Bureau of Statistics, the industry sector and the electricity sector consumed around 5.343 Peta Joules of energy, or around 40% of total industry energy consumption, with coal and oil making up the highest energy consumed. On the energy supply side, the mining sector is the primary sector that meets total energy demand; approximately 85% of total energy demand is met by the mining sector. Those conditions emphasized the role of the mining sector as a primary energy source, posing delicate challenges in the transition pathway, as energy is an indispensable part of the production process. According to these data, the industry sector, the electricity sector, and the mining sector are anticipated to be the most affected by transition policies.

## 3.2 Indonesia's Social Accounting Matrix

The Social Accounting Matrix is a necessary input to estimate the CGE model, which contains complete information on all transactions and transfers between different production activities, factors of production, and institutions, providing insight into the economic structure. This research utilizes the latest Indonesia SAM in 2022 for modelling input with additional adjustments conducted by regrouping the sectors from 17 sectors to 7 sectors, namely Agriculture, Mining, Industry, Electricity, Construction, Trade, and Services. In the expenditure side, consumption accounted for 53.79% of the total economy, followed by investment for around 36.23%. In terms of global trade, Indonesia recorded a trade surplus, with its exports accounting for 23.45% of the total economy, compared to imports of 21.26%. Indonesia's exports are primarily reliant on commodity exports such as coal briquettes and palm oil, consistent with SAM data, which shows that the manufacturing sector and the mining sector exported around 70% of total exports. In the industrial origin side, the manufacturing sector and the services sector contributed to the economy by 19.18% and 25.02% respectively, while high-emission sectors, such as the manufacturing and electricity sectors, accounted for 12.78% and 1.16% respectively.

## 3.3 Carbon Tax Scenarios

This research utilizes the NGFS phase V scenario specific to Indonesia, with a few adjustments to capture Indonesia's stylized facts better, including Indonesia's current development. In examining transition risk, delayed transition and net zero emission scenarios are incorporated to assess the impact of carbon tax implementation. As mentioned in the NGFS phase V scenario, the delayed transition scenario assumes the implementation of the carbon tax being delayed until 2030. This delayed implementation leads to an aggressive policy with the aim of reaching Net Zero by 2050. This aggressive policy tends to impact sectors with high emissions, indicated by rising production costs and a sharp decline in demand. Regarding carbon tax implementation, it is assumed that in the initial year of implementation, the carbon tax is priced at Rp30,000 per tonne $CO_2$e and follows the NGFS carbon tax scenario pathways afterward.

## 3.4 Computable General Equilibrium (CGE) Model to Capture Impact of Carbon Tax

We augment the standard CGE model by adding a carbon tax mechanism in intermediate use and household consumption. An imposing carbon tax in the intermediate market aims to reduce dependency on fossil-based energy input. The CES function serves as an aggregation function to capture the substitutability between inputs and goods. In the primary factors bundle, we assume inelastic substitution between labor and capital, representing a complementary relation between labor and capital in the Indonesian context. Conversely, we assume elastic substitution between goods in a bundle of intermediate use to accommodate shifting in input as a result of implementing the carbon tax. Aggregation between primary factors and intermediate use leads to final production goods that will be allocated to the domestic market and export using the CET function. The total supply of commodities in the economy originates from imports and domestic output after deducting exports. These available commodities are then allocated across household consumption, government consumption, investment, and intermediate use according to the solution of the maximization problem (Fig. 9.2).

The carbon tax is incorporated in the CGE model by taking into account the total emissions released. This study applies the following formula to estimate total emissions for each economic sector

$$Emission_{c,i} = cci_{c,i}\, x\, s_{c,i}\, x\, \alpha_{c,i} x\, INTM_i$$

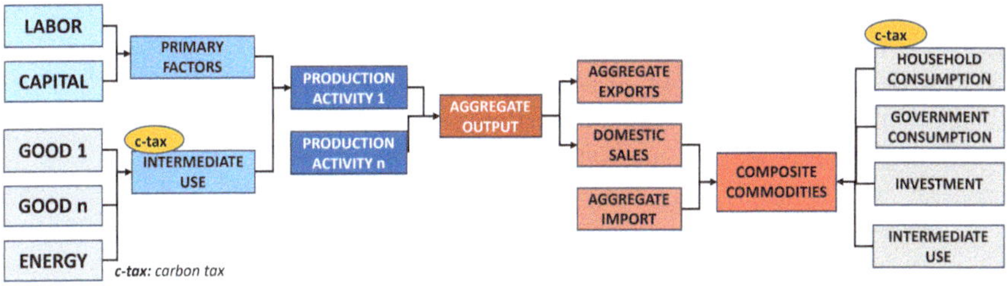


**Fig. 9.2** Computable general equilibrium with carbon tax

where subscript $c$ refers to the commodity that releases emissions and subscript $i$ refers to the economic sector. According to the equation above, the total emissions produced for a commodity in a sector depend on the carbon content intensity ($cci$), the share of fossil-based energy of the total intermediate input ($s$), the share of total intermediate input obtained from SAM ($\alpha$), and the total intermediate input for each sector (INTM). Since the CGE model endogenously computes INTM, the total emission pathway can be derived as the dynamic-recursive CGE model projected forward. In order to ensure the total emission decline as economic capacity grows, $cci$ requires calibration in a downward pattern over time, representing adoption of new technologies, to attain the net-zero emission condition. High-emission sectors will be obliged to incur carbon taxation, further depleting the sector's value added. A similar approach is also applied to generate the household's emission pathway by substituting INTM with the household's consumption.

## 3.5 Macro-financial Model to Connect Macro and Financial Variables

In translating the impact of macro on financial variables, an econometrics-based model connects a set of macroeconomic variables to the sector's non-performing loan ratio through a logit regression. The regression is conducted on a sectoral basis, thus each macroeconomic variable exhibits a heterogeneous effect on the sector's non-performing loan. Macro-financial model comprises several macroeconomic variables as predictors in a model as follows:

$$\ln\left(\frac{npl_t^i}{1-npl_t^i}\right) = \beta_0 + \beta_1 \ln\left(\frac{npl_{t-1}^i}{1-npl_{t-1}^i}\right) + \beta_2 gGDP_{i,t-k_i} + \beta_3 BIRATE_{t-k_i}$$
$$+\beta_4 gEXR_{t-k_i} + \beta_5 gPCOM_{t-k_i}$$

where $gGDP_{i,t-k_i}$ is the year-on-year growth of Gross Domestic Product, $BIRATE_{t-k_i}$ is the policy rate, $gEXR_{t-k_i}$ is the year-on-year growth of the exchange rate, g $PCOM_{t-k_i}$ is the year-on-year growth of the commodity price, and $k_i$ is the optimum predictor lag for each sector. The macro-financial model enables us to generate a projection path of non-performing loans for each sector. In consequence, the bank is required to allocate additional provisions to cover credit losses based on its credit exposure in each sector.

## 3.6 Bayesian Network Analysis

In conducting simulation-based physical risk through BNs, this study collects the Regional GDP consists of 17 sectors for each province in Indonesia, and historical data from various sources to determine prior probabilities of nodes in BNs. For example, historical data of *Sea Level Rise, Drought, Floods, Cyclones, Landslides, and Forest Fires* are collected from the Central Bureau of Statistics. After gathering the required data, the next step is to apply the data to the modelling process below:

a. The construction of the graph of risk transmission, including specifying how risk is transmitted from climate events, is constructed.
b. Scenario selection defined the scope of the scenario in terms of time frame, complexity, and geographic area.
c. Risk analysis conducted based on chosen scenarios and historical data.
d. Policy impact analysis and pathways, analyzing the impact of policies and developing pathways, with a focus on sectors vulnerable to climate risks under extreme but plausible scenarios

The prior probabilities of the variables come from historical data, climate projections, hypothetical judgment, or combinations of both. In order to map physical risks across sectors in the Indonesian economy, three sectors with the largest contributions to provincial GDP over three years were selected. For instance, the three largest sectors in the Special Capital Region of Jakarta cover Trade, Information, and Manufacturing.

## 3.7 TRISK Methodologies

As mentioned before, the TRISK framework consists of three main layers: scenarios, calculation of the real economic impact, and estimation of the impact on financial institutions. Layer one of the TRISK framework translates the climate scenarios data into sector-level decarbonization pathways, which are subsequently translated into technology-level impacts to individual company production capacity. The second layer examines the company's decarbonization pathways with real economic projections on costs, prices, as well as the company's financial risk profile. In this bottom-up approach, the carbon tax is incorporated through the following equation:

$$Net\,\text{Profit}_t = \text{Production Volume}_t \text{ x}\left(\text{Unit Price}_t - \left(\text{Unit Cost}_t + \text{Carbon Tax}_t\right)\right)$$

The net present value (NPV) of a company is represented as a cumulative sum of discounted future net profit. It is used to calculate the equity value change compared to the NPV without a climate shock. In the next step, we calculated expected losses for each economic sector using the multiplication between Probability of Default, Exposure, and LGD as follows:

$$EL_{sector} = PD \;\; x\, Exposure_{company} \; x\, lgd_{company}$$

where $EL_{sector}$ is the expected loss of the sector calculated based on the Merton Structural Credit Risk Model, *PD* is the probability of default under a shock

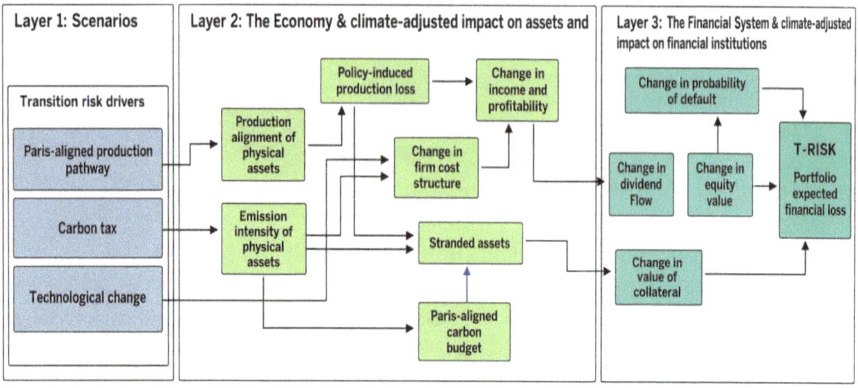


**Fig. 9.3** TRISK methodology

scenario, $Exposure_{company}$ is the loan exposure value of each company, $lgd_{company}$ is the loss given default of the company.

Three types of data are needed to assess financial resilience through the TRISK methodology. The first type of input data is the climate scenario, which provides a projection of a wide set of macroeconomic variables. The climate scenarios used in this study are taken from well-established scenario providers, namely the Network for Greening the Financial System (NGFS MESSAGE and NGFS GCAM), the International Energy Agency (IEA WEO, 2022), and the European Commission's Joint Research Centre (Global Energy and Climate Outlook). The second type of input data includes financial and economic data of individual firms, specific requirements of individual firms, and information on emission intensities and production capacity. The third type of input is the information on corporate loan book exposures, including credit outstanding of covered sectors from the 13 banks with the highest asset value as of December 2022, which was selected for the non-automotive sectors (Fig. 9.3).

This approach comprises six scenarios derived from several scenario providers, namely NGFS, IEA, and the European Commission's Joint Research Centre. These scenarios were selected due to their widespread recognition among policymakers and financial institutions. Each scenario is characterized by distinct assumptions and parameters, encompassing the shock year, start year, geographical coverage, and the carbon price model. By default, the year 2030 is set as the "shock" year. All selected shock scenarios are designed to achieve targets that aim to limit global warming to well below 2 °C.

Regarding the carbon price model, it relies on the projected global carbon prices from NGFS GCAM 5.3+ for Nationally Determined Contribution (NDC) and Net Zero 2050 (NZ2050) scenarios. These scenarios have been tailored to align their implementation within the Indonesian context. In this case, both scenarios have been adjusted to incorporate a carbon price specific to Indonesia. Concerning sector coverage, this study covers lending to high-emitting sectors, which include oil and gas, coal, power generation, and automotive.

# 4 Discussion

## 4.1 Top-Down Transition Risk Result

Impact of implementing carbon tax on GDP differs across two scenarios: net zero emission and delayed transition. In a net-zero emission scenario, where a carbon tax is introduced in 2025 to reach the net-zero emission target by 2050, the GDP growth trajectory is projected to fall below the baseline in the short term, before surpassing the baseline scenario in the long term. This result emphasizes the nature of the transition process toward greener economy, which requires transition effort, especially for sectors with high emissions. However, once new energy sources and technology are adopted, economic growth can be ramped up without accumulating emissions. In the case of a net-zero emission scenario, early and strong commitment to reach the net-zero condition attracts investment inflows to support various green infrastructures and green investment projects, which prop up the development of the renewable energy ecosystem. In the short run, economic growth is projected to fall below the baseline as firms incur financial losses in the initial transition phase due to stranded fossil fuel-based capital and a shift in demand. Several challenges need to be resolved in order to ensure the smooth transition, including financing for infrastructure, large subsidies, geographical challenges, capacity building to support green job opportunities, and excess capacity in fossil power plants (Rishanty et al., 2022a, b).

As investment inflows increase to support the transition, firms begin the sustainable production process by adopting new technologies. This condition aligns with the simulation result that GDP growth in the net zero emission scenario is projected to exceed the baseline after 2035, while in the delayed transition scenario, it is expected to start to outstrip the baseline after 2045 due to the disruptive nature of the delayed policy measure. Although at the end of the period, both GDP growth in the net-zero scenario and the delayed transition outperform the baseline scenario, the economic size in the delayed transition is projected to dip below the baseline scenario by 3%, constituting permanent losses from being delayed in the transition pathway. Conversely, economic size in transition risk is projected to rise above the baseline scenario by 1%, signaling a permanent gain from early implementation of transition policy. Due to the consequences of implementing the transition policy, the economic structure is also projected to morph toward a greener economy, signified by a decline in the mining sector's contribution and a rise in the electricity sector's contribution. The growing contribution of the electricity sector and the shrinking mining sector indicate that the mining sector no longer acts as a central node in the intermediate energy input market. According to Indonesia's blueprint toward net zero emissions (IEA, 2022), the blueprint envisions the electricity sector to serve as the primary energy supplier to support the economic production process, as coal-based fuel is phased out and various forms of renewable

**Table 9.1** GDP growth pathways comparison

| GDP Growth compared to baseline | Net Zero Emission (%) | | Delayed Transition (%) | |
|---|---|---|---|---|
| | With Investment | Without Investment | With Investment | Without Investment |
| The Highest Growth | +0.38 | −0.18 | +0.31 | −0.35 |
| The Lowest Growth | −0.28 | −0.81 | −0.55 | −1.35 |

energy (e.g., geothermal, solar, modern solid bioenergy, wind) emerge as the primary energy source.

From the perspective of sectoral GDP, the mining sector, industry, and electricity sector are foreseen to inflict the brunt of the impact among all other sectors due to their high emissions profile. In the initial transition phase, these economic sectors are compelled to bear a high carbon tax, which significantly erodes the sector's value added. However, in the long run, these economic sectors will be charged only a small amount of carbon tax since the production process has already shifted toward a sustainable way, generating GDP growth that surpasses the baseline scenario. A surge of green investment is necessary for GDP growth in both net-zero emission and delayed transition to surpass the baseline scenario. If investment is absent during the transition process, then GDP growth for both the net-zero emission scenario and the delayed transition scenario will fall below the baseline scenario, as depicted in Table 9.1. The result emphasizes the importance and role of investment in fostering greener production practices as well as strengthening Indonesia export competitiveness through adoption of circular economy as global green standard rise (Rishanty et al., 2022a, b).

Aligning with the GDP growth trajectory, the exchange rate is projected to depreciate compared to the baseline in the delayed transition scenario. Meanwhile, in a net-zero emission scenario, the exchange rate is expected to depreciate in the short run and appreciate in the long run. In the short run, exchange rate depreciation occurs due to the impact of capital outflow as investors seek better risk-return investments. However, once the transition is well-established, capital inflows from investors are expected to surge, leading to exchange rate appreciation over the long run. This result highlights the transition's impact on the current accounts and aligns with findings that the transition may improve or mitigate the ill-effects of oil price shocks on oil-importing countries and the improvement in the current account position (Juhro et al., 2024).

Proceeding to the macro-financial model, GDP growth and exchange rate pathways are deployed to generate a trajectory of non-performing loans for each sector. In line with sectoral GDP output, non-performing loan trajectories for the mining, electricity, and industry sectors witness the highest increase compared to all other sectors due to high exposure in high-emitter sectors. Meanwhile, other sectors exhibit a negligible impact due to low emissions released. At the aggregate level, the resilience of the financial system remains strong, with a non-performing loan ratio staying below 5%.

## 4.2 Bottom-Up Transition Risk Result: Expected Loss and Probability of Default

The coal sector exhibits the highest increase in PD (45.2%), followed by power (41.5%), and oil & gas (0.1%). The change in PD in the oil & gas sector shows a notably low increase since, in this exercise, loan and PD for oil & gas extraction activities are calculated together, due to the loan book data categorization. Most companies in the oil & gas dataset also show that the same companies are involved in both oil and gas extraction. The expected increase in gas extraction as transitional measures might counteract the high increase in PD in the oil sector, resulting in a very low change in oil and gas PD. Given these estimated PDs, we calculate the expected loss from the transition risk shock. The higher the expected loss value of a bank's portfolio, the higher the risk of loss if it is exposed to the climate transition shocks.

Most banks recorded a significant increase in expected loss for all sectors. For all sectors, banks that give loans to the power sector have the highest magnitude of increase in expected loss. The high loan exposure can explain the banks' significant power sector exposure. Meanwhile, banks that give loans to oil and gas companies have the lowest increase in expected loss. This is likely since the oil & gas sector bundles both oil & gas extraction. In contrast, oil extraction is a technology predicted to be at risk of climate transition; gas, in the context of the Indonesian economy, is a technology that the climate scenario project predicts will benefit from climate transition due to its lower emission intensity. Therefore, the positive production shock on gas offsets any drop in the oil technology production.

The significant increase in expected credit loss can be attributed to the change in probability of default (PD). The most substantial increase in PD is observed in banks that provide loans to the power sector in most scenarios, consistent with the expected loss result. Conversely, a slight decrease is observed in the oil & gas sector, particularly in the NGFS GCAM scenario, NGFS GCAM with three main different shock years, and NGFS GCAM with the NDC carbon price model. Furthermore, the expected loss results under the baseline scenario reveal that 4 of 13 banks have the highest expected loss value in the coal, oil & gas, power, and automotive sectors, respectively. Compared to the coal, oil & gas, and power sectors, banks providing loans to companies in the power sector exhibit relatively high expected losses in all scenarios. However, the bank with the highest expected loss varies across scenarios and configurations.

The PD differences exhibit a more diverse range of results when constructing the PD under baseline and shock scenarios. All expected loss values are positive in the WEO and NGFS GCAM scenarios with the NZ20250 carbon model. Moreover, in the NGFS GCAM scenario, specifically in the scenario with shock years and the NDC carbon price model, positive expected loss values are observed for banks involved in loans to the coal and power sector. Conversely, banks extending loans to the oil and gas sector exhibit negative expected loss values.

## 4.3 Bayesian Network Result of Physical Risk

The five primary physical risks selected as ultimate parent nodes—sea level rise, heat waves, droughts, floods, and typhoons—are identified as the most significant climate risks for Indonesia (World Bank, 2021). These risks impact productivity, property damage, and other secondary physical risks, including forest fires, biodiversity loss, landslides, and heat stress. Property damage and productivity losses disrupt business and consumer demand, which leads to inflation, stranded assets, and employment shifts. Meanwhile, forest fires, biodiversity loss, landslides, and heat stress affect health through mortality, declining air quality, and the emergence of new diseases. The impact on health and employment influences fiscal expenditure and income. Changes in revenue, stranded assets, and business disruptions then materialize as credit risk, market risk, underwriting risk, and operational risk. These four financial risks, along with fiscal changes, are collectively transmitted to shift in Gross Domestic Product (GDP).

From the network below, we can create an influence diagram to examine the most influential arc between a parent and a child, noted with the thicker arc indicating more influence. Based on the influence diagram of physical risks below, three of the most influential arcs are between *Business Disruption* and *Operational Risk*, *Property Damage and Market Risk*, and *Forest Fires* and *Air Quality*. In order to assess the sensitivity of each node to GDP, the Tornado diagram enables us to examine the influence of various other variables on each state of GDP. For instance, our result exhibits that an increase in probability of the variable *Underwriting Risk* with the state *High Risk* and Income with the state *LowChangeBAU* causes a decrease in the probability of *GDP = LowChangeBAU* suggesting that a high underwriting risk and a small change in income can decrease the probability of having a low change in GDP and into having a moderate or high change in it. Conversely, the second most influential variable is *Operational Risk* with the state *LowRiskBAU* and *BusinessDisruption* with the state *LowDisruptionBAU*. The increased probability of both of these variables causes the probability of GDP having a low change to also increase. This means that an increase in the probability of having a low operational risk and a low business disruption helps maintain only a small change in GDP (Fig. 9.4).

The BNs are capable of conveying scenario analysis by selecting the state of various variables to be realized. We select two scenarios of cyclones, floods, drought, sea level rise, heatwaves, landslides, heat stress, and forest fires, once in their low state and once in their high state. When events of these physical risks are kept low, we found that the probability of GDP having a low change increase from 40% to 43% and the probability of GDP having a high change decreases from 26% to 24%. When all the physical risks are high, the probability of GDP experiencing a high change increases from 26% to 29%.

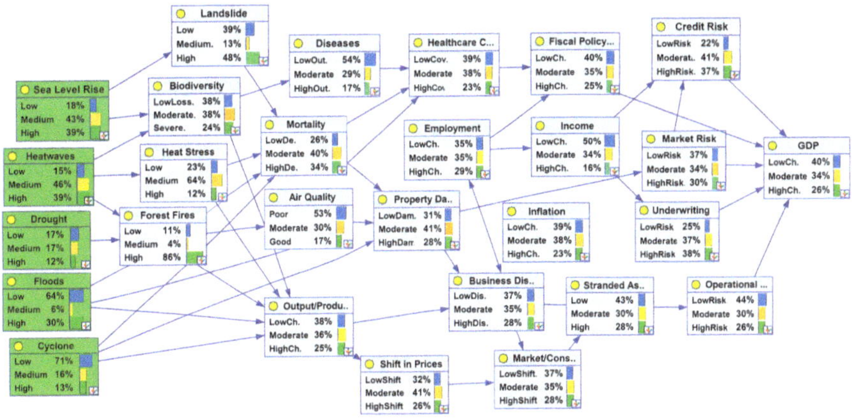


**Fig. 9.4** Physical risks transmission in BNs

## 5 Conclusion

This research explores the implications of macroeconomic and financial instability arising from transition risk (top-down and bottom-up) and physical risk. Key takeaways from these complementary approaches are, transition and physical risks are required to be mitigated early and gradually, followed by upswing in investment inflows to boost economic growth during the transition pathway, ensuring the GDP growth exceeds the baseline scenario. When efforts toward transition falter, heightening the intensity of physical risks is ineluctable and leading to staggering economic costs. Timing and commitment to achieve net zero emissions determine macroeconomic trajectories, which are subsequently translated into a macro-financial model to assess the resilience of the financial system. The delayed implementation of the carbon tax leads to lower GDP growth compared to the baseline scenario, representing permanent GDP losses of around 3% at the end of 2050. Conversely, in a net-zero emission scenario, as a carbon tax is implemented early and followed by a surge of investment inflows, GDP growth is projected to outrun the baseline in the long run after experiencing lower GDP growth in the short run. Adhering to a net-zero emission scenario leads to a permanent GDP gain of around 1% above the baseline scenario. In conclusion, the financial system's resilience is projected to remain strong as the non-performing loans ratio stays below 5% and ample capital adequacy ratio in Indonesia.

From a bottom-up perspective (Rishanty et al., 2023a, b), this study reveals a notable increase in expected losses for most banks' lending to coal, oil & gas, power, and automotive sectors. Notably, banks' lending to the power sector experiences the most significant increase in expected loss, while banks' financing of oil & gas companies exhibits the smallest increase in expected loss. Banks also witness an increase in expected losses in the automotive sector, though the magnitude is not as pronounced as in other sectors. Results based on the average of the Probability of Default (PD) differences suggest that, in most scenarios, banks' lending to the coal sector has the highest PD compared to other sectors associated with the coal phase-out plan. This is particularly relevant as the coal phase-out commitment is more advanced compared to the oil and gas sector, where there is still reliance on natural gas as a viable alternative option. The study signifies the role of banks, central banks, financial supervisors, and the financial sector in facilitating the transition to a low-carbon economy and supporting the sectoral rebalancing process of high-risk sector exposures in banks' portfolios.

In assessing impact of physical risk using Bayesian Network, it is found that physical risk phenomenon—sea level rise, heat waves, droughts, floods, and typhoons—can significantly influence GDP through several interconnected transmission channels with different climate scenarios can affect different economic outcomes with low levels of risks can increase the probability of achieving stable economic condition while high level if risks lead to the opposite. This finding suggests to policymakers that proactive policy measures are essential to achieve net-zero emissions and transition away from a carbon-intensive economy for the long term, mitigating the transition risks and stabilizing the economy in the short term. Moreover, a complete risk assessment when formulating a policy is very important.

From the results, several implications and policy recommendations can be found as developing a climate risk assessment tool appropriate to Indonesia's stylized facts should be prioritized to support more granular and accurate decision-making and resource allocation for sustainable investment and development. The implementation of a carbon tax also needs to be initiated early and gradually, allowing firms particularly those in high-emitting sectors to prepare and adjust their business processes toward a sustainable future. In addition, investment in green infrastructure and projects is crucial to strengthen the development of a sustainable ecosystem by providing firms with the capacity to transition away from fossil fuel-based technologies and inputs. Reinforcing a Paris-aligned macroprudential framework and instruments is also necessary, including enhancing existing macroprudential policy instruments to incentivize financing toward low-carbon emission activities and disincentivize financing toward high-emitting activities. In this regard, Bank Indonesia issued an incentive mechanism linked to the reserve requirement secondary policy in 2023, and similar measures could be applied to disincentivize banks in mitigating harmful transition risks, as well as to limit banks' portfolio concentration in activities and sectors most exposed and vulnerable to climate transition. Finally, macroprudential policies should complement impactful microprudential measures, particularly through the implementation of capital buffers for banks heavily exposed to high-emitting industries.

## References


Abe, N., Kawasumi, Y., Takano, Y., Naka, T., Hirakata, N., Matsumura, K., & Munakata, K. (2023). Top-Down scenario analysis of climate-related financial risks: perspective from time horizon and inter-industry spillovers. *Bank of Japan, BOJ Reports & Research Papers, Tokyo, Japan.*

Acharya, V. V., Berner, R., Engle, R., Jung, H., Stroebel, J., Zeng, X., & Zhao, Y. (2023). Climate stress testing. *Annual Review of Financial Economics, 15*(1), 291–326.

Allen, T., Dees, S., Caicedo Graciano, C. M., Chouard, V., Clerc, L., de Gaye, A., ... & Vernet, L. (2020). *Climate-related scenarios for financial stability assessment: An application to France.*

Ashizawa, T., Furukawa, K., Hashimoto, R., Koide, Y., Naka, T., Nishizaki, K., ... & Suzuki, G. (2022). *Physical risks from climate change faced by Japan's financial institutions: Impact of floods on real economy, land prices, and FIs' financial conditions* (No. 22-E-2). Bank of Japan.

Babatunde, K. A., Begum, R. A., & Said, F. F. (2017). Application of computable general equilibrium (CGE) to climate change mitigation policy: A systematic review. *Renewable and Sustainable Energy Reviews, 78*, 61–71.

Battiston, S., Mandel, A., Monasterolo, I., Schütze, F., & Visentin, G. (2017). A climate stress-test of the financial system. *Nature Climate Change, 7*(4), 283–288.

Borio, C., Drehmann, M., & Tsatsaronis, K. (2014). Stress-testing macro stress testing: Does it live up to expectations?. *Journal of Financial Stability, 12*, 3–15.

Bolton, P., Despres, M., Da Silva, L. A. P., Samama, F., & Svartzman, R. (2020). *The green swan.* BIS Books.

Burns, A., Zebaze, C. D., & Prihardini, D. (2018). Modeling Macroeconomic Impacts and Global externalities. *Energy Subsidy Reform Assessment Framework (ESRAF) Good Practice Note, 7.*

Burns, A., Jooste, C., & Schwerhoff, G. (2021). Climate Modeling for Macroeconomic Policy.

Desnos, B., Le Guenedal, T., Morais, P., & Roncalli, T. (2023). From climate stress testing to climate value-at-risk: A stochastic approach. *Available at SSRN 4497124.*

Dunz, N., Emambakhsh, T., Hennig, T., Kaijser, M., Kouratzoglou, C., & Salleo, C. (2021). ECB's economy-wide climate stress test. ECB Occasional Paper, (2021/281).

IEA. (2022). An Energy Sector Roadmap to Net Zero Emissions in Indonesia. In International Energy Agency Special Report. https://doi.org/10.1787/4a9e9439-en

Grippa, P., & Mann, S. (2020). *Climate-related stress testing: Transition risks in norway.*

Grippa, P., Schmittmann, J., & Suntheim, F. (2019). *Financial risk.* Finance & Development.

Guth, M., Hesse, J., Königswieser, C., Krenn, G., Lipp, C., Neudorfer, B., ... & Weiss, P. (2021). OeNB climate risk stress test–modeling a carbon price shock for the Austrian banking sector. *Financial Stability Report, 42*, 27–45.

Juhro, S. M., Narayan, P. K., Garg, B., & Anugrah, D. F. (2024). Transition to a green economy, oil prices and the current account. *Energy Economics, 139*, 107916.

Juhro, S., Robinson, I., Rahadyan, H., & Rishanty, A. (2025). *Climate Risks, Just Transition, and Central Bank Policy for Sustainable Economic Growth.* Retrieved from Jurnal Ekonomi Indonesia: https://jurnal.isei.or.id/index.php/isei/article/view/587

Jung, H., Engle, R. F., & Berner, R. (2021). Climate stress testing. *FRB of New York Staff Report*, (977).

Kohei, M., Naka, T., & Sudo, N. (2024). Analysis of the transmission of carbon taxes using a multisector DSGE. *Energy Economics, 136*, 107642. https://doi.org/10.1016/j.eneco.2024.107642

Malahayati, M., & Masui, T. (2021). Potential impact of introducing emission mitigation policies in Indonesia: how much will Indonesia have to spend? Mitigation and Adaptation Strategies for Global Change, 26(8), 37. https://doi.org/10.1007/s11027-021-09973-2

NGFS, - Network for Greening The Financial System. (2024). NGFS Climate Scenarios: for central banks and supervisors.

Reinders, H. J., Regelink, M. G. J., Calice, P., & Uribe, M. E. (2021). *Not-So-Magical Realism: A Climate Stress Test of the Colombian Banking System.*

Reinders, H. J., Schoenmaker, D., & Van Dijk, M. (2023). A finance approach to climate stress testing. *Journal of International Money and Finance*, *131*, 102797.
Reinders, H. J., Schoenmaker, D., & van Dijk, M. (2025). Climate risk stress testing: A critical survey and classification. *Journal of Climate Finance*, *10*, 100061.
Rishanty, A., Sambodo, M. T., Anugrah, D. F., & Wicaksono, R. P. K. (2022a). Energy transition: Prospect and Challenges at ASEAN Plus Three Countries (WP/08/2022). https://www.bi.go.id/en/publikasi/kajian/Documents/WP_08_2022.pdf
Rishanty, A., Sambodo, M. T., & Wicaksono, R. P. K. (2022b). *Green Transition Risks on Export Competitiveness: Circular Economy Approach* (No. WP/14/2022).
Rishanty et al. (2023a), "*Navigating climate transition: evaluating exposure and resilience of Indonesian banks*". Bank Indonesia working papers 2023. https://ideas.repec.org/p/idn/wpaper/wp052023.html
Rishanty, A., Anugrah, D. F., & Rahmawati, D. (2023b). *Coal Phase-Out: Socioeconomic Impact In Achieving Just Energy Transition In Indonesia* (No. WP/04/2023).
Rishanty, A., Setiastuti, S. U., & Purwanto, N. M. A. (2021), "The Growth Agenda and Financing green projects: Environmental DSGE". Bank Indonesia working papers 2021, https://ideas.repec.org/p/idn/wpaper/wp132021.html
Vermeulen, R., Schets, E., Lohuis, M., Kölbl, B., Jansen, D.-J., & Heeringa, W. (2018). DNB Occasional Studies: An energy transition risk stress test for the financial system of the Netherlands. www.dnb.nl
Zhang, D., Guo, Y., & Taghizadeh-Hesary, F. (2023). Green finance and energy transition to achieve net-zero emission target. *Energy Economics*, *126*, 106936.

# Part III
# Just Transition and Sustainability

# Chapter 10
# Just Transition and Sustainable Growth

**Solikin M. Juhro, Bambang Arianto, Arnita Rishanty, and Maxensius Tri Sambodo**

**Abstract** This study aims to present a cross-country assessment of the transition dynamics for the ASEAN+3 countries (the ASEAN countries plus Japan, China, and South Korea). Our research shows that economic activity has a significant impact on $CO_2$ emissions rise and that there may be asymmetries between energy diversity and efficiency. It is argued that Indonesia's use of renewable energy is low given its enormous potential. It is associated with the financial viability of state-owned firms, human and capital resources, misdirected subsidies, geographic settings, and the structural stale of the economic energy basis.

**Keywords** Just transition · Sustainable growth · Transition dynamics of the ASEAN+3 countries

## 1 Introduction

The energy transition is an important process to reduce the increase in the earth's temperature due to carbon emissions that have grown very rapidly since the industrial revolution. However, Salomon and Krishna (2011) show the experience of several countries, not all transitions to more sustainable energy systems can be successful.[1] They mentioned that globally the energy transition will be slow, this is because the political economy context in each country will determine the attention of each country such as on the energy efficiency side, the development of smart grids, as well as the presence of new

[1] 1 https://www.sciencedirect.com/science/article/abs/pii/S0301421511006987

S. M. Juhro (✉) · B. Arianto · A. Rishanty
Bank Indonesia, Jakarta, Indonesia
e-mail: solikin@bi.go.id; bambang_a@bi.go.id; Arnita_rishanty@bi.go.id

M. T. Sambodo
National Research and Innovation Agency of Indonesia (BRIN), Jakarta, Indonesia



S. M. Juhro et al. (eds.), *Sustainable Economy: The Indonesian Pathways*,
https://doi.org/10.1007/978-981-92-1215-6_10

agreements. Further, Juhro et al. (2024) highlights that a transition to a greener economy mitigates the negative impacts of an oil price rise more so for deficit countries than surplus countries. Salomon and Krishna (2011) also concluded that paying greater attention to the energy efficiency side would lead to a better acceleration of the energy transition. Therefore, the efficiency of energy use is not too difficult to do.

Learning from the energy transition carried out by Brazil, Lazaro et al. (2022) concluded two important things.[2] First, the energy transition is not only a technological process, but also involves the construction of political, social, environmental, and economic sides for the purpose of energy production and consumption. Second, energy policy is still the domain of the central government, this will certainly have an impact on the debate on policy solutions, regulations, and governance, especially if it is faced with the interests of local governments (decentralization perspective). Thus, their views show that the dimensions of governance starting from the side of planning, utilization and impact of energy use, as well as the domain of energy policy at the central and local government levels are important things to consider in the energy transition process.

What is interesting is the finding of York and Bell (2019) that a larger role of renewable energy in the energy production mix does not mean replacing fossil fuels, but rather adding to total energy production.[3] They said this is not a 'transition', in fact it will hinder the implementation of policies aimed at reducing the use of fossil fuels. Thus, it appears that the transition requires not only a greater role for renewable energy, but also more supportive policies for the use of renewable energy, to substitute the use of fossil energy.

Furthermore, Miller et al. (2013) provide the view that the energy transition is a complex technological social transformation process and requires major changes in many communities.[4] However, they are optimistic about the ongoing energy transition process for four reasons. First, this effort has received great support from the community. Second, there is greater concern from the public over the extraction and production of existing energy, rather than fear over energy supply. Third, the development of many new infrastructures for alternative energy systems has provided many opportunities to pay greater attention to the social dimensions of the energy transition. Fourth, greater social participation in the realization of democracy in technological change. Thus, the social impacts or risks of the energy transition process need to be managed properly by building good literacy on this process, including support for infrastructure development and greater community involvement in the energy transition.

Likewise, Sovacool (2016) stated that energy transitions are complex.[5] He also gave his six views. First, the energy transition can be driven by endogenous factors that exist within the country driven by political will and stakeholder involvement, or

[2] https://www.sciencedirect.com/science/article/abs/pii/S2214629621004916

[3] https://www.sciencedirect.com/science/article/abs/pii/S2214629618312246

[4] https://www.tandfonline.com/doi/pdf/10.1080/09505431.2013.786989?src=getftr

[5] https://www.sciencedirect.com/science/article/pii/S2214629615300827

factors from outside the country such as military conflicts, energy disasters such as nuclear, or global crises. Second, another transition has also occurred because it is market driven with better offers of financial and social benefits. One case study illustrating this situation is reviewed in Rishanty et al. (2024), which examines how energy transition risks in Indonesia can be reduced by leveraging circular economy practices through methane capture in biogas production within the palm oil sector. Third, some transitions may occur quickly due to management or incentives, or in other conditions they occur more naturally due to changes in technology, prices, or demand. Fourth, he also said there was no magical formula for energy transitions, but learned from history, the transitions that have occurred are based on new discoveries, with great impact, and in widely accessible forms of energy. Furthermore, in the future, scarcity and 'stranded assets', compared to abundance will influence decision making. Finally, energy transitions are path dependent versus revolutionary, cumulative versus fully substitutive. Sovacool's view shows that the complexity of the transition requires a more gradual approach and is full of in-depth reflection on institutional memory policies that have been running, including experiences in many places.

From an economic perspective, price is an important determinant for determining the demand for energy and Fouquet (2016),[6] said that energy prices have a major influence in creating incentives to stimulate the energy transition, but energy price fluctuations are only a catalyst to stimulate processes that will lead to more definite energy transitions. Furthermore, he also said that the new technology offered is also an important factor, especially if the technology can provide value to consumers, and is able to create a market even though the price is still relatively expensive. However, he also conveyed an important factor that could delay the transition, namely the reaction from the incumbent and the declining industry. This condition will certainly have an impact on economic transformation and inequality. Likewise, the role of the government is very important to build institutional settings that can stimulate the energy transition, but this can only happen if there is political will and alternative energy sources are available. The interesting thing from Fouquet's argument is that the risk will come from the position of the incumbent who has enjoyed economic rent from the use of fossil energy. Thus, it is important to see how the incumbent is also able to transform to green energy, and what is also important is the development of large sunk costs to start a fossil-based production system.

The World Energy Outlook (2021) and IEA (2021) provides three important notes related to the energy transition.[7] First, the transition risk will be faced with a choice of scenarios. There are at least four possible energy transition scenarios, namely: (1) Net Zero Emissions by 2050 Scenario (NZE); (2) Announced Pledges Scenario (APS); (3) Stated Policies Scenario (STEPS); and (4) Sustainable Development Scenario (SDS). NZE is the most radical carbon emission reduction

[6] https://www.sciencedirect.com/science/article/abs/pii/S2214629616301979

[7] https://iea.blob.core.windows.net/assets/4ed140c1-c3f3-4fd9-acae-789a4e14a23c/WorldEnergyOutlook2021.pdf

scenario, where by 2050, the world will no longer emit carbon emissions. Meanwhile, STEPS is the mildest scenario because it is more about stabilizing carbon emissions with a reduction rate that tends to be marginal. Meanwhile, APS and SDS tend to be more moderate, but SDS is the second highest emission reduction scenario after NZE. Second, the risk does not only reflect the national interest (internal) but also concerns other countries either in the individual or group (external) scope. Third, the risks are interconnected and interact to find a compromise point. For example, the Indonesian government's policy to secure the supply of coal for domestic electricity needs, makes coal exports temporarily need to be stopped. However, this policy has led to protests from other countries, such as Japan, South Korea, and the Philippines, which view that the Indonesian government's policies will threaten the energy security conditions in their countries.[8]

Furthermore, examining the search for the world risk in the World Energy Outlook (2021), there are several things that need attention in relation to the energy transition. For example, climate change will have an impact on increasing the vulnerability of energy infrastructure in the form of the threat of damage, jobs, cyber security, air pollution and health. Moreover, the effects are mismatches of supply and demand, tension on global trade and constraints on technology transfer, pandemic and energy, volatility of energy prices, finances, gap between the early and late adopters of clean technologies, and over-investment. This condition shows that the risk is very complex. The current challenge is how to make the energy transition reduce these risks or at least make many of them easier to control.

Thus, the energy transition stands in a plural conception, and from a risk perspective it is also complex. This is of course interesting because when measuring the risk of energy transitions it will contain various combinations. In the energy transition literature, Sovacool (2016) mentions that Indonesia has succeeded in converting from kerosene to LPG in a fairly fast time. On the other hand, considering the volatility of energy prices, it seems that it also needs to be viewed critically, because the Indonesian government is still actively implementing energy subsidies and compensation policies.

The energy transition is characterized by structural changes in the composition of the mixed energy both in terms of consumption and production. This has an impact on changes in energy-related CO2 emissions. Furthermore, the energy transition cannot be separated from the condition of energy security, which includes (i) self-sufficiency and diversification; (2) energy sustainability which includes energy efficiency and low carbon emissions, and finally (3) energy (electricity) affordability which is measured as the ratio of electricity costs to income per capita (Fueyo et al., 2015).[9] Thus, the energy transition process can be captured from the decomposition of energy-related CO2 emissions.

---

[8] https://www.thejakartapost.com/business/2022/01/10/philippines-urges-indonesia-to-lift-coal-export-ban-as-talks-proceed.html

[9] Fueyo, N., Gomez, A., and Dopazo, C. (2015). Energy security, sustainability, and affordability in Asia and the Pacific, in Asia's Energy Challenge: Key issues and policy options, Minsoo Lee, Donghyun Park, and Harry D. Saunders (Eds), Routledge, 81–131, Manila.

In their study, Zhang et al. (2009)[10] performed a complete decomposition technique to identify the factors that influence sectoral changes in CO2 emissions. In their study, they concluded that between 1991–2006, the decline in CO2 emissions in China was due to the role of the energy intensity effect, while the increase in CO2 emissions was caused by the intensity of CO2 emissions and economic activity. In general, decomposition techniques are divided into two major groups, namely structural decomposition analysis (SDA) and index decomposition analysis (IDA). SDA uses input-output model in doing decomposition. Meanwhile, IDA can be applied based on Laspeyres IDA and Divisia IDA. The advantage of using IDA is that this technique can be applied to any available data at the aggregate level, therefore IDA is widely applied in many publications.

This study aims to present a cross-country assessment of the transition dynamics for the ASEAN+3 countries. It is organized as follows. The next two sections review methodology and data, followed a cross-country assessment of the ASEAN+3. Section 4 specifically discusses just transition from macroeconomic stability perspective and the achievement of Golden Indonesia 2045. Section 5 concludes.

## 2 Data and Methodology

This study aims to measure the transition risk of energy-related CO2 emissions in two stages. In the first stage, an analysis of the direction of investment is carried out, which is captured from indicators of production and consumption in the energy sector that runs between 2000 and 2020, whether in the span of that year, the mixed energy structure has led to a stronger grip on the fossil energy base or has it tended to be loosening grip on fossil-based energy. Second, based on the energy transition that has taken place in the last twenty years, what about the risk conditions faced, and in this case the risk will be measured in the dimensions of energy security, sustainability, and affordability. Furthermore, through these two stages of analysis, it will be mapped whether the transition has been, is being, and will be running with the dynamics of the risks that will be faced. By illustrating the dynamics of the transition and risk in the quadrant analysis, it is possible to map the direction of the energy transition that has been going on so far. Interestingly, this study makes a comparison, not only in Indonesia, but also at the level of ASEAN plus three countries (Japan, China, and South Korea).

This study uses mixed-methods. A qualitative approach is taken to explore the potential, challenges, and risks of the energy transition. In-depth interviews were conducted by several resource persons representing the government (Ministry of Energy and Mineral Resources), state-owned enterprises in the electricity sector (PLN), the Indonesian electricity community (MKI), and the ASEAN Energy

[10] Zhang, M., Mu, H., Ning, Y., and Song, Y. (2009). Decomposition of energy-related CO2 emissions over 1991–2006 in China, Ecological Economics, 68:2122–2128.

Center (AEC). Furthermore, a quantitative approach is taken to measure the dynamics of energy transitions that have occurred, so that the patterns of changes that occur can be understood.

Next, four quadrants of the energy transition matrix are constructed. The four transitional quadrants reflect changes in terms of energy, economy, emissions, and equity. These four aspects, both directly and indirectly, are able to capture the risk side of the transition. The ability to maintain the performance of these four aspects indicates the country's ability to carry out the energy transition optimally.

Two years of observation, namely 2000 and 2019, are considered sufficient to see the energy transition in terms of energy diversity and efficiency. Considering the risk of fossil energy availability, countries that are able to improve their energy diversity position towards using renewable energy and becoming more efficient are considered to be better at carrying out the energy transition. This is an effort made in the first stage. Thus, based on the energy transition matrix, countries in clusters A and C, in the context of energy transition, are in a better position than those in clusters B and D. To get a more in-depth mapping, then in the second stage, mapping is carried out based on the results of the decomposition of carbon emissions. In the third stage, countries which have increasing Energy Self Sufficiency (ESS) for renewable energy will be kept in the matrices. Final step, countries which have increasing energy equity will be kept on the matrices (Table 10.1).

The quantitative process built in several stages, namely (1) decomposition of carbon emissions; (2) energy efficiency self-sufficiency; (3) energy diversity; and (4) energy equity (to capture affordability conditions).

Energy use data per sector and the type of energy used, obtained from https://www.iea.org/data-and-statistics/data-tables/?country=WORLD&energy=Balances. The data indicated that 'total final energy consumption' was carried out by the industrial sector; transports; residential; commerce and public services; agriculture/forestry; fishing; non-specified; and non-energy used. Furthermore, the units of energy used are converted into carbon emissions. The figure below shows the final total energy consumption by sector for the case in Indonesia (TJ). Furthermore, this information becomes the basis for calculating carbon emissions by sector. GDP data for the economic sector will be divided into three major groups, namely: agriculture; industry; and services. The data source was obtained from the Asian Development Bank (ADB) Key Indicators for Asia and the Pacific 2021 https://kidb.adb.org/kidb/. GDP data is calculated at constant 2010 prices. Calculation of Energy self-sufficiency is carried out using production, import, export and consumption

**Table 10.1** First stage in mapping energy transition

| | | Energy Diversity | |
|---|---|---|---|
| | | Diversify to Renewable Energy | Less Diversify |
| Energy Efficiency | Less Energy Intensity (to emissions)—CI: Emission/Energy Used | A | B |
| | Less Energy Intensity (to GDP)—EI: Energy/GDP | C | D |

data. Data obtained from the IEA whose aggregation includes hydro; wind, solar, etc.; biofuels and waste; coal; crude oil; oil products; and natural gas. With the same data source, energy diversification can also be calculated. Data for calculating energy equity, obtained from the source https://trilemma.worldenergy.org/#!/energy-index.

## 3 A Cross-Country Assessment

CE is the total carbon emissions generated from the industrial, transportation, residential, commercial, and public sectors, as well as agriculture and fisheries. In absolute value, China has provided the highest emission level, from around 1.3 billion tons in 2000 and increased to about 3.5 billion tons of carbon in 2019. In 2019, Japan had the second largest carbon emission level after China and followed by Indonesia and South Korea. However, the changing in carbon emission levels between 2000 and 2019, it appears that only Japan and Korea experienced a reduction in emissions, by around 163 million tons and 7.3 million tons, respectively. The reduction in carbon emissions that occurred in Japan occurred in all sectors, and in Korea there was still an increase in emissions in the transportation and residential sectors. As the largest emitter, the industrial and transportation sectors in China contributed to the largest increase in emissions in the country, reaching 58.6 percent and 30 percent respectively. Meanwhile, the increase in emissions from Singapore is the smallest compared to other countries. Considering the role of changes in emissions in 2000 and 2019, it appears that Singapore, Viet Nam, and China have shown an increasing role, respectively 0.1 percent, 1.2 percent, and 19 percent (Table 10.2).

**Table 10.2** Carbon emissions

| | CE 2019 | | CE 2000 | | 2019–2000 | |
|---|---|---|---|---|---|---|
| Country | Total | Share | Total | Share | Absolute Change | Change in share |
| Indonesia | 301.097.630 | 0,061 | 159.906.167 | 0,062 | 141.191.462 | −0,001 |
| Malaysia | 107.860.809 | 0,022 | 62.134.218 | 0,024 | 45.726.591 | −0,002 |
| Philippines | 61.330.524 | 0,012 | 41.382.427 | 0,016 | 19.948.097 | −0,004 |
| Singapore | 22.766.949 | 0,005 | 9.511.526 | 0,004 | 13.255.423 | 0,001 |
| Thailand | 130.873.637 | 0,027 | 86.690.989 | 0,034 | 44.182.648 | −0,007 |
| Viet Nam | 119.394.549 | 0,024 | 30.725.306 | 0,012 | 88.669.243 | 0,012 |
| Japan | 473.423.104 | 0,096 | 636.485.600 | 0,247 | (163.062.496) | −0,151 |
| People's Republic of China | 3.506.409.217 | 0,710 | 1.328.960.908 | 0,516 | 2.177.448.309 | 0,194 |
| Korea | 212.107.740 | 0,043 | 219.437.047 | 0,085 | (7.329.307) | −0,042 |
| Total | 4.935.264.159 | 1000 | 2.575.234.188 | 1000 | 2.360.029.971 | |

Source: authors' calculation

The findings show changes in the decomposition of carbon emissions (CE) as seen from the magnitude of changes in CI, EI, and ES both in 2000 and 2019. In general, it can be concluded that economic activity (G Effect) has the greatest influence on the increase in CO2 emissions. Furthermore, the CI Effect shows a negative magnitude for all countries except the Philippines. This means that the energy used is relatively more carbon intensive. This condition reflects the resources and capacity, which need to be optimized to develop the use of renewable energy at an increasingly efficient level. The results of the EI Effect, require negative conditions. This indicates that to produce one unit of GDP, the less energy sources are used. However, a positive value was found for Singapore. Furthermore, from indications of structural changes effect (ES) it has a negative effect on carbon emissions in many countries except Indonesia and Viet Nam. This condition shows changes in the structure of the economy, still driving up carbon emissions.

A mapping of the important conditions of the transition process was carried out, namely, the position in terms of conditions of energy diversification and energy efficiency. Regarding energy efficiency, the references used are the conditions of CI and EI (Tables 10.3, 10.4, 10.5).

Thus, based on the results of the mapping based on these criteria, it appears that three countries, namely Indonesia, Malaysia, and Korea, which in the last twenty years have shown relatively good energy transition conditions, and furthermore, if we pay attention to countries with conditions of diversity to renewable energy, then two countries are selected, namely Indonesia and Korea. Thus, in terms of transition risk, both Indonesia and Korea have relatively low transition risks (Table 10.6).

**Table 10.3** Transition Matrix—Step I

| | | | Energy Diversity | |
|---|---|---|---|---|
| | | | Diversify to Renewable energy | Less Diversify |
| | | | Indonesia; Philippines; Thailand; Japan; China; Korea | Malaysia; Singapore; Viet Nam; |
| Energy Efficiency | Less Energy Intensity (to emissions)—CI: Emission/ Energy Used | Indonesia<br>Malaysia<br>Singapore<br>Thailand<br>Viet Nam<br>Japan<br>China<br>Korea | Indonesia; Thailand; Japan; China; Korea | Malaysia; Singapore; Viet Nam |
| | Less Energy Intensity (to GDP)—EI: Energy/GDP | Indonesia<br>Malaysia<br>Philippines<br>Thailand<br>Viet Nam<br>Japan<br>China<br>Korea | Indonesia; Philipines; Thailand; Japan; China; Korea | Malaysia; Viet Nam |

**Table 10.4** Transition Matrix—Step II

| | | | Energy Diversity | |
|---|---|---|---|---|
| | | | Diversify to Renewable energy | Less Diversify |
| | | | Indonesia; Philippines; Thailand; Japan; China; Korea | Malaysia; Singapore; Viet Nam; |
| Energy Efficiency | Less Energy Intensity (to emissions)—CI: Emission/Energy Used | Indonesia Malaysia Singapore Thailand Viet Nam Japan China Korea | Indonesia; Thailand; Japan; China; Korea | Malaysia; Viet Nam |
| | Less Energy Intensity (to GDP)—EI: Energy/GDP | Indonesia Malaysia Philippines Thailand Viet Nam Japan China Korea | | |

Step II In the context of efficiency; choose a country that has both CI and EI negative values

**Table 10.5** Transition Matrix—Step III

| | | | Energy Diversity | |
|---|---|---|---|---|
| | | | Diversify to Renewable energy | Less Diversify |
| | | | Indonesia; Philippines; Thailand; Japan; China; Korea | Malaysia; Singapore; Viet Nam; |
| Energy Efficiency | Less Energy Intensity (to emissions)—CI: Emission/Energy Used | Indonesia Malaysia Singapore Thailand Viet Nam Japan China Korea | Indonesia; Korea | Malaysia |
| | Less Energy Intensity (to GDP)—EI: Energy/GDP | Indonesia Malaysia Philippines Thailand Viet Nam Japan China Korea | | |

Step III We dropped countries that have declining ESS in Renewable Energy

**Table 10.6** Transition Matrix—Step IV

| | | | Energy Diversity | |
|---|---|---|---|---|
| | | | Diversify to Renewable energy | Less Diversify |
| | | | Indonesia; Philippines; Thailand; Japan; China; Korea | Malaysia; Singapore; Viet Nam; |
| Energy Efficiency | Less Energy Intensity (to emissions)—CI: Emission/Energy Used | Indonesia<br>Malaysia<br>Singapore<br>Thailand<br>Viet Nam<br>Japan<br>China<br>Korea | Indonesia; Korea | Malaysia |
| | Less Energy Intensity (to GDP)—EI: Energy/GDP | Indonesia<br>Malaysia<br>Philippines<br>Thailand<br>Viet Nam<br>Japan<br>China<br>Korea | | |

Step IV We dropped countries that showed declining energy equity—none dropped

The finding shows the relative position between countries for several energy intensity and emission indicators. The lower the intensity value, the better. Comparing Indonesia with Korea, it appears that Korea's position is relatively better in terms of CO2 intensity of energy mix, and Indonesia is relatively better in terms of energy intensity economy and CO2 emissions per unit of real GDP PPP (Table 10.7).

The awareness of energy transition in the ASEAN, Japan, China, and South Korea cannot be separated from the global action of climate change in COP 26 conference. In recent years, the renewable energy mix in ASEAN regionals is significantly increasing. The target share of utilized renewable energy in 2025 for whole ASEAN is set to 33 percent. The energy transition is a dynamic process and developments in the last twenty years have shown that many countries have been quite successful in improving their state of energy efficiency, although in terms of energy diversification, it has not been running optimally. In other words, the efficiency and energy diversification side are still running asymmetrically. It is not easy to justify that one country is superior in the energy transition because of the unequal condition of resources and capabilities. The energy transition should ideally not hamper economic development, and on the contrary, be able to direct development to be greener and more inclusive.

As stated by Lazaro et al. (2022), policy direction will determine the energy transition. As discussed by the National Development Planning Agency, Republic of Indonesia (Badan Perencana Pembangunan Nasional/Bappenas), it appears that

**Table 10.7** Low-carbon electricity generation share by sources, 2019 (%)

| Type | China | Korea | Japan | Thailand | Indonesia | Singapore | Total (%) |
|---|---|---|---|---|---|---|---|
| Nuclear | 4.7 | 25.2 | 6.2 | 3.4 | – | – | 39.5 |
| Hydro | 17 | 0.5 | 7.7 | – | 7.2 | – | 32.4 |
| Biomass | 1.6 | 1.6 | 4.3 | 9.7 | 4.6 | 2.6 | 24.4 |
| Wind | 5.4 | 0.5 | 0.7 | 1.9 | 0.2 | – | 8.7 |
| Solar PV | 3 | 2.3 | 6.7 | 2.7 | – | 0.8 | 15.5 |
| Solar TH | – | – | | – | – | – | – |
| Geothermal | – | – | 0.3 | – | 4.8 | – | 5.1 |
| Marine | – | 0.1 | | – | – | – | 0.1 |
| Total 2 | 31.7 | 30.2 | 25.9 | 17.7 | 16.8 | 3.4 | |

Source: International Energy Agency

there are three low-carbon policies to support the GEI (Green Economy Index), namely: decreasing energy intensity (energy efficiency), gradually by 1–2% per year until 2030 for all demand sectors; the role of new and renewable energy (EBT) to close to 100% by 2060; full transition to electricity and hydrogen from fuel. Likewise, Bappenas conveyed 8 (eight) challenges that will be in the transition to a green economy, namely the amount of investment needs, policy reforms to manage stranded asset risk, technology and innovation gaps, preparation for migration to green jobs, creation of green jobs, decarbonization of the energy sector and transportation, implementation of carbon pricing, increasing trend of ESG (Environmental, Social, and Governance) in the industry.

Although in terms of energy mix, Indonesia has huge potential of renewable energy compared to other ASEAN countries, but the utilisation is considerably low. According to Ministry of Energy and Mineral Resources (2022a), the potential of renewable energy is 3686 GW, but only 0.3 percent of it have been utilized, and fossil fuel has still become the main energy resources. Table 10.8 shows Indonesia's renewable energy potentials and how many it has been utilized. Hydro power is the most utilized renewable energy, although it is still small number, followed by the utilization of bioenergy and geothermal power for energy sources.

Although Indonesia, in fact, has huge potential of renewable energy, and huge amount of nickel mining for battery material, but the utilisation of renewable-resource-based power faces some obstacles. The coal power plant in Indonesia is still considerably new, which have not reached its economical state yet. Moreover, the electricity supply in Java and Bali are oversupply, therefore it will be a high cost to invest the renewable-resource-based power plant. In fact, the use of coal power plant contributes in higher carbon emissions. So, even though we realize that switching to more environmentally friendly energy sources is more profitable in the long run, the high cost will become a barrier.

Another major obstacle to utilize the renewable energy in Indonesia is the high economical cost due to social and environmental issues. This is also why the electricity distribution in the country is considered exclusive. This constraint is

**Table 10.8** Indonesia's Renewable Energy Potential 2021

| Energy | Potential (GW) | Utilization (MW) |
|---|---|---|
| Solar | 3295 | 229 |
| Hydro | 95 | 6602 |
| Bioenergy | 57 | 2284 |
| Wind | 155 | 154 |
| Geothermal | 24 | 2286 |
| Ocean | 60 | 0 |
| Total | 3686 | 11,555 |

Source: Ministry of Energy and Mineral Resources (2022b)

**Fig. 10.1** The Distribution Planning of Nusantara GRID. Source: Masyarakat Ketenagalistrikan (2022)

supported by several factors. First, Indonesia is the largest archipelagic country with thousands of islands, but the economic activity is located in bigger islands, mostly in Java. Most of the coal plants located in Java and Bali to power the industrial areas, and currently Java becomes oversupply in electricity. Meanwhile, the other small islands, or even in remote areas, are still lack of it. In order to distribute the electricity evenly, Ministry of Energy and Mineral Resources plans to build the smart grid system, called Nusantara grid, to connect the power plants that located in Java and Bali to the grid in remote areas (Fig. 10.1). However, the investment of this project will be expensive. Another option is to build micro grid in each smaller local area, such as wards or cluster areas, although it needs more skilled-labor to do the maintenance (Masyarakat Ketenagalistrikan Indonesia, 2022). Second, most of Indonesia's lands covered by forests and difficult terrains, making it more challenging to build electricity or power facility in those areas. Moreover, the development will also have a trade off with the environment issue, where many of the trees will be cut down and threatening the biodiversity. Third, lack of awareness and low education of local people, especially in remote areas, resulting in higher risks of rejection from the people or not well-maintained by them.

Indonesia is expected to have net zero emission in 2060. However, in order to shift from fossil-based energy to renewable energy, Indonesia needs a lot of investment. Financing will be one of the major obstacles to the energy transition process. The Ministry of Energy and Mineral Resources said that a budget of around USD 1 trillion is needed to achieve the EBT target in 2060 and this amount could increase if efforts to accelerate early retirement coal are carried out. On the other hand, information from the IEA, shows that both Indonesia and China provide subsidies on fossil energy, respectively 0.2% and 0.6% of GDP in 2020. The IEA said that oil and electricity subsidies in China reached USD 25.5 billion, while oil subsidies in Indonesia reached USD 6.9 billion. Thus, taking part in the financing of NRE investment will be a big challenge from a policy perspective and a great political commitment from the government is needed (Salomon & Krishna, 2011).

Further, in the discussion with the Indonesian state own enterprises in power sector (PLN), it was stated that the transition to carbon neutral 2060 is divided into two parts, namely (i) power plants that are more environmentally friendly; (ii) new technologies and businesses. In the short-term (2021–2030), PLTN aims to achieve the enhance NDC; and long-term (2031–2060), the carbon neutral 2060 becomes the objectives. The short goals such as, new and renewable energy (NRE) development, diesel power plant (PLTD) conversion, steam coal power plant (PLTU) phase I retirement, PLTU cofiring, energy efficiency and grid loss improvement; gas expansion; and clean coal. Meanwhile, the long-term goals include development of NRE + battery + interconnection; hydrogen cofiring; retirement steam coal power plant stage 2, carbon capture storage (CCS) /carbon capture storage and utilisation (CCSU). Furthermore, in the context of new technologies and businesses, including electric vehicles, roof top solar panels, induction cookers, carbon credits, and emissions trading. As seen from Table 10.9, the shifting demand based on the energy resources, and in 2060 targets to shift from majority using coal and fossil oil in 2020 to more than 50 percent using electricity and other renewable resources to generate the energy.

Energy transition from fossil-based resource to renewable energy also will potentially create a new job. However, according to a discussant from ASEAN Center for Energy, majority of universities and colleges in ASEAN member countries do not have specific curriculum about energy transition, even the technicality of the renewable energy. They only found one curriculum in Bandung Institute of Technology (ITB), but it is taught in master's degree. It results in the availability of current labour's skill in renewable energy. Although in terms of technicality may not need high-skilled labour, but universities, colleges, and even vocational schools, have to soon create relevant curriculum, so that the energy transition process through investments and power plant establishments are in the same track with the labour's skills.

While in Vietnam, most of its energy resources sourced by solar energy and becomes the largest contributor country for renewable energy mix in the regional. In Fig. 10.2, Vietnam is contributing almost 56 percent of its renewable energy, or about 12 GW, and solar power has a significant contribution. However, the success story of renewable energy in Vietnam also bring another side effect. The Vietnam

**Table 10.9** Energy transition planning based on energy demand

| Jenis Energi | 2020 | 2025 | 2030 | 2035 | 2040 | 2045 | 2050 | 2055 | 2060 |
|---|---|---|---|---|---|---|---|---|---|
| Batubara | 16.06 | 18.04 | 19.42 | 19.83 | 18.77 | 16.62 | 13.72 | 10.67 | 7.33 |
| Gas | 26.36 | 21.37 | 26.21 | 30.91 | 35.37 | 37.51 | 38.12 | 39.52 | 40.88 |
| Minyak | 67.22 | 78.46 | 91.74 | 98.81 | 92.33 | 80.25 | 72.76 | 71.13 | 73.59 |
| EBT | 6.18 | 10.68 | 12.55 | 15.12 | 17.53 | 21.83 | 26.47 | 31.52 | 37.53 |
| Listrik | 26.06 | 35.24 | 49.68 | 67.92 | 89.55 | 111.62 | 129.64 | 142.14 | 150.36 |
| Total | 142 | 164 | 200 | 233 | 254 | 268 | 281 | 295 | 310 |

Source: Ministry of Energy and Mineral Resources (2022a)

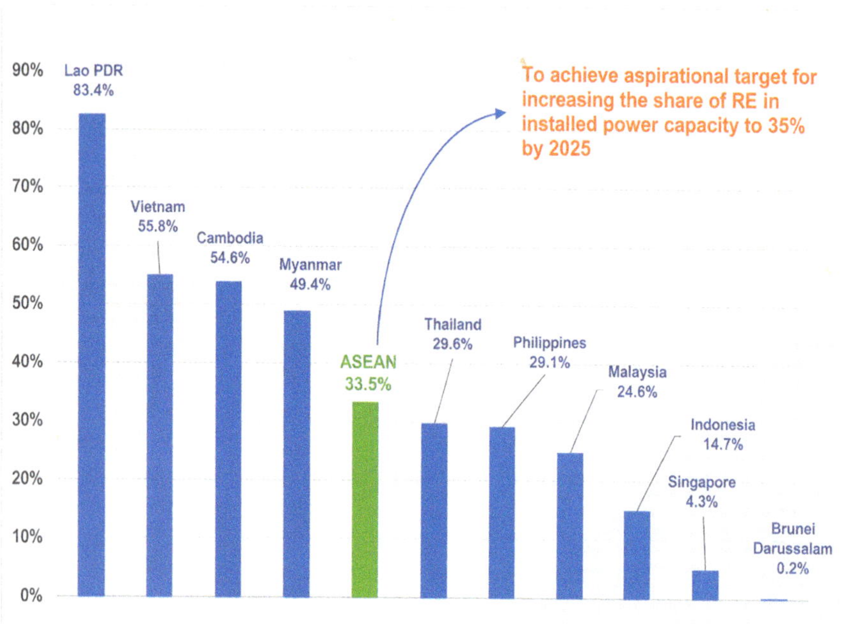


**Fig. 10.2** Renewable Energy Share in ASEAN Member's Installed Power Capacity 2020. Source: ASEAN Center for Energy (2022)

government regulates the price of solar energy, but not regulating the quota of selling the excess energy. This regulation results in many private companies that want to invest in solar panel. While the investment cost is considerably low due to using local manufactured-tools, the investors can sell their excess energy with a good price. The selling of excess of solar energy makes the Vietnam's state electricity company, the one who is regulated to buy the excess energy, to buy the energy from the private companies, although they already have excess energy supply. This results in their financial failure of the state own enterprises.

Meanwhile, Singapore becomes an important key for energy sectoral in ASEAN. It is known to had severe limitations in adopting renewable energy and was heavily dependent on fossil fuels (Masyarakat Ketenagalistrikan Indonesia, 2022). Currently, 90 percent of its electricity is generated from LNG, although its energy mix is considered low compared to the other ASEAN Members. Singapore is planning to invest on sun cable project that will be the longest submarine solar cable to bring the power from Australia to Singapore. The estimated cable is 4200 km long (Sun Cable Energy, 2022), and potentially enough to "close" the whole cable industries to fulfil its needs. This investment could increase the energy mix of renewable energy in the regional. However, since the cable will pass through the Indonesia's territories, the government still find the best way to join this project. The Government of Indonesia plans to join, through their investment, to build a station in Bali, discharge the energy to PLN's grid in Java, and then connect to Singapore through Jakarta. This investment will also benefit PLN. Another plan is that Singapore should invest the solar power plant in Sumatera instead of investing in this sun cable. According a discussant from ASEAN Centre for Energy, Sumatra's solar panel plant will be enough to power electricity from Aceh to Lampung and export some of them to Singapore.

Compared to ASEAN member countries, China, Japan, and Korea seem have planned their own transition to renewable energy (ASEAN Center For Energy, 2022). China targeted to achieve lower their carbon emissions to 65 percent of GDP in 2030, as well as increasing forest stock by 6 billion cubic meters, increasing the consumption renewable-based power plant to around 25 percent, and installing both wind and solar power to over 1200 GW in the same year. Meanwhile in the same year, Japan declared to aim net zero emissions in 2050 by using Green Growth Strategy, which incorporates policies in budgeting, taxation, financing, and regulatory reforms. They also declare to shift to electricity fuels that powered by offshore wind/solar/geothermal power to total 30–45 GW, hydrogen to 20 million tons, next-generation heat energy by injecting synthetic methane to 90 percent of their infrastructures and lastly using nuclear power. Still in the same year, South Korea targeted to cut the carbon emission to more than 40 percent by increasing their share of renewable energy power to 20 percent and accelerating the use of electric vehicle (EV). They also set different goals of carbon emission reduction for each sector, which the significant reduction is set to power sector (44.4 percent) and transportation (37.8 percent).

Indonesia needs to consider including nuclear in its energy mixed. One interesting option is PLN to build a nuclear power plant. It is relatively more environmentally friendly even though the cost is expensive, but the power generated can be very large. However, the use of nuclear power is not easy because of an internationally sensitive issue. Developed countries that produce nuclear strongly object if we try to use nuclear power for electricity generation. This is because the potential abuse of nuclear power will be very easy for countries that have it.

## 4 Just Transition, Macroeconomic Stability, and Golden Indonesia 2045

From a macroeconomic perspective, a just transition is not merely a social safeguard accompanying climate policy, but a central pillar for sustaining long-term growth, macroeconomic stability, and political feasibility of structural transformation. In emerging economies such as Indonesia, where growth remains closely tied to resource extraction, fossil energy, and labor-intensive sectors, an unmanaged transition risks amplifying unemployment, regional inequality, and fiscal stress—outcomes that could undermine development objectives rather than advance them. Conversely, a well-designed just transition framework aligns decarbonization with productivity growth, labor reallocation, and social cohesion, thereby reinforcing the foundations of sustainable growth consistent with the vision of Golden Indonesia (Indonesia Emas) 2045 (ILO, 2015; IMF, 2022).

At the macro level, the core challenge of the green transition lies in reallocating capital and labor away from carbon-intensive activities toward low-carbon and climate-resilient sectors without triggering growth slowdowns or social dislocation. Indonesia's economic structure remains heterogeneous: fossil fuel–dependent regions, energy-intensive industries, and informal labor markets coexist with rapidly expanding green opportunities in renewable energy, electric vehicles, circular economy activities, and nature-based solutions. Without compensatory mechanisms, carbon pricing, subsidy reforms, and regulatory tightening may generate asymmetric adjustment costs, particularly for lower-income households and regions reliant on coal mining, conventional agriculture, and energy-intensive manufacturing. These distributional effects, if left unaddressed, can erode aggregate demand, increase inequality, and provoke political resistance that weakens policy credibility and investment certainty (Stiglitz et al., 2017; OECD, 2021).

A just transition mitigates these macroeconomic risks by smoothing adjustment pathways and stabilizing expectations. From a Keynesian and structuralist perspective, redistributive mechanisms—such as recycling carbon revenues into social protection, retraining programs, and regional development—help maintain consumption and employment during the transition, preventing demand-side contractions. At the same time, targeted public investment in green infrastructure, skills development, and innovation generates multiplier effects that crowd in private investment and enhance total factor productivity (TFP) over time (Aghion et al., 2016; IMF, 2023). In this sense, just transition policies are not a drag on growth but a macroeconomic stabilizer that supports both short-term demand management and long-term supply-side transformation.

For Golden Indonesia 2045, which aspires to high-income status alongside environmental sustainability, labor market dynamics are particularly critical. Indonesia is projected to enjoy a demographic dividend over the coming decades, but this dividend can only be realized if labor is productively absorbed into higher value-added sectors. A disorderly transition risks creating pockets of structural unemployment among workers displaced from fossil fuel-related industries, informal agriculture, and carbon-intensive manufacturing. A just transition framework—combining active labor market policies, reskilling, and mobility support—facilitates the reallocation of labor toward emerging green sectors such as renewable energy, sustainable manufacturing, waste management, ecosystem restoration, and green services. Empirical evidence suggests that such sectors are often more labor-intensive and geographically dispersed, offering opportunities for inclusive growth and regional convergence when supported by appropriate policies (ILO, 2018; World Bank, 2022).

From a fiscal and financial stability standpoint, just transition considerations are equally salient. Indonesia faces rising climate-related fiscal risks, including disaster response costs, infrastructure damage, and contingent liabilities from stranded assets. Abrupt transitions that neglect social and regional impacts can exacerbate these risks by triggering asset write-downs, banking sector stress, and public pressure for ad hoc fiscal interventions. Integrating just transition principles into fiscal planning—through climate budget tagging, medium-term expenditure frameworks, and social expenditure prioritization—enhances fiscal credibility and reduces long-term liabilities. Moreover, predictable and socially embedded transition pathways lower policy uncertainty, which is a key determinant of private investment decisions in capital-intensive green sectors (NGFS, 2023; IMF, 2022).

Importantly, just transition also strengthens Indonesia's external competitiveness and growth resilience. As global markets increasingly impose carbon-related trade measures and sustainability standards, economies that fail to manage transition risks may experience declining export competitiveness and capital outflows. By contrast, embedding just transition into industrial and labor policies enables Indonesia to upgrade its export structure, develop green value chains, and position itself advantageously within the evolving global economy. This is particularly relevant for Indonesia's ambitions in electric vehicles, battery ecosystems, sustainable agriculture, and the circular economy, where social legitimacy and workforce readiness are critical complements to technological and financial investments (OECD, 2022).

Finally, from a political economy perspective, just transition is indispensable for sustaining reform momentum over the long horizon required to reach Golden Indonesia 2045. Structural transformation unfolds over decades, not electoral cycles. Policies perceived as inequitable or exclusionary are vulnerable to reversal, weakening long-term growth prospects. By explicitly addressing fairness, regional balance, and intergenerational equity, just transition frameworks build durable social contracts that anchor climate and development policies across administrations. This institutional continuity is a key macroeconomic asset, enhancing credibility, lowering risk premia, and supporting sustained investment-led growth (Rodrik, 2014; Stiglitz, 2019).

## 5 Conclusion

This study aims to measure the transition risk of energy-related CO2 emissions in two stages. First, an analysis of the direction of investment is carried out which is captured from indicators of production and consumption in the energy sector that runs between 2000 and 2019. In the span of that year, the mixed energy structure has led to a stronger grip on the fossil energy base or has it tended to be loosening grip on fossil-based energy. Second, based on the energy transition that has taken place in the last twenty years, what about the risk conditions faced, and in this case the risk will be measured in the dimensions of energy security, sustainability, and affordability. Furthermore, through these two stages of analysis, it will be mapped whether the transition has been, is being, and will be running with the dynamics of the risks that will be faced. By illustrating the dynamics of the transition and risk in the quadrant analysis, it is possible to map the direction of the energy transition that has been going on so far. This study makes a comparison, not only in Indonesia, but also at the level of ASEAN plus three countries (Japan, China, and South Korea). This study also uses a qualitative approach to elaborate on the findings of quantitative approach.

From the analysis, we find that economic activity has the greatest influence on the increase in CO2 emissions. The CI Effect shows that the energy used is relatively more carbon intensive. This condition reflects the resources and capacity, which need to be optimized to develop the use of renewable energy at an increasingly efficient level. The results of the EI Effect indicates that to produce one unit of GDP, the less energy sources are used. However, a positive value was found for Singapore. Furthermore, from the ES Effect aspect, only Indonesia and Viet Nam have positive values. In the context of the theoretical increase, it appears that China made the largest contribution, followed by Indonesia and Viet Nam. However, it is important to note that the rate of theoretical decrease shows a decrease for all countries, and Viet Nam shows the largest decline. While the transition matrix shows how the combination of energy diversity and efficiency is established, the results indicates that Indonesia and Korea have more energy diversity than the other countries, and Malaysia has less energy diversity.

Through quadrant analysis, there are two general patterns of energy transition, energy efficiency and the development of new and renewable energy. The results of the analysis show that both can run asymmetrically. Countries that are able to achieve better conditions in terms of energy intensity and emissions, can achieve it without significant changes in terms of the renewable energy mix or even a decrease in the renewable energy mix. Thus, a good transition needs to do both symmetrically.

The results of this study are also supported by the results of discussions with experts in the energy field. From the results of discussions with experts, it is known that although the energy transition has taken place, various risks still need to be considered. First, related to financing for infrastructure to support the development of new and renewable energy. This includes network related. Second, the bias in supporting large subsidies for fossil fuels. Third, geographical challenges that require network support and system reliability. Fourth, green job opportunities that also need to be supported by capacity building through certification. Fifth, excess capacity in fossil power plants (particularly coal) which makes the choice of transition not easy and costly. Sixth, the feed in tariff policy, which if not managed properly can jeopardize the business resilience of many states electricity companies that have to buy renewable energy.

From a macroeconomic perspective, just transition is not an auxiliary social policy but a growth-enabling strategy that aligns decarbonization with productivity, fiscal sustainability, and social cohesion. For Indonesia, integrating just transition into the broader green economy agenda strengthens the pathway toward high and sustainable growth, ensuring that the pursuit of Golden Indonesia (Indonesia Emas) 2045 is both economically robust and socially inclusive. By managing adjustment costs, mobilizing human capital, and reinforcing policy credibility, a just transition transforms climate action from a perceived constraint into a central driver of long-term national prosperity.

## References


Aghion, P., Dechezleprêtre, A., Hémous, D., Martin, R., & Van Reenen, J. (2016). Carbon taxes, path dependency, and directed technical change. Journal of Political Economy.

Fouquet, R. (2016). Historical energy transitions: Speed, prices and system transformation. *Energy Research & Social Science, 22*, 7–12. https://doi.org/10.1016/j.erss.2016.08.014

Fueyo, N., Gomez, A., & Dopazo, C. (2015). Energy security, sustainability, and affordability in Asia and the Pacific. In Donghyun Park, & Harry D. Saunders (Eds.) *Asia's Energy Challenge: Key issues and policy options*. Routledge, 81–131, Manila.

IEA. (2021). https://iea.blob.core.windows.net/assets/4ed140c1-c3f3-4fd9-acae-789a4e14a23c/WorldEnergyOutlook2021.pdf

International Labour Organization (ILO). (2015). Guidelines for a just transition towards environmentally sustainable economies and societies. Geneva: ILO.

International Labour Organization (ILO). (2018). World employment and social outlook: Greening with jobs. Geneva: ILO.

International Monetary Fund (IMF). (2022). Fiscal policies for climate change mitigation and adaptation. Washington, DC: IMF.

International Monetary Fund (IMF). (2023). Transition risks and macro-financial stability. Washington, DC: IMF.

Lazaro, L. L. B., Soares, R. S., Bermann, C., Collaço, F. M. A., Giatti, L. L., & Abram, S. (2022). Energy transition in Brazil: Is there a role for multilevel governance in a centralized energy regime? *Energy Research & Social Science, 85*, 102404. https://doi.org/10.1016/j.erss.2021.102404

Masyarakat Ketenagalistrikan Indonesia. (2022). Seri manajemen pengetahuan ketenagalistrikan: Mewujudkan ketenagalistrikan nasional yang berkelanjutan.

Miller, C. A., Iles, A., & Jones, C. F. (2013). The social dimensions of energy transitions. *Science as Culture, 22*(2), 135–148. https://doi.org/10.1080/09505431.2013.786989

Network for Greening the Financial System (NGFS). (2023). Climate-related risks and transition pathways. Paris: NGFS.

Organisation for Economic Co-operation and Development (OECD). (2021). Towards a green recovery. Paris: OECD Publishing.

Organisation for Economic Co-operation and Development (OECD). (2022). Inclusive transitions for net zero. Paris: OECD Publishing.

Rishanty, A., Sambodo, M.T., Silalahi, M. et al. Zero-Waste Bioenergy to Lower Energy Transition Risks in Indonesia — A Circular Economy Practice on Methane Capture in Biogas Production from POME. Bioenergy. Res. 17, 1930–1942 (2024). https://doi.org/10.1007/s12155-024-10754-3

Rodrik, D. (2014). The past, present, and future of economic growth. Global Citizen Foundation.

Salomon, B. D., & Krishna, K. (2011). The coming sustainable energy transition: History, strategies, and outlook. *Energy Policy, 39*(11), 7422–7431. https://doi.org/10.1016/j.enpol.2011.09.009

Sovacool, B. K. (2016). How long will it take? Conceptualizing the temporal dynamics of energy transitions. *Energy Research & Social Science, 13*, 202–215. https://doi.org/10.1016/j.erss.2015.12.020

Juhro, S. M., Narayan, P. K., Garg, B., Anugrah, D. A., (2024). Transition to a green economy, oil prices and the current account. Energy Economics. Volume 139, 2024, 107916, ISSN 0140-9883, https://doi.org/10.1016/j.eneco.2024.107916

Stiglitz, J. (2019). People, power, and profits: Progressive capitalism for an age of discontent. New York, NY: W. W. Norton & Company.

Stiglitz, J., Stern, N., Duan, M., et al. (2017). Report of the High-Level Commission on Carbon Prices. Washington, DC: World Bank Group.

World Bank. (2022). Inclusive green growth in emerging economies. Washington, DC: World Bank.

York, R., & Bell, S. E. (2019). Energy transitions or additions?: Why a transition from fossil fuels requires more than the growth of renewable energy. *Energy Research & Social Science, 51*, 40–43. https://doi.org/10.1016/j.erss.2019.01.008

Zhang, M., Mu, H., Ning, Y., & Song, Y. (2009). Decomposition of energy-related CO2 emissions over 1991–2006 in China. *Ecological Economics, 68*, 2122–2128.

# Chapter 11
# Energy Subsidies and the Quest for Fairness in Indonesia

**Maxensius Tri Sambodo, Rio Novandra, Egi Suarga, and Rizky Wibisono**

**Abstract** Indonesia has allocated heavily in fossil fuel subsidies, yet reform is politically difficult. Although energy access is improving, it remains unfair in remote areas. This study analyses how these subsidies affect inequality. It finds that current policies often miss the intended targets and are distributed unevenly across provinces. Crucially, both keeping and removing subsidies can widen the wealth gap. The study proposes a new framework to ensure a fairer energy transformation for everyone.

**Keywords** Energy subsidies · Regional inequality · Subsidy reform · Equitable energy transition

## 1 Introduction

Many countries have increasingly emphasized the affordability of energy prices. In its 2024 report, the IEA (2024) stated that affordability and fairness lie at the core of today's energy debates. The IEA further noted that, to the extent possible, the transition to green energy can help reduce household energy bills, although it requires substantial investment and targeted support for those unable to bear the higher upfront costs of certain green technologies. The report also highlighted that nearly 750 million people still lack access to electricity, while 2 billion people lack access to clean cooking methods.

In an effort to enhance both the affordability and accessibility of energy, the government provides subsidies. The latest report from the International Monetary Fund (IMF) (Black, 2023) highlights four key points. First, total fossil fuel subsidies in 2022 reached approximately USD 7 trillion, equivalent to 7.1% of global gross domestic product (GDP). Second, implicit subsidies were found to be larger

M. T. Sambodo (✉) · R. Novandra
National Research and Innovation Agency of Indonesia (BRIN), Jakarta, Indonesia

E. Suarga · R. Wibisono
World Resources Institute, Jakarta, Indonesia



S. M. Juhro et al. (eds.), *Sustainable Economy: The Indonesian Pathways*,
https://doi.org/10.1007/978-981-92-1215-6_11

than explicit subsidies.[1] This reflects the significant opportunity costs of fossil fuel subsidies, including air pollution, global warming, traffic congestion, and lost consumption tax revenues. Third, nearly half of global fossil fuel subsidies occur in East Asia and the Pacific, with China, the United States, Russia, the European Union, and India being the largest providers. A pressing challenge is the need to explicitly phase out these subsidies and implement carbon taxation to ensure global temperature increases remain below 2 degrees Celsius. Fourth, fossil fuel price reform has the potential to generate additional tax revenue, reduce premature deaths, and enhance social welfare through improved environmental conditions. Given the substantial external costs of fossil fuels, fossil energy consumption should be regulated through taxation policies. While energy subsidies may still be necessary, they should be directed toward the appropriate target groups, namely low-income households (OECD, 2024), rather than toward commodities whose distribution and oversight are difficult to control.

Indonesia exhibits a pattern consistent with global trends, wherein implicit subsidies surpass explicit subsidies. The share of subsidies reached 15.4% of GDP—higher than the global average and greater than that of several major economies such as China and India (Table 11.1). This demonstrates that the burden of energy subsidies in Indonesia is considerable, not only in terms of their proportion of GDP but also when assessed on a per capita basis at constant prices. When the fiscal deficit expands as a result of rising energy subsidies, the government is more inclined to resort to borrowing (new debt issuance). For instance, during the administration

**Table 11.1** Total (Explicit and Implicit) Energy Subsidies, Top 10 Selected Countries, 2022

| | | Explicit Subsidies | | Implicit subsidies | | Total subsidies | |
|---|---|---|---|---|---|---|---|
| No | Country | % GDP | capita USD | % GDP | capita USD | % GDP | capita USD |
| 1 | Iran | 10.5 | 711 | 16.7 | 1131 | 27.2 | 1842 |
| 2 | Saudi Arabia | 13.8 | 3579 | 13.2 | 3418 | 27.0 | 6997 |
| 3 | Russia | 4.0 | 488 | 19.6 | 2423 | 23.6 | 2911 |
| 4 | Indonesia | 6.2 | 285 | 9.2 | 422 | 15.4 | 707 |
| 5 | Türkiye | 5.9 | 696 | 9.3 | 1089 | 15.2 | 1785 |
| 6 | Viet Nam | 1.7 | 67 | 12.6 | 507 | 14.3 | 574 |
| 7 | South Africa | 1.2 | 85 | 12.8 | 934 | 14.0 | 1019 |
| 8 | China | 1.5 | 189 | 11.0 | 1379 | 12.5 | 1568 |
| 9 | India | 1.0 | 23 | 9.6 | 223 | 10.6 | 246 |
| 10 | Morocco | 1.0 | 38 | 8.9 | 340 | 9.9 | 378 |

Notes: Estimates for energy subsidies in other countries are available here: https://www.imf.org/-/media/Files/Topics/energysubsidies/EXTERNALfuelsubsidiestemplate2023new.ashx
Source: IMF staff calculations

[1] The IMF has a method for calculating subsidies in two categories, namely implicit and explicit. Explicit subsidies (undercharging for fossil fuel supply costs) and implicit subsidies (undercharging for environmental costs and loss of consumption tax revenue). The full gap between the efficient price (the sum of supply, environmental costs, and other costs) and the retail price multiplied by consumption equals total fossil fuel subsidies.

of President Susilo Bambang Yudhoyono, the government allocated a substantial budget for energy subsidies. As documented in the *Financial Note and Draft State Budget (Nota Keuangan dan RAPBN) 2025*, between 2010 and 2014, energy subsidy expenditures increased from approximately IDR 140 trillion to IDR 350.3 trillion,[2] representing an average annual growth rate of 25.8%. In parallel, the state budget (APBN) deficit relative to GDP in 2014 reached 2.4%, or approximately IDR 214.49 trillion, with the debt-to-GDP ratio amounting to 25.6%.

Moreover, fossil fuel subsidies risk locking countries into long-term fossil fuel dependence. Seto et al. (2016) note that Carbon lock-in is highly vulnerable to several risks, including substantial capital costs, the long lifespan of infrastructure, and the complex interrelations between socio-economic and technical systems. Likewise, they demonstrate that for countries with abundant oil and gas resources and higher income levels, eliminating subsidies would reduce $CO_2$ emissions—potentially surpassing the region's climate pledges—while affecting fewer people living below the poverty line compared to low-income regions.

In terms of achieving sustainable development targets in the energy sector, Indonesia demonstrates notable progress. Affordability and clean energy are integral components of the Sustainable Development Goals (SDGs). According to the most recent report on SDG 7, Indonesia's position is classified as "quite improved," with its strongest performance falling under the category of "on track or maintaining SDG achievement" (UN, 2024). Looking at the four sub-indicators of SDG 7, Indonesia remains on track in terms of electricity access and clean energy access[3]. However, persistent challenges remain, particularly in reducing emission intensity in the power generation sector and in strengthening the role of renewable energy.

Energy subsidy policy has been a crucial element of social protection programs designed to mitigate the impacts of the COVID-19 pandemic. Between April and June 2020, the government eliminated electricity bills for households using 450 VA power, while those in the 900 VA category and classified as poor received a 50% discount on their bills. This policy was extended until February 2021. Notably, Indonesia was not alone; many ASEAN countries also introduced similar subsidy measures (Lee et al., 2020).

While progress in electricity and clean cooking access appears to be on track, significant challenges remain. According to official statistics (Ministry of Energy and Mineral Resources, 2023b), Indonesia's electrification ratio has reached 99.79%, leaving around 177,732 households without access to electricity. Moreover, the data reveal that nearly 1.2 million households do not receive electricity from PLN (the state-owned utility). Another challenge lies in the uneven distribution of electrification, particularly in access to PLN-supplied electricity. For instance, Central Papua has a PLN electrification ratio of only 56%, while Papua Highlands

[2] Such a subsidy allocation amounts to approximately 29% of total domestic tax revenues, or about 2.7 times the central government's expenditure on education.

[3] It covers: Population with access to electricity (%); Population with access to clean fuels and technology for cooking (%); CO2 emissions from fuel combustion per total electricity output (MtCO2/TWh); and Renewable energy share in total final energy consumption (%).

Province stands at just 15%. This suggests that many households still depend on electricity provided by local groups or individuals. For many residents, gaining access to PLN's electricity represents freedom from the constraints of limited supply, unreliable service, and unaffordable costs (Sambodo, 2015).

At the same time, while many families still lack adequate electricity access, the government allocates substantial energy subsidies. As a result, these subsidies are disproportionately enjoyed by those who already have access to energy. The state budget acknowledges this risk of misdirected subsidies. Furthermore, rising energy consumption, higher energy prices, and currency depreciation have significantly increased subsidy expenditures. Subsidies are provided for three main commodities: specific types of fuel (diesel and kerosene), 3-kg LPG cylinders, and electricity. Over the last five years (2020–2025)[4], energy subsidies have grown from IDR 108.8 trillion to IDR 183.8 trillion, an increase of approximately IDR 75 trillion. Acknowledging these challenges, the government has announced that future energy subsidy policies will be integrated into broader social protection efforts. The aim is to ensure that subsidies are more targeted, efficient, and equitable.

In addition to the provision of energy subsidies, due to the lack of periodic adjustments to energy tariffs, the government must also allocate a budget for unwanted subsidies or what can be termed compensation. The amount of compensation continues to increase, even the 'compensation' item has exceeded the number of subsidies for electricity and LPG fuel. This has occurred since 2021. The amount of electricity compensation has increased significantly, from approximately IDR 18 trillion in 2020 to around IDR 100 trillion in 2024. This indicates that energy policy is not only trapped in the number of subsidies, but also compensation. The provision of compensation is intended as an effort by the government to maintain people's purchasing power, but compensation is enjoyed more by PLN customers who are not included in the category of poor families. Thus, the provision of subsidies that are not on target and compensation both have problems in terms of justice.

This paper seeks to address two central questions. First, what are the costs of energy subsidy policies, and what are the consequences of adopting different targeted subsidy options? Second, drawing on the empirical evidence presented in the previous section, which frameworks are most appropriate for analyzing policy reforms necessary to support a more just energy transition in Indonesia?

## 2 Data and Methodology

To address those two central questions, the analysis offers an in-depth analysis of inclusion and exclusion errors, with particular attention to the 3-kg LPG and electricity subsidies. It also employs the Williamson inequality index to assess the extent

[4]Author's compilation from various national budged; *PLN's Financial Report; **first semester 2025.

to which the distribution of energy subsidies and per capita income across provinces in Indonesia has become more equitable or remains uneven. In addition, it analyzes compensation variations to evaluate the impacts of different subsidy reduction policy scenarios on inequality, as measured by the Gini index, and on poverty levels. The analysis is based on Susenas Dataset 2023 and is built with two main commodities, namely LPG and Electricity. We did not conduct calculations for fuel subsidies due to the limited availability of household-level information on fuel consumption, particularly for products such as diesel and Pertalite (RON 90).

## 3 The Cost of Action and Inaction: Economic and Social Implications of Energy Subsidy

This section examines the costs of both action and inaction associated with energy subsidy policies.

### *3.1 Inclusion: Exclusion Errors in LPG Subsidies and Fuel Stacking*

The 3-kg LPG subsidy is frequently captured by non-target households, particularly non-poor groups, as the fuel is easily accessible and monitoring mechanisms for subsidy allocation remain weak. Evidence indicates that a substantial portion of the subsidized 3-kg LPG, intended for the bottom 40 percent of households, is disproportionately consumed by wealthier groups. Estimates suggest that approximately IDR 8.8 trillion per month—or IDR 106 trillion annually—of LPG subsidies are absorbed by higher-income households.

Reflecting on the current subsidy design, about 74 percent of benefits accrue to non-target households (beyond the bottom 40 percent), while in many regions outside Java, households remain highly dependent on traditional fuels such as firewood. The concentration of subsidy consumption in Java—driven largely by its population size—further constrains fiscal space for expanding clean energy access in more remote areas. This competition between subsidies and infrastructure investment unintentionally reinforces marginalization and exacerbates interregional inequality.

It is estimated that wealthy households in Java capture around IDR 7 trillion in misallocated subsidies per month, compared to only about IDR 100 million per month in Papua and Maluku. In addition, more than 50 percent of households in Papua and Maluku still rely on firewood for cooking. Interestingly, among households in the eighth to tenth expenditure deciles, the consumption of 3-kg LPG declines. This trend warrants further investigation to assess whether it reflects a shift in preferences, differences in cooking practices, growing awareness, barriers to access, or other influencing factors. The issue of inclusion error also stems from substitution with non-subsidized cylinders. Although the 3-kg LPG cylinder is lighter than the 12-kg cylinder, consumers perceive it as more expensive on a per-kilogram basis. Practicality and habitual factors also influence choices, as the 12-kg cylinder lasts longer than the 5.5-kg cylinder and is relatively easier to obtain in retail markets.

In the context of exclusion error, data indicate that approximately 7.1 million households still rely on firewood and around 1.7 million households continue to use kerosene for cooking. Spatial patterns of household energy consumption reveal that in the Papua and Maluku regions, dependence on traditional energy sources such as firewood and kerosene remain particularly pronounced. This persistence reflects the incomplete implementation of the 2007 kerosene-to-LPG conversion program, which has not been fully realized across several major islands, including Papua, Maluku, Bali, Nusa Tenggara, Sulawesi, and Sumatra.

An important aspect of the Indonesian context is the persistence of fuel stacking behavior at the household level.[5] On the island of Java, for example, a substantial number of households—approximately 3.6 million—continue to rely on firewood. This reliance is likely influenced by the relatively low cost and availability of firewood, frequent disruptions in LPG supply, ingrained cooking habits shaped by cultural preferences, and safety concerns associated with LPG use. The practice of households maintaining three types of stoves (LPG, induction, and firewood) reflects both adaptive capacity and strategies for risk mitigation (Fig. 11.1). Such behavior may also be viewed as a form of local wisdom, representing the integration of modern and traditional practices. The inability to completely separate these technologies highlights the heterogeneity of household capacities and technological capabilities in achieving equitable energy access across diverse social groups.

**Fig. 11.1** Fuel Stacking Behaviour. Note: This picture was taken from a household in Kesiman, South Denpasar, Bali (30 April 2024). This household participated in the LPG-to-induction stove conversion program. The program was implemented by PLN as part of the showcase project for the G20 Summit in Bali on 15–16 November 2022

[5]Fuel stacking refers to the practice of households using multiple fuels simultaneously for cooking, heating, or other domestic energy needs, rather than fully transitioning from traditional fuels to modern energy sources.

An important aspect to note concerns the use of the National Socio-Economic Unified Database (DTSEN). Recently, a debate emerged between the Minister of Finance and the Minister of Energy and Mineral Resources. The Minister of Finance, Purbaya Yudhi Sadewa, stated that the Government of Indonesia could not yet terminate the subsidy program, given that domestic economic growth has not been sufficiently robust. The application of the DTSEN in the distribution of fuel subsidies has not yet been adopted by the Ministry of Energy and Mineral Resources (MEMR), whereas the Ministry of Social Affairs has already utilized the DTSEN for social program targeting.[6] On the other hand, the Minister of Energy and Mineral Resources argued that the Minister of Finance had misinterpreted the data and had not received complete information from his subordinates.[7] The government further noted that the MEMR is currently designing a new LPG subsidy scheme aimed at improving targeting accuracy.

### *3.2 Inclusion: Exclusion Errors in Electricity Subsidy*

Exclusion error can be examined across two dimensions. First, community-level portraits of electricity access reveal that many households continue to obtain electricity from PLN without having individual meters. The largest concentration is in Java, with more than 1.8 million households affected. Under such conditions, households face limited access to electricity because they must share connections with other families that already have PLN meters.

Households without meters should be encouraged to obtain them. According to the Regulation of the Minister of Energy and Mineral Resources (ESDM) No. 27/2017, the connection cost for new electricity access with 450 Volt Ampere (VA) capacity is IDR 421,000. Through the *Memberi Terang Membangun Negeri* program, a 50% discount is provided for underprivileged households in Frontier, Outermost, and Disadvantaged (3T) regions. These conditions suggest that the cost of new connections remains one of the barriers to expanding electricity access.

Second, approximately one million households obtain electricity from sources other than PLN. Notably, most of these households are located outside Java, highlighting that significant populations in these regions still lack reliable access to electricity. This situation is largely attributed to the high investment costs required to expand grid services, combined with the financial constraints faced by PLN (*Perusahaan Listrik Negara*, the state-owned electricity company). Furthermore, an estimated 456,800 households have no access to electricity at all. To meet their lighting needs, these households rely on alternative energy sources. Overall, around 4.65 million households require attention to improve access to adequate and affordable electricity.

---

[6] https://www.cnnindonesia.com/ekonomi/20250930170450-532-1279385/purbaya-sentil-bahlil-tak-pakai-dtsen-untuk-salurkan-subsidi-bbm

[7] https://money.kompas.com/read/2025/10/04/081927926/duduk-perkara-bahlil-purbaya-saling-jawab-soal-data-subsidi-lpg-3-kg

Inclusion error in electricity subsidies is largely associated with households connected to 450-watt electricity. Currently, around 30 million households are connected at this level, making them eligible for electricity subsidies. Meanwhile, among 900-watt customers, approximately 3.8 million poor households—or around 13.8% of the total 900-watt customer base—are recipients of the Family Hope Program (Program Keluarga Harapan, PKH). However, having low connected power does not necessarily indicate that a household is poor. This is also evident in the case of 900-watt customers, and data show that 450-watt customers are distributed across all expenditure deciles, meaning that many of them are not poor.

Therefore, the policy of providing subsidies to 450-watt households needs to be better targeted, distinguishing between poor and better-off households. A similar re-sorting strategy has already been applied to the 900-watt customer group. The total electricity subsidy allocated for 450-watt and 900-watt PKH customer groups is estimated at IDR 19 trillion. Furthermore, if subsidies were restricted to households in the bottom 40 percent, the required amount would be approximately IDR 8.4 trillion per month. In other words, there remains potential savings of around IDR 10.57 trillion within household subsidy allocations.

In addition to issues of inclusion and exclusion errors, another important aspect that warrants attention is household expenditure on electricity consumption. Relatively, the share of electricity spending in total household expenditure among the bottom three deciles increased between 2022 and 2023, while for other deciles it declined. This development is concerning, as rising electricity costs may reduce spending on more essential needs such as food, education, and health. It may also indicate that the energy expenditure burden on poor households requires closer government monitoring to ensure that subsidy policies remain attentive to principles of equity and justice.

# 4 Discussion

## *4.1 Energy Subsidy Policy in the Context of the Williamson Index*

The Williamson inequality index is particularly useful for assessing disparities in the allocation of per capita energy subsidies (electricity, LPG, and fuel). In this context, inequality is analyzed across provinces in Indonesia.[8] Since energy subsidies are still provided on an untargeted basis, measuring per capita subsidy levels serves as an appropriate proxy, although it does not fully capture the dimension of equity. In comparison, electricity subsidy policies are generally considered to be more accurately targeted than those for LPG and fuel.

[8] If this inequality index approaches zero, it indicates lower regional disparities (a more equitable distribution of subsidies). Conversely, a higher index value reflects greater inequality across regions.

Table 11.2 highlights three important patterns related to inequality. First, inequality in electricity subsidies is relatively higher and more pronounced compared to other forms of energy, indicating that access to electricity remains uneven across provinces. Second, as noted in the previous section, within the 450 VA customer group receiving subsidies, a considerable proportion of households are non-poor.

**Table 11.2** Inequality of electricity subsidy across the province (in per capita)

| Province | Electricity Subsidy Inequality | LPG Subsidy Inequality | Oil Subsidy Inequality |
|---|---|---|---|
| Aceh | 0.07 | 0.00 | 0.02 |
| Sumatera Utara | **0.13** | 0.01 | **0.06** |
| Sumatera Barat | 0.03 | 0.01 | 0.05 |
| Riau | 0.09 | 0.05 | **0.19** |
| Jambi | 0.01 | 0.00 | 0.04 |
| Sumatera Selatan | 0.02 | 0.00 | 0.02 |
| Bengkulu | 0.02 | 0.01 | 0.02 |
| Lampung | 0.01 | 0.02 | **0.07** |
| Kep. Bangka Belitung | 0.05 | 0.03 | 0.05 |
| Kep. Riau | 0.03 | **0.07** | 0.01 |
| DKI Jakarta | 0.07 | 0.05 | 0.03 |
| Jawa Barat | **0.21** | 0.01 | **0.13** |
| Jawa Tengah | **0.13** | 0.03 | 0.02 |
| DI Yogyakarta | 0.06 | 0.05 | 0.03 |
| Jawa Timur | **0.32** | 0.01 | 0.01 |
| Banten | **0.17** | **0.06** | 0.03 |
| Bali | 0.03 | **0.07** | 0.02 |
| Nusa Tenggara Barat | **0.10** | 0.04 | **0.06** |
| Nusa Tenggara Timur | **0.10** | 0.04 | 0.03 |
| Kalimantan Barat | 0.02 | 0.00 | 0.01 |
| Kalimantan Tengah | 0.01 | 0.02 | 0.05 |
| Kalimantan Selatan | 0.07 | 0.00 | 0.00 |
| Kalimantan Timur | 0.02 | 0.00 | 0.01 |
| Kalimantan Utara | 0.04 | 0.03 | 0.00 |
| Sulawesi Utara | 0.04 | 0.01 | 0.02 |
| Sulawesi Tengah | 0.08 | 0.03 | 0.02 |
| Sulawesi Selatan | **0.14** | 0.00 | **0.13** |
| Sulawesi Tenggara | 0.06 | 0.03 | **0.31** |
| Gorontalo | 0.03 | 0.01 | 0.03 |
| Sulawesi Barat | 0.06 | 0.02 | 0.02 |
| Maluku | 0.06 | 0.00 | 0.01 |
| Maluku Utara | 0.06 | **0.06** | 0.01 |
| Papua | 0.07 | **0.13** | 0.04 |
| Papua Barat | 0.02 | **0.07** | 0.03 |

Moreover, inequality in fuel (BBM) subsidies is also relatively high, with disparities in access, infrastructure conditions, and the availability of transportation modes contributing to this outcome. Third, inequality in LPG subsidies appears relatively lower than for other energy sources. This may partly be explained by the success of the stove conversion program from kerosene to LPG, with data showing that nearly 84% of Indonesian households use LPG for cooking. The relatively equitable access to LPG across provinces has contributed to the lower measured inequality in LPG subsidies. It is important to note, however, that Papua records a high inequality index, largely due to the continued reliance of many households on kerosene and firewood for cooking.

Figure 11.2 illustrates the correlation between inequality in Gross Regional Domestic Product (GRDP) and inequality in per capita energy subsidies. The findings indicate that inequality in energy subsidies is more pronounced than inequality in GRDP, suggesting that the distribution of per capita energy subsidies tends to be uneven across provinces. This also underscores the risk that energy subsidy policies may exacerbate interprovincial disparities.

By contrast, inequality in per capita GRDP is less severe than inequality in per capita energy subsidies. The Province of DKI Jakarta exhibits the highest level of GRDP inequality. However, when using DKI Jakarta's energy subsidy inequality as a benchmark, several provinces—namely Papua, Banten, Riau, and North Maluku—display even higher levels of energy subsidy inequality. This indicates that the

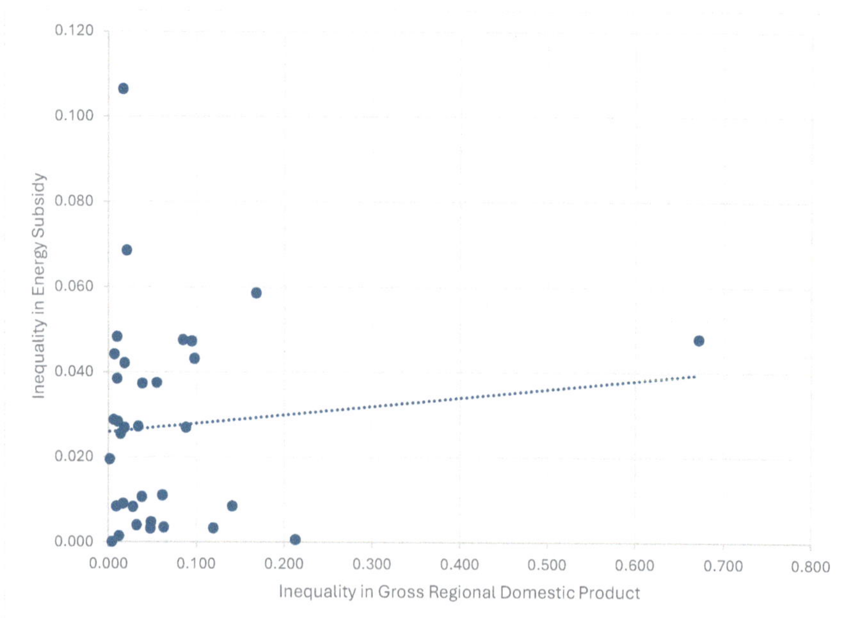


**Fig. 11.2** Correlation between Inequality in Gross Regional Domestic Product and Inequality in Energy Subsidy Across Provinces in Indonesia

distribution of per capita energy subsidies is more unequal in these provinces compared to DKI Jakarta.

Several factors may contribute to this outcome, including disparities in energy access, geographical conditions, infrastructure, population distribution, and uneven economic structures (Kanbur & Venables, 2005; Yusuf & Resosudarmo 2008). In light of these realities, it is essential to incorporate these factors into the design and allocation of energy subsidy policies.

### 4.2 Evaluating Compensation Variation Analysis

It is important to explore various scenarios concerning policy options that may be considered to reduce subsidy pressures. The general idea of raising energy prices (by removing subsidies) is followed by the provision of compensation to poor and vulnerable groups. This study analyzes three scenarios: (i) Price Adjustment on LPG; (ii) Price Adjustment on LPG and Electricity; and (iii) Price Adjustment on LPG and Electricity combined with a Give Up Program.

The analysis in this section reveals three important findings. First, energy subsidies increase the Gini ratio, while the removal of such subsidies also leads to a higher Gini ratio. This highlights the dual effects of subsidies. Second, rural and urban areas demonstrate different responses to compensation policies in terms of inequality outcomes, even though compensation measures contribute to reducing poverty rates. It is therefore essential to design differentiated interventions for each income decile, as these measures produce varying impacts on inequality and poverty. Third, alongside formal subsidy reduction policies, it is equally important for the government to encourage households with sufficient capacity to voluntarily abstain from consuming subsidized fuels. In this context, particular attention should be given to the study by Yusuf and Sumner (2015), which underscores the importance of timing in compensation interventions following subsidy reform, in order to avoid adverse effects on vulnerable population groups.

### 4.3 Price Adjustment on LPG[9]

The storyline that is being developed is that if the income from subsidies that can be saved in part or in full is given to the 40% decile group below, meanwhile those in the decile above them pay economic prices (market prices or subsidies are removed 100%). Based on the analysis in the previous section, it is known that around IDR 8.8 trillion per month of subsidy budget can be saved or around IDR 105.6 trillion per year. Next, based on three scenarios, namely: 25%; 50%; and 100% of the total

[9] Data for this analysis please refer to Table 11.2 at raw A and B.

LPG subsidy that can be saved is returned in the form of a social protection program to target households (the bottom 40%) on a pro-rata basis or IDR 75,000 per month; IDR 150,000 per month and IDR 300,000 per month, then the impact on the Gini ratio indicator will be different.

Looking at these scenarios, it appears that energy subsidies have an impact on increasing income inequality (Gini ratio) and the removal of energy subsidies will have an impact on increasing Gini ratio. However, the increase in the Gini indicator can be avoided or reduced by continuing to provide subsidies to the 'bottom 40%' group and providing compensation to them. If the government wants the Gini ratio condition not to change after the subsidy reform is carried out, then the amount of compensation can be given in the 25% scenario. The interesting thing is to see the condition of inequality in rural areas which turns out (Table 11.3 Raw A), even though 100% compensation has been given, the condition of inequality has only decreased marginally compared to the condition where price reform was not carried out. Taking into account the conditions of inequality which are relatively more 'persistent' in rural areas, this indicates the need to provide other programs that are able to reduce conditions of inequality in society. Furthermore, Table 11.3 Raw B shows that providing compensation has an impact on reducing poverty rates. Thus, the policy of eliminating LPG subsidies for the well-off group and accompanied by providing compensation to the 'bottom 40%' group, not only has an impact on softening conditions of inequality, but also on reducing the percentage of the poor population.

## 4.4 Price Adjustment on LPG and Electricity

In this scenario, researchers make adjustments to LPG and electricity prices. Furthermore, 50% and 100% of the total subsidies that can be saved are returned to the bottom 40 decile groups with decile I to IV scenarios, each receiving a compensation allocation of 40%; 30%; 20%; and 10%. The consideration for this scenario is that the impact of the increase will be more pronounced in the poorest groups, therefore compensation needs to be given in a different way, compared to the scenario where the amount of compensation is given the same for all decile groups I to IV. By comparing Table 11.3 Raw A and Raw C, it can be seen that differences in compensation in decile groups provide conditions of lower inequality, both in the total scope (rural and urban), urban and rural. These findings also confirm that the form of intervention for each decile group should be different to reduce conditions of inequality. The same thing can also be seen from the poverty conditions which are much lower (Table 11.3 Raw D) compared to the previous scenario described in Table 11.3 Raw B.

**Table 11.3** Compensation variation analysis

| A. Conditions of Expenditure Inequality with Compensation Scenario from LPG (Gini Ratio) | | | | | |
|---|---|---|---|---|---|
| Area | Initial—2023 | Subsidy removal | 25% | 50% | 100% |
| Urban & Rural | 0.388 | 0.393 | 0.388 | 0.382 | 0.372 |
| Urban | 0.409 | 0.418 | 0.414 | 0.411 | 0.403 |
| Rural | 0.313 | 0.339 | 0.332 | 0.325 | 0.312 |
| B. Poverty Rate with Compensation Scenario from LPG | | | | | |
| Area | Initial—2023 | 25% | 50% | 100% | |
| Urban & Rural | 8.1% | 7.1% | 5.8% | 3.8% | |
| Rural | 10.8% | 9.3% | 7.6% | 5.1% | |
| Urban | 6.3% | 5.6% | 4.6% | 3.0% | |
| C. Conditions of Expenditure Inequality with Compensation Scenario (Gini Ratio) | | | | | |
| Area | Initial—2023 | 50% | 100% | | |
| Urban & Rural | 38.8% | 36.8% | 36.8% | | |
| Rural | 0.313 | 0.323 | 0.307 | | |
| Urban | 0.409 | 0.4095 | 0.4015 | | |
| D. Poverty Rate with Compensation Scenario | | | | | |
| Area | Initial—2023 | 50% | 100% | | |
| Urban & Rural | 8.1% | 4.4% | 2.2% | | |
| Rural | 10.8% | 4.4% | 2.2% | | |
| Urban | 6.3% | 3.5% | 1.7% | | |
| E. Conditions of Expenditure Inequality with Incorporating Give Up program | | | | | |
| Area | Initial—2023 | Give-Up program | 50% | 100% | |
| Urban & Rural | 0.388 | 0.385 | 0.380 | 0.368 | |
| Urban | 0.409 | 0.414 | 0.409 | 0.401 | |
| Rural | 0.313 | 0.332 | 0.323 | 0.307 | |
| F. Poverty Rate with Incorporating Give Up program | | | | | |
| Area | 2003 | Give up program | 50% | 100% | |
| Urban & Rural | 8.14% | 8.14% | 4.40% | 2.16% | |
| Rural | 10.76% | 10.76% | 5.70% | 2.78% | |
| Urban | 6.34% | 6.34% | 3.49% | 1.71% | |

Source: Authors' calculation

## 4.5 *Price Adjustment on LPG and Electricity with Give Up Program*

In this scenario, we proposed the opportunity to carry out a 'give up' program. Households in deciles 5 to 10 are given the opportunity to 'give up'. In the 'give up' scenario it is assumed that for each decile, namely 5 to 10, there is around 10%; 20%; 30%; 40%; 50%; and 60% of total households voluntarily gave up. The Gini ratio results show that the Gini ratio (combined rural and urban) has experienced a decline, but it appears that for the 50% and 100% scenarios the condition of inequality is in a lower position (Table 11.3 Raw E). In Table 11.3 Raw F, it appears that poverty conditions do not change in the give up scenario. Thus, the 'give up' policy does not have a significant impact on the poverty side, and in terms of the Gini ratio there appears to be a decline. Thus, this policy is worthy of consideration as a step to reduce the burden of subsidies and improve conditions of inequality.

## 4.6 Seeking an Appropriate Subsidy Reform Design

The policy of phasing out energy subsidies remains a challenging task to implement. This observation remains highly relevant today for two reasons McCulloch et al. (2022). First, in the context of price reform, studies demonstrate that the tendency to halt gradual subsidy reductions often results in unsustainable subsidy levels. Second, when large-scale adjustments to energy prices are implemented abruptly, they tend to provoke strong public protests.

Chipangamate and Nwaila (2024) proposed the "energy transition cycle". They emphasize the financing dimension, addressing various dilemmas that may arise, and the need to foster behavioral change. This indicates that policy reform need to enhance public awareness. Studies indicate three main factors that shape the rejection or acceptance of fuel price reform policies (McCulloch et al., 2021). First, individuals or groups who expect to bear higher costs, or who frequently experience disruptions in fuel availability, may support reform in the hope of achieving greater stability. Second, those who perceive the government as corrupt or incapable of implementing compensation programs transparently are more likely to oppose reform. Third, acceptance of fuel price reform tends to increase when governance is perceived as more accountable, when religious and ethical values are emphasized, and when governments demonstrate the ability to deliver better public services at both local and national levels.

In Indonesia, the energy subsidy policy is stipulated in Law No. 30 of 2007 on Energy. Article 7(1) of the law states that energy prices must be determined based on a *fair economic value*. The accompanying explanation clarifies that "fair economic value" refers to a value or cost that reflects the cost of energy production, including environmental and conservation costs and benefits, assessed according to the community's ability to pay, and ultimately determined by the government. Furthermore, Article 7(2) specifies that *"the government and regional governments shall provide subsidy funds for underprivileged community groups"*.

Despite this legal framework, energy pricing policy remains problematic. The reference to community ability is a grey area that often opens space for pragmatic debate. From a fairness perspective, the policy is difficult to justify, as the highest-income group receives, in absolute terms, six times more in subsidies than the lowest-income group. A similar view is expressed by Davis (2014), who emphasizes that fuel subsidies generate significant welfare losses (deadweight loss) and drain fiscal space, diverting public funds away from more productive investments such as health, education, and green infrastructure.

In the context of better subsidy targeting, government plans in 2026 to utilize the *National Socio-Economic Unified Database* (DTSEN) to ensure that energy subsidies and compensation policies are more accurately targeted toward low-income households.[10] On the other hand, the government's budget statement continues to frame energy subsidies as a means of strengthening energy, social, and economic security. Arzel et al. (2012) argue that the potential for significant energy subsidy leakage, combined with the government's efforts to protect the poor, makes this policy highly costly.

More challenge is further compounded by Government Regulation No. 14 of 2012,[11] which requires parliamentary (DPR) approval for electricity tariffs. This renders pricing policy an increasingly complex decision-making process. According to Sambodo (2014), because energy price adjustments in Indonesia are often delayed for political reasons, the country could consider adopting a model similar to the Independent Oil Price Review Committee (IOPRC), established in 2017 by the Philippine Department of Energy. The IOPRC is a multi-sectoral body, composed of representatives from academia, business, consumers, and the public transport sector, tasked with conducting independent reviews to ensure fair and transparent pricing.

In the Medium-Term Development Plan (RPJMN) 2025–2029, under National Priority 6—Building from Villages and from the Ground Up for Economic Growth, Equity, and Poverty Alleviation—one of the activities outlined is the distribution of adaptive social assistance and targeted subsidies through a welfare card. This welfare card is envisioned as a tool to integrate various social assistance and subsidy programs. Nevertheless, the government itself acknowledges that establishing such a system is far from straightforward. The key challenges include inaccurate targeting and fragmented social assistance programs that fail to adequately meet beneficiaries' needs, demonstrate limited responsiveness to crises, and remain underdeveloped in terms of digitalization. Moreover, limited inclusiveness, unequal access to services, the absence of graduation mechanisms, and insufficient monitoring further constrain effectiveness, leaving vulnerable groups inadequately supported within social protection systems.

The implementation of this priority activity involves 13 ministries, 2 national agencies, state-owned enterprises, and local governments. Interestingly, the Ministry of Administrative and Bureaucratic Reform (PANRB)—which is not explicitly mentioned in the RPJMN document for this priority activity—was present at a meeting on the Welfare Card Planning held in early September 2025. Given the large number of institutions involved, and the possibility of additional actors being included, it is essential to clarify how the coordination process for this preparation

[10] As stated by the Minister of Finance, Purbaya Yudhi Sadewa, during a Working Meeting with Commission XI of the House of Representatives of the Republic of Indonesia on Tuesday, 30 September 2025, the DTSEN system is already operational and has been utilized by the Ministry of Social Affairs but has not yet been adopted by the Ministry of Energy and Mineral Resources. It was also noted that, to date, the system has never been audited. The Financial and Development Supervisory Agency (BPKP) has therefore been requested to conduct oversight in order to prevent potential misuse

[11] Amended by Government Regulation Number 23 of 2014.

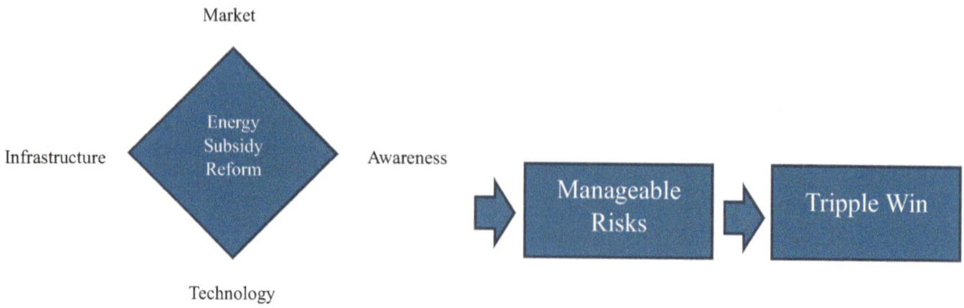


**Fig. 11.3** Framework for equitable energy transformation

is to be conducted and which institution will be held accountable for the welfare card's development as a key performance indicator. Such issues highlight the challenges the government faces in ensuring the readiness to implement more effectively targeted energy subsidies.

Building on the empirical and preceding discussion, we propose a *Framework for Equitable Energy Transformation* (Fig. 11.3). Policy reform must be understood as a comprehensive policy package. As the World Bank notes, policy implementation can fail for two general reasons (Loayza & Woolcock, 2020): (1) the absence of complementary measures needed for the chosen policy to be effective; and (2) the inadequacy of existing institutional and administrative capacities. In this regard, it is important to recall the perspective of Boediono (2019), who observed that what has been missing in policymaking in Indonesia is "order, focus, coherence, rationality, and continuity." Similarly we adopted North (1994) that said institutions and the technology employed determine the transaction and transformation cost that add up to the costs of production. We argued that energy subsidy reform encompass markets, public awareness, technology, and infrastructure.[12] This approach is broader and deeper than the energy transition framework proposed under the "energy transition cycle".

*Market* refers to the consistent, transparent, and accountable implementation of price adjustment mechanisms. *Public awareness* refers to the shift in subsidy provision from a commodity-based scheme to a household-targeted approach, which can be promoted under the social voluntary movement from the rich (non-target group). Building public awareness inevitably requires time, and in this context the government must make genuine efforts to foster public trust.

The *technological dimension* points to efforts to strengthen both hard and soft systems for updating beneficiary data, as well as developing techniques that enhance reliability. In this way, the likelihood of inclusion and exclusion errors can be minimized. Finally, *infrastructure* entails efforts to expand energy access, including logistics systems, to ensure that clean energy can also be accessed by those living in remote, frontier, and outermost regions. This also encompasses efforts to promote the development of green energy infrastructure.

[12] This conceptual framework was developed by Sambodo et al. (2025) in a report prepared for discussion at the G20 meeting in Brazil. This report is part of joint project with International Institute for Sustainable Development (IISD).

Well-designed energy subsidy reforms can significantly reduce the risks associated with energy transition. These risks can be mitigated through four key elements: effective leadership, alignment of goals, mutual trust, and the establishment of a robust social security system. Leadership and strong governance are widely recognized as critical preconditions for successful adaptation to energy policy reform. A just energy transition, in turn, enables the simultaneous achievement of economic, social, and environmental objectives (triple win). At the macro level, this can be reflected in a more controlled current account and fiscal deficit, accelerated economic growth, higher productivity and competitiveness, stronger social protection institutions, and carbon emissions targeting.

## 5 Conclusion

Many countries still provide fossil energy subsidies. Indonesia's position is in the fourth largest position in terms of the proportion of total subsidies (implicit and explicit) to gross domestic product of the 25 countries that have been evaluated by the IMF. An important reason behind the difficulty of removing energy subsidies is that this policy affects many people and from a politician's point of view makes it unpopular with their constituents.

Even though the achievement of Indonesia's seventh SDG target is on track in the context of access, the intensity of emissions and the role of renewable energy are still below the target. Even though the condition of energy access appears to be moving according to expectations, in terms of fairness it is still a challenge, especially in remote areas and with limited infrastructure access. Thus, the quality of access to electricity and clean energy for cooking still needs to continue to be improved.

This study presents four important findings. First, subsidy policies remain closely linked to the challenges of inclusion and exclusion errors. This arises because subsidies are still commodity-based and insufficiently targeted at poor households. The role of infrastructure, such as the National Socio-Economic Unified Database (DTSEN), should be further optimized to enhance both the efficiency and equity of subsidy distribution.

Second, the Williamson index analysis reveals three critical points. First, inequality in per capita energy subsidy allocation at the provincial level is more pronounced than inequality in Gross Regional Domestic Product (GRDP). Second, there are indications of a negative correlation between subsidy allocation inequality and GRDP inequality. Based on these findings, subsidy allocation must account for disparities in energy access, geographical conditions, infrastructure, population distribution, and uneven economic structures.

Third, in the context of policy scenarios, this study identifies three key findings: (1) both the provision and removal of energy subsidies increase the Gini ratio, underscoring their dual effects; (2) rural and urban areas respond differently to compensation policies, demonstrating the need for tailored interventions across income deciles, as compensation reduces poverty but affects inequality unevenly; and (3) subsidy reforms should be accompanied by voluntary withdrawal from subsidized fuel among capable households, with careful consideration of compensation timing to mitigate adverse impacts on vulnerable groups. Finally, based on empirical analysis and conceptual studies of transition and policy, the author proposes a *Framework for Equitable Energy Transformation* as an extension of the earlier *energy transition cycle* model.

## References


Arze del Granado, F. J., Coady, D., & Gillingham, R. (2012). The unequal benefits of fuel subsidies: A review of evidence for developing countries. *World Development, 40*(11), 2234–2248 https://doi.org/10.1016/j.worlddev.2012.05.005

Black, S. (2023) *IMF Fossil Fuel Subsidies Data: 2023 Update, IMF Working Papers*. Available at: https://doi.org/10.5089/9798400249006.001.

Boediono. (2019). Foreword: Lessons for Indonesia from East Asia. In H. Hill & S. D. Negara (Eds.), *The Indonesian economy in transition: Policy challenges in the Jokowi era and beyond* (pp. vii–xiii). ISEAS Publishing.

Chipangamate, N.S. and Nwaila, G.T. (2024) 'Assessment of challenges and strategies for driving energy transitions in emerging markets: A socio-technological systems perspective', *Energy Geoscience*. Available at: https://doi.org/10.1016/j.engeos.2023.100257.

Davis, Lucas W. 2014. "The Economic Cost of Global Fuel Subsidies." *American Economic Review* 104 (5): 581–85

IEA. (2024). *Security, affordability and sustainability – World Energy Outlook 2024 – Analysis - IEA*. Available at: https://www.iea.org/reports/world-energy-outlook-2024/security-affordability-and-sustainability (Accessed: 23 January 2025).

International Monetary Fund (2022) *Saudi Arabia- Selected Issues*.

Kanbur, R., & Venables, A. J. (Eds.). (2005). *Spatial Inequality and Development*. Oxford University Press; ADB (2015). *Fossil-Fuel Subsidies in Indonesia: Trends, Impacts, and Reforms*. Asian Development Bank

Lee, C., Negara, D. and Sambodo, M.T. (2020) *iseas perspective 2020: Covid-19's Economic Reckoning in Southeast Asia*. Available at: https://covid19.who.int/table.

Loayza, N. and Woolcock, M. (2020) *Designing good policies is one thing, implementing them is another*. Available at: https://blogs.worldbank.org/en/developmenttalk/designing-good-policies-one-thing-implementing-them-another (Accessed: 23 January 2025)

McCulloch, N. et al. (2022) 'An exploration of the association between fuel subsidies and fuel riots', *World Development*, 157. Available at: https://doi.org/10.1016/j.worlddev.2022.105935.

McCulloch, N., Moerenhout, T. and Yang, J. (2021) 'Fuel subsidy reform and the social contract in Nigeria: A micro-economic analysis', *Energy Policy*, 156. Available at: https://doi.org/10.1016/j.enpol.2021.112336.

Ministry of Energy and Mineral Resources (2023a) *Kementerian ESDM RI - Media Center - Arsip Berita - Pemerintah Tegaskan Subsidi LPG 3 Kg Tepat Sasaran Bermanfaat bagi Masyarakat Miskin*. Available at: https://www.esdm.go.id/id/media-center/arsip-berita/pemerintah-tegaskan-subsidi-lpg-3-kg-tepat-sasaran-bermanfaat-bagi-masyarakat-miskin (Accessed: 23 January 2025).

Ministry of Energy and Mineral Resources (2023b) *Statistik Ketenagalistrikan 2023*. Available at: https://gatrik.esdm.go.id/assets/uploads/download_index/files/e6394-buku-statistik-ketenagalistrikan-2023-esdm-revised.pdf (Accessed: 23 January 2025).

Ministry of Finance (2024) *Nota Keuangan beserta RAPBN Tahun Anggaran 2025*. Available at: https://berkas.dpr.go.id/setjen/dokumen/persipar-Naskah-Pidato-Buku-II-Nota-Keuangan-RAPBN-TA-2025-1724054085.pdf (Accessed: 23 January 2025).

North, D. 1994. Economic Performance Through Time, *The American Economic Review*, Vol 84(3):359-368

OECD (2024) *OECD Inventory of Support Measures for Fossil Fuels 2024*. OECD Publishing. Available at: https://doi.org/10.1787/a2f063fe-en.

Sambodo, M. T. (2015) *Kemiskinan Energi Listrik Memberi Terang Wilayah Terpencil Indonesia, LIPI Press, anggota Ikapi.*

Sambodo, M. T. (2014) *LPG Price Adjustments in Indonesia: An Unfinished Reform EXECUTIVE SUMMARY.* Available at: https://www.iseas.edu.sg/wp-content/uploads/pdfs/ISEAS_Perspective_2014_30.pdf (Accessed: 23 January 2025).

Sambodo, M. T., Silalahi, M., Sharma, S., Laan, T., Farandy, A. R., Nurjati, E., Inayah, I., Suardi, I., Handoyo, F. W., & Septania, I. (2025, November 18). Clean cooking means moving beyond fossil fuels: G20 countries must lead the way. *International Institute for Sustainable Development*. https://www.iisd.org/articles/deep-dive/clean-cooking-beyondfossil-fuels-g20.

Seto, K. C., et al. (2016). Carbon lock-in: Types, causes, and policy implications. *Annual Review of Environment and Resources, 41*, 425–452

UN (2024) *Sustainable Development Report 2024*. Available at: https://dashboards.sdgindex.org/static/profiles/pdfs/SDR-2024-indonesia.pdf (Accessed: 23 January 2025).

Yusuf, A. A., & Resosudarmo, B. P. (2008). Mitigating distributional impact of fuel pricing reform: The Indonesian experience. *ASEAN Economic Bulletin, 25*(1), 32–47. doi:https://doi.org/10.1355/ae25-1d

Yusuf, A.A. and Sumner, A. (2015) 'Growth, Poverty and Inequality under Jokowi', *Bulletin of Indonesian Economic Studies*, 51(3), pp. 323–348. Available at: https://doi.org/10.1080/00074918.2015.1110685.

# Chapter 12
# Identifying Strategic Service Sectors for Inclusive and Green Development in Indonesia: Input–Output Analysis

**Muhammad Handry Imansyah, Djoni Hartono, Titi Muswati Putranti, and Muzdalifah**

**Abstract** This study evaluates service subsectors along four dimensions: value-added multipliers, employment multipliers, carbon elasticity, and distributional effects. The findings indicate that six subsectors, including transport, construction-related services, and health, hold strong potential to deliver a "triple win" by generating output, creating jobs, and reducing carbon intensity. Nevertheless, the benefits remain uneven, with higher-income households capturing a disproportionate share. This provides new insights into the opportunities and limitations of positioning services at the core of Indonesia's development strategy. It points to policy directions that emphasize sector-specific efficiency, stronger social inclusion, and greener investment pathways.

**Keywords** Green development · Structural transformation · Inclusive green services · Input–output analysis · Strategic service sectors

## 1 Introduction

Economic development typically unfolds through a structural transition beginning with agriculture (primary), moving into manufacturing (secondary), and eventually advancing toward services (tertiary) (Kuznets, 1971; Chenery & Syrquin, 1975). Seminal theories by Lewis (1954) and later by Chenery and Taylor (1968) emphasize the decisive importance of sectoral shifts in enabling surplus labor to move into higher-productivity activities. In the classical dual economy model, the trajectory of

M. H. Imansyah (✉) · Muzdalifah
Universitas Lambung Mangkurat, Kalimantan, Indonesia
e-mail: mhimansyah@ulm.ac.id; muzdalifah.feb@ulm.ac.id

D. Hartono · T. M. Putranti
Universitas Indonesia, Jakarta, Indonesia
e-mail: djoni.hartono@ui.ac.id; titi.muswati09@ui.ac.id



S. M. Juhro et al. (eds.), *Sustainable Economy: The Indonesian Pathways*,
https://doi.org/10.1007/978-981-92-1215-6_12

development is determined by the capacity of economies to reallocate labor and capital away from low-productivity subsistence agriculture and into value-generating sectors that sustain growth over the long term.

Indonesia, however, has not followed this trajectory in a conventional way. The country is currently experiencing premature deindustrialization, a process in which the share of manufacturing in GDP and employment begins to decline at a stage when high-income status has not yet been reached (Rodrik, 2016). This premature contraction of the manufacturing base has elevated the role of the service sector as a central driver of Indonesia's ongoing structural transformation and positioned services at the forefront of debates on the country's long-term growth strategy.

Nevertheless, it is important to recognize that service subsectors do not all contribute in the same way to sustainable development. Some are capital-intensive, concentrated in metropolitan areas, and disproportionately capture benefits among higher-income groups, while others are labor-intensive, exhibit relatively low carbon intensity, and are distributed more evenly across rural regions. The crucial policy challenge is to identify which service subsectors provide the most strategic opportunities for advancing inclusive and green development within the Indonesian context, and to differentiate them from those with narrower or unequal developmental effects.

This study responds to that challenge by addressing a key research gap. It evaluates the role of different service subsectors against four structural criteria: their contribution to value added, their capacity for employment generation, their level of environmental sustainability, and their impact on income equity. Unlike earlier studies that largely relied on gross output multipliers, this paper employs value-added multipliers to better reflect net contributions to GDP, which are more consistent with national accounts and with the metrics used in sustainability-oriented development frameworks (Oosterhaven & Stelder, 2002; Miller & Blair, 2009). The purpose is to identify subsectors that are already aligned with the objectives of structural transformation and that can serve as leverage points for promoting sustainable and inclusive economic growth.

## 2 Literature Review

### *2.1 Structural Transformation and the Role of Services*

The classical theory of structural transformation suggests that economic development is characterized by a progressive movement of labor and resources from sectors with low productivity, predominantly agriculture, into sectors with higher productivity, initially manufacturing and ultimately services. This gradual reallocation of economic activity is widely considered essential for raising aggregate productivity levels and improving overall living standards (Lewis, 1954; Chenery & Syrquin, 1975). Building on this conceptual foundation, Chenery and Taylor (1968) further elaborated how sectoral dynamics evolve in response to economic maturation, showing that structural change follows identifiable patterns across different stages of development.

Indonesia's development trajectory illustrates a marked deviation from this traditional framework. The country has been experiencing premature deindustrialization, a phenomenon in which the share of industrial employment and manufacturing output declines before the economy attains a high-income level (Rodrik, 2016).

In this context, an increasing number of scholars and policymakers advocate for a reframing of services, not as peripheral activities, but as strategic sectors capable of advancing inclusive and environmentally sustainable growth. This perspective has been institutionalized in policy frameworks such as Indonesia's National. At the same time, regional studies on inclusive green growth highlight that inefficiencies in public expenditure allocation can significantly undermine the developmental capacity of services, reinforcing the importance of targeted and well-prioritized sectoral planning (Asyrof & Rizaldi, 2025).

## *2.2 Value-Added Contribution of Services*

Traditional reliance on gross output multipliers in input–output analysis has often been criticized for overstating the apparent contribution of sectors characterized by high levels of intermediate consumption. Oosterhaven and Stelder (2002) argue that conventional gross multipliers often overstate sectoral impacts due to double counting, and propose net multipliers that adjust for the ratio of final demand to output—thus yielding unbiased aggregate effects when applied across sectors. This perspective reinforces the case for using value-added multipliers, which more directly align with GDP and sustainability considerations. In this regard, service subsectors such as tourism and finance frequently appear to be highly productive when measured in terms of gross output. However, once intermediate inputs are properly accounted for, their net contributions prove to be significantly lower. Joppe and Li (2016) emphasized the importance of adopting assessment approaches that incorporate ecological and social dimensions of value creation alongside economic measures, thereby offering a more comprehensive evaluation of sectoral performance.

The need for this value-based perspective is particularly evident in Indonesia, where service subsectors demonstrate wide variation in terms of productivity and efficiency. Input–output analyses have shown that even though services now employ a larger share of the workforce than manufacturing, their net value-added contribution to the economy remains relatively limited. These findings highlight the critical importance of identifying which subsectors within services exhibit the greatest efficiency and potential for supporting national development (Hassan & Rehman, 2021). This leaves room for further inquiry into how service-based growth interacts with employment and sustainability.

## 2.3 Employment Potential and Labor Absorption

The employment intensity of service sectors is well established, yet the quality and inclusivity of the jobs created vary substantially across subsectors. Tourism, for instance, has long been recognized as a significant generator of employment opportunities; however, it is frequently criticized for relying on precarious and seasonal work arrangements that undermine long-term security for employees (Baum et al., 2016). The fragility of service employment was made visible during the COVID-19 crisis, when global tourism and hospitality sectors collapsed almost overnight, leading to widespread job and income losses (Baum & Hai, 2020). Earlier scholarship had already emphasized systemic employment issues in tourism, including job precarity, low wages, and limited career progression, suggesting persistent vulnerabilities in service labor markets (Baum et al., 2016). These concerns have been reinforced by recent evidence of persistent labor shortages in the hospitality sector, where imbalances between labor supply and demand continue to constrain industry recovery (Kwok, 2022). Service sector resilience has also been challenged by global health emergencies, with Gössling et al. (2020) documenting how pandemic-induced travel restrictions reshaped labor relations and forced structural adjustments in tourism industries. The International Labour Organization (2021) similarly highlights that service employment accounts for the largest share of global labor, yet remains marked by informality and vulnerability, particularly in developing economies.

The International Labour Organization (ILO, 2021) further notes that service activities absorb a disproportionate share of women and youth within labor markets, particularly in economies characterized by large informal sectors. Persistent labor shortages in hospitality indicate untapped employment capacity that could be addressed through targeted workforce development and stronger industry-academia collaboration (Kwok, 2022). Strategies aimed at enhancing inclusivity therefore become essential for ensuring that service-led growth contributes meaningfully to broader development objectives. Addressing this intersection could offer a fuller perspective on services' role in inclusive transformation.

## 2.4 Environmental Footprint and Carbon Efficiency

Although service sectors are often perceived as relatively low-carbon compared to energy-intensive manufacturing and heavy industries, an expanding body of research demonstrates that their contribution to climate change is both direct and indirect and therefore cannot be dismissed as negligible. In hospitality and restaurant-related activities, for instance, supply chain studies reveal that emissions are generated not only from operational energy consumption but also from upstream food production and distribution. These findings underscore the importance of adopting sustainability benchmarks as a central element of long-term sectoral planning (Di Pierro et al., 2023). Tourism-related services provide another clear example: high levels of emissions are produced through the combined impacts of travel, accommodation, and infrastructure development, indicating that so-called "soft" industries also exert substantial environmental pressures (Gössling et al., 2020).

A particularly important challenge lies in recognizing the significance of indirect emissions embedded within service activities. Alcántara and Padilla (2009), applying an input–output subsystems approach to the Spanish economy, demonstrate that services—commonly labeled as clean—are in fact responsible for a considerable share of national $CO_2$ emissions once upstream production linkages are taken into account. This analysis suggests that an exclusive focus on direct emissions risks underestimating the true environmental footprint of services. Their work highlights that the service sector is deeply interlinked with energy-intensive industries through consumption and production linkages, making it an integral driver of overall emissions. Recent cross-country evidence confirms this dynamic, with global service-sector emissions rising by more than 60 percent between 1995 and 2021, particularly in transportation, communication, and commercial services (Liang & Wang, 2025).

Sector-specific research further complicates the picture by revealing the heterogeneity of service impacts. For instance, Gan et al. (2022) show that China's service sector exhibits only weak decoupling from emissions, while full decoupling remains elusive due to structural reliance on fossil fuel inputs. In Malaysia, trade, communication, and public services generate substantial proportions of $CO_2$, $NO_n$, and $SO_2$, indicating that services are neither uniformly low-carbon nor homogeneous in their ecological effects (Al-Amin et al., 2007). Historical research on OECD economies also demonstrates that rising electricity demand in commercial buildings has offset efficiency improvements, thereby sustaining upward trajectories of emissions (Krackeler et al., 1998).

Despite these challenges, a variety of targeted strategies demonstrate that emissions in services can indeed be mitigated. Within hospitality, reductions in both operational and embodied carbon can be achieved through innovations in green building design, renewable energy adoption, and sustainable management practices (Legrand et al., 2022). In public-sector organisations, circular economy practices are increasingly promoted to improve resource efficiency and support a transition away from linear consumption patterns (Klein et al., 2022). Taken together, this body of literature makes clear that the service sector, though often overlooked in climate policy debates, plays a pivotal role in shaping national carbon trajectories. Addressing both its direct emissions and the indirect effects captured by input–output analysis is therefore indispensable for achieving comprehensive decarbonization strategies.

Yet the environmental dimension cannot be considered in isolation from issues of social equity. The distribution of emissions across different regions and population groups demonstrates that the ecological burdens of services are often unequally shared, raising questions of justice and inclusivity. In many instances, carbon-intensive service industries displace environmental costs onto vulnerable communities, thereby linking ecological sustainability directly to wider challenges of income distribution and social well-being. This recognition provides a natural conceptual bridge to examining how services affect equity and inclusive spillovers within development processes. A broader integration with employment and distributional aspects is still limited, pointing to the need for more comprehensive approaches.

## 2.5 *Equity, Distribution, and Inclusive Spillovers*

Equity continues to stand as a central pillar in assessing the developmental role of services, since their expansion simultaneously offers opportunities for inclusion while also creating risks of widening inequality. The rise of digital platforms and finance-based services, for instance, has been instrumental in facilitating access to markets, credit, and information. Yet a growing body of evidence demonstrates that, without deliberate inclusivity measures, such sectors often exacerbate existing divides, as benefits tend to accrue disproportionately to high-income groups and urban populations that already possess stronger economic and digital capacities (Imansyah et al., 2023). This inherent tension underscores the need to embed equity considerations into the governance and regulatory frameworks of service-sector growth, ensuring that technological and financial innovations do not merely deepen preexisting disparities but instead serve as vehicles for broader social inclusion.

The role of services in shaping labor market inclusion has been particularly highlighted in tourism and hospitality. Scholars argue that equitable access to employment in these subsectors, coupled with investments in vocational training and skills development, is critical for enabling upward social mobility (Baum et al., 2016). By opening opportunities for low-skilled and rural workers to participate in service-based employment, these industries can act as powerful pathways for reducing poverty and narrowing inequalities across regions. Parallel to this, financial inclusion has emerged as another cornerstone of inclusive regional development. Evidence indicates that expanding access to credit, savings instruments, and financial services for low-income households not only enhances resilience but also mitigates vulnerability, thereby reducing inequality across communities and strengthening local economies (Rumbogo et al., 2021).

Beyond labor markets and financial systems, broader structural reforms strongly influence the distributive impacts of service-sector expansion. Evidence from developing-country models indicates that services liberalization can generate broad welfare gains, expand economic activity, and increase the real returns to both labor and capital (Konan & Maskus, 2006). At the same time, the equitable provision of essential public services—particularly in healthcare and education—has consistently been identified as one of the most effective strategies for reducing regional disparities and fostering long-term inclusive development pathways (UNDP, 2024). These findings suggest that equity-oriented policies and institutions are decisive in determining whether the benefits of service expansion are broadly shared or narrowly concentrated.

The financial sector further illustrates how equity, sustainability, and efficiency can be integrated in practice. In the Indonesian context, the expansion of green lending initiatives, microfinance programs, and digital banking services demonstrates that sustainability-oriented financial innovations can simultaneously enhance firm performance and promote financial inclusion. These developments reinforce the argument that equitable access to finance, when combined with environmental responsibility, is not only compatible with but also essential to achieving sustainable economic growth (Khoirrudin & Utami, 2023).

Importantly, the distributive implications of services extend well beyond the sphere of economic inclusion and into the environmental domain. Carbon-intensive service industries—such as logistics, aviation, and increasingly data-driven digital services—impose ecological costs that disproportionately fall on vulnerable social groups and less developed regions. Moreover, cross-border outsourcing of emissions from advanced economies to developing countries, as documented by Liang and Wang (2025), illustrates how service-based globalization can externalize environmental burdens, thereby aggravating inequalities between nations. These dual dynamic reveals that the service economy functions both as a potential equalizer and as a source of inequity. When inclusivity, sustainability, and social safeguards are embedded in its governance, services can foster equitable development and strengthen social cohesion. Conversely, when such safeguards are absent, service-sector growth risks reinforcing inequality, entrenching uneven development, and displacing environmental costs onto the most vulnerable. Exploring this nexus could enrich the debate on inclusive and sustainable service development.

## 3 Data and Methodology

This study employs the 2016 Indonesian Input–Output (I-O) table published by Statistics Indonesia (BPS), which disaggregates the economy into 73 sectors. The dataset contains detailed information on energy use, labour income, and household consumption differentiated by rural and urban income deciles. Sectoral energy use is converted into $CO_2$ emissions using standard emission factors, with calculations standardized by BPS to ensure consistency across sectors. This study adopts an input–output methodological framework that follows the seminal approach of Alcántara and Padilla (2006), who demonstrated how identifying 'key' sectors of $CO_2$ emissions allows researchers to link production structures with environmental externalities in the Spanish economy, providing a solid analytical base for subsequent applications in emerging economies.

The analytical framework is based on a modified Input–Output (I-O) model. This approach systematically traces intersectoral linkages by examining how the output of one industry becomes the input for another, thereby identifying sectors that act as key drivers of economic growth. The fundamental structure of the I-O model can be expressed as $AX+Y = Y = AX+Y = X$, where A is the technical coefficient matrix, X represents gross output, and Y denotes final demand. The Leontief inverse,

$B = (I - A)^{-1}$, is derived to capture both direct and indirect requirements in production.

Using this framework, two types of multipliers are estimated. The Type I multiplier incorporates only direct and indirect effects, while the Type II multiplier extends the analysis to include induced effects by treating households as an endogenous sector. This distinction is important for understanding not only sectoral production linkages but also how income and consumption feedback amplify economic impacts.

Environmental implications are analysed through the estimation of carbon emission elasticities, following the approach of Alcántara and Padilla (2006). Emission elasticity measures the responsiveness of $CO_2$ emissions to changes in value added, quantifying how a 1% increase in sectoral output affects emissions. The elasticity matrix highlights which sectors are more carbon-intensive, thereby providing an evidence base for designing mitigation policies without undermining economic growth.

Finally, to address distributional concerns, the model incorporates household-level detail using the Miyazawa (1976) extension. Income and consumption accounts are disaggregated into ten household deciles using data from the National Socio-Economic Survey (SUSENAS) and the National Labor Force Survey (SAKERNAS). This allows the study to simulate how sectoral expansion affects income distribution across different social groups, thus identifying which household categories gain the most from structural change in the economy.

Despite extensive contributions, prior Indonesian studies remain fragmented. Athukorala and Patunru (2023) largely emphasized manufacturing without integrating environmental or equity considerations, while Kurniawan and Managi (2018) narrowed their focus to emissions and productivity, leaving distributional aspects unexplored. Recent IO-based studies have expanded into service-related sectors. For example, multiplier effects of transportation development in Indonesia have been analyzed through an IO framework (Marpaung et al., 2025), offering insights into how service subsectors can generate significant linkages across the economy. This complements the equity dimension discussed through financial inclusion in services (Rumbogo et al., 2021). This study therefore fills a clear research gap by systematically applying an extended input–output framework to assess the "triple-win" potential across Indonesian service subsectors.

# 4 Discussion

## *4.1 Value-Added Multiplier Type II*

The value-added multiplier Type II reflects the degree to which an increase in final demand for a sector's goods or services induces total output expansion across the wider economy, including both indirect effects through inter-industry linkages and induced effects via household income and expenditure. In practice, it captures not only the immediate supply chain responses but also the secondary rounds of demand generated as households spend their additional income. This makes the output multiplier a crucial indicator for identifying sectors that serve as engines of broad-based economic growth (Miller & Blair, 2009).

Table 12.1 presents the ten sectors with the highest Type II value-added multipliers. The results indicate substantial variations across sectors, highlighting the uneven capacity of industries to generate system-wide impacts. Thermal power emerges as the sector with the highest multiplier at 2.75, meaning that one unit of additional demand can generate nearly three units of total output in the economy. This reflects the extensive backward linkages of energy supply, which serves as a fundamental input across industries. However, as the literature emphasizes, sectors with high multipliers are not automatically sustainable, especially when their expansion is associated with significant energy consumption and environmental costs (Kurniawan & Managi, 2018).

Other high-performing sectors include water transport (2.25), eating and drinking places (2.12), civil engineering (2.05), and buildings (2.02). These sectors underscore the pivotal role of both infrastructure-related activities and mobility- or consumption-driven services in stimulating intersectoral linkages. For instance, eating and drinking places show strong output effects due to their connections with agriculture, trade, and small-scale services, resonating with UNDP (2024) which highlights the importance of food and hospitality in strengthening local supply chains. Similarly, civil engineering and buildings confirm the argument of Athukorala and Patunru (2023) that infrastructure remains a central driver of Indonesia's industrial transition.

Meanwhile, air transport (2.01) also demonstrates a strong multiplier effect, consistent with its wide linkages to fuel, logistics, catering, and tourism services. Railway transport (1.90), though slightly lower, still contributes significantly, reinforcing the importance of diversified transport infrastructure.

Beyond transportation and construction, medical and health services (1.77) and road transport (1.76) also appear within the top ten, showing that social services and conventional mobility systems play important roles in generating broader output spillovers. Empirical evidence supports this view that research on China's health

**Table 12.1** Value Added Multipliers Type II by Sector (Top 10)

| Rank | Sector | Type II VA Multiplier |
|---|---|---|
| 1 | Thermal power | 2.7465 |
| 2 | Water transport | 2.2502 |
| 3 | Eating and drinking | 2.1207 |
| 4 | Civil engineering | 2.0481 |
| 5 | Buildings | 2.0195 |
| 6 | Air transport | 2.0130 |
| 7 | Railway transport | 1.9046 |
| 8 | Medical and health | 1.7710 |
| 9 | Road transport | 1.7606 |
| 10 | Public administration | 1.6980 |

sector demonstrates that medical and health services produce not only direct impacts but also significant spatial spillover effects across regions, thereby enhancing the efficiency and accessibility of healthcare systems beyond local boundaries (Fu et al., 2021; Yang et al., 2022; Wang et al., 2016). Similarly, studies of road and transport infrastructure confirm that conventional mobility networks generate substantial spillover effects, stimulating wider economic and social benefits. For instance, Gong et al. (2023) reveal that road transport exerts positive spillovers on sustainable tourism development, while Álvarez-Ayuso et al. (2016) and He et al. (2021) highlight that investments in road infrastructure foster regional economic linkages and inter-city growth through multiplier and spillover mechanisms. Together, these findings reinforce the notion that both health services and road transport act as pivotal channels for amplifying broader output spillovers within national economies.

Although public administration shows lower multiplier effects compared to infrastructure or transport sectors, studies confirm its systemic role in sustaining economic linkages. Fiscal policy analyses indicate that government spending generates modest but stabilizing spillovers across regions (Auerbach et al., 2019), while evidence from multi-regional models highlights how governance reforms and fiscal decentralization enhance public administration quality and intersectoral linkages (Dinh Thanh et al., 2023; Kratena & Streicher, 2017).

Overall, the findings confirm the mixed nature of Indonesia's economy: sectors with strong physical and consumption linkages, such as energy, construction, transport, and food services, dominate in their ability to stimulate system-wide activity, while administrative and governance-related services remain less catalytic in driving broad-based output expansion (Table 12.1).

## Employment Multiplier Type II

The employment multiplier Type II provides a comprehensive perspective on how increases in final demand stimulate job creation not only within the focal sector but also throughout the economy, incorporating both indirect and induced employment effects. Sectors with high employment multipliers are central to inclusive growth strategies, as they create widespread opportunities for labor absorption and directly influence the inclusivity of development outcomes. The fragility of service employment was made visible during the COVID-19 crisis, when global tourism and hospitality sectors collapsed almost overnight, leading to widespread job and income losses (Baum & Hai, 2020). Earlier scholarship had already emphasized systemic employment issues in tourism, including job precarity, low wages, and limited career progression, suggesting persistent vulnerabilities in service labor markets (Baum et al., 2016). These concerns have been reinforced by recent evidence of persistent labor shortages in the hospitality sector, where imbalances between labor supply and demand continue to constrain industry recovery (Kwok, 2022). Service sector resilience has also been challenged by global health emergencies, with Gössling et al. (2020) documenting how pandemic-induced travel restrictions reshaped labor relations and forced structural adjustments in tourism industries. The International Labour Organization (2021) similarly highlights that service employment accounts for the largest share of global labor, yet remains marked by informality and vulnerability, particularly in developing economies.

Table 12.2 reports the Type II employment multipliers for the twelve selected sectors. The results reveal considerable variation across industries. Air transport records the highest employment multiplier at 18.21, far surpassing other sectors. This striking result reflects the sector's dense linkages with tourism, logistics, catering, and trade, which amplify both direct and induced labor demand. While this indicates tremendous potential for job creation, scholars such as Kurniawan and Managi (2018) caution that employment expansion in transport sectors raises sustainability concerns due to heavy reliance on fossil fuels and the associated rise in carbon emissions.

Beyond infrastructure and construction, both health services and road transport emerge as key drivers of broader output spillovers. Research on China's health sector shows that medical services generate not only direct benefits but also significant cross-regional effects, improving accessibility and efficiency beyond local boundaries (Fu et al., 2021; Yang et al., 2022). Similarly, investments in road transport stimulate tourism development and strengthen regional linkages, reinforcing its role in spreading economic benefits across cities and industries (Gong et al., 2023; Álvarez-Ayuso et al., 2016; He et al., 2021). These findings highlight how social services and conventional mobility systems extend their influence well beyond their immediate sectors, amplifying growth through intersectoral linkages. In contrast, public administration ranks lower in multiplier strength, yet its systemic role remains essential. Although its spillover potential is more modest, governance and fiscal policies provide stability and coordination across sectors, ensuring that economic linkages function effectively (Auerbach et al., 2019; Dinh Thanh et al., 2023).

Construction-related activities, including buildings (2.40) and civil engineering (2.12), also register robust multipliers, underscoring their capacity to generate wide-ranging employment effects across supply chains. Similarly, eating and drinking

**Table 12.2** Employment Multiplier Type II (Top 12 Selected Sectors)

| Sector | Employment Multiplier (Type II) |
|---|---|
| Air transport | 18.2076 |
| Real estate services | 3.4257 |
| Water transport | 2.9590 |
| Buildings | 2.3951 |
| Civil engineering | 2.1195 |
| Eating & drinking place | 2.0172 |
| Business services | 2.0666 |
| Railway transport | 1.8577 |
| Gas supply | 1.8123 |
| Medical & health | 1.5438 |
| Public administration | 1.4254 |
| Other services | 1.1631 |

places (2.02) show strong job-creating potential because of their reliance on agricultural inputs, small and medium enterprises, and labor-intensive service delivery. More broadly, services liberalization in developing economies can generate welfare gains and raise real returns to labor and capital (Konan & Maskus, 2006).

Interestingly, business services (2.07), while not among the very top performers, still display a notable capacity for job creation. This reflects their role in linking professional services, information systems, and administrative support across sectors. However, their contribution to inclusive employment depends heavily on skill levels and access to education, which may limit the participation of low-income groups. This highlights the need for policies that expand human capital formation and ensure equitable access to jobs in knowledge-intensive services.

Other sectors with moderate multipliers also carry strategic significance. Railway transport (1.86) remains an important job creator, providing mid-skill employment and supporting regional mobility, while the gas supply sector (1.81) offers moderate employment effects but is constrained by its high fossil fuel intensity (Bouwmeester & Scholtens, 2014; Rahko, 2025). Socially oriented sectors such as medical and health services (1.54) generate consistent job opportunities with high social returns, consistent with Bishop (2009), who emphasizes the role of localized knowledge spillovers and labor-related factors in supporting employment growth in service industries. At the lower end, public administration (1.43) and other services (1.16) exhibit weaker employment spillovers, reflecting their limited production linkages and narrower contributions to systemic labor absorption (Bishop, 2009).

Taken together, these findings highlight a dual challenge. On one hand, sectors such as air transport, real estate, and construction-related activities possess remarkable job creation potential. On the other, their environmental burdens and skill-biased employment patterns raise questions of long-term sustainability and equity. As Imansyah et al. (2023) stress, the sectors that generate the most jobs are not always those aligned with sustainable development pathways. Policymaking must therefore strike a careful balance—supporting labor-intensive industries that absorb large numbers of workers while ensuring that such growth does not exacerbate carbon dependency or deepen inequality (Table 12.2).

## Carbon Elasticity

While multipliers measure economic linkages, carbon elasticity captures the environmental dimension by indicating how responsive $CO_2$ emissions are to marginal increases in sectoral value-added. Low elasticities suggest that a sector can expand with minimal environmental impact, whereas high elasticities signal carbon-intensive growth. Integrating this measure with multiplier analysis allows for a balanced view of economic and environmental outcomes, a priority emphasized in green industrial policy debates (UNDP, 2024). An application to the Malaysian economy shows that selected service subsectors, far from being carbon-neutral, actually drive significant shares of $CO_2$ emissions through indirect linkages (Al-Amin et al., 2007). Evidence from Tunisia by Chaouali et al. (2024) reveals that value added in services has a statistically significant elasticity with respect to $CO_2$ emissions, raising concerns for sustainable growth strategies. Supply chain assessments in Europe show that restaurants and food services carry high embedded carbon, pointing to the importance of accounting for indirect emissions in service sector evaluations (Di Pierro et al., 2023). A detailed input–output analysis for China demonstrates the considerable contribution of service industries to national $CO_2$ growth, suggesting that energy transitions must include tertiary sectors (Gan et al., 2022). City-level case studies, such as Beijing, highlight how expansion in service demand directly translates into higher energy use and carbon emissions, particularly in transport, trade, and real estate (Ge & Lei, 2014). Revisiting the Environmental Kuznets Curve, Yassin and Aralas (2020) find that the service sector plays a central role in the non-linear relationship between economic growth and emissions, complicating traditional assumptions that services are environmentally benign. Hospitality and tourism services also face rising pressure to adopt low-carbon operational practices, with Legrand et al. (2022) showing how green hotel management can significantly cut emissions while maintaining competitiveness. The rising energy demand of digital services has been widely identified as a source of new carbon pressures. Recent peer-reviewed assessments show that ICT already accounts for a non-trivial share of global GHG emissions and—without strong efficiency improvements and clean power—its footprint can grow further despite device-level gains (Belkhir & Elmeligi, 2018; Freitag et al., 2021; Lange et al., 2020; Masanet et al., 2020; Mytton & Ashtine, 2022). The rising energy demand of digital services has been widely identified as a source of new carbon pressures. Recent peer-reviewed assessments show that ICT already accounts for a non-trivial share of global GHG emissions and—without strong efficiency improvements and clean power—its footprint can grow further despite device-level gains (Belkhir & Elmeligi, 2018; Lange et al., 2020; Masanet et al., 2020). National assessments in Indonesia reveal that real estate and construction services generate sizable embodied emissions, underlining the importance of sector-specific policies. Economy-wide and building-scale studies consistently indicate that construction products are among the largest contributors to consumption-based emissions (Rum et al., 2024; Agustiningtyas et al., 2024).

Using input–output and decomposition evidence, prior studies show that shifting consumption toward services does not automatically reduce carbon footprints because service activities carry substantial indirect emissions through electricity, transport, buildings, and manufactured inputs; only rapid efficiency gains and power-sector decarbonization prevent overall emissions from rising (Barrett et al., 2013).

The results reveal a cluster of sectors with the lowest carbon elasticities, which are summarized in Table 12.3. At the most favorable end, railway transport (0.0006) and medical and health services (0.0006) record the lowest values, implying virtually no incremental emissions burden from value-added expansion. This aligns with findings in global literature that highlight rail as an energy-efficient transport mode and healthcare as a comparatively low-carbon service sector. Studies show that high-speed rail can achieve the lowest life-cycle emissions among passenger modes

**Table 12.3** $CO_2$ Elasticities by Sector (Top 10 Lowest)

| Rank | Sector | Elasticity |
|---|---|---|
| 1 | Railway transport | 0.0006 |
| 2 | Medical and health services | 0.0006 |
| 3 | Civil engineering | 0.0016 |
| 4 | Eating and drinking | 0.0017 |
| 5 | Buildings | 0.0032 |
| 6 | Water transport | 0.0037 |
| 7 | Air transport | 0.0047 |
| 8 | Education | 0.0064 |
| 9 | Public administration | 0.0069 |
| 10 | Real estate services | 0.0085 |

when supported by clean energy and high occupancy (Chester & Horvath, 2010; IEA, 2021), while input–output analyses confirm that healthcare consistently exhibits lower carbon intensity relative to industrial sectors (Liang et al., 2025). Other sectors with similarly low elasticities include civil engineering (0.0016), eating and drinking places (0.0017), and buildings (0.0032). These results demonstrate that even construction and consumer-service activities can achieve relatively efficient energy use per unit of value-added growth.

A second cluster of sectors shows slightly higher but still manageable carbon intensities. Water transport (0.0037) and air transport (0.0047) both generate emissions, though shipping remains relatively more efficient than aviation on a per-unit basis. Education (0.0064) and public administration (0.0069) largely reflect emissions from building energy use rather than production processes, while real estate services (0.0085) capture embodied carbon from property development. Together, these ten sectors represent the least carbon-intensive industries in the economy, and they are explicitly reported in Table 12.3.

Beyond these, the analysis also identifies sectors with high elasticities that fall outside the table, as the table is restricted to the lowest values. Thermal power (0.0160) and gas supply (0.0172) predictably dominate this group due to their dependence on fossil fuels. Road transport (0.0130) also contributes heavily, consistent with its reliance on private vehicles and inefficient fuel use. Postal and telecommunications (0.0148) register unexpectedly high elasticity, likely linked to the rising energy demands of digital infrastructure. The commerce sector (0.0879) shows the highest elasticity overall, indicating disproportionate sensitivity of retail and wholesale activities to $CO_2$ emissions.

Taken together, these findings highlight two important insights. First, the sectors listed in Table 12.3 represent the most environmentally efficient industries, offering opportunities for growth with minimal carbon trade-offs. Second, other service sectors not in the table but with high elasticities illustrate the risks of environmentally intensive development. This dual perspective reinforces the conclusion of Athukorala and Patunru (2023) that structural transformation in services must explicitly account for environmental burdens if it is to align with Indonesia's long-term green growth strategy.

## Intersection of Three Criteria: High Value-Added, High Employment, and Low $CO_2$ Elasticity

A more nuanced perspective arises when combining the three criteria—high value-added multiplier, high employment multiplier, and low carbon elasticity. This intersection identifies the "green growth" sectors where economic expansion generates both value-added and jobs without imposing excessive environmental costs, an approach consistent with the "triple-win" framework discussed in Kurniawan and Managi (2018).

The results, summarized in Table 12.4, classify sectors into four categories: strong candidates, borderline candidates, moderate elasticity, and high or very high elasticity. This classification provides a clearer picture of which service industries can drive inclusive and sustainable growth, and which ones pose environmental or distributional risks.

Six sectors emerge as the most promising: water transport, eating and drinking places, railway transport, medical and health services, and hotels and lodging are identified as strong candidates, while real estate services is considered a borderline case. These sectors combine strong economic linkages with relatively sustainable environmental performance. For instance, water transport (VA 2.25, employment 2.96, elasticity 0.07) and eating and drinking places (VA 2.12, employment 2.02, elasticity 0.009) deliver both output and job creation with manageable environmental costs. Railway transport (VA 1.90, employment 1.86, elasticity 0.048) and medical and health services (VA 1.77, employment 1.54, elasticity 0.009) represent socially vital sectors aligned with low-carbon development. Hotels and lodging (VA 1.51, employment 1.96, elasticity 0.004) provide further opportunities in tourism, provided safeguards are in place. Real estate services (VA 1.28, employment 3.43,

**Table 12.4** Strategic service sectors at the intersection of value-added, employment, and carbon efficiency

| Sector | VA Multiplier (Type II) | Employment Multiplier (Type II) | $CO_2$ Elasticity | Status |
|---|---|---|---|---|
| Water transport | 2.2502 | 2.9590 | 0.0688 | ■ Strong candidate |
| Eating & drinking place | 2.1207 | 2.0172 | 0.0086 | ■ Strong candidate |
| Railway transport | 1.9046 | 1.8577 | 0.0476 | ■ Strong candidate |
| Medical & health | 1.7710 | 1.5438 | 0.0087 | ■ Strong candidate |
| Hotels & lodging | 1.5149 | 1.9604 | 0.0037 | ■ Strong candidate |
| Real estate services | 1.2801 | 3.4257 | 0.0544 | ■ Candidate (borderline) |
| Civil engineering | 2.0481 | 2.1195 | 0.1154 | ⚠□ Moderate elasticity |
| Buildings | 2.0195 | 2.3951 | 0.0992 | ⚠□ Moderate elasticity |
| Air transport | 2.0130 | 18.2076 | 0.0970 | × High elasticity |
| Gas supply | 1.5225 | 1.8123 | 1.3799 | × Very high elasticity |
| Business services | 1.6209 | 2.0666 | 0.5295 | × High elasticity |

elasticity 0.054), though marked as borderline, remains important given its exceptionally high employment effects despite modest value-added performance.

By contrast, civil engineering (VA 2.05, employment 2.12, elasticity 0.115) and buildings (VA 2.02, employment 2.40, elasticity 0.099) fall into the moderate elasticity group. Their strong multipliers are offset by higher environmental costs, which limit their sustainability. Air transport, despite an outstanding employment multiplier (18.21) and strong value-added linkages (2.01), belongs to the high elasticity category due to its heavy dependence on fossil fuels and significant carbon intensity.

At the least sustainable end, gas supply (VA 1.52, employment 1.81, elasticity 1.38) represents very high elasticity, reflecting its overwhelming reliance on fossil fuel inputs. Business services (VA 1.62, employment 2.07, elasticity 0.53) also fall into the high elasticity group, highlighting that even knowledge- and office-based activities can be carbon-intensive once their indirect energy requirements are accounted for.

This classification underscores two important insights. First, the sectors that truly represent "green growth" are not necessarily those with the absolute highest multipliers, but rather those that combine competitiveness with environmental efficiency, as shown by the strong candidates in Table 12.4. Second, sectors in the borderline, moderate, or high-elasticity categories should not be dismissed outright but require carefully designed policies—such as clean energy adoption, carbon pricing, or inclusive governance frameworks—to reduce their environmental costs and improve inclusivity.

Overall, Table 12.4 highlights that water transport, hospitality, healthcare, and railways represent the most balanced pathways toward sustainable and inclusive growth. Real estate, although borderline, remains a significant employment generator. Conversely, infrastructure-heavy and energy-intensive services must undergo green transformation before they can play a comparable role in Indonesia's long-term transition.

This intersection analysis emphasizes that true green growth does not arise from sectors with the absolute highest multipliers, but rather from those that combine competitiveness with environmental efficiency. The findings highlight that water transport, eating and drinking places, railway transport, medical and health services, hotels and lodging, and real estate services together represent a balanced path forward. These sectors not only generate significant value-added and employment but also maintain relatively low carbon intensities, thereby enabling inclusive job creation while staying aligned with climate goals.

In this sense, green growth requires deliberate prioritization of sectors that balance productivity with sustainability. As Imansyah et al. (2023) underline, inclusive strategies demand explicit attention to both distributional and ecological outcomes. Without such attention, even sectors with strong linkages may risk reinforcing inequality or environmental burdens. By contrast, the six identified service subsectors provide a strategic opportunity to advance Indonesia's transition toward a more resilient, inclusive, and low-carbon economy.

## Distributional Implications of Investment

Six Strategic Sectors

Figure 12.1 illustrates the distributional impact of investment in six strategic service sectors identified as the most sustainable "triple-win" candidates: water transport, eating and drinking places, railway transport, medical and health services, hotels and lodging, and real estate services. These sectors combine strong value-added and employment multipliers with relatively low carbon intensities.

The results show that inequality remains persistent. Under the **HHU (Household Urban)** scenario, the richest 10 percent of households capture around 25 percent of the total gains, while under the **HHR (Household Rural)** scenario this rises to 36 percent, reflecting weaker capacity of rural households to capture induced effects. Middle-income groups (deciles 7–9) also benefit, but their shares decline once consumption effects are considered. The ninth decile, for example, drops from over 20 percent under HHU to 14 percent under HHR. By contrast, the bottom three deciles together receive less than 5 percent of total benefits, reflecting structural barriers

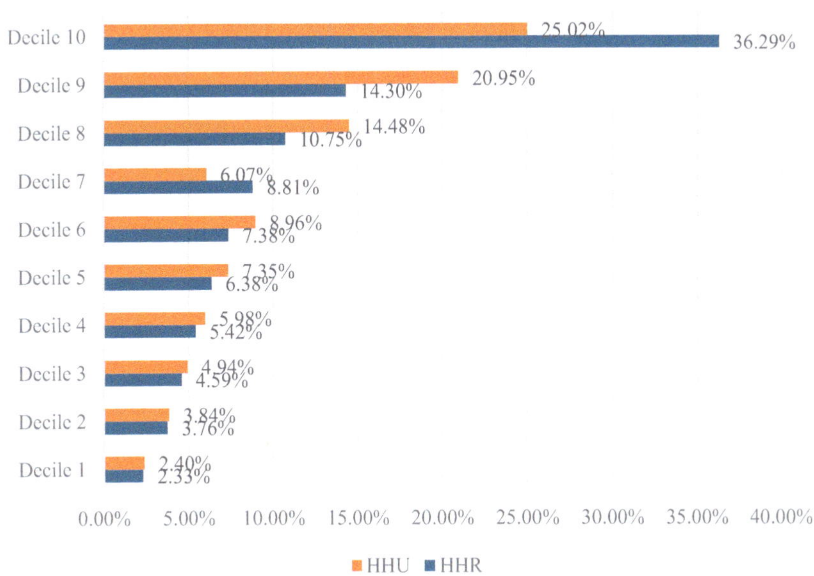


**Fig. 12.1** Distributional impact of investment in six strategic sectors

such as limited capital ownership, lack of skilled jobs, and informality in labor markets.

Sector-specific dynamics further explain this skew. Real estate and hotels, while high in employment or value-added, are capital-intensive, channelling returns to wealthier households. Real estate in particular stands as a borderline sector: it creates jobs but contributes less in value-added terms and carries higher carbon intensity than other triple-win sectors. Medical and health services largely reward highly educated professionals, while transport sectors (railway and water) have stronger potential for inclusivity but remain dominated by large-scale operators. Only eating and drinking places show clearer potential for broad-based participation, but this requires supportive measures such as SME financing and inclusive procurement.

Overall, while the six strategic sectors deliver strong multipliers and low carbon intensities, the distributional outcomes remain skewed toward wealthier households. Policies such as skills upgrading, credit support for SMEs, and community-based participation in real estate projects are crucial to redirect gains toward middle- and lower-income groups.

## Eight Strategic Sectors

Figure 12.2 extends the analysis by including **civil engineering** and **buildings** alongside the six sectors above. While these two sectors display strong multipliers, they are characterized by moderate carbon elasticities, meaning that they are less environmentally sustainable compared to the six primary triple-win sectors.

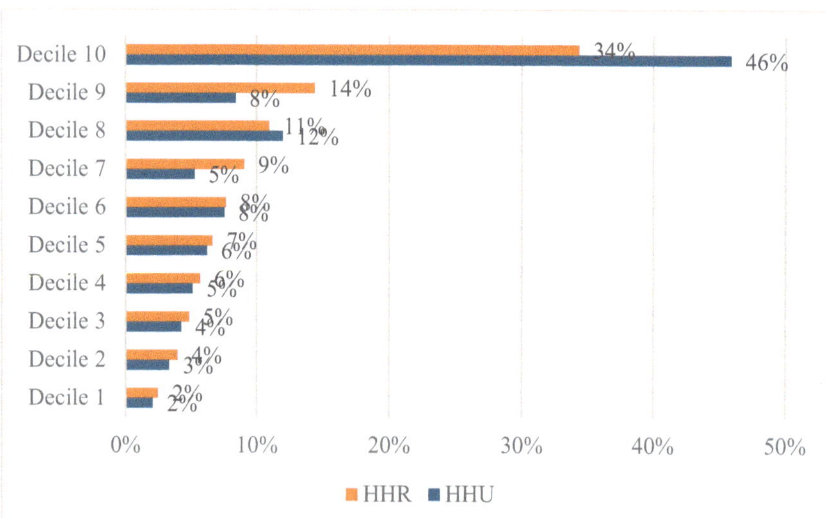


**Fig. 12.2** Distributional impact of investment in eight strategic sectors

The distributional results show an even sharper inequality pattern. Under the HHU scenario, the richest 10 percent secure more than one-third of the total gains, while under the HHR scenario their share rises to nearly one-half. This indicates that when household consumption effects are incorporated, benefits are heavily concentrated at the very top. Middle-income households gain but see their shares decline once induced effects are considered, while the bottom four deciles remain almost excluded.

Sectoral characteristics shape these outcomes. Real estate, hotels, civil engineering, and buildings are capital- and asset-intensive, with income flowing to property developers, large construction firms, and highly skilled professionals concentrated in urban areas. Medical and health services reward educated professionals, reinforcing inequalities in access. By contrast, railway and water transport could create mid-skill jobs and linkages with local suppliers and eating and drinking places remain an important entry point for small-scale entrepreneurship. Without inclusive measures, however, these opportunities remain underutilized.

This distributional skew reveals a paradox: investment in eight sectors delivers growth, jobs, and—at least for six of them—low-carbon outcomes, but it also intensifies inequality. The inclusion of civil engineering and buildings highlights that environmental and distributional trade-offs often move in tandem.

## 5 Conclusion

This study highlights the central role of services in Indonesia's economic transformation. Six subsectors—water transport, eating and drinking places, railway transport, medical and health services, hotels and lodging, and real estate services—stand out as the most promising because they combined strong contributions to growth and employment with relatively low carbon intensity. Civil engineering and buildings also contribute significantly, but their higher environmental costs make them less compatible with long-term green growth objectives.

The distributional analysis, however, reveals a persistent imbalance. The gains from service-sector expansion are captured largely by the wealthiest households, while poorer groups—particularly in rural areas—remain sidelined. When household consumption effects are taken into account, inequality becomes even sharper, with additional demand reinforcing existing advantages for those at the top. Without deliberate policy action, service-led growth risks deepening inequality even as it strengthens the economy and reduces environmental pressure.

The policy direction that emerges from these findings is clear. The development of the service sector must not only aim for growth but also ensure that the benefits are distributed more fairly and achieved in an environmentally responsible manner. Strengthening human capital is a priority. Through vocational training, skills upgrading, and certification, workers from diverse backgrounds can gain access to better jobs, including in modern service industries that demand higher competencies. Expanding financial access is equally crucial, especially for small and medium enterprises in hospitality, food services, and transport. With improved credit facilities, microfinance schemes, and business support, these labor-intensive subsectors can become more effective channels for inclusive employment.

At the same time, governance frameworks must be redesigned to support inclusivity. Procurement systems should provide opportunities not only for large firms but also for smaller businesses. In real estate and infrastructure projects, community participation should be integrated from planning to implementation to prevent benefits from being captured solely by capital owners. By combining investments in human capacity, broader financial inclusion, and more equitable governance, Indonesia can ensure that its service sector evolves not just into a driver of competitiveness but also into a foundation for shared prosperity and long-term sustainability.

This study adds to the literature by systematically integrating output, employment, carbon, and distributional dimensions for services in Indonesia, thereby offering a comprehensive framework that has been largely absent in previous analyses.

## References

Agustiningtyas, R. S., Pratiwi, A. A., & Hidayat, A. (2024). Embodied energy and carbon assessment of existing affordable apartments in Indonesia. Journal of Asian Architecture and Building Engineering. Advance online publication. https://doi.org/10.1080/13467581.2023.2278481

Al-Amin, A. Q., Jaafar, A. H., & Siwar, C. (2007). The services sector's contribution as well as pollution implication in the Malaysian economy: Input-output approach. Paper SSRN, https://papers.ssrn.com/sol3/Delivery.cfm/SSRN_ID1017181_code845927.pdf?abstractid=1017181&mirid=1

Alcantara Escolano, V., & Padilla Rosa, E. (2006). An input-output analysis of the "key" sectors in CO2 emissions from a production perspective: an application to the Spanish economy. *Working papers (Universitat Autònoma de Barcelona. Departament d'Economia Aplicada)*, (1). https://portalrecerca.uab.cat/en/publications/an-input-output-analysis-of-the-quotkeyquot-sectors-in-co2-emissi

Alcántara, V., & Padilla, E. (2009). Input–output subsystems and pollution: An application to the service sector and $CO_2$ emissions in Spain. *Ecological Economics, 68*(3), 905–914. https://www.sciencedirect.com/science/article/abs/pii/S0921800908003157

Álvarez-Ayuso, I. C., Condeço-Melhorado, A. M., & Gutiérrez, J. (2016). Integrating network analysis with the production function approach to study the spillover effects of transport infrastructure. Regional Studies, 50(8), 1303–1315. https://www.tandfonline.com/doi/abs/10.1080/00343404.2014.953472

Asyrof, F., & Rizaldi, A. (2025). Regional inclusive green growth in Indonesia: A framework using IGGI. *Economics and Policy of Energy and the Environment, 67*(1), 89–105. https://www.ije--pyc.org/IJE/article/download/220/88?

Athukorala, Prema-Chandra & Patunru, Arianto A., (2023). Domestic Value Added, Exports, and Employment: An Input–Output Analysis of Indonesian Manufacturing, Bulletin of Indonesian Economic Studies Volume 59, 2023 - Issue 3, https://www.tandfonline.com/doi/abs/10.1080/00074918.2022.2134554

Auerbach, A. J., Gorodnichenko, Y., & Murphy, D. (2019). Local fiscal multipliers and fiscal spillovers in the United States. NBER Working Paper, No. 25457. https://www.nber.org/papers/w25457

Barrett, J., Peters, G., Wiedmann, T., Scott, K., Lenzen, M., Roelich, K., & Le Quéré, C. (2013). Consumption-based GHG emission accounting: A UK case study. Climate Policy, 13(4), 451–470. https://doi.org/10.1080/14693062.2013.788858

Baum, T., & Hai, N. T. T. (2020). Hospitality, tourism, human rights and the impact of COVID-19. *International Journal of Contemporary Hospitality Management, 32*(7), 2397–2407. https://doi.org/10.1108/IJCHM-03-2020-0242

Baum, T., Kralj, A., Robinson, R. N., & Solnet, D. J. (2016). Tourism workforce research: A review, taxonomy and agenda. *Annals of Tourism Research, 60*, 1–22. https://doi.org/10.1016/j.annals.2016.04.003

Belkhir, L., & Elmeligi, A. (2018). Assessing ICT global emissions footprint: Trends to 2040 & recommendations. Journal of Cleaner Production, 177, 448–463. https://doi.org/10.1016/j.jclepro.2017.12.239

Bishop, P. (2009). Spatial spillovers and employment growth in the service sector. *The Service Industries Journal, 29*(6), 791–803. https://doi.org/10.1080/02642060902749310

Bouwmeester, M., & Scholtens, B. (2014). Cross-border spillovers from European gas infrastructure investment. https://pure.rug.nl/ws/portalfiles/portal/19400337/14028_EEF_def.pdf

Chaouali, I., Jebli, M. B., & Ghazouani, T. (2024). Investigating the dynamic effects of service value added on $CO_2$ emissions: Novel insights from a non-parametric approach. *Journal of Environmental Management, 349*, Article 121553. https://doi.org/10.1016/j.jenvman.2024.121553

Chenery, H. B., & Syrquin, M. (1975). *Patterns of development, 1950–1970.* Oxford University Press for the World Bank. https://documents1.worldbank.org/curated/en/482491468328816108/pdf/11913.pdf

Chenery, H. B., & Taylor, L. (1968). Development patterns among countries and over time. *Review of Economics and Statistics, 50*(4), 391–416. https://doi.org/10.2307/1926806

Chester, M., & Horvath, A. (2010). Life-cycle assessment of high-speed rail: The case of California. Environmental Research Letters, 5(1), 014003. https://doi.org/10.1088/1748-9326/5/1/014003

Di Pierro, R., Frasnetti, E., Bianchi, L., Bisagni, M., Capri, E., & Lamastra, L. (2023). Setting the sustainable development targets for restaurants and Italian HoReCa sector. *Science of the Total Environment, 855*, 158908. https://doi.org/10.1016/j.scitotenv.2022.158908

Dinh T. S., Nguyen, C. P., Duy-Tung, B., & Binh, N. Q. (2023). Spatial spillover effects of fiscal decentralization on governance and public administration quality. Regional Studies, 57(5), 789–804. https://www.tandfonline.com/doi/abs/10.1080/00343404.2022.2078801

Freitag, C., Berners-Lee, M., Widdicks, K., Knowles, B., Blair, G. S., & Friday, A. (2021). The real climate and transformative impact of ICT: A critique of estimates, trends, and regulations. *Patterns, 2*(9), 100340. https://doi.org/10.1016/j.patter.2021.100340

Fu, L., Xu, K., Liu, F., Liang, L., & Wang, Z. (2021). Regional disparity and patients mobility: benefits and spillover effects of the spatial network structure of the health services in China. International Journal of Environmental Research and Public Health, 18(3), 1096. https://www.mdpi.com/1660-4601/18/3/1096

Gan, C., Wang, K., & Voda, M. (2022). Decoupling relationship between carbon emission and economic development in the service sector: Case of 30 provinces in China. *Environmental Science and Pollution Research, 29*(42), 63846–63858. https://doi.org/10.1007/s11356-022-20032-4

Ge, J., & Lei, Y. (2014). Carbon emissions from the service sector: An input–output application to Beijing, China. *Climate Research, 60*(1), 13–24. https://doi.org/10.3354/cr01224

Gong, H., Zheng, Y., Shi, J., Wang, J., Yang, H., & Sibalo, S. (2023). An examination of the spatial spillover effects of tourism transportation on sustainable development. Sustainability, 15(5), 4522. https://www.mdpi.com/2071-1050/15/5/4522

Gössling, S., Scott, D., & Hall, C. M. (2020). Pandemics, tourism and global change: A rapid assessment of COVID-19. *Journal of Sustainable Tourism, 29*(1), 1–20. https://doi.org/10.1080/09669582.2020.1758708

Hassan, N., & Rehman, A. ur. (2021). Examining the inter-sectoral relationship, productivity and inclusive growth of Pakistani and Indonesian economies. *IRASD Journal of Economics, 3*(1), 38–57. https://doi.org/10.52131/joe.2021.0301.0024

He, S., Yu, S., & Wang, L. (2021). The nexus of transport infrastructure and economic output in city-level China: a heterogeneous panel causality analysis. The Annals of Regional Science, 67, 115–136. https://link.springer.com/article/10.1007/s00168-020-01012-3

Imansyah, M. H., Hartono, D., Putranti, T., & Muzdalifah. (2023). The impacts of digital economy on green economy: The Indonesian Miyazawa Model. *Polish Journal of Environmental Studies, 32*(2), 1609–1619. https://doi.org/10.15244/pjoes/159123

International Energy Agency (IEA). (2021). The future of rail: Opportunities for energy and the environment. OECD/IEA. https://www.iea.org/reports/the-future-of-rail

International Labour Organization. (2021). *World Employment and Social Outlook 2021: The role of services in the global recovery*. ILO. https://www.ilo.org/sites/default/files/wcmsp5/groups/public/%40dgreports/%40dcomm/%40publ/documents/publication/wcms_795453.pdf

Joppe, M., & Li, X. (2016). Productivity measurement in tourism and services: Value-added versus gross output. Journal of Travel Research, Volume 55, Issue 2, 1–11, https://doi.org/10.1177/00472875145462

Khoirrudin, M., & Utami, N. R. T. (2023). Analysis of sustainability and inclusive strategies in achieving profitability: Studies on banking listed on the Indonesia Stock Exchange. *International Journal of Multidisciplinary Research and Analysis, 6*(8), 3869–3878. https://doi.org/10.47191/ijmra/v6-i8-62

Klein, N., Deutz, P., & Ramos, T. B. (2022). A survey of circular economy initiatives in Portuguese central public sector organisations: National outlook for implementation. *Journal of Environmental Management, 314*, 114982. https://doi.org/10.1016/j.jenvman.2022.114982

Konan, D. E., & Maskus, K. E. (2006). Quantifying the impact of services liberalization in a developing country. *Journal of Development Economics, 81*(1), 142–162. https://doi.org/10.1016/j.jdeveco.2005.05.009

Krackeler, T., Schipper, L., & Sezgen, O. (1998). Carbon dioxide emissions in OECD service sectors: Trends and drivers. *Energy Policy, 26*(15), 1139–1156. https://doi.org/10.1016/S0301-4215(98)00055-X

Kratena, K., & Streicher, G. (2017). Fiscal policy multipliers and spillovers in a multi-regional macroeconomic input–output model. Economic Systems Research, 29(1), 45–66. https://www.econstor.eu/bitstream/10419/179294/1/wp_2017_540.pdf

Kurniawan, R., & Managi, S. (2018). Economic growth and sustainable development in Indonesia: An assessment. *Bulletin of Indonesian Economic Studies*, 54(3), 339–361. https://www.tandfonline.com/doi/full/10.1080/00074918.2018.1450962

Kuznets, S. (1971). *Economic growth of nations: Total output and production structure.* Harvard University Press. https://doi.org/10.4159/harvard.9780674493490

Kwok, L. (2022). Labor shortage: A critical reflection and a call for industry–academia collaboration. *International Journal of Contemporary Hospitality Management, 34*(11), 3929–3943. https://doi.org/10.1108/IJCHM-01-2022-0103

Lange, S., Pohl, J., & Santarius, T. (2020). Digitalization and energy consumption: Does ICT reduce energy demand? Ecological Economics, 176, 106760. https://doi.org/10.1016/j.ecolecon.2020.106760

Legrand, W., Chen, J. S., & Laeis, G. C. M. (2022). *Sustainability in the hospitality industry: Principles of sustainable operations* (4th ed.). Routledge.

Lewis, W. A. (1954). Economic development with unlimited supplies of labour. *The Manchester School, 22*(2), 139–191. https://doi.org/10.1111/j.1467-9957.1954.tb00021.x

Liang, J., & Wang, H. (2025). Cross-border emissions in the service sector: A global analysis. Energy Economics, (forthcoming). https://research.rug.nl/en/publications/cross-border-emissions-in-the-service-sector-a-global-analysis-of

Liang, J., Wang, S., Zhao, Y., Fang, C., & Feng, K. (2025). Cross-border emissions in the service sector: A global analysis of environmental and economic linkages. The Innovation: Global Sustainability, 2(2), 100133. https://doi.org/10.59717/j.xinn-geo.2025.100133

Marpaung, E., Wunas, S., Jinca, M. Y., & Siahaan, L. D. (2025). Multiplier effects of ferry transportation development on Indonesia's medium-term economy by using input-output approach: A case study of Samosir Island. *Economies, 13*(6), 169. https://doi.org/10.3390/economies13060169

Masanet, E., Shehabi, A., Lei, N., Smith, S., & Koomey, J. (2020). Recalibrating global data center energy-use estimates. Science, 367(6481), 984–986. https://doi.org/10.1126/science.aba3758

Miller, R. E., & Blair, P. D. (2009). Input–Output analysis: Foundations and extensions (2nd ed.). Cambridge University Press.

Miyazawa, K. (1976). Input–Output analysis and the structure of income distribution. Springer. https://link.springer.com/book/10.1007/978-3-642-48146-8

Mytton, D., & Ashtine, M. (2022). Sources of data center energy estimates: A comprehensive review. *Joule, 6*(9), 2032–2056. https://doi.org/10.1016/j.joule.2022.07.011

Oosterhaven, J., & Stelder, D. (2002). Net multipliers avoid exaggerating impacts: With a bi-regional illustration for the Dutch transportation sector. Journal of Regional Science, 42(3), 533–543. https://doi.org/10.1111/1467-9787.00270

Rahko, J. (2025). Vertical spillovers and the energy intensity of European industries. *Energy Economics*. https://doi.org/10.1016/j.eneco.2024.108053

Rodrik, D. (2016). Premature deindustrialization. *Journal of Economic Growth, 21*(1), 1–33. https://doi.org/10.1007/s10887-015-9122-3

Rum, I. A., Nasrudin, R. A., Lestari, P. K., Handayani, W., & Widianingsih, I. (2024). Exploring carbon footprints and carbon intensities of Indonesia's provinces: A multi-scale input–output approach. Frontiers in Environmental Science, 12, 1325089. https://doi.org/10.3389/fenvs.2024.1325089

Rumbogo, T., McCann, P., Hermes, N., & Venhorst, V. (2021). Financial inclusion and inclusive development in Indonesia. In R. L. Holzhacker & W. G. Z. Tan (Eds.), *Challenges of Governance: Development and Regional Integration in Southeast Asia and ASEAN* (pp. 161–181). Springer Nature. https://doi.org/10.1007/978-3-030-59054-3_8

United Nations Development Programme. (2024). *Human development report 2023/24: Breaking the gridlock – Reimagining cooperation in a polarized world.* UNDP. https://hdr.undp.org/system/files/documents/global-report-document/hdr2023-24reporten.pdf

Wang, L., Wang, J., Xu, C., & Liu, T. (2016). Modelling input–output flows of severe acute respiratory syndrome in mainland China. BMC Public Health, 16, 86. https://link.springer.com/article/10.1186/s12889-016-2867-6

Yang, Y., Zhang, L., Zhang, X., Yang, M., & Zou, W. (2022). Efficiency measurement and spatial spillover effect of provincial health systems in China: based on the two-stage network DEA model. Frontiers in Public Health, 10, 952975. https://www.frontiersin.org/articles/10.3389/fpubh.2022.952975/full

Yassin, J., & Aralas, S. (2020). The service sector and carbon emission nexus: Revisiting Environmental Kuznets Curve. *Jurnal Ekonomi Malaysia, 54*(2), 145–159. https://www.ukm.my/jem/wp-content/uploads/2021/05/jeko_542-10.pdf

# Chapter 13
# Cultivating Circular Economy for Sustainability

**Arnita Rishanty, Solikin M. Juhro, Evie Sylviani, Asep Suryahadi, and Dong Li**

**Abstract** This chapter examines how circular economy practices enhance business productivity in Indonesia. Using large-scale local data, it finds that higher circularity is consistently associated with improved firm productivity, with the strongest effects observed in agriculture, particularly in value added and labour productivity. The findings suggest that scaling circular models in agri-food systems should be prioritised, as the circular economy offers a productivity-enhancing and resilience-building pathway for Indonesia's development.

**Keywords** Circular economy · Supply chain finance · Sustainability · Sustainable growth

## 1 Introduction

The current global economic system, in its pursuit of creating value to meet human needs for welfare, prosperity, and satisfaction, primarily operates in a linear manner—take–make–waste. Humans extract raw materials from nature, whether renewable or non-renewable resources (take), process them into goods and services for consumption (make), and after a certain period of use—whether brief or extended—most of these products eventually end up discarded as waste (waste). This economic system structurally and continuously generates inefficiencies in the form of wasted resources, energy, and labor. While such economic inefficiencies can be minimized,

A. Rishanty (✉) · S. M. Juhro · E. Sylviani
Bank Indonesia, Jakarta, Indonesia
e-mail: Arnita_rishanty@bi.go.id; evie@bi.go.id

A. Suryahadi
The SMERU Research Institute, Jakarta, Indonesia

D. Li
University of Liverpool, Liverpool, England
e-mail: Dongli@liverpool.ac.uk



S. M. Juhro et al. (eds.), *Sustainable Economy: The Indonesian Pathways*,
https://doi.org/10.1007/978-981-92-1215-6_13

they are often overlooked. Therefore, the paradigm of sustainable economic growth is critical for policymakers and economic actors to understand.

The wastefulness inherent in the current take–make–waste economic paradigm significantly contributes to global emissions, accelerating climate change and global warming. Wackernagel et al. (2002) argues that human activities could still be supported by natural ecosystems until the 1980s, yet by 2002, humanity had already exceeded the Earth's ecological capacity by 20%. While the concerns on sustainability can be traced back as far as to the year 1849 (Ruskin, 1849), up until now the general awareness of sustainability is still very limited. The idea of the earth has physical limits in the form of depletable natural resources and that the earth has a finite capacity to absorb emissions (Daly, 1972; Meadows et al., 2005) up until now is still rarely to be considered as first priority in business decisions. The circular economy arises as the opposing concept of linear economy. Whilst the concept of the circular economy is a relatively new focus of research,[1] very limited research has been done that focuses on the relationship between circular economy practices and firm productivity empirically. That makes this paper to be the first empirically researching the impact of circular economy practices on firms productivity in Indonesia.

Mathis Wackernagel et al. (2002) argued that human is currently overused the earth's resources by around 20 percent above the global carrying capacity. Responding to that notion, the circular economy concept arises to transform products to create self-sustaining production systems and workable relationships between ecological systems and economic growth, by using cyclical materials flows, renewable energy sources and cascading-type energy flows (Geissdoerfer et al., 2017; Korhonen et al., 2018; Prieto-Sandoval et al., 2018; Winans et al., 2017).

Circular economy paradigm has an open paradigm that is non-restrictive and adaptable to the social and ecological environment depending on the availability of resources (low-tech to high-tech) and markets (small to large). That also includes a wide range of firm styles and earnings models (Wageningen, 2018; Winans et al., 2017). This makes circular economy approach, theoretically, is effective to improve productivity sustainably with limited resources available as in developing economies such as Indonesia (Rishanty, 2021).

Indonesia is widely acknowledged as being a unique and diverse country that is extremely rich in socio-cultural elements. Leyden et al. (2014) find that social capital (social networks) enhances innovation and reduces uncertainty. Given Indonesia's socio-cultural endowment, social capital could be an important source of the country's progress as it influences behaviour and the decision to innovate (Juhro et al., 2022), including efforts to build a circular economy ecosystem for sustainable growth. Thus, based on this construct, we are motivated to empirically examine the impact of circular economy practices on manufacturing firms' productivity.

---

[1] The term was introduced by policy makers of China in mid-2008 and European Union in 2015 (Geissdoerfer et al., 2017; Mathews & Tan, 2011; Prieto-Sandoval et al., 2018).

The nature of empirical circular economy research that encounters challenges in data limitation, more so in developing countries due to poor administration and instution. This study confronts the similar problem. This research focuses on capturing the flow of materials within sectors and exclude the inter-sectoral material flows (further research) due data limitation. However, we extend what previous research have done by adopting circularity level variable (Haas et al., 2015) instead of using the circular economy innovation dummy variable as in Horbach and Rammer's (2019), and other revenue as the circular economy measurements. The firm's circularity level is the value of production of goods (in Indonesian Rupiah) produced by firms whose raw materials are from the waste of other firms in one sector devided by the total value of production of goods (in Indonesian Rupiah) in that sector. The other circular economy measurement is firm's other revenue (profits from the sale of unprocessed goods, sales of waste/production waste). We employ a large database of the Indonesian Survey of Large and Medium Manufacturing (SIBS)[2] that provides a complete enumeration of all manufacturing industry firms in Indonesia which have a workforce of 20 or more people (medium and large sized industries). The findings of this research suggest the evidence in support of circular economy practices positively affecting the increase of firms' productivity. However, the effects differs in different sectors.

The rest of the paper is organized as follows. Section 2 reviews the literature on the relationships between social capital and economic development. Section 3 discusses the data analyzed in this study. Section 4 elaborates the empirical method to analyze the data. Section 5 presents the results of the estimations. Section 6 provides a discussion of the findings. Section 7 concludes.

## 2 Literature Review

The circular economy concept is the opposing concept of linear economy concept. Linear economy concept is where we only concern on how to collect the raw materials, and then transformed into products that are used (take-make-use) until they are finally discarded as waste. While in circular economy, we assume that the planet is a closed circular system, where the amount of resources depleted in a period is equal to the amount of waste generated in the same period. Although limited by some basic physical laws, circular economy seeks continually sustain the circulation of resources and energy within a closed system thus reducing the need for new raw material inputs into production systems (Genovese et al., 2017). Circular economy presents as the structural fixes of the currently overused earth's resources to strengthen the sustainability revolution (Ansell & Cayzer, 2018; D'Amato et al., 2017; Meadows et al., 2005). In a circular economy ecosystem, the resource input and waste, are minimised by slowing, closing, and narrowing material and energy

[2] https://www.bps.go.id/subject/9/industri-besar-dan-sedang.html

loops. This can be achieved through reuse, recycle, redesign/enduring design, maintenance, remanufacture, reduce, recover, refurbish (Geissdoerfer et al., 2017; Winans et al., 2017).

## 2.1 The "Limits to Growth" Theory

Sustainable development challenges conventional growth models. Daly (1972, 1991) argued that natural capital imposes binding limits on growth, as man-made capital cannot substitute natural systems. Economic growth becomes uneconomic when additional production reduces overall welfare by depleting resources, eroding leisure, or increasing pollution more than the benefits generated. The theory stresses the importance of balancing marginal utility (gains in well-being from additional consumption) with marginal disutility (costs such as labor, congestion, or pollution). Growth beyond this optimal point results in declining net welfare and potential ecological collapse. Thus, policies should aim for "good growth"—economic expansion compatible with ecological boundaries (Paehlke, 2001).

By adopting the circular economic perspective, the notion of sustainability in supply-focused industries can broaden the role of the industries not only as the producers that are required to implement sustainable production, but also as consumers (of the producers) that are required to implement sustainable consumption (Genovese et al., 2017). The circular economy pushes the limits of environmental sustainability by inducing the idea of product transformation and partnership so that ecological systems can be sustained along with economic growth (Genovese et al., 2017). Circular economy limits the throughput flow to a level that nature tolerates and utilises ecosystem cycles in economic cycles by respecting their natural reproduction rates." (Korhonen et al., 2018). In a circular economy ecosystem, the resource input and waste, are minimised by slowing, closing, and narrowing material and energy loops. This can be achieved through reuse, recycle, redesign/enduring design, maintenance, remanufacture, reduce, recover, refurbish (Geissdoerfer et al., 2017; Winans et al., 2017).

Many literature focuses on the conceptual level such as the evolution of terms related to circular economy concept such as "Industrial Symbiosis" (Amato et al., 2018; Domenech et al., 2019), "Cleaner Production" (Hens et al., 2018), "Finnish bio-economy" (Takala et al., 2019), and "EU's transition efforts towards circular economy" (Brears, 2015). Other research such as Nasiri et al. (2018) reviews the concept of sustainability and existing approaches to find sustainable solutions for firms, while Wreford et al. (2019) proposes an assessment framework to analyse where New Zealand's current position for bioeconomy-based wealth creation and solutions to enable New Zealand to transform into a fully functioning bioeconomy. Cooper et al. (2017) analysed the effect on the energy use of applying a wide range of circular economy approaches using Thermodynamic insights. Other research discussed ethical framework of circular economy (Dicks, 2017) and role of media to promote awareness of biogas as a potential renewable energy solution in Finland

(Lyytimäki et al., 2018). Brears (2015) reviews EU's transition efforts history towards circular economy. Foschi and Bonoli (2019) shows how European Commission has worked to regulate production and consumption of plastic carrier bags and packaging including food packaging, while Swagemakers et al. (2018) discussed experience in developing a biomass waste conversion that is challenged by questions of scale, administrative and regulatory barriers, conflicting land-use claims and financial cutbacks from public sector. Most literature in circular economy is focused on valorisation and waste management technologies, environmental benefits measurements.

The circular economy (CE) has emerged alongside concepts like the green economy and bioeconomy, but with distinct emphases. While the green economy addresses broad sustainability issues, and the bioeconomy emphasizes renewable biological resources, the CE focuses on optimizing resource efficiency, minimizing waste, and closing production–consumption loops (D'Amato et al., 2017).

Unlike the linear economy, CE seeks to design waste out of the system by reducing, reusing, recycling, refurbishing, and regenerating resources (Geissdoerfer et al., 2017). CE not only minimizes environmental harm but can also generate negative-waste outcomes, such as carbon sequestration. In food systems, CE practices could cut emissions by 49% (5.6 billion tons $CO_2e$) by 2050 (Ellen MacArthur Foundation, 2019). Soil carbon retention through organic fertilizers and compost, methane capture from manure, and sustainable biomass use exemplify CE's role in enhancing food security while mitigating climate change.

Similarly, in manufacturing, CE reduces emissions, enhances firm competitiveness through byproduct valorization, and meets rising consumer demand for sustainable goods. Successful CE ecosystems require trust, cooperation, and collaboration across suppliers, producers, and consumers (Ritzén & Sandström, 2017).

Measuring the impact of circular economy, some papers developed assessments on the circularity level of each research unit. Bala et al. (2014) presents food security modelling in Malaysia that models the circular causality between variables in the paddy and rice production system using computer model system dynamics methodology to improve food security, while Didenko et al. (2018) empirically presented the environmental impact of linear economy in comparison with circular economy from macro perspectives. Haas et al. (2015) assessed the circularity of global material flows with an interesting fact of Europe despite having a higher end of life recycling rate, yet low circularity level. Learning from these articles, then we developed a simple circularity measurement of a firm that is a percentage of reuse or recycle as input of total input and (if any) a percentage of circularity level of total waste.

Further, we did literature search in February 2020 using Scopus website with the keyword of "circular economy AND firm productivity" for all years available. The search is limited to final published articles to ensure the reliability of the literature search and to English literature. We obtained 6 literature from the literature search, and after removing duplication, applying inclusion and exclusion criteria to title, abstract, keywords and full papers, we only obtained 1 literature. It was a paper by Horbach and Rammer (2019). They questioned whether firms with circular economy innovations perform better or worse in terms of sales growth and employment using quantile regression (shrinking, stable, slowly growing, fast growing firms) with panel data of German community innovation survey wave 2014 and 2016. They found that circular economy innovations are positively linked to turnover and employment growth. While there is no statistically significant impact on labour productivity, at the same time, firms with CE innovations show a significantly better financial standing.

Horbach and Rammer (2019) employ a circular economy variable as a dummy variable of the firms that introduced circular economy innovations during the period of year 2012–2014[3] with a significant impact on the environment and the firms that did not introduce any circular economy innovations during the period. They defined the circular economy innovation by firms as process-related circular economy innovation, reduced energy use per unit of output, recycled waste, water, or materials for own use or sale, reduced material use/use of water per unit of output, replaced fossil energy sources by renewable energy sources, replaced materials by less hazardous substitutes, product-related CE innovation, reduced energy use, extended product life through longer-lasting/more durable products, and improved recycling of product after use. This approach is the most feasible since the most challenging part of estimating the circular economy variable empirically in firm level, is the data availability.

In this chapter, we succeeded to extend the circular economy variable using the circularity level variable adopted from Haas et al. (2015), instead of using the circular economy innovation dummy variable as in Horbach and Rammer's (2019). On top of it, we lengthen further by using the variable of firm's other revenue (profits from the sale of unprocessed goods, sales of waste/production waste) as the second circular economy variables.

The hypothesis of our study is that *an increase in circular economy variables increase the firm's productivity indicators*. It is grounded on the theoretical and empirical works constructed by previous literature supporting the importance of circular economy approach on productivity (Bala et al., 2014; Didenko et al., 2018; Haas et al., 2015; Horbach & Rammer, 2019).

## 3 Data and Methodology

The circular economy data was obtained from the Indonesian Survey of Large and Medium Manufacturing (SIBS) database from Statistics Indonesia (BPS).[4] The **SIBS** database provides a complete enumeration of all manufacturing industry firms in Indonesia which have a workforce of 20 or more people (medium and large sized industries). The SIBS database covers more than 20,000 manufacturing firms in 34

[3] German community innovation survey (CIS).

[4] https://www.bps.go.id/subject/9/industri-besar-dan-sedang.html

province in Indonesia covering the period of 2000–2015 annually. SIBS categorize each manufacturing industry firms into different sectors and sub-sectors based on the Indonesian Standard Industrial Classification (KBLI) that follows the International Standard Industrial Classification of All Economic Activities (ISIC). As the buildings of the datasets unevitably is constraint by limited data availability, we chose manufacturing sector since it is the only sector in Indonesia with extensive data series available. For a detailed data treatments and method refer to Rishanty and Suryahadi (2020).

## 3.1 The Circular Economy Variables

We used the Circularity Level variable and the Other Revenue[5] variable as proxies from circular economy activities. We adopted a purpose sampling method to capture the circularity level in a firm. The circularity level data is defined as the production of goods (in Indonesian Rupiah) produced by firms whose raw materials are from the waste of other firms in one sector divided by the total production of goods (in Indonesian Rupiah) in that sector. This research focuses on capturing the flow of materials within sectors and exclude the inter-sectoral material flows. We calculated the Circularity Level as follows:

$$CL_{it} = \frac{Output\_Prod_{it}}{Total\_ProdSector_{mt}} \tag{13.1}$$

where $CL_t$ is the circularity level of firm i in period t, $Output\_Prod_t$ is production output of firms i in period t, $Total\_ProdSector_t$ is the total production output of sector m in period t.

## 3.2 The Other Variables

The dependent variables representing firm's productivity is measured by the value of output production, value of total revenue, value of value added, value added productivity (ratio of value added to total labor), and labor productivity (ratio of output production to total labor) adopting from Horbach and Rammer (2019). The other variables explaining productivity, are foreign investment, the market concentration measure, size of the firms, used installed capacity, import share of inputs and export share of outputs, ratio of R&D expenditure, capital ratio, and non-production labor ratio as in Horbach and Rammer (2019). Foreign investment is considered as firm that has foreign investment might have more access to new technology that will

[5] Profits from the sale of unprocessed goods, sales of waste/production waste.

increase its productivity. The market concentration indicator used is the Herfindahl-Hirschman Index (HHI) which is a measure of the size of firms in relation to the industry. It is defined as the sum of the squares of the market shares of the firms within the industry. The result is proportional to the average market share, weighted by market share (Schaeck & Čihák, 2007). Higher values indicate greater concentration, while a decrease in the HHI indicates an increase in competition in the industry or lower concentration.

Size of the firms used installed capacity, ratio of R&D expenditure, capital ratio, non-production labor ratio, import share of inputs and export share of outputs are perceived as indicators that may affect the productivity of a firm. Larger firms tend to be more productive and unused installed capacity hinders the productivity to improve. Firms with R&D may have more productivity due to better technology. A better technology may also represent in high capital ratio (ratio of machines price to total labor expenditure) (Wacker et al., 2006). Non-production labor ratio is defined as a ratio of non-production labor to total labor. Non-production labor includes engineers, product designer, quality inspectors, administrators and other non-production roles. In general, the more headcounts of non-production labor hinder the productivity improvement. Therefore, the more bureaucratic a firm is, the more possible it is as the bottleneck for productivity. However, non-production labor are required to control production through supervising workers (Fu & Balasubramanyam, 2003) reported the critical role of non-production and supervisory workers in Chinese manufacturing plants. Effective administration is critical to the productivity of many medium-sized enterprises. Engineering labor may play a significant role in these plants by implementing process improvements to improve output. No large-scale empirical studies have been conducted to verify the effect of non-production labor on a manufacturing plant's productivity since country differences in productivity generally can be attributed to difference in social, cultural, political, or economic differences (Wacker et al., 2006). Thus, the effect can be vary in each firm. A few researchers have confirmed the effect of national culture on manufacturing decisions (e.g., Pagell et al., 2005).

Import share of inputs may positively affect firm's productivity due to better quality of inputs and more cost-effective (Halpern et al., 2005). Export share of outputs may positively affect firm's productivity related to participation in knowledge-intensive activities (Benkovskis et al., 2017). Benkovskis et al. (2017) argue that the relationships are reciprocal, since exporting firms tend to be more productive, larger, pay higher wages and are more capital intensive than non-exporting firms. While this is partly because firms that are originally more productive and have better performances are more likely to enter export, those firms realize higher labour productivity level as the result of export entry. We estimate the R&D data using the variable named as the "other of other expenditure" that contains R&D expenditure together with other expenses (such as management fee, promotion, telephone, prevention of environment pollution, and human resource development cost).

# 4 Empirical Method

This study aims to establish the impact of circular economy activities on productivity in Indonesia within the period of 2000–2015 annually by using panel regression. By using panel estimations, we aim to: (1) control individual heterogeneity; (2) get more informative, variability, and efficient data, but less colinear; (3) study the dynamics adjustment better, especially in economic development outcome; (4) identify and measure effects better; (5) construct and test more complicated behavioral model; (6) measure the micro data more accurately (Baltagi, 2005). First, we estimated the datasets using both fixed effect model (FE) and random effect model (RE), then tested each model by using Hausman Test.

# 5 Estimation Results

The result suggests that the circularity level positively affecting the five productivity indicators (output production, total revenue, value added, value added productivity and labor productivity) especially for firms of 5 subsectors implementing circular economy practices. As for firms from agriculture sectors implementing circular economy practices, the results also indicate that circularity level positively affecting the three out of five productivity indicators (value added, value added productivity and labor productivity). As for all set of firms included in the SIBS database, the result imply that circularity level positively affecting the four out of five productivity indicators (output production, total revenue, value added productivity and labor productivity). By observing the magnitude of the parameters, we can analyze that the effects of circularity level on productivity vary across sectors. Agriculture sectors implementing circular economy practices shows the highest positive impact on productivity. While all firms in the SIBS database shows lowest positive impact of circularity level on productivity. The firms implementing circular economy practices shows medium positive impact of circularity level on productivity.

As for other circular economy variables (other revenue or profits from the sale of unprocessed goods, other non-industrial services, sales of waste/production waste), its effect on productivity less feasible compared to that of circularity level's. Yet we can still observe the impact' difference on productivity across sectors. Similar with the phenomena of circularity level, the other revenue variable's impact on productivity for firms of agriculture sector implementing circular economy practices is the highest, while the impact on productivity for firms implementing circular economy practices is relatively the same with that of for all firms in the SIBS database.

## 6 Discussion

Figures 13.1, 13.2, 13.3, 13.4, 13.5 summarize the estimation results on the effects of circularity level and other determinants on firms' productivity. From the figures we can see that the effects of circularity level on productivity vary across sectors. Agriculture sectors implementing circular economy practices shows the highest positive impact on productivity. While all firms in the SIBS database shows the lowest positive impact of circularity level on productivity. The firms implementing circular economy practices shows medium positive impact of circularity level on productivity. While the impact of other circular economy variables (other revenue) on productivity is less tangible.

For other determinant variables, the degree of competition measure in the industry has negative impact on productivity indicators for all firms in the SIBS database, meaning a decrease in HHI or less concentration (more competition) in the industry increases the productivity indicators. However, the estimation result suggests the opposite findings specifically for the firms implementing circular economy practices and for the firms in agriculture sectors implementing circular economy practices. It may be related with the uniqueness of circular economy ecosystem that encourages the producers to have a coordinated capacity to be able to make a circular business flow. Thus, the less market competition or the more market concentration, the easier for firms to establish the circular ecosystem and gain more value added productivity measurements. This is inline with the arguments of Wacker et al. (2006) that conducted an international study on productivity that productivity generally can be attributed to differences in social, cultural, political, or economic differences.

For import share, export share, and R&D ratio, they all have positive impacts on productivity for all datasets. For firm size, the effects are positive on productivity measurements of total output, total revenue, value added for all datasets, while the effects are negative on productivity measurements of value added productivity (value added per labor) and labor productivity (output per labor). This may be due to the larger the firm, the larger its total output, total revenue, value added. However, when we look at the increment per labor, the effects become negative, as the more headcounts work in the firm, the less marginal productivity per labor and more costs.

The capital ratio (ratio of machines price to total labor expenditure) has negative effects on productivity measurements of total output and labor productivity (output per labor) for all datasets, while it has positive effects on productivity measurements of total revenue, value added and value added productivity for all datasets. This may be due to high capital ratio means that the firm is capital intensive which invites value added and revenue, and capital intensive firm with high capital ratio invites better economies of scale gained by the firm during the production process. Thus, the firm can produce goods with less costs (less value or price for total output and output per labor).

Non-production labor ratio has positive effects on productivity measurements of value added and value added productivity for firms in agriculture sectors

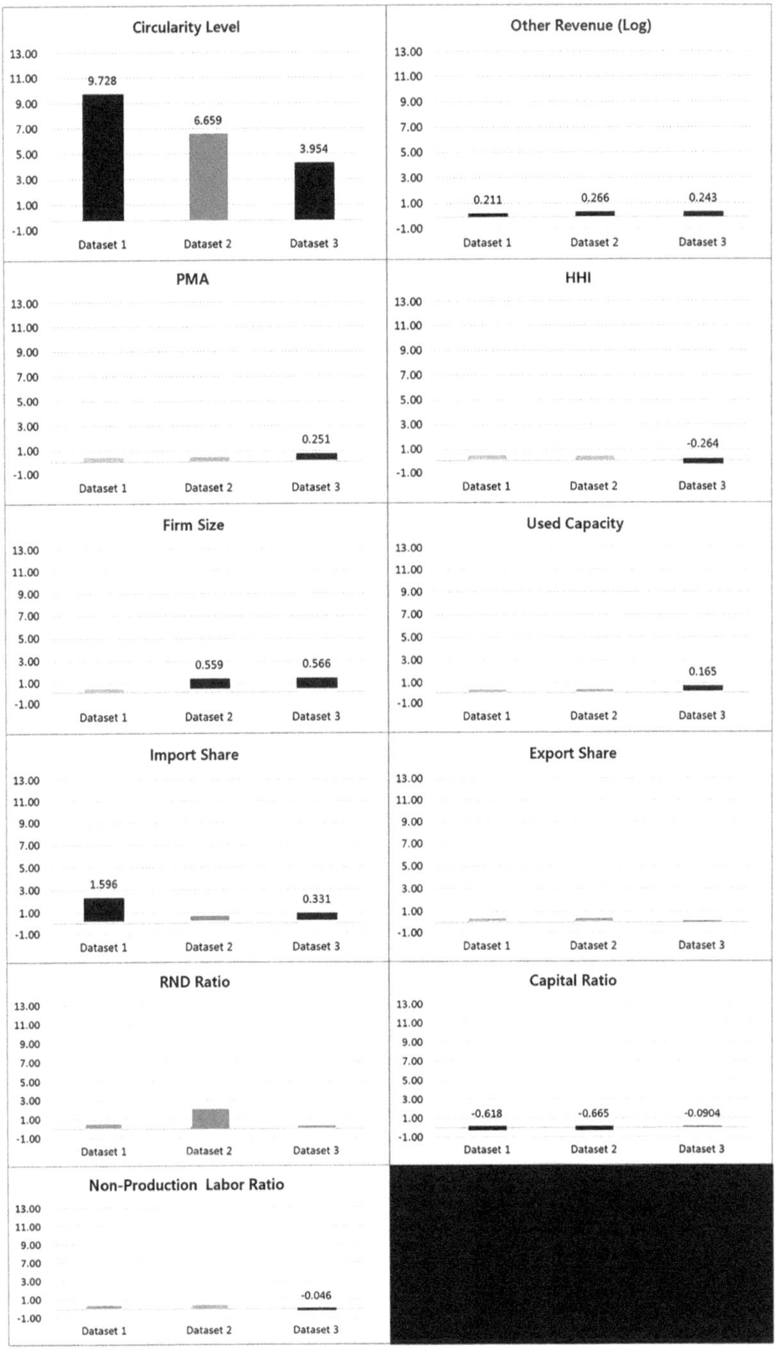


**Fig. 13.1** The effect of circular economy and other determinants on log production output

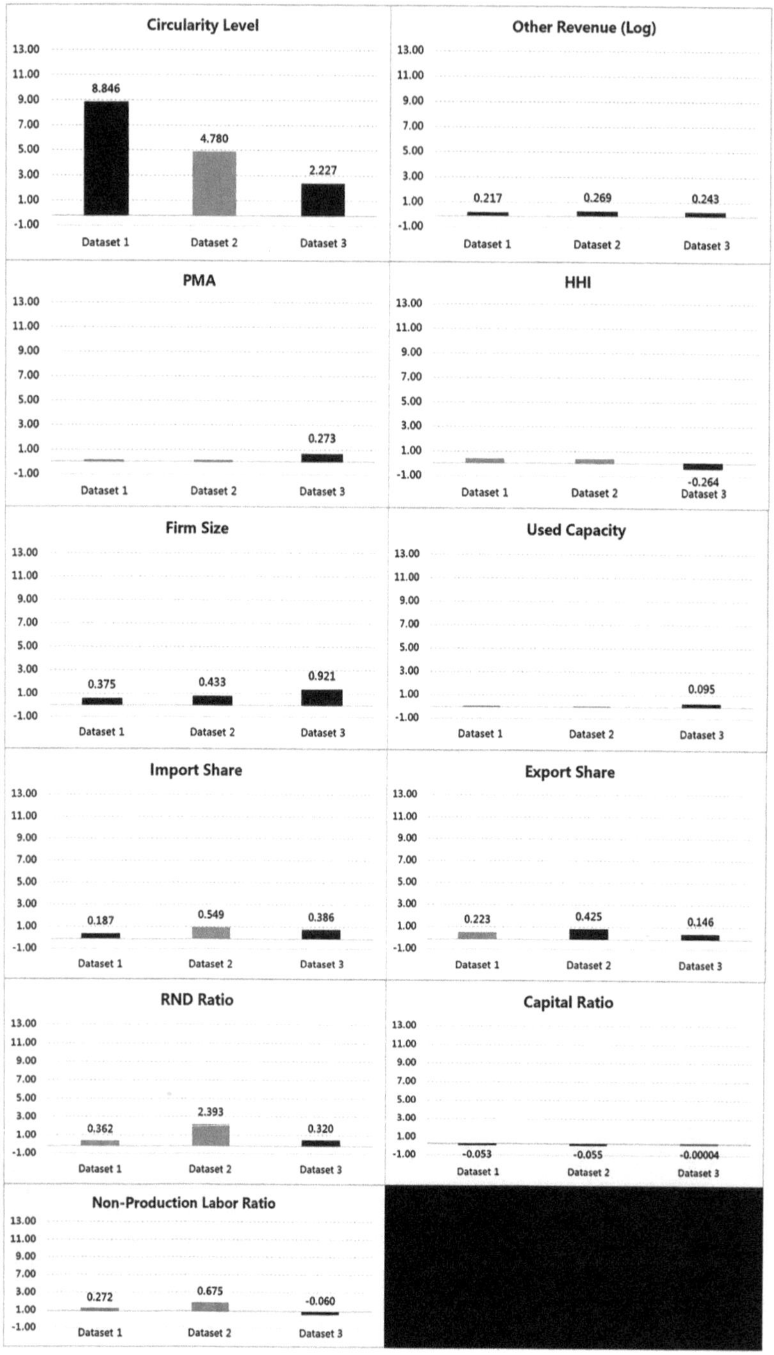


**Fig. 13.2** The effect of circular economy and other determinants on log total revenue

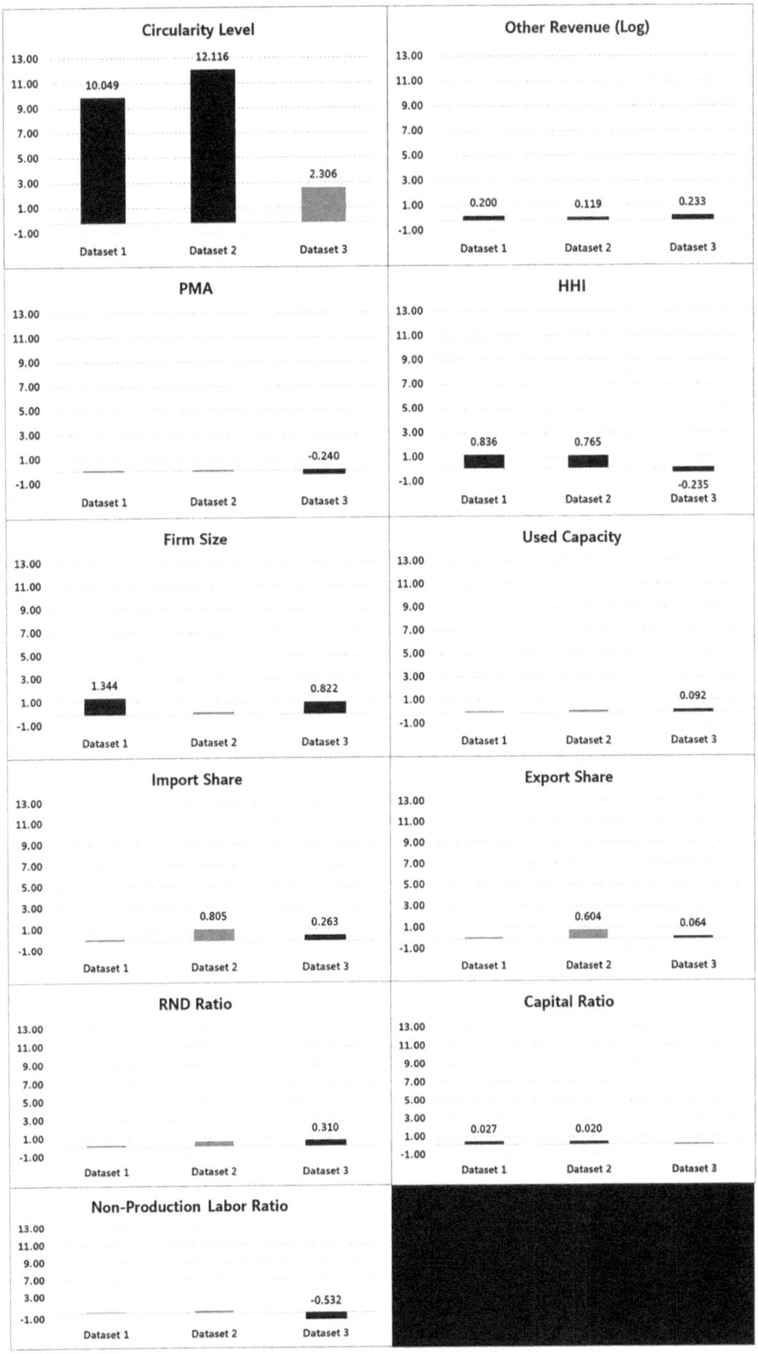


**Fig. 13.3** The effect of circular economy and other determinants on log value-added

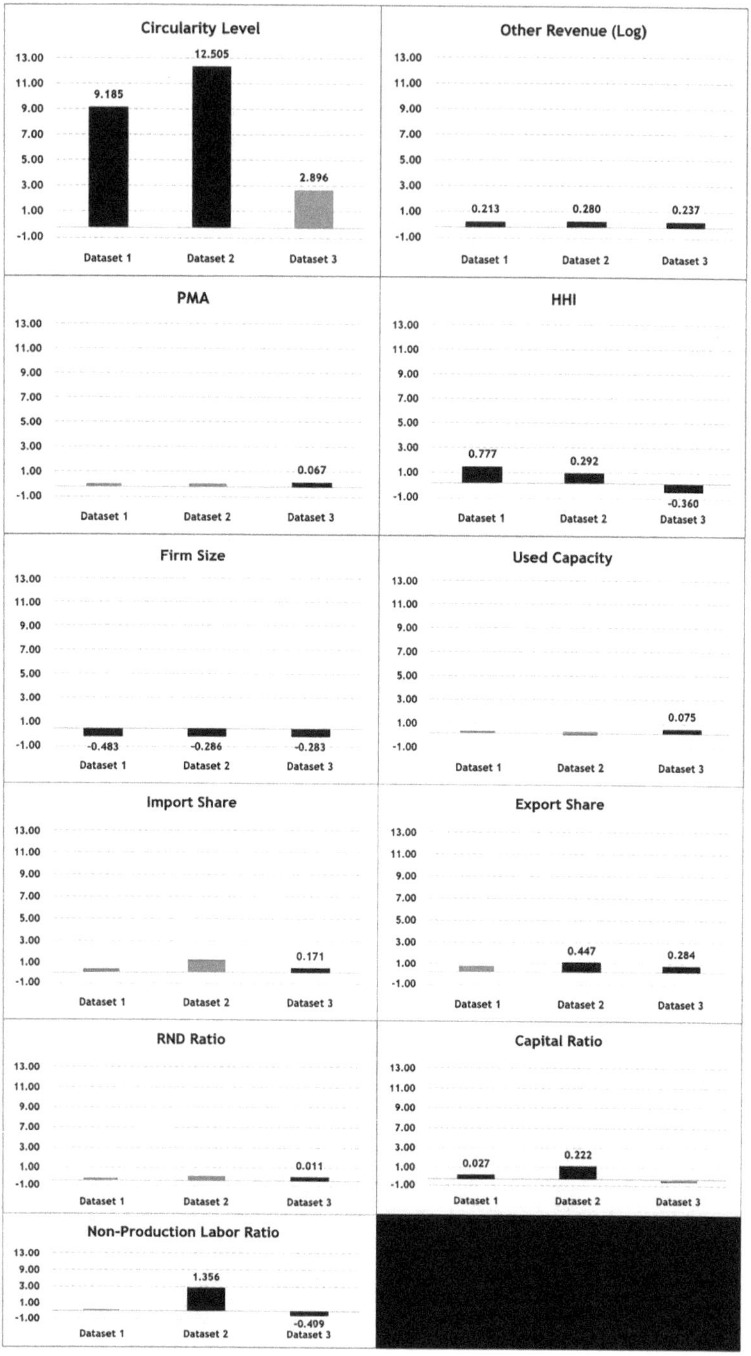


Fig. 13.4 The effect of circular economy and other determinants on log value-added productivity

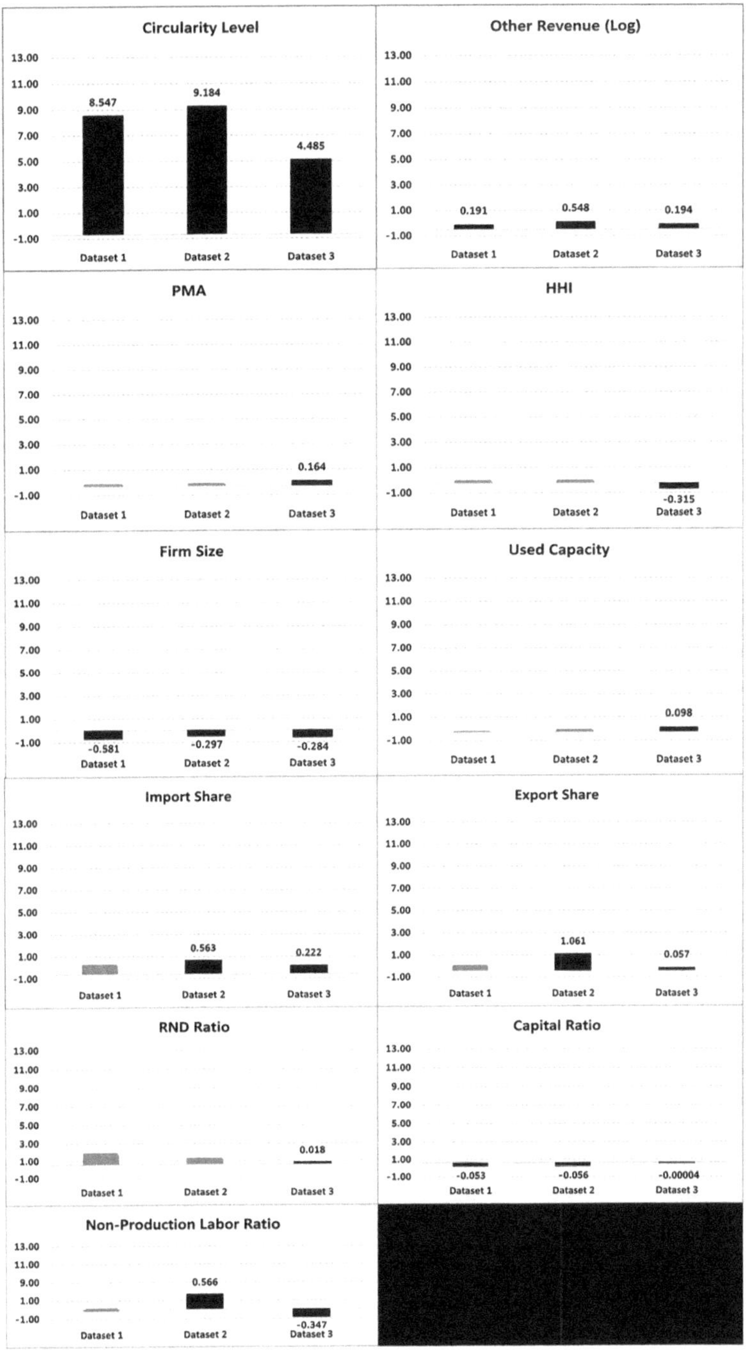


**Fig. 13.5** The effect of various circular economy and other determinants on log labor productivity. Note: = statistically significant; = statistically insignificant

implementing circular economy practices, while it has negative effects on productivity measurements of output production, value added, value added productivity and labor productivity for all firms in the SIBS database. For the firms implementing circular economy practices, it has no significant effects. This may be due to there is a difference between non-production labor's role importance specifically in firms in agriculture sectors implementing circular economy practices with that of all general firms in the SIBS database. For agriculture sectors, administration skills is important to obtain certificates (for instance, organic certificate) as well as market expansion which will increase the productivity, while in all sectors, generally an increase in non-production labor means more costs to bear for the firm. Green transition efforts in export-oriented industries open opportunities for circular economy adoption (Rishanty et al., 2022).

Foreign ownership does not play a significant role in increasing productivity for firms implementing circular economy practices, while it has significant positive impact on productivity for all general firms in the SIBS database. Similar case with that of used capacity variable. This may be due to circular economy ecosystem encourages producers to go local, to empower local, to shorten the supply chain, produce with coordinated capacity with other producers to build the circular business flows. Thus, foreign ownership and used capacity do not contribute to the increase in productivity. This makes firms implementing circular economy practices more resilient to global shocks.

The findings suggest that agricultural firms implementing circular economy practices experience the strongest positive effects on productivity, which is consistent with the case study of a farming community in Java, Indonesia, comprising 627 farmers (Rishanty, 2021).

The case study highlights a farming community that has successfully adopted circular economy practices through organic rice production, supported by certification, diversified marketing channels, and farmer training programs. With an average yield of 6 tonnes per hectare across 28 hectares, the community produces up to 168 tonnes of organic rice per harvest and supplies both local and national markets. The transition to organic farming is conducted gradually through structured training and reduced chemical input, with temporary yield declines that recover after several planting seasons. Youth involvement and improved education have played a critical role in modernising operations, overcoming the challenge of ageing farmers, and strengthening the community's capacity to integrate circular practices sustainably.

However, the transition remains constrained by structural challenges, including limited government support, low competitiveness of organic rice, and persistent skill gaps among farmers. The ageing farmer demographic exacerbates these challenges, as older farmers often face difficulties in adopting new technologies, organisational practices, and certification requirements, while youth participation in agriculture remains limited without targeted incentives. Inadequate infrastructure, misdirected chemical fertiliser subsidies, and dependence on middlemen further weaken farmers' bargaining power and income stability. Skills gaps—particularly in organisation, administration, certification, and technology adoption—further constrain competitiveness. The findings suggest that policy responses should focus on reallocating subsidies toward circular economy practices (shifting subsidies from chemical fertilisers to circular economy practices), strengthening infrastructure and training, and actively attracting and empowering younger farmers. Such measures would enhance productivity, competitiveness, and environmental sustainability while ensuring long-term food security and resilience in Indonesia's agricultural sector.

## 7 Conclusion

The circular economy arises as the opposing concept of linear economy based on the awareness of sustainability. Since the concept of the circular economy is a relatively new focus of research, very limited research has been done that focuses on the relationship between circular economy practices and firm productivity empirically. Circular economy paradigm has an open paradigm that is non-restrictive and adaptable to the social and ecological environment depending on the availability of resources (low-tech to high-tech) and markets (small to large). This makes circular economy approach, theoretically, is effective to improve productivity sustainably with limited resources available as in developing economies such as Indonesia (Rishanty, 2021; Rishanty & Suryahadi, 2020).

This study brings implication that to fully realize the potential of the circular economy—where environmental sustainability and economic growth can progress in harmony (Genovese et al., 2017)—the model is framed within a non-restrictive and adaptive paradigm, contingent upon the availability of resources (including technological capacity) and market conditions (Wageningen University, 2018; Winans et al., 2017). This paradigm allows firms the flexibility to transition toward circular practices incrementally, in accordance with their respective capacities.

The principle of circularity emphasizes the use of inputs derived increasingly from by-products or waste streams, while minimizing waste outputs. Over time, this can evolve into a fully closed-cycle circular economy ecosystem. Such cycles can be established at different scales, ranging from the level of individual farmers, to regional systems, and even global networks, depending on the specific needs and available potentials (Borrello et al., 2016; Ghisellini et al., 2016; Scheel, 2016; Wageningen University, 2018; Winans et al., 2017).

This study contributes to circular economy and productivity literature by examining the dynamics and the importance of circular economy variables (circularity level and profit from the sale of byproducts and waste) on firm's productivity using large datasets from Indonesia. The study shows that a higher level of circularity is consistently associated with better firm productivity, although the magnitude of the impact varies across sectors. Firms in agriculture that implement circular economy practices experience the strongest positive effects, particularly in value added, value-added productivity, and labor productivity. Firms in five non-agricultural subsectors implementing circular practices also benefit across all five productivity indicators, while the impact is more modest when considering all firms in the SIBS database. Overall, circularity level emerges as a more influential driver of productivity than other circular economy-related variables, such as additional revenues from waste or non-industrial services, whose effects are weaker and less consistent across sectors.

What also important is that the dynamics of other determinant variables of productivity shows that there is unique treats of firms that implement circular economy practices. The study highlights that productivity outcomes depend not only on circularity but also on firm and market characteristics. Greater competition (lower market concentration) generally enhances productivity for all firms, but the opposite holds for firms implementing circular economy practices, suggesting that more concentrated markets may facilitate coordination and ecosystem building required for circular business models. Trade openness (import and export shares) and R&D intensity positively affect productivity across datasets, while firm size increases total output and revenue but reduces productivity per worker. Capital intensity raises value added and revenue but lowers output-based productivity, reflecting scale efficiencies alongside higher capital costs. The dynamics of firms implementing circular economy is also consistent with Gusmerotti et al. (2019) and Lusiantoro et al. (2025), who find that firms motivated by economic benefits are more likely to adopt circular economy practices. Notably, foreign ownership and capacity utilization do not significantly improve productivity for circular economy firms, indicating a stronger reliance on local ecosystems and shorter supply chains, which may enhance resilience to global shocks.

The study findings bring insights to policy recommendations as follows. First, given the strongest productivity gains are observed in agriculture firms implementing circular economy practices, policies should prioritise scaling circular models in agri-food systems. This includes support for organic inputs, waste-to-value processes, and localised circular supply chains that enhance value added and labour productivity. Policy responses should prioritise reforming agricultural subsidies by shifting support from industrialised chemical fertilisers to circular economy practices, alongside strengthening infrastructure and farmer skills to improve productivity and competitiveness. At the same time, targeted incentives are needed to attract and empower younger farmers and strengthen farmer organisations, reducing reliance on middlemen while enhancing environmental sustainability, food security, and long-term resilience. Second, since the *level of circularity* has a stronger and more consistent impact on productivity than auxiliary circular revenues (e.g. waste sales), policy instruments should focus on deepening circular integration. Standards, certification schemes, and performance-based incentives can encourage firms to embed circular practices throughout production rather than treat them as side activities. Third, the finding shows that market concentration can enhance productivity for circular economy firms suggests the need for policies that facilitate coordination. Government can play a catalytic role by supporting industrial symbiosis platforms, cluster-based development, and cooperative arrangements—particularly at the regional level—while maintaining safeguards against anti-competitive behaviour. The urgent need of government support in infrastructure has been shown in a case study of a circular economy practice in palm oil industry which beneficial for energy security in remote areas (Rishanty et al., 2024).

Next, the positive role of R&D intensity and trade exposure indicates that innovation and openness remain critical. Targeted fiscal incentives, green financing, and technical assistance should be directed toward R&D in circular technologies, as well as export facilitation for circular products that meet international sustainability standards. The differing role of non-production labour highlights the importance of sector-specific skill development. In agriculture, administrative and certification-related skills should be strengthened through training programs, as these can directly raise productivity. For other sectors, policies should aim to balance efficiency and cost management. Last, the limited role of foreign ownership and capacity utilisation in circular firms suggests that locally rooted business models are central to productivity gains. Policies should therefore support MSMEs, local financing mechanisms, and domestic supply chains to reinforce resilience against global shocks and external volatility.

Thus, the study underscores that circular economy can serve as a productivity-enhancing and resilience-building development pathway for Indonesia when supported by well-targeted policies. By prioritising deep circular integration, fostering coordinated ecosystems, strengthening innovation and skills, and anchoring circular business models in domestic value chains, policymakers can simultaneously advance value-added industrialisation, environmental sustainability, and long-term economic resilience. These measures are particularly relevant for supporting MSMEs and the agri-food sector, positioning the circular economy as a strategic instrument for achieving Golden Indonesia 2045 while mitigating structural and external risks.

## References

Amato, F., Privitera, G., Serrano, C., Trimarchi, E. G., Giuliana, C., & Vescera, F. (2018). Assessment of the energetic value of ancient sicilian wheat in the industrial symbiosis perspective. Procedia Environmental Science, Engineering and Management, 5, 1–9.

Ansell, T., & Cayzer, S. (2018). Limits to growth redux: A system dynamics model for assessing energy and climate change constraints to global growth. Energy Policy, 120(June), 514–525. https://doi.org/10.1016/j.enpol.2018.05.053

Bala, B. K., Alias, E. F., Arshad, F. M., Noh, K. M., & Hadi, A. H. A. (2014). Modelling of food security in Malaysia. Simulation Modelling Practice and Theory, 47, 152–164. https://doi.org/10.1016/j.simpat.2014.06.001

Baltagi, B. H. (2005). Econometric Analysis of Panel Data (3rd ed.). Chicester: John Wiley & Sons.

Benkovskis, K., Masso, J., Tkacevs, O., Vahter, P., & Yashiro, N. (2017). Export and productivity in global value chains: Comparative evidence from Latvia and Estonia (No. 1448). https://doi.org/10.1787/cd5710c4-en

Brears, R. C. (2015). The circular economy and the water-food nexus. Journal on Food, Agriculture and Society, 3(2), 53–59.

Cooper, S. J. G., Giesekam, J., Hammond, G. P., Norman, J. B., Owen, A., Rogers, J. G., & Scott, K. (2017). Thermodynamic insights and assessment of the 'circular economy'. Journal of Cleaner Production, 162, 1356–1367. https://doi.org/10.1016/j.jclepro.2017.06.169

D'Amato, D., Droste, N., Allen, B., Kettunen, M., Lähtinen, K., Korhonen, J., … Toppinen, A. (2017). Green, circular, bio economy: A comparative analysis of sustainability avenues. Journal of Cleaner Production, 168, 716–734. https://doi.org/10.1016/j.jclepro.2017.09.053

Daly, H. E. (1972). Limits to growth. Ecological Economics and Sustainable Development, 9–11.

Dicks, H. (2017). Environmental Ethics and Biomimetic Ethics: Nature as Object of Ethics and Nature as Source of Ethics. Journal of Agricultural and Environmental Ethics, 30(2), 255–274. https://doi.org/10.1007/s10806-017-9667-6

Didenko, N., Klochkov, Y., & Skripnuk, D. (2018). Ecological Criteria for Comparing Linear and Circular Economies. Resources, 7(3), 48. https://doi.org/10.3390/resources7030048

Domenech, T., Bleischwitz, R., Doranova, A., Panayotopoulos, D., & Roman, L. (2019). Mapping Industrial Symbiosis Development in Europe_ typologies of networks, characteristics, performance and contribution to the Circular Economy. Resources, Conservation and Recycling, 141(October 2018), 76–98. https://doi.org/10.1016/j.resconrec.2018.09.016

Foschi, E., & Bonoli, A. (2019). The Commitment of Packaging Industry in the Framework of the European Strategy for Plastics in a Circular Economy. Administrative Sciences, 9(1), 18. https://doi.org/10.3390/admsci9010018

Fu, X., & Balasubramanyam, V. N. (2003). Township and Village Enterprises in China. Journal of Development Studies, 39(4), 27–46. https://doi.org/10.1080/713869424

Geissdoerfer, M., Savaget, P., Bocken, N. M. P., & Hultink, E. J. (2017). The Circular Economy – A new sustainability paradigm? Journal of Cleaner Production, 143, 757–768. https://doi.org/10.1016/j.jclepro.2016.12.048

Genovese, A., Acquaye, A. A., Figueroa, A., & Koh, S. C. L. (2017). Sustainable supply chain management and the transition towards a circular economy: Evidence and some applications. Omega (United Kingdom), 66, 344–357. https://doi.org/10.1016/j.omega.2015.05.015

Gusmerotti, N. M., Testa, F., Corsini, F., Pretner, G., & Iraldo, F. (2019). Drivers and approaches to the circular economy in manufacturing firms. Journal of Cleaner Production, 230, 314-327. ISSN 0959-6526. https://doi.org/10.1016/j.jclepro.2019.05.044

Haas, W., Krausmann, F., Wiedenhofer, D., & Heinz, M. (2015). How circular is the global economy?: An assessment of material flows, waste production, and recycling in the European union and the world in 2005. Journal of Industrial Ecology, 19(5), 765–777. https://doi.org/10.1111/jiec.12244

Halpern, L., Koren, M., & Szeidl, ´Ad'am. (2005). Imports and Productivity. CEPR Discussion Paper No. 5139, (November). Retrieved from https://ssrn.com/abstract=785127

Hens, L., Block, C., Cabello-Eras, J. J., Sagastume-Gutierez, A., Garcia-Lorenzo, D., Chamorro, C., … Vandecasteele, C. (2018). On the evolution of "Cleaner Production" as a concept and a practice. Journal of Cleaner Production, 172, 3323–3333. https://doi.org/10.1016/j.jclepro.2017.11.082

Horbach, J., & Rammer, C. (2019). Circular economy innovations, growth and employment: At the firm level Empirical evidence from Germany. *Journal of Industrial Ecology*, 1–11. https://doi.org/10.1111/jiec.12977

Juhro, S. M., Narayan, P. K., Iyke, B. N., & Trisnanto, B. (2022). Social capital, R&D and provincial growth in Indonesia. *Regional Studies*, *56*(12), 2117–2132. https://doi.org/10.1080/00343404.2022.2042469

Korhonen, J., Honkasalo, A., & Seppälä, J. (2018). Circular Economy: The Concept and its Limitations. Ecological Economics, 143, 37–46. https://doi.org/10.1016/j.ecolecon.2017.06.041

Leyden, D. P., Link, A. N., & Siegel, D. S. (2014). A theoretical analysis of the role of social networks in entrepreneurship. Research Policy, 43(7), 1157–1163. https://doi.org/10.1016/j.respol.2014.04.010

Lusiantoro, L., Caselli, G., & Rishanty, A. (2025). Circular economy practices of SMEs: do business survivability and supply chain finance matter? Production, vol.35, e20240126, 2025. https://doi.org/10.1590/0103-6513.20240126

Lyytimäki, J., Nygrén, N. A., Pulkka, A., & Rantala, S. (2018). Energy transition looming behind the headlines? Newspaper coverage of biogas production in Finland. Energy, Sustainability and Society, 8(1), 1–11. https://doi.org/10.1186/s13705-018-0158-z

Mathews, J. A., & Tan, H. (2011). Progress toward a circular economy in China: The drivers (and inhibitors) of eco-industrial initiative. Journal of Industrial Ecology, 15(3), 435–457. https://doi.org/10.1111/j.1530-9290.2011.00332.x

Meadows, D., Randers, J., & Meadows, D. (2005). Limits to growth: the 30-year update (3rd ed.). Retrieved from www.earthscan.co.uk

Nasiri, M., Rantala, T., Saunila, M., Ukko, J., & Rantanen, H. (2018). Transition towards sustainable solutions: Product, service, technology, and business model. Sustainability (Switzerland), 10(2). https://doi.org/10.3390/su10020358

Paehlke, R. (2001). Environmental Politics, Sustainability and Social Science. Environmental Politics, 10(4), 1–22.

Pagell M, Katz JP, Sheu C (2005), The importance of national culture in operations management research. International Journal of Operations & Production Management, Vol. 25 No. 4 pp. 371–394, https://doi.org/10.1108/01443570510585552

Prieto-Sandoval, V., Jaca, C., & Ormazabal, M. (2018). Towards a consensus on the circular economy. Journal of Cleaner Production, 179, 605–615. https://doi.org/10.1016/j.jclepro.2017.12.224

Rishanty, A. (2021). The Transition Towards a Circular Economy in Developing Countries: A Firm-level Perspective. Retrieved from https://books.google.co.id/books?id=0ZsgzwEACAAJ. University of Liverpool.

Rishanty, A., Sambodo, M. T., & Wicaksono, R. P. K. (2022). Green Transition Risks On Export Competitiveness: Circular Economy Approach, Working Papers WP/14/2022, Bank Indonesia. https://ideas.repec.org/p/idn/wpaper/wp142022.html

Rishanty, A., Sambodo, M. T., Silalahi, M. & Hambali E. (2024). Zero-Waste Bioenergy to Lower Energy Transition Risks in Indonesia—A Circular Economy Practice on Methane Capture in Biogas Production from POME. Bioenergy Research, April 2024 17(3):1–13. https://doi.org/10.1007/s12155-024-10754-3

Rishanty, A. & Suryahadi, A., (2020). Circular Economy And Productivity In A Large Developing Country: Empirical Evidence From Indonesia. Working Papers WP/10/2020, Bank Indonesia. https://ideas.repec.org/p/idn/wpaper/wp102020.html

Ritzén, S., & Sandström, G. Ö. (2017). Barriers to the Circular Economy - Integration of Perspectives and Domains. *Procedia CIRP, 64*, 7–12. https://doi.org/10.1016/j.procir.2017.03.005

Ruskin, J. (1849). The Seven Lamps of Architecture. Retrieved from https://books.google.co.uk/books/about/The_Seven_Lamps_of_Architecture.html?id=MFwJAAAAQAAJ&printsec=frontcover&source=kp_read_button&redir_esc=y#v=onepage&q&f=false

Schaeck, K., & Čihák, M. (2007). Banking competition and capital ratios (IMF Working Paper No. 2007/216). International Monetary Fund. https://doi.org/10.5089/9781451867800.001

Swagemakers, P., Garcia, M. D. D., & Wiskerke, J. S. C. (2018). Socially-inclusive development and value creation: How a composting project in Galicia (Spain) "Hit the Rocks". Sustainability (Switzerland), 10(6). https://doi.org/10.3390/su10062040

Takala, T., Tikkanen, J., Haapala, A., Pitkänen, S., Torssonen, P., Valkeavirta, R., & Pöykkö, T. (2019). Shaping the concept of bioeconomy in participatory projects – An example from the post-graduate education in Finland. Journal of Cleaner Production, 221, 176–188. https://doi.org/10.1016/j.jclepro.2019.02.007

Wacker, J. G., Yang, C., & Sheu, C. (2006). Productivity of production labor, non-production labor, and capital: An international study. 103, 863–872. https://doi.org/10.1016/j.ijpe.2005.12.012

Wackernagel, M., Schulz, N. B., Deumling, D., Linares, A. C., Jenkins, M., Kapos, V., … Randers, J. (2002). Tracking the ecological overshoot of the human economy. Proceedings of the National Academy of Sciences of the United States of America, 99(14), 9266–9271. https://doi.org/10.1073/pnas.142033699

Wageningen, U. (2018). Circular agriculture: a new perspective for Dutch agriculture - WUR. Retrieved May 19, 2019, from https://www.wur.nl/en/newsarticle/Circular-agriculture-a-new-perspective-for-Dutch-agriculture-1.htm

Winans, K., Kendall, A., & Deng, H. (2017). The history and current applications of the circular economy concept. Renewable and Sustainable Energy Reviews, 68(October 2015), 825–833. https://doi.org/10.1016/j.rser.2016.09.123

Wreford, A., Bayne, K., Edwards, P., & Renwick, A. (2019). Enabling a transformation to a bioeconomy in New Zealand. Environmental Innovation and Societal Transitions, 31(November 2017), 184–199. https://doi.org/10.1016/j.eist.2018.11.005

# Chapter 14
# Green Human Capital and Economic Growth

**Donni Fajar Anugrah, Anastuty Kusumowardhani, and Mohammad Marza Naufal**

**Abstract** This chapter explores how green job skills drive eco-friendly economic growth in Indonesia. By looking at key industries like manufacturing and energy, we found that improving these skills directly boosts sustainable growth. To succeed, Indonesia must invest more in vocational training and encourage schools to work with businesses. Preparing workers with the right skills is crucial for the country's shift toward a greener future.

**Keywords** Green human capital · Green economic growth · Green skill

## 1 Introduction

Green growth is the concept that fostering economic growth and development while ensuring that natural assets continue to provide the resources and environmental services on which our well-being relies (OECD, 2017). For instance, cultivating a circular economy could promote sustainability by fostering economic growth while protecting the environment. From 2010 to 2023, Indonesia's economy grew at an average rate of 4.72% per year. This rate is slower than Vietnam's (6.02%) and the Philippines' (5.22%). A major structural weakness that limits economic growth is the presence of low labor productivity, with Indonesia's average productivity growth being only 2.97% per year (CEIC, 2023). This rate is slower than the growth rates in Vietnam and the Philippines, which are 5.38% and 3.11%, respectively. The slower growth in productivity makes it hard for Indonesia to help the economy grow, which limits Indonesia's long-term growth potential.

D. F. Anugrah (✉) · A. Kusumowardhani
Bank Indonesia, Jakarta, Indonesia
e-mail: donni@bi.go.id; nita@bi.go.id

M. M. Naufal
Universitas Indonesia, Jakarta, Indonesia
e-mail: mohammad.marza@ui.ac.id


S. M. Juhro et al. (eds.), *Sustainable Economy: The Indonesian Pathways*,
https://doi.org/10.1007/978-981-92-1215-6_14

Climate change also plays an important role in the economy because it increases Indonesia's vulnerability to various types of risks, which leads to economic losses. For example, climate change is projected to raise surface temperatures due to an increased level of greenhouse gas emissions (SSP5-8.5), which might exceed 29 °C by 2100 (World Bank, 2025). The higher temperature will influence changes in weather patterns around Indonesia, which have also led to an increase in extreme weather occurrences and hydrometeorological disasters over recent years (BNPB, 2025). As a result, Bappenas (2021) projects that due to climate change, economic losses may exceed 100 trillion rupiahs per year. However, it can even reach 40% of GDP if there is no serious attention. Moreover, climate change may also reduce productivity by 2.97% in working hours by 2030 due to an increased risk of workplace accidents (ILO, 2018).

Enhancing labor productivity is crucial for promoting green growth through labor capability enhancement strategies, which involve attending to technical vocational education and training (TVET) that are integrated with green skills. Along with the growth of the green economy, the demand for green labor in green industries remains on an increasing trend, requiring the workforce to be equipped with the necessary skills (ILO, 2019). By building workforce capacity in these areas, Indonesia can increase economic competitiveness while accelerating the transformation towards more inclusive and sustainable economic growth. However, accessibility, affordability, and infrastructure remain the main challenges in the education sector that must be addressed as a priority. One way to do this is to increase private investment and government spending in the education sector (Ministry of Education and Culture, 2024).

Several priority sectors have been identified as key areas of green growth for Indonesia (Bappenas, 2025). First, sustainable agriculture and marine management are equally essential for achieving sustainable, longer-term food security (FAO, 2023). The forestry and other land-use (FOLU) sector is also central to Indonesia's climate plan (FAO, 2023). In the manufacturing and construction sectors, low-carbon growth requires the adoption of green buildings and green industries that emphasize the aspect of resource efficiency (Ellen MacArthur Foundation, 2020; World Green Building Council, 2021). Sustainable tourism is a possibility through ecotourism projects, although programs to this end are yet small-scale (UNEP, 2020). In the energy sector, renewable energy (RE) and energy efficiency (EE) play important roles in reducing dependence on fossil fuels that have high levels of emissions (IEA, 2021). The waste management sector, including the circular economy, relies on effective systems for waste reduction and recycling, as well as the scaling up of waste-to-energy plants (UNEP, 2020). Finally, the transport sector presents both challenges of accelerating vehicle electrification and expanding low-carbon public transport (IEA, 2021).

Study by Acemoglu et al. (2012) have explained that clean energy investment, resource efficiency, and the improvement of green workforce skills are necessary to enhance industrial innovation and reduce environmental pressure. Lin (2024) stated that human capital is essential to support the green growth in China. Lu et al. (2024) described that misallocating human capital could harm green development in China.

However, research on the role of green human capital in driving green economic growth in Indonesia is still minimal. Therefore, this chapter aims to analyze the impact of increasing green human capital on green growth in Indonesia, both at the national level and at the sectoral level. Indonesia was chosen as the object of research because this country has great potential to develop a green economy.

This chapter is divided into five main sections. The first section provides an introduction that explains the background, its objectives, and the contribution to previous studies. The second is a review of related literature studies to comprehend the theoretical foundation, and the last is empirical evidence. The third is on data and methods utilized, together with the analytical model implemented to capture the influence of green human capital on green growth. The fourth section presents the analysis findings and a discussion, including an analysis of their impact on Indonesia's sectoral economy. The last is on conclusions and recommendations to enhance inclusive and sustainable green economic growth.

# 2 Literature Review

## *2.1 Theoretical Framework*

The Mankiw, Romer, and Weil (MRW) model (1992) is an extension of the Solow growth model, which incorporates human capital as a separate input within the production function and assumes technology as labor-augmenting. Human capital within this model is a vital determinant of economic growth, as skills and the quality of labor significantly contribute to output. A labor force with higher levels of human capital can produce more output than one with lower skill levels. The following equation represents the MRW model:

$$Y_t = K_t^a H_t^b \left(A_t L_t\right)^{1-a-b} \tag{14.1}$$

The $Y$ stands for Real GDP, $K$ for Physical Capital Stock, $H$ for Human Capital Stock, $A$ for Total Factor Productivity, $L$ for labor, and $t$ for time. The condition $a + b < 1$ is introduced to ensure that Decreasing Returns to Scale (DRS) prevails with diminishing marginal returns for all inputs. The parameters a and b denote the marginal productivity (MP) of physical capital and human capital, respectively. The revised equation can be expressed as a function of output per effective labor (productivity) by dividing both sides by $A_tL_t$:

$$y_t = k_t^a h_t^b \text{; where } y_t = \frac{Y_t}{A_t L_t} \tag{14.2}$$

The MRW model assumes that individuals distribute their income between investments in human capital ($s_H$) and physical capital ($s_K$). It also posits that both physical and human capital have the same rate of depreciation, represented by $\delta$. Additionally, it is assumed that population and technology grow at consistent rates, $n$ and $g$, respectively, as described in the Solow Growth Model. In equilibrium, the productivity of human capital per effective unit of labor ($h_t$) remains unchanged. To explore the differences in human capital accumulation, we can derive the following equation:

$$h^* = \left( \frac{s_K^a s_H^{1-a}}{n+g+\delta} \right)^{\frac{1}{1-a-b}} \tag{14.3}$$

Equation (14.3) demonstrates that higher investment in human capital leads to greater accumulation of human capital. Under steady-state conditions, this accumulation enhances output, thereby promoting long-term economic growth. To assess the effect of human capital on productivity and growth, we can substitute the steady-state value of human capital from Eq. (14.3) into the production function presented in Eq. (14.2). This results in the following expression:

$$\ln\left[\frac{Y_t}{L_t}\right] = \ln A(0) + g_t - \frac{a}{1-a}\ln(n+g+\delta) + \frac{a}{1-a}\ln s_K + \frac{b}{1-a}\ln(h)^* \tag{14.4}$$

## 2.2 Previous Studies

Previous research on human capital and its relationship to economic growth has shown that human capital is crucial for driving economic progress. Vu et al. (2012) noted that workers with vocational education contribute significantly more to productivity than those with university or secondary education. Shamzzuzoha et al. (2022) explained that technical vocational education and training (TVET) is essential to develop both specific technical skills and broader competencies that encourage green innovation. The finding is also supported by the World Economic Forum (2025), which emphasizes the importance of green skills within vocational education in preparing workers for emerging green job opportunities, including positions such as environmental engineers and renewable energy professionals, which are forecasted to grow the most from 2025 to 2030.

The relationship between human capital and the environment in general shows that human capital plays a positive role in mitigating environmental damage and supporting ecological sustainability. Bano et al. (2018) used an autoregressive distributed lag model and found that human capital has a significant long-term effect on reducing carbon emissions in Pakistan (1971–2014). Additionally, Ahmed et al. (2020) found that human capital could mitigate environmental degradation and promote sustainable urbanization in China.

Liu et al. (2023) investigated the impact of green human capital on green growth in China from the onset of digitalization (1991–2019) using the ARDL approach.

They determined that green human capital is crucial in driving both short-term and long-term green growth, with better education, renewable energy use, and digitalization serving as the primary engines. Ecological consciousness and environmental efficiency during production and consumption were also vital to its success. Crifo (2024) applied an endogenous model of growth to investigate the link between green human capital, innovation, and inequality. The findings were that innovation by green human capital boosts economic growth at a rapid pace and also widens the gap between skilled and unskilled labor, underlining the importance of ensuring a fair energy transition that generates new economic opportunities without sacrificing people's justice. In the case of Indonesia, Affandi et al. (2024) show that increasing human capital both in quality and quantity has a positive influence on economic growth, with STEM expertise that can encourage increased worker productivity.

# 3 Data and Methodology

## *3.1 Data and Methodology*

The methodology of this chapter is mixed methods that include qualitative and quantitative methods. Qualitative methods optimize focus group discussion and interviews. While quantitative methods will optimize the use of panel data regression (FEM as baseline & System GMM) and descriptive statistics to analyze the impact of green human capital on green growth. This analysis uses primary and secondary data. Primary data is obtained through FGD and interviews. Secondary data is obtained through national sources such as the Central Bureau of Statistics (BPS), SAKERNAS, and SUSENAS. The object of observation is Indonesia at the provincial level from 2010 to 2023 with annual data frequency. This chapter employs four types of variables: dependent variables, independent variables, control variables, and instrument variables. A summary of the research variables is as follows (Table 14.1).

In this model, green growth is defined as economic growth achieved while minimizing the negative environmental impacts. This method is a modification of Hickel (2020), which calculates the Gross Domestic Regional Product (GDRP) divided by the ecological footprint. The Ecological Footprint quantifies the amount of biologically productive land and water necessary for an individual, population, or activity to generate all the resources it consumes, manage its urban infrastructure, and process the waste it produces, utilizing current technology and resource management practices, and is represented in global hectares (Global Footprint Network, 2023). The formula for calculating green growth is as follows:

$$GreenGDRP_{it} = \frac{GDRP_{it}}{Ecological\,Footprint_{it}} \tag{14.8}$$

**Table 14.1** Summary of variables

| No | Variable | Code | Unit | Hypo | Source |
|---|---|---|---|---|---|
| 1. | Gross Domestic Regional Product | $GDRP_{it}$ | Billion Rupiah | | BPS |
| 2. | Ecological Footprint | $EcoFP_{it}$ | Global ha | | GFN |
| 3. | Green Growth | $GDPG_{it}$ | Billion Rupiah | | Hickel (2020) |
| 4. | Green Human Capital | $GHC_{it}$ | Person | + | SAKERNAS |
| 5. | Technology | $ICT_{it}$ | % of Population | + | SUSENAS |
| 6. | Green Jobs | $Labor_{it}$ | Person | + | SAKERNAS |
| 7. | Domestic investment | $Inv_{it}$ | Billion Rupiah | +/– | BPS |
| 8. | Innovation | $Patent_{it}$ | Unit | +/– | DJKI |
| 9. | Foreign Direct Investment | $FDI_{it}$ | Million USD | +/– | BPS/WB |
| 10. | ICT Skill | $ICTskill_{it}$ | % of Population | | SUSENAS |
| 11. | Productive Ages | $Age_{it}$ | % of Population | | SAKERNAS |

$$GreenGrowth_{it} = \frac{GreenGDRP_{it} - GreenGDRP_{it-1}}{GreenGDRP_{it-1}} \tag{14.9}$$

Green human capital is a variable of interest in this chapter. The green human capital in this study refers to the definition of Ahakwa et al. (2023), namely the number of workers who possess the skills or education necessary to fulfill green tasks or tasks with green potential, as defined by Granata and Posadas (2024). Green human capital data is taken from SAKERNAS. According to the Cobb-Douglas model, technology and domestic investment are other variables that affect GDRP. The control variables are foreign direct investment and innovation. In comparison, ICT Skills and productive ages are instrumental variables. The details of the green human capital data used in this study are as follows.

## 3.2 Model

Green growth adopts the green principles and requires more innovative and sustainable practices. To optimize the development of the green economy and green growth, significant productivity increases are required, especially in green economy sectors. Therefore, TVET with a green curriculum forms the solution as it equips the workforce with the necessary capacity to enhance productivity in greener economic activity. Moreover, investment within the education sector is key to improving the quality of education, especially TVET. Investment is necessary to strengthen infrastructure and increase learning capacity. Investment also raises the quality of training programs to ensure that the workforce is well-equipped to respond to the green economy. The following is the conceptual framework for this study (Fig. 14.1):

This chapter applies the Cobb-Douglas model modified by Hall et al. (2010) and Inekwe (2015) to analyze the impact of green human capital on green growth in Indonesia. This study modifies the Cobb-Douglas model by incorporating

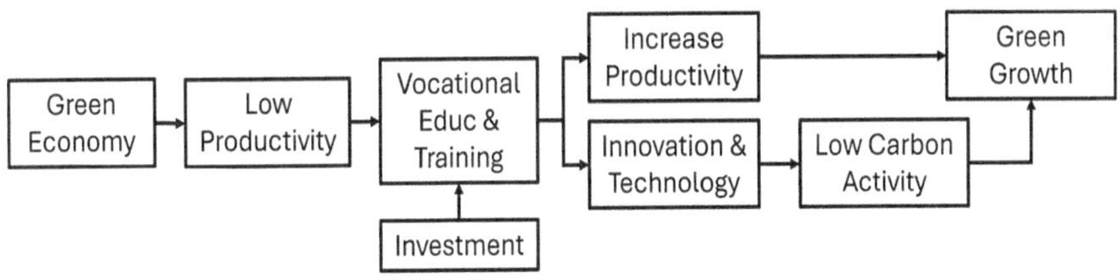


**Fig. 14.1** Conceptual framework

innovation and human capital as additional factors that influence green growth. This study assumes that the capital stock variable (K) can be separated into domestic capital (Domestic Investment) and the external capital variable (FDI). The variables representing innovation and technology are represented by patents and ICT adoption, respectively. Based on the framework above, this study formulates the following empirical model:

$$GDPG_{it} = a_0 + a_1 ICT_{it} + a_2 GHC_{it} + a_3 Inv_{it} + a_4 Gjobs_{it} + a_5 X_{it} + v_t + \gamma_i + \varepsilon_{it} \quad (14.10)$$

Equation (14.13) represents the model for estimating Green Gross Domestic Regional Product (Green GDRP) for region/sector $i$ at time $t$. In this equation, Green GDRP is affected by a number of important elements: *ICT* (Information and Communication Technology) signifies the technological progress in the area, *GHC* (Green Human Capital) refers to the expertise and knowledge of the workforce regarding environmental sustainability, *Inv* (Investment) represents the financial resources allocated for sustainable development, and *Gjobs* indicates the green jobs available in the region, which play a crucial role in enhancing economic output. Additionally, $X$ includes other relevant explanatory variables that might affect green growth. $v_t$ and $\gamma_i$ respectively are the time specific effect and sector specific effect. An error term (ε) completes the equation, which captures unobserved factors influencing Green GDRP.

The empirical model (10) above is a log-log regression model to see the elasticity between the dependent and independent variables. To overcome the possibility of endogeneity problems due to omitted variable bias and reverse causality in the data, this chapter employs the System Generalized Method of Moments (GMM) regression approach, which aligns with the study by Hickel (2020) on Sustainable Development research. This approach is suitable for capturing the dynamics of economic variables while ensuring that the estimation results are not affected by endogeneity problems. The following Eqs. (14.11) and (14.12) are the System GMM equations in level and difference, respectively.

$$GDPG_{it} = a_0 + a_1 GDPG_{i(t-\tau)} + a_2 GHC_{it} + \sum\nolimits_{h=1}^{k} \delta_h X_{h,i(t-\tau)} + v_t + \gamma_i + \varepsilon_{it} \quad (14.11)$$

$$GDPG_{it} - GDPG_{i(t-\tau)} = a_1\left(GDPG_{i(t-\tau)} - GDPG_{i(t-2\tau)}\right) + a_2\left(GHC_{it} - GHC_{i(t-\tau)}\right) + \sum_{h=1}^{k}\delta_h\left(X_{h,i(t-\tau)} - X_{h,i(t-2\tau)}\right) + \left(v_t - v_{t-\tau}\right) + \varepsilon_{i(t-\tau)} \quad (14.12)$$

# 4 Discussion

## 4.1 Descriptive and Regression Analysis

This study conducted baseline regression using the Pooled Least Squared (PLS) and Fixed Effect Model (FEM) approaches based on Eq. (14.10). Although both models provide a valuable overview of the relationship between variables, the potential endogeneity problem makes the empirical results uninterpretable and leads to bias in the estimation. Therefore, it is necessary to employ a more robust GMM model that accounts for endogeneity and provides more robust and interpretable estimates (Table 14.2).

The estimation results applying system GMM show that GHC (lnghc) has a positive and significant effect on green economic growth (lngdpg), with a significant coefficient value at the 1% level (0.010). This finding aligns with the research of Liu

**Table 14.2** Baseline regression dan system GMM estimation

| | PLS | FEM | SYSGMM |
|---|---|---|---|
| | (1) | (2) | (3) |
| VARIABLES | Lngdpg | Lngdpg | Lngdpg |
| l.lngdpg | 0.982*** | 0.858*** | 0.967*** |
| Ict | 0.013*** | 0.009 | 0.016*** |
| Lnghc | 0.003*** | 0.013** | 0.010*** |
| Lngjobs | 0.023** | 0.075*** | 0.033*** |
| Lninvdom | 0.000 | 0.001 | 0.002** |
| Lnfdi | 0.003*** | 0.005* | 0.004*** |
| Lnpaten | 0.007*** | 0.008* | 0.009*** |
| Constant | 0.115*** | 1.192* | 0.192*** |
| AR (1) | | | (0.001) |
| AR (2) | | | (0.335) |
| Hansen | | | (0.013) |
| Observations | 402 | 402 | 400 |
| Instruments | | | 24 |
| R-squared | 0.999 | 0.981 | |
| Number of id | | 34 | 34 |

Robust standard errors in parentheses
*** $p < 0.01$, ** $p < 0.05$, * $p < 0.1$

et al. (2023), which demonstrates that green human capital makes a significant contribution to green growth in China. Furthermore, Vu, Hammes, and Im (2012) explain that vocational education can increase productivity, affecting GDP growth. In addition, research by Ahmed et al. (2020) emphasizes that education encourages higher environmental awareness, which can contribute to increasing low-carbon activity that reduces carbon emissions.

The System GMM estimation shows different results for other variables. ICT has a positive effect on green economic growth, albeit with a smaller coefficient and significance at the 10% level (0.016***). These findings are in line with the trend of the ICT sector's contribution to GDP that has continued to increase in the last 14 years in Indonesia (Rohman et al., 2025). Labor and domestic investment have a positive but weaker impact than other variables. In contrast, foreign direct investment (FDI) shows a significant effect at the 5% level, although the effect is slightly smaller. Patents (number of patents) also have a significant, albeit small, effect, indicating a positive relationship between innovation and green economic growth, although not as strong as the effect of GHC.

Regarding the diagnostic test, the System GMM estimation results meet the assumptions required for validity of the model. The AR (1) test yields significant results (p-value <0.01), indicating that autocorrelation in the model needs to be considered. Nonetheless, the AR (2) test is not significant (p-value >0.1), which shows that there is no second-order autocorrelation and verifies the validity of the model. Moreover, the Hansen test is also found to be insignificant (p-value >0.1), indicating that the instruments used in the model are valid and do not suffer from overidentification issues. The consistency test also shows that the lag of the dependent variable is between the PLS and FEM results, further confirming that the System GMM estimation results are consistent and reliable.

Nowadays, the development of vocational education in Indonesia has shown significant progress. PDDIKTI (2023) reported that the number of vocational education graduates in 2023 reached approximately 285,221 people. However, only a small portion acquired skills related to sustainability and the green economy. The main challenge is green skills have not yet become a priority agenda in the revision of the national curriculum. In addition, access to vocational education that is more relevant to the demands of the green jobs in the market is still limited, especially in areas outside Java. However, the opportunities are significant if the government and the private sector can collaborate to develop green skills and expand access to relevant vocational education.

On the other hand, Indonesia's education quality suffers from several problems related to its low Gross Participation Rate (GPR) at higher and vocational schools. BPS (2024) shows that GPR tends to continue to decline at each higher level. This problem threatens the sustainability of education in Indonesia because students cannot study for at least 13 years due to inadequate educational capacity. Moreover, the low APK rate is influenced by several factors, namely the relatively high costs of education. This problem affects 50,000 registered pupils who are unable to afford higher schooling expenses (Ministry of Education and Culture, 2024). In addition, the capacity of educational institutions is not yet optimal, and the quality of the curriculum does not always match the needs of the labor market, which are also significant problems.

The opportunity to develop a green-based TVET model first was introduced by UNESCO-UNEVOC (2018) to encourage the creation of a mature education ecosystem for sustainable development (ESD) in various countries. The TVET model aims to integrate green concepts into the campus environment, curriculum and training, research, community, and institutional culture. Various countries have adopted this model, such as Malaysia, which has modified its diploma program in electrical engineering at the Port Dickson Polytechnic to include energy efficiency and renewable energy in the curriculum (UNESCO-UNEVOC, 2015). Furthermore, the implementation of a green curriculum was implemented earlier in Canada at the high school level (UNESCO-UNEVOC, 2018).

Incorporating extra skills into Indonesia's curriculum and training programs will be a challenging task. Consequently, three levels that can aid this process should be examined. At the macro level, green skills regulations and curricula are systemic because they encourage the introduction of new knowledge and skills across various educational programs. At the institutional level, the adoption of green skills is more geared toward matching industry needs with those of educational institutions to increase labor market efficiency. Lastly, at the micro level, improving bootcamps for teachers and instructors, along with providing relevant learning materials, is vital to enhance the quality of green based TVET.

## *4.2 Sectoral Analysis*

This chapter also analyzes the sectoral impact of green human capital, focusing on six main sectors: agriculture, manufacturing, waste management, construction, transportation, and energy. These sectors are selected considering their relevance to their association with the green economy and carbon reduction based on Bappenas green economy priority sectors; for example, the farming sector directly comes under natural resource management and emissions from farming practices. The manufacturing sector contains high reduction potential by adopting environmentally sound technology. The waste and construction sectors also contribute to emission management through environmentally friendly practices in waste management toward a circular economy. Transportation and energy, as one of the sectors with the most significant emissions, is also a key sector in reducing carbon emissions through innovation and the transition to environmentally friendly vehicles. The following are the results of sectoral estimations (Table 14.3).

All diagnostic tests in the System GMM model show results that follow the assumptions: the AR (1) test is significant, the AR (2) test is insignificant, and the Hansen test shows insignificant results, indicating that this model is valid, and the instruments used are appropriate. Based on the sectoral estimation results, GHC significantly affects green economic growth in all sectors. The most significant impact is observed in the manufacturing sectors, energy, and waste management sector with coefficients of 0.183, 0.158 and 0.138, respectively. These sectors, which are major contributors to carbon emissions, demonstrate that developing

**Table 14.3** Sectoral estimation

| | (1) | (2) | (3) | (4) | (5) | (6) |
|---|---|---|---|---|---|---|
| | Agriculture | Manufacture | Energy | Waste | Construction | Transport |
| Variables | lngdpg | lngdpg | lngdpg | lngdpg | lngdpg | lngdpg |
| l.lngdpg (−1) | 0.960*** | 0.331*** | 0.031*** | 0.137*** | 0.022*** | 0.208*** |
| ict | 0.030*** | 0.263*** | 0.084*** | 0.031*** | 0.018*** | 0.095*** |
| lnghc | 0.011** | 0.183** | 0.158*** | 0.138*** | 0.031*** | 0.070*** |
| lngjobs | 0.039*** | 0.049*** | 0.021*** | 0.045*** | 0.036*** | 0.019 |
| lnfdi | 0.030** | 0.070*** | 0.055*** | 0.025** | 0.058*** | 0.046*** |
| lninvdom | 0.004** | 0.019* | 0.067*** | 0.005** | 0.079*** | 0.062*** |
| lnpatent | 0.013** | 0.073 | 0.059*** | 0.019*** | 0.064*** | 0.316 |
| Constant | 0.162*** | 6.883*** | 2.426*** | 2.227*** | 3.883*** | 1.924 |
| AR (1) | (0.049) | (0.045) | (0.000) | (0.000) | (0.001) | (0.033) |
| AR (2) | (0.397) | (0.299) | (0.323) | (0.864) | (0.140) | (0.530) |
| Hansen | (0.428) | (0.564) | (0.056) | (0.073) | (0.135) | (0.193) |
| Time effect | Yes | Yes | Yes | Yes | Yes | Yes |
| Fixed effect | Yes | Yes | Yes | Yes | Yes | Yes |
| Obs | 399 | 402 | 402 | 398 | 402 | 408 |
| Instruments | 23 | 21 | 22 | 24 | 19 | 16 |
| Ids | 34 | 34 | 34 | 34 | 34 | 34 |

Robust standard errors in parentheses
*** $p < 0.01$, ** $p < 0.05$, * $p < 0.1$

green human capital can play a crucial role in accelerating the transition to more sustainable practices.

## 4.3 *Agriculture Sector*

The Indonesian agricultural sector can lead to green growth by embracing sustainable approaches that combine economic productivity with environmental conservation. While the previous estimation reveals that green human capital exhibits the lowest coefficient within this sector, vocational schooling remains a key factor within this transition since it endows farmers with green skills to apply approaches such as organic farming and agroforestry, efficient water usage and irrigation, and the adoption of ICT in agriculture (UNESCO-UNEVOC, 2018). Green skills also contribute to the greening agenda in the food sector, as green human capital provides employees with the knowledge of sustainable waste treatment, advanced packaging, and improved sensors and process control to increase productivity. Those green skills lead to improvements in water and soil health, as well as a decrease in reliance on chemical inputs that are destructive to ecosystems.

Although many farmers are aware of the benefits of sustainable agriculture, a significant number still do not adopt it and continue to use pesticides. In 2022, FAO (2022) noted that Indonesia became the third-largest country using pesticides. This harmful habit persists because approximately 75% of farmers in Indonesia only hold an elementary school education and are not aware of the harm caused by chemical pesticides (Dhiaswari et al., 2019). The situation worsens due to inadequate large-scale training programs, particularly among smallholder farmers. The situation has led to the persistence of conventional, resource-using farming practices with limited productivity and environmental sustainability.

Investment also plays an equally essential role in this sector. Nevertheless, Indonesia struggles to attract foreign direct investment (FDI) in its agricultural sector due to several challenges and the condition of the agricultural sector, which has a low level of productivity (Ryandiansyah & Azis, 2018). The realization of domestic investment in this sector is still directed towards palm oil downstream, which tends to be less environmentally friendly and has reached IDR 130 trillion in the last 5 years. (BKPM, 2024). ICT integration, such as IoT-based water management systems, can help modernize farming operations, optimize resource use, and reduce waste, yet its use is still minimal in Indonesia.

## 4.4 Manufacturing Sector

The manufacturing industry in Indonesia holds the greatest potential to benefit from the production of GHC due to its key function in economic activity and its high environmental influence. GHC equips employees with knowledge of energy-efficient technology, sustainable material and production system, and waste reduction practices as a basis for sustainable industry operations (UNESCO-UNEVOC, 2018). For example, vocational schools can educate employees to apply sustainable materials to production and recycling systems that convert scrap metals and plastic materials to usable inputs. These approaches decrease reliance on limited resources and accelerate innovation and competitiveness within the industry. Albeit with this high potential, we are yet to witness an integrated and related curriculum for meeting the needs of the green job (manufacturing industry) as an inhibiting factor (Ministry of Manpower, 2024).

One of the greatest opportunities among manufacturers is found within the food and beverages sector, which is the biggest beneficiary of domestic investment as well as the third-biggest beneficiary of FDI in Indonesia (BKPM, 2024). This situation matches the estimation findings above, with the manufacturing industry experiencing the highest FDI coefficient. The finding shows high international interest in sectoral potential. Using sustainable approaches like responsible sourcing of ingredients, water usage optimization, and substituting conventional packaging with biodegradable packaging materials, the sector can provide a green manufacturing benchmark. IoT-based technology usage, for instance, real-time tracking of energy and resource consumption, is essential towards increased efficiency as well as waste reduction and is especially effective within this industry. Through channeling domestic as well as foreign investment into green technology as well as human capital training specific to the food as well as beverages industry, Indonesia's manufacturing industry can become a green industry leader with green growth as well as lowered environmental footprint.

## 4.5 Construction Sector

Construction forms a pillar of Indonesia's green growth, with skilled green human capital (GHC) playing a crucial role in driving environmentally friendly and resilient infrastructure development. This condition has become even more important because of the construction sector, which also includes the energy used to build, heat, cool, and illuminate homes and businesses, as well as the equipment and equipment installed in them. Moreover, the construction sector accounts for about one-third or 32% of global energy demand and 34% of $CO_2$ emissions, with operational emissions reaching a record 9.8 Gt CO2, while the carbon contained is around 2.9 Gt CO2 (UNEP, 2025).

Green-skilled workers play a crucial role in constructing infrastructure with comprehensive green building knowledge that utilizes sustainable materials, incorporates sustainable building practices, ensures water and sanitation, promotes energy efficiency, and adopts renewable energy sources, as well as manages solid waste effectively (UNESCO-UNEVOC, 2018). Those skills are required to optimize national construction projects such as green buildings, flood-resistant infrastructure, and city developments with renewable energy integration. Efficient urban planning is also crucial to developing livable and sustainable cities that align with Indonesia's broader environmental objectives. Green building reduces carbon footprints and maximizes the long-term economic and social value of infrastructure.

## 4.6 Transportation Sector

Transportation is among Indonesia's key contributors to green growth and serves a two-fold function as an enabler of economic activity as well as a catalyst for sustainable environmental functioning. ICCT (2023) report describes the current target of net-zero greenhouse gas (GHG) emissions by 2060 in transportation sector will depend in part on the decarbonization of the transportation sector, which today is responsible for about 15% of the country's GHG emissions. Green transition is necessary to create an eco-friendly transportation ecosystem through the adoption of electric vehicles (EVs) and sustainable finance. In 2024, transportation sector experienced its highest investment from foreign direct investment (FDI) as well as domestic investment, with a strong emphasis on EVs and their downstream sectors, with investment reaching an amount of IDR 19.14 trillion during the past half-decade (BKPM, 2024). The situation presents the central role of the transportation sector in encouraging greener solutions to mobility (IESR, 2024). Nevertheless, challenges persist with a focus on those of a workforce role that has not yet been optimized to enable green growth.

On the other hand, ICT proved to be a transformative force within the transport sector and exerted a bigger influence relative to other sectors. Internet-based platforms connecting riders with drivers increase efficiency on the operations level and open avenues for integrating more environmentally friendly options, including ride-hailing services via electric vehicles (EVs) (McKinsey & Company, 2024). The transformation requires growing support, especially the improvement of workforce capabilities. Although, TVET is vital to enhance employees' capacity on proper digital skills and competencies required for assembling and maintaining EVs.

## 4.7 *Energy Sector*

The energy sector makes a significant contribution to the green transition agenda, with green human capital (GHC) also making a substantial contribution in this transition. Green-skilled workers are particularly needed to assess the technical knowledge required for the application of RE and EE (UNESCO-UNEVOC, 2018). The economic opportunities of RE are enormous, from decreasing fossil fuel reliance to generating sustainable employment and energy self-sufficiency. Nevertheless, filling these labor market needs requires substantial investment in training human resources with advanced technology implementation capabilities. The LinkedIn Economic Graph (2024) reveals a distinct trend: shrinking labor demand within the fossil fuel sector is being offset by growing opportunities within the renewable energy industry, which underscores the need to scale up GHC building projects.

ICT integration further amplifies the efficiency and scalability of renewable energy systems, with technologies such as smart grids and predictive analytics optimizing energy generation, distribution, and consumption. To make the energy sector more efficient, however, it requires a skilled workforce capable of leveraging digital tools to maximize sector performance. To sustain and accelerate growth in the energy sector, both FDI and domestic investments must be targeted at green skills development and infrastructure enhancement. The development of RE in Indonesia is estimated to require funds of up to USD 163.5 billion by 2030 (OJK, 2024). In fact, the potential of RE in Indonesia also includes Indonesian waters with investment needs of up to 101.8 billion USD by 2060 to build solar panels along Indonesia's coastline and ocean current energy (Damanik et al., 2023). Those investments may improve economic returns and align with Indonesia's long-term sustainability goals, making them a critical driver of the country's green economy.

## 4.8 Waste Management Sector

The waste management industry in Indonesia plays a crucial role in driving green growth, minimizing pollution, and creating economic value from waste. This condition is expected to occur because, by 2024, food waste in Indonesia will account for 41.60% of total waste, and plastic waste will account for 18.71% (MoEF, 2024). In addition, households contribute to the accumulation of waste by 44.37% of total waste (MoEF, 2024). This situation is exacerbated by the observation that more than 40% of Indonesia's waste remains unmanaged in landfills. In fact, as many as 3.2 million metric tons of plastic waste are dumped in the sea with terrible consequences for marine ecosystems (MoEF, 2024).

Vocational training is essential for developing workforces that can apply high-end recycling, upcycling, and waste-to-energy technologies for reducing existing waste. For instance, organic waste can be converted into biogas or compost. Innovative methods, such as Black Soldier Fly (BSF) farming and maggot farming, can convert organic waste into high-value animal protein feed. The 3R values (Reduce, Reuse, Recycle) add to the industry's applicability to circular economy objectives by converting waste into usable resources. Investment in waste management, particularly foreign direct investment (FDI), is low due to limited awareness among citizens regarding waste management among members of society (MoEF, 2024). Widespread improper waste sorting among households restricts the development of waste banks and the effectiveness of domestic investment. ICT-based technology solutions, such as IoT-based waste tracking systems and automatic separation technology, can substantially elevate efficiency and recover resources. However, its adoption in Indonesia and especially in waste banks remains limited.

## 4.9 Green Human Capital and Green Jobs

Green human capital and green jobs are closely related, as Granata & Posadas (2024) suggest that green jobs can be measured through the green skills and green tasks approach, which serves as a proxy for green human capital. This approach refers to the International Standard Classification of Occupations 2008 (ISCO-08), which has been adjusted to the 2020 Indonesian Standard Classification of Occupations (KBJI), by defining every task in the job related to green tasks or green potential tasks. In the case of Indonesia, as many as 329 skills are classified as green human capital, with 84 skills as green skills and 246 as green potential skills. There are five main classifications of green skills mastered by Indonesian workers, such as machinery maintenance and repair, natural resource management, data management and environmental analysis, as well as technical consulting for environmental impact reduction.

The trend of green skill development globally is quite diverse. The figures below illustrate the rapid growth of green skills in the United States and the European

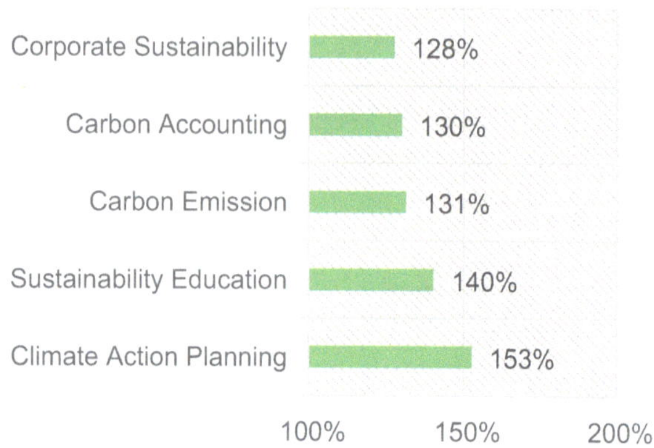


**Fig. 14.2** Fastest growing green skills in the European Union Source: LinkedIn Economic Graph (2024)

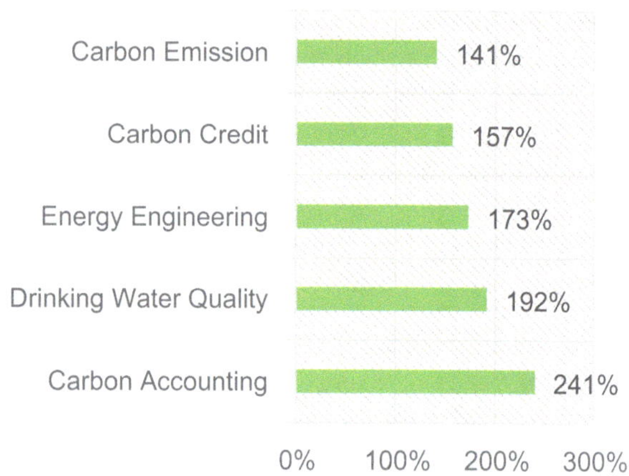


**Fig. 14.3** Fastest growing green skills in the United States. Source: LinkedIn Economic Graph (2024)

Union, driven by the increasing need for businesses to employ individuals with sustainability expertise. The EU focuses on learning about sustainability and planning for climate action to stay true to its firm policy commitments to environmental goals. The US is putting more emphasis on carbon accounting, water quality management, and energy engineering to demonstrate its commitment to clean energy infrastructure and improved environmental protection. The emphasis on carbon-based abilities in both places indicates an international need to achieve carbon neutrality by a specific date. These trends make it clear that vocational training and workforce upskilling must be in line with industry demand to make sure that professionals have the skills they need to help the industry make the switch to green (Figs. 14.2 and 14.3).

The increase in green human capital in various countries is also a driver of increasing green jobs. The LinkedIn Economic Graph (2024) notes a growth in green jobs, reaching around 20% from 2016 to 2021, with green jobs hiring rates reaching around 55% in 2024. However, green jobs have also shown much faster growth than jobs in the emitting sector in many countries. Developed countries such as the United States, the United Kingdom, and Sweden have experienced significant

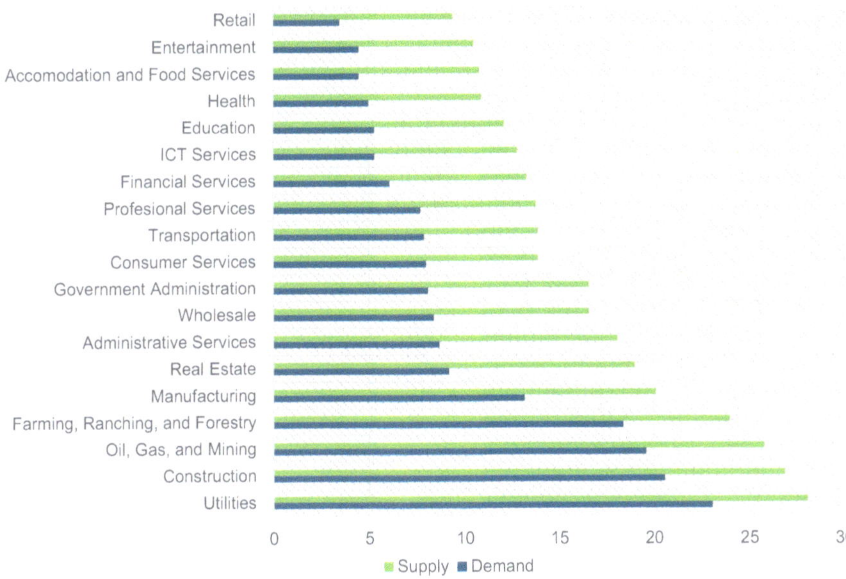


**Fig. 14.4** Share of 2024 job postings requiring green skills in 2024. Source: LinkedIn Economic Graph (2024)

growth in green jobs. In developed countries, the renewable energy sector has been growing rapidly, supported by strong investments and policies supporting the transition to a green economy. This condition is also supported by the increasing public awareness of environmental issues, as well as the commitment of the local government to reduce carbon emissions and dependence on fossil energy. Environmentally friendly technological innovations and fiscal incentives are also accelerating the development of the sector, making green jobs an important part of sustainable economic transformation (da Costa et al., 2025; Stanef-Puică et al., 2022; van der Ree, 2019).

Meanwhile, developing countries, such as Indonesia, India, and Brazil, tend to still rely on fossil energy and show slower growth in green jobs than developed countries. In Indonesia, despite initiatives to switch to renewable energy, the fossil energy sector, such as coal and oil, still plays a vital role in the economy. Nevertheless, Indonesia has begun to show a declining trend in the fossil energy sector with the fastest rate of decline compared to other countries (Lieuw-Kie-Song & Lal, 2010; Mathieu, 2024). However, it is still very important to improve TVET because the number of green jobs in Indonesia is growing to 2.5% of the overall workforce (Bappenas, 2025). Indonesia can align with the global trend toward sustainability by making it easier for people to access green skills training. This condition will prepare the workforce for changes in the job market and make the country more competitive in the global green economy (Fig. 14.4).

On the other hand, globally, there is an imbalance in the supply of workers with green skills in various green economy sectors (Apostel & Barslund, 2024;

Stanef-Puică et al., 2022). Although the LinkedIn Economic Graph (2024) shows that many workers already have the skills needed for sustainable sectors, the jobs that lead to green jobs are still limited. Sectors such as renewable energy, sustainable agriculture, and green technology have grown. However, the number of jobs created in these sectors has not been commensurate with the number of skilled workers available. Alternatively, new jobs that appear are not decent work because wages are not appropriate, or other workers' rights, such as social protection and insurance, are not available. This situation indicates that even though the supply of labor is available, green jobs need to grow more rapidly to absorb the workforce with green skills that already exist.

## 5 Conclusion

This chapter analyzes how enhancing green human capital through vocational education and training substantially influences green economic growth in both national and sectoral, particularly with the highest impact on manufacturing and waste sectors. These results indicate that green skills obtained through vocational education can expedite the shift towards more sustainable practices, including the integration of green technologies and the establishment of a circular economy.

This chapter collaborates with the existing evidence that vocational education increases environmental awareness, boosts production, and lowers carbon emissions. This chapter also highlights the important role of investment in the development of green human capital to facilitate vocational education oriented towards sustainability, ensuring a proficient workforce capable of advancing the green transition. Sectoral hiring trends show that there is a growing need for green skills, especially in consumer goods, manufacturing, and finance. This condition highlights the need for the government and private sector to collaborate in enhancing green curricula and infrastructure, thereby keeping pace with the evolving job market.

Based on our findings, this chapter advises the government to enhance investment in Green-Based TVET by financing programs to meet the increasing need for green skills, especially in the manufacturing and waste (including circular economy) sectors. Investments should prioritize curriculum enhancements, infrastructure upgrades, and increased access to training, particularly in areas with few vocational education options.

To increase Public-Private Partnerships (PPP) in Green Skills Development, improvement in collaboration between government, industry, and educational institutions is needed to align workforce skills with market needs. Incentives toward the green transition should encourage all stakeholders in the ecosystem, mainly businesses, to participate in green training programs, corporate sustainability education, and sector-specific apprenticeships in areas such as finance, manufacturing, and waste management. The partnership also develops sector-specific GHC Programs that align with industry suggestions to ensure educational institutions teach students with the right green skills, enabling workers to promote low-carbon technologies and sustainable practices.

## References


Acemoglu, D., Aghion, P., Bursztyn, L., & Hemous, D. (2012). *The environment and directed technical change.* American Economic Review, 102(1), 131–166. https://doi.org/10.1257/aer.102.1.131

Affandi, Y., Anugrah, D. F., Harun, C. A., Naufal, M. M., Tasijawa, J., & Kuntoadji, P. (2024). *Optimizing Human Capital Capacity To Drive Growth Above 5%* (No. WP/04/2024).

Ahakwa, I., Xu, Y., Tackie, E. A., Tackie, F. K., Mangudhla, T., & Sarpong, F. A. (2023). How different levels of education affect individuals' attitudes and actions toward carbon neutrality? A novel quantile-on-quantile regression approach. *Energy & Environment*, 0958305X231217648.

Ahmed, Z., Asghar, M. M., Malik, M. N., & Nawaz, K. (2020). Moving towards a sustainable environment: the dynamic linkage between natural resources, human capital, urbanization, economic growth, and ecological footprint in China. *Resources Policy*, *67*, 101677.

Apostel, A., & Barslund, M. (2024). Measuring and characterising green jobs: A literature review. *Energy Research & Social Science*, *111*, 103477. https://doi.org/10.1016/j.erss.2024.103477

Bano, S., Zhao, Y., Ahmad, A., Wang, S., & Liu, Y. (2018). Identifying the impacts of human capital on carbon emissions in Pakistan. *Journal of Cleaner Production*, *183*, 1082-1092.

Bappenas. (2021). *Kebijakan Pembangunan Berketahanan Iklim.* Bappenas. Jakarta

Bappenas. (2025). *Peta Jalan Pengembangan Tenaga Kerja Hijau Indonesia.* Bappenas. Jakarta

BKPM. (2024). *Capaian Kinerja Investasi 2024.* Retrieved from https://www.bkpm.go.id/id/info/realisasi-investasi/2024

BNPB. (2025). *Data Bencana Indonesia 2024.* Retrieved from https://bnpb.go.id/storage/app/media/Buletin%20Info%20Bencana/Buku%20Data%20Bencana%202024/20250613_Buku%20Data%202024.pdf

BPS. (2024). *Angka Partisipasi Kasar (APK) Menurut Provinsi dan Jenjang Pendidikan.* Retrieved from https://www.bps.go.id/id/statistics-table/2/MzAzIzI=/angka-partisipasi-kasar%2D%2Dapk%2D%2Dmenurut-provinsi-dan-jenjang-pendidikan.html

CEIC. (2023). *Indonesia Economic Indicators.* CEIC Data. Retrieved from https://www.ceicdata.com

Crifo, P. (2024). Green human capital, Innovation and Growth. *Environmental Modeling & Assessment*, *29*(1), 1-18.

da Costa, T., Aranda Lopez, L. I., Perussello, C., Quinn, F., Crowley, Q. G., McMahon, H., & Holden, N. M. (2025). Addressing the Demand for Green Skills: Bridging the Gap Between University Outcomes and Industry Requirements. *Sustainability*, *17*(6), Article 6. https://doi.org/10.3390/su17062732

Damanik, R., Noor, R., Muliawan, I., Arman, M. S., & Nasir, M. (2023). Proyek Strategis Ekonomi Biru Menuju Negara Maju 2045. *Jakarta: Laboratorium Indonesia, 2045.*

Dhiaswari, D. R., Santoso, A. B., & Banowati, E. (2019). Pengaruh perilaku petani bawang merah dan penggunaan pestisida terhadap dampak bagi lingkungan hidup di desa klampok kecamatan wanasari kabupaten brebes. *Edu Geography*, *7*(3), 204-211.

Ellen MacArthur Foundation. (2020). *Completing the Picture: How the Circular Economy Tackles Climate Change.* Retrieved from https://ellenmacarthurfoundation.org/

FAO. (2022). *Pesticides use and trade.* Retrieved from https://www.fao.org/statistics/highlights-archive/highlights-detail/pesticides-use-and-trade-1990-2022/en

FAO. (2023). *The state of food and agriculture 2023: Leveraging green growth for food security.* Food and Agriculture Organization. https://www.fao.org/

Global Footprint Network. (2023). *National Footprint and Biocapacity Accounts 2023.* Retrieved from https://data.footprintnetwork.org/
Granata, J., & Posadas, J. (2024). Why look at tasks when designing skills policy for the green transition. *World Bank Policy Research Working Paper*, 10753.
Hall, B. H., J. Mairesse, & Mohnen, P. (2010). Measuring the returns to R&D. *The Economics of Innovation*.1033–1082. Burlington: Academic Press.
Hickel, J. (2020). The sustainable development index: Measuring the ecological efficiency of human development in the anthropocene. *Ecological economics*, *167*, 106331.
ICCT. (2023). *Annual Report 2023.* Retrieved from https://theicct.org/wp-content/uploads/2024/12/ICCT-Annual-Report-2023-v5-1.pdf
IEA. (2021). *Net Zero by 2050: A roadmap for the global energy sector.* International Energy Agency. https://www.iea.org/reports/net-zero-by-2050
IESR. (2024). *Indonesia Energy Transition Outlook (IETO) 2024.* Jakarta
ILO. (2018). *The Employment Impact of Climate Change Adaption.* Retrieved from https://www.ilo.org/sites/default/files/wcmsp5/groups/public/@ed_emp/documents/publication/wcms_645572.pdf
ILO. (2019). *Skills for a greener future: A global view.* International Labor Organization. Retrieved from https://www.ilo.org/global/publications/books/WCMS_732214/lang%2D%2Den/index.htm
Inekwe, J. N. (2015). The contribution of R&D expenditure to economic growth in developing economies. *Social indicators research*, *124*(3), 727-745.
Lieuw-Kie-Song, M., & Lal, R. (2010). Green Jobs for the Poor. *International Policy Centre for Inclusive Growth, One Pager.*
Lin, X. (2024). The impact of innovative human capital on green growth convergence in China's regions from the perspective of space. *Heliyon, 10*(15).
LinkedIn Economic Graph. (2024). *Global Green Skills Report 2024.* Retrieved from https://economicgraph.linkedin.com/research/global-green-skills-report
Liu, D., Wang, G., Sun, C., Majeed, M. T., & Andlib, Z. (2023). An analysis of the effects of human capital on green growth: effects and transmission channels. *Environmental Science and Pollution Research*, *30*(4), 10149-10156.
Lu, W., Peng, L., & Fang, N. (2024). The Impact of Human Capital Misallocation on Green Economy Efficiency: Empirical Analysis of Chinese Urban Agglomerations. *Heliyon.*
Mankiw, N. G., Romer, D., & Weil, D. N. (1992). A contribution to the empirics of economic growth. *The Quarterly Journal of Economics*, 107(2): 407-437. https://doi.org/10.2307/2118477
Mathieu, A. (2024). Foundations and conditions of green jobs in developing economies: Systematic literature review and bibliometric analysis. *Development and Sustainability in Economics and Finance*, *2–4*, 100016. https://doi.org/10.1016/j.dsef.2024.100016
McKinsey & Company. (2024). *Spotlight on mobility trends.* Retrieved from https://www.mckinsey.com/industries/automotive-and-assembly/our-insights/spotlight-on-mobility-trends
Ministry of Education and Culture. (2024). *Pendanaan dan Peningkatan Kualitas Pendidikan*
Ministry of Manpower. (2024). *Analisis Pasar Kerja dan Kebutuhan Pelatihan Kerja Dalam Negeri.* Kementerian Ketenagakerjaan. Jakarta
MoEF. (2024). *Laporan Inventarisasi Gas Rumah Kaca Indonesia 2023.* Kementerian Lingkungan Hidup dan Kehutanan Indonesia.
OECD. (2017). *Green Growth Indicators 2017.* OECD Green Growth Studies, OECD Publishing, Paris, https://doi.org/10.1787/9789264268586-en.
OJK. (2024). *Outlook Investasi Energi Terbarukan di Indonesia 2023.* Retrieved from https://keuanganberkelanjutan.ojk.go.id/keuanganberkelanjutan/id/NewsMedia/detailnews/3655
PDDIKTI. (2023). *Statistik Perguruan Tinggi Di Indonesia.* Retrieved from https://pddikti.kemdiktisaintek.go.id/statistik
Rohman, I. K., Naufal, M. M., & Naufal, I. (2025). Indonesian Service Sector Review: Telecommunications. *ERIA Discussion Paper Series*, (552).

Ryandiansyah, N. R. & Aziz, I.J. (2018). Structural change, productivity, and the shift to services: the case of Indonesia. *Economics and Finance in Indonesia, 64*(2), 1.

Shamzzuzoha, A., Chavira, P. C., Kekäle, T., Kuusniemi, H., & Jovanovski, B. (2022). Identified necessary skills to establish a center of excellence in vocational education for green innovation. *Cleaner Environmental Systems, 7*, 100100.

Stanef-Puică, M.-R., Badea, L., Şerban-Oprescu, G.-L., Şerban-Oprescu, A.-T., Frâncu, L.-G., & Creţu, A. (2022). Green Jobs—A Literature Review. *International Journal of Environmental Research and Public Health, 19*(13), Article 13. https://doi.org/10.3390/ijerph19137998

UNEP. (2020). *Waste Management Outlook for Asia.* United Nations Environment Programme. Retrieved from https://www.unep.org/resources/report/waste-management-outlook-asia

UNEP. (2025). *Global Status Report for Buildings and Construction 2024/2025*. Retrieved from https://www.unep.org/resources/report/global-status-report-buildings-and-construction-20242025

UNESCO-UNEVOC. (2015*). Case study submitted by the Department of Polytechnic Malaysia, Ministry of Higher Education for the UNEVOC Green Skills research project.* Bonn, Germany, UNESCO-UNEVOC.

UNESCO-UNEVOC. (2018). *Greening technical and vocational education and training: A practical guide for institutions.* Bonn, Germany, UNESCO-UNEVOC.

van der Ree, K. (2019). Promoting Green Jobs: Decent Work in the Transition to Low-Carbon, Green Economies. *International Development Policy | Revue Internationale de Politique de Développement, 11*, Article 11. https://doi.org/10.4000/poldev.3107

Vu, T. B., Hammes, D. L., & Im, E. I. (2012). Vocational or university education? A new look at their effects on economic growth. *Economics Letters, 117*(2), 426-428.

World Bank. (2025). *Climate Mean Projections (CMIP6).* Retrieved from https://climateknowledgeportal.worldbank.org/country/indonesia/climate-data-projections

World Economic Forum. (2025). *The Future of Jobs Report 2024*

World Green Building Council. (2021). *Bringing embodied carbon upfront: Coordinated action for the building and construction sector.* Retrieved from https://www.worldgbc.org/

# Part IV
# Policy Strategy

# Chapter 15
# Indonesia's Green Economy

**Vivi Yulaswati**

**Abstract** Indonesia has positioned the green economy as a central pillar of its long-term development strategy, aligned with "Golden Indonesia 2045" vision and commitments to the Sustainable Development Goals and Net Zero Emissions by 2060 or sooner. This chapter outlines Indonesia's green economy framework, encompassing low-carbon and climate-resilient development, supported by energy transition, circular economy, green industry, and low-carbon initiatives. An integrated policy simulations highlights that ambitious green economy policies can simultaneously boost economic growth, reduce emissions, create green jobs, and enhance productivity. The chapter also discusses the Green Economy Index as a tool to monitor progress and critically examines key challenges.

**Keywords** Green economy · Low carbon development · SDGs · Net zero emission

## 1 Introduction

Indonesia has committed to global agenda of the Sustainable Development Goals (SDGs) and ratified the Paris Agreement through Law No. 6/2016. The Government has pledged to achieve Net Zero Emissions by 2060 or sooner during the COP 26 in 2021. However, Indonesia's dependency on fossil fuel-based resources still remains and has led to adverse effects of development. It has resulted to substantial fiscal burden through energy subsidies as well as increased greenhouse gas (GHG) emissions. Based on Our World Data, Indonesia's emission in has reached 733.2 million tones CO2e in 2023 (Fig. 15.1).

The impact of climate change has posed a threat to the environment, economy, and well-being of societies. The Intergovernmental Panel on Climate Change (IPCC) reported that the current global temperatures are approximately 1.47 °C to

V. Yulaswati (✉)
The Ministry of National Development Planning (BAPPENAS), Jakarta, Indonesia
e-mail: viviyulaswati@bappenas.go.id



S. M. Juhro et al. (eds.), *Sustainable Economy: The Indonesian Pathways*,
https://doi.org/10.1007/978-981-92-1215-6_15

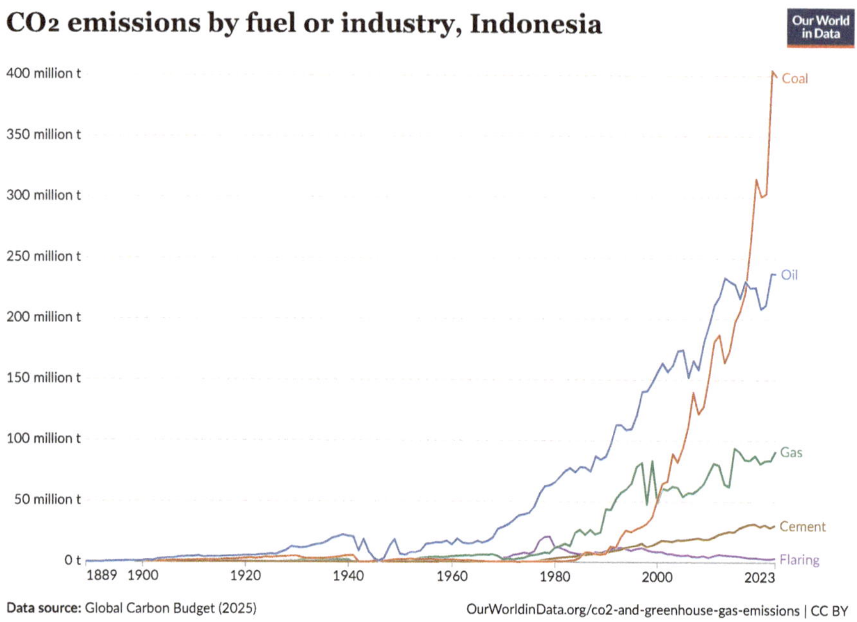


**Fig. 15.1** Indonesia's CO2 emissions by fuel. Source: Global Carbon Budget (2024) in ourworldindata.org

1.5 °C above the pre-industrial average. The increased temperature has impacted to the increased ocean's temperatures causing higher sea levels as well as the intensity of rainfall and storms. The rise of sea level has been 3 times compare to 1901–1971. The increased intensity of the hydrometeorological disasters brought to economic losses, which was estimated to reach an average of IDR 22.8 trillion per year (Ministry of Finance, 2022). The climate change that causes more intense and extreme disaster events have serious consequences for economy and threatening our ability to meet the SDGs. The climate change demands our immediate attention and action. Obama said (2015), *"We are the first generation to feel the impact of climate change, and the last generation that can do something about it."*

Considering the unsustainable of current development, Indonesia has paved a tangible target that cannot rely on *business as usual*. The Long-term Development Plan (RPJPN)2025-2045, along with a vision of "Golden Indonesia 2045," and the Mid-term Development Plan (RPJMN)2025-2029 have stated consciously that sustained GNI per capita on par with developed nations is not possible to be achieved if the environment quality continues to degrade and the detrimental impact of climate change harms our lives. Subsequently, development targets have been set to fulfill global commitments, synergize the economic growth that balance with the environment protection and tackle the climate change issues, and achieve the green economy.

# 2 Understanding the Green Economy for Indonesian Context

The term Green Economy was first introduced in the Blueprint for a Green Economy of the United Kingdom in 1989. Furthermore in 2012, following series of earlier studies, UNEP launched a document "Towards a Green Economy: Pathways to Sustainable Development and Poverty Eradication" at the UN Conference on Sustainable Development in Rio de Janeiro. In this document, Green Economy was defined as "activities that results in improved human wellbeing and social equity, while significantly reducing environmental risks and ecological sacrifices." As an alternative to the neo-classical growth models, the green economy proposed mix policy actions that would stimulate economic growth and at the same time improve the sustainability of the earth.

The evolution of technology, climate, politics and economics open the possibility of interconnected understanding and practices that bring balance between the good of nature, citizens, and businesses. The green economy is not just about the ability to produce clean energy, but also technologies that allow cleaner production processes, the growing market for products which consume less energy, from fluorescent light bulbs to organic and locally produced food, use recycled packaging, as well as change to electric vehicles and **electrifying cooking.** The **importance of green economy** is it encourages economies to become more low-carbon, ensures that nature continue to provide the resources and environmental services for our resilience and continued **wellbeing**. The green economy for sure requires transformation from brown-based to green based economic investment, activities, and infrastructure.

Considering Indonesia is the maritime country, it is necessary to understand that the green economy cover activities both at the terrestrial and marine. The later often refer as the blue economy, which emphasize the sustainable use of ocean resources for economic growth, while also maintaining the health of marine ecosystems and improving people's livelihoods. It includes, among others, sustainable fisheries, costal tourism, renewable ocean energy, and marine biotechnology. The blue economy for Indonesia is considered as a new source of growth as it has huge potential of emerging sectors including for super food, bio pharmaceuticals, and biofuel. The goal of both green and blue economy is to create a new engine of high and green growth, foster social cohesion, and improve the carrying capacity of the environment or economic development that ensures the long-term well-being of both the ocean and the communities. Figure 15.2 describes the transition from the brown toward green economy.

## *2.1 Indonesia's Green Economy Policy*

Indonesia has been as a middle-income country for more than 30 years. To avoid from a middle-income trap—condition that make a country could not become an advance country thus stay forever as a middle-income country—the Government of Indonesia has set a Golden Vision of 2045, in which Indonesia will become an advance country by its centennial independence year. This Golden Vision has been

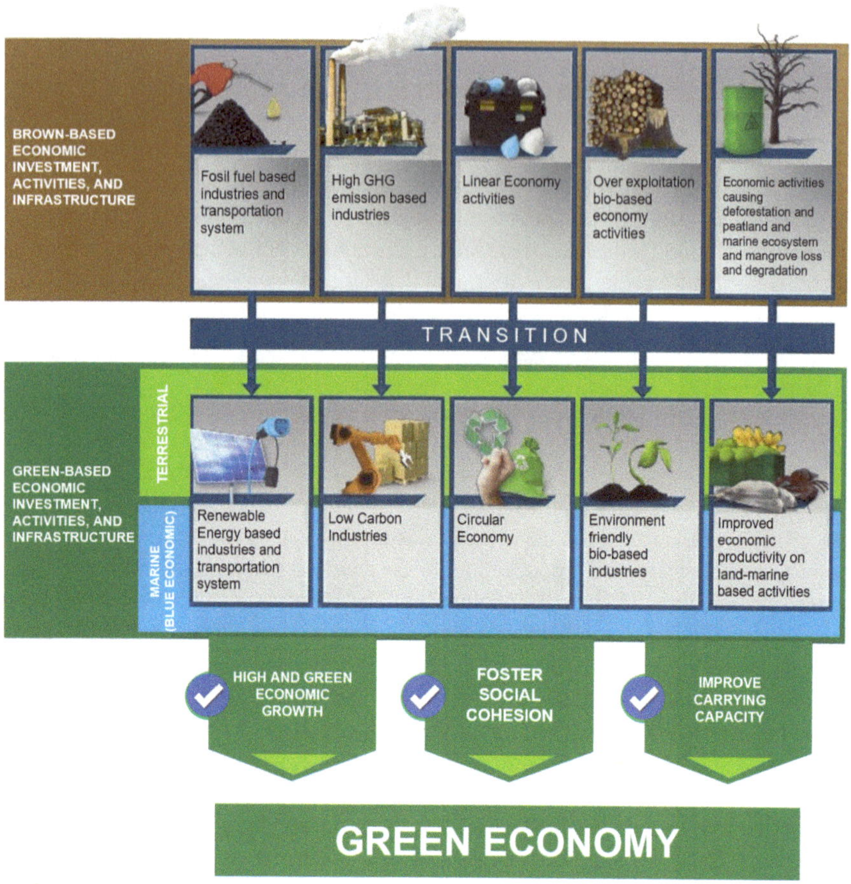


**Fig. 15.2** Green Economy Transformation. Source: Indonesia's Ministry of National Development Planning (Bappenas)

elaborated into transformation strategies within the RPJPN 2025–2045, which was enacted by the Law No. 59/2024.

As part of the economy transformation, green economy has been one of the game changers to pursue the golden vision. Using integrated analysis under the Low Carbon Development Initiative model (LCDI, 2021), Bappenas carried out policy scenario exercises signaled that Green Economy policies with ambitious low-carbon and climate-resilient development policy can support Indonesia to achieve the golden vision by 2045 as well as the commitment for the Net Zero Emissions in 2060 or sooner. The intervention of the green economy policies will benefit the economy, boosting the average GDP growth at least by 6.1–6.5% between 2025–2045 (Fig. 15.3).

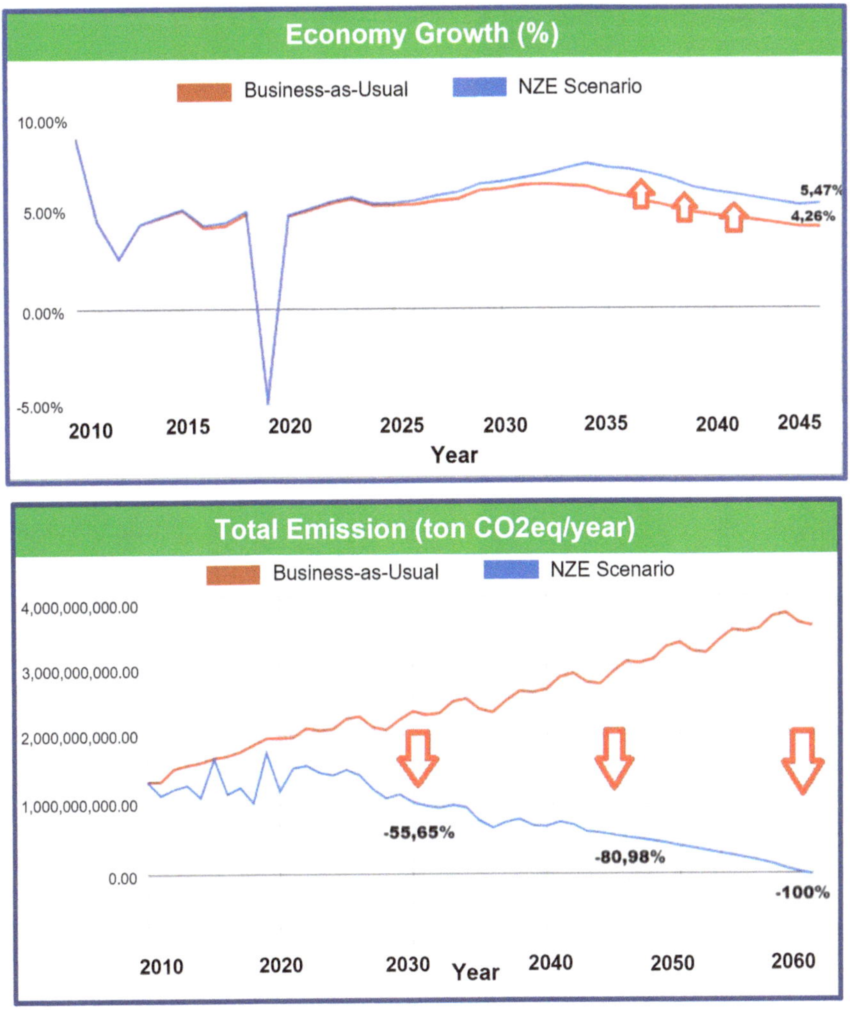


**Fig. 15.3** The Trajectory of Growth and Net Zero Emission. Source: Indonesia's Ministry of National Development Planning (Bappenas)

The NDC targets of Indonesia have recently been made more ambitious by the Enhanced Nationally Determined Contribution (E-NDC) in 2025. The E-NDC 2025 is the Second Nationally Determined Contribution (SNDC) that consist of ambitious climate commitment with the target of absolute emission peak in 2030 by 1.34–1.49 GtCO2e. The This target has been along the line with the National Mid-term Development Plan (RPJMN) 2025–2029 as well as with the long strategy to achieve the Net Zero Emission (NZE) by 2060 or sooner. The current RPJMN is accordance with the President Prabowo vision of Asta Cita. To achieve the above targets, there are 5 major strategies that have to be pursued:

### Increase Renewable Energy Mix Off and on Grid in the Power Sector

Based on the Government Regulation No. 79/2014, the new and renewable energy was set at least 23% in 2025 and 31% in 2050. However, its realization was only half of the target. The new electricity master plan reveals the intention to increase coal capacity by 26.8 GW in seven years, showing that the captive coal is the main driver of the expansion. Renewables, however, could play a bigger role in meeting captive demand, as increasing coal generation beyond 2030 is incompatible with the Net Zero Emission target. Hence, Indonesia's energy transition pathway must decarbonize the power sector through retirement or phase-out of coal-fired power plants, acceleration of the development of dispatchable and variable renewables, and expansion and enhancement of the transmission grid. Furthermore, Indonesia has actually significant geothermal potential to develop clean electricity. Despite having an enormous amount of untapped energy reserves from the "Ring of Fire," the utilization rate remains low. Indonesia holds about 40% of the world's geothermal potential, with total reserves estimated between 23.7 and 29.5 GW. The government has implemented regulations and targets to promote geothermal development, aiming for over 5% of the national energy mix and a significant increase in installed capacity by 2025.

### Peatland Restoration and Degraded Land Rehabilitation

Indonesia is the world's largest tropical peatland, which has over 15 million hectares of peatlands, accounting more than 12% of the country's forest land. Peatlands store carbon for thousands of years because crop production and peatlands accumulation outpace the rate of organic matter decomposition. Apart from carbon storage, natural peatlands provide various ecosystem and regulate water flow beyond the peatlands. Over time, the peatland ecosystem has undergone significant changes to accommodate other land uses and become the root of forest fires and frequent haze disasters in Indonesia. Therefore, peatland restoration is among of the priority strategy to achieve the SNDC target in 2030. It is targeted the peatland for about 2 million hectares and degraded land rehabilitation for about 12 million hectares.

### Green Industries

As Indonesia continues its industrialization initiatives across multiple sectors, emission is expected to grow in line with the increased energy use if pursuing the conventional growth path. Hence, Indonesia needs to be coupled with the decarbonization of end-use industries through energy efficiency, electrification, and demand response as well as development of green industries. As many industries still relies on fossil fuels as their energy resource, Indonesia has to be aware and monitor the global competitiveness. Indonesia's exported goods could decrease the value and competitiveness of Indonesia's goods, should it lag in decarbonization efforts compared to other countries exporting the same goods. An example of a policy emerging is the Carbon Border Adjustment Mechanism (CBAM), which will be effectively implemented in the European Union by 2026. This policy encourages other countries exporting to the European Union to report their emissions and take mitigation actions to avoid heavy penalties. This policy encourages export-focus Indonesian corporations to take mitigation action and report on the carbon content of their products. It also provides additional impetus to carbon pricing as an instrument to promote decarbonization in Indonesia, as carbon prices paid domestically can be deducted from the CBAM obligation. Currently, Indonesia's industrial sectors that are most impacted due to the European Union's EU's) CBAM is iron and steel. Prices of iron and steel could increase by 16.8% after adjustment, according to the Ministry of Trade Indonesia. It is important for Indonesia to prepare its industries to compete in a decarbonization pathway, also in view of similar mechanisms being introduced, or additional sectors included.

Indonesia has also introduced the green industry certification and eco-industrial park. The green industry certification requires assessment of the energy efficiency and emission reduction aspect. On the other hand, eco industrial park regulates environmental management, including the aspects of energy efficiency and renewable energy. The industry that can produce and supply sustainable products will surely have additional competitive advantage in the market. Moreover, with the implementation of carbon tax and carbon border adjustment mechanism, decarbonization of industry has become crucial to meet the international requirement to reduce CO2 emission in the industrial processes. The focus needs more on the utilization of fossil fuel in the heating process, not only on the electricity.

## Low Carbon Development Initiative Policies

The green economy development is also implemented through a set of integrated policies known as low carbon development initiatives, both at the national as well as at the local levels. Through this initiatives, BAPPENAS and development partners conducted a systematic and comprehensive analyses and modelling in the business solutions in selected sectors (forestry, agriculture, peatland, energy, transport, fisheries, and water). Engagement and constituency building at the local level involve at least 10 provinces that have joined as pilot to formulate their Regional Low Carbon Development Plan as a reference for regional low carbon development initiatives.

One of fundamental policies of the LCDI is the implementation of a circular economy that currently not only in the matters of waste reduction, but also resource efficiency. Implementing a circular economy in the industry sector will generate more economic benefit by maintaining the value of products, materials, and resources in the economy as long as possible and by offering restorative, regenerative, as well as high quality product designs. In 2024, Bappenas has launched the National Roadmap and Action Plan on Circular Economy, which outlines strategies across five priority sectors: food & beverage, textile, construction, retail (focus on plastic packaging), and Electronics. The focus within these sectors is on improving resource use intensity, product usage rates, and recycling rates. These aspects are defined as indicators that will support the achievement of Indonesia's Net-Zero Emissions target by 2060 or sooner.

The other important policy under LCDI is about food loss and waste (FLW). Globally, one-third of the food produced for consumption is lost or wasted in between the harvesting and consumption process. Each year, FLW contributes to approximately 4.4 gigatons of greenhouse gas emissions. According to Bappenas study on FLW (2021), it is estimated that Indonesia's FLW in 2045 will reach to 49 million ton/year or 166 kg/capita/year. The assumptions of strategy scenario consist of: (1) % food loss production decreases from 4.37% in 2022 to 3% in 2045; (2) food spoilage time in storage increases from 8 months in 2022 to 10 months in 2045; (3) shipping to processing delays decreased from 5 days in 2022 to 4 days in 2045; (4) % food loss in processing and packaging decreased from 1.2% in 202 to 08% in 2045; (5) food spoilage time in distribution increases from 18 months in 2022 to 24 months in 2045; (6) food supply chain delays decrease from 7 days in 2022 to 4 days in 2045; and (7) food waste consumption is decreased as 355 from 2022 to 2030. Understand the FLW issues and its targets will bring the program like school meal of the President Prabowo more efficient and effective (Fig. 15.4).

## Green Financing

At the 2019 UN General Assembly Indonesia committed to operationalize an Integrated National Financing Framework (INFF). Globally, there are around 86 countries who are establishing their INFF. The INFF was first coined at the Addis Ababa Action Agenda 2015, which recognized that public and private finance had important and differentiated roles to play in advancing sustainable development. Sustainable Development Strategy together with financing strategy will close the gap in SDGs financing gap by optimizing different sources of finance and other means of implementation. Indonesia continues to be one of the world's leading innovators in the SDG financing domain, which leaves it well placed to overcome

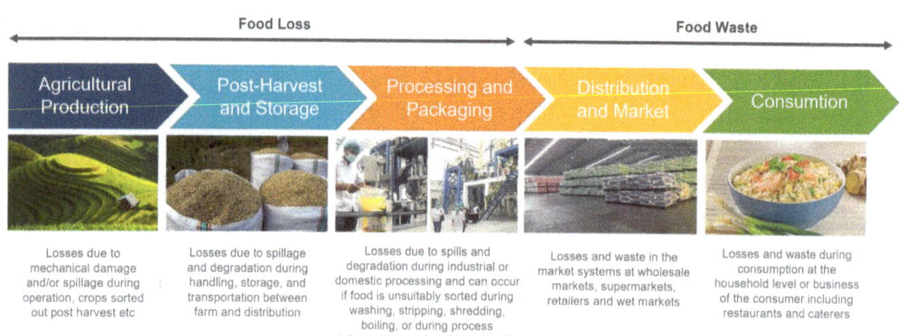


**Fig. 15.4** Food Loss and Waste Scope on Food Supply Chain. Source: Indonesia's Ministry of National Development Planning (Bappenas)

the annual gap in SDG financing, projected to increase from US$10 billion–$21 billion in 2020 to US$175 billion–US$355 billion by 2030. As part of the INFF roadmap, Indonesia focuses on the consolidation of gains made, expansion of innovative SDG financing instruments and the adoption of new approaches. The financing strategy also articulates how government will use the policies and instruments at its disposal to mobilize, invest in, and influence public and private financing from both domestic and international sources, by focusing on three areas of integration: (1) planning and financing policies, public and private financing policies, and collaboration across government and partners.

Sustaining private sector activity, and increasing economic efficiency and productivity are critical to sustaining growth. Blended financing tends to be narrowly defined as PPPs, but with the new current significant trend provides considerably broader potential for engaging the domestic private sector. Like many advanced economies, there is need for considerable investment in digitalization, Industry 4.0, towards developing the digital economy as a tool to transform labor and financial markets, while also reducing credit market asymmetries. Moreover, given the considerable potential for innovative and sustainable financing solutions including the from the ESG revolution. One initiative that are prepared by Ministry of Industry, working together with Bappenas and the World Bank is developing the Green Industry Service Company (GISCO), that will facilitate industry players to transition toward green industries.

## Carbon Market as Indonesia Development Strategy

Carbon markets constitute an increasingly important instrument within Indonesia's development strategy by aligning climate mitigation objectives with economic efficiency and fiscal sustainability. As a market-based mechanism, carbon pricing—through emissions trading systems and carbon taxes—internalizes the negative externalities of greenhouse gas emissions while allowing firms flexibility in meeting abatement targets at least cost (Stiglitz & Stern, 2017). For Indonesia, carbon markets complement existing development planning frameworks by supporting the transition toward a low-carbon growth model without undermining macroeconomic stability. When designed credibly and implemented gradually, carbon markets can stimulate investment in clean technologies, enhance resource allocation efficiency, and generate fiscal revenues that may be recycled toward priority development goals, including green infrastructure, human capital development, and social protection. In this sense, carbon markets function not merely as environmental instruments but as macroeconomic tools that reinforce productivity growth and long-term competitiveness.

From a structural perspective, carbon markets also support Indonesia's broader industrial transformation and integration into global value chains. As international trade increasingly incorporates carbon-related standards—such as carbon border adjustment mechanisms—domestic carbon pricing can help Indonesian firms reduce exposure to external trade risks and maintain export competitiveness (OECD, 2023). Moreover, carbon market revenues can be strategically used to finance just transition measures, mitigating distributional impacts on vulnerable households, regions, and workers in carbon-intensive sectors. By encouraging gradual sectoral rebalancing and fostering innovation, carbon markets can strengthen financial system resilience and reduce the risk of stranded assets. Overall, embedding carbon markets within Indonesia's development strategy enhances policy coherence between climate commitments and the long-term vision of inclusive and sustainable growth, consistent with the objectives of "Golden Indonesia 2045."

## 2.2 *How to Measure the Green Economy?*

In the long run, green economy will encourage a capital generation that ensures inclusiveness, containing low carbon natural capital, resource efficient physical capital, and human capital with green skills (PAGE, 2017). Therefore, the Green Economy Index (GEI) was launched during Indonesia's G20 Presidency in 2022. Indonesia's GEI has a set of multidimensional indicators covering the interlinkages between environment, society, and economy as three main pillars of sustainability. The index has been including in the development plans as a measuring tool for green economy progress (Fig. 15.5).

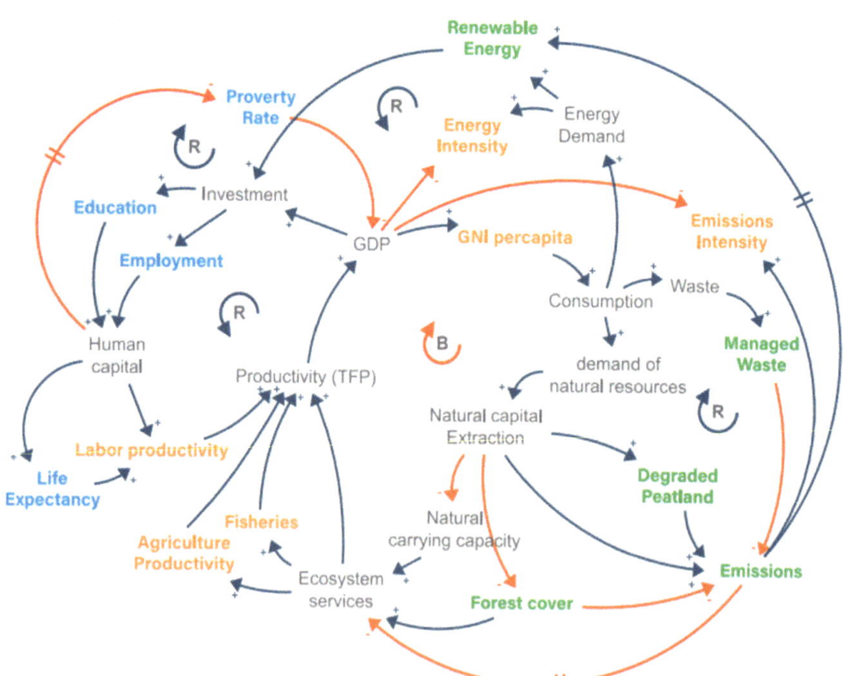


**Fig. 15.5** Interlinkages between Selected Environment (*green*), Economy (*orange*), and Social (*blue*) Indicators. Source: Indonesia's Ministry of National Development Planning (Bappenas)

The above Causal Loop Diagram illustrates the correlation and feedback loop between three sustainable pillars of the SDGs and 15 selected indicators. For instance, growth in GDP that is aligned with GNI per capita growth will cause higher consumption and encourage more energy needed to provide the demand. This surging energy demand gives opportunity to deploy more renewables, increase share of renewable energy and promote larger green investment. Following that, rise in investment will foster more employment in green jobs, which also reduce unemployment rate. Improvement on employment as well as education combined will increase labour productivity and quality of life. Series of these increment will add Total Factor Productivity (TFP) and loop back to and increase the GDP over time. On the other side, consumption will generate demand of natural resources that will create pressure to the natural carrying capacity as well as degradation of environment quality. Negative externalities are created from these feedback loop, including increase of GHG emissions and waste. In the last decade, Indonesia's GEI shows the right track of the green economic growth, with the composite score increasing from 47.20 (2011) to 59.17 (2020). With this trend, along with the alarming climate change, it is our responsibility to ensure that all green economy strategies are implemented well.

## 3 Discussion

### *3.1 Decoupling Growth from Environmental Pressure*

A central premise of Indonesia's green economy strategy is the feasibility of sustaining high economic growth while reducing environmental degradation and greenhouse gas (GHG) emissions. The simulation results presented in the RPJPN 2025–2045 suggest that ambitious green economy policies can raise average GDP growth to above 6% while substantially lowering emissions intensity. From an analytical perspective, this implies a transition from relative to partial absolute decoupling, whereby emissions growth slows and potentially declines even as economic output expands.

However, international experience indicates that achieving durable absolute decoupling remains challenging for emerging economies with growing consumption and industrial bases (OECD, 2019; UNEP, 2023). In Indonesia, structural pressures persist in energy-intensive sectors such as transport, manufacturing, and buildings, which together account for more than half of national $CO_2$ emissions. Rising incomes and urbanization may further induce rebound effects, whereby efficiency gains are offset by increased demand for energy and materials (Sorrell et al., 2020). This suggests that technological improvements alone will be insufficient without complementary demand-side measures, including urban planning, behavioral change, and pricing instruments that internalize environmental externalities.

Indonesia's approach—combining energy transition, circular economy, and land-based mitigation—reflects an integrated strategy consistent with the "green growth" paradigm. Yet, the credibility of decoupling will ultimately depend on the speed of coal phase-out, electrification of transport and industry, and the extent to which renewable energy displaces fossil fuels rather than merely supplements them. Continuous monitoring of emissions in absolute terms, rather than intensity metrics alone, is therefore critical to validate the long-term decoupling trajectory.

### *3.2 Political Economy and Implementation Capacity*

While Indonesia's green economy framework is robust at the strategic and planning level, its implementation is shaped by political economy constraints and institutional capacity. The transition away from fossil fuels, particularly coal, poses significant distributional and political challenges. Coal-producing regions, state-owned enterprises, and workers embedded in the fossil fuel value chain have vested interests that may resist rapid transition, potentially slowing policy execution (Averchenkova, 2019).

Moreover, Indonesia's decentralized governance structure adds complexity to implementation. Provincial and local governments vary widely in fiscal capacity, technical expertise, and political commitment to green development. Although low-carbon development initiatives have been piloted in selected provinces, scaling these efforts nationwide requires stronger vertical coordination, clearer fiscal incentives, and capacity-building at the subnational level. Without these, there is a risk that national green economy targets remain aspirational while local development priorities continue to favor conventional growth models.

Policy coherence also remains a critical issue. Aligning industrial policy, energy policy, labor policy, and land-use regulation is essential to avoid conflicting signals. For instance, incentives for downstream mineral processing and industrial expansion must be carefully synchronized with decarbonization pathways to prevent carbon-intensive lock-in. This underscores the importance of adaptive governance, where policies are periodically reviewed and adjusted based on implementation feedback and evolving economic conditions.

### *3.3 Green Jobs and Just Transition Challenges*

The promise of green job creation is a key political and economic justification for Indonesia's green economy strategy. Projections of 1.8 million additional green jobs by 2030 highlight the potential of renewable energy, waste management, electric vehicles, and land restoration to absorb labor and enhance productivity. Nevertheless, the transition raises critical questions about job quality, skills alignment, and regional equity.

Green jobs are not automatically inclusive. Many require technical skills that are currently scarce in the domestic labor market, while workers displaced from fossil fuel–based sectors may lack the qualifications needed to transition smoothly. This creates a risk of labor market segmentation, where high-quality green jobs coexist with informal or declining employment in carbon-intensive sectors (ILO, 2018). Without proactive reskilling and social protection measures, the transition could exacerbate inequality rather than reduce it.

A just transition framework is therefore essential. This includes targeted training programs, regional transition strategies for coal-dependent areas, and mechanisms to protect vulnerable workers and communities. Integrating green job planning into education, vocational training, and industrial policy would enhance labor mobility and ensure that the benefits of green growth are broadly shared. In this sense, human capital development is as critical as physical investment in determining the success of Indonesia's green economy transformation.

### 3.4 Circular Economy and Competitiveness

Indonesia's circular economy agenda represents a strategic shift from linear, resource-intensive growth toward a model that emphasizes efficiency, value retention, and waste reduction. Beyond its environmental benefits, the circular economy has significant implications for industrial competitiveness. By improving resource productivity and reducing dependence on imported raw materials, circular practices can strengthen domestic value chains and enhance resilience to global supply shocks.

The focus on five priority sectors—food and beverage, textiles, construction, retail (plastic packaging), and electronics—reflects a pragmatic approach, targeting sectors with high material intensity and economic relevance. International evidence suggests that firms adopting circular business models can gain competitive advantages, particularly as global markets increasingly impose environmental standards through mechanisms such as carbon border adjustment measures (OECD, 2020).

However, the transition entails short-term adjustment costs, including higher upfront investment and the need for new technologies and business models. Small and medium-sized enterprises (SMEs), which dominate Indonesia's industrial landscape, may face disproportionate barriers to adoption. Policy support, including access to finance, technical assistance, and regulatory clarity, is therefore essential to prevent uneven implementation that could undermine competitiveness gains.

### 3.5 Measuring Green Economy Progress

The introduction of the Green Economy Index (GEI) marks an important innovation in Indonesia's development planning, providing a multidimensional framework to track the interlinkages between economic, social, and environmental outcomes. By embedding the GEI within national planning documents, Indonesia signals a shift away from GDP-centric evaluation toward a more holistic assessment of progress.

Nevertheless, composite indices face inherent limitations. Data availability and quality remain uneven across regions and sectors, and causal attribution between policies and outcomes is often difficult. Moreover, indices may mask trade-offs between dimensions, such as short-term economic gains versus long-term environmental costs. To address these challenges, the GEI should be complemented by sector-specific indicators, emissions accounting, and distributional metrics that capture equity and regional disparities.

Continuous refinement and transparency in methodology will be crucial to maintain the credibility and policy relevance of the GEI. When used as part of a broader monitoring and evaluation framework, the index can support evidence-based policymaking and facilitate learning across regions and sectors.

## *3.6 The Challenges*

The transition toward green economy, however, has several challenges. They include, among others:

**Technology and Knowledge Gap**

Technological innovation is vital to reversing climate impacts. Globally, there is a growing trend in innovation and technology to create environmentally friendly products and services as well as its production process and supply chain. Some key features include utilizing solar, hydro, and wind power for renewable energy; reducing pollution and waste through circular economy; smart agricultural practices; and promoting green data center to support AI application. As the technology and innovation progress so fast, Indonesia needs to embrace international collaboration to catch up the wide gap with local technology and skills. Bringing foreign green in investment, research, and other collaborations is not always easy. It usually requires such enable environment as clear land and regulation, fair business climate, skilled labor, and fiscal incentives.

**High Investment**

The investment needs for the green economy are often identified as very high. Economic modeling of the Low Carbon Development Initiative (LCDI) by Bappenas (2022), an annual capital investment of USD 145 million is needed to support green transition in sectors such as renewable energy, transportation, agriculture, land-use, and waste management sectors. The industry's decarbonization, for example, will require huge investment from changing machinery, source of energy, adapt business model, as well as preparing its green job transition. Meanwhile, finance in public and private sectors currently are still dominated by high-carbon investments. Apparently, the green investment needs cannot be covered solely by the government nor the businesses. Exploring an alternative or innovative financial resources as well as green fund mobilization mechanisms have been the main issues in many meetings and seminars within the last 5 years.

#### Green Jobs Transition

Shifting human resources toward green jobs need a comprehensive preparation. Following the RPJPN 2025–2045, Bappenas together with ILO launched the Road Map of Green Job, which has identified the occupation map of green job, best practices of some countries, the need for regulations and institutional frameworks, and estimated the number of green job and priority sectors such as environment protection, circular economy, renewable energy, as well as decarbonization in transport and industries. Other study by Global Green Growth Institute (2020) estimated that large hydropower generates 3.8 times more job-years per electricity output than coal, followed by small hydro at 3.2 times more than coal, and geothermal and solar both at 2.8 and 2.5 times more jobs per GWh respectively compared to coal. However, there are a lot of homework to be done, including revise education and training curriculum to fill in the huge gap for medium-high skill in green jobs; insufficient funding and investment for green technologies; weak institutional support and policy frameworks particularly at local level; limited market demand, enable regulations; and the difficulty of ensuring the quality and decent working conditions of green jobs.

#### Major Policy Reforms Required

The transition process to a green economy will require policy alignment in the area of macroeconomy, employment, environment, natural resources, industry and many other sectors. This includes policies to manage the risk of stranded assets (early retirement of coal-fired power plants must be carefully managed and regulated), workforce migration to green jobs, the willingness of industries to decarbonize, and other transitional consequences. The coherence includes alignment of existing related policies. Therefore, policies and regulation must be prepared inclusively among related stakeholders and expertise.

## 3.7 *Comparative Insights and Global Relevance*

In comparative perspective, Indonesia's green economy strategy exhibits several distinctive features. As a large archipelagic, resource-rich middle-income country, Indonesia integrates terrestrial and marine (blue economy) dimensions more explicitly than many peers. Its strong linkage between long-term development planning and climate objectives also differentiates it from countries where climate policy is treated as a separate domain.

Compared to China's state-led green industrial policy or the European Union's regulation-driven transition, Indonesia's approach emphasizes planning coherence and gradual transformation, reflecting its institutional context and development stage. These features offer valuable lessons for other emerging economies seeking to balance growth, equity, and sustainability under fiscal and institutional constraints.

At the same time, Indonesia's experience underscores the universal challenges of green transformation: managing political resistance, mobilizing investment, ensuring social inclusion, and maintaining policy credibility over long time horizons. As such, Indonesia's green economy strategy contributes to the global discourse on sustainable development by illustrating both the opportunities and constraints faced by middle-income countries in the climate transition.

## 4 Conclusion

Indonesia's green economy strategy represents a comprehensive attempt to reconcile economic growth with environmental sustainability and social inclusion. The analysis suggests that while the potential for decoupling growth from environmental pressure exists, its realization depends on effective implementation, political economy management, and sustained investment in human and institutional capacity. Addressing green jobs and just transition challenges, leveraging the circular economy for competitiveness, and strengthening measurement frameworks are all critical to ensuring that the transition is both credible and inclusive. In a global context, Indonesia's experience offers important insights for other developing and emerging economies navigating similar structural transformations, reinforcing the notion that green growth is not merely an environmental agenda but a central development strategy for the twenty-first century.

Success transition toward Green Economy requires collaboration of all development stakeholders. The challenges we face transcend all boundaries—sectors, regional, and nationalities. It is imperative for all of us to put efforts for regional cooperation and even more the global communities to work together, share knowledge, and build partnerships to unlock the full potential of the Green Economy.

Green economy business opportunities emphasize creating a healthy environment and promoting the well-being of all by promoting the use of low-carbon technologies and practices and using technologies that rely on clean and renewable energy. To attract more industries to achieve the NZE, an incentive schemes for industries adopting the green economy approach is necessary. While achieving a green economy through such efforts as decarbonization is time consuming and requires capital spending, it is increasingly being seen by businesses themselves as creating **green economy business opportunities.**

Innovation and technology is the main source of all economic growth and the green economy is no different. McKinsey estimates that green economy business opportunities could generate between $9 trillion and$12 trillion in new revenue by 2030 in sectors including transport, power, and hydrogen. According to the OECD, some sectors will grow more than others, but within each sector, companies using resources more efficiently will have a competitive advantage.

Lastly, Green Economy is not only about environmental stewardship but also a strategic imperative for creating the overall supply chain of decarbonization, business sustainability and a moral responsibility. Let's commit to this cause, and work together to create a sustainable, resilient, and prosperous future for Indonesia and the world.

## References


Averchenkova, A. (2019). Legislating for a Low Carbon and Climate Resilient Transition: Learning from International Experiences. *Elcano Policy Paper*, Real Instituto Elcano, Madrid

Global Carbon Budget (2024). Indonesia's CO2 emissions by fuel. https://ourworldindata.org/profile/co2/indonesia.

Government Indonesia's Long-term National Development Plan (RPJPN) 2025-2045 (Law No. 59/2024)

Indonesia's Mid-term National Development Plan (RPJMN) 2025-2029 (Presidential Decree No. 12/2025).

Indonesia's Ministry of National Development Planning (Bappenas), *Green Economy Index to Measure the Progress of Low Carbon & Green Economy In Indonesia,* 2022.

International Labour Office (ILO). (2018). World employment and social outlook 2018: Greening with jobs. *International Labour Organization*. https://researchrepository.ilo.org/esploro/outputs/report/World-employment-social-outlook-2018-Greening/995218839002676

Low Carbon Development Initiative (LCDI). (2021). The economic, social, and environmental benefits of a circular economy in Indonesia. *Ministry of National Development Planning/Bappenas*. https://lcdi-indonesia.id/wp-content/uploads/2026/07/ESR-003.pdf

Organisation for Economic Co-operation and Development (OECD). (2023). *Climate change mitigation, trade, and global value chains*. OECD Publishing.

Organisation for Economic Co-operation and Development (OECD). (2019). Innovation, Productivity and Sustainability in Food and Agriculture: Main Findings from Country Reviews and Policy Lessons, *OECD Food and Agricultural Reviews*, OECD Publishing, Paris. https://doi.org/10.1787/c9c4ec1d-en

Organisation for Economic Co-operation and Development (OECD). (2020). *Climate policy leadership in an interconnected world: What role for border carbon adjustments?* OECD Publishing. https://doi.org/10.1787/8008e7f4-en

Partnership for Action on Green Economy (PAGE). (2017). *PAGE annual report 2017*. https://archive.un-page.org/files/public/20170618_page_ar2017_online.pdf

Stiglitz, J. E., & Stern, N. (2017). *Report of the High-Level Commission on Carbon Prices*. World Bank.

Sorrell, S., Gatersleben, B., & Druckman, A. (2020). The limits of energy sufficiency: A review of the evidence for rebound effects and negative spillovers from behavioural change. *Energy Research & Social Science, 64*, 101439.

United Nations Environment Programme (UNEP). (2023). Emissions gap report 2023. *United Nations Environment Programme*. https://www.unep.org/resources/emissions-gap-report-2023

# Chapter 16
# Fiscal Policy for Green Growth in Indonesia

**Gerry Pramudya Sulaiman and Prama Wiratama**

**Abstract** This chapter examines the role of fiscal policy as a catalytic instrument for green growth. It documents Indonesia's comprehensive fiscal toolkit, including targeted tax incentives, climate budget tagging, public–private partnership schemes, innovative thematic bonds, special mission vehicles, and the gradual implementation of carbon pricing. While public finance covers only a limited share of Indonesia's climate investment needs, fiscal policy has been effective in crowding in private and international capital and de-risking green investments. Coherent alignment between fiscal, financial, and regulatory policies is essential to support the country's net-zero ambition.

**Keywords** Sustainable economy · Sustainable finance · Fiscal policy for green economy

## 1 Introduction

Indonesia is entering a decisive phase in its development journey, marked by a strong commitment to align sustained economic growth with environmental stewardship. As one of the world's largest emerging economies, Indonesia recognizes that long-term prosperity depends on safeguarding natural capital, enhancing resilience to climate risks, and modernizing its growth model. The government's green economy blueprint reflects this strategic vision, positioning sustainability not as a constraint but as an enabler of higher-quality growth, improved welfare, and greater economic resilience.

This transition is integral to Indonesia's ambition to achieve "Golden Indonesia 2045" and to move decisively beyond the middle-income threshold. Forward-looking projections indicate that green economy policies can serve as a powerful engine of growth, supporting robust GDP expansion, generating millions of new

G. P. Sulaiman (✉) · P. Wiratama
Ministry of Finance (Kemenkeu), Jakarta, Indonesia
e-mail: gerry.sulaiman@kemenkeu.go.id; prama.wiratama@kemenkeu.go.id


S. M. Juhro et al. (eds.), *Sustainable Economy: The Indonesian Pathways*,
https://doi.org/10.1007/978-981-92-1215-6_16

jobs in future-oriented sectors, and significantly reducing greenhouse gas emissions. Improvements in national green growth indicators further suggest that Indonesia has made tangible progress in embedding sustainability into its development trajectory. While challenges remain, these trends point to a credible and increasingly coherent pathway toward green and inclusive growth.

Fiscal policy has emerged as a central pillar in operationalizing this transition. Indonesia has progressively transformed its fiscal framework to actively shape market behavior, redirect investment flows, and accelerate the adoption of clean technologies. Recognizing these constraints, the government has repositioned fiscal policy from a passive budgetary function to an active lever for behavioral change and investment reallocation. Through a combination of green tax incentives, targeted public expenditures, carbon pricing instruments, and innovative financing mechanisms, fiscal policy is increasingly used to internalize environmental externalities, lower investment risks, and catalyze private capital toward sustainable activities.

Crucially, Indonesia's green fiscal strategy is embedded within a broader and increasingly integrated policy ecosystem. Public finance is used strategically to catalyze, rather than substitute for, private investment, supported by financial sector reforms, institutional coordination, and long-term planning frameworks. This chapter examines how Indonesia's green fiscal policies contribute to high and sustainable growth, highlighting their role in strengthening economic competitiveness, promoting social inclusion, and enhancing resilience to climate risks. In doing so, the analysis offers constructive insights into how emerging economies can harness fiscal policy as a powerful instrument for sustainable development while preserving macroeconomic stability and policy credibility.

## 2 The Imperative for Sustainable Development in Indonesia

Indonesia's green economic blueprint is strategically designed to reconcile robust economic expansion with stringent environmental stewardship, confronting pressing challenges including climate change and the considerable fiscal encumbrance of fossil fuel subsidies. The pivot towards a green economy is of paramount importance, as it concurrently augments societal well-being and mitigates ecological perils. Consequently, the nation is embarking on a strategic transition from a carbon-intensive, "brown" economic model to a resilient, low-carbon, and ecologically sustainable "green" paradigm.

This structural transformation is a critical linchpin for Indonesia to circumvent the middle-income trap and realize its "Golden Indonesia 2045" vision. Projections indicate that the green economy could serve as a primary growth engine, propelling average GDP growth to 6.22% between 2025 and 2045, while simultaneously generating an incremental 1.8 million green jobs by 2030 and achieving a substantial abatement in greenhouse gas emissions (Government of Indonesia, 2024). The trajectory of this transition is quantitatively assessed through the Green Economy

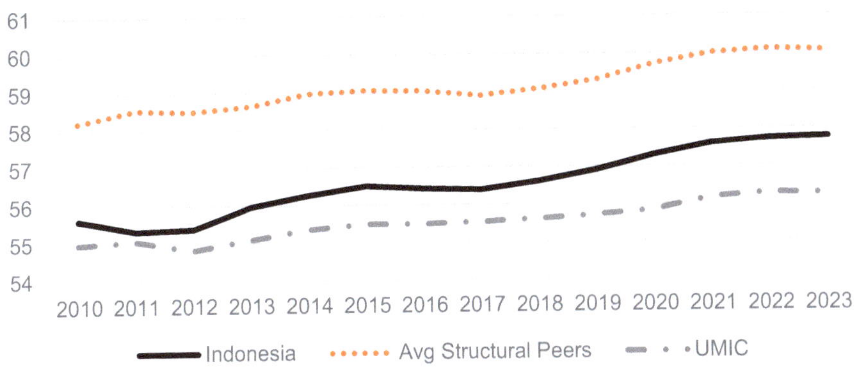


**Fig. 16.1** Green Growth Index (GGI)

Index (GEI), which has demonstrated a marked ascent from 47.20 in 2011 to 59.17 in 2020, signaling that the nation is on a promising course (Ministry of National Development Planning, 2022). From another vantage point, Indonesia's performance on the Green Growth Index (GGI) is comparatively strong among upper-middle-income countries. Nevertheless, the nation cannot afford complacency, as it continues to trail behind its structural peers in BRICS and ASEAN, despite a gradual trend that indicates it is slowly closing the gap (Fig. 16.1).[1]

To orchestrate this paradigm shift, the Indonesian government has promulgated a multifaceted policy framework. Cornerstone strategies involve accelerating the renewable energy mix, phasing out coal-fired power plants, championing energy efficiency, and pioneering nascent energy sources such as green hydrogen and nuclear power (Government of Indonesia, 2025). These measures are underpinned by robust regulatory instruments, notably Presidential Regulation No. 112/2022, which imposes a moratorium on new coal-fired power plants, and Government Regulation No. 23/2021, which governs forest utilization permits.

Furthermore, the policy arsenal includes the adoption of green industry certification and the development of eco-industrial parks, which prioritize energy conservation and emission mitigation. A fundamental tenet of this strategy is the institutionalization of a circular economy, aimed at optimizing resource productivity across five priority sectors: food and beverage, textiles, construction, retail, and electronics. Collectively, these integrated policies, complemented by carbon pricing mechanisms, arc instrumental in ensuring Indonesia can honor its international commitments, including its ambitious Net Zero Emissions target by 2060 or sooner.

[1] The Green Growth Index is publicly accessible via the Global Green Growth Institute's platform https://greengrowthindex.gggi.org/. The determination of structural peers is conducted through a comparative analysis of relevant economies within the ASEAN region and BRICS member states, based on analogous economic structures.

### 2.1 The Strategic Lever of Fiscal Policy: Catalyze Behavioral Shifts and Green Investment

In an era of escalating environmental imperatives and palpable climate risks, Indonesia confronts a pivotal juncture. The pursuit of robust, inclusive economic growth must be intrinsically aligned with an unwavering commitment to ecological preservation. The entrenched reliance on fossil fuel-based resources has engendered a significant fiscal drag through pervasive energy subsidies, simultaneously exacerbating greenhouse gas emissions that jeopardize both public well-being and long-term economic stability. Acknowledging this exigency, the Indonesian government is leveraging fiscal policy instruments, thereby transforming its role from a mere custodian of the public purse into a principal architect of the transition towards a sustainable, green economy.

Fiscal policy serves as a strategic lever to change behavior and direct investment flows. By deploying a suite of market-based incentives, it strategically steers private sector actors and the public away from ecologically detrimental practices and towards sustainable economic paradigms. From the institution of carbon pricing to internalize the cost of emissions, to the provision of targeted tax credits for green industries, each policy measure is deliberately calibrated to cultivate a fertile ecosystem for green growth. Consequently, fiscal policy lays the foundational groundwork for a future Indonesia that is not only economically prosperous but also environmentally resilient and sustainable.

## 3 State Revenue and Expenditure Policy for Climate Action

### 3.1 State Revenue Policy for Climate Action

The Indonesian government has strategically calibrated its state revenue policies to serve a triple objective: safeguarding the sustainability of natural resources and environmental management, incentivizing investment in renewable energy and clean technology, and ensuring a just and affordable transition.

A robust suite of tax expenditures has been deployed to catalyze private capital towards strategic green sectors. These fiscal instruments are designed to enhance the investment appeal of renewable energy, electric vehicles (EVs), and other clean technologies. Reduction of corporate income tax by 100% for up to 20 years for pioneer industries: the motor vehicles manufactures and their main components (including electric cars and motorcycles, electric motors for electric vehicles, and electric vehicle batteries) and upstream basic metal industries of iron and steel or non-iron and steel, with or without integrated downstream industries, including nickel smelters for battery production. Income Tax Borne by the Government for Geothermal Energy (Ministry of Finance of Indonesia, 2020a). Tax facilities for certain businesses in certain areas, including nickel mining, battery industry, and motorized vehicles (Government of Indonesia, 2019).

Tax facilities of up to 200% for industrial vocational activities, with competencies that encourage the electric vehicle ecosystem (Ministry of Finance of Indonesia, 2019). Tax facilities of up to 300% for R&D activities in Indonesia, including R&D on electric vehicles and their components (Ministry of Finance of Indonesia, 2020b). Exemption of import duty for investment and development of the power generation industry. Import duty of 0% for import of electric vehicles incompletely knocked down (IKD) and import duty of 0% for import of electric vehicles completely knocked down (CKD) through several FTA/CEPA cooperations, including Korea and China. Waived import duties on imports of goods for geothermal business activities and the prevention of environmental pollution activities (Ministry of Finance of Indonesia, 2022).

VAT is exempted for mining goods including nickel ore as a raw material for electric vehicle batteries, import and acquisition of factory machines and equipment (including the automotive industry). VAT is borne by the government for electric cars and buses, at 11%/10%/5% of the selling price according to the product's domestic content level (TKDN) value (Ministry of Finance of Indonesia, 2023). Luxury tax of 0% for electric vehicles that use battery electric vehicles or fuel cell electric vehicles technology. Reduction of land and building tax for mining/geothermal business activities at the exploration stage (Ministry of Finance of Indonesia, 2021). Regional tax incentives in the form of a reduction in the vehicle registration tax (BBN-KB) and motor vehicle tax of 0% (Ministry of Domestic Affairs, 2023).

From 2019 to 2024, tax expenditure on climate-related facilities reached 36.7 trillion rupiah (USD 2.43 billion). It is predicted to reach 48.4 trillion rupiah (USD 3.14 billion) by the end of 2025. Indonesia is also preparing to implement a carbon tax, which is believed to accelerate domestic emissions reductions (Ministry of Finance of Indonesia, 2024a). The legal foundation for implementing a carbon tax is firmly established under Law No. 7 of 2021 concerning the Harmonization of Tax Regulations. Nevertheless, its rollout is being pursued with deliberate caution and a phased approach. Presently, the Indonesian government is prioritizing the establishment of an Emission Trading Scheme (ETS) as the prevailing mandatory carbon pricing instrument.

### 3.2 *State Expenditure Policy for Climate Action*

Formally, Indonesia has institutionalized a climate budget tagging mechanism to systematically track and classify public expenditures that support climate change mitigation and adaptation actions. Currently, the mechanism's scope remains confined to the expenditures of line ministries, with ongoing efforts to expand its purview to subnational government spending and treasury fund allocations.

Within the governance framework, this mechanism operates on a voluntary basis, utilizing a self-assessment methodology conducted by line ministries. The Ministry of Finance provides comprehensive guidelines to enable line ministries to identify and designate budgetary allocations for climate change mitigation and adaptation actions, which are aligned with the overarching framework established by the Ministry of Environment. Throughout the planning and budgeting cycle, line ministries are systematically encouraged to perform this tagging exercise on an annual basis.

Since 2016, Indonesia has systematically tracked and classified climate-related expenditures within its national budget, encompassing both mitigation and adaptation initiatives. These allocations have demonstrated volatility over the 2016–2024 period, experiencing notable pressure during the 2019–2020 COVID-19 pandemic, which necessitated a strategic reallocation of central government funds towards emergency health and economic response.

On average, public climate expenditures accounted for 3% of the annual state budget (APBN) during this period, translating to an average of IDR 73.5 trillion (approximately USD 4.4 billion) per year. The sectoral distribution of this funding was heavily skewed, with the energy and transportation sector commanding a predominant 78% share. This was followed by agriculture (10%), waste management (7%), forestry (4%), and the IPPU sector constituting the remainder. In terms of expenditure type, capital expenditure formed the bulk of the outlay at 76%, with operational expenditure covering the balance. A disaggregation by action type revealed that mitigation actions accounted for 53.4% of the spending, adaptation for 43.1%, and cross-cutting co-benefit actions for the remaining 3.5%.

When contextualized against the projected funding requirements for climate change mitigation—estimated at IDR 4002 trillion (USD 281 billion) in Indonesia's Third Biennial Update Report (third BUR) (Government of Indonesia, 2021), the state budget can only cover 12.3% of the annual needs. Therefore, the gap must be filled by private sector and other external financing.

To catalyze private sector financing, Public-Private Partnership (PPP) schemes have been adopted as a strategic instrument. In a significant move, Indonesia established an ESG Manual for Public-Private Partnership in 2023 to ensure that all PPP projects are aligned with sustainable development objectives. The government has deployed de-risking mechanisms and financial viability support, particularly for drinking water provision projects, through instruments such as the Viability Gap Funding (VGF), Project Development Facility (PDF), and guarantees.

Substantial public capital has been committed to leverage private investment. Approximately IDR 1.2 trillion (equivalent to USD 75.5 million) in Viability Gap Funding has been allocated to three ESG-compliant drinking water projects. This injection of public funds directly supported the Umbulan Drinking Water Supply System with IDR 818 billion (USD 51.4 million), successfully leveraging IDR 2.4 trillion in total capital expenditure for a 2.9x leverage ratio. A further IDR 258.8 billion (USD 16.3 million) was allocated to the Bandar Lampung Drinking Water Supply System, which achieved an identical 2.9x leverage ratio against a IDR 750 billion project capex. Most notably, the Pekanbaru Drinking Water Supply System demonstrated the highest capital efficiency; with a VGF of IDR 118.07 billion (USD

7.4 million), it mobilized a project capex of IDR 499.5 billion, resulting in a superior leverage ratio of 4.2x.

Strategic project preparation is also being funded through the Project Development Facility (PDF), which is currently facilitating the development of three critical projects: the Kamijoro Water Supply System (IDR 347 billion), the Merangin Dam Project (IDR 4.8 trillion), and the Jatigede Regional Drinking Water Supply System (IDR 2.04 trillion). Concurrently, one project, the **West Semarang Drinking Water Supply System** with a total capex of approximately IDR 417.3 billion (USD 26.2 million), has utilized a guaranteed instrument to secure financing.

## 3.3 *Below the Line Budget Financing*

Recognizing the limitations of the traditional budget, Indonesia has proactively leveraged innovative financing instruments 'below-the-line'. Since 2018, the Indonesian government has strategically leveraged the global capital markets by issuing Sovereign Global Green Sukuk, establishing itself as a pioneering issuer in the sustainable finance landscape. To date, these instruments have successfully mobilized a cumulative USD 6.6 billion. Complementing this international effort, the domestic Retail Green Sukuk has garnered IDR 44.6 trillion from local investors, demonstrating robust domestic market appetite.

The allocation of these proceeds is strategically targeted, with the majority (74%) directed towards sustainable water and wastewater management. A significant portion (25%) is earmarked for climate change resilience, with the remainder financing a diversified portfolio including sustainable transportation, resource management, green buildings, renewable energy, and energy efficiency. Funded projects are tangible and wide-ranging, encompassing dam construction, lake revitalization, irrigation and railway systems, green buildings, and flood mitigation infrastructure (Ministry of Finance of Indonesia, 2024b).

Building upon the sukuk's success, Indonesia has diversified its thematic bond offerings. Indonesia introduced another innovative funding instrument in 2021 with a EUR 500 million Global SDGs Bond. This was followed by the issuance of Domestic SDGs Bonds in 2022 and 2023, which collectively raised IDR 10.5 trillion. The proceeds from these bonds are exclusively dedicated to public sector projects that directly advance the Sustainable Development Goals (SDGs), such as enhancing healthcare and educational facilities, improving sanitation, upgrading agricultural infrastructure, and providing vocational training (Ministry of Finance of Indonesia, 2024c).

In a further diversification of its sustainable finance toolkit, the government also issued Blue Bonds (denominated in JPY as Samurai Bonds) in 2023. As of the latest data, this issuance has raised JPY 49.4 billion, earmarked for development in the blue economy and coastal resilience. Projects include the construction of breakwaters, climate-adaptive coastal infrastructure, flood control systems, mangrove rehabilitation, biodiversity conservation, and waste management in coastal and insular regions (Ministry of Finance of Indonesia, 2024c).

Venturing beyond capital markets, Indonesia is also pioneering groundbreaking financial mechanisms such as debt-for-nature swaps. Initial precedents were set with the German government in 2002 and 2004, where EUR 12.5 million in debt service payments were redirected to fund environmental initiatives, including a project for environmental investments in micro-enterprises and the strengthening of national parks in fragile ecosystems. Most recently, a landmark 2024 agreement with the United States, valued at USD 106.2 million, will channel funds towards the Tropical Forest Conservation Act in Sumatra and Borneo, and the Tropical Forest and Coral-Reef Conservation Act in the Sunda-Banda Kecil and Kepala Burung regions.

Concurrently, access to multilateral climate finance is being aggressively optimized. Indonesia is actively optimizing access to multilateral climate funds, including the Green Climate Fund (GCF), the Global Environment Facility (GEF), and the Adaptation Fund. The Ministry of Finance, in its capacity as the National Designated Authority for the GCF, currently oversees a portfolio of 19 GCF-funded projects—four of which are Indonesia-specific and 15 are multi-country initiatives—with a total allocation of USD 578.2 million for Indonesia.

### *3.4 Special Mission Vehicle*

To orchestrate this complex financial ecosystem, the government has architected a suite of specialized financial institutions, or Special Mission Vehicles (SMVs). The Indonesia Climate Change Trust Fund (ICCTF) was established to act as a catalytic financial intermediary, strategically designed to attract, manage, and channel climate finance towards mitigation and adaptation programs.

Complementing this, the Indonesia Environment Fund (IEF), structured as a Public Service Agency, operates with a broader environmental mandate encompassing waste management, biodiversity, and disaster resilience. Its funding base is more diversified than that of a traditional trust fund; beyond grants and endowments, the IEF is empowered to manage state budget allocations and revenue streams from carbon pricing mechanisms, including carbon trading and levies.

The centerpiece of this architecture is PT Sarana Multi Infrastruktur (PT SMI). PT SMI operates as the government's pivotal infrastructure finance company, with a core mandate to bridge the financing gap for strategic projects often deemed non-bankable by commercial lenders. Its operational model is underpinned by three synergistic pillars. Firstly, in Financing and Investment, it functions as a complementary or "alternative financier," providing flexible debt and equity instruments for infrastructure projects across both public and private sectors. Secondly, through its Advisory Services, the entity delivers critical transaction advisory to enhance project bankability, ensuring robust financial structuring and preparation for a diverse clientele including investors, local governments, and developers. Lastly, in Project

Development, PT SMI actively engages in early-stage development to de-risk innovative ventures—particularly Public-Private Partnerships (PPPs)—thereby improving governance and catalyzing the mobilization of essential private capital.

Beyond its core functions, PT SMI also stewards two strategic country platforms: SDGs Indonesia One (SIO), which accelerates investment in projects aligned with the Sustainable Development Goals, and the Energy Transition Mechanism (ETM), a blended finance platform designed to catalyze the shift towards clean energy.

To address sector-specific barriers, the government established PT Geo Dipa Energi with a threefold mission: (1) to assume the high-risk, capital-intensive exploration phase of geothermal development; (2) to de-risk the sector and crowd-in investment from other public and private developers; and (3) to accelerate the deployment of geothermal capacity to meet national renewable energy targets.

Finally, to complete the risk mitigation ecosystem for PPPs, PT Penjaminan Infrastruktur Indonesia (PII) was formed. It provides credit enhancement and guarantees for risks that are deemed unmanageable by the private sector within PPP contracts, thereby unlocking otherwise stalled investments.

## 3.5 Carbon Pricing

Completing this multi-faceted strategy is the methodical establishment of a carbon pricing framework. Indonesia has methodically established a carbon pricing framework since 2021, instituting a dual-pronged approach comprising both market-based and non-market-based mechanisms. The former encompasses an Emissions Trading System (ETS) and a carbon offset mechanism, while the latter includes carbon taxation and results-based climate finance.

The nation has operationalized a cap-and-trade system, an ETS initially confined to the power generation subsector since 2023. This pilot phase is a strategic precursor to a significant scaling; by 2025, the scheme is projected to encompass 615 generation units with a collective capacity of 84.5 Gigawatts, representing 83.6% of Indonesia's total installed capacity. Concurrently, on the offset front, Indonesia launched the Indonesian Carbon Exchange (IDXCarbon) on September 26, 2023. Market activity has been demonstrable, with 336 transactions executed by December 1, 2025—facilitating the trade of approximately 1.6 million tons of CO2e at a total value of USD 4.7 million. Through the newest regulation of carbon pricing, Presidential Regulation (Perpres) 110 year 2025, Indonesia is poised to solidify its position as a leading global supplier of high-integrity carbon credits.

Complementing these market initiatives, the government is advancing the non-market-based pillar by formulating regulations for a carbon tax and defining non-tax state revenue from carbon trading. This critical policy layer is designed to fortify the foundational ecosystem for low-carbon development across the Indonesian economy.

## 4 Discussion: Towards a High and Sustainable Growth

The global economy is navigating a Triple Planetary Crisis, where the externalities of traditional growth are starkly quantified. The costs are staggering: USD 8.1 trillion in annual healthcare costs from pollution, a climate bill exploding at USD 14 million per hour, and USD 25 trillion in annual losses from biodiversity erosion. For Indonesia, this is not a distant abstraction but an immediate fiscal and existential threat. Our coasts are receding at an alarming 1.2 cm annually, imperiling the 65% of our population who live in coastal zones. With over 30,000 km$^2$ of land at risk by 2050 and 115 islands projected to vanish, the cost of inaction is measured in lost homes, livelihoods, and national heritage.

In this context, high and sustainable growth is our indispensable North Star. Indonesia is not merely aiming to break free from the middle-income trap, it is shifting gears to catalyze a structural transformation targeting 8% growth by 2029. This ambition, aligned with the Golden Indonesia 2045 vision, is audaciously coupled with a commitment to achieve net-zero emissions by 2060 or sooner (Fig. 16.2). The paradigm is clear: the old trade-off between economic expansion and environmental stewardship is obsolete.

Forging this new path requires a holistic and synergistic policy architecture. The Ministry of Finance is committed to optimizing the fiscal arm and, orchestrating the entire financial sector towards this dual objective. While a dedicated fiscal policy for green finance is still evolving, the financial regulators—Bank Indonesia and the Financial Services Authority (OJK)—have been proactive. Through a suite of microprudential, macroprudential, and monetary instruments—including the Indonesian Taxonomy for Sustainable Finance, mandatory sustainability reporting, and macroprudential liquidity incentives—they are systematically embedding sustainability into the financial sector's DNA.

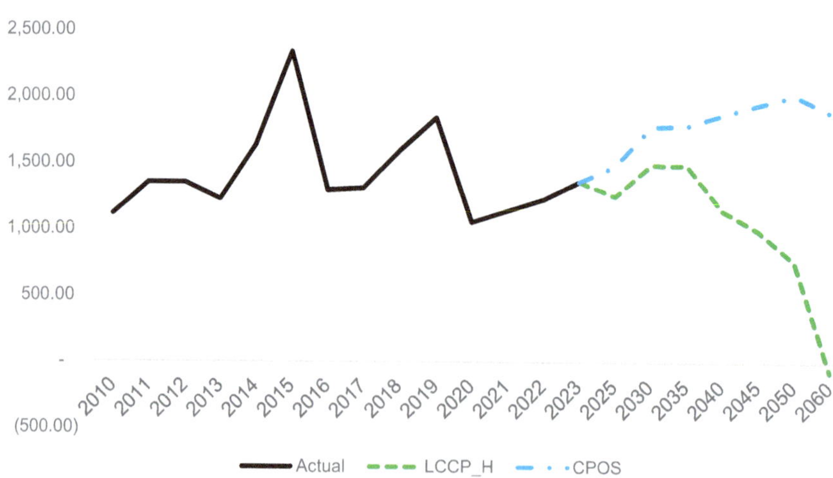


**Fig. 16.2** Net Zero Emission's Pathway

**Fig. 16.3** Closing the gap of climate finance required (USD billion)

However, a chain is only as strong as its most vulnerable link. While decarbonization forges our future, building systemic climate resilience is what fortifies the entire economic and financial chain. The ultimate success of this transition hinges on a whole-of-society shift. Given that Indonesia's growth is predominantly consumption-driven, catalyzing climate-conscious household behavior is paramount. Businesses play a crucial role as educators, illuminating the carbon footprint of goods and services to shape consumer demand. This rising demand will, in turn, create a powerful pull factor, ensuring that green and sustainable investments thrive, while brown assets are progressively stranded.

Looking ahead, the integrated force of public finance and private capital will be our engine. With public climate budgets—including strategic tax expenditures—serving as a springboard, we must mobilize sustainable finance to bridge the USD 254 billion chasm to our NDC targets (Fig. 16.3).[2] This is not merely about funding projects; it is about future-proofing our nation's financial stability and building a wider runway for climate investments to achieve scale and velocity. By aligning fiscal, financial, and regulatory policies, Indonesia will not only secure its economic ascent but also build a legacy of resilience and prosperity for generations to come.

### *4.1 Effectiveness of Green Fiscal Incentives in Indonesia*

Indonesia has deployed a wide range of green fiscal incentives, including tax holidays, VAT exemptions, import duty relief, and super deductions for renewable energy, electric vehicles (EVs), and energy-efficient technologies. From a policy

[2] The climate financing needs estimation is derived from Indonesia's Third Biennial Update Report (BUR). The mitigation requirements are projected at USD 281 billion, complemented by adaptation needs estimated at USD 12.14 billion—a conservative figure that requires further calibration against current climate mitigation and resilience dynamics. The public climate finance estimate comprises direct climate-related expenditures in the State Budget (APBN) and forgone revenue from tax expenditures, excluding fiscal contributions channeled through Public-Private Partnership (PPP) schemes.

design perspective, these instruments aim to correct market failures related to environmental externalities, high upfront capital costs, and technology risks. Empirical evidence suggests that green fiscal incentives in Indonesia have been more effective in scaling deployment in downstream sectors—such as EV manufacturing and battery ecosystems—than in accelerating upstream renewable energy generation, where regulatory uncertainty, tariff structures, and off-taker risks remain binding constraints (Asian Development Bank, 2023). This pattern mirrors findings from other emerging economies, where fiscal incentives alone are insufficient to overcome structural and institutional barriers in infrastructure-heavy sectors (World Bank, 2022).

Moreover, green tax expenditures tend to be more accessible to large firms with strong balance sheets and tax planning capacity, potentially limiting their impact on MSMEs and local innovators. Without robust ex-post evaluation mechanisms, there is also a risk that incentives primarily subsidize investments that are already commercially viable, leading to fiscal leakage rather than transformational change (International Monetary Fund, 2023a). These considerations suggest that the effectiveness of Indonesia's green fiscal incentives depends critically on complementary regulatory reforms, sunset clauses, and systematic impact evaluation.

## 4.2 *Fiscal Space, Trade-offs, and Sustainability*

While green fiscal policy is essential for Indonesia's low-carbon transition, it operates within finite fiscal space and must compete with other development priorities such as health, education, and social protection. Indonesia's experience highlights a fundamental trade-off between short-term fiscal costs and long-term economic and environmental benefits. On the one hand, green incentives reduce government revenue and increase contingent liabilities; on the other hand, they can lower future climate-related fiscal risks by reducing exposure to physical damage, stranded assets, and transition shocks (International Monetary Fund, 2023b). The challenge lies in sequencing: incentives should be front-loaded where market failures are most severe, while carbon pricing and subsidy reform gradually strengthen the revenue base.

The gradual reform of fossil fuel subsidies is therefore a critical component of fiscal sustainability. Without meaningful reallocation of expenditure away from carbon-intensive activities, green fiscal incentives risk being fiscally neutralized. International experience suggests that integrating green objectives into medium-term fiscal frameworks and climate budget tagging can improve transparency and help governments manage these trade-offs more effectively (OECD, 2021).

## 4.3 Mobilizing Private Capital and Managing Risk

Given that public finance can cover only a fraction of Indonesia's estimated climate investment needs, the primary role of fiscal policy is to *crowd in* private capital by reducing risks rather than substituting for private investment. Instruments such as viability gap funding, guarantees, blended finance facilities, and thematic bonds have been central to this strategy.

Evidence indicates that risk-sharing mechanisms—particularly guarantees and first-loss capital provided through special mission vehicles—have higher leverage effects than direct subsidies, especially in renewable energy and transport projects (Mazzucato & Semieniuk, 2018). However, their effectiveness depends on credible project pipelines, regulatory stability, and transparent governance. This highlights the need for differentiated fiscal strategies across mitigation and adaptation domains, as well as stronger coordination with financial regulators and development finance institutions to address non-fiscal barriers (World Bank, 2023).

## 4.4 Equity, Inclusion, and Just Transition

Green fiscal policy has important distributional implications that shape its political feasibility and long-term sustainability. While green incentives tend to benefit capital-intensive firms and urban consumers in the short term, carbon pricing and subsidy reforms may impose disproportionate burdens on low-income households if not carefully designed (International Monetary Fund, 2022). Hence, Indonesia's approach underscores the importance of recycling fiscal revenues and savings toward social protection, targeted subsidies, and support for affected workers and regions. Fiscal transfers, retraining programs, and MSME financing are essential to ensure that the transition does not exacerbate existing regional and income inequalities. Without such measures, green fiscal policy risks undermining social cohesion and public support for climate action.

From a fiscal perspective, equity considerations are not merely normative but instrumental: policies perceived as unfair are more likely to face resistance, policy reversals, and credibility loss. Integrating just transition principles into fiscal design therefore strengthens both economic efficiency and policy durability.

## 4.5 Governance and Institutional Coordination

The breadth of Indonesia's green fiscal toolkit increases the importance of strong governance and inter-institutional coordination. Fragmentation across ministries and agencies can lead to overlapping incentives, inconsistent policy signals, and suboptimal resource allocation. Climate budget tagging has improved transparency, but ex-post evaluation and accountability mechanisms remain uneven.

Effective green fiscal policy requires alignment between fiscal authorities, financial regulators, and sectoral ministries, particularly in areas such as taxonomy development, disclosure standards, and project eligibility criteria. Without such coordination, fiscal incentives may inadvertently conflict with prudential objectives or financial sector regulations, reducing overall effectiveness (Network for Greening the Financial System, 2023). Strengthening institutional coordination also enhances policy credibility, which is critical for mobilizing long-term private investment. Clear mandates, data-sharing frameworks, and performance evaluation systems are therefore central to scaling up green fiscal policy.

### *4.6 Comparative Insights and Lessons Learned from a Fiscal Perspective*

In comparative perspective, Indonesia's green fiscal strategy shares similarities with other emerging economies but also reflects important contextual differences. Compared to Chile, which relies more heavily on explicit carbon taxation and revenue earmarking, Indonesia has prioritized incentives and market-based mechanisms to manage political economy constraints. Relative to China, Indonesia's fiscal interventions are smaller in scale but more reliant on blended finance and international partnerships.

These comparisons suggest that there is no one-size-fits-all model for green fiscal policy. Institutional capacity, political economy, and economic structure shape feasible policy choices. Indonesia's experience illustrates that gradualism, policy experimentation, and coordination with financial sector reforms can be effective in contexts with limited fiscal space and high development needs.

At the same time, international experience highlights the importance of moving beyond incentive-heavy approaches toward more robust carbon pricing and regulatory frameworks over time. Fiscal policy is most effective when it evolves from subsidizing early adoption to reinforcing market discipline and long-term price signals.

## 5 Conclusions

Fiscal policy has emerged as the cornerstone instrument for the Indonesian government to orchestrate a transition towards balanced, resilient, and sustainable economic growth. By strategically deploying a multifaceted arsenal—including targeted tax expenditures, calibrated public spending, and innovative sovereign debt instruments—the government is actively shaping market incentives, catalyzing job creation in future-proof sectors, and safeguarding long-term macroeconomic stability. This reflects a profound paradigm shift in economic development, moving beyond the myopic pursuit of GDP figures towards a holistic model that values natural capital and intergenerational prosperity.

Indonesia's commitment is embodied in its comprehensive green economy strategy, which seeks to reconcile robust economic expansion with stringent environmental stewardship. To navigate pressing challenges such as climate change and entrenched fossil fuel dependency, the government has proactively implemented a coherent policy framework. Within this framework, fiscal instruments serve as strategic levers to fundamentally reorient behavior and redirect capital flows towards a sustainable trajectory.

The government's approach is both granular and strategic. On the revenue side, it has engineered a sophisticated system of tax incentives, including exemptions and allowances for the electric vehicle and renewable energy industries, designed to enhance their investment appeal and competitive parity. This is complemented by the ongoing development of carbon pricing mechanisms, which aim to internalize environmental costs and create a powerful price signal against emissions. On the expenditure front, the institutionalization of climate budget tagging ensures that public spending is systematically aligned with climate objectives, with an average of 3% of the state budget (APBN) annually dedicated to climate action.

Acknowledging that public finance alone cannot bridge the substantial funding gap, Indonesia has demonstrated remarkable ingenuity in mobilizing non-public capital. The government has successfully positioned itself as a pioneer in the thematic debt market, leveraging instruments like the Global Green Sukuk, SDGs Bonds, and Blue Bonds to tap into global pools of sustainable capital. This "crowding-in" strategy is further amplified by a sophisticated financial architecture of Special Mission Vehicles (SMVs). Institutions such as the Indonesia Climate Change Trust Fund (ICCTF), the Indonesia Environment Fund (IEF), PT Sarana Multi Infrastruktur (PT SMI), and PT Penjaminan Infrastruktur Indonesia (PII) act as catalytic intermediaries, de-risking investments and addressing critical funding gaps in strategic infrastructure and climate projects.

This discussion underscores that Indonesia's green fiscal policy plays a catalytic rather than dominant role in the country's transition toward sustainable growth. While fiscal incentives and public financing instruments have been effective in reducing investment barriers and mobilizing private capital in selected sectors, their long-term success depends on careful management of fiscal trade-offs, institutional coordination, and equity considerations. The Indonesian case demonstrates that green growth is not solely a question of fiscal scale, but of policy coherence, credibility, and sequencing. For emerging economies facing similar constraints, Indonesia offers a valuable illustration of how fiscal policy can support climate objectives while remaining consistent with macroeconomic stability and development priorities.

In conclusion, Indonesia's fiscal policy narrative powerfully refutes the antiquated dichotomy between economic growth and environmental sustainability. They are not a trade-off but two synergistic sides of the same coin. The ongoing calibration of fiscal measures and financial architecture demonstrates a clear recognition that future economic competitiveness is inextricably linked to ecological resilience. These policies possess the transformative power to forge a new economic paradigm for Indonesia—one of inclusive growth, embedded sustainability, and lasting prosperity.

## References

Asian Development Bank. (2023). *Indonesia Energy Transition Outlook*. ADB.
Government of Indonesia. (2019). *Government Regulation Number 78/2019 on Tax Allowance.*
Government of Indonesia. (2021). *Indonesia Biennial Update Report 3.*
Government of Indonesia. (2024). *Government Indonesia's Long-term National Development Plan (RPJPN) 2025-2045.*
Government of Indonesia. (2025). *Indonesia's Mid-term National Development Plan (RPJMN) 2025-2029.*
International Monetary Fund. (2022). *Distributional Effects of Carbon Pricing*. IMF.
International Monetary Fund. (2023a). *Climate-Related Fiscal Risks*. IMF.
International Monetary Fund. (2023b). *Fiscal Policy and Climate Change*. IMF.
Mazzucato, M., & Semieniuk, G. (2018). Financing renewable energy: Who is financing what and why it matters. *Technological Forecasting and Social Change, 127*, 8–22. https://doi.org/10.1016/j.techfore.2017.05.021.
Ministry of Domestic Affairs. (2023). *Ministry of Domestic Affairs Number 6/2023.*
Ministry of Finance of Indonesia. (2019). *Ministry of Finance Regulation Number 128/2019 on Vocational Income Tax Super Deduction.*
Ministry of Finance of Indonesia. (2020a). *Finance Minister Regulation Number 130/2020 on Tax Holiday.*
Ministry of Finance of Indonesia. (2020b). *Ministry of Finance Regulation Number 153/2020 on R&D Income Tax Super Deduction.*
Ministry of Finance of Indonesia. (2021). *Government Regulation Number 74/2021 on Luxury Tax Waive.*
Ministry of Finance of Indonesia. (2022). *Finance Minister Regulation Number 26/2022 on Excise Waive.*
Ministry of Finance of Indonesia. (2023). *Finance Minister Regulation Number 38/2023 on Waived VAT.*
Ministry of Finance of Indonesia. (2024a). *Green Sukuk Allocation and Impact Report 2024.*
Ministry of Finance of Indonesia. (2024b). *SDG Bond and Blue Bond Allocaion and Impact Report 2024.*
Ministry of Finance of Indonesia. (2024c). *Tax Expenditure Report 2023.*
Ministry of National Development Planning. (2022). *Green Economy Index.*
Network for Greening the Financial System. (2023). *Central Banking and Climate Change*. NGFS.
OECD. (2021). *Climate Change and Long-Term Fiscal Sustainability*. OECD Publishing.
World Bank. (2022). *Fiscal Policies for Low-Carbon Development*. World Bank.
World Bank. (2023). *Mobilizing Private Finance for Climate Action*. World Bank.

# Chapter 17
# Bank Indonesia's Climate Policy Strategy

**Solikin M. Juhro, Irman Robinson, Dhaha Praviandi Kuantan, Satwika Lulu, and Ratna Oktriyani**

**Abstract** Climate change challenges financial system stability in Indonesia as an archipelagic country, demanding an integrated central banking response. Anchored in the Act No. 4 of 2023, this chapter examines Bank Indonesia's policy strategies in responding the climate-related challenges, specifically to leverage monetary, macroprudential, and payment system policies for mobilizing and accelerating sustainable finance in Indonesia. It underscores the necessity of national and global coordination, including through ASEAN and G20 engagements. Our analysis suggests that effective climate policy actions by a central bank requires targeted instruments, robust data frameworks, and strong institutional coordination across fiscal, macroprudential, microprudential and sectoral authorities to support a low-carbon transition.

**Keywords** Climate change challenges · Sustainable finance · Bank Indonesia climate policy · Climate policy coordination

## 1 Introduction

Climate change has emerged as a defining challenge of the twenty-first century, not only as an environmental crisis but also as a profound threat to global financial system stability as it is strongly linked to the financial institution's exposures. As Mark Carney (2015) famously warned, climate change represents a "tragedy of the horizon"—a systemic risk that lies beyond the typical planning cycles of financial institutions and policymakers (Bank of England, 2015). This risk is transmitted directly through physical risks, such as extreme weather events, sea-level rise, and flooding, and transition risks associated with the market preference shift to a low-carbon economic activities. As an archipelagic nation, Indonesia is highly exposed

S. M. Juhro (✉) · I. Robinson · D. P. Kuantan · S. Lulu · R. Oktriyani
Bank Indonesia, Jakarta, Indonesia
e-mail: solikin@bi.go.id; irman_r@bi.go.id; dhaha@bi.go.id; lulu@bi.go.id; Ratna_o@bi.go.id


S. M. Juhro et al. (eds.), *Sustainable Economy: The Indonesian Pathways*,
https://doi.org/10.1007/978-981-92-1215-6_17

to climate-related hazards, making Indonesia significantly vulnerable to encounter multiple physical risks from climate change and other natural hazards due to its geographical location on the Pacific Ring of Fire and coastal areas. These events can damage infrastructure, disrupt livelihoods, and impair the financial health of households and businesses, thereby transmitting shocks to the broader financial system. At the macroeconomic level, physical risks may lead to reduced production output—particularly in agriculture and fisheries—and disruptions in distribution and supply chains, thereby increasing food price volatility and complicate monetary policy formulation. Meanwhile, transition risks typically lead to decreased businesses' revenue associated with the shift of market demands to more sustainable businesses' practices.

Indonesia's economic structure further compounds these vulnerabilities. The country remains heavily reliant on fossil fuels and carbon-intensive sectors, with coal and palm oil each contributing around 15% of net exports in 2020 (International Energy Agency, 2022). Coal alone accounts for over a third of the national energy supply in 2023 (International Energy Agency, 2023). As global markets shift toward decarbonization, Indonesia faces significant transition risks, including declining demand for fossil fuels and changing global preferences for sustainable products or projects. This shift demands a meaningful progress in adopting renewable energy and circular economy to maintain economic competitiveness. In turn, global demands for sustainable financing is increasingly strong, necessitating a robust due diligence to verify sustainable claims and mitigate greenwashing risks. These transitions threaten financial viability of key industries, including financial institutions, and, at broader scale, the stability of financial system.

As concerns on climate risks growing, the role of a central bank has evolved. The central bank is no longer confined to traditional mandates of price and financial system stability. Instead, more central banks are now increasingly called upon to respond climate-related risks in ensuring financial system stability. Likewise, Bank Indonesia has been mandated by the Act No. 4 of 2023 on the Development and Strengthening of the Financial Sector to regulate and develop sustainable finance, in addition to the main mandate in maintaining Rupiah stability, preserving payment system stability, and supporting to financial system stability in achieving a sustainable economic growth. As Dikau and Volz (2018) argue, central banks possess powerful regulatory and monetary tools that can be leveraged to align financial flows with sustainability goals. This includes integrating climate risks into macroprudential policy frameworks, promoting green financial instruments, and guiding credit allocation toward low-carbon sectors (Dikau & Volz, 2018).

As Indonesia has committed in the Paris Agreement to contribute in reducing carbon emission, a significant amount of financing is needed for transition to a lower carbon economy. Concerning this issue, Indonesian related authority has estimated total funding needs of USD281.18 billion for mitigation efforts and USD816.52 billion for adaptation efforts to meet the Indonesia's Nationally Determined Contribution (NDC) targets in 2030 (Ministry of Environment Republic of Indonesia, 2025). However, public funding source alone is insufficient, as the state budget is only able to cover around 34% of the total financing needs to achieve the NDC targets in 2030 (Ministry of Finance). Hence, source of financing from the nonstate budget, i.e. international financial markets, is crucial. Yet, financing from global markets is not easy to tap due to complex and lengthy due diligence processes as required by the investors. On the other hand, financing from domestic banking sector is still limited due to the still-low banking's risk appetite on green projects. At this stage, there is an urgency to accelerate and mobilize sustainable financing to support climate mitigation and adaptation efforts in Indonesia.

Under these circumstances, Bank Indonesia's contribution is pivotal in bridging the financing gap and ensuring a just and orderly transition for financial system stability. Therefore, Bank Indonesia's policy strategies for sustainable finance—through monetary, macroprudential, and payment system policies—are expected to: (i) mobilize global and domestic sustainable financing (supply side) to finance the transition to a low-carbon economy, and (ii) foster the development of the low-carbon economy (demand side). The central bank policies would ideally work in coordination with other Government Ministries' policies who lead sectoral transition. Consequently, the success of sustainable finance implementation in navigating the Indonesia's transition toward net zero emissions hinges on a comprehensive regulatory framework and robust institutional coordination between Bank Indonesia, the Financial Services Authority (OJK), and the Ministry of Finance, as well as other relevant stakeholders, both domestically and globally (Juhro et al., 2025).

This chapter presents Bank Indonesia's policy strategy in delivering a sound climate regulatory framework to support financial system stability, thus enabling sustainable economic growth. It also explores how Bank Indonesia manages coordination with related Government Ministries as well as international cooperation bodies on climate-related financing policy nexus, navigating changing and complex landscape to achieve a resilient, inclusive, and sustainable economy.

## 2 Perspectives on Central Bank's Climate Policy Strategy

### 2.1 *Policy Framework*

The concepts of welfare and economic sustainability are fundamentally intertwined with the role of central bank in fulfilling its mandate to achieve and maintain price stability such as economic growth, full employment, equitable income distribution, and environmental and climate issue. From a central bank policy perspective, the meaning of achieving stability needs to be directed in the context of supporting sustainable economic growth, "stability for sustainability" (Juhro, 2025).

Figure 17.1 exhibits a central bank's integrated climate regulatory framework aimed at ensuring financial system stability to support sustainable economic growth through macroprudential policy. The primary objective of macroprudential policy is to ensure stability of the financial system. In Indonesia's context, Bank Indonesia adopts

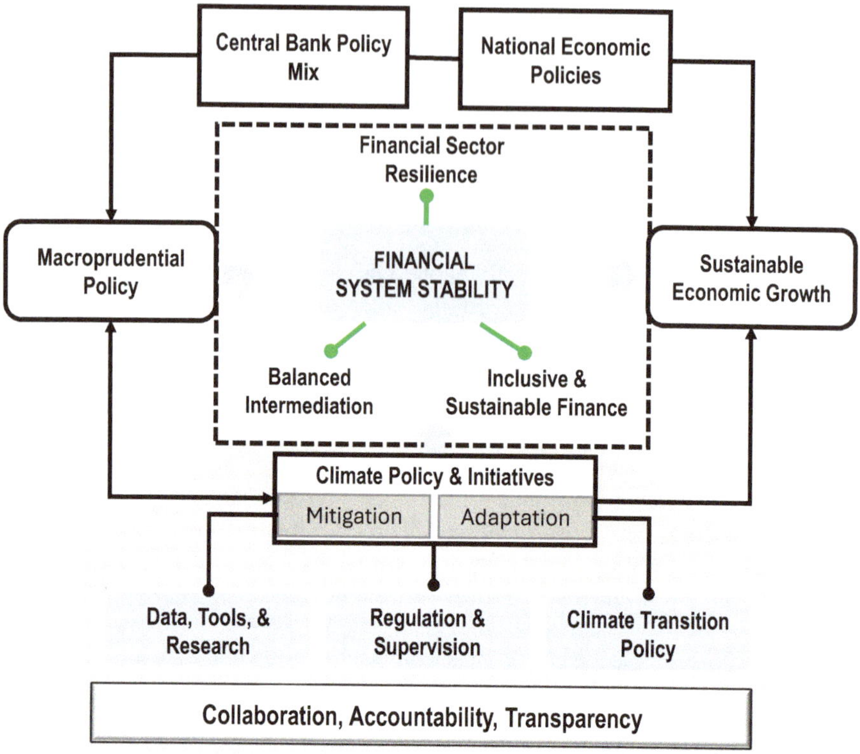


**Fig. 17.1** Central Bank's Sustainable Finance Policy Framework. Source: Juhro et al. (2025)

a three-pronged macroprudential policy strategy tailored to the dynamics of emerging market economies, which includes: (i) preserving financial sector resilience by mitigating the transmission of risks stemming from institutional interconnectedness and systemic contagion; (ii) managing balanced and sustainable intermediation to address procyclicality; and (iii) supporting financial inclusion and sustainable finance. These three strategic pillars are designed to be complementary, reinforcing one another in pursuit of the overarching goal of financial system stability.

In connection with climate change, two main strategies take the spotlight, namely climate mitigation and climate adaptation. Climate mitigation involves the active reduction or prevention of greenhouse gas emissions to curb the impact of climate change (IPCC, 2022b). On the other side, climate adaptation calls for adjustments in process, practices, and structures to either cushion potential damages or seize opportunities arising from the changing climate (IPCC, 2022a). In this regard, the framework outlines three fundamental policy strategies for addressing climate-related risks: (i) data, tools, and research; (ii) regulation and supervision; and (iii) climate-related transition policies. Operationalizing these strategies requires a shift beyond the traditional scope of central banking. It demands a coordinated and collaborative approach among regulators, financial institutions, and industry stakeholders to guide the economy toward a sustainable and resilient future (Juhro et al., 2025).

## 2.2 Regulation and Supervision

Presuming that central banks are endowed with a climate mandate; they can implement three distinct types of regulations as depicted below (Fig. 17.2).

*Firstly,* it is imperative to enhance the macroprudential instruments to bolster climate mitigation and adaptation strategies, including both price and non-price instruments. The instruments such as liquidity incentives, in terms of reducing reserve requirements for banks that lend to the green sector, are examples of instruments that relate to the pricing of credit. Other instruments such as Green Loan-To-Value (LTV), Green Down Payment, and Green Credit Allocation, are prevalent as non-price instruments in this domain. The Green LTV serves as an incentive mechanism instituted by central banks that permits banks to offer mortgages for eco-friendly houses with a higher loan-to-value ratio than mortgages for non-green properties. Similarly, a Green Down Payment allows a lower down payment for electric vehicle ownership loans than automotive ownership loans for non-green alternatives. Green Credit Allocation mandates banks to designate a specific fraction of their loans towards environmentally friendly activities. This instrument is frequently incorporated as a component of a more extensive credit allocation scheme, typically associated with priority sector lending. This approach encourages financial institutions to increase their green lending practices, thereby promoting environmentally sustainable activities.

*Secondly*, the optimization of monetary instruments to bolster climate mitigation and adaptation is crucial. The Green Reserve Requirement, Green Central Bank Repo Operations, and Green Quantitative Easing are typical examples of such instruments. The Green Reserve Requirement serves as an incentive, offering a relaxation

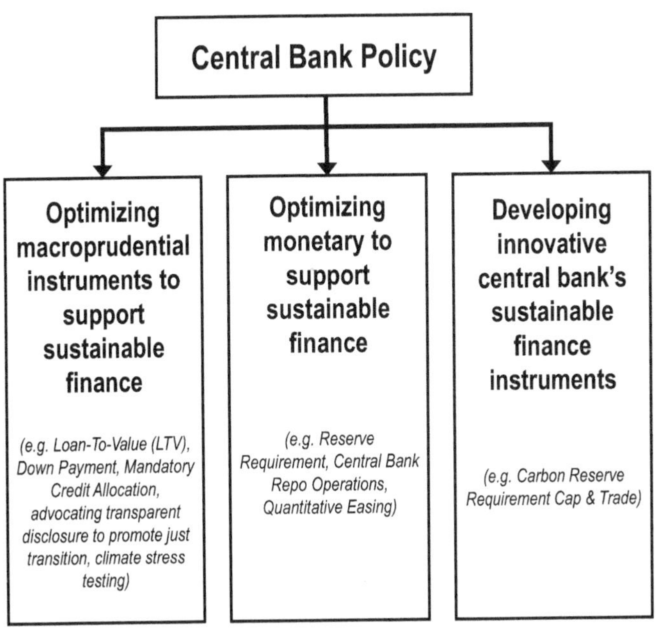


**Fig. 17.2** Central Bank Policy Options. Source: Juhro et al. (2025)

of reserve requirements for banks engaged in green lending. On the other hand, Green Central Bank Repo Operations incentivize the banks by providing lower repo rates for those involved in green lending. In the context of Green Repo Operations, central banks can also consider green bonds as collateral that are subject to a favorable rate. Incorporating climate-related criteria into collateral eligibility frameworks can encourage financial institutions to hold more sustainable assets. In another case, central banks may permit the refinancing of green mortgages, combined with standard central bank repo collaterals, with lower rates. Other variations of Green Repo Operations are employed by limiting brown securities as eligible repo transactions. Furthermore, central banks can conduct Green Quantitative Easing by prioritizing the purchase of green bonds and other sustainable assets as part of their quantitative easing programs, supporting the growth of green finance markets.

*Thirdly*, the introduction of an innovative mechanism to enhance green lending is imperative. Currently, the amalgamation of a carbon tax and carbon trading is perceived as a fundamental component of climate mitigation strategies. This regulatory framework can be adapted and implemented within the financial sector. In this regard, central banks could instigate a carbon reserve requirement cap and trade as the primary climate instrument. Under this proposed initiative, the banks would be mandated to maintain a reserve in central banks, calculated on the basis of their environmental sustainability. This reserve could be diminished by purchasing credit points from other banks, which have been awarded by central banks for their green initiatives. Given the comparative financial advantage of acquiring credit points as opposed to maintaining a non-interest-bearing carbon reserve, the envisaged model envisions the establishment of a novel carbon reserve market. The functioning of this market, in conjunction with a transparent central bank roadmap governing the cap (e.g., gradual reduction of the cap each year), is anticipated to exert a guiding influence on banks' lending preferences. Furthermore, it is expected to foster heightened competition among banks, resulting in more favorable interest rates for loans extended in support of environmentally sustainable initiatives.

While the green initiatives of central banks could significantly contribute to the attainment of climate targets, it is crucial to recognize that poorly crafted initiatives may yield adverse consequences. Such initiatives could disrupt the prevailing business model and increase non-performing loans. Consequently, central banks must strive to uphold a balance between quality and sustainable financing. Moreover, the adoption of robust climate supervision principles, as outlined by the Basel Committee on Banking Supervision (BIS, 2022), is also recommended.

## 3 Benchmarking

Climate change poses both physical and transition risks with various level of impact to countries, depending on the geographical location and economical position within global value chain of each country. This condition affects a central bank's position in responding the climate change issues which may impact a central bank's key objective, typically in achieving its inflation targets and financial system stability. Recognizing the multifaceted nature of these risks, Dikau and Volz (2018) identify five strategic areas where central banks can meaningfully contribute to sustainability goals—green microprudential policies, green macroprudential policies, green financial market development, green credit allocation, and other central bank's green initiatives such as soft power and guidelines (Table 17.1).

These strategies reflect a growing understanding that central banks must expand their traditional roles to address climate-related challenges effectively. As evidently found in the 2021 Asia-Pacific (APAC) Central Bank Sustainability Survey, 26 Central Banks and Financial Supervisors (CBFS) in the region have either implemented or are in the process of implementing sustainable finance measures. These

**Table 17.1** Central Bank Policy Strategies

| Policy | Instrument | Example |
|---|---|---|
| Green Micro-prudential Regulation | • Disclosure Requirements<br>• Environmental & Social Risk-management Standards<br>• Reserve Requirements | The People' Bank of China (PBOC), the Ministry of Environmental Protection, and the China Banking Regulatory Commission has jointly launched The Green Credit Policy in 2007 |
| Green Macro-prudential Regulation | • Climate-related Stress Testing<br>• Counter-cyclical Capital Buffers<br>• Differentiated Capital Requirements<br>• Loan-to-value and Loan-to-income Caps<br>• Large Exposure Restrictions<br>• Identification of Systemically Important Financial Institutions and Capital Surcharges | The Banco Central do Brasil requires commercial banks to take the exposure to environmental damages and risks into account |
| Green Financial Market Development | • Information Disclosure Requirements<br>• Green Bond Guidelines | The PBOC has launched green bond guidelines in 2015 |
| Green Credit Allocation | • Targeted Refinancing Lines<br>• Minimum and Maximum Credit Quotas to specified classes of assets, industries, or geographical areas<br>• Preferred Interest Rates for Priority Sectors<br>Central Bank Assistance to Development Banks | The Bangladesh Bank has introduced targeted refinancing lines in 2009. |
| Other Supportive Central Bank's Green Initiatives | • Green Finance Guidelines and Frameworks<br>• Soft Power (e.g. research, workshop, seminar) | |

Source: Dikau and Volz (2018)

measures span the full scope of their institutional mandates, with the most common area of intervention being governance and strategy—including the development of climate strategies, participation in international initiatives, and capacity building for financial institutions. As a foundational step, this area naturally encompasses a broader range of actions than others and plays a critical role in the early stages of integrating climate and environmental objectives. In addition to governance efforts, the survey highlights a stronger emphasis on microprudential measures compared to macroprudential ones, suggesting that CBFS are prioritizing institution-level risk management tools to address climate risks (BIS, 2021; Table 17.2).

However, despite growing awareness and initial progress, the central banks and financial supervisors still face challenges in translating climate ambition into impactful actions. The Green Central Banking Scorecard 2024 reveals that while notable advancements have been made in research, advocacy, and financial policy, significant gaps remain in monetary policy and leading by example. Many institutions have yet to deploy high-impact monetary tools or align their own portfolios

**Table 17.2** Measures Implemented by CBFS to Address Climate and Environmental Issue

| Type of intervention area | Total # of measures currently implemented | Number of associated CBFS | Total # of measures to be implemented in the future | Number of associated CBFS | Total # of measures implemented either currently or in the future | Number of associated CBFS |
|---|---|---|---|---|---|---|
| Macro-prudential instruments | 15 | 11 | 20 | 14 | 25 | 16 |
| Micro-prudential instruments | 52 | 17 | 51 | 15 | 72 | 19 |
| Portfolio management | 16 | 10 | 17 | 11 | 26 | 14 |
| Credit allocation instruments | 18 | 10 | 19 | 9 | 24 | 11 |
| Own governance and strategy | 117 | 24 | 107 | 23 | 135 | 24 |
| Dev./eval. Of gov. policies and measures* | 23 | 12 | 19 | 10 | 23 | 12 |
| Monetary policy | 25 | 14 | 22 | 11 | 29 | 14 |
| Standard setting for sustainable finance | 27 | 17 | 34 | 18 | 41 | 18 |

Source: BIS (2021)

with environmental goals, underscoring a persistent disconnection between climate awareness and meaningful implementation (Positive Money, 2024).

This trend is also reflected in the ASEAN region, where the central banks are increasingly integrating climate-related and environmental risk management into their mandates. Institutions such as Bank Indonesia, the State Bank of Vietnam, and the Monetary Authority of Singapore are taking proactive steps through macroprudential incentives, regulatory guidelines, and green investment programs. These efforts demonstrate a growing regional commitment to sustainability, even amid varying levels of financial sector maturity. Crucially, the ASEAN central banks are not working in isolation. They are actively engaging with global platforms such as the Sustainable Banking Network and the Network for Greening the Financial System (NGFS), which provide frameworks, technical support, and allow peer learning opportunities. These collaborations are instrumental in building institutional capacity, harmonizing strategies and policies, and enhancing the resilience of financial systems across the region—ensuring that ASEAN economies are better equipped to navigate the transition toward a low-carbon future.

## *3.1 The Monetary Authority of Singapore*

The Monetary Authority of Singapore (MAS) has placed sustainability as one of the key priorities in its financial policy strategy. In 2023, MAS launched the Finance for Net Zero (FiNZ) Action Plan, building upon the Green Finance Action Plan introduced in 2019 (MAS, 2023a). The FiNZ Action Plan focuses on four strategic areas: (i) data, definitions, and disclosures; (ii) fostering a climate-resilient financial sector; (iii) supporting credible transition plans; and (iv) promoting green market solutions and transitions. These strategies are underpinned by two key enablers—green fintech and skills and capabilities—which are essential for driving innovation and building institutional capacity. To further support this agenda, MAS provides catalytic funding through the Green Investments Programme (GIP) in 2019, channeling capital to asset managers committed to advancing regional green initiatives from Singapore (MAS, 2019). These efforts align with MAS' broader goals of developing green financial markets and managing environmental risks.

To strengthen policy coordination and industry engagement, MAS established the Green Finance Industry Taskforce (GFIT) in 2019. Comprising representatives from financial institutions, corporates, NGOs, and industry associations, GFIT exemplifies the importance of public-private collaboration in mainstreaming green finance. Over its mandate, GFIT delivered key outputs across four domains: (i) Developing Taxonomy, with the publication of the Singapore-Asia Taxonomy for Sustainable Finance in 2023 (MAS, 2023b); (ii) Improving Disclosures, through the Climate-Related Disclosure Document for Financial Institutions in 2021 (MAS, 2021); (iii) Driving Green Finance Solutions, via the White Paper on Fostering Green Finance Solutions in 2021; and (iv) Enhancing Environmental Risk Management, with the release of the Handbook on Implementing Environmental Risk Management in 2021.

Internationally, MAS plays an active role in regional and global platforms. Within ASEAN, it contributes to the ASEAN Taxonomy for Sustainable Finance, developed by the ASEAN Taxonomy Board (ATB) established in 2021 (SFIA, 2021). MAS also collaborates with global institutions such as the Bank for International Settlements (BIS) and the Network for Greening the Financial System (NGFS) to harmonize sustainability reporting standards, strengthen green market infrastructure, and support ASEAN financial market integration.

## *3.2 The Bank Negara Malaysia*

In line with its mandate to maintain monetary and financial stability, the Bank Negara Malaysia (BNM) has proactively prepared national financial system to be more resilient and sustainable in the face of climate change impacts. To support the development of sustainable finance, BNM has implemented several strategic initiatives (BNM, 2025). First, BNM developed the Climate Data Catalogue, designed as a central reference for climate and environmental data relevant to the financial sector. This initiative also serves as a collaborative call to stakeholders to jointly improve the availability and accessibility of climate data. The catalogue classifies data into categories—available, partially available, and unavailable—while identifying existing data gaps. To ensure its relevance and reliability, the Climate Data Catalogue is updated annually, taking into account evolving data standards and sources.

Second, BNM introduced the Climate Change and Principle-based Taxonomy (CCPT) in 2021, which provides guidance for financial institutions to identify and classify economic activities that contribute to climate mitigation and adaptation. The CCPT offers a systematic approach that enables consistent and comprehensive assessment of economic activities and their broader environmental impacts. It also considers Malaysia's national development context and the readiness of economic actors in transitioning toward a low-carbon economy. The taxonomy supports the transformation of activities that currently do not contribute to climate goals into more sustainable practices.

Third, BNM established the Joint Committee on Climate Change (JC3) in 2019, a collaborative platform between financial authorities and industry players aimed at strengthening the financial sector's resilience to climate risks. JC3 has several key mandates: (i) enhancing capacity through knowledge exchange, expertise sharing, and best practices in climate risk assessment and management; (ii) identifying strategic issues, challenges, and priorities faced by the financial sector in the transition to a low-carbon economy; (iii) facilitating cross-stakeholder collaboration to develop coordinated solutions to address these challenges; and (iv) supporting the integration of climate solutions into financial institutions' operations and business models.

Fourth, BNM actively participates in the NGFS, a global network of central banks and financial supervisors committed to strengthening the financial system's response to climate risks. Through this membership, BNM contributes to global efforts to: (i) enhance collective responses to meet the goals of the Paris Agreement; (ii) elevate the role of the financial system in identifying and managing climate risks; and (iii) mobilize financing toward sustainable, green, and low-carbon investments within an inclusive and environmentally responsible development framework.

## 3.3 *Bangko Sentral ng Pilipinas (BSP)*

The BSP acknowledges the vital role of the financial services sector in promoting sustainable and resilient development by supporting environmentally and socially responsible business decisions aligned with national goals. To support this initiative, the BSP introduced the Philippine Sustainable Finance Roadmap and Guiding Principles in 2022, developed by the Inter-Agency Technical Working Group on Sustainable Finance (ITSF), also known as the 'Green Force'. These documents provide a comprehensive framework to guide effective strategies for mainstreaming sustainable finance within the Philippine financial system (BSP, 2022).

The pillars of the Philippine Sustainable Finance Roadmap are:

(i) Creating a conducive environment (the Policy Pillar). This pillar recognizes the importance of creating an environment of transparency on climate-related finance and risk management, including reporting of green and climate finance flows.

(ii) Mainstreaming sustainable finance (the Financing Pillar). This pillar aims to promote sustainable financial products through incentives and penalties, leverage on available financing, and establishing a sustainable insurance mechanism. Under this pillar, BSP has issued Philippine Sustainable Finance Taxonomy Guidelines in 2024, as a tool to classify whether an economic activity is environmentally and socially sustainable and guides different stakeholders in making informed investment and financing decisions.

(iii) Developing a sustainable pipeline (the Investment Pillar). This pillar acknowledges that in achieving the goals of sustainable finance, a whole of nation effort is needed. This pillar aims to establish a sustainable pipeline database for the public and private sector and monitor progress and provide for regular updating, including linking the sustainable pipeline to SDGs, the Philippine Development Plan (PDP), and NDC targets.

The Green Force is a crucial body for the Philippines' sustainable finance agenda, supporting the country's commitment to a sustainable and low-carbon economy by providing focused leadership and coordinating efforts across different government agencies. It is co-chaired by the Department of Finance (DOF) and the Climate Change Commission (CCC) and includes participation from various critical government agencies such as BSP, the Securities and Exchange Commission (SEC), the Insurance Commission (IC), the Department of Energy, the Department of Environment and Natural Resources, and the National Economic and Development Authority (NEDA).

# 4 Bank Indonesia's Climate Policy Strategy

## *4.1 Bank Indonesia's Policy Framework*

As stipulated in the Bank Indonesia Act as lastly amended by the Act No. 4 of 2023 (the Development and Strengthening of Financial Sector), Bank Indonesia is mandated to achieve rupiah stability, maintain payment system stability, and contribute in safeguarding financial system stability in order to support sustainable economic growth. Furthermore, the Act No. 4 of 2023 also mandates Bank Indonesia to formulate and implement macroprudential policies aimed at supporting financial system stability through efforts to encourage balanced, quality, and sustainable intermediation; mitigates and manages systemic risks; and elevates economic inclusion, financial inclusion, and sustainable finance. Following this mandate, Bank Indonesia has developed a policy framework on economic inclusion, financial inclusion, and sustainable finance to pursue its objective in supporting sustainable economic growth.

From Bank Indonesia's point of view, the policy framework on economic inclusion, financial inclusion, and sustainable finance (Fig. 17.3) is developed to facilitate the attainment of Bank Indonesia's key objectives by advancing these three pillars, thereby promoting sustainable economic growth. The framework encompasses three key strategies to achieve: (i) an integrated and competitive inclusive economic ecosystem (**the 1st pillar**); (ii) an optimal inclusive financing and sustainable finance (**the 2nd pillar**); and (iii) a widespread literacy and synergy in inclusive and sustainable finance and economy (**the 3rd pillar**). While the first strategy focus in empowering and expanding inclusive businesses as well as facilitating the most-needed infrastructures, the second strategy is designed to facilitate Bank Indonesia's critical role in assisting national approach for strengthening inclusive financing as well as mobilizing and accelerating sustainable finance. At last, the third strategy is presented to put emphasis on the literacy and synergy for the economic and financial inclusive and sustainable finance to complement the other two strategies. It recognizes the importance of interagency coordinated approach in promoting inclusive and sustainable finance.

Essentially, Bank Indonesia's sustainable finance policy is carried out to ensure the resilience and stability of financial system against the intensifying climate-related risks. This is well reflected from the second strategy which highlight Bank Indonesia's role in promoting higher access to financing for high-emission and hard-to-abate sectors, including vulnerable sectors such as the MSMEs, which serve as key drivers of national target in transition toward a low-carbon economy. In general, Bank Indonesia's sustainable finance policy is developed for two groups:

**First,** the financial institution (banks and nonbank) through macroprudential policy—such as macroprudential liquidity incentive policy (widely known as the KLM), loan-to-value policy for green building and down payment policy for electrical vehicle; monetary policy; and payment system policy. These policies aim to promote sustainable financial products development through incentives and

**Fig. 17.3** Bank Indonesia's Climate Policy Strategy. Source: Bank Indonesia., 2025

mobilization of the banks' available financing to sustainable economic activities, including those conducted by the MSMEs.

**Second**, the MSMEs as the vital backbone of the economy through other initiatives—such as guidelines or business model for sustainable MSME, classification for sustainable MSME. This policy aims to support the MSMEs in transitioning to a low-carbon business practice, both financially and operationally.

At the implementation level, Bank Indonesia's policy framework on economic inclusion, financial inclusion, and sustainable finance is supported by data, tools, and research as well as regulation and supervision. In terms of data, tools, and research, Bank Indonesia has several initiatives reflecting its commitment in advancing sustainable finance:

**First**, Bank Indonesia has launched Green Calculator as a tool to calculate greenhouse gas emission in 2024. In this respect, Bank Indonesia—together with the Coordinating Ministry for Maritime Affairs and Investment, the Ministry of Environment and Forestry, and the Ministry of Energy and Mineral Resources—has taken the initiative to develop the Green Calculator, as a tool which is designed to be user-friendly, internationally standardized, and utilizing national emission factors to ensure reliable calculations for domestic player. The Green Calculator—widely known for its user-friendly apps—is accessible and intended for use by all economic entities, including micro, small, and medium enterprises (MSMEs) as well as individuals. By providing a practical and inclusive solution, the application supports broader participation in environmental accountability and helps promote low-carbon practices across sectors.

**Second**, Bank Indonesia carries out the climate risk stress testing for the banking sector, jointly conducted with the banks to allow an updated and rigorous assessment on the potential impact of climate-related risks on the financial system stability, which is the ultimate concern of Bank Indonesia. This stress test is highly relevant for a country with inherent specific geographical characteristic like Indonesia—an archipelagic country with numerous volcanic mountain.

**Third,** Bank Indonesia also conducted various research and reviews regarding the sustainable economy and finance, highlighting its concern in addressing climate-related risks. Recently, Bank Indonesia just launched the study on "Green Financing Ecosystem for MSMEs: Supply and Demand Perspectives", in collaboration with the Research and Training Unit for Economics and Business, Gadjah Mada University. The study is part of the ongoing push to help the MSMEs transition toward truly sustainable business practices by making financing more accessible.

As for the regulation and supervision, Bank Indonesia thus far has contributed in strengthening the sustainable ecosystem by instituting three macroprudential policies:

**First**, Bank Indonesia has issued loan-to-value (LTV) policy for green property loans and down payment requirements on green automotive loans since December 2019. This policy differentiates the LTV ratios and minimum down payment requirements for financing of green and non-green products. The LTV for financing green buildings is set at up to 100%, while the minimum down payment requirement on electric vehicles has been reduced to 0% in accordance with risk assessments conducted by the lending banks. These accommodative LTV and down payment policies are expected to increase demand and access to green loans and encourage consumer preferences for green property and vehicles. The policies are also intended to accelerate the growth of green finance and stimulate the economy while addressing the environmental risks.

**Second**, Bank Indonesia formulated the Macroprudential Inclusive Financing Ratio (RPIM) under Bank Indonesia Regulation No. 24/3/PBI/2022 to enhance inclusive financing and ensure financial system stability. The banks determine their own RPIM target based on a self-assessment and are obligated to achieve that target with evaluations conducted at the end of each year. The RPIM policy expands the modalities of inclusive financing to include: (i) direct financing and supply chain financing; (ii) financing through financial service institutions, public service agencies, and business entities; and (iii) inclusive financing securities. To support sustainable finance growth, the types of securities in the 3rd modality have been expanded to include securities for development or sustainability purposes. The banks, therefore, can purchase sustainable finance instruments to meet their RPIM target.

**Third**, Bank Indonesia has implemented Macroprudential Liquidity Incentive Policy (KLM) by relaxing the average reserve requirements for banks that extend loans to specific sectors, including inclusive sectors, such as ultra micro enterprises, green sectors and other sectors designated by Bank Indonesia. As of 1 April 2025, Bank Indonesia expanded the scope of green sectors of the KLM from only green property and green automotive to include subsectors dealing with waste management, remediation activities and recycling.

Interestingly, the Positive Money's Green Central Banking Scorecard 2024 places Indonesia 9th among G20 countries. The report credits Bank Indonesia for incorporating green considerations in foreign reserves management, for supporting and investing in the government's green sukuk, and for operational support that mobilizes capital for domestic green projects. However, it also notes that high-impact monetary policy tools (e.g., green lending facilities at scale, robust collateral screens, or explicit limits on dirty lending) remain under-utilized (Positive Money, 2024). Furthermore, as part of Bank Indonesia's commitment in integrating sustainability principle into central bank's operations, Bank Indonesia's policy framework is also reinforced by instituting sustainable working culture such as green commuting and green consumption.

## *4.2 Policy Coordination on Sustainable Finance*

To ensure the effective implementation of inclusive and sustainable finance, continuous series of synergy and coordination are being carried out between Bank Indonesia, the Financial Services Authority (OJK), the Ministry of Finance, and other relevant ministries and institutions. These collaborative efforts are in line with the mandate of the Act No.4 Year 2023, authorizing Bank Indonesia to regulate and promote inclusive financing and sustainable financial practices.

As part of this mandate, Bank Indonesia, together with the Ministry of Finance and OJK, is tasked with formulating and establishing strategies, policies, and programs that support sustainable finance. This tripartite coordination is not only strategic but also essential in optimizing policy support across various domains—monetary, payment systems, macroprudential, fiscal, and microprudential. To strengthen the foundation for sustainable finance, the three institutions are also working together to develop robust data systems and supporting infrastructure. This includes the development of a sustainable taxonomy, as mandated by the Act No.4 Year 2023, which requires close coordination among Bank Indonesia, the Ministry of Finance, and OJK.

In the context of advancing sustainable finance, Bank Indonesia undertakes several forms of interagency policy coordination at the national level as well as international level.

## 4.3 Sustainable Finance Committee (SFC)

The Law No. 4 of 2023 stipulates explicitly that Bank Indonesia, in collaboration with the Ministry of Finance (MoF) and the Financial Services Authority (OJK), shall undertake coordinated efforts in promoting and developing the implementation of sustainable finance. This includes: (i) the harmonization of strategies, policies, and programs for sustainable finance; (ii) the optimization of policy support across fiscal, monetary, microprudential, macroprudential, and payment system areas; (iii) the development of databases and enabling infrastructure[1] to support the implementation of sustainable finance; and (iv) the coordinated efforts to develop and establish sustainable taxonomy. In addition, Bank Indonesia, the Ministry of Finance (MoF) and the Financial Services Authority (OJK) are also required to establish the Sustainable Finance Committee (SFC) which serves as a national platform to synergize, align, and coordinate policy strategies accross the three main agencies (financial sector authorities and fiscal authority) to enhance the sustainable finance ecosystem. This mandate reflects government target at national level to facilitate smooth transitioning society to a low-carbon economy, suggesting a well-coordinated policies formulation across related authorities. Within the SFC, Bank Indonesia's role is to facilitate the implementation of sustainable finance through monetary, macroprudential, and payment system policies formulation. Meanwhile, the OJK's support is to optimize its microprudential policy and the MoF is to advancing sustainable finance through fiscal policy support.

## 4.4 Sustainable Finance Committee (SFC) and Other Sectoral Ministries or Stakeholders

To ensure that sustainable finance policies are aligned with national policy directions and consistent with the initiatives formulated or developed by other sectoral ministries and government agencies, Bank Indonesia, the Ministry of Finance, and the Financial Services Authority (OJK) actively coordinate with a wide range of sectoral stakeholders, including the Ministry of Agriculture, the Ministry of Industry, the Ministry of Environment and Forestry, and the Ministry of Energy and Mineral Resources. This strategy is important to allow policy harmonization and coordination beyond financial sector regulation, where Bank Indonesia is also actively collaborating with certain ministry to address specific sectoral issues such as renewable energy, sustainable agriculture, and waste management.

These interagency efforts reflect a broader Bank Indonesia's commitment to integrating sustainability into Indonesia's economic development strategy. Thus far,

[1] Infrastructure for the implementation of sustainable finance include verification, certification, development of related professional competencies, development of sustainable reporting standards, and securities rating agencies.

policy coordination among Bank Indonesia, the Ministry of Finance, and OJK—as members of the Sustainable Finance Committee—has been conducted regularly with various ministries and stakeholders, particularly in the development of the Indonesia's Sustainable Finance Taxonomy (TKBI). TKBI provides a classification of economic activities that support Indonesia's efforts to achieve its Sustainable Development Goals (SDGs), encompassing economic, environmental, and social dimensions. It serves as a guiding framework to improve capital allocation and promote sustainable financing, thereby fostering low-carbon and inclusive economic growth. This coordination effort is reflected in the completion of TKBI Version 1 and Version 2, as well as the ongoing development of TKBI Version 3. Moreover, the interagency coordination is also frequently conducted by any authority who has ongoing concern to mobilize and boost green finance, sustainable finance, or blue finance, depending on certain sector to be promoted. For instance, the National Development Planning Agency calls for interagency coordination with Bank Indonesia and other related sectoral Ministries to undertake policy dialogue and promote blue financing for marine sector.

Furthermore, interagency policy coordination is also conducted through the involvement of Bank Indonesia, the Ministry of Finance, and the Financial Services Authority (OJK) as ex-officio members of the Sustainability Standards Board of the Institute of Indonesia Chartered Accountants (DSK IAI). It reflects a cross-institutional coordination aimed at building a transparent, accountable, and internationally aligned sustainability reporting ecosystem. A major milestone in this journey was achieved on July 1, 2025, when DSK IAI officially launched the Sustainability Disclosure Standards 1 on General Disclosure Requirements and Sustainability Disclosure Standards 2 on Climate-Related Disclosures by DSK IAI (Institute of Indonesia Chartered Accountants, 2025). These standards, which refer to the International Financial Reporting Standards (IFRS S1 and S2) issued by the ISSB, will take effect on January 1, 2027, marking a significant step toward harmonizing Indonesia's sustainability reporting framework with global practices. The implementation of these standards is expected to have strategic impact on the business sector, allowing the companies to be perceived as better prepared to meet global expectations from investors, trading partners, and international institutions. Moreover, the due diligence process for green financing and cross-border investments is anticipated to become faster, more efficient, and more cost-effective. This progress underscores Indonesia's proactive role in advancing sustainable finance and enhancing its competitiveness in the global market.

### 4.5 *Bilateral Coordination*

Apart from what has been established through a platform, policy coordination is also carried out by Bank Indonesia bilaterally with several sectoral Ministries/Agencies, such as the Ministry of Finance, the Financial Services Authority, the Ministry of Industry, and the National Development Planning Agency, in relation to the development of a sustainable finance ecosystem. This cooperation is driven by the need to address specific cross-institutional issues, including data and information exchange, capacity building, and the joint formulation of policies that require alignment and coordination between the involving authority/ministry.

### 4.6 International Policy Coordination

At international level, policy coordination to advance sustainable finance agenda is strengthened through Bank Indonesia's active engagement in international and regional fora. At the regional fora, Bank Indonesia's leadership and actve coordination are reflected in its role as Co-Chair—alongside the State Bank of Vietnam—of the ASEAN Senior Level Committee on Financial Integration—Task Force on Sustainable Finance (SLC-TF) for the 2024–2026 period. In 2024, the ASEAN SLC-TF has finalized the ASEAN Green Map,[2] a strategic document that: (i) articulates ASEAN's vision for a comprehensive sustainable finance ecosystem; (ii) outlines the key building blocks to realize that vision; and (iii) provides targeted, non-duplicative recommendations for regional action.

At the international fora, Bank Indonesia is an active member of the G20 Sustainable Finance Working Group (G20-SFWG), where it consistently raises concerns about barriers to sustainable finance and voices strategy to mobilize and scale up sustainable finance, particularly in emerging markets. Currently, the G20-SFWG commits the 2025 G20 Sustainable Finance Report, which outlines three strategic priorities: (i) strengthening the global sustainable finance architecture, (ii) scaling up financing for climate adaptation, and (iii) unlocking the financing potential of carbon markets. The report highlights collaborative efforts to mobilize public and private capital, enhance policy coherence, and support just transitions, especially in emerging markets and developing economies.

Since early 2025, following Indonesia's accession to the BRICS forum, Bank Indonesia has become a member of the BRICS Transition-Sustainable Finance initiative, allowing Bank Indonesia's active engagement with other BRICS' central banks in promoting sustainable finance. In this capacity, Bank Indonesia actively contributes to the development of the BRICS report on Transition-Sustainable Finance, particularly by providing input on approaches to climate-related financial risks and stress testing in the financial sector as well as strengthening the initiatives

[2] The ASEAN Green Map presents a set of strategic recommendations aimed at advancing sustainable finance across ASEAN's financial sectors. It focuses on establishing a robust and interoperable framework that supports the region's transition toward a greener economy, while addressing the diverse challenges faced by financial markets at varying stages of development. These recommendations cover the banking, capital market, and insurance sectors, and are structured around four key dimensions: (i) Financial Products and Services; (ii) Development Finance and Incentives; (iii) Transparency and Disclosure; and (iv) Risk Management and Supervision.

going forward. Moreover, as a member of the OECD, Bank Indonesia is also joining the Network for Greening the Financial System (NGFS) to actively contribute in shaping the research, data development, and climate-related scenario and to voice main concerns with respect to emerging market condition. In short, Bank Indonesia's active participation in international forums has enhanced policy synergy and coordination for sustainable finance.

## 5 Conclusion

Climate change has fundamentally reshaped the risk landscape faced by Indonesia's economy and financial system, transforming environmental challenges into systemic macro-financial risks. As a climate-vulnerable, resource-dependent economy, Indonesia faces both physical risks from climate change impacts and transition risks arising from global decarbonization. These risks directly affect price stability, financial intermediation, and long-term growth prospects, underscoring that climate change can no longer be treated as peripheral to macroeconomic and financial system stability. In this context, sustainable finance emerges not only as an environmental agenda, but as a core component of economic resilience and financial system soundness.

This chapter demonstrates that Bank Indonesia has progressively adapted its policy framework to respond these challenges by integrating sustainability into its monetary, macroprudential, payment system, and inclusiveness mandates. Through data development, research, macroprudential incentives, and coordinated regulatory actions, Bank Indonesia plays a pivotal role in mobilizing sustainable financing and managing climate-related financial risks. These efforts are strengthened by close coordination with the Ministry of Finance, the Financial Services Authority (OJK), and sectoral ministries, as well as active engagement in regional and global forums. Such coordination is essential to align policies in financial sector with sectoral transition pathways to ensure consistency, credibility, and effectiveness in sustainable finance implementation.

Looking ahead, the success of Indonesia's transition toward a low-carbon and inclusive economy will highly depend on deepening policy coherence, strengthening data and disclosure frameworks, and scaling up private sector participation in promoting sustainable finance. While public resources remain constrained, credible regulatory frameworks, robust institutional coordination, and solid international coordination aligned with the global standards can help mobilizing domestic and global capital better. Ultimately, Bank Indonesia's evolving role illustrates how central banks in emerging economies can support a just and orderly transition—preserving financial system stability while enabling sustainable economic growth that is resilient, inclusive, and aligned with Indonesia's long-term development goals.

## References


Bank of England. (2015, September 29). *Breaking the tragedy of the horizon - climate change and financial stability - speech by Mark Carney*. Retrieved from Bank of England: https://www.bankofengland.co.uk/speech/2015/breaking-the-tragedy-of-the-horizon-climate-change-and-financial-stability

BIS. (2021, September). *Assessing the effectiveness and impact of central bank and supervisory policies in greening the financial system across the Asia-Pacific*. Retrieved from Bank for International Settlements: https://www.bis.org/ifc/publ/ifcb56_06.pdf

BIS. (2022). *Principles for the Effective Management and Supervision of Climate-related Financial Risks*. Basel: BIS

BNM. (2025). *Preparing Our Financial Sector for Risks from Climate Change*. Retrieved from Bank Negara Malaysia: https://www.bnm.gov.my/climatechange#:~:text=Starting%20from%202021%2C%20we%20are,Engagement%20%26%20capacity%20building

BSP. (2022, February). *The Philippine Sustainable Finance Roadmap and Guiding Principles*. Retrieved from Bangko Sentral NG Pilipinas: https://www.bsp.gov.ph/Regulations/Issuances/2022/CL-2022-011.pdf

Dikau, S., & Volz, U. (2018, September). *Central Banking, Climate Change, and Green Finance*. Retrieved from ADBInstitute: https://www.adb.org/publications/central-banking-climate-change-and-green-finance

Institute of Indonesia Chartered Accountants. (2025, August 7). *Indonesia Launches Sustainability Disclosure Standards based on IFRS S1 and S2*. Retrieved from Institute of Indonesia Chartered Accountants: https://web.iaiglobal.or.id/Berita-IAI/detail/indonesia_launches_sustainability_disclosure_standards_based_on_ifrs_s1_and_s2#gsc.tab=0

International Energy Agency. (2022, September). *An Energy Sector Roadmap to Net Zero Emissions in Indonesia*. Retrieved from International Energy Agency: https://iea.blob.core.windows.net/assets/b496b141-8c3b-47fc-adb2-90740eb0b3b8/AnEnergySectorRoadmaptoNetZeroEmissionsinIndonesia.pdf

International Energy Agency. (2023). *Where does Indonesia get its energy?* Retrieved from International Energy Agency: https://www.iea.org/countries/indonesia/energy-mix#where-does-indonesia-get-its-energy

IPCC. (2022a). Climate Change 2022: Impacts, Adaptation and Vulnerability. Contribution of Working Group II to the Sixth Assessment Report of the Intergovernmental Panel on Climate Change. Cambridge University Press. https://doi.org/10.1017/9781009325844

IPCC. (2022b). Climate Change 2022: Mitigation of Climate Change. Contribution of Working Group III to the Sixth Assessment Report of the Intergovernmental Panel on Climate Change. Cambridge University Press. https://doi.org/10.1017/9781009157926

Juhro, S.M. (2025) 'Future central banking in emerging market economies', in *Encyclopedia of Monetary Policy, Financial Markets and Banking*. Elsevier, pp. 189–198. https://doi.org/10.1016/B978-0-44-313776-1.00118-5

Juhro, S., Robinson, I., Rahadyan, H., & Rishanty, A. (2025). *Climate Risks, Just Transition, and Central Bank Policy for Sustainable Economic Growth*. Retrieved from Jurnal Ekonomi Indonesia: https://jurnal.isei.or.id/index.php/isei/article/view/587

MAS. (2019, November 11). *New US$2 billion Investments Programme to Support Growth of Green Finance in Singapore*. Retrieved from Monetary Authority of Singapore: https://www.mas.gov.sg/news/media-releases/2019/new-us$2-billion-investments-programme-to-support-growth-of-green-finance-in-singapore

MAS. (2021, May 19). *Accelerating Green Finance - Guide for climate-related disclosures and framework for green trade finance*. Retrieved from Monetary Authority of Singapore: https://www.mas.gov.sg/news/media-releases/2021/accelerating-green-finance

MAS. (2023a, April 20). *MAS Launches Finance for Net Zero Action Plan*. Retrieved from Monetary Authority of Singapore: https://www.mas.gov.sg/news/media-releases/2023/mas-launches-finance-for-net-zero-action-plan#

MAS. (2023b, December). *Singapore-Asia Taxonomy for Sustainable Finance*. Retrieved from Monetary Authority of Singapore: https://www.mas.gov.sg/-/media/mas-media-library/development/sustainable-finance/singaporeasia-taxonomy-updated.pdf

Ministry of Environment Republic of Indonesia. (2025, May 6). *Indonesia First Biennial Transparency Report (BTR1)*. Retrieved from United Nations Climate Change: https://unfccc.int/sites/default/files/resource/INDONESIA%20BTR1_SUBMIT%20FINAL.pdf

Positive Money. (2024, September). *The Green Central Banking Scorecard: 2024 Edition*. Retrieved from Green Central Banking: https://www.datocms-assets.com/132494/1736848825-positive-money-green-central-banking-scorecard-report-2024-v8.pdf

SFIA. (2021). *The ASEAN Taxonomy Board*. Retrieved from Sustainable Finance Institute Asia: https://www.sfinstitute.asia/asean-taxonomy/asean-taxonomy-board/

# Chapter 18
# Indonesia Taxonomy for Sustainable Finance

**Henry Rialdi, Joko Siswanto, Jarot Suroyo, Yuki Yasarani, and Amanda Sarina Rumbaf**

**Abstract** The global urgency to address climate change has intensified the demand for robust frameworks that channel financial resources into sustainable development. The taxonomy for sustainable finance a classification system to identify, define, and standardize sustainable economic activities. The Indonesia Financial Services Authority, in collaboration with relevant ministries and stakeholders, has launched the Indonesia Taxonomy for Sustainable Finance/*Taksonomi untuk Keuangan Berkelanjutan Indonesia* (TKBI) since 2023, drawing from the ASEAN Taxonomy for Sustainable Finance (ATSF) and national policies. The TKBI provides guidance for sustainable projects that support Indonesia's long-term goal of achieving net-zero emissions (NZE) by 2060 or earlier.

**Keywords** Sustainable finance · Green taxonomy · Indonesian taxonomy for sustainable finance (TKBI) · Environment, social, and governance (ESG) · Net zero emissions (NZE)

## 1 Introduction

Amidst current climate change and the challenges of global and geopolitical dynamics, sustainable economic development remains a fundamental problem, requiring a coherent approach that balances economic, environmental, and social considerations. This process undoubtedly requires tangible activities that are carried out gradually and tailored to each jurisdiction's unique conditions and readiness, while also safeguarding future generations' economic and environmental well being.

The global implementation of policies, regulations, and initiatives aimed at advancing sustainable finance reflects a unanimous commitment to achieving net-zero emissions. As countries advance their sustainable development agendas, the

H. Rialdi (✉) · J. Siswanto · J. Suroyo · Y. Yasarani · A. S. Rumbaf
Financial Services Authority (OJK), Jakarta, Indonesia
e-mail: Henry.Rialdi@ojk.go.id; jarot_s@ojk.go.id; Yuki.Yasarani@ojk.go.id; amanda.sarina@ojk.go.id



S. M. Juhro et al. (eds.), *Sustainable Economy: The Indonesian Pathways*,
https://doi.org/10.1007/978-981-92-1215-6_18

need for a standardized framework to classify sustainable activities has become increasingly urgent to maintain consistency and establish a shared "common language." Taxonomies—classification systems defining what constitutes "sustainable" activities—have emerged globally as critical policy tools. Taxonomies serve to guide investors, prevent greenwashing, and strengthen disclosure regimes. Sustainable finance taxonomies have become the "operating system" that links corporate reporting, product labelling, and financial-sector metrics into a coherent policy stack (Hummel & Bauernhofer, 2024).

By 2024, over 60 national and regional taxonomies have been developed or are currently in development (SBFN, 2024). The number is anticipated to increase into the hundreds, encompassing both privately developed taxonomies and widely recognized official taxonomies. With the proliferation of taxonomy guidelines for sustainable finance over the past 4 years, prioritizing interoperability is essential to prevent fragmentation and ensure consistent advancement toward the Net Zero Emissions (NZE).

The development of taxonomies is accelerating globally due to cross-border initiatives initiated by establishment of the Common Ground Taxonomy (CGT) by the European Union and China, followed by Singapore's participation in 2024 which evolves into the Multi-Jurisdiction Common Ground Taxonomy (M-CGT). This collaboration aims to improve interoperability of jurisdictions and produce a technical reference document for stakeholders. Efforts to support climate change adaptation financing and strengthen sustainable taxonomy implementation are also underway (IPSF, 2024).

Indonesia's vast natural resources and biodiversity, which are often referred to as the "lungs of the world" offers a strategic role. The Government of Indonesia (GoI) has implemented various policies aimed at promoting long-term sustainable economic development. The 1945 Constitution of the Republic of Indonesia has set the foundation of the fundamental principle of the country's sustainable development which ensures the provision of good and healthy living environment as well as utilization of the land and waters for the optimal welfare of the people (Republic of Indonesia, 1945). Following the Paris Agreement ratification under Law No. 16 of 2016 (Republic of Indonesia, 2016), commitments to reduce greenhouse gas emissions are set in the Nationally Determined Contributions (NDCs), as well as the establishment of a Net Zero target for 2060 or earlier, and strengthened by Presidential Regulation No. 111 of 2022 concerning the Implementation of the Sustainable Development Goals (Republic of Indonesia, 2022).

The legal framework for sustainable finance has been enhanced through the enactment of Law No. 4 of 2023 on the Development and Strengthening of the Financial Sector (FSOL) (Republic of Indonesia, 2023), which emphasize the requirements for financial sector business actors to implement sustainable finance. This legislation expands the definition of sustainable finance to encompass transition finance and requires the coordinated development of a sustainable taxonomy. Furthermore, Law No. 59 of 2024 concerning the National Long-Term Development Plan for 2024–2045 incorporates the Sustainable Development Goals (SDGs) and highlights the importance of environmentally sustainable growth (Republic of Indonesia, 2024).

The early trajectory of sustainable finance in Indonesia has been shaped predominantly by the Financial Services Authority/*Otoritas Jasa Keuangan* (OJK), which, in its capacity as regulator and supervisor of the financial sector, has introduced a series of policies designed to align financial markets with the GoI's climate objectives. Within this institutional framework, the Indonesia Taxonomy for Sustainable Finance /*Taksonomi Keuangan Berkelanjutan Indonesia* (TKBI) occupies a pivotal role. Conceived as a collaborative initiative involving multiple stakeholders, TKBI provides a structured classification of economic activities that integrates environmental, economic, and social considerations. In doing so, it anchors national sustainability goals to operational financial practice. More specifically, the taxonomy is intended to channel investment flows and capital allocation toward projects and activities that substantively contribute to Indonesia's commitments under the SDGs and long-term climate strategies, thereby reinforcing the country's transition pathway to net-zero emissions by 2060 or earlier.

# 2 Literature Review

## *2.1 Definition*

Taxonomy, in the context of sustainable finance, denotes a structured classification system designed to identify economic activities that make a substantial contribution to internationally and nationally determined environmental objectives, while simultaneously ensuring that such activities do not inflict significant harm on other environmental or social priorities (World Bank, 2021). Among existing frameworks, the European Union (EU) Taxonomy has emerged as a global benchmark, formally embedded within the Sustainable Finance Disclosure Regulation (SFDR) and interlinked with corporate reporting obligations such as the Non-Financial Reporting Directive (NFRD) and the Corporate Sustainability Reporting Directive (CSRD). Beyond the European experience, China's "Green Bond Endorsed Project Catalogue" and the ASEAN Taxonomy for Sustainable Finance (ATSF) initiatives illustrate regional approaches that seek to harmonize definitional standards while maintaining sensitivity to local economic, environmental, and institutional contexts. Furthermore, several jurisdictions, including Singapore and South Africa, have developed taxonomies that explicitly recognize transition activities, thereby underscoring the importance of flexibility and pragmatism in accommodating the developmental trajectories of emerging and middle-income economies.

Comparative analyses of sustainable finance frameworks reveal a proliferation of taxonomies and related guidance instruments worldwide. These range from publicly mandated frameworks—such as those established in the European Union, China, Colombia, Mexico, and Russia—to regional initiatives like the ASEAN Taxonomy, as well as voluntary market-based standards including the International Capital Market Association (ICMA) Green Bond Principles and the Climate Bonds

Initiative. Despite differences in institutional design, scope, and sectoral emphasis, a striking degree of convergence is observable: most taxonomies prioritize core sectors such as energy, transport, buildings, and industry, and advance objectives linked to climate change mitigation, adaptation, biodiversity conservation, and circular economy principles. A central feature across these instruments is the incorporation of "do no significant harm" (DNSH) safeguards, which function to ensure that activities making positive contributions to one objective do not simultaneously undermine others (Bhattacharyya, 2025).

An important emerging trend is the incorporation of transition-sensitive provisions. For instance, the European Union's Complementary Climate Delegated Act conditionally includes activities such as natural gas and nuclear power under strict technical criteria, thereby acknowledging the role of intermediate solutions in facilitating orderly transitions. Similar transition-oriented elements are evident in other jurisdictions, suggesting the gradual formation of a global consensus: financially viable and socially acceptable transition pathways are as essential as "dark-green" activities in steering economies toward net-zero trajectories (Tettamanzi et al., 2024). This recognition reflects an evolving scientific and policy understanding that sustainability is a dynamic continuum rather than a binary categorization, necessitating frameworks that can accommodate incremental progress while upholding environmental integrity.

The academic literature offers several critical insights into the functional role of taxonomies in advancing sustainable finance. A central contribution lies in their capacity to reduce divergence across environmental, social, and governance (ESG) ratings, an issue that has long undermined comparability and investor confidence. By providing a science-based and transparent classification of economic activities, taxonomies furnish investors and financial institutions with more robust and reliable benchmarks for evaluating sustainability performance. Beyond harmonization, taxonomies also serve as regulatory safeguards against greenwashing. In the absence of clear and enforceable standards, markets are susceptible to a "race to the bottom," wherein financial products may be rebranded as sustainable without delivering measurable environmental impact (greenwashing). By establishing minimum thresholds for sustainability, mandatory taxonomies mitigate this risk, thereby enhancing market credibility, strengthening investor confidence, and fostering the legitimacy of sustainable finance instruments (Inderst & Opp, 2025).

The empirical evidence from the European Union further illustrates that taxonomies can function as catalysts for corporate transformation. The requirement to evaluate and disclose alignment with taxonomy criteria has stimulated strategic reflection within firms, encouraging them to reconfigure long-term business models and operational practices in pursuit of low-carbon pathways. This process has fostered a competitive "race to the top," in which corporations actively seek to demonstrate superior sustainability performance, not merely for regulatory compliance but also as a means of securing market differentiation and reputational capital (Hummel & Bauernhofer, 2024).

Theoretical contribution complement these empirical findings by situating taxonomies within broader welfare economics debates. Inderst and Opp (2025) emphasize that a taxonomy enhance social welfare under conditions where environmental regulations are insufficiently stringent or where financial frictions inhibit the flow of capital into green investments. In such contexts, taxonomies do not substitute for core instruments like carbon pricing but rather function as complementary mechanisms that improve capital allocation and accelerate the transition to a sustainable economy. This insights underscore the importance of embedding taxonomies within a comprehensive policy mix that integrates fiscal, regulatory, and market-based instruments to maximize systemic effectiveness.

## 2.2 *Principles of Taxonomies*

The scientific and regulatory literature identifies a set of foundational principles that underpin the design and legitimacy of sustainable finance taxonomies. The Climate Bonds Initiative (CBI) emphasizes three essential elements: a binary system of classification in which activities are clearly identified as eligible or non-eligible; an evidentiary basis grounded in robust scientific research; and the recognition of taxonomies as living instruments that require periodic revision to reflect technological and policy advancements (CBI, 2021). Expanding on these insights, the Bank for International Settlements (BIS, 2021) together with the CBI delineates four broader principles. First, a taxonomy must articulate a clear objective, explicitly linking classification criteria to sustainability goals and levels of ambition. Second, it should define its scope and sectoral coverage, specifying industries, economic activities, or entities to which the framework applies. Third, the taxonomy should operationalize objectives into quantifiable benchmarks by identifying activities that make substantial contributions and setting measurable targets. Fourth, the framework must employ scientifically validated screening criteria to ensure rigor, credibility, and transparency in its application.

Comparative observations of taxonomies developed in other jurisdictions—including the EU, Canada, Australia, South Korea, Malaysia, Singapore, Thailand, as well as Latin America and the Caribbean—reveal a striking convergence around several scientific and policy-oriented principles. These include reliance on rigorous scientific evidence, interoperability with globally recognized frameworks, measurable contributions to environmental objectives, adherence to social safeguards, alignment with national NZE strategies, provisions for credible transition activities, and adaptability as living documents. Taken together, these principles underscore an emerging global consensus on the essential features of effective taxonomies, while allowing for context-specific modifications to address the distinct developmental and institutional challenges faced by individual economies.

At the regional level, the ATSF provides a guiding framework for ASEAN Member States (AMS) balancing ambition with the diverse economic structures and levels of readiness across the region. The ATSF rests on five main principles: 1) it serves as an overarching guide and common language for member states, complementing existing sustainability initiatives within members' jurisdictions; 2) it contextualizes international taxonomies to regional realities towards a sustainable ASEAN; 3) it ensures inclusivity by accommodating varying levels development and transition pathways of members; 4) it upholds scientific credibility; and 5) it maintains cross-sectoral alignment on sustainability initiatives across banking, insurance, and capital markets.

At the national level, TKBI exemplifies the localization of these global and regional principles. TKBI integrates environmental, economic, and social dimensions into its classification of economic activities, aligning Indonesia's sustainable development agenda and Net Zero Emission (NZE) commitments. Its design is anchored in three guiding principles: 1) scientific and credible, achieved by embedding national and international best practices in science, technology, and policy, science, and technology; 2) interoperable while safeguarding national interests and enabling Indonesia's gradual and just transition; and 3) inclusive, ensuring applicability across multiple user scales, from large corporations to Small, and Medium Enterprises/SMEs. This framework reflects Indonesia's commitment to both ambition and accessibility in driving sustainable finance.

## 2.3 *Global Developments in Taxonomy for Sustainable Finance*

Taxonomies provide a scientifically grounded and structured mechanism through which countries can ensure that assets, activities, projects, and entities designated as green, social, or sustainable demonstrably contribute to international environmental commitments while and simultaneously advancing national development priorities. Functioning as a shared conceptual and operational language, taxonomies link sustainability labels to measurable impact and outcomes. To date, more than 60 sustainable finance taxonomies have either been developed or are underway across national jurisdictions, regional, and multilateral platforms. According to the Sustainable Banking and Finance Network (SBFN) Toolkit on Sustainable Finance Taxonomies, this figure is expected to grow substantially, potentially reaching into the hundreds as both official and market-driven frameworks proliferate globally (Fig. 18.1).

The CBI identifies three principal methodological approaches to defining sustainable categories within taxonomies. The first is the whitelist-based approach, which specifies eligible projects or activities within particular sectors or sub-sectors. This model has been adopted in jurisdictions such as China, Russia, and Mongolia. The second is the technical screening criteria (TSC) based taxonomy, which establishes quantitative thresholds and detailed criteria that activities must meet to be classified as sustainable. Examples include the EU Taxonomy, ASEAN Plus Standards, and frameworks in Singapore, Thailand, Colombia, and South Africa. The third is the principle-based taxonomy, which formulates high-level guiding principles without prescribing specific activities, requirements, or thresholds. Japan,

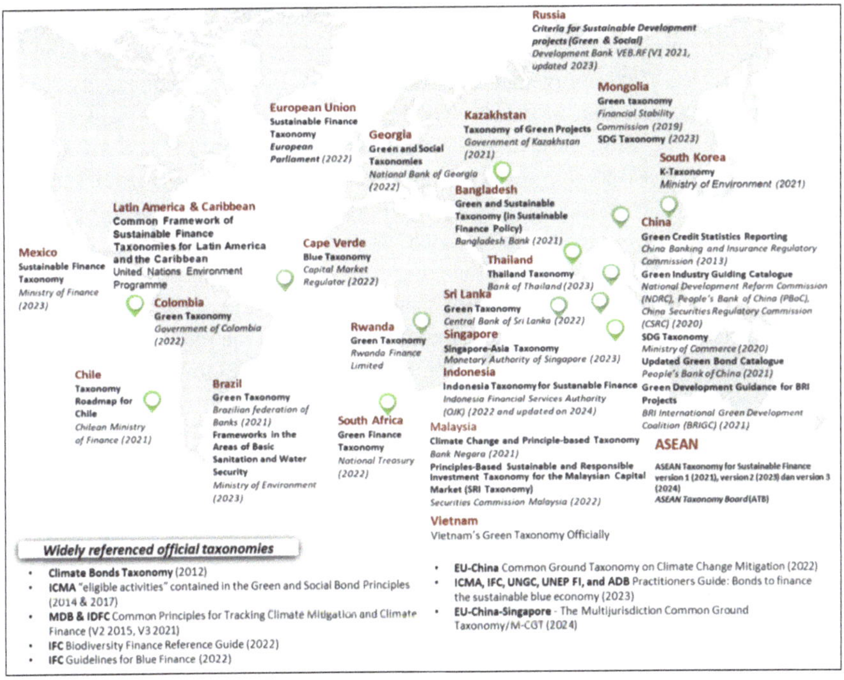


**Fig. 18.1** Examples of green/sustainable taxonomy (SBFN, 2024 and various sources)

Malaysia, the ASEAN Foundation Framework, and the ICMA Green Bond Principles exemplify this category. In practice, many taxonomies operationalize sustainability classifications through hybrid approaches, combining principle-based rules with detailed technical thresholds for priority sectors. Such blended methodologies allow for both economy-wide applicability and sector-specific precision.

The ATSF illustrates this hybrid model. It employs a multi-tier framework: a foundational framework built on principle-based guidance, complemented by "plus standards" that incorporate technical screening criteria for sectors where specificity is required. Similarly, Indonesia's TKBI distinguishes between user scales, applying a sector-agnostic decision tree (SDT) for medium-sized enterprises, while imposing detailed TSCs on larger corporates and non-SME activities. This design underscores the importance of inclusivity, ensuring accessibility for smaller enterprises while maintaining scientific rigor for larger institutions.

Recent developments in sustainable finance taxonomies at the global, regional, and national levels highlight not only strong commitment but also growing opportunities to mobilise capital and direct financing toward sustainability goals. These frameworks are increasingly viewed as indispensable instruments for accelerating the transition to net-zero emissions and for aligning financial systems with both international climate agreements and domestic development priorities.

The development of sustainable finance taxonomies is also characterized by intensifying cross-border collaboration. A prominent example is the M-CGT, which seeks to enhance interoperability across diverse framework. In 2022, the European Union and China jointly established the Common Ground Taxonomy (CGT), building upon the EU Taxonomy and the China Green Bond Catalogue. By 2024, Singapore has joined this initiative, leading to the publication of the Common Ground Taxonomy Multi-Jurisdiction Activity. Anticipated future expansions will further broaden its scope, providing technical reference points for financial institutions, corporations, investors, and regulators. Parallel to these interoperability initiatives, several reports and studies have advanced adaptation and resilience taxonomies, intended to facilitate financing for climate change adaptation and to strengthen the global implementation of sustainable finance frameworks. These collective efforts reflect a growing international consensus on the role of taxonomies as both scientific and policy tools in guiding the financial sector toward sustainability transformation.

## 2.4 Indonesia Taxonomy for Sustainable Finance (TKBI)

The development of Indonesia's sustainable finance taxonomy reflects both domestic imperatives and the broader global momentum toward establishing standardized classification systems for sustainable activities. Responding to advances in international sustainable finance policies and the market's growing demand for a standardized classification for sustainable activities, OJK initiated the formulation of a national taxonomy in 2021. This initiative was embedded within the Indonesia Sustainable Finance Roadmap Phase II, a comprehensive policy framework designed to cultivate a resilient and inclusive sustainable finance ecosystem.

## 2.5 TKBI Framework

The developmental trajectory of Indonesia's taxonomy began with the Indonesian Green Taxonomy (THI), which was initially confined to environmental objectives. Over time, the scope was expanded and institutionalized into the TKBI (OJK, 2024), reflecting a more comprehensive integration of economic, environmental, and social dimensions. TKBI thus functions as a national classification framework for economic activities that substantively advance Indonesia's Sustainable Development Goals (SDGs) and long-term climate commitments, particularly the net-zero emissions (NZE) target by 2060 or earlier. By aligning economic activities definitional standards with the SDGs, TKBI reinforces the harmonization of economic performance with ecological integrity and social equity.

The TKBI is primarily anchored in the ATSF, while integrating key national policies and sectoral regulations. Established by the ASEAN Taxonomy Board under the mandate of ASEAN Finance Ministers and Central Bank Governors, the ATSF articulates a collective regional approach to sustainable economic activities and

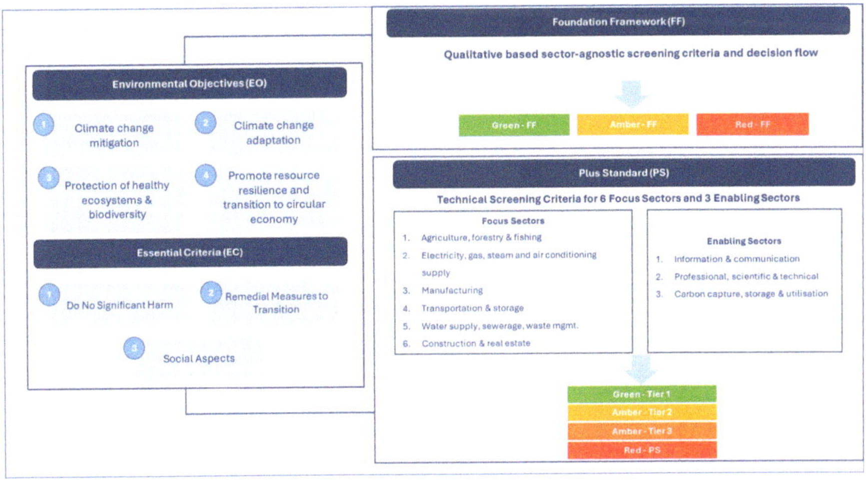


**Fig. 18.2** ASEAN Taxonomy Framework (ATSF, 2024)

investment. Whereas regional taxonomies promote consistency and interoperability across markets, national frameworks tailor classification systems to reflect distinct development priorities and policy objectives. Within this context, the ATSF functions as an overarching guide, fostering alignment, minimizing fragmentation, and consolidating the region's credibility in global sustainable finance.

The ATSF holds particular significance for its role in providing a unified ASEAN voice, thereby reducing definitional inconsistencies and enhancing investor confidence. By promoting clarity and comparability, it lays the foundation for capital allocation and transition finance at scale, establishing the contours of a sustainable ASEAN asset class capable of attracting regional and international investment.

The ATSF is structured as a multi-tiered framework composed of two layers (Fig. 18.2): the Foundation Framework, which employs a principle-based, sector-agnostic approach relying on guiding questions, decision trees, and qualitative criteria; and the Plus Standard, which introduces detailed technical screening criteria for six focus sectors and three enabling sectors, benchmarked against Paris Agreement objectives. Underpinned by Environmental Objectives (EOs) and Essential Criteria (ECs), activities are classified through a "traffic-light" system, indicating their degree of sustainability relative to environmental objectives. This tiered design accommodates the heterogeneity of readiness levels across ASEAN Member States, thereby enhancing both inclusivity and scientific credibility.

Building upon the ATSF, Indonesia's TKBI incorporates several distinctive features (Fig. 18.3), as its scope is selective, focusing not on all economic activities enumerated in the Indonesian Standard Industrial Classification (KBLI), but rather on those that make demonstrable contributions to environmental goals (NDC) while accounting for economic and social dimensions. Enabling activities that facilitate broader transitions are also considered, reflecting a pragmatic recognition of the interconnectedness of sectors. In this respect, TKBI represents both a technical

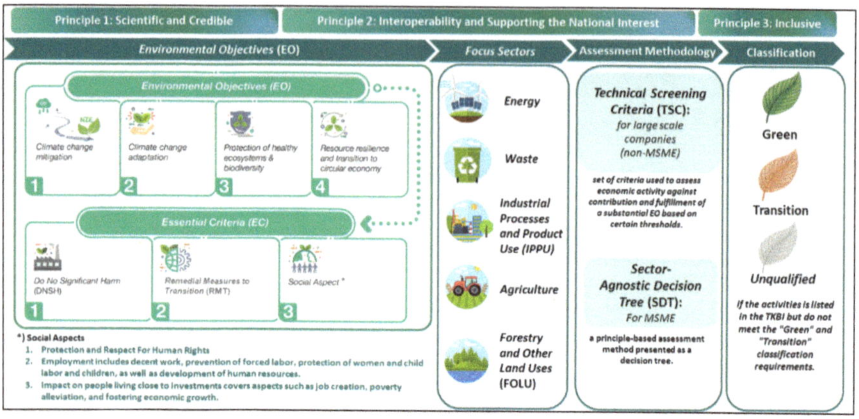


**Fig. 18.3** Conceptual Framework of Indonesia Taxonomy for Sustainable Finance

classification instrument and a strategic policy lever for aligning financial flows with Indonesia's sustainable development trajectory.

The TKBI has been designed with several strategic objectives. First, it aims to minimize risks of interpretive ambiguity, greenwashing, social washing, and impact washing through the application of a scientifically credible framework. Second, TKBI provides the foundational basis for policy formulation, including sustainability reporting requirements, incentive and disincentive mechanisms, and the innovation of sustainable financial products and services. Third, the framework promotes inclusivity by expanding access to sustainable finance for both medium-sized enterprises and larger corporations, thereby fostering financial literacy, deepening market participation, and stimulating economic growth. Fourth, TKBI strengthens inter-sectoral collaboration by fostering synergies across regulators, ministries, industry associations, and other stakeholders, thereby embedding sustainable finance principles into Indonesia's broader development architecture.

The formulation of TKBI has been inherently collaborative, spearheaded by OJK in coordination with relevant ministries, institutions, and private sector actors. Stakeholder engagement has been extensive, encompassing courtesy meetings, technical workshops, focus group discussions, and public consultations, thereby ensuring that the taxonomy reflects diverse perspectives and policy priorities while maintaining scientific rigor.

TKBI is designed with an emphasis on the principles of scientific and credible, interoperable, and in favor of national interests, and inclusive for users of all scales. The ATSF and national policy serve as the primary references for the TKBI framework (Fig. 18.4), elements, and criteria, in addition to the taxonomies of other relevant countries. The TKBI has adopted four environmental objectives (EO): EO1-Climate Change Mitigation, EO2-Climate Change Adaptation, EO3-Protection of Healthy Ecosystems and Biodiversity, and EO4-Resource Resilience and the Transition to a Circular Economy; and three Essential Criteria (EC), namely

**Table 18.1** Environmental Objectives (EO)

| Environmental Objectives (EO) | Description |
|---|---|
| EO1-Climate Change Mitigation | Focuses on the decarbonization pathway, which refers to an activity aligned with the commitment to limit the global temperature rise to well below 2 °C and striving to limit the increase to 1.5 °C, as outlined in the Paris agreement. An activity is considered to fulfill EO1 if it contributes to one or more of the following: avoids GHG emissions; reduces GHG emissions; or enables others to avoid or reduce GHG emissions |
| EO2-Climate Change Adaptation | To reduce the negative effects caused by climate change and increase resilience to the adverse physical impacts of current and future climate change. Resilience is defined as the ability of an activity to remain functional over time in the event of disruptions/disasters caused by climate change |
| EO3-Protection Of Healthy Ecosystems and Biodiversity | Focuses on the incorporation of conservation, restoration, and protection mechanisms of natural ecosystem and biodiversity. EO3 is location and context-specific, typically relevant for activities related to the agriculture, forestry and fisheries, real estate, and manufacturing sectors. EO3 aims to promote positive impacts and minimize or eliminate negative impacts of an activity on natural ecosystems and biodiversity. |
| EO4-Resource Resilience and the Transition to a Circular Economy | Focuses on the materiality of activities, and their impacts to business operations, through adoption of the following principles of circularity: a) Minimising resource use; b) Optimising resource yield; c) Closing resource loops through effective waste management. |

**Table 18.2** Essential Criteria (EC)

| Essential Criteria (EC) | Description |
|---|---|
| Do No Significant Harm (DNSH) | Refers to the principle that an activity contributing to one EO should not negatively affect, cause harm, or cause damage to other EOs. |
| Remedial Measures to Transition (RMT) | Measures to ensure that any significant actual or potential damage or loss can be eliminated or minimized, so that the impact becomes insignificant. If, after a DNSH assessment, it is found that an activity causes significant harm to other EOs, RMT must be undertaken. The implementation of RMT needs to be planned effectively to eliminate all significant harm within 5 years of the assessment date. |
| Social Aspects (SA) | SA relates to the condition where an activity potentially causes harm or negative impact on the social conditions within an environment. The essential part for the SA assessment is compliance with relevant social aspect regulations. |

EC1-Do No Significant Harm (DNSH), EC2-Remedial Measures to Transition (RMT), and EC3-Social Aspect (SA) (Tables 18.1 and 18.2).

The TKBI employs a dual methodological approach tailored to the scale and nature of economic entities, thereby ensuring both scientific rigor and inclusivity. For larger corporations and non-SMEs, the framework utilizes Technical Screening Criteria (TSC). These criteria consist of threshold-based, quantifiable benchmarks

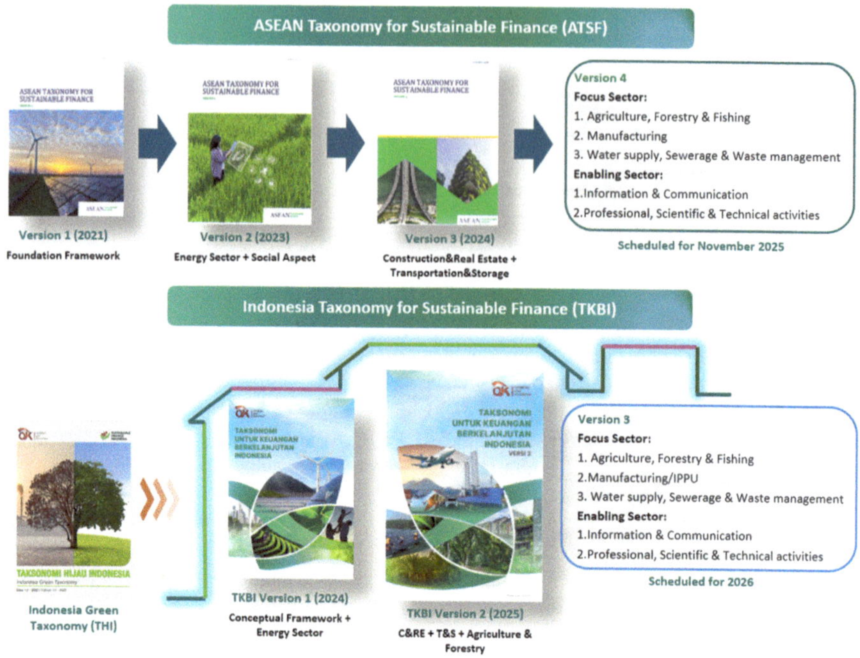


**Fig. 18.4** Alignment of TKBI and ATSF Development

designed to determine whether a given activity makes a substantial contribution to specific EOs. The TSC provides detailed parameters that align corporate-level activities with sustainability outcomes, thereby reducing ambiguity and enhancing comparability across sectors.

For small, and medium-sized enterprises, TKBI applies SDT, which takes the form of a principle-based assessment tool structured as a decision tree, incorporating guiding questions that directly relate to the taxonomy's environmental objectives. The SDT acknowledges the capacity constraints often faced by medium-sized enterprises, providing an accessible yet systematic mechanism for evaluating sustainability contributions without imposing disproportionate reporting burdens.

Upon completion of the TKBI assessment, activities are classified into one of three classifications. "Green" activities are those that fully satisfy the technical or principle-based criteria, demonstrating a substantial contribution to environmental and sustainability goals. "Transition" activities denote economic actions that are not yet fully aligned with green thresholds but are demonstrably on a credible pathway toward achieving sustainability. Activities that fail to meet either of these thresholds are designated "Unqualified". This classification underscores the taxonomy's role not only in validating best practices but also in facilitating progressive transitions across diverse sectors of the economy.

In general, the taxonomy's classification process can be illustrated conceptually in the figure below (Fig. 18.5):

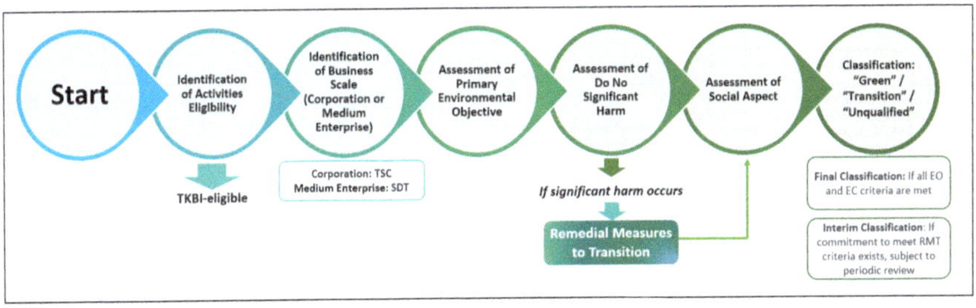


**Fig. 18.5** TKBI Assessment Flow

If an economic activity falls within the defined scope of TKBI, it is designated as "TKBI-eligible." The assessment process then proceeds by differentiating the evaluation approach according to the scale of the business entity. Corporate entities and other entities larger than medium size enterprises as defined by Law are assessed using TSC, which establish thresholds for determining substantial contributions to specified EOs. Medium-sized enterprises, by contrast, are evaluated through the SDT, which employs principle-based guiding questions to assess alignment with sustainability objectives in a more accessible and capacity-sensitive manner.

Once the segment-specific pathway has been identified, the activity undergoes a multi-layered evaluation. First, it is examined for its direct contribution to one or more primary EOs. This is followed by a DNSH assessment to ensure that, while contributing positively to one EO, the activity does not generate adverse effects on others. In instances where potential harm is identified, a RMT must be applied to address or offset the negative impacts. Finally, a social safeguard assessment is conducted to ensure that activities uphold minimum social standards and do not exacerbate inequality or exclusion. Based on this comprehensive evaluation, activities are classified into one of three categories: "Green," for activities that fully align with sustainability criteria; "Transition," for those that are credibly advancing toward green thresholds; and "Unqualified," for activities that do not meet the established requirements.

The TKBI framework is intended for application by a wide range of actors, including corporations, financial institutions, investors, and regulators, providing each with a scientifically grounded tool for assessing the sustainability profile of economic activities. Importantly, TKBI is being developed in phases (Table 18.3), allowing for gradual expansion and refinement over time. This staged approach ensures that coverage progressively encompasses sectors identified in Indonesia's NDC, along with enabling sectors critical for decarbonization and resilience. Through its phased and adaptive design, TKBI seeks to balance scientific rigor with practical feasibility, ensuring its relevance and usability across a diverse national economy.

In its initial phase (Version 1), TKBI concentrated on activities within the energy sector, grouping them into two broad categories. The first category addresses the procurement of electricity, gas, steam/hot water, and chilled air, encompassing

Table 18.3 The development of TKBI and possible future work

| TKBI version 1 (2024) | TKBI version 2 (2025) | TKBI version 3 (2026) |
|---|---|---|
| • The conceptual framework of the TKBI<br>• Focus sector: Energy sector<br>• Enabling sectors:<br>- CCS (Carbon Capture Storage)<br>- Research, development, and innovation for CCS technology<br>- Energy efficiency | Focus sectors:<br>- Construction and Real Estate (C&RE);<br>- Transportation and Storage (T&S); and<br>- some of Agriculture, Forestry and Fishing (AFF) sectors (forestry and palm oil plantation).<br>Enabling sectors: embedded in all three activities in the focus sector<br>Additional Annex:<br>- Annex 8 Use Case of Taxonomy: consumptive use of proceeds, including credit/financing/ insurance; and<br>- Annex 12—The Climate Risk Vulnerability Assessment (CRVA). | Focus sectors:<br>- Agriculture, Forestry and Fishing (AFF);<br>- Manufacturing/ IPPU; and<br>- Water Supply, Sewerage & Waste Management (WSSWM)<br>Enabling sectors:<br>- Information and communication; and<br>- Professional, scientific & technical activities |
| Future work:<br>Development of TSC for updated NDC and other enabling sectors. | | |

electricity generation from new and renewable energy sources, the early retirement of coal-fired power plants, and the extraction of critical minerals essential for clean energy technologies. The second category focuses on the broader transition toward NZE, capturing enabling activities such as energy conservation and efficiency services, as well as research, development, and innovation in carbon capture and storage (CCS) technologies. This dual structure reflects both the immediate priorities of decarbonization and the enabling pathways required to sustain long-term systemic transformation.

Version 2, formally launched in February 2025, significantly expanded TKBI's sectoral scope to include the Construction and Real Estate (C&RE) sector, the Transportation and Storage (T&S) sector, and selected activities within the Agriculture, Forestry, and Fishing (AFF) sector, with a particular emphasis on forestry and oil palm plantations. Within C&RE, covered activities now include the construction of new buildings, retrofitting of existing buildings, acquisition and ownership of residential and civil structures, land preparation, installation of renewable energy systems, deployment of energy-efficient technologies, and adoption of performance monitoring and regulatory systems. In T&S, the taxonomy incorporates land, maritime, and aviation transport, together with related infrastructure and enabling services. The AFF coverage extends to sustainable forest management, plantation forestry, development of non-timber forest products, conservation and restoration practices, supply chain governance, and sustainable palm oil plantation management. Collectively, these expansions reflect the taxonomy's progressive incorporation of high-emission and high-impact sectors central to Indonesia's development trajectory.

Preparation is currently underway for Version 3, anticipated in early 2026, which will align with ATSF Version 4. This iteration is expected to introduce TSC for three additional NDC-related sectors: Agriculture, Forestry, and Fishing (AFF); Manufacturing / Industrial Processes/Product Use (IPPU); and Waste, Sanitation, Sewerage, and Waste Management (WSSWM). Furthermore, Version 3 will extend coverage to two enabling sectors—Information and Communication (IC), and Professional, Scientific, and Technical Activities (PST)—underscoring the taxonomy's recognition of cross-cutting services that enable decarbonization, innovation, and systemic resilience.

The TKBI is explicitly designed as a dynamic, evolving instrument. It is subject to regular review and updating in order to incorporate scientific and technological advances, as well as policy developments at both the national and international levels. Over time, this iterative process is expected to solidify TKBI as a central regulatory and market-oriented framework consistent with Indonesia's Financial Sector Omnibus Law (FSOL). By maintaining adaptability, scientific integrity, and alignment with global standards, TKBI is positioned to remain both credible and effective in steering Indonesia's financial system toward long-term sustainability and climate objectives.

## 2.6 *The Unique Features of TKBI*

A defining characteristic of TKBI lies in its emphasis on interoperability. For a taxonomy to be effective in mobilizing sustainable finance across borders, it must conform to international best practices and provide a standardized "common language" that enhances interoperability and credibility among global investors. TKBI incorporates this principle by aligning its "Green" classification with internationally recognized benchmarks, including trajectories consistent with the 1.5 °C pathway and net-zero emissions (NZE) by 2050. At the same time, it innovatively introduces a "Transition" classification to capture the specificities of Indonesia's economic structure and developmental stage. This dual classification acknowledges both the global imperative of decarbonization and the national context and demand for a just and gradual transition (Fig. 18.6).

Furthermore, the TKBI introduces several new initiatives that are tailored to Indonesia's national interests and policies priorities. For example, it establishes TSC for the mining and quarrying of critical minerals that are essential for clean energy technologies and NZE, with certain requirements and classified as a "transition". It also incorporates TSC for the construction of new buildings and residential areas for Low Income Communities /Masyarakat Berpenghasilan Rendah (MBR); the adoption of Sustainable Aviation Fuel (SAF) in accordance with the Ministry Roadmap; and includes carbon capture and storage (CCS) activities in both production and protected forests.

Beyond these core classifications, TKBI integrates several novel features designed to reflect Indonesia's national interests and policy priorities. Among these

| | EU Taxonomy | ASEAN Taxonomy | Australia Taxonomy | Singapore Taxonomy | Thailand Taxonomy | TKBI | |
|---|---|---|---|---|---|---|---|
| Green | **Lifecycle GHG emissions** from the generation of electricity by the entire facility **<100 gCO2 eq/kWh** | Lifecycle GHG emissions from the generation of electricity by the entire facility **<100 gCO2e/kWh.** | Until 2030 the emission intensity measured during the **life cycle of the power plant is less than 100g CO2e/kWh** | **Lifecycle GHG emissions <100 gCO2e/kWh.** | **Lifecycle GHG emissions <100 gCO2e/kWh.** | Lifecycle GHG emissions from the generation of electricity by the entire facility **<100 gCO2e/kWh.** | ***Interoperable*** *There are similarities across the taxonomy* |
| Transition | N/A | Lifecycle GHG emissions from the generation of electricity by the entire facility<br>• **Amber T2:** ≥100 and <425 gCO2e/kWh.<br>• **Amber T3:** ≥425 and <510 gCO2e/kWh. | N/A | **Direct emissions <220 gCO2e/kWh.** | **Lifecycle GHG emissions <381 gCO2e/kWh.** | Lifecycle GHG emissions from the generation of electricity by the entire facility **≥100 gCO2e/kWh dan <510 gCO2e/kWh.** | *There are variations tailored to jurisdictional policies in the transition to sustainability* |

**Fig. 18.6** Example of TSC for Power Generation Activities

is the establishment of TSC for the mining and quarrying of critical minerals that are indispensable to clean energy technologies and thus central to Indonesia's pathway toward NZE. Such activities are categorized under the "Transition" label, recognizing their enabling role while acknowledging their environmental trade-offs.

Indonesia holds a strategic position in the global supply of critical minerals, particularly nickel, copper, bauxite, and tin. According to the U.S. Department of Commerce, Indonesia's critical mineral resources include approximately 1.5 billion tonnes of nickel, 640 million tonnes of copper, 927 million tonnes of bauxite, and 1.2 billion tonnes of tin in 2023. More notably, Indonesia controls upwards of 42% of global nickel reserves, making it arguably the dominant node in the global nickel ecosystem. In 2023, Indonesia produced about 1.6 million tonnes of nickel metal (International Trade Administration, 2023), solidifying its position as the world's largest nickel producer. Export revenues tied to nickel and downstream nickel-based products have surged: prior to the ban on raw ore exports, nickel export receipts accounted for roughly 10% of Indonesia's nickel ore export value (eq. USD 1.1 billion). Following the implementation of strict domestic processing requirements, some estimates suggest downstream nickel and battery-related exports have generated tens of billions of dollars in foreign direct investment and export revenue. These figures highlight not only the economic weight of critical minerals in Indonesia's export portfolio but also the significance of policy interventions in reshaping value chains toward higher-value processing and manufacturing.

Similarly, TKBI introduces TSC for the construction of new buildings and residential areas targeted at Low-Income Communities (MBR) thereby embedding social equity considerations into the taxonomy. Sustainable housing for low-income communities represents a crucial social dimension of sustainable finance. Affordable, energy-efficient housing not only contributes to inclusive urban development but also reduces long-term environmental footprints through the use of green construction materials and technologies. Embedding such projects within TKBI ensures that sustainability transitions do not exacerbate inequality but instead expand social welfare.

Moreover, social forestry initiatives—programs that devolve forest management rights to local communities—constitute an important mechanism for reconciling ecological protection with livelihood security. By empowering communities in forest stewardship, these programs enhance biodiversity conservation, absorbing carbon emissions, promote sustainable land use, and generate income opportunities. Integrating housing for low-income groups and social forestry into Indonesia's sustainable finance framework exemplifies a holistic approach that simultaneously advances environmental integrity, social equity, and economic resilience.

Other distinctive provisions include the recognition of Sustainable Aviation Fuel (SAF) in accordance with the national aviation roadmap, and the incorporation of carbon capture and storage (CCS) activities within both production and protected forest areas. These initiatives underscore TKBI's integrative approach, combining environmental ambition, social inclusivity, and technological innovation within a framework tailored to Indonesia's national development trajectory.

## 3 Discussion

### *3.1 Linkage of TKBI to Sustainable Finance Policy*

A taxonomy is most effective as part of a building blocks: it underpins disclosure regimes (ie. NFRD/CSRD in Europe), product regulations (ie. SFDR), and prudential metrics (ie. EU banks' Green Asset Ratio). By linking these elements, a taxonomy creates consistent incentives that cascades from issuer to intermediary to ultimately to end-investor (Oliveira Neves, 2022; Hummel & Bauernhofer, 2024; Garcia-Torea et al., 2024).

In Indonesia, the implementation of TKBI is closely integrated with other sustainable finance policies. In response to the FSOL mandate, the TKBI is expected to serve as the basis for the forthcoming Government Regulation on sustainable finance development, currently being drafted by members of the Sustainable Finance Committee (Indonesia Ministry of Finance, OJK, Bank Indonesia). This regulation will provide a robust legal foundation for TKBI to enhance its enforcement and consistency.

The TKBI framework can also function as a criterion for identifying and classifying sustainable activities within the broader development of sustainable finance policies across ministries and state institutions. For instance, it may serve as a qualifying benchmark for renewable energy projects seeking access to financing under the Energy Transition Platform. This role is formally codified in the Minister of Finance Regulation No. 103 of 2023 on the Provision of Fiscal Support through a Financing and Funding Framework for the Acceleration of Energy Transition in the Electricity Sector.

Moreover, the Technical Screening Criteria (TSC) of TKBI explicitly integrates requirements that correspond with, and reinforce, existing regulatory frameworks issued by various government ministries, particularly in relation to priority sectors. In the case of the energy sector, for example, the TSC provisions concerning energy conservation and efficiency are directly aligned with the stipulations of Government Regulation of the Republic of Indonesia No. 33 of 2023 on Energy. This regulatory coherence underscores TKBI's function as a harmonizing instrument, ensuring that sustainable finance mechanisms remain consistent with sectoral policy objectives and legal mandates.

In the Construction and Real Estate sector, the TKBI framework advances the adoption of Green Building Certification, in accordance with Government Regulation No. 16 of 2021 on the Implementing Regulation of Law No. 28 of 2002 regarding Green Buildings, as well as the Ministry of Public Works and Housing Regulation No. 21 of 2021 on the Assessment of Green Building Performance. In the transportation and storage sector, aviation activities are guided by the national Sustainable Aviation Fuel Roadmap, while other industries operate under established national sustainability frameworks, such as the Timber Legality and Sustainability Verification System (SVLK) in forestry and the Indonesian Sustainable Palm Oil (ISPO) certification for palm oil plantations.

From the perspective of industry and investors, TKBI provides a reference point for corporate budgeting in the real sector, the establishment of sustainable equity labeling, and the design of sustainable financing portfolios, including the formulation of sustainability indices and investment strategies. For the OJK, TKBI constitutes a critical regulatory instrument for fostering comprehensive sustainable finance policies. In particular, TKBI supports the integration of green and sustainable performance indicators into corporate sustainability disclosures, aligning with the Metrics and Targets Pillars under IFRS S1 and S2. This alignment is expected to be institutionalized through the forthcoming OJK Regulation on Sustainable Finance Implementation, which will apply to financial sector institutions, issuers, and publicly listed companies.

Furthermore, TKBI plays a role in the calculation of sustainable finance portfolios within the framework of Climate Risk Management & Scenario Analysis (CRMS). CRMS provides an integrated structure encompassing governance, strategy, risk management, and disclosure dimensions to evaluate the resilience of banking business models and strategic plans under climate change scenarios in the short, medium, and long term. In addition, TKBI facilitates the allocation of proceeds from Sustainable Bonds and Sukuk, ensuring their proper channeling toward environmentally and socially sustainable activities.

At a broader policy level, TKBI—together with the granular data it generates—can serve as an empirical foundation for future sustainability policy formulation by regulators and other relevant government ministries. This highlights TKBI's dual function as both a technical screening criterion for specific sectors and a strategic policy instrument for the long-term advancement of sustainable finance in Indonesia.

## 3.2 *Gradual Implementation of TKBI*

The implementation of the TKBI is deliberately designed as a phased process, reflecting both the complexity of sustainable finance integration and the need to balance regulatory ambition with market readiness. The initial phase, scheduled for

2024, will be launched as a pilot program in the banking sector, allowing banks to develop familiarity with the taxonomy before its full-scale adoption. This staged entry point serves as a capacity-building mechanism, reducing potential compliance frictions and facilitating institutional learning across diverse banking actors.

During the pilot phase, the coverage of corporate and medium enterprises portfolios reported under TKBI version 2 will expand progressively, with incremental increases introduced on a quarterly basis. This gradual escalation is designed to ensure an orderly transition, providing banks and other market participants with sufficient time to adapt their internal systems, risk assessment frameworks, and reporting infrastructures. Such a stepwise approach is consistent with international best practices in regulatory rollout, where the sequencing of implementation functions as a strategy to mitigate market disruption and enhance long-term compliance.

Simultaneously, the progress of sustainable finance implementation will be evaluated through sustainability reports, with a specific emphasis on monitoring financial flows directed toward environmentally friendly business activities Environmentally Friendly Business Activities/KUBL (Table 18.4). By embedding continuous monitoring within the implementation architecture, TKBI not only enhances transparency and accountability but also generates empirical data necessary for iterative policy refinement. This data-driven feedback loop is essential for regulators to recalibrate thresholds, adjust sectoral benchmarks, and identify systemic challenges in the evolving landscape of sustainable finance.

The data presented in the table illustrate the trajectory of sustainable financing by commercial banks in Indonesia, as reported in publicly available sustainability disclosures. Between 2019 and 2024, the volume of financing allocated to environmentally responsible business activities increased markedly, rising from IDR 705 trillion in 2019 to IDR 2047 trillion in 2024. This represents nearly a threefold expansion over a 5-year period, signifying a structural shift in the allocation of financial resources toward green and sustainable economic activities. The steady upward trajectory underscores the evolving role of financial institutions as pivotal actors in Indonesia's broader transition toward a low-carbon and climate-resilient economy. This trend is not only aligned with the country's national sustainability and energy transition objectives but also reflects Indonesia's increasing integration into the architecture of global climate finance and Paris Agreement commitments.

Looking ahead, the TKBI is expected to emerge as the primary performance metric for assessing financial institutions' contributions to sustainable development. By systematically capturing banks' financing flows toward Paris-aligned activities and transition-related investments, TKBI offers both a standardized measurement framework and a benchmark for accountability. Furthermore, the granularity of TKBI-based data provides a scientific foundation for sectoral ministries and regulatory authorities to design evidence-based incentive and disincentive mechanisms, thereby accelerating the pace and scale of sustainable finance.

Ultimately, the phased implementation strategy strengthens both the credibility and practicality of TKBI. It ensures that market actors can internalize sustainability principles without undermining financial stability, while regulators accumulate robust evidence to inform future policy development and market deepening. In this

**Table 18.4** Financing Growth for Environmentally Friendly Business Activities

| Commercial banks | | | | | | |
|---|---|---|---|---|---|---|
| Environmentally responsible business practices | 2019 | 2020 | 2021 | 2022 | 2023 | 2024 |
| Renewable energy | 16,141 | 19,578 | 30,802 | 38,196 | 19,185 | 22,827 |
| Energy efficiency | 14,859 | 9567 | 24,141 | 18,299 | 18,749 | 32,964 |
| Pollution prevention and control | 12,174 | 1828 | 7304 | 10,254 | 9369 | 12,093 |
| Natural resources management and sustainable land use | 120,155 | 187,330 | 232,784 | 270,145 | 302,258 | 340,107 |
| Land and water biodiversity conservation | 513 | 725 | 755 | 1413 | 1173 | 916 |
| Environmentally friendly transportation | 20,845 | 28,948 | 28,884 | 31,303 | 39,544 | 32,262 |
| Sustainable water and wastewater management | 6451 | 9614 | 11,357 | 10,481 | 14,384 | 41,791 |
| Climate change adaptation | – | – | – | – | – | – |
| Ecoefficient products that reduce resource use and generate less pollution | 17,833 | 18,138 | 22,523 | 33,284 | 44,196 | 50,871 |
| Certified green buildings | 29,155 | 20,934 | 16,857 | 19,891 | 30,053 | 32,903 |
| Other environmentally responsible business practices | 15,395 | 34,845 | 36,914 | 49,125 | 65,298 | 68,657 |
| MSMEs | 451,633 | 937,576 | 1,108,076 | 1,271,176 | 1,371,381 | 1,411,974 |
| Total (IDR billion) | 705,154 | 1,269,082 | 1,520,396 | 1,753,566 | 1,915,591 | 2,047,366 |

Source: OJK, 2025

regard, TKBI's rollout functions not merely as a compliance exercise but as a dynamic governance process, aligning institutional practices with the broader objectives of climate resilience, financial system stability, and sustainable economic transformation.

## 3.3 *Challenges and Opportunities*

The implementation of sustainable finance in Indonesia is marked by both significant challenges and promising opportunities. These complexities are deeply rooted in the country's institutional capacity, market structure, and socio-economic priorities. One of the primary challenges is institutional readiness. Many Indonesian financial institutions, particularly smaller banks and MSMEs, face limited technical and human resource capacity to implement taxonomy-aligned reporting and sustainable financing practices. This lack of preparedness could slow down adoption rates and hinder consistency in implementation. Moreover, gaps in data availability and quality exacerbate this challenge. Comprehensive and standardized data on emissions, biodiversity, and social safeguards remain scarce, making it difficult to measure and monitor alignment with TKBI's criteria.

Another major obstacle lies in the preparation of the TSC, especially in relation to the national decarbonization pathway. In some cases, in certain sectors, national guidelines on quantitative emission reduction targets and trajectory plans are still under development. To address this, the best regional and global approaches can be adopted, while simultaneously adjusting them to reflect national progress—a necessary approach given the taxonomy's design as a "living document". TSC will be updated periodically to maintain quality and interoperability.

Conversely, the TKBI also creates a broad array of opportunities that can significantly reshape Indonesia's financial and economic landscape. One of the most compelling opportunities is the mobilization of capital. By providing a credible and standardized framework, TKBI enhances investor confidence and unlocks international green finance flows into Indonesia's economy. This is particularly crucial as the country seeks to finance large-scale renewable energy projects, infrastructure for climate resilience, and biodiversity conservation initiatives. The taxonomy also encourages financial innovation. It creates the foundation for the development of new financial products such as sustainability-linked bonds, sukuk, and blended finance instruments tailored to Indonesia's unique socio-economic and cultural contexts. Furthermore, TKBI's inclusive design enables small and medium enterprises to participate in sustainable finance markets, broadening economic participation and fostering equitable growth. Its alignment with Indonesia's NDCs and the National Long-Term Development Plan ensures policy coherence, creating synergies between climate goals and development priorities. Furthermore, regulators and policy makers may benefit from data gathered from TKBI in developing data-driven policy.

On a global scale, TKBI positions Indonesia as an integral player in sustainable finance dialogues. Its interoperability with multi-jurisdictional frameworks strengthens Indonesia's role in regional and international sustainable finance platforms, thereby expanding the country's integration into global green value chains. This creates long-term benefits in terms of capital flows, knowledge sharing, and international recognition of Indonesia's commitment to sustainability.

## 4 Conclusion

Taxonomies for sustainable finance allow countries to ensure that local green, social, and sustainable assets and activities meaningfully contribute to both international goals and national development strategies. OJK, through TKBI, has implemented a balance between the principle of "interoperability" and efforts to transition to NZE. The criteria for "Green" are set to be consistent with other international taxonomies. "Transition" efforts are in line with national commitments towards sustainable goals, enabling Indonesia to pursue ambitious climate goals through pathways that remain feasible and context-specific.

The TKBI was developed using a framework that conforms to both global and regional taxonomies. The TKBI serves as a reference to promote the sustainable capital allocation and financing to facilitate the achievement of Indonesia's NZE, while enhancing the standard definition of economic activities to align with the SDGs, which integrate harmonize economic, environmental and social aspects. Emerging evidence from the financial sector, including increased allocations to environmentally sustainable business activities, indicates a growing institutional readiness to operationalize TKBI. As regulatory integration deepens across ministries and financial institutions, TKBI is poised to become the cornerstone of Indonesia's sustainable finance ecosystem. The taxonomy not only strengthens market credibility and reduces risks of greenwashing but also establishes the basis for coherent, quantifiable capital flows that directly support Indonesia's NZE commitments and broader sustainable development agenda.

The latest developments related to taxonomy for sustainable finance demonstrate strong attention and commitment from global, regional, and national levels, as well as various future opportunities to increase capital allocation and financing for sustainability and the achievement of NZE. In line with global developments related to M-CGT and taxonomy for resilience and adaptation, Indonesian regulators must anticipate and define an appropriate role for TKBI to maintain interoperability while fulfilling national interests and responding to global challenges.

Looking ahead, the continued refinement of TKBI, informed by advances in science, technology, and global best practices, offers significant potential to enhance Indonesia's role as a leader in sustainable finance within ASEAN and beyond. With strong stakeholder engagement and policy coherence, TKBI can serve as both a national instrument of transformation and a bridge to international capital markets, underscoring Indonesia's commitment to achieving a just, inclusive, and resilient transition toward sustainability.

To ensure the sustained relevance of the TKBI framework, future work must address several critical dimensions. This includes the development of grandfathering and sunsetting mechanisms to manage transition criteria, as well as the continuous refinement of the TSC in order to better align with evolving NDC and priority sectors. Such efforts will not only maintain TKBI's applicability but also strengthen its role as a dynamic tool for guiding evidence-based transitions in complex policy environments.

## References

ASEAN Taxonomy Board (ATB). "ASEAN Taxonomy for Sustainable Finance Version 1", 2021. https://asean.org/wp-content/uploads/2021/11/ASEAN-Taxonomy.pdf

Bank for International Settlements (BIS). "A Taxonomy of Sustainable Finance Taxonomies", 2021. https://www.bis.org/publ/bppdf/bispap118.pdf

Bhattacharyya, Rupsha. (2025). Enabling the clean energy transition: An assessment of the role of sustainable and green finance taxonomies. https://www.researchgate.net/publication/374213156_Enabling_the_clean_energy_transition_An_assessment_of_the_role_of_sustainable_and_green_finance_taxonomies

Climate Bonds Initiative (2021). Taxonomy. [online] Climate Bonds Initiative. Available at: https://www.climatebonds.net/standard/taxonomy.

Climate Policy Initiative. "Tracking and Mobilizing Private Sector Climate Adaptation Finance, 2024", https://www.climatepolicyinitiative.org/wp-content/uploads/2024/09/Tracking-and-Mobilizing-Private-Sector-Climate-Adaptation-Finance-2.pdf

Garcia-Torea, N., Alessi, L., Cojoianu, T., Hoepner, A. G. F., & Michelon, G. (2024). The EU Taxonomy, sustainability reporting and financial institutions: Understanding the elements driving regulatory uncertainty. *Accounting Forum, 48*(3), 427–454.

Hummel, K., & Bauernhofer, D. (2024). Consequences of sustainability reporting mandates: Evidence from the EU taxonomy regulation. *Accounting Forum, 48*(3), 374–400.

Inderst, R. and Opp, M. M. (2025) 'Sustainable finance versus environmental policy: Does greenwashing justify a taxonomy for sustainable investments?', Journal of Financial Economics, 163, Article 103954. https://doi.org/10.1016/j.jfineco.2024.103954

International Trade Administration. (2023). Indonesia Critical Minerals. [online] www.trade.gov Available at: https://www.trade.gov/market-intelligence/indonesia-critical-minerals

Oliveira Neves, R. (2022). The EU Taxonomy Regulation and Its Implications for Companies. In P. Câmara & F. Morais (Eds.), *The Palgrave Handbook of ESG and Corporate Governance* (pp. 249–265). Springer.

Otoritas Jasa Keuangan (OJK). "Taksonomi untuk Keuangan Berkelanjutan Indonesia", 2024. http://gapura.ojk.go.id/tkbi2024

OJK. (2025). Sustainable Finance OJK. [online] Ojk.go.id. Available at: https://keuanganberkelanjutan.ojk.go.id/keuanganberkelanjutan/id/statistik [Accessed 3 Oct. 2025]

Republic of Indonesia. (1945). The 1945 Constitution of the Republic of Indonesia (n.d.) https://www.mkri.id/public/content/infoumum/regulation/pdf/UUD45%20ASLI.pdf

Republic of Indonesia. (2016). Law No 16 Year 2016 concerning Ratification of the Paris Agreement to the United Nations Framework Convention on Climate Change (n.d.). https://peraturan.bpk.go.id/Details/37573/uu-no-16-tahun-2016

Republic of Indonesia. (2022). President Regulation No 111 Year 2022 concerning the Implementation of Sustainable Development Goals (n.d.) https://sdgs.bappenas.go.id/product/perpres-no-111-2022/

Republic of Indonesia. (2023). Minister of Finance Regulation No. 103 of 2023 on the Provision of Fiscal Support through a Financing and Funding Framework for the Acceleration of Energy Transition in the Electricity Sector.

Republic of Indonesia. (2023). Law Number 4 of 2023 concerning the Development and Strengthening of the Financial Sector (n.d.), https://jdih-old.kemenkeu.go.id/download/58fac07c-7165-4c55-882d-965687f8090b/UU4TAHUN2023.pdf

Republic of Indonesia. (2024). Law No. 59 of 2024 on the National Long-Term Development Plan for 2024–2045 (n.d.), https://peraturan.bpk.go.id/Details/299728/uu-no-59-tahun-2024

Sustainable Banking and Finance Network (2024). Sustainable Finance Taxonomies. https://www.sbfnetwork.org/sbfn-toolkit-sustainable-finance-taxonomies.

Tettamanzi, P. et al. (2024). The European Union (EU) green taxonomy: Codifying sustainability to provide certainty to the markets. *Environment, Development and Sustainability, 26*, 27111–27136. https://doi.org/10.1007/s10668-023-03798-6

The International Platform for Sustainable Finance (IPSF). "Common Ground Taxonomy Multi-Jurisdiction Activity Tables", 2024, https://finance.ec.europa.eu/document/download/e83394d0-daf1-487e-b1bf-922731767a10_en?filename=241113-common-ground-taxonomy-multi-jurisdiction-activity-tables_en.pdf

The Sustainable Banking and Finance Network (SBFN). "SBFN Toolkit: Sustainable Finance Taxonomies", 2024, https://www.sbfnetwork.org/sbfn-toolkit-sustainable-finance-taxonomies/

World Bank. "Guidance on Developing a National Green Taxonomy", 2021. https://documents1.worldbank.org/curated/en/953011593410423487/pdf/Developing-a-National-Green-Taxonomy-A-World-Bank-Guide.pdf

# Chapter 19
# Green Economy Transformation Through Islamic Green Financing

**Ferry Syarifuddin**

**Abstract** This study investigates the preferences of various Islamic Financing Instruments to promote green economy transformation adopting ANP-BOCR (Benefit, Opportunity, Cost, Risk) approach, with academicians and practitioners as the respondents. The first finding shows that 'Benefit' aspect is the most preferred urgency to conduct green economy transformation withnatural resource damage prevention and reduction as the primary issues, in line with maqasid al-Syari'ah. Using standard formula, the second finding shows that Islamic Asset Management is the most preferred Islamic financial instrument to perform green economy transition. Meanwhile, the third finding shows that in the short-term, Islamic Asset Management is more preferred financial instrument.

**Keywords** Green economy transformation · Islamic green financing · ANP · BOCR · JEL

## 1 Introduction

A clear relationship exists between environmental issues and economic performance (Tienhaara, 2016). In recent years, ecological imbalances, resource depletion, and the threat of environmental contamination have entered economic and political discourses, as they are inextricably linked to the issue of social progress and human survival (Liu et al., 2020). Furthermore, the brown economy will increase poverty and inequalities (Kousar et al., 2022). To address these difficulties, various fundamental conceptions of development have emerged. "Green Economy" has been commonly used as an "umbrella term lacking operationalisation" among various ideas (Loiseau et al., 2016). UNEP (2011) described the green economy

F. Syarifuddin (✉)
Bank Indonesia, Jakarta, Indonesia



S. M. Juhro et al. (eds.), *Sustainable Economy: The Indonesian Pathways*,
https://doi.org/10.1007/978-981-92-1215-6_19

idea as "… one that improves human well-being and social fairness while substantially decreasing environmental risk and ecological scarcities."

In transitioning to a green economy, economies are likely to face various economic and financial risks coming from a) the different strands of the global decarbonisation trend and b) the accelerating effects of physical climate risk, transition risk, and biodiversity loss. Green economic transformation requires government intervention to ensure its successful and efficient implementation (Borel-Saladin & Turok, 2013). Different policies have been implemented in developing and developed nations; however, differences in political and economic frameworks have resulted in considerable variation in policies between nations (Megwai et al., 2016). Regulatory institutions, indeed, play important roles in facilitating the transition to a green economy. However, significant policy-incentive frameworks are required for a more effective transition (Berensmann & Lindenberg, 2016).

Financial institutions can shift investments away "from greenhouse gas, fossil fuel, and natural resource-intensive industries towards more resource-efficient technologies and business models" (Volz, 2018); that is, the financial sector can promote green economy transformation by channelling financial resources towards greener, more sustainable pathways. Green finance refers to the concept of sustaining the green economy through the actions of financial institutions (Berensmann & Lindenberg, 2016). The current market system has led to the misallocation of capital resources to "fossil-fuel-dependent and energy-inefficient" businesses and business practices (Borel-Saladin & Turok, 2013). It has been demonstrated that the regulation of financial institutions promoting green finance transformation greatly reduces the negative environmental impact of corporate operations (Akomea-Frimpong et al., 2021; Muganyi et al., 2021; Raberto et al., 2019; Zhang et al., 2021). However, various obstacles accompany the use of green financing for green economic transformation. Financial institutions must internalise environmental externalities and reduce risk perception to attract investments that provide environmental benefits (Berensmann & Lindenberg, 2016). While green technologies are somewhat inefficient when the economic structure is predominantly brown (the current state), they will become comparatively efficient once a predominantly green economic structure has been achieved (Kemp-Benedict, 2014).

Indonesia is also the most populous Muslim-majority nation in the world. The size of the country's Muslim population has led to the rapid expansion of its Islamic banking infrastructure. As such, the precise mechanism of how to finance the transition from a predominantly brown economy to a green economy for the Muslim majority remains an open subject, which, alongside Islamic financial tools, is difficult for Indonesia to address, as it is for other growing economies. However, Indonesia was the only nation to issue green Islamic bonds in 2018, thereby laying the groundwork for other Islamic green finance instruments (Siswantoro & Surya, 2021). Yet it is feared that the limitation of Islamic financial instruments will hinder the economic transformation. Scholars have claimed that "Islamic finance is naturally compatible with the concepts of green finance, which seek to direct investments toward environmental-benefitting ends" (Liu & Lai, 2021). The existence of an Islamic financial infrastructure in Indonesia enables policymakers to further push the green transformation goal by utilising Islamic finance tools, including retail Islamic banking, business and investment banking, asset management, insurance, weather derivatives, sukuk, and social finance. The availability of Islamic finance infrastructure in Indonesia enables policymakers to promote the transformation to a green economy through the use of Islamic financing instruments. Thus far, however, no research has been conducted into how Islamic financing will support the green economy transformation goal.

The main objective of this chapter is to assess the preferences for alternative Islamic financing instruments that promote green economy transformation in relation to socio-economic and institutional-political challenges, its impact on the overall economic performance of the real and financial sectors, and possible risks in the process of transitioning to a green economy, along with policies related to green economy transformation. We built an Analytic Network Process Benefits, Opportunities, Costs, and Risks—ANP BOCR (Saaty & Vargas, 2013)—model and gathered primary data to conduct the assessment. The primary data, in the form of expert opinion, were gathered from related stakeholders (academicians and NGOs) for the ANP model (pair-wise comparison questionnaire) between June and July 2022. During this time, we also conducted several in-depth interviews to deepen the analysis of the ANP results, especially concerning the merits and shortcomings of Islamic green financing instruments. After the quantification of the ANP BOCR model, we will also conduct a sensitivity analysis to assess how the preference for the respective Islamic green financing instrument changes in response to the changes in other key factors in the model. To the best of our knowledge, this is the first study to undertake such an evaluation. The findings of this study will assist the relevant authorities, particularly in Indonesia, in developing a road map for the transition to a green economy through regulation of the Islamic finance system. The outcomes of this research can also be analyzed by other economic bodies for their green economy transformation roadmaps. Therefore, a green economy can have a positive effect on reducing emissions, fossil fuel dependency, particularly in the energy sector, and contributing to more sustainable use of natural resources. Given by the background above, this research has three objectives to be accomplished. First, this research wants to identify the scale of priority among benefits, opportunities, costs, and risk aspects toward green economy transformation. Second, to identify the scale of priority among Islamic green financing (IGF) alternatives to promote green economy transformation. Lastly, identifying the IGF Scale of priority among Islamic green financing related to short or long-term strategy toward green economy transformation.

This chapter provides several benefits, including first, contribution to the literature on green economy transformation through Islamic green financing. Second, the proposal of suitable Islamic green finance alternatives, taking into account constraints and expert viewpoints. Third, as input for governments and related parties to propose the grand design of green economy transformation through Islamic financing instruments. Using ANP-BOCR (Benefit, Opportunity, Cost, Risk) approach, this study finds that 'Benefit' aspect is the most preferred, urgency to conduct green economy transformation. Among criteria in the benefit aspect, natural resource damage prevention and reduction are the primary issues which is in line with maqasid al-Syari'ah (objectives of Islamic law). Using standard formula, this study finds that Islamic Asset Management is the most preferred Islamic financial instrument to perform green economy transition. Meanwhile, in the short-term, Islamic Asset Management is more preferred financial instrument. Whereas, Islamic corporate and investment banking is the most preferred and crucial for long-term when transforming economy to green. Therefore, this study is divided into five sections. The first section is the background, which describes the significance of the subject and the study problems identified. The second section examines relevant theories and previous literature. Through the Delphi-ANP BOCR method mentioned in Sect. 3, the research methodology employs a qualitative approach. The results are detailed in Sect. 4, while in Sect. 5, conclusions are drawn and policy recommendation assessed.

## 2 Literature Review

Several relevant concepts to the study issues will be discussed in this section. First, concept regarding to green economy transformation and second, theories related to Green Finance and Islamic Green Financing.

### *2.1 Green Economy*

The green economy is an alternative vision for growth and development; one that can generate economic development and improvements in people's lives in ways consistent with advancing both environmental and social well-being (Söderholm, 2020). According to UNEP (2011), the green economy is supported by three major pillars: low-carbon, resource efficiency, and social inclusion. It is further clarified that the focus is on the economy itself: "The concept of a green economy does not replace sustainable development, but it is becoming increasingly apparent that attaining sustainability depends almost entirely on getting the economy right." Decades of creating new wealth through a "brown economy" model centred on fossil fuels have done little to address social marginalisation, environmental degradation, and resource depletion (UNEP, 2011).

Law et al. (2016) suggested other definitions for the green economy, green growth, and low-carbon development. Green economy and green growth principles intersect in their holistic approach with growth and economic development, environmental protection, low-carbon development, resilience, resource efficiency, ecological sustainability, human well-being, inclusivity, and equity (Law et al., 2016). Therefore, a green economy can have a positive effect on reducing emissions, fossil fuel dependency, particularly in the energy sector, and contributing to more sustainable use of natural resources. Moreover, it has been found that investments in low-carbon development and the management of ecosystem services promote more robust economic expansion over the medium and long term (Musango et al., 2014).

Green and circular economies aim to reduce resource inputs, waste, and emissions through the reduction, reuse, recycling, recovery, and remanufacturing of resources.

In addition, the 2030 Agenda for Sustainable Development and its 17 Sustainable Development Goals (SDGs) recognise that eradicating global poverty requires strategies that not only promote economic growth but also address a variety of social needs, such as education, health, social protection, and job creation, while also addressing environmental pollution and climate change. Thus, the SDGs provide a genuine connection between the ecological and economic systems. The imperative of transitioning to a green economy, i.e. enacting a fundamental shift toward more sustainable production and consumption practices, must therefore be emphasised (Söderholm, 2020).

According to Kaggwa et al. (2013), a green economy is "a system of economic activities related to the production, distribution, and consumption of goods and services that enhances the long-term human welfare without exposing future generations to significant environmental risks or ecological scarcities." They also highlighted that the green economy is intended to facilitate the separation of resource use and environmental impact from economic growth. The green economy is characterised by significantly increasing investment in green manufacturing sectors, supported by policy reforms (Kaggwa et al., 2013).

Therefore, the green economy perspective focuses on the root cause of environmental degradation, namely the current economic structure. In this manner, it may offer solutions that are moderately resistant to potential setbacks such as rebound effects (Droste et al., 2016). At the same time, however, the green economy model presents political implementation difficulties (Barbier, 2012) and significant transaction costs (Barbier, 2011). Transforming the economy requires innovation in terms of available technology, organisational support, market conditions, the broader social backdrop, and overarching governance (Barbier, 2011; Droste et al., 2016; UNEP, 2011).

## 2.2 *Green Economy Transformation: Appropriate Policies*

Green economy transformation can be defined as the shift from a conventional economic system (brown economy) to an environmentally friendly economic framework. It requires an all-encompassing policy framework, including the integration and coordination of relevant policies. A green economy transformation requires public investment in the green economy, risk coverage, economically sustainable green technology, risk coverage management, climate pricing, and knowledge and awareness of the green economy.

In addition to these types of regulations, industry-specific policies can be employed to advance the green economy transformation agenda. To prevent government failure, however, a comprehensive risk analysis is required for the execution of industrial policies to promote the transition. A combination of regulation, procurement, and financial incentives, in addition to private incentives, increases the likelihood of implementing environmentally beneficial innovations.

Various studies have demonstrated the effectiveness of financial policies in promoting green economy transformation. The two most effective policy mechanisms for promoting private investment are feed-in tariffs and loans (Azhgaliyeva et al., 2019). Central banks play a significant role in accelerating the transition to a green economy and have a variety of tools at their disposal (Dikau & Volz, 2019). By incorporating the agenda into their missions, central banks can play a vital role in the transition to a green economy.

However, only a minority of central banks have taken such action to date (Dikau & Volz, 2021). The primary and secondary responsibilities of central banks enable them to directly assist in the transition to a green economy (Alexander & Fisher, 2020). Financial and banking policies have been found to significantly impact the extent to which banks have adopted the green economy (Akomea-Frimpong et al., 2021). Regulators must encourage a competitive banking industry to increase finance for green enterprises. One of the most important factors in success is the coherence of the approach for integrating the policies aimed at driving the green economy transformation. Transformation to a green economy requires incentive programmes since new green investments offer a lower rate of return than conventional investments. To accelerate the shift to a green economy, banking regulators and other stakeholders must harmonise their policies. Thus, in supporting a specific means of promoting green economy transformation, i.e. through the promotion of Islamic green financing instruments/products, coherence is required with existing or planned policies and other types of instruments, especially financial instruments.

## 2.3 Green Economy Transformation Risks and Green Islamic Financing

Islamic finance is defined as a system "based on Sharia law that prohibits interest, uncertainty, and investment in unlawful sectors defined by Islam". Basically, the principles of Islamic finance align with the concept of a green economy. The latter attempts to promote human well-being and equity, and reduce environmental degradation (UNEP, 2011). Based on the similarity between the two concepts, scholars have argued that "Islamic finance is inherently compatible with principles of green finance that seeks to channel investments towards purposes that bring environmental benefits" (Liu & Lai, 2021).

Various Islamic green financing instruments have been developed over the years. Noh (2019) in Sachs et al. (2019) outlined five forms of Islamic green financing instruments. They cover retail banking, corporate and investment banking, asset management, insurance, and weather derivatives. Retail banking products and instruments include green mortgages, home equity loans, commercial building loans, auto loans, and green cards. The corporate and investment banking measures include green project finance, green securitisation, green venture capital and private equity, green indexes, and carbon commodities. The asset management category includes green fiscal funds, green investment funds, and carbon funds, while the insurance industry provides green insurance and carbon insurance products. The final instrument type is weather derivatives, which the authorities can utilise and promote to push the green economy transformation.

The transition to a green economy is not without risk. On the contrary, green economic policies are often associated with increased risk for the real and financial sectors, at least in the short term (where brown industries dominate the economic structure). The risks of green economy transformation tend to be more pronounced in developing countries, where it remains common practice to rely on brown industries in the quest for high economic growth. The uncertainties associated with a low-carbon transition mirror those that investors, business owners, entrepreneurs, consumers, and workers face in any intentional socio-technological transition; they include whether government policies will be sustained; the actions that competitors and trading partners will take; whether one's current job is in danger; and whether good jobs will be available. Within a socio-ecological regime and in stable times it is sometimes possible to assign probabilities to these sorts of questions; however, it is not possible when the economy is in flux, particularly in the middle of a major transition (Kemp-Benedict, 2014). One of the core principles of Islamic finance is to mitigate uncertainty. Hence, the use of Islamic green financing instruments can help in mitigating the risks involved in transitioning toward a green economy.

# 3 Data and Methodology

## *3.1 Data*

The study utilises primary data from in-depth interviews with a number of academicians and practitioners, which were conducted to collect in-depth information about the benefits, opportunities, costs, and risks associated with the transition to a green economy through Islamic green financing. 25 green economy experts were involved (Table 19.1).

The respondents from a group of experts were selected based on the following criteria:

a. The expert has in-depth knowledge and understanding of the theory and practice of conventional economics.
b. The expert has in-depth knowledge and understanding of the theory and practice of Islamic economics.
c. The practitioner expert is equipped with in-depth knowledge and understanding of the theory and practice of green economy/finance and deals directly to the green economy agenda.
d. The expert from academics is prolific in publishing their research on green economy/green finance.

**Table 19.1** List of Respondents

| No | Name | Background |
|---|---|---|
| 1 | RE | Economics employee of the Wali Nanggroe Darussalam government (Academician) |
| 2 | HF | State Islamic University in Ar-Raniry (Academician) |
| 3 | AS | Syiah Kuala university (Academician) |
| 4 | TD | Syiah Kuala university (Academician) |
| 5 | WR | Aceh's regional development planning agency (BAPPEDA) (Practitioner) |
| 6 | JN | Environment and forestry department, Aceh Province (Practitioner) |
| 7 | AM | Brawijaya university (Academician) |
| 8 | HP | Malang state university (Academician) |
| 9 | AY | Bukittinggi state Islamic university (Academician) |
| 10 | IZ | Bukittingg state Islamic college (Academician) |
| 11 | DW | Mataram University (Academician) |
| 12 | MA | Mataram University (Academician) |
| 13 | KA | Bogor Forest Waqf (Practitioner) |
| 14 | SW | Penabulu foundation (Practitioner) |
| 15 | NA | Malang Islamic university (Practitioner) |
| 16 | MA | Islamic boarding school Riyadul Jannah (Practitioner) |
| 17 | BP | Malang heritage society (Practitioner) |
| 18 | FA | Andalas university (Practitioner) |
| 19 | AB | Organic farmer, Foundation for Penabulu (Practitioner) |
| 20 | RH | Organic farmer, Foundation for Penabulu (Practitioner) |
| 21 | NH | Department of Cooperatives, SMEs, and trade employee located in Bukittinggi (Practitioner) |
| 22 | RS | Regional secretary for the province of West Nusa Tenggara (Practitioner) |
| 23 | MW | Organic farmer, Foundation for Penabulu (Practitioner) |
| 24 | AW | Organic farmer, Foundation for Penabulu (Practitioner) |
| 25 | RM | Educational and empowerment Center for Independent Agriculture (Practitioner) |

*Source: created by authors*

As we involve some experts from various regions in Indonesia such as Aceh, West Sumatra, East Java, and West Nusa Tenggara, this is due to these areas have green economy projects such as the practice of the Banda Aceh Green City Initiation 2034 by the Banda Aceh City Bappeda. Second, the practice of waqf plantations and green agriculture in the East Java area. Third, sustainable agricultural practices by millennial farmers in West Sumatra and West Nusa Tenggara.

The experts as shown in Table 19.1. included Islamic economics and conventional economics academicians. The green economy practitioners included organic farmers from selected samples. The experts were from the Regional Development Planning Agency for Banda Aceh City (Bappeda), the Department of Environment and Forestry Aceh Province, the Waqf Forest Practitioner, the Bukittinggi Department of Cooperatives, SMEs, and trade. The remaining respondents were agricultural and environmental specialists. In-depth interviews were conducted with these respondents in order to obtain their viewpoints on the green economy research subject. It is preferable to conduct such interviews as respondents can openly express their thoughts on the particular topic.

Using a questionnaire adopting a Likert scale from 1 to 9 and the ANP approach, the responses in the in-depth interviews were measured. In the form of a framework model, data and information regarding the viewpoints of the academicians and practitioners were assembled. When the questionnaire responses and/or opinions had been collected, the next step was to evaluate their opinions using the Super Decision and Microsoft Excel programmes.

### 3.2 Research Design

A qualitative methodology was employed, adopting the Delphi-ANP model based on BOCR (Benefits, Opportunities, Costs, and Risks). This model can be used to evaluate the benefits, opportunities, costs, and risks of transitioning to a green economy utilising Islamic green financing as a viable alternative that could be employed for the benefit of society.

### 3.3 Research Steps

With the use of ANP-BOCR, the study necessitated multiple phases (three steps) for completion, as shown in Fig. 19.1. The first step is ANP-BOCR model construction. Literature review and in-depth interview are used to construct ANP-BOCR model. Furthermore, the model will be validated to the most appropriate expert. With regards to second step, this study will design pair-wise questionnaire and followed

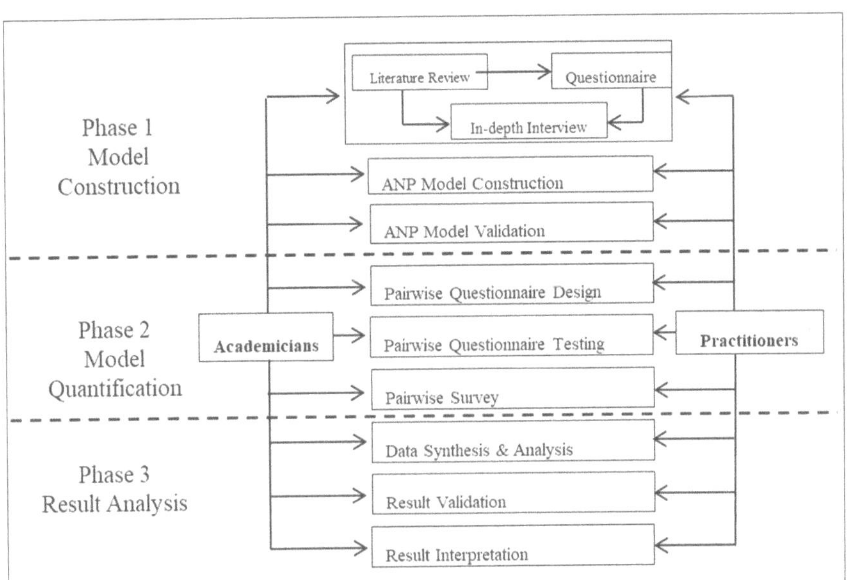


**Fig. 19.1** Research Stages. Source: Ascarya, 2013

by distribution to the respective expert amounting 25 experts (10 academicians and 15 green economy practitioners). Lastly, data synthesis and analysis will be conducted to obtain the priority result of BOCR and alternative cluster in relation to green economy transformation via Islamic green financing.

### 3.4 Data Processing

In the form of a model framework, the data and information regarding the viewpoints of the academicians and practitioners were assembled. If the results of the opinion survey have been gathered, the next step is to process the obtained data with Microsoft Excel and Super Decision software. The questionnaire was processed into a type of comparison (pair-wise) both between elements within the cluster and between clusters themselves, in order to determine which has the most impact on one side.

### 3.5 Model Construction and Decomposition

Figure 19.2 illustrates the ANP-BOCR framework of green economy transformation through Islamic Green Financing.

This study adopts the ANP two-layer model to identify short or long term suitable Islam green financing. In this step, the first layer consists of two primary clusters: (i) the goal cluster and (ii) BOCR cluster. BOCR cluster consists of benefit,

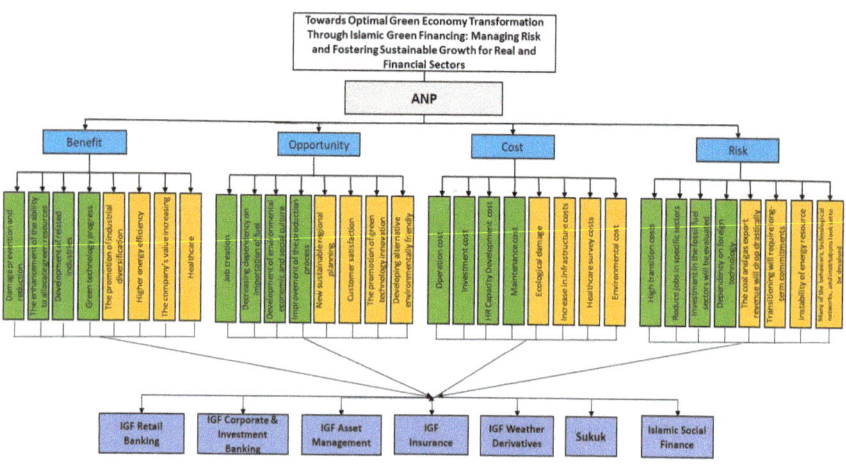


*Source: created by authors*

**Fig. 19.2** ANP-BOCR Two-Layer Model. *Source: created by authors*

opportunity, cost, and risk. Meanwhile, the second layer consists of four sub-network, namely sub-network benefit, sub-network opportunity, sub-network cost, and sub-network risk. For each sub-network, there are two clusters: (i) Benefit—Opportunity—Cost—and Risk cluster, and (ii) Alternative cluster.

# 4 Discussion

This chapter describes the stages of data processing and analysis of the results to conclude the priority by considering of benefits, opportunities, costs, and risks of Islamic green financing alternatives when transforming economy from brown to green. Briefly, the results of the in-depth interviews with 25 experts (academicians and practitioners) were processed with two-layer ANP BOCR to establishing the importance/priority value of each cluster and the elements that have been formed in the construction of the ANP BOCR model.

## *4.1 Delphi-ANP Results*

The Delphi-ANP data gathered from the two types of respondents converged with a significant Kendall's W value as the metric used to determine rater agreement. Delphi and ANP use the 10% significance threshold as an inconsistency condition in (Shweta et al., 2015). The findings of the rater agreement (Kendall's W) and the p-value as an indicator of robustness indicate that all respondents and practitioners group agreed on all sub-network criteria clusters (benefit, opportunity, cost, risk) with different levels of agreement. According to Schmidt, (1997), it becomes increasingly harder to achieve high W scores when the number of raters increases, and consequently, low W scores can become significant.

In spite of practitioners group, academia group has a slightly different conclusion, whereby only two aspects are significant in this context, namely benefit and opportunity, while cost and risk are insignificant. From the above W-score and its value discussion, we can conclude that all sub-network criteria clusters are important to be included in the model, and also significant to be included as considerable factors in choosing Islamic Green Financing Instrument as alternatives in this research model. The opinions of all respondents converged on all criteria: benefit, opportunity, cost, and risk. The Delphi and ANP results demonstrate 100% convergence and 0 divergence, which is acceptable for qualitative techniques.

## 4.2 First Layer—BOCR Cluster Priority

The ANP-BOCR results in the first layer for the BOCR cluster that were processed and analysed indicate that the highest priority, or most important clusters, in the transformation of the green economy through Islam green financing are 1) Benefit (0.424), followed by 2) Opportunity (0.227); 3) Cost (0.277); and 4) Risk (0.122). The analysis result also shows the highest levels of inconsistency for pairwise comparisons of the respondents' responses regarding the relationships between clusters in the ANP network. Because the inconsistency value is less than 10%, it can be concluded that the ANP BOCR cluster consistency test results for the ANP first-layer using the BOCR approach match the consistency requirements of the respondents' responses.

According to all the respondents, the benefit is the most essential component of the BOCR cluster, as the transition to a green economy may generate advantages for present and future generations and assure sustainability. In addition, the value of opportunity and benefit exceeds that of cost and risk, indicating that the green economic transformation model could be implemented in Indonesia.

## 4.3 Second Layer—BOCR Sub-Network Cluster Priority

The second layer of ANP-BOCR analysis describes the priority value for each sub-network (benefit, opportunity, cost & risk) for two groups of respondents and the overall value. In order to obtain a comprehensive understanding of BOCR sub-network cluster priority, therefore the sub-network priority discussion will be divided into four sub-discussion.

## 4.4 Sub-Network Benefit Cluster Priority

The final weights of the Benefit sub-network cluster indicates that respondents generally agreed that 1) Damage prevention and reduction was the most important element in the benefit cluster (0.255), followed by 2) The enhancement of the ability to allocate green resources (0.147) and 6) Higher energy efficiency (0.147); 8) Healthcare (0.145); 3) Development of related industries (0.082); 4) Green technology progress (0.082); 5) The promotion of industrial diversification (0.082) and finally 7) The company's value increasing (0.059). The rater agreement shows 0.300 which means that all respondents have a fair/medium level of agreement and significant on the benefit cluster's priority scale. The benefit cluster priority's analysis also shows the highest levels of inconsistency for pairwise comparisons of the respondents' responses in the ANP network. Because the inconsistency value is less than 10%, it can be concluded that the Sub-network benefit cluster is consistent.

According to all the respondents, damage prevention and reduction was the most essential element in the benefit cluster, as prevention and reduction are central concepts in *maqāṣid al Syariah* and will bring substantial benefits for future generations. This is consistent with the rules of *ushul fiqh*, according to which preventing harm takes precedence over gaining benefits; in the words of God: "…And seek not corruption in the land" (Q.S. 28: 77). In accordance with Felice and Petrillo, (2013), the benefits of 1) Damage prevention and reduction show the social and individual benefits attained via the creation of a sustainability level or standard. According to practitioner respondents, the top three priorities in the benefit cluster are 1) Damage prevention and reduction (0.160) and 2) Enhancement of the ability to allocate green resources (0.160), with 8) Healthcare being the third most important (0.160). The rater agreement value is 0.343, represent that the agreement among practitioner respondents is fair/medium and significant.

Based on survey result on academician respondents, the benefit cluster top priority is 1) Damage prevention and reduction (0.236), followed by 2) The enhancement of the ability to allocate green resource; 3) Development of related industries; 4) Green technology progress; 6) Higher energy efficiency and 8) Healthcare with the same value of priority (0.126). In addition, they have a rater agreement value of 0.332 showing a fair/medium level of agreement and significant on the benefit cluster's priority scale.

## 4.5 *Sub-Network Opportunity Cluster Priority*

All the respondents agreed that 8) Developing alternative environmentally friendly (0.160) was the top priority of the opportunity cluster, followed by 2) Decreasing dependence on importation of fuel (0.158); 7) The promotion of green technology innovation (0.157); 3) Development of environmental economic and social culture (0.155); 5) New sustainable regional planning (0.132); 1) Job creation (0.086); 4) Improvement of the production process (0.086); and finally, 6) Customer satisfaction (0.065). The rater agreement shows 0.165 which means that all respondents have a low level of the agreement but significant on the opportunity cluster's priority scale. The opportunity cluster priority's analysis also shows the highest levels of inconsistency for pairwise comparisons of the respondents' responses in the ANP network. Because the inconsistency value is less than 10%, it can be concluded that the Sub-network opportunity cluster is consistent.

As developing alternative environmentally friendly was the top priority of the opportunity cluster, it is understandable that an environmentally based program has become a global priority program. The G20 reaffirmed its commitment to the Paris Agreement and the SDGs by releasing the Climate and Energy Action Plan for Growth and placing sustainable renewables at the forefront of revitalizing the global economy. The action plan calls for close collaboration among G20 members to address several critical issues, including environmental protection and energy access (Kamil et al., 2019). In addition, International Financial Institutions (IFIs) and

Inter-Governmental Organizations (IGOs) have been involved in developing principles and implementing environmental and awareness programs. Developing environmentally friendly businesses could be in the form of activities that cover atmospheric protection, defense against water pollution, land degradation, etc. (Islam et al., 2014). Thus, this finding is in line with the government's commitment to achieving zero emissions by 2060.

According to the practitioners, the top two priorities in the opportunity cluster are: 8) Developing alternative environmentally friendly, meanwhile, 1) Job creation; 2) Decreasing dependency on the importance of fuel; 3) Development of environmental economic and social culture, and 7) The promotion of green technology innovation have the same value of priority (0.130). According to the responses from the practitioners, the rater agreement value is 0.197. This shows that the majority of practitioner respondents concur fell into the low category. In addition, according to the academic respondents, the top priority in the opportunity cluster was 3) Development of environmental economic and social culture (0.256), followed by 2) Decreasing dependency on the importation of fuel; 4) Improvement of the production process and 5) New sustainable regional planning with the same weight of 0.147. The rater agreement value of priority ranking is 0.231, indicating a low to medium level of agreement on the priority scale for the opportunity cluster among the academic respondents.

## 4.6 Sub-Network Cost Cluster Priority

The final weight of the BOCR sub-network in the cost cluster demonstrates that the academics and practitioners held divergent opinions. Nevertheless, all agreed that 2) Investment cost (0.226); 3) HR Capacity Development Cost (0.226); 1) Operation cost (0.129); 8) Environmental cost (0.129); 4) Maintenance cost (0.073); 5) Ecological damage (0.073); 6) Increase in infrastructure costs (0.073); and 7) Healthcare survey costs (0.073). The rater agreement shows 0.127 which means that all respondents have a low level of the agreement but significant on the cost cluster's priority scale. The cost cluster priority's analysis also shows the highest levels of inconsistency for pairwise comparisons of the respondents' responses in the ANP network. Because the inconsistency value is less than 10%, it can be concluded that the Sub-network cost cluster is consistent.

The sub-network cost cluster priority shows that Investment cost & HR Capacity Development Cost are the most important cost sub-criterion, given that sustainability requires adequate human resources to ensure the implementation of the green economy, and that training employees to become aware of and committed to sustainability initiatives is an important step towards developing human capital, in line with the UN Sustainable Development Goals (Liu & Yin, 2019; Felice & Petrillo, 2013). The academicians and practitioners agreed that 3) HR Capacity Development Cost is the highest priority, with a value of 0.212 and 0.177, respectively, followed by 2) Investment cost, with a value of 0.211 and 0.177, respectively. According to the responses of rater agreement from both groups of respondents, the rater agreement of academicians was 0.104, while the rater agreement of practitioners was 0.188. This indicates that both groups of respondents have a low-level agreement but significant except academician.

## 4.7 Sub-Network Risk Cluster Priority

The other final weights of the BOCR sub-network indicates that all the respondents agree that 1) High transition cost (0.245) is the most important risk cluster factor, followed by 2) Reduce jobs in specific sectors, especially for lower-skilled manual labor (0.136); 3) The legacy investment of financial institutions in the fossil fuel sectors will be evaluated (0.136); 5) The coal and gas export revenue will drop dramatically (0.136); 6) Transitioning will require revenue will drop drastically (0.136); 4) Dependency on foreign technology (0.075); 7) Instability of energy resources (0.069); and 8) Many of the behaviors, technological networks, and institutions look set to be devalued or stranded (0.069). The rater agreement shows 0.153 which means that all respondents have a low level of the agreement but significant on the risk cluster's priority scale. The risk cluster priority's analysis also shows the highest levels of inconsistency for pairwise comparisons of the respondents' responses in the ANP network. Because the inconsistency value is less than 10%, it can be concluded that the Sub-network risk cluster is consistent.

According to all the respondents, High transition costs is the most significant aspect of the risk cluster, since institutional change, governance, legislation, and other policies increase the cost of transitioning to a green economy. Funding may cover the cost of a feasibility study, investment, infrastructure, the operationalization of infrastructure, the cost of maintenance, the cost of human resources, and initiatives to increase society awareness regarding the significance of energy consumption or the green economy. According to Ekins and Zenghelis (2021), economies that are disproportionately dependent on fossil fuels for production and commerce may incur greater transition costs.

Based on survey on the practitioners, the top three priorities in the risk cluster are 5) The coal and gas export revenue will drop dramatically (0.164); 6) Transitioning will require revenue will drop drastically (0.164); and 1) High transition costs (0.164). The practitioner respondents' agreement for this order is 0.172, which shows that the agreement falls within the low range. On the other hand, according to the academic respondents, the primary priorities in the risk cluster are 1) High transition costs, and 2) Reduce jobs in specific sectors, particularly for less-skilled manual labor, both with a value of 0.239. According to respondents, the third priority is evaluating the legacy investments of financial institutions in fossil fuel sectors, which has a weight of 0.145. The respondent's agreement with this risk cluster is 0.163, which places it in the category of low agreement.

## 4.8 Robustness Test in BOCR

The ANP BOCR robustness test is demonstrated by the level of inconsistency in respondents' responses to the pair-wise comparison questionnaire.

Table 19.2 reveals that the maximum levels of inconsistency among the academicians and practitioners are 0.0432 for cost cluster and 0.04588 for benefit cluster, respectively, significantly below the 10% threshold for statistical significance. The inconsistency value is considered excellent when it is near zero. In contrast, an inconsistency rating near 0.1 suggests that the level of consistency is decreasing.

## 4.9 Selected Islamic Green Financing: A Synthesis of Standard Formula

This session interpret the alternative priority result of ANP-BOCR using standard formula (B/C) computations. The priority of Islamic Green Financing according to standard formula can be seen through the Fig. 19.3 below. Saaty and Vargas describe the outcomes of a number of prioritised choices based on three results: general (standard) conditions derived from B/C computations, meanwhile pessimistic conditions B/(CxR), and realistic conditions (BxO)/(CxR). Figure 19.3 displays the findings of the Islamic green financing priorities with standards formula. The Islamic green financing choice with the highest projected value has the best specification.

According to Fig. 19.3, it reveals that choice of 3 Islamic asset management is the most popular instrument chosen by the respondents, followed by alternative 1 Islamic retail banking and 4 Islamic insurance, 2 Islamic corporate and investment banking; 6 Sukuk and 7 Islamic social finance; and 5 Weather derivatives stand as the last priority.

**Table 19.2** Inconsistency Level

| | | Academician | | Practitioner | | All | |
|---|---|---|---|---|---|---|---|
| No. | Cluster | Lowest | Highest | Lowest | Highest | Lowest | Highest |
| 1 | Benefit | 0.00000 | 0.00132 | 0.00000 | 0.04588 | 0.00000 | 0.00397 |
| 2 | Opportunity | 0.00000 | 0.00159 | 0.00000 | 0.00423 | 0.00000 | 0.03746 |
| 3 | Cost | 0.00000 | 0.0432 | 0.00000 | 0.0025 | 0.00000 | 0.00985 |
| 4 | Risk | 0.00000 | 0.00132 | 0.00000 | 0.00159 | 0.00000 | 0.00250 |

Note: The level of inconsistency level must not be higher than 10%
Source: calculated by authors

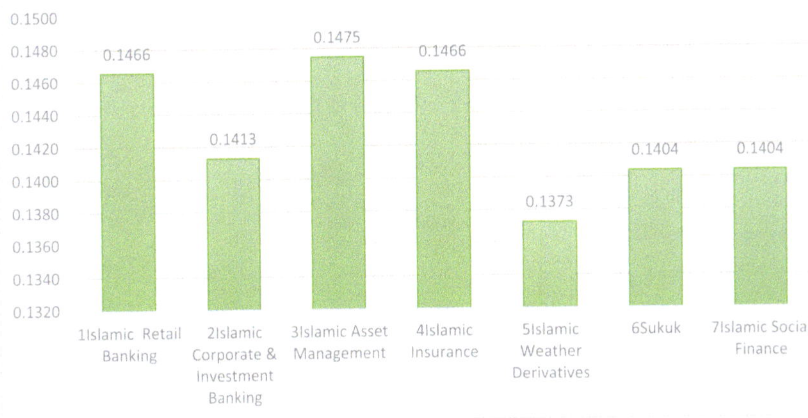


**Fig. 19.3** *Islamic Green Financing Priority using Standard Formula*. Source: calculated by authors

## 4.10 Selected Islamic Green Financing: A Synthesis of Short and Long Term

In place of a supermatrix, this study adopts the approach of Saaty and Vargas, which compares benefits and costs, in order to choose the optimal type of Islamic green finance for green economic transformation. The benefits–costs ratio of the green economy transformation is modified by incorporating opportunity and risk. In addition, BOCR-based formulas are employed based on Saaty (2001) and Emanuel and Cefalu (2002) to evaluate the best model for the BOCR approach, namely (1) the additive probabilistic formula, which is typically used to determine long-term priorities with the formula bB + oO + c(1-C) + r(1-R), and (2) the multiplicative formula, which is equivalent to marginal cost or benefit analysis and is typically used to determine short-term priorities with the BO/CR. The outcomes of the short-term alternative to the Islamic Green Financing alternatives are displayed in Fig. 19.4.

Based on Fig. 19.4, it reveals that choice 3) Islamic asset management is the most popular solution chosen by the respondents for short-term priorities, followed by alternative 1) Islamic retail banking; 4) Islamic insurance; 2) Corporate and investment banking; 6) Sukuk; 7) Islamic social finance; and 5) Islamic weather derivatives stands as the last priority. Islamic asset management is by far the most relevant kind of Islamic green financing for the transition to a green economy in Indonesia in the short term. This is due to the fact that the potential of natural resources and the environment in the country continues to ensure the growth of Islamic green financing through environmental development services, ecology transfer, and carbon tax. In addition, industrialised nations must reduce their emissions by purchasing carbon credits, which can be used to construct a green economy. In this matter, the government plays a significant role; for instance, it can control expenditures to fund the green economy and serve as a model for launching green economy operations. This is consistent with Speck and Zoboli's (2017) research on environmental

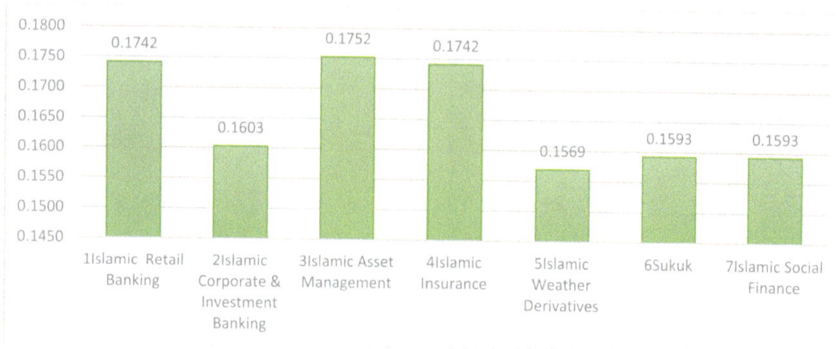


**Fig. 19.4** *ANP Results–Short-Term Alternative*. Source: calculated by authors

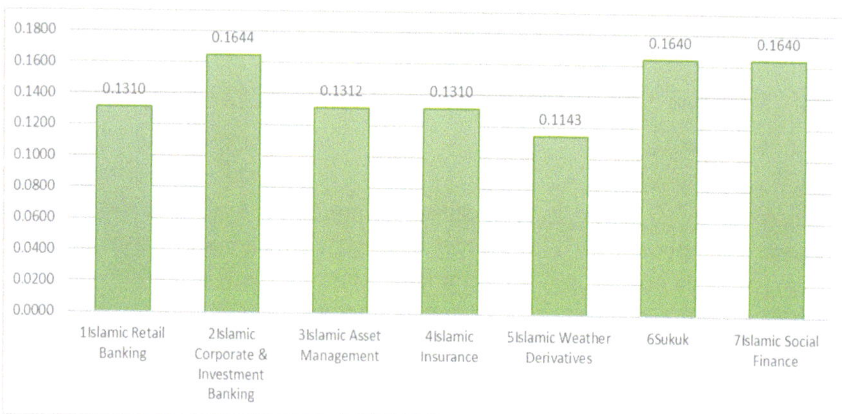


**Fig. 19.5** *ANP Results–Long-Term Alternative*. Source: calculated by authors

taxation and fiscal reforms for a transition to a green economy, such as a carbon fund that can accept investor funds to purchase CO2 emission reduction projects, or investment in new projects that will produce a flow of CO2 emission reduction credits Noh (2019) in Sachs et al. (2019).

Figure 19.5 shows the best alternative in the long term based on the additive (probabilistic) formula. It is concluded that 2) Islamic corporate and investment banking is the most popular long-term alternative among all the respondents, followed by 7) Islamic social finance; 6) Sukuk; 3) Islamic asset management; 1) Islamic retail banking; 4) Islamic insurance; and 5) Islamic weather derivatives. Islamic corporate and investment banking is by far the most relevant Islamic green finance option for the long-term transition to a green economy in Indonesia. This is due to the fact that banking is a financial institution that plays a major role in financing large-scale clean fuel and renewable energy initiatives, in line with Noh (2019) in Sachs et al. (2019). Moreover, because the corporate ecosystem and investors have a broad reach, the opportunity to fund green projects through this scheme is considerably more promising and plays a significant role in mobilising the private capital required for the energy transition (Geddes & Schmidt, 2020). This outcome is consistent with Asiyanbi's (2018) assertion that carbon commodity finance will result in emissions reductions that would not have occurred otherwise.

The second most preferred Islamic green financing alternative for the long term according to all the respondents is Islamic social finance (ISF), as it can promote sustainable economy including agricultural sector which is significant in emerging economies through *Ihya al-Mawat*[1] and *al-Iqta*[2] (Abduh, 2019). The social sector's role in the Islamic economic system to support inclusive economic development is proven as significant, relegated to merely complementing and supporting commercial finances. The growth of Islamic social finance institutions to manage inclusive wealth in accordance with sharia law is increasing and becoming more important, complementing sharia financial services targeting all social strata in Indonesia. Generally, Islamic commercial finance sector tends to serve small, medium, and large enterprises. Meanwhile, islamic microfinance sector serves micro and small enterprises. Furthermore, ISF dedicated especially tp the poor (*duafa*) and the supermicro (nano) enterprises or households To accelerate Islamic social finance (ISF), ISF activity shoul be digitalised as it give benefits such as financial performance improvement, corporate establishment, transperancy, and stability. ISF, e.g. *zakat, infaq, alms, and waqf*, is a financial instrument based on Islamic principles and aims to promote inclusive welfare (Juhro et al., 2025).

The third preferred Islamic green financing for the long term for all respondents is Sukuk. This is in accordanc with Al-Jayyousi et al. (2022), who proposed mission-led sustainability models manifested through Islamic social finance (including *zakat* and *waqf*) and sukuk, which are founded on community-based natural resource governance, an ownership-based approach, and technology for sustainable development. Therefore, Sukuk can contribute to green, social, or sustainable economic activities including green economy transition (Richardson, 2020).

According to all the respondents, Islamic asset management and Islamic retail banking are the fourth and fifth preferred long-term alternatives for Islamic green finance. These will encourage banks and corporations to establish strategic policy and action objectives for the transition to a green economy. Banks and enterprises could emphasise the potential business benefits of a systematic and proactive approach to environmental challenges. Once a retail bank or asset management company has determined the scope and determinants of sustainability, the next step is to understand how to build and implement a sustainable entrepreneurial plan. Authentic stakeholder involvement and successful cross-sector collaboration are vital in this regard (Kupakuwana, 2012). Islamic weather derivatives are the lowest priority in Islamic green financing for the transformation to a green economy. The use of these for agricultural risk transfer is a new insurance product established in

[1] *Ihya al-mawat* is revive the dead land or putting an unused piece of land to be used by an individual and acquiring proprietary rights over it (Abduh, 2019).

[2] *Al-iqtā'* is a type of grant to cultivate land issued by the state to certain people for the common interest of the society at large (Abduh, 2019).

recent years, but underdeveloped nations still lack the ability to use the mechanism to achieve the diversification and transfer of climate change risk (Kong & Sun, 2021).

(i) **Advantages of Islamic Asset Management in Financing the Green Economy Transition**

A strategy known as "green finance" has emerged that includes not only tools to reduce greenhouse gas emissions and adapt to climate change, but also financial services and products that address broader environmental issues, such as industrial pollution control, waste management, hygienic and sanitary conditions, and ecological protection. Green finance is an area of interest to policymakers targeting sustainable economic and environmental growth, which is significantly unexplored compared to areas of carbon dioxide (CO2) and climate change policy explored extensively in recent decades. Nonetheless, green finance and other variables have a significant relationship with economic and environmental growth.

Green finance has a positive effect on improving the environment and increasing corporate social responsibility. Better funding for environmental planning, as well as financial instruments designed specifically for climate-friendly projects, can help achieve environmental, social, and governance (ESG) goals. Green finance has three main functions. The first is to mobilize savings to form green investments. The second is to encourage companies to improve their green performance, and promote green consumption. Additionally, it provides a solid base for long-term growth and sustainable development. Among the Islamic green financing instruments relevant for the transition in Indonesia to a green economy are based on the results of this study namely Islamic asset management and Islamic corporate and investment banking.

Islamic asset management is by far the most relevant kind of Islamic green financing for the transition to a green economy in Indonesia in the short term. This is due to the fact that the potential of natural resources and the environment in the country continues to ensure the growth of Islamic green financing through environmental development services, ecology transfer, and carbon tax. In addition, industrialised nations must reduce their emissions by purchasing carbon credits, which can be used to construct a green economy. In this matter, the government plays a significant role; for instance, it can control expenditures to fund the green economy and serve as a model for launching green economy operations. This is consistent with Speck and Zoboli's (2017) research on environmental taxation and fiscal reforms for a transition to a green economy, such as a carbon fund that can accept investor funds to purchase CO2 emission reduction projects, or investment in new projects that will produce a flow of CO2 emission reduction credits Noh (2019) in Sachs et al. (2019).

According to Dulal et al., the carbon tax has the potential to significantly reduce carbon emissions and result in positive welfare benefits. Regarding the transmission mechanism of the carbon tax, it is generally accepted that the collection of carbon taxes could promote innovation and development of green technology in place of more conventional ones, prompting the transition to a low-carbon economy. In addition, Islamic asset management with green fiscal fund instruments can support the development of industries that reduce carbon emissions. This is done through green investment and the renewable energy transition. Fiscal decentralization, green investment, and the use of renewable energy can contribute significantly to reducing the ecological footprint. In addition, Islamic asset management with fiscal instruments can also encourage the private sector to reduce forest-based emissions and improve governance of the forestry sector.

According to H. Sun & Chen's research, the only option to deal with the current weak economic growth and worsening environment is through green investment. Investing in green sectors may not only save the environment but also foster long-term regional economic growth. The bigger the province's investment in environmental protection as a percentage of GDP, the higher its level of environmental protection, and the greater its capacity for sustainable economic growth. On the other hand, the provision of financing for investment in environmentally friendly activities encourages business activities to reduce their environmental pollution emissions. Thus, Islamic asset management with green fiscal fund instruments can encourage green economic growth by expanding the green sector, providing incentives to remove the "brown economy" and changing consumption habits. Sachs et al. (2019) emphasize the importance of green investment and promote green projects to achieve the SDGs included in the United Nations 2030 Agenda and emphasize the creation of green bonds and green fund markets to achieve this goal. Thus, Islamic asset management through green investment funds can encourage green growth.

(ii) **Advantages Of Islamic Corporate and Investment Banking In Financing The Green Economy Transition**

Islamic corporate and investment banking is by far the most relevant Islamic green finance option for the long-term transition to a green economy in Indonesia. This is due to the fact that banking is a financial institution that plays a major role in financing large-scale clean fuel and renewable energy initiatives, in line with Noh (2019) in Sachs et al. (2019). In the study of Chen et al., it is explained that banks can play an important role in helping to achieve the broader goals of sustainable development and green recovery. On the other hand, banks can also provide the benefits of uninterrupted capital availability for corporations. Thus, these findings have important implications for regulators, monetary authorities, and the banking sector because green financing (among them Islamic corporate and investment banking) can result in a more efficient and resilient financial system.

Moreover, because the corporate ecosystem and investors have a broad reach, the opportunity to fund green projects through this scheme is considerably more promising and plays a significant role in mobilising the private capital required for the energy transition (Geddes & Schmidt, 2020). This outcome is consistent with Asiyanbi's (2018) assertion that carbon commodity finance will result in emissions reductions that would not have occurred otherwise. In addition, Islamic corporate and investment banking instruments, such as green bonds and green stocks, and private green investment are effective ways to guide investment capital to climate change reduction and conformation projects. Many companies have increased investment in green projects due to reputational and social responsibility benefits. In addition, international organizations and governments are actively responding to the requirements of the sustainable development goals and providing signals and strategic policy frameworks that can reduce the uncertainty of green investment policies.

On the other hand, by providing long-term financial support, Islamic corporate and investment banking with venture capital instruments can contribute to urban green innovation (GI). Other studies have demonstrated that venture capital influences the creativity of new energy (NE) businesses positively and significantly, with the effects of government-sponsored innovation incentives and joint venture capital being more important. Therefore, there is no doubt that corporate investment can have a significant impact on the upcoming paradigm transition in the utilities industry; but, in order to achieve overall success, many investors at various levels would be needed. Corporate venture capital (CVC) initiatives also have an advantageous effect on CSR performance because they improve the environmental and social results for the organization. Thus, Islamic corporate and investment banking with venture capital instruments can aid in the creation and expansion of a sustainable firm. Besides, Islamic corporate and investment banking with its green indices instruments can improve the environmental sustainability of the economic system. In line with the research conducted by Noh (2019), that banks have created an index that considers environmental risks as well as potential future opportunities. As an illustration, Merrill Lynch has created an energy efficiency index that only considers demand-side optimization and energy saving (Noh, 2019).

Thus, green financing is becoming a potent tool in the industrialisation of low-carbon technologies and green economies. Green financing through investments in renewable energy sources encourages the growth of high-quality businesses while supporting technological innovation and enhancing the industry's structural composition. Green financing is crucial for stabilizing industrial infrastructure in terms of both quality and quantity in areas where natural resources are abundant. Recent investigations by Y. Wang et al., Lee and Lee, support similar findings. The findings of this study are supported by research by Ronaldo and Suryanto, which found that green finance with green financing instruments, such as Islamic corporate and investment banking and Islamic asset management, can support the progress of the SDGs in terms of environmental sustainability and economic sustainability, including by reducing CO2 in the environment. Sustainable development goals (SDGs) can be achieved through economic and environmental sustainability, which can be supported by green business by fostering the development of green micro-enterprises and green technological innovation.

## 5 Conclusion

The purpose of this study was to analyse the benefits, opportunities, costs, risks, and alternatives of green economy transformation through Islamic green finance, as well as to identify the best suggested Islamic green financing alternatives.

Based on deep assesment this study confirms three main findings as shown below:

a. On the basis of the ANP BOCR approach model, the study demonstrates that the most important criterion in green economy transformation through Islam green finance is beneficial, particularly in connection with damage prevention and mitigation. This is followed by opportunity (mostly associated with developing alternative environmentally friendly); cost (the expense of developing human resource capability, and investment cost); and risk (high transition costs). In the study, the value of benefit and opportunity is shown to exceed that of cost and risk. This demonstrates that a green economy transition can be implemented in Indonesia.
b. According to the standard formula, it is reveals that the best priority of Islamic Green Financing is Islamic asset management and then followed by Islamic retail banking, insurance, Islamic corporate and investment banking, Sukuk, Islamic social finance, and Weather derivatives stand as the last priority.
c. The alternative long-term strategy for Islamic green financing in a green economy transformation comprises (in order of priority) namely: Islamic corporate and investment banking; Islamic social finance; Sukuk; Islamic asset management; Islamic retail banking; Islamic insurance; and Islamic weather derivatives. Islamic corporate and investment banking is by far the most relevant type of Islamic green financing for Indonesia's long-term green economy transition. This is due to the fact that banking is a financial institution that plays a major role in financing large-scale clean fuel and renewable energy initiatives. Moreover, because the corporate ecosystem and investors have a broad reach, the opportunity to fund green projects through this scheme is considerably more promising and plays a significant role in mobilising the private capital required for energy transition.

Due to the study's use of BOCR analysis as a synthesis technique, the output is approximated using additive and realistic approaches. Islamic asset management is identified as a short-term option, followed by Islamic retail banking; Islamic insurance; Islamic weather derivatives; Islamic corporate and investment banking; Islamic social finance; and Sukuk. Islamic asset management is the most important option for Islamic green finance in Indonesia's transition to a green economy in the short term. This is because the country's natural resources and environment continue to support the growth of Islamic green financing through environmental development services, ecological transfer, and carbon tax. In order to minimize their emissions, industrialized nations must also purchase carbon credits, which can be utilized to construct a green economy. The government plays a key role in this regard; for instance, it can supervise green economy funding expenditures and serve as a model for establishing green economy activities.

### 5.1 Recommendations

On the basis of the research findings, it is suggested that Islamic asset management is the most relevant short-term Islamic green financing solution for the transition to a green economy in Indonesia. The potential of natural resources and the environment in the country, environmental development services, the transfer of ecology, and carbon tax will continue to foster the growth of Islamic green financing. In addition, developed nations must purchase carbon credits to reduce their emissions, which can be utilized to build a green economy. Thus, all stakeholders consist of government, corporate, financial institutions, academicians and etc. should promote Islamic asset management to finance short term green economy transformation.

It is widely believed that through the green economy financing, the application of sharia principles in Islamic Asset Management such as private equity, asset-backed securities represents a significant new milestone. It able to provide a wider choice of investment, broader portfolio diversification and more attractive risk and reward potential, while at the same time to ensure that the underlying investment are structured to satisfy the Environmental and Social Governance (ESG) agenda.

Meanwhile, the Islamic corporate and investment banking alternative is by far the most pertinent Islamic green finance alternative for Indonesia's long-term green economy transition. This is based on the role of the banking industry in facilitating large-scale clean fuel and renewable energy initiatives. Moreover, the corporate ecosystem and investors have important parts to play. The opportunity to finance green projects through this alternative is far more promising then other alternatives, and it plays a crucial role in mobilizing the private capital required for the energy transition. Therefore, it is urgent for all stakeholders to motivate all banks, especially Islamic corporate and Investment banking in the sense that maintaining profitabiliy to serve the environment and focus on environmental issue busines as the way to achieve the 2030 agenda for sustainable development.

Among them, Islamic social finance (ISF) should be considered more as it can promote inclusive and sustainable economy. Islamic social finance instrument to manage inclusive wealth in accordance with sharia law is increasing and becoming more important, complementing sharia financial services targeting all social strata. To accelerate Islamic social finance (ISF), ISF activity should be digitalised to enhance the developments of ISF as it give benefits such as financial performance improvement, corporate establishment, transperancy, and stability. ISF, e.g. *zakat, infaq, alms, and waqf*, is a financial instrument based on Islamic principles and aims to promote inclusive welfare (Juhro et al., 2025).

## References

Abduh, M. (2019). The role of islamic social finance in achieving sdg number 2: End hunger, achieve food security and improved nutrition and promote sustainable agriculture. *Al-Shajarah, 2019* (Special Issue Islamic Banking and Finance 2019), 185–206.

Akomea-Frimpong, I., Adeabah, D., Ofosu, D., & Tenakwah, E. J. (2021). A review of studies on green finance of banks, research gaps and future directions. *Journal of Sustainable Finance and Investment*, 1–24.

Al-Jayyousi, O., Tok, E., Saniff, S. M., Wan Hasan, W. N., Janahi, N. A., & Yesuf, A. J. (2022). Re-Thinking Sustainable Development within Islamic Worldviews: A Systematic Literature Review. *Sustainability (Switzerland)*, *14*(12).

Alexander, K., & Fisher, P. G. (2020). Central Banking and Climate Change. *Making the Financial System Sustainable*, 49–74.

Ascarya. (2013). The root causes of financial crisis in Islamic economic perspective using structural equation modeling. *10th International Conference on Tawhidi and World-System: God Conscious Organization and Conscious Social Order.*

Asiyanbi, A. P. (2018). Financialisation in the green economy: Material connections, markets-in-the-making and Foucauldian organising actions. *Environment and Planning A*, *50*(3), 531–548.

Azhgaliyeva, D., Kapsalyamova, Z., & Low, L. (2019). Implications of Fiscal and Financial Policies on Unlocking Green Finance and Green Investment. *Handbook of Green Finance.*

Barbier, E. (2011). The policy challenges for green economy and sustainable economic development. *Natural Resources Forum*, *35*(3), 233–245.

Barbier, E. B. (2012). The green economy post Rio+20. *Science*, *338*(6109), 887–888.

Berensmann, K., & Lindenberg, N. (2016). *Green finance: actors, challenges and policy recommendations.*

Borel-Saladin, J. M., & Turok, I. N. (2013). The green economy: Incremental change or transformation? *Environmental Policy and Governance*, *23*(4), 209–220.

Dikau, S., & Volz, U. (2019). Central Banking, Climate Change, and Green Finance. *Handbook of Green Finance*, *867*, 81–102.

Dikau, S., & Volz, U. (2021). Central bank mandates, sustainability objectives and the promotion of green finance. *Ecological Economics*, *184* (August 2020), 107022.

Droste, N., Hansjürgens, B., Kuikman, P., Otter, N., Antikainen, R., Leskinen, P., Pitkänen, K., Saikku, L., Loiseau, E., & Thomsen, M. (2016). Steering innovations towards a green economy: Understanding government intervention. *Journal of Cleaner Production*, *135*, 426–434.

Ekins, P., & Zenghelis, D. (2021). The Costs And Benefits Of Environmental Sustainability. *Sustainability Science*, *16*(3), 949–965.

Emanuel, J., & Cefalu, P. (2002). Drilling for oil in the artic national wildlife refuge. *A Project in a graduate class: decision making in complex environments. University of Pittsburgh.*

Felice, D. F., & Petrillo, A. (2013). An integrated conceptual model to promote green policies. *International Journal of Innovation and Sustainable Development*, *7*(4), 333–355.

Geddes, A., & Schmidt, T. S. (2020). Integrating finance into the multi-level perspective: Technology niche-finance regime interactions and financial policy interventions. *Research Policy*, *49*(6), 103985.

Islam, M. A., Yousuf, S., Hossain, K. F., & Islam, M. R. (2014). Green financing in Bangladesh: Challenges and opportunities—A descriptive approach. *International Journal of Green Economics*, *8*(1), 74–91.

Juhro, S.M., Syarifuddin, F., Sakti, A. (2025). Inclusive Welfare: On the Role of Islamic Social-Public Finance and Monetary Economics. *Springer International Publishing Switzerland.*

Kaggwa, M., Savious, S., & Nhamo, G. (2013). *South Africa' s Green Economy Transition: Implications for Reorienting the Economy Towards a Low-Carbon Growth Trajectory*. 1–20.

Kamil, W. A. R., Bakhor, S. A. S. M. (SC), Martinez, J. D. L.-, Zhan, W., & Aziz, A. H. A. (2019). Islamic green finance. *Islamic Social Finance*, 144–172.

Kemp-Benedict, E. (2014). *Shifting to a green economy: Lock-in, path dependence, and policy options* (SEI Working Paper 2014-08.).

Kong, F., & Sun, S. (2021). Better understanding insurance mechanism in dealing with climate change risk, with special reference to China. *International Journal of Environmental Research and Public Health*, *18*(6), 1–14.

Kousar, S., Bhutta, A. I., Ullah, M. R., & Shabbir, A. (2022). *Why is the Shift from Brown Economy to Green Economy Important in South Asian Economies? A Panel Cointegration Analysis.*

Kupakuwana, P. S. (2012). Sustainable Retail Banking and Asset Management: Lessons from Challenges Faced by Entrepreneurs in African Economies. In Prof. Thierry Burger-Helmchen (Ed.), *Intechopen.* Entrepreneurship-Gender, Geographies and Social Contex.

Law, A., De Lacy, T., Lipman, G., & Jiang, M. (2016). Transitioning to a green economy: The case of tourism in Bali, Indonesia. *Journal of Cleaner Production, 111*, 295–305.

Liu, F. H. M., & Lai, K. P. Y. (2021). Ecologies of green finance: Green sukuk and development of green Islamic finance in Malaysia. *Environment and Planning A, 53*(8), 1896–1914.

Liu, J., & Yin, Y. (2019). An integrated method for sustainable energy storing node optimization selection in China. *Energy Conversion and Management, 199*(May), 112049.

Liu, N., Liu, C., Xia, Y., Ren, Y., & Liang, J. (2020). Examining the coordination between green finance and green economy aiming for sustainable development: A case study of China. *Sustainability (Switzerland), 12*(9).

Loiseau, E., Saikku, L., Antikainen, R., Droste, N., Hansjürgens, B., Pitkänen, K., Leskinen, P., Kuikman, P., & Thomsen, M. (2016). Green economy and related concepts: An overview. *Journal of Cleaner Production, 139*, 361–371.

Megwai, G., Njie, N. I., & Richards, T. (2016). Exploring green economy strategies and policies in developing countries. *International Journal of Green Economics, 10*(3–4), 338–357.

Muganyi, T., Yan, L., & Sun, H. ping. (2021). Green finance, fintech and environmental protection: Evidence from China. *Environmental Science and Ecotechnology, 7*, 100107.

Musango, J. K., Brent, A. C., & Tshangela, M. (2014). Green economy transitioning of the South African power sector: A system dynamics analysis approach. *Development Southern Africa, 31*(5), 744–758.

Noh, H. J. (2019). Financial strategis to accelerate green growth. In J. D. Sachs, W. T. Woo, N. Yoshino, & F. T. Hesary (Eds.), *Handbook of Green Finance* (Sustainable). Springer International Publishing Switzerland.

Raberto, M., Ozel, B., Ponta, L., Teglio, A., & Cincotti, S. (2019). From financial instability to green finance: the role of banking and credit market regulation in the Eurace model. In *Journal of Evolutionary Economics* (Vol. 29, Issue 1). Journal of Evolutionary Economics.

Richardson, E. (2020). The UAE and responsible finance-Can responsible finance sukūk help the UAE in fulfilling its sustainability ambitions? *Arab Law Quarterly, 34*(4), 313–355.

Roy C. Schmidt. (1997). Managing Delphi Surveys Using Nonparametric Statisical Techniques. *Decision Sciences, 28*(3), 736–774.

Saaty, T., & Vargas, L. G. (2013). *Decision making with the analytic network process (Vol. 282)* (second ed.). *Springer Science Business Media.*

Saaty, T. L. (2001). *Theory and Applications of the ANalytic Network Proccess.*

Shweta, Bajpai, R. C., & Chaturvedi, H. K. (2015). Evaluation of inter-rater agreement and inter-rater reliability for observational data: An overview of concepts and methods. *Journal of the Indian Academy of Applied Psychology, 41*(Special Issue 3), 20–27.

Siswantoro, D., & Surya, H. V. (2021). Indonesian Green Sukuk (Islamic Bond) of climate change: A revisited analysis. *IOP Conference Series: Earth and Environmental Science, 716*(1).

Söderholm, P. (2020). The green economy transition: the challenges of technological change for sustainability. *Sustainable Earth, 3*(1).

Speck, S., & Zoboli, R. (2017). *The Green Economy in Europe: In Search for a Successful Transition* (S. Shmelev (ed.); Volume 6, Issue September). *Springer International Publishing Switzerland.*

Tienhaara, K. (2016). Governing the Global Green Economy. *Global Policy, 7*(4), 481–490.

UNEP. (2011). *Pathways to Sustainable Development and Poverty Eradication—A Synthesis for Policy Makers.: Vol. Towar. a G.*

Volz, U. (2018). Fostering Green Finance For Asian Development Bank Institute. *Ssrn, 814.*

Zhang, S., Wu, Z., Wang, Y., & Hao, Y. (2021). Fostering green development with green finance: An empirical study on the environmental effect of green credit policy in China. *Journal of Environmental Management, 296*(July), 113159.

# Part V
# Epilogue

# Chapter 20
# Achieving Sustainable Growth: Lessons Learned and Way Forward

**Solikin M. Juhro**

**Abstract** This final chapter synthesizes the core lessons learned on achieving sustainable growth and articulates a forward-looking agenda for developing and emerging economies, with Indonesia as a central reference. Drawing together insights from macroeconomic management, structural transformation, environmental sustainability, and financial system stability, it highlights that growth and stability are mutually reinforcing rather than competing objectives in delivering sustainable development. The chapter underscores the importance of policy coherence, institutional credibility, and a just transition in sustaining long-term welfare gains, and outlines strategic priorities for translating sustainability commitments into resilient, inclusive, and sustainable development pathways.

**Keywords** Sustainable growth · Sustainability · Structural transformation

## 1 Introduction

Achieving sustainable growth has emerged as one of the most pressing challenges for developing and emerging economies in the twenty-first century. Economic development has hitherto failed to generate a significant impact on poverty alleviation and the reduction of social inequality, thereby motivating the adoption of development strategies that place social welfare at their core. The global initiative of the Millennium Development Goals (MDGs), followed by the Sustainable Development Goals (SDGs), represent a response to the shortcomings of the traditional trickle-down theory of development. The MDG/SDG framework adopts a modern development approach that directly targets poverty reduction, inequality alleviation, and ameliorating welfare for all through economic empowerment.

Moreover, growth trajectories that rely heavily on natural resource extraction, fossil fuels, and environmental externalization have delivered short-term economic

S. M. Juhro (✉)
Bank Indonesia, Jakarta, Indonesia
e-mail: solikin@bi.go.id



S. M. Juhro et al. (eds.), *Sustainable Economy: The Indonesian Pathways*,
https://doi.org/10.1007/978-981-92-1215-6_20

gains but have proven increasingly incompatible with long-term prosperity, macroeconomic stability, and social welfare. For Indonesia, this challenge is particularly salient. As a large, resource-rich, and climate-vulnerable archipelagic nation, Indonesia's aspiration to achieve high-income status by 2045—popularly articulated as Golden Indonesia (Indonesia Emas) 2045—cannot be realized through conventional growth models alone.

The implementation of strong and consistent structural reform policies, along with a new growth paradigm, are sufficiently required. The structural reforms are expected to not only accelerate Indonesia's transition into developed economies and avoid the middle-income trap, but also make the Indonesian economy grows in a sustainable level, in order to further reduce poverty and social inequality. To achieve these ideal conditions, Indonesia is required to be able to further optimize the natural resource management, build reliability in the industrial sectors, build resilience in energy and foods, strengthen the financing structure of the economy, develop inclusive economic activities and strengthen the basic capital of national development.

These strategic steps require pre-requisite of macroeconomic and financial system stability, as elements of continuity in supporting the implementation of sustainable growth. Sustainable growth, in this context, extends beyond maintaining positive GDP growth rates. It encompasses the capacity to generate rising productivity, inclusive employment, and social welfare while preserving ecological systems and ensuring macro-financial system stability (Stiglitz, 2019).

This chapter synthesizes lessons learned from Indonesia's development trajectory, comparative country experiences, and recent empirical evidence across macroeconomics, climate risk, fiscal and financial policy, and structural transformation. It argues that sustainability is not a constraint on growth, but rather a precondition for durable, resilient, and equitable development.

## 2 Conceptual

### 2.1 *Growth, Stability, and Environmental Sustainability: A Reinforced Nexus*

A central lesson emerging from Indonesia's experience is that growth, stability, and environmental sustainability are deeply interdependent. Traditional macroeconomic frameworks often treat environmental sustainability as external to core economic objectives. However, mounting evidence suggests that environmental degradation feeds directly into macroeconomic volatility through multiple channels, including productivity losses, fiscal pressures, health costs, and financial instability (NGFS, 2019; Dasgupta, 2023).

Indonesia's development vision recognizes this interdependence through four mutually reinforcing pillars: human development and science and technology, sustainable economic development, equitable development, and national resilience and governance (Bappenas, 2024). Empirically, these pillars do not operate in isolation. Improvements in human capital raise productivity and innovation capacity; sustainable economic development reduces exposure to climate and resource shocks; equitable development strengthens social cohesion; and strong institutions enhance policy credibility and investment confidence.

The experience of repeated external shocks—including commodity price cycles, the COVID-19 pandemic, and climate-related disasters—has underscored that macroeconomic stability cannot be sustained without addressing environmental risks. Physical climate risks such as floods, droughts, and sea-level rise disrupt production, infrastructure, and financial intermediation, while transition risks associated with global decarbonization affect export demand, asset values, and employment in carbon-intensive sectors. These dynamics reinforce the insight that sustainability functions as a "guardrail" for growth: without it, economic expansion becomes increasingly fragile.

## 2.2 *The Triple Planetary Crisis and Development Externalities*

The concept of the triple planetary crisis—climate change, biodiversity loss, and pollution—offers a powerful framework for understanding why unsustainable development undermines long-term growth (UN, 2022). These crises interact through reinforcing feedback loops, generating externalities that are not priced by markets but impose substantial social and economic costs.

For Indonesia, climate change manifests in rising temperatures, increased frequency of extreme weather events, and heightened exposure to sea-level rise, particularly in coastal and low-lying regions. Biodiversity loss threatens agricultural productivity, fisheries, and ecosystem services that underpin food security and livelihoods. Pollution, including air pollution and plastic waste, imposes health costs and undermines labor productivity. Together, these externalities translate into fiscal burdens, inflationary pressures, and heightened financial risks (Pigou, 1920; D'Orazio, 2025).

It is worth noting that the planetary crisis has profound implications for economic inclusion, particularly in terms of poverty and unemployment. Climate change increases the frequency of extreme weather events, which disproportionately affect low-income communities that depend on climate-sensitive sectors such as agriculture, fisheries, and informal labor, thereby deepening vulnerability and income instability. Biodiversity loss undermines ecosystem services—such as food security, water availability, and livelihoods—on which millions of poor households rely, reducing productivity and long-term economic opportunities. Meanwhile, pollution (air, water, and land) worsens public health outcomes, raises healthcare costs, and lowers labor productivity, often affecting marginalized populations most severely. Together, these crises risk widening inequality, increasing structural unemployment, and trapping vulnerable groups in cycles of poverty unless accompanied by inclusive green transition policies, strengthened social protection, and investment in sustainable job creation.

Another key lesson is that environmental externalities, when left unaddressed, evolve into systemic macro-financial risks. Physical risks generate sudden output losses and fiscal shocks, while transition risks—if poorly managed—can create persistent drags on growth. This insight justifies the expanding role of fiscal, financial, and monetary authorities in integrating sustainability considerations into macroeconomic management, not as mission creep, but as risk mitigation (Juhro et al., 2025).

## 2.3 *Institutional Strengthening, Collaboration, and Sustainability*

Institutional strengthening is a critical determinant of successful national development. Acemoglu and Robinson (2012) argue that a country's long-term success or failure is largely shaped by its ability to design and manage effective economic and political institutions. In this regard, sustainable economic growth is more likely to emerge in countries characterized by inclusive institutional frameworks, rather than extractive ones.

A key institutional factor in achieving sustainable growth is catalytic collaboration among all stakeholders, including government, the public, and the private sector, at both domestic and international levels. Such collaborative interactions are underpinned by several essential elements: shared long-term objectives, symmetrical governance structures with shared responsibilities, and high levels of negotiation, interactivity, and interdependence. These conditions foster the generation of ideas and innovations, serving as key drivers of improved living standards and societal well-being (Juhro & Aulia, 2019).

Consistent with this perspective, strong institutional development is indispensable for the success of sustainability initiatives—defined as strategic actions undertaken by individuals and organizations to promote environmental, social, and economic well-being for both current and future generations. Robust institutions ensure effective coordination, implementation, and oversight across all levels of governance: from the central government's role in policy formulation and accountability, to local governments' responsibilities in operational execution and community empowerment, and to the contributions of academia and the private sector in innovation, education, and partnership. Together, these actors form an inclusive and accountable sustainable development ecosystem that is essential for achieving national objectives and global sustainability targets.

## 3 Discussion on Indonesia Context

### *3.1 Structural Transformation and the Middle-Income Trap*

Indonesia's prolonged experience in the middle-income trap highlights the limits of growth models based on factor accumulation and resource extraction. While structural transformation toward services and manufacturing has progressed, productivity growth remains uneven, and environmental pressures have intensified. Lessons from comparative country experiences demonstrate that sustainable growth requires deliberate policy sequencing and institutional capacity.

Chile, South Korea, and China offer instructive contrasts. Chile's experience shows how resource-based economies can upgrade through industrial policy, fiscal incentives, and export diversification, but also reveals the risks of regulatory capture and limited technological upgrading without strong institutions (Sato et al., 2020; OECD, 2021). South Korea illustrates how innovation-led growth, green stimulus, and coordinated industrial policy can align environmental regulation with competitiveness (Hille et al., 2021; Han & Lee, 2023). China demonstrates the power of large-scale policy experimentation, green subsidies, and institutional learning, while also highlighting the challenges of uneven implementation across regions (Wu et al., 2019; Cai et al., 2023).

The lesson for Indonesia is that sustainable growth is not automatic; it requires active state capacity to guide structural transformation, mobilize finance, and manage distributional impacts during the low-carbon transition (IMF, 2022). Green industrial policy, when aligned with human capital development and institutional reform, can support productivity growth while reducing environmental intensity.

### *3.2 Fiscal and Financial Policy as Catalysts for Sustainable Growth*

Fiscal and financial policies play a pivotal role in internalizing environmental externalities and crowding in private investment. Indonesia's experience with climate budget tagging, green sukuk, tax incentives for renewable energy and electric vehicles, and gradual carbon pricing demonstrates how public finance can act as a catalyst rather than the sole funding source.

Empirical evidence from climate stress testing suggests that early and credible climate policy action yields superior macroeconomic outcomes. IMF (2023) argues that managing climate risks can support financial stability. Delayed transition increases physical risks and locks in carbon-intensive assets, resulting in permanent output losses. Conversely, early carbon pricing combined with investment surges can generate long-term GDP gains despite short-term adjustment costs. Importantly, Indonesia's financial system is projected to remain resilient under orderly transition scenarios, provided that risks are identified and managed proactively.

A key lesson is that fiscal space is limited, particularly in developing economies. Sustainable growth therefore depends on policy coherence: aligning fiscal incentives, financial regulation, and development planning to mobilize private capital while safeguarding stability. Instruments such as sustainable finance taxonomies, disclosure standards, and blended finance mechanisms enhance market credibility and reduce greenwashing risks, thereby lowering the cost of capital for sustainable investments.

### 3.3 Just Transition: Growth with Equity and Social Legitimacy

One of the most critical lessons emerging from Indonesia's experience is the centrality of a just transition. Structural transformation and decarbonization inevitably create winners and losers across sectors, regions, and income groups. Without deliberate policies to manage distributional impacts, sustainability transitions risk social resistance, political backlash, and policy reversal.

Energy subsidy reform illustrates this challenge vividly. While fossil fuel subsidies are regressive and environmentally harmful, their removal can increase inequality and poverty if compensation mechanisms are inadequate. Empirical evidence shows that both subsidy provision and removal can raise inequality, underscoring the need for targeted social protection and inclusive design.

Just transition principles emphasize employment creation, skills development, regional support, and stakeholder participation (ILO, 2018). Investments in green human capital—through education, training, and vocational programs—emerge as a powerful driver of green growth, particularly in manufacturing and energy sectors. Youth engagement, as evidenced in circular economy and agricultural case studies, can modernize production systems while addressing demographic challenges such as aging workforces.

The lesson is clear: sustainable growth must be socially legitimate. Equity is not merely an ethical concern but a functional requirement for maintaining political support and policy credibility over long transition horizons.

### 3.4 Measurement, Data, and Governance: From Vision to Implementation

Another key lesson concerns the importance of measurement and data governance. Sustainable growth strategies are only as effective as the metrics used to guide and monitor them. Indonesia's development of a Green Economy Index and mandatory sustainability reporting represents significant progress, yet challenges remain in data consistency, assurance, and interoperability with global standards.

Fragmented data systems, limited firm-level information, and uneven subnational capacity constrain evidence-based policymaking. Strengthening data governance—across climate risk, emissions, biodiversity, and social indicators—is essential for aligning public and private decision-making. From a governance perspective, coordination across ministries, financial regulators, and subnational governments is critical to avoid policy fragmentation and ensure coherent implementation.

Comparative experiences suggest that institutional adaptability and learning are as important as policy design. Pilot programs, phased implementation, and feedback mechanisms allow policymakers to adjust strategies while minimizing systemic risks.

### *3.5 Global Relevance and Indonesia's Strategic Position*

Indonesia's experience offers broader lessons for other developing and emerging economies. First, sustainable growth pathways must be context-specific; there is no one-size-fits-all model. Second, sustainability transitions are most effective when embedded in long-term national visions rather than treated as standalone environmental agendas. Third, macroeconomic stability and sustainability are mutually reinforcing, not competing objectives.

As global trade becomes more fragmented and climate policies increasingly shape market access, sustainability is also a competitiveness issue. Countries that align growth strategies with decarbonization, innovation, and human capital development are better positioned to integrate into future value chains. For Indonesia, this alignment strengthens its aspiration not only to achieve high-income status, but also to emerge as a resilient and influential global actor.

The overarching lesson from Indonesia's journey toward sustainable growth is that sustainability is a strategic economic choice, not a luxury. Growth that undermines ecological systems, social cohesion, and financial stability ultimately erodes its own foundations. Conversely, growth strategies that internalize environmental externalities, invest in human capital, and ensure social inclusion are more resilient, adaptive, and durable.

Achieving Golden Indonesia 2045 requires orchestrating macroeconomic stability, structural transformation, and sustainability through coherent policy mixes and strong institutions. The experiences reviewed in this chapter demonstrate that while the transition entails costs and trade-offs, the long-term benefits—in terms of productivity, resilience, and welfare—far outweigh them. Sustainable growth is therefore not only compatible with development ambitions; it is indispensable to realizing them.

# 4 What's Next?

Looking ahead, the challenge for Indonesia is no longer whether sustainable growth is necessary, but how to operationalize it at scale, pace, and depth consistent with the ambition of Golden Indonesia 2045. The lessons identified in this chapter point to a set of strategic priorities that will determine whether sustainability transitions translate into durable productivity gains, social cohesion, and macroeconomic resilience. These priorities span policy sequencing, institutional strengthening, financing architecture, and societal engagement.

## *4.1 From Policy Commitment to Policy Credibility*

A critical next step is strengthening policy credibility. Indonesia has articulated ambitious long-term goals—including net-zero emissions by 2060 or sooner and a green economy transformation embedded in national development planning. However, international and domestic evidence suggests that the effectiveness of such commitments depends less on headline targets than on the credibility of intermediate milestones, enforcement mechanisms, and institutional coordination (Rodrik, 2014; OECD, 2023).

Moving forward, greater emphasis should be placed on translating long-term visions into binding medium-term frameworks, such as sectoral decarbonization pathways, time-bound subsidy reform schedules, and investment pipelines aligned with climate and development objectives. Clear signaling reduces policy uncertainty, lowers risk premia, and encourages private investment in green technologies and infrastructure. In this sense, policy credibility functions as a macroeconomic asset, reinforcing stability and growth rather than constraining them.

## *4.2 Deepening Green Structural Transformation*

Sustainable growth in the next phase will hinge on deepening structural transformation rather than relying on incremental efficiency gains alone. While energy efficiency and emissions intensity improvements are necessary, they are insufficient without parallel shifts in production structures, value chains, and innovation systems. Indonesia's industrial strategy will need to increasingly prioritize green manufacturing, circular economy models, and nature-based industries that combine value addition with environmental stewardship.

This implies a more strategic integration of industrial, trade, and climate policies. Green industrial policy—when transparent, time-bound, and performance-based—can support learning-by-doing, technology diffusion, and export competitiveness, particularly in emerging sectors such as electric vehicles, batteries, sustainable bioeconomy products, and green services (Aghion et al., 2016; UNIDO, 2022). Importantly, future policies should emphasize dynamic efficiency and upgrading rather than static protection, ensuring that green transformation remains growth-enhancing.

## 4.3 *Scaling Sustainable Finance and Managing Systemic Risk*

Another key priority is scaling sustainable finance while safeguarding financial stability. Indonesia has made notable progress through green sukuk issuance, climate budget tagging, and sustainable finance taxonomies. The next phase requires moving from pilot instruments to system-wide integration of climate and sustainability risks into financial decision-making.

This includes embedding climate risk assessment into prudential supervision, stress testing, and capital allocation frameworks, as well as improving data availability and disclosure quality. As global financial markets increasingly price climate risk, domestic financial systems that fail to adapt may face capital misallocation, stranded assets, and heightened volatility (NGFS, 2023). Conversely, proactive integration of sustainability considerations can enhance resilience and position Indonesia as a credible destination for long-term green investment.

Equally important is ensuring that sustainable finance supports real-economy transformation rather than remaining concentrated in a narrow set of low-risk projects. Blended finance mechanisms, guarantees, and public–private partnerships will be essential to crowd in private capital for infrastructure, adaptation, and innovation, particularly in regions and sectors facing higher transition risks.

## 4.4 *Investing in Human Capital and a Just Transition*

Looking ahead, human capital development emerges as a decisive factor for sustaining growth during the transition. Indonesia's demographic dividend presents a unique opportunity, but only if education, training, and labor market policies are aligned with emerging green sectors. Without such alignment, structural transformation risks generating skills mismatches, unemployment, and inequality that undermine growth and social cohesion.

A forward-looking just transition strategy should therefore move beyond compensation toward capability building. This includes expanding green skills curricula in vocational schools and universities, supporting lifelong learning, and facilitating labor mobility across sectors and regions (ILO, 2018; World Bank, 2022). Integrating just transition principles into development planning also strengthens political feasibility, ensuring that sustainability reforms are socially embedded and durable across political cycles.

## *4.5 Strengthening Data, Measurement, and Adaptive Governance*

Another pressing agenda is strengthening measurement and adaptive governance systems. As sustainable growth increasingly relies on complex policy interactions—across climate, finance, trade, and social policy—robust data and monitoring frameworks become indispensable. Indonesia's Green Economy Index and sustainability reporting initiatives provide a strong foundation, but future progress will require greater harmonization, assurance, and subnational coverage.

Adaptive governance—characterized by experimentation, feedback loops, and institutional learning—should be institutionalized rather than treated as ad hoc. Pilot programs, regional experimentation, and phased implementation allow policymakers to manage uncertainty while minimizing systemic risks (Mazzucato, 2018). In this sense, governance capacity becomes as important as policy ambition in determining long-term growth outcomes.

### Promoting Leadership dan Innovation

Leadership and innovation are central pillars in delivering sustainable economic growth, as sustainability requires not only adequate resources and sound policies, but also clear vision, effective coordination, and continuous adaptation. Sustainable growth cannot be achieved through market mechanisms or technological progress alone; it requires visionary leadership to steer innovation toward economic prosperity, social equity, and environmental sustainability. Innovation enables economies to grow qualitatively rather than merely quantitatively by enhancing productivity without depleting natural resources, thereby strengthening economic resilience.

From this perspective, leadership and innovation should be orchestrated in an integrated manner so that they mutually reinforce one another and generate more powerful development outcomes. Juhro et al. (2020) demonstrate that innovation quality and leadership competence constitute new sources of growth, facilitating economic breakthroughs and supporting long-term sustainability.

Accordingly, to deliver sustainable growth, Indonesia needs to establish an integrated institutional framework that promotes both leadership and innovation. This strategy should encompass investment in human capital and leadership capacity; the strengthening of integrated innovation ecosystems—including education, research and development, and digital infrastructure; the deepening of financial markets to support innovation and green investment; the expansion of inclusive access to technology and finance; and the reinforcement of institutional quality and governance. Together, these elements provide a coherent foundation for sustainable and inclusive economic transformation.

### 4.6 *Strengthening Indonesia's Strategic Position in a Fragmented Global Economy*

The global context underscores the urgency of forward-looking strategy. Climate policies, carbon border measures, and sustainability standards are reshaping global trade and investment patterns. Countries that delay adaptation risk marginalization, while those that align domestic reforms with global trends can enhance competitiveness and strategic autonomy.

For Indonesia, sustainable growth offers a pathway to reposition itself within evolving global value chains—not merely as a supplier of raw materials, but as a producer of higher value-added, low-carbon goods and services. This requires proactive engagement in international cooperation, standards-setting, and regional initiatives, particularly within ASEAN and the G20, to ensure that sustainability transitions are inclusive and development-friendly.

## 5 Conclusion

Drawing together insights from macroeconomic management, structural transformation, environmental sustainability, and financial system stability, it highlights that growth, stability, and inclusivity are mutually reinforcing rather than competing objectives in delivering sustainable development. This perspective underscores the importance of policy coherence, institutional credibility, and a just transition in sustaining long-term welfare gains, and outlines strategic priorities for translating sustainability commitments into resilient, inclusive, and sustainable development pathways.

The next phase of Indonesia's development will be defined by its ability to convert sustainability commitments into credible, coordinated, and inclusive action. The lessons of the past suggest that sustainable growth is not achieved through isolated policies, but through coherent systems that align macroeconomic stability, structural transformation, social equity, and environmental stewardship. What comes next is therefore not a single reform, but a sustained process of institutional strengthening, investment, and learning—one that will ultimately determine whether Golden Indonesia (Indonesia Emas) 2045 becomes a realized outcome or an unfulfilled aspiration.

## References

Afshan, S., et al. (2024). *Environmental taxes, financial development, and green growth in emerging economies.*

Aghion, P., Dechezleprêtre, A., Hémous, D., Martin, R., & Van Reenen, J. (2016). Carbon taxes, path dependency, and directed technical change: Evidence from the auto industry. *Journal of Political Economy, 124*(1), 1–51.

Bappenas. (2024). National Long-Term Development Plan 2025–2045.
Cai, Q., Ji, Z., Ma, F., & Liang, H. (2023). The green effects of industrial policy: Evidence from China's NEV subsidies. *Energies, 16*(19).
Dasgupta, P. (2023). *The Economics of Biodiversity.*
D'Orazio, P. (2025). Climate risks and financial stability: Evidence on the effectiveness of climate-related financial policies. *International Review of Financial Analysis, 105*, 104304. https://doi.org/10.1016/j.irfa.2025.104304
Han, H., & Lee, T. (2023). Varieties of green stimulus policies in South Korea. *Journal of Environment & Development.*
Hille, E., Lambernd, B., & Tiwari, A. K. (2021). Any signs of green growth? *Environmental and Resource Economics, 80*(3).
International Labour Organization (ILO). (2015). *Guidelines for a just transition towards environmentally sustainable economies and societies for all.* ILO.
International Labour Organization (ILO). (2018). *World employment and social outlook 2018: Greening with jobs.* ILO.
International Monetary Fund (IMF). (2022). *Fiscal policies for climate change mitigation.* IMF.
International Monetary Fund (IMF). (2023). *Climate change and financial stability.* IMF Global Financial Stability Report.
Juhro, Solikin M. and Aulia, A. Farid (2019) "New Sources of Growth: The Role of Frugal Innovation and Transformational Leadership, Bulletin of Monetary Economics and Banking: Vol. 22: No. 3, Article 2. https://doi.org/10.21098/bemp.v22i3.1195. Available at: https://bulletin.bmeb-bi.org/bmeb/vol22/iss3/2
Juhro, S. M., Aulia, A. F., Hadiwaluyo, D., Aliandrina, D., & Lavika, E. (2020), The Role of Catalytic Collaboration in Leveraging Transformational Leadership Competencies to Generate Sustainable Innovation. *International Journal of Organizational Leadership.* https://doi.org/10.2139/ssrn.3786739.
Juhro, S. M., Robinson, I., Rahadyan, H., & Rishanty, A. (2025). Climate Risks, Just Transition, and Central Bank Policy for Sustainable Economic Growth. *Jurnal Ekonomi Indonesia, 13*(3), 215–248. https://doi.org/10.52813/jei.v13i3.587
Mazzucato, M. (2018). *The value of everything: Making and taking in the global economy.* Penguin Random House.
Network for Greening the Financial System (NGFS). (2023). *NGFS climate scenarios for central banks and supervisors.* NGFS.
NGFS. (2019). *A Call for Action: Climate Change as a Source of Financial Risk.*
Organisation for Economic Co-operation and Development (OECD). (2021). *Aligning finance with climate goals.* OECD Publishing.
Organisation for Economic Co-operation and Development (OECD). (2023). *Green growth and sustainable development.* OECD Publishing.
Pigou, A. C. (1920). *The Economics of Welfare.*
Rodrik, D. (2014). Green industrial policy. *Oxford Review of Economic Policy, 30*(3), 469–491.
Sato, T., et al. (2020). Resource-based development and industrial policy. *Journal of Technology Transfer.*
Stiglitz, J. E. (2019). *People, power, and profits: Progressive capitalism for an age of discontent.* W. W. Norton & Company.
UN. (2022). *Making Peace with Nature.*
United Nations Industrial Development Organization (UNIDO). (2022). *Industrial development report 2022: The future of industrialization in a post-pandemic world.* UNIDO.
World Bank. (2022). *Inclusive green growth: The pathway to sustainable development.* World Bank.
Wu, Y., Zhu, X., & Groenewold, N. (2019). *Industrial policy in China.* China Economic Review.

FSC
www.fsc.org
MIX
Papier | Fördert
gute Waldnutzung
FSC® C083411

Kolibri 360 GmbH
Ferdinand-Jühlke-Straße 7
99095 Erfurt, Deutschland
produktsicherheit@kolibri360.de